C000272245

WHEN THE GODS CAME DOWN

Also by Alan F. Alford

GODS OF THE NEW MILLENNIUM
THE PHOENIX SOLUTION

WHEN THE GODS CAME DOWN

The Catastrophic Roots
of Religion Revealed

Alan F. Alford

Hodder & Stoughton

Copyright © 2000 by Alan F. Alford

First Published in Great Britain in 2000
by Hodder and Stoughton
A division of Hodder Headline

The right of Alan F. Alford to be identified as the Author of
this Work has been asserted to him in accordance with the
Copyright, Designs and Patents Act 1988.

10 9 8 7 6 5 4 3 2 1

All rights reserved. No part of this publication may be
reproduced, stored in a retrieval system, or transmitted,
in any form or by any means without the prior written
permission of the publisher, nor be otherwise circulated
in any form of binding or cover other than that in which
it is published and without a similar condition being
imposed on the subsequent purchaser.

British Library Cataloguing in Publication Data

A CIP catalogue record of this title is available from the British Library

ISBN 0 340 69616 8

Printed and bound in Great Britain by
Mackays of Chatham plc, Chatham, Kent

Hodder and Stoughton
A division of Hodder Headline
338 Euston Road
London NW1 3BH

To the Lady of Life

Though you are Poor [in spirit or wisdom], do *not* say:

"I am penniless, so I cannot seek out Knowledge."

Instead, bend your back to all discipline,
Purify your heart through all Wisdom,
And in the abundance of your intellectual potential,
Investigate the Mystery of Existence.

— *The Dead Sea Scrolls*

CONTENTS

PREFACE

What *is* religion? Most people in the Western world today would identify one or more of three things: a moral code, a faith in a supreme being, and an obedience to the Church. Or, to state it succinctly: morals, faith and obedience. But should there not be something more to religion?

It is a fact that the word 'religion' stems from the word *religare*, which means literally 'to bind back'. In the Latin language, this term was equated with the mooring fast of a boat, as if to emphasise that religion should somehow provide a mooring post or anchor for our existence – a kind of safe haven, not just in this life but also in the next. Strictly speaking, then, religion should not only be instilling in us essential moral values, but should also be binding us back to where we came from, in order to give us some sense of who we are and why we are here. Or, to put it succinctly once again, religion should also be teaching us about ancestry, history and, ultimately, *origins*.

Does the Bible do this? Well, yes, but only in a manner of speaking. We are told that God created Adam from clay (or soil) and then created Eve from the rib of Adam, and that finally God expelled both Adam and Eve from the Garden of Eden. But even if we understand this tale as an allegory for a paradise lost, it does not tell us *where* this paradise was, and it provides us with only the barest details concerning *who* our ancestors, Adam and Eve, actually were. Thus the biblical story, as it stands, fails to satisfy our yearning to know who we are and where we came from. And it leaves us with no alternative but to suspend our disbelief concerning Adam and Eve, and place our faith in the 'fact' that the first man was created from clay *by God*. It is thus God who should be regarded as our ultimate ancestor, mooring post and safe haven.

But who, or what, is God? It is at this point that *faith* traditionally enters the equation. We are not supposed to know who or what God is, or where he came from, for God is supposed to be a mysterious and unknowable being. Instead, we are told that the essence of religion is to have *faith* in this elusive being, and *faith*, too, in the Church as the sole intermediary between man and God. Thus we are steered away from the *knowledge* of origins, and are instead sold *faith* as a substitute for it.

Ironically, as we enter the 21st century AD, it is science rather than religion which is providing the necessary insights into our past. It is science which has determined the age of the Earth as 4.6 billion years. It is science which has explained how we evolved from earlier creatures by a process of natural selection (now accepted by the Church after a 140-year period of reflection). It is science which has dated the first hominids to several million years ago and *Homo sapiens* to less than 200,000 years ago. And it is science which has introduced us (via genetic studies) to a 'most recent common ancestor' of all mankind, known as 'mitochondrial Eve'. In all of these matters, science has begun to bind us back to our long lost past, and has thus become more religious than religion itself.

The Church, in contrast, binds us back only to *the mystery* of God. There is the mystery of how he created mankind and then destroyed mankind with the Flood of Noah; there is the mystery of the Immaculate Conception of Jesus Christ within the womb of the Virgin Mary, and there is the mystery of how Christ's body rose from the tomb after three days. All of these mysteries are supposed to be beyond the human ken – unfathomable and irresolvable. And logic thus dictates that faith in God is the 'be all and end all' of the religious quest.

This combination of faith and mystery has worked extremely well for the Church during the past two thousand years, but only because of poor education and superstition among the masses. As Isaac Newton once famously remarked: 'tis the temper of the hot and superstitious part of mankind in matters of religion ever to be fond of mysteries, and for that reason to like best what they understand least.'

But such simple-mindedness is no longer in the ascendancy today. On the contrary, the 21st century attitude – even among regular Churchgoers – is one of rationality, scepticism and materialism. In this consumer age, everything is seen as a commodity to be purchased – even religion – and we will buy nothing unless we know what it is and where it came from. For example, when we go to buy a new car, we expect to be told what type of engine is under the bonnet, where it was manufactured and how it works; we do not expect to be told "sorry, but it's a mystery."

The Church, then, has a 'product' which is becoming increasingly difficult to sell to a sceptical public – a public which sees no need for further lessons about morals but instead demands that religion live up to the literal meaning of its name and bind us all back to our origins. The rational man of the 21st century wants to know who he is and where he came from, and he expects to be told exactly how God created mankind. He does not want to be told "sorry, but it's a mystery".

At issue here are the mysteries which lie at the heart of the Church, the Bible and God. Rational man is no longer prepared to buy into these mysteries on the basis of faith alone. He wants to know how the Church was founded, when the Bible was written, and how the ideas therein evolved during the many centuries which preceded the writing of it.

This is where this book enters the equation. Although I am not an apologist for modern consumerism, it is right in this instance that one of the world's most sacrosanct religious texts should be regarded as a product to be inspected with all due diligence. The Bible is, after all, only a 'fragment of the writings of the Bible World', as the eminent scholar Cyrus H. Gordon once put it, and its roots can be traced back to the earlier religions of the ancient Near East – in particular to the beliefs of the ancient Egyptians and Sumerians, who founded civilisation as we know it some six thousand years ago.

In 1956, Samuel N. Kramer, one of the world's foremost translators of the Sumerian texts, listed thirty-nine Sumerian 'firsts' in man's recorded history, including the first cosmogony (similar to Genesis) and the first 'Noah'. In his book *History Begins at Sumer*, Kramer spelled out in no uncertain terms just how important was the connection between the Bible and the earlier writings of the ancient Near East:

> Archaeological discoveries made in Egypt and in the Near East in the past hundred years have opened our eyes to a spiritual and cultural heritage undreamed of by earlier generations... a bright and revealing light has been shed on the background and origin of the Bible itself. We can now see that this greatest of literary classics did not come upon the scene full-blown, like an artificial flower in a vacuum; its roots reach deep into the distant past and spread wide across the surrounding lands. Both in form and content, the biblical books bear no little resemblance to the literatures created by earlier civilisations in the Near East.

According to this paradigm – of a religion conceived by the mind of man – it should be possible to trace the roots of Judaism and Christianity back to the earliest known religions of ancient Egypt and Mesopotamia, and thus shine a light on the origins of the Bible. Our quest in this book, in a nutshell, is to *understand* the Bible by *standing under* it.

This, it must be said, is not a new approach, but rather a redoubling of the efforts made by many earlier scholars. It must be stressed, however, that earlier scholars hit a stumbling block which could not be overcome, namely a preponderance of obscure metaphors and idioms in the ancient Egyptian and Sumerian texts. This book is different in the sense that these metaphors and idioms *can* now be decoded, thus allowing us to see the world through the eyes of the ancients for the first time. The result, I am pleased to report, is a religion which not only makes perfect sense but was also truly religious, for it bound the ancients back to the place whence they said they had come – a great mooring post *in the Sky* which we today know only vaguely as 'Heaven' or 'God'.

In the chapters which follow, you, the reader, will learn all about the Heaven of the ancients, and you will learn exactly how and why the writers of the Old Testament occulted the secrets of mankind's oldest known religion. Furthermore, you will see why the New Testament story of Jesus Christ marked a renaissance of the old pagan philosophy, and you will come to understand why this story was written in the form of an ingenious esoteric parable – a parable which only made sense to those who had been initiated into the secrets of the ancient Mysteries.

Finally, I would remind readers that it does not follow automatically that the beliefs of the ancients are necessarily true, scientifically, and we must therefore try to moderate our excitement at the revelations in this book. Ultimately, it is to modern science that we must turn if we are to judge whether the secret 'truth' of the ancients is, or is not, a Truth with a capital 'T'. It is in the depths of space that NASA and the Vatican must seek scientific knowledge concerning the lost paradise of man and the fingerprints of God.

Reading Notes

I have used male pronouns throughout this book, along with sporadic references to 'man' and 'men' which are obviously intended to refer to the human population of both men *and women*. No offence is intended towards women, and I do not in any way wish to suggest an inequality between the sexes. I have followed this practice purely to avoid the constant clumsiness of 'he or she', 'himself or herself', 'his or her' and so on. Readers should assume the alternatives whenever appropriate.

In all quotations, the emphasis is *mine* and not the original, except where clearly indicated with the words 'original emphasis'.

Where quotations include dots thus: '...', this indicates a section of the passage which has been omitted for the sake of being concise.

Where quotations include dots thus: ' . . . ', this indicates a lacuna in the original text, i.e. a section which is damaged and illegible.

CHAPTER ONE

WHAT'S THE SECRET?

**I will open my mouth in parables, I will utter things
hidden since the creation of the world.**

(Jesus Christ, in the Gospel of Matthew)

In 1903, a team of German archaeologists, led by Walter Andrae, began excavations at the site of Assur, the oldest capital of the ancient Assyrian empire.[1] The site, situated on the western bank of the river Tigris, 300 kilometres north of modern Baghdad, had once been the pride and joy of the Assyrian empire; its palaces, temples and ziggurats had been among the most impressive wonders of the ancient world. Now, however, the 'city' was just a vast shapeless mound, covered with grass. The only signs of its former glory were potsherds and baked mudbricks, the latter stamped with the distinctive wedge-shaped writing of the Assyrians.

Nevertheless, what came out of these ruins was very special indeed. Walter Andrae and his men soon managed to discover the ruins of the city's temple and palace libraries, and between 1903 and 1914 they recovered thousands of small clay tablets, which told the story of Assur and its resident deities, who had founded the city in an age long ago.

One of these clay tablets proved to have especial significance. Its text, divided into three columns, told the story of the creation of mankind by the gods. One column told the story in the Sumerian language (then regarded as a classical language, as Greek and Latin are regarded today). Another column told the same story in the Akkadian language of those times (*c.* 800 BC per the best estimates). But the remaining column – the first of the three – contained a series of symbols which was unlike any text previously encountered (see Plate 24). These symbols could not be translated, and they remain undeciphered to this day.

This tablet – first translated in 1916 by the German Assyriologist Erich Ebeling – was later published in English by Alexander Heidel, an

Assyriologist at the University of Chicago, who gave it the rather innocuous title *Another Account of the Creation of Man*.[2] As for the mysterious and indecipherable symbols, Heidel commented that: '(they) are most likely symbols of some kind of secret writing'.

Why would the ancient scribes of Assur have wished to annotate a legend of the creation of man with an esoteric commentary? Before we read Heidel's further intriguing comment on this, let us first take a look at what the translatable portion of the text actually says.

The Assyrian creation story begins, rather like the biblical book of Genesis, by referring to the very beginning of time, 'when Heaven had been separated from Earth – its distant trusty twin'. Then it relates how the great gods – Anu, Enlil, Shamash and Ea – seated themselves in the assembly of the gods, and decided what to do next. Enlil said:

> "Now that the destinies of Heaven and Earth have been fixed,
> Trench and canal have been given their right courses,
> The banks of the Tigris and the Euphrates have been established,
> What else shall we do?
> What else shall we create?"
> The great gods who were present... gave Enlil this answer:
> "In Uzumua, the Bond of Heaven-and-Earth,
> Let us slay two Lamga-gods.
> With their blood let us create mankind,
> The service of the gods to be their lot...
> Let their names [i.e. the Lamga-gods] be Ulligarra and Zalgarra..."[3]

Who were Ulligarra and Zalgarra? According to Alexander Heidel, they were 'the first two human beings'. The text, however, identifies them as fully fledged gods.[4]

What happened next is even more intriguing. Ulligarra and Zalgarra proceeded to create mankind, apparently in their own image – the same means used by the Hebrew God, Elohim, in the first chapter of the book of Genesis. The relevant part of the text reads:

> Aruru, the great lady of the gods, who is fit for rulership,
> Ordained for them [Ulligarra and Zalgarra] great destinies:
> Skilled worker to produce for skilled worker,
> And unskilled worker for unskilled worker,
> Springing up by themselves like grain from the ground.
> A thing which, like the stars of the heavens, shall not be changed
>   forever.[5]

Thus was mankind created from divine blood. And it all happened at a place called Uzumua, meaning 'Flesh-Producer', which was also known as 'the Bond of Heaven-and-Earth'.[6]

What is the meaning of this legend? How could mankind be created from divine 'blood'? What was the significance of the sacred Bond of Heaven-and-Earth? Why had Heaven been 'separated' from Earth in the beginning? And how was it that Earth was 'the distant trusty twin' of Heaven?

The questions arising from this tablet – not to mention many other tablets like it – are endless. But satisfactory answers there are none, just a deafening silence from academics, even after the passage of nearly a hundred years since the translation of the text.

Are we perhaps missing some significant, deeper import? It would appear that the ancient scribes might well have thought so, for the two translatable sections of the tablet were brought to a close with the following enigmatic words:

> These great destinies did Anu, Enlil, Ea and Ninmah – the great gods – decree for them [Ulligarra and Zalgarra].
> In the place where mankind was created, there was Nisaba [the goddess of writing and wisdom] firmly established.
> *Let the wise teach the mystery to the wise.*[7]

What was the significance of this cryptic last line? Alexander Heidel offered the following intriguing comment:

> This legend was meant *only for the initiated*, which may account for the mysterious signs on the first column of the tablet.[8]

So, what we appear to have in this tiny tablet is a strong indication of a *mystery school* which was in existence some 2,800 years ago – a mystery school which preserved an esoteric meaning concerning the so-called 'myth' of the creation.

But as for what that esoteric meaning might be, we, the common folk of today, are no wiser than the common populace in Assur of 800 BC, for such is the nature of mystery schools that the uninitiated (the vast majority) have always been excluded from knowledge of the inner secrets. That, dear reader, means: "the likes of you and I".

The Lips are Sealed

Much of what we know about the past has been handed down to us by Greek historians and philosophers, such as Pythagoras, Herodotus, Plato, Aristotle and Plutarch, several of whom travelled widely throughout the ancient world. But it is often overlooked that these authorities were not allowed to speak freely about everything they learned. They could write about the 'lesser mysteries' (the public rituals), which were open to all-comers, but they were forbidden to write about the so-called 'greater mysteries'.[9]

Take Herodotus, for example. During the 5th century BC, the 'Father of History' travelled through the Nile Valley, where he won the trust of the Egyptian priests, and was thus permitted to learn something of the mysteries of the Egyptian gods. But whatever it was that this eminent historian saw and heard, we will never know. Instead, Herodotus wrote:

> On this lake it is that the Egyptians represent by night his suffering –
> he whose name I refrain from mentioning – and this representation
> they call their Mysteries. I know well the whole course of the
> proceedings in these ceremonies, but they shall not pass my lips.[10]

This was secrecy taken to an extreme, and a more relaxed approach is evident in the work of later Greek writers. For example, by the time of Plutarch, a philosopher of the 1st century AD, the name of the suffering Egyptian god had become well-known – it was Osiris – and it had also become acceptable to describe certain aspects of the Egyptian Mysteries. But even then, only the barest outline of the Mysteries was revealed, as in the following statement by Plutarch:

> When the Sun was in Scorpio, in the month of *Athyr*, the Egyptians
> enclosed the body of their god Osiris in an ark or chest, and during this
> ceremony a great annual festival was celebrated. Three days after the
> priests had enclosed Osiris in the ark, they pretended to have found
> him again.[11]

Elsewhere in his writings, however, Plutarch displayed a remarkable coyness. For example, when he presented the various explanations of the Osiris Mysteries, he was notably shy concerning the legend of Osiris as a cleaved tree-trunk, stating that this was 'intermixed with such of their mysteries as may not be revealed'.[12] Once again it becomes evident that the greater mysteries were withheld deliberately, for fear of breaking a vow of silence. And our knowledge of ancient religious belief systems has consequently been impoverished to a very serious extent.

The Mysteries of Eleusis

This distinction between the greater mysteries and the lesser mysteries is particularly evident in the Eleusinian Mysteries – perhaps the most famous of all the ancient Mysteries – which were performed at the Greek city of Eleusis from *c.* 1500 BC. The eminent mythologist Mircea Eliade summarised the various levels of initiation into the Eleusinian Mysteries as follows:

> There were the Lesser Mysteries, the rites of the Greater Mysteries (the *teletai*) and the final experience, the *epopteia*. The true secrets of the *teletai* and *epopteia* have never been divulged.[13]

It is indeed quite amazing that these secrets were never revealed despite the fact that the Eleusinian Mysteries were performed every year for approximately *two thousand years* (ending *c.* 500 AD). Let it never be said that ancient mystery schools were incapable of safeguarding their secrets.

Modern scholars have, nevertheless, made attempts to synthesise the little that we do know and speculate as to the nature and meaning of the secret rites. What emerges is a most intriguing picture. Allow me, briefly, to paint a picture of what the Eleusinian rituals were all about.

At the heart of the Eleusinian Mysteries was the story of Persephone, the daughter of the goddess Demeter. Persephone had been kidnapped by the god Hades, and dragged off to his domain in the underworld (i.e. the subterranean region). Demeter, it was said, had then set off in search of Persephone. She came down from Mount Olympus to Eleusis and demanded that a great temple be built for her, with an altar beneath it. Then, she retired inside the temple, causing a terrible drought on the Earth.[14]

Eventually, Demeter was reunited with Persephone, but only through the intervention of Zeus, who ordered Hades to return the kidnapped daughter. Even then, Hades tricked Persephone into eating a pomegranate seed, and this – the food of the underworld – caused Persephone to have to return to the underworld for four months every year. Despite this setback, Demeter was delighted to have her daughter back, and thus left her temple and went back up to Mount Olympus. Before she did so, however, she revealed her rites and taught all her mysteries to mankind.

Scholars believe that the *lesser* mysteries of Eleusis revolved around a public re-enactment of the story as related above – the loss of the daughter, the wanderings of Demeter in search of her, and the eventual reunion of mother and daughter.

But what of the *greater* mysteries? In the 3rd century AD, Hippolytus wrote that the *epopteia* – the final experience – consisted of the solemn presentation of an ear of wheat to the candidates. This, we might surmise, marked the miraculous beginning of agriculture on the Earth, but perhaps a great deal more besides. Hippolytus added that:

> During the night, in the midst of a brilliant fire... the hierophant [high priest] cries out: "Holy Brimo [i.e. the Queen of the Dead] has borne a sacred child, Brimos!". That is: the Powerful One [feminine] has given birth to the Powerful One [masculine].[15]

This account rings true with other sources, which confirm that the final vision – the *epopteia* – took place in the presence of a fire, or a dazzling light.[16]

But what should we make of the claim of the 5th century Greek philosopher Proclus? He claimed that initiates into the greater Eleusinian Mysteries would look skywards and cry "Rain!", and then look to the Earth and cry "Conceive!". According to Hippolytus, these two words – 'rain' and 'conceive' – together constituted the great secret of the Mysteries.[17]

It is not to be doubted that certain words (e.g. rain, conceive), certain symbols (e.g. the ear of wheat) and certain rituals (e.g. the fire in the night) did carry a profound esoteric meaning to initiates in the Eleusinian Mysteries, just as the sliced apple carried a profound meaning to initiates in the Pythagorean Mysteries. But the whole point is that these words, symbols and rituals revealed everything and nothing simultaneously; they revealed *everything* to one who had seen the light (and had the knowledge), and they revealed *nothing* to the one who was in darkness (and had ignorance). Hence initiates such as Hippolytus and Proclus could say what they did, safe in the knowledge that they were not betraying their vows of secrecy.

It is indeed noticeable that, despite all the tantalising clues outlined above, modern scholars have never penetrated the esoteric meaning of the Eleusinian symbolism. There could not be a clearer indication of the yawning gap which exists between our way of thinking and that of the ancients.

The Christian Mysteries

The Eleusinian Mysteries were by no means the only Mysteries in ancient Greece. To cite but a few examples, there were the Mysteries of the Cabiri (otherwise known as the Samothracian Mysteries), the Mysteries of Sabazius, the Mysteries of Apollo, the Mysteries of Orpheus, the Mysteries of Hecate and the Mysteries of Dionysus. In addition, the Mysteries of Demeter were celebrated at towns other than Eleusis.

At the same time, in the rest of the world, there were mystery schools in lands as far apart as Egypt, India, Mesopotamia (modern-day Iraq), and doubtless in many other places of which we are only dimly aware.

In all of these mystery schools, there were lesser mysteries and greater mysteries; and in respect of the latter, the initiates maintained unfailingly their strict code of silence. Today, we have an astonishingly sparse knowledge of what the whole thing was about.

Which brings us to the subject of Christianity. When this religion emerged in the 1st century AD, it did so against furious competition from other religions, cults and mystery schools, including some of those mentioned above. One of the biggest threats came from a religion called Mithraism, which had been imported from Persia into the Roman empire. But a more immediate threat came from within – from the so-called 'gnostic' Christians – who rejected the authority of the Church, and promoted their own independent ideas about the teachings of Jesus Christ.

One of the most famous gnostic teachers was Valentinus, who taught at Alexandria, and came to Rome in AD 140. According to Tertullian (an early Christian theologian), the followers of Valentinus underwent initiations which were comparable to those of the Eleusinian Mysteries. Tertullian claimed that:

> (They) first beset all access to their group with tormenting conditions; and they require a long initiation before they enroll their members, even instruction for five years for their adept students, so that they may educate their opinions by the suspension of full knowledge, and, apparently, raise the value of their Mysteries in proportion to the longing for them which they have created. Then follows the duty of silence...[18]

According to Bishop Irenaeus, one of the early leaders of the Christian Church, the gnostic followers of Valentinus would hold meetings at which they would flout openly the authority of the Church, by alleging that the Church's sacraments of baptism and the Eucharist were not a complete initiation into the Christian faith, but only the first steps.[19] In other words, the gnostics were suggesting that the Church taught *only the elementary doctrines*, whilst the initiations of Valentinus offered much greater revelations concerning the mysteries of Christ – i.e. the secret mysteries and higher teachings, which were forbidden to the masses.

These higher teachings were never written down – for the ancient mystery schools were paranoid about secrecy – but the gnostics did maintain various books which criticised many aspects of the official Church dogma, such as the virgin birth and the bodily resurrection of Christ, which the gnostics claimed were naive misunderstandings.[20] Some of these books alluded to a great secret, which was being withheld deliberately from Christians. The *Secret Book of John*, for example, opened with an offer to reveal 'the mysteries and the things hidden in silence' which had been taught to John by Jesus himself.[21] These secrets, needless to say, were not spelled out for the uneducated eye, but were instead conveyed by means of enigmatic metaphors and parables.

Might there be some truth in the gnostics' accusation that the Church was withholding its higher teachings? Indeed there might be, according to a letter from Clement, one of the early Church fathers, to a man named Theodore, who had written to him complaining about a certain gnostic sect known as the Carpocratians. In his letter of reply, Clement referred to 'things not to be uttered', and acknowledged the existence of a 'truth hidden by seven veils'. He also displayed his familiarity with initiations and the greater mysteries of religion. Here is the text of this amazing passage in Clement's letter:

> He [Mark] composed a more spiritual Gospel for the use of those who were being perfected. Nevertheless, he yet did not divulge *the things not to be uttered*, nor did he write down the hierophantic teachings of the Lord, but to the stories already written he added yet others and, moreover, brought in certain sayings of which he knew the interpretation would, as a mystagogue, *lead the hearers into the innermost sanctuary of that truth hidden by seven (veils)*. Thus, in sum, he prearranged matters, neither grudgingly nor incautiously, in my opinion, and, dying, he left his composition to the church in Alexandria, where it even yet is most carefully guarded, *being read only to those who are being initiated into the great mysteries.*[22]

Did the early Church leaders know far more than they let on? Were they themselves initiated into the greater mysteries of Jesus Christ – mysteries which, by definition, had to be restricted to the few, and withheld from the masses? Was this the purpose of the 'seven veils'?

From what we know of early Christianity, entrance into it was not unlike an initiation into a mystery school. Prospective candidates had to go through a probationary period, a doctrinal instruction, a memorising of words, and a ritual baptism – all things which were characteristic of mystery schools at the time.

The Lion Handbook on *The History of Christianity* (an authoritative source on this subject) summarises the process of entry into the Church community as follows:

> From an early period, considerable preparation was considered necessary before baptism took place. Candidates often had a period of

three years' probation, to see if they were of good character. Then came a period of intensive instruction in Christian doctrine, often involving memorising a short statement of Christian belief (the 'creed'). It was very likely that the creed began in the form of questions put to the candidate when he was baptised...[23]

When we think about it, this induction into Christianity sounds very much like a first-stage induction into a mystery school. And such a thought is not altogether implausible when Christianity is viewed in the context of the early centuries of our era, when virtually all religions in the West were essentially mystery schools at heart.

Of course, a great deal of water has passed under the bridge during the last two thousand years, and Christianity can hardly be called a mystery school today. And yet it cannot be denied that mysteries are at the very heart of modern Christianity. In the Catholic Mass, for example, the bread and the wine are supposedly transformed into the body and the blood of Jesus Christ by the supernatural presence of Jesus Christ. This is a great mystery. In addition, it should be stressed that the entire Christian theology is a mystery from start to finish – from the mystery of Christ's birth (to the Virgin Mary), to the mystery of Christ's miracles, to the ultimate mystery of Christ's bodily resurrection following his death by crucifixion. And above all, there is the mystery of how the shedding of Christ's blood managed to wash away the sins of mankind and offer us all access to the blessed kingdom of God.

Furthermore, in the New Testament letters of Paul – the Christian missionary whom many regard as the true founder of Christianity – the word 'mystery' appears no less than seventeen times.[24] For example, in his 'Letter to the Corinthians', Paul wrote:

Behold, I show you a mystery – we shall not all sleep, but we shall all be changed [i.e. resurrected to life in spiritual bodies].[25]

Elsewhere, Paul claimed to have knowledge of the 'mystery of Christ', the 'mystery of Christ and the Church', the 'mystery of the gospel', and the 'mystery of God and Christ'.[26]

Are these the same kind of mysteries as were being taught by the mystery schools of the early centuries AD? The word translated as 'mystery' in the New Testament is the Greek term *mysterion*, and an authoritative modern source on biblical scripture states that:

The Greek word *mysterion*, [sometimes] translated 'sacred secret', has reference primarily to *that which is known by those who are initiated*. In the ancient mystery religions that flourished in the time of the early

Christian congregation, those who wished to take part in the mystery celebrations had to undergo initiation... Those initiated into them were bound by a vow of silence, not to reveal the secrets.[27]

It is also pertinent to note that the Greek term *mysterion* was derived from the verb *musteion*, meaning 'to close the eyes or the mouth'.[28] Such was the nature of the ancient Mysteries that it was indeed required of initiates to *close their eyes* at certain parts of their initiation, and *close their mouths* (concerning the revelations) for ever afterwards.

Some authorities, it must be said, claim that the mysteries known to Paul were different from the pagan or gnostic Mysteries, on the basis that the mysteries were being revealed and proclaimed openly to the world, rather than being withheld and kept secret from the masses. But this is not entirely true, for there is a huge difference between making *the existence* of a mystery manifest (which Paul certainly *did* do) and making *the esoteric meaning* of a mystery manifest (which Paul certainly *did not* do).

All of this means that we are fully entitled to ask whether Paul was an initiate into certain mysteries of Christ – *the meaning of which has never been revealed to the wider congregation of Christians.*

Immediately, one thinks of the account of Paul's conversion on the road to Damascus. In the New Testament's Acts of Apostles, we read:

Suddenly there shined round about him [Saul, i.e. Paul] a light from Heaven. And he fell to the ground, and heard a voice [the spiritual Jesus] saying: "Saul, Saul, why are you persecuting me?".[29]

As we shall see in a short while, the sudden appearance of a bright light is a classic characteristic of a mystery school initiation. Did Saul really have a supernatural encounter? Or does this account preserve a reference to his initiation, written in a coded language?

There are indeed several further clues to suggest that the road-to-Damascus incident was an initiation.

Firstly, it is interesting to note that Saul suffered blindness after the vision of the light. Such blindness, symbolising darkness, was followed by an opening of the eyes three days later (Acts 9:9 & 9:18). The three-day period was widely used for ancient initiations, especially those where the candidate was deprived of light. The closing of the eyes is indeed the root meaning of the term 'mystery', as explained earlier. Overall, the road-to-Damascus incident is highly evocative of a mystery school initiate acquiring esoteric wisdom.

Secondly, we are told that Saul went without food or drink for the same three days during which he lost his sight. Fasting, too, is a feature of many ancient mystery school initiations, and seems to be referred to as such in Paul's 'Letter to the Philippians', in which he wrote:

> Everywhere and in all things, I have been *initiated into the secret* of being full and being hungry – having an abundance and suffering need.[30]

Thirdly, it is surely significant that Paul was baptised immediately after his eyes were opened (Acts 9:18). Baptism marked the entry into the Christian cult, and was also a purification rite in many other ancient mystery traditions.

Fourthly, we should not miss the point that this incident marked the sudden transformation of Saul from persecutor of Christians to one of their greatest spokesmen. Such a transformation – equivalent to a personal *rebirth* – was a crucial element in ancient initiations. It would thus seem likely that Saul's change of name to 'Paul' dates to this very incident, especially as the name Paul, meaning 'small', seems to evoke the mystery of the resurrection to Heaven through Christ. I am referring here to the gnostic text written by Valentinus, in which Jesus stated that: "I became very small, so that through my humility I might take you up to the great height, whence you had fallen."[31] The change of name from Saul to Paul would thus have been highly symbolic, and would be typical of the new names which were often given to initiates into the ancient mystery schools.

Fifthly, the gnostic teacher Valentinus confirmed that Paul had indeed been initiated into a secret doctrine of God, and had initiated others, but only the select few who were 'spiritually mature' and ready to receive it.[32] One of these initiates, named Theudas, had apparently initiated Valentinus. And Valentinus offered, in turn, to initiate others – but again only those who were mature, for the immature would not be able to comprehend the wisdom.[33]

Sixthly, and finally, we return to the words of Paul himself. In his first letter to the Corinthians, he wrote 'we speak the wisdom of God in a mystery', whilst in his second letter to the Corinthians he wrote of himself as one who had been 'caught up' (initiated?) to the Third Heaven (the third 'degree' of the Mysteries?) where he heard 'unspeakable words, which it is unlawful for a man to utter'.[34] Modern scholars are indeed inclined to think that Paul *was* privy to some kind of secret knowledge.[35]

In summary, a very strong case can be made that Paul – the man whom many regard as the founder of Christianity – was initiated into secrets which were not fully divulged in his letters, and which have never been spelled out clearly in Christian texts and rituals. On the contrary, the very nature of these secrets would have meant that they could only be passed on safely (discreetly) by means of verbal instruction to the chosen few, or by esoteric code-words and parables, which could only be understood by the chosen few.

You and I, dear readers, with very few (if any) exceptions, are *not* among this 'chosen few'.

The Mystery of the Gospels

So, we now know all about the secret wisdom of Paul, but what about that other founder of Christianity – Jesus Christ himself? What about the gospels which described his teachings? Might they, too, contain a hidden wisdom of Christ, and a hidden wisdom of God – *for initiates only*?

One of the most remarkable things about the gospels, which is not widely appreciated, is that they constitute one huge riddle or mystery play concerning *the identity of Jesus Christ*. All of the characters in this mystery play seemed to spend their time speculating on the question of who Jesus actually was. Was he the Son of God? The Son of David? The Messiah called Christ? The reincarnation of Elijah? Just another prophet? Who was he?

These questions of Jesus's identity, which are repeated in numerous and diverse scenarios throughout the gospels, highlight a fact the importance of which has never been fully recognised – namely that Jesus claimed not to be the Son of *God*, but rather the Son of *Man*.

True, Jesus did on some occasions seem to acknowledge that he was the Son of God, but he did so only in roundabout ways. For example, one such roundabout way was for Jesus to *fail to contradict an assertion* by someone else that he was the Son of God, as occurs in Matthew 14:33, John 6:69, and John 11:27.

A second roundabout way was for Jesus to utter words suggestive that he was the Son of God, but *only by assenting to words which were spoken by someone else*. For example, in Matthew 16:16, Simon Peter suggested that Jesus was 'the Son of the living God', and Jesus indicated that Simon Peter was correct (notably, Simon Peter had worked this out for himself rather than being told).[36] Then, in Matthew 26:63, the high priest asked Jesus whether he was the Son of God, and Jesus simply replied: "Thou hast said it." As a third example, in Luke 22:70, the Jewish elders accused Jesus of claiming to be the Son of God, and Jesus simply replied: "Ye say that I am."

On the other hand, as mentioned earlier, Jesus referred to himself *frequently and explicitly* as the Son of Man; there was no evasiveness at all with this title. *Why* was Jesus so *evasive* about being the Son of God? And *why* was he so *explicit* in acknowledging himself to be the Son of Man? And what did the title Son of Man actually mean?

According to one biblical expert, the title Son of Man 'simply stressed the weakness and mortality of the human condition', and therefore emphasised that Jesus had incarnated into *human* flesh.[37] But this makes no sense when we read passages such as the following one from the gospel of John:

> No man has ever gone up to Heaven except he that came down from Heaven – the Son of Man.[38]

If the title Son of Man 'simply stressed the weakness and mortality of the human condition', as has been suggested, how was it that this same Son of Man was one who had come down from Heaven, and one who would return to Heaven? It makes no sense.

Nor did it make sense to the disciples. In the gospel of Mark, when Jesus told his disciples that he, the Son of Man, would be delivered into the hands of men, be killed, and then rise on the third day, the disciples 'understood not that saying, and were afraid to ask him'.[39] The gospel of Luke adds that the meaning of the saying was 'hidden from them, so that they perceived it not'.[40]

Is the meaning hidden from us, too? Do we really understand who Jesus Christ was, and how he rose from the dead? It is, after all, a mystery, that much is for certain. And if it is a mystery, then it surely follows, according to the rules of the ancient mysteries, that we – the common folk – *are not supposed to know the secret of the esoteric meaning*.

Consider, now, the following quotation from the gospel of Mark, where Jesus said to his disciples:

> To you, the mystery of the kingdom of God has been given. But to those who are on the outside, all things are done in parables; so that they may indeed see but not perceive, and may indeed hear but not understand.[41]

This is, of course, the classic stratagem of the mystery schools, in order to keep the profane from understanding the mysteries. Note the references in this passage to '*mystery*', and '*those on the outside*'. The parables of Jesus Christ are surely no different in nature from the symbols and code-words of mystery schools, such as the ear of wheat, or the cries of "Rain" and "Conceive" in the Eleusinian Mysteries.

The big question, of course, is this: if the disciples of Jesus were given a secret knowledge (as is attested by the early Church writers), would that knowledge end up being recorded for posterity in the gospels of Matthew, Mark, Luke and John?

The simple answer is: *"Of course not!"*. The whole point was that such knowledge was *secret* – and should be transmitted only to the select few who had been prepared by the necessary degrees of initiation. And this transmission was always *verbal*. The last place we would expect to find the secret wisdom spelled out is in the *written* gospels.

Hence, in the 4th century AD, Chrysostom, Bishop of Constantinople, wrote:

> I wish to speak openly: but I dare not, on account of those who are not initiated. I shall therefore avail myself of disguised terms, discoursing in a shadowy manner...[42]

Similarly, in the 4th century AD, Cyril, the Bishop of Jerusalem, wrote:

> The Lord spoke in parables to his hearers in general; but to his disciples he explained in private the parables and allegories which he spoke in public... the Church reveals its mysteries to those who have advanced beyond the class of Catechumens [initiates for baptism]: we employ obscure terms with others.[43]

It would thus seem that the disciples were the select few who received the teachings of Jesus, whilst outsiders were excluded. This point is confirmed, incidentally, by the writings of the gnostic teacher Valentinus, who alleged that the disciples kept the esoteric meaning of the parables secret, and transmitted them only to those who had proven themselves to be spiritually mature, thus qualifying for 'initiation into gnosis'.[44]

It thus behoves us to ask whether we really understand the meaning of the parables in the gospels, not to mention the various stories of Jesus walking on water, turning water into wine, and feeding thousands of people with bread and fishes. We might like to think that we understand, but do we really? After completing the remainder of this book, readers might well wish to pause and reconsider.

It is of especial significance that the parables of Jesus related to *things which had been hidden since the beginning of the world*. Hence the famous quotation of Jesus from the gospel of Matthew that was cited at the beginning of this chapter:

> I will open my mouth in parables, I will utter things hidden since the creation of the world.[45]

This same thought was echoed repeatedly by Saul/Paul, who received his initiation-like vision of Christ on the road to Damascus. In his writings, Paul stressed frequently the idea of a secret relating to the beginning of the world, as the following examples demonstrate very clearly:

But we speak the wisdom of God in *a mystery* – that which was hidden – which God ordained for our glory *before the world began.*[46]

And to make all men see what is the fellowship of *the mystery*, which has been hidden in God *since the beginning of the world.*[47]

Now to him who is able to establish you according to my gospel, and the preaching of Jesus Christ, according to the revelation of *the mystery which was kept secret since the world began...*[48]

Jesus and Paul, then, were insistent that the mysteries of Christianity referred to the beginning of the world. Which, rather curiously, brings us back to where we started – to ancient Assur eight centuries before Christ. It was then that the scribes recorded a tale of the creation of Heaven and Earth at the beginning of time, and appended to it a commentary in secret writing. It was a tale which related the creation of mankind by Ulligarra and Zalgarra, who created men in their own image, causing them to 'spring up like grain from the ground'.

Perhaps it is no coincidence that Jesus Christ also taught the parable of God the sower, and man the seed.[49]

The Secret-of-Secrets

At this point, many readers will be growing impatient to know what the fuss was all about. Was there really some ultimate secret which was revealed at the end of the arduous initiations?

Doubtless the same questions were asked by outsiders in ancient times. In the *Bacchae*, the Greek dramatist Euripides (5th century BC) made Pentheus ask about the Mysteries of Dionysus: "These Mysteries, what are they?" In response, the god Dionysus replied: "Their secrecy forbids communicating them to those who are not Bacchants." Pentheus, persisting, then asked: "What use are they to those who celebrate them?" To which Dionysus replied: "It is not permitted thee to learn that, but they are things worthy to be known."[50]

A similar vagueness was used to refer to the Mysteries of Demeter. According to one report, they were 'awful mysteries which no-one may in any way transgress or pry into or utter, for deep awe of the gods checks the voice.'[51] Other ancient writers, however, dropped hints which were much more revealing. Isocrates (4th century BC) stated that initiation into the Mysteries of Demeter brought hope in regard to 'the end of life and all eternity'.[52]

Whatever the secret was, we know that it had something to do with the gods, or – in the case of the Eleusinian Mysteries – the goddesses, Demeter and Persephone. Somehow, the revelations concerning these goddesses would enable the initiate to overcome the obstacles of the underworld and achieve some kind of blissful life after death. Hence the author of the *Homeric Hymn to Demeter* wrote:

> Happy is he among men on Earth who has seen these mysteries! But he who is uninitiate, and who has no part in them, never has a chance of such happiness once he is dead, down in the darkness and gloom.[53]

Aristotle (4th century BC) said something similar – that the main point of initiations into the various mystery religions was to enable candidates 'to experience certain emotions and to be put in a certain disposition', specifically with regard to the experience of death and rebirth.[54] The implication is obvious – that the initiatory experience was a trial run, which would prepare the candidate for the real thing, when he would eventually leave this world for the next.

The gnostic Christians would have agreed. According to the teacher Theodotus (2nd century AD), the aim of gnosticism was to create understanding of:

> ... who we were, and what we have become. Where we were... whither we are hastening. From what we are being released. What birth is, and what is rebirth.[55]

Ultimately, this amounted to a knowledge of God, or the gods, and their creation of mankind. Hence, with regard to the Orphic Mysteries, we know that the final level of initiation comprised a 'Secret-of-secrets' which was 'a knowledge of the true God'.[56] Such was the nature of this Secret-of-secrets that it came as a total surprise, even to the initiate who was fully prepared. The revelation, we are told, 'startled their ears' and 'overturned their preconceived opinions'.[57]

Today, it is easy to scoff at these claims, and dismiss the ancient mystery schools as a collection of crackpot cults. We are, after all, brought up in a very sceptical world, and there is no solid evidence that the mystery schools really knew of any great secret whatsoever. Moreover, it would have been perfectly possible for them to *pretend* that they knew rather more than they did.

The sceptic might even suggest that if there was some great secret, it would most likely have applied to some superstitious belief in life after death. Thus, it might be argued that the secret would be irrelevant to the hard-headed, scientific man of the 21st century.

This, however, would be taking scepticism too far, for even if we take a worst-case scenario, an unveiling of the ancient secrets would provide historians with a fascinating insight into the development of European culture. In this respect, we should mark the words of Mircea Eliade, who wrote in 1978:

> Very little is known about the Eleusinian Mysteries and the earliest manifestations of Orphism; yet the fascination that they have exercised over the best minds of Europe for more than twenty centuries constitutes a *religious fact* that is highly significant and whose consequences have not yet been properly understood.[58]

As Eliade pointed out, the mystery schools were effectively mystery *religions*, and an unveiling of their secrets would thus have much to teach us about the religious baggage which we carry into the 21st century and beyond. And this would be especially true if Christianity started out as a mystery school, as I suggested earlier. If we could decode an esoteric meaning behind the New Testament gospels, would it not be a priceless discovery?

It thus behoves us to dig deeper into these ancient mysteries, and to renew our attempts to crack the code. Who knows, the Secret-of-secrets might even turn out to be the most profound truth imaginable.

Seeing the Light

In the 2nd century AD, the Roman philosopher and author Lucius Apuleius described his initiation into the Mysteries of Isis (the Egyptian goddess) as follows:

> I saw the Sun at midnight shining with its brilliant light, and I approached the presence of the gods beneath, and the gods of Heaven, and stood near and worshipped them.[59]

How could the Sun be seen 'at midnight', in the middle of the night? The answer to this mystery will become apparent in due course, but suffice to say for now that Apuleius was evoking a very common theme among ancient mystery schools initiations, namely that the candidate should be confined in darkness and then struck suddenly by a bright light. Thus was the candidate *illuminated* with knowledge.

According to Robert Hewitt Brown, a high-ranking freemason of the thirty-second degree of initiation, the secret of the Mysteries indeed related to the bright light of the Sun, or of the Sun-god, and in particular to the idea that the Sun had somehow died but had been resurrected. Brown wrote:

> The ritual of the Mysteries in Egypt, India and Greece, was founded upon this legend, in some form, of the death and resurrection of the personified Sun-god... The crowning secret was a knowledge of the true God, and the disclosure of the fact that the Sun was only a symbol of the great Creator, and not itself a divine being.[60]

Robert Hewitt Brown's words should be noted carefully. The Sun-god, he said, was at the heart of the ancient mysteries, but it was only a *symbol* for the hidden God – the great architect of Heaven and Earth.

Let's look at some examples, in order to underline the fundamental importance of Brown's statement.

Firstly, as regards the Eleusinian initiations, several ancient writers commented that the candidates were required *to wander in darkness* and experience various terrors, prior to being struck *by a marvellous light*.[61]

Secondly, in the Mysteries at Samothrace, the candidate was required *to enter a dark cavern* and experience various horrors, before being immersed *in a dazzling light*.[62]

Thirdly, in the Persian mystery school initiations, the candidate was required to undergo a five-day fast, followed by a symbolic wounding of the candidate's breast, and various other tests of fortitude against the powers of darkness. All of these experiences were enacted *in gloomy caverns*, from which the candidate would eventually emerge to witness the *victory of the Sun-god* over the powers of darkness.[63]

Fourthly, in the Egyptian mystery schools initiations, the candidate had to struggle through *a dark and mysterious labyrinth*, but at the end of the ordeal, he would experience *the dazzling light of the subterranean Sun*.[64]

From these brief examples, we can see that Brown identified correctly a recurring motif in the ancient mystery school initiations – the Sun in the underworld, shining its light into darkness. It is a motif which turns up in some surprisingly diverse places.

In Christianity, for example, the gospel of John identified Jesus Christ himself as the light in the darkness:

> In him [the Word, i.e. Jesus Christ] was life, and that life was the light of men. And the light shone in the darkness, but the darkness comprehended it not.[65]

Similarly, in the gospel of Luke, we read of Jesus Christ that:

The dayspring [Sun] from on high has visited us, to give light to them that sit in darkness, and in the shadow of death, to guide our feet into the path of peace.[66]

And, returning to the gospel of John, Jesus Christ compared himself to the light which would be with men for a short time, saying:

"Believe in the light while you have the light, so that you may become the children of light."[67]

This theme was picked up by early Church leaders such as Clement, who referred to Christians as being 'the children of light', who had been 'illuminated by the dayspring of the Spirit of the Lord from on high.'[68]

But this is not just a theme of Christianity. It also turns up in freemasonry, the earliest initiates of which were known as 'Sons of Light'.[69] Some masons have even claimed that the term 'freemason' derived from the ancient Egyptian *Phre*, 'Sun', and *mas*, 'child', thus meaning 'Child of the Light'.[70] This seems to be consistent with the fact that freemasons have a sacred calendar known as *Anno Lucis*, the 'Year of the Light', which began its count in the year 4000 BC.[71]

Furthermore, the 'light' turns out to be a very significant symbol in the masonic rituals of initiation. For example, in freemasonry's first level of initiation, the candidate is blindfolded and becomes a 'poor candidate in a state of darkness'. Then, the candidate requests to see 'the light', at which point the blindfold is removed, certain objects are revealed, and the candidate becomes an Entered Apprentice Freemason.[72] This – the first of three degrees of initiation within the English lodges – is very reminiscent of the Eleusinian, Samothracian, Persian and Egyptian Mysteries cited earlier, where the light of the Sun-god appeared in the darkness of the underworld.

What does it mean to be sons of the light, or sons of the Sun-god who appeared in the underworld? Was this darkness of the underworld merely symbolic of man's state of ignorance, or was there more to it?

It is a curious fact that the early freemasons also called themselves 'the Widow's Son' – a name which is widely recognised as referring to the Egyptian god-child Horus, whose mother, the goddess Isis, was widowed by the death of her husband, the god Osiris.[73]

It is now widely known that Osiris was the god of the dead, the Lord of the Underworld (the subterranean region), and that Isis had joined him there, in the mysterious darkness. This explains why Isis was known as a 'dark' goddess, while Osiris was also a 'dark' god, who was sometimes referred to as 'the Lord in the perfect black'.[74]

It is also known from the ancient Egyptian books of the afterlife that the darkness of the underworld could be dispelled by the light of the Sun-god (Re), who would unite with Osiris in the bottommost caverns of the underworld, and hence resurrect the dead god to life.

In ancient Egypt, then, all of the ancient mysteries seem to come together. We have the light-in-the-underworld motif (Re). We have the divine child motif (Horus). And we have the life after death, or rebirth, motif (Osiris).

Unfortunately, we also have once again the forbidden knowledge motif. The secrets of Re, Osiris, Isis and Horus are mysteries which have been preserved intact for thousands of years, and they are not going to yield their secrets easily. Isis, for example, was the goddess whose temple at Sais boasted the following enigmatic inscription:

> I, Isis, am all that has been, that is, or shall be. No mortal man hath ever unveiled me.[75]

These words seem intended to be not so much a statement of historical fact, but rather a warning to the initiated: "Will you dare to unveil my secrets?"

A similar theme involving Isis was picked up by a Hermetic text, which was written in Alexandria some two thousand years ago. The text, entitled *The Virgin of the World*, is a typical example of what we have to deal with – it is full of metaphors, allegories and code-words. It states, for example, that the highest level of initiation into the Egyptian Mysteries was the 'Black Rite' of Isis, which was connected to a mysterious something called 'Night' – not night as in the mundane sense of the night sky, but rather to Night as a higher power, which moved in Heaven, and 'weaved her web with rapid light'.[76] This Night, whatever it was, supposedly honoured Isis and 'gave her perfection'.[77]

What could this mean? How could *Night* be associated with *light*? The text informs us that the 'rapid light' of Night was 'less than the Sun's', i.e. the light was *not* that of the Sun. One is reminded of the words of Robert Hewitt Brown cited earlier – the Sun was 'only a *symbol* of the great Creator'. This, he said, was the crowning secret, along with a knowledge of what the true God really was.

'Night', then, was a code-word. So was 'light'. And so was 'Sun'. The uninitiated were not supposed to know what any of this meant.

The mystery is summed up perfectly in one of the most famous passages of *The Virgin of the World*, where Horus was made to ask Isis about the secret of his divine birth:

> And Horus said: "How was it, mother, then, that Earth received God's Efflux?" And Isis said: "I may not tell the story of (this) birth; for it is

not permitted to describe the origin of thy descent, O Horus (son) of mighty power, lest afterwards the way of birth of the immortal gods should be known unto men – except so far that God the Monarch, the universal Orderer and Architect, sent for a little while the mighty sire Osiris, and the mightiest goddess Isis, that they might help the world, for all things needed them."[78]

Who were Osiris and Isis? Why was the world in need of them? What was 'the way of birth of the immortal gods'? What was the 'Efflux of God'? Why was a divine child born in the underworld? The questions raised by this enigmatic passage are endless.

One thing, however, is certain. We cannot ignore the parallels between the birth of the Egyptian divine child, Horus, and the birth of the divine child in the Eleusinian Mysteries – 'the Powerful One' – who would be born in the midst of a brilliant fire, to the cry of "Holy Brimo has borne a sacred child!". This advent (*eleusis*) was at the very heart of the Eleusinian Mysteries. And it is a theme which is echoed in the Christian mystery of the Virgin Mary and her miraculous conception of the Son of God.

Five centuries before the Christian era, the Greek poet Pindar wrote about the Mysteries, saying:

Happy is he who has seen this before descending underground!... He knows the end of life! He also knows its beginning![79]

Is this the key to it all – *the beginning of life*? Once again we are reminded of the mysterious tablet with the secret writing, excavated at Assur by Walter Andrae during the early part of the 20th century. It was a tablet which contained a great secret – known only to Assyrian initiates – concerning the beginning of life for *Homo sapiens*:

In the place where mankind was created, there was Nisaba [the goddess of writing and wisdom] firmly established.
Let the wise teach the mystery to the wise.[80]

Who were the Gods?

If we wish to solve the ancient Mysteries, we must ultimately unveil the identities of the gods. Who, or what, were these strange entities? Why did they come down from Heaven to Earth? And how did they create mankind in their own image?

The most popular theory of the gods, certainly in academic circles at any rate, is that they were a jumbled mixture of celestial gods and terrestrial gods. The former comprised gods of the Sun, Moon and stars, the worship of which is perfectly understandable. The latter generally comprised nature-gods, weather-gods, agriculture and fertility gods, as well as mythical giants and demons. Again, the worship of such deities is perfectly understandable.

A further theory, known as 'euhemerism', suggests that some of the ancient gods might have been human beings, who were deified on account of their heroic achievements.[81]

Another theory, which might be termed 'historicism', suggests that some myths, in particular the battles of the gods, might be allegories concerning the overthrow of one people, or one cultural system, by another.

Then there is the Jungian school of thought, which holds that the gods might in many cases represent expressions of the archetypes which have always existed within that part of the human mind called the 'collective unconscious'.[82]

All of these various theories seem entirely plausible at first sight, and they are not necessarily mutually exclusive. Thus we have a situation where scholars can pick and choose from a veritable armoury of theories, to explain away the meaning of the gods in any particular myth. This is indeed what scholars do, picking and choosing from the armoury almost whimsically, and arguing back and forth between themselves concerning each and every legend. The result is not only a lack of consensus on any one particular legend, but also a complete lack of any sensible framework concerning the corpus of mythology as a whole.

Most concerning of all, the vast majority of scholars seem entirely satisfied with this state of affairs, and pin the blame for any confusion on the ancients themselves, who are generally presumed to have been of a primitive psychological state of mind.

All in all, scholars seem to take the view that anything worth saying on this subject has already been said – by the founding fathers of modern academia, back in the 19th and early 20th centuries. The bottom line is that further study of the gods is discouraged, and no need is seen for a better theory, particularly not a higher, unifying theory.

As the reader can probably judge, I am sceptical of the conventional theories, and the reason for my scepticism is very straightforward: *the conventional theories do not explain adequately why the gods came down from Heaven to Earth.* This, it must be emphasised, is *the* most fundamental trait of the gods, both in the religion of ancient Egypt, and also in the religion of ancient Mesopotamia.

What was the 'Heaven' whence the gods came down to the Earth? In the opinion of scholars, this Heaven was no higher than the troposphere, i.e. the place where the Earth's weather is produced. The gods of Heaven are thus seen as weather-gods – storm-gods, rain-gods, thunder-gods, lightning-gods and hailstone-gods, who descended to the Earth in the form of rain, lightning and hailstones. It is a theory which admittedly makes a neat fit with the fertility theory of the gods, implying that the sky-gods fertilised Mother Earth with floods of rainwater.

But I beg to disagree. To me, it seems entirely obvious, from reading the legends of the ancient Near East (Egypt and Mesopotamia), that the Heaven of the ancients was where the planets and stars were to be found – *in the distant depths of space*. It was from this region – *outside the Earth's atmosphere* – that the gods descended to the Earth.

The strength of evidence for my argument will become increasingly apparent in the chapters which follow, where ample citations will be provided to demonstrate what the ancients themselves actually said concerning their 'universe' of Heaven and Earth. One fact, however, may be stated at the outset, since it strikes a fatal blow to the orthodox theory, and it is this: *the gods who came down from Heaven to Earth entered into the underworld* (i.e. into the subterranean region), almost as a matter of course.

Let us look at some examples. Firstly, there was Nergal, the famous Mesopotamian god of the underworld. But according to the legend entitled *Nergal and Ereshkigal*, Nergal was originally a god of Heaven, and he arrived in the underworld only by descending the long staircase of the heavens.[83] The translation of the legend is not in question. The only question is why scholars have ignored the obvious implication of a Sky-god going down into the underworld.

Secondly, there was Osiris, the ancient Egyptian god of the underworld. But the Pyramid Texts (those inscribed inside the 5th and 6th Dynasty pyramids) assert that Osiris was born in Heaven, and split open the Earth when he descended in fire.[84] Once again, the translations of the texts are not in question, but the judgement of scholars certainly is.

Here is another example. The Greek god Adonis is supposed to be nothing more than a vegetation deity. If this were so, why would there be traditions of his resurrection to Heaven? And why would the annual Adonis rites at Aphaca (in Syria) have been initiated by the flashing symbol of a meteorite, which was supposed to have fallen like a star from the top of Mount Lebanon into the river Adonis?[85]

A meteorite, of course, *does* have sufficient mass and velocity to split open the Earth and enter the underworld, as all the major deities of Egypt and Mesopotamia were said to have done. The products of a rain-god or a hailstone-god, on the contrary, *do not* have sufficient mass and velocity to enter the underworld.

Why, then, have scholars neglected this crucial point, and stuck to their rather mundane theory of terrestrial weather-gods, and a Heaven in the troposphere?

One possible reason is that the early scholars of ancient Near Eastern mythology were educated under a paradigm of uniformitarianism (the opposite of catastrophism), which virtually denied the existence of things falling from the sky. As recently as two hundred years ago, the American president Thomas Jefferson, on hearing reports of meteorites, said: "I would sooner believe that two Yankee professors lied, than that stones fell from the sky."[86] At that time also, the French Academy of Sciences issued a report which observed that 'in our enlightened age there can still be people so superstitious as to believe stones fall from the sky.'[87] Just a few centuries ago, anyone who witnessed a meteorite streaking down from the sky like a ball of fire was thought to have lost leave of their senses. The authorities even debunked the physical evidence (i.e. the meteorites themselves) by asserting that these objects were terrestrial stones which had been struck by lightning.

Let us return, however, to the subject of the gods. It cannot be denied that there is an intriguing connection between meteorites and the mystery school initiations which I described earlier. All over the ancient world, candidates in these rites would be confined in darkness (symbolising the underworld) and would then be illuminated by a sudden, dazzling light. Could this light indeed signify the fiery meteorite, splitting open the surface of the Earth and entering into the underworld?

According to my understanding, the underworld, as stated earlier, was the *subterranean region*. This means that the *Sun* which entered the underworld had to be a *symbol* of the meteorite. If we extrapolate this symbolism a little further, and look at the movements of the *real* Sun, we find that it sinks over the western horizon in the evening, as if to embark on a journey by night in a mythical abode of darkness. Hence the ancient Egyptians believed that the underworld (the land of the dead) could *also* lie beyond the western horizon. Of course, this was merely *symbolic*. Everyone knew that the real land of the dead lay beneath their feet – in the ground – where the bodies of the ancestors were buried.

In summary, then, there was a *real* underworld (beneath the ground) and a symbolic underworld (over the horizon). The *real* underworld was entered by a *symbolic* Sun (symbolising the meteorite). The *symbolic* underworld was entered by the *real* Sun.

How odd, then, that early Egyptologists such as Sir Ernest Alfred Wallis Budge and James Henry Breasted conveyed exactly the opposite idea. The Sun was not a symbol of the meteorite, they said, but the meteorite was a symbol of the Sun (this in reference to the Benben Stone – see chapter three). And because the Sun was all-important, the real underworld, they said, was the one over the western horizon. In other words, Wallis Budge and Breasted succeeded in turning the real into the symbolic, and the symbolic into the real.

And as if this was not enough, Wallis Budge then set about destroying the ancient Egyptian concept of the *Duat*. According to the Egyptians, the *Duat* was an invisible (metaphysical) envelope of space-time, which stretched all the way from the underworld to Heaven. It can best be imagined as taking the form of a letter J. In order for the kings to enter Heaven, they had to take an indirect route, by *first descending* into the underworld, and *then ascending* out of the underworld, up towards Heaven. Thus the first, short leg was to go down the short curve of the J, whilst the second, longer leg was to go up the pillar of the J to reach the uppermost perch or plateau, representing Heaven. This, overall, was the *Duat* – and it is a remarkably simple concept once one appreciates the metaphysical nature of the journeys undertaken by the souls of the dead kings.[88]

Wallis Budge's description of the *Duat*, on the other hand, was unbelievably complex. By taking symbolic depictions literally, he wrote of the *Duat* as if it were a two-dimensional, almost geographical region:

> In inventing a situation for the *Duat*, the Egyptians appear to have believed that the whole of the habitable world, that is to say Egypt, was surrounded by a chain of mountains... from one hole in this mountain (range) the Sun rose, and in another he set. Outside this chain of mountains, but presumably quite close to them, was the region of the *Duat*; it ran parallel with the mountains, and was on the plane either of the land of Egypt or of the sky above it. On the outside of the *Duat* was a chain of mountains also, similar to that which encompassed the earth, and so we may say that the *Duat* had the shape of a valley; and... was nearly circular in form.[89]

Thus was the real *Duat* destroyed by Wallis Budge with a nonsensical description, which was totally divorced from the wider context of Egyptian religion. But worse was to come.

As intimated earlier, the real *Duat* was not two-dimensional but four-dimensional, and its basic shape, moreover, was not a valley but the form of a letter J – incorporating *both the underworld and the metaphysical heavens*. Wallis Budge, however, presented a translation of *Duat* as 'The Underworld', whilst at the same time emphasising that '*it was not under the ground*', and 'the Egyptians *never believed it to be under the earth*'.[90]

Thus it was that Sir Ernest Alfred Wallis Budge – one of the founding fathers of Egyptology at the beginning of the 20th century – occulted the true meaning of the underworld and the symbolic Sun, and – more to the point – wittingly or unwittingly perpetuated the millennia-old secrets of the ancient mystery schools.[91]

The result of such confusion was that nearly a century later, the British Museum Press published their authoritative *British Museum Dictionary of Ancient Egypt* (effectively a vast A-Z) and did not even include an entry under the subject of 'Underworld' or '*Duat*'.[92]

The underworld – the key to ancient Egyptian religion, and once the shining edifice of ancient theology – had barely even made it into the footnotes.

It is an extraordinary and almost unbelievable fact.

* * * * *

CHAPTER TWO

LOVE ON THE MOUNTAIN

Great is the mystery of marriage!
For without it the world would not have existed.
(The Gospel of Philip)

We begin this chapter with a brief look at two legends which will be familiar to many readers. The first comes from the Hebrew Old Testament and involves the enigmatic Sons-of-God and their offspring, the Nephilim. The second legend comes from ancient Greek mythology, and involves the descent of the Sky-god Uranus, who caused Mother Earth to bear the infamous Titans.

These legends, as we shall see, share a common theme, and set the scene most aptly for the Mesopotamian legends which form the core of this chapter.

Let us begin with the Hebrew legend. According to the book of Genesis, the reason God decided to destroy mankind with the Flood was the sexual mixing which had taken place in the Earth between the daughters-of-men and the Sons-of-God. The unfortunate situation is recorded in chapter 6 of Genesis:

> And it came to pass, when men began to multiply on the face of
> the Earth and daughters were born unto them, that the Sons-of-God
> saw that the daughters-of-men were beautiful, and they married any
> of them they chose...
> There were Nephilim in the Earth in those days, and also afterwards,
> the Sons-of-God having ravaged the daughters-of-men, who had
> children by them. The same [children, i.e. the Nephilim] were the
> mighty men of old, the men of the *Shem*.[1]

Needless to say, the existence of this passage in the Bible has caused considerable discomfort to theologians, who are repeatedly asked to explain how God could have 'Sons', when Jesus Christ was supposedly his *only-begotten* son.

The standard answer from theologians is that the Sons-of-God were wicked spiritual entities, who descended from Heaven and interfered in human affairs. In other words, the Sons-of-God were not real, solid-bodied characters, and consequently we should not worry too much about them.

Nevertheless, there are many of us who *do* worry about these Sons-of-God. We note, for example, that they 'shouted for joy' at the moment of creation (Job 38:7) and we wonder how exactly that creation came about. We also note with puzzlement that the presence of these Sons-of-God on the Earth caused the birth of the Nephilim.

Who were the Nephilim? The book of Genesis tells us only that they were 'the mighty men of old, the men of the *Shem*'. But the Ethiopian holy book, the *Kebra Nagast*, expands on this laconic statement and reveals that the Nephilim were supernatural giants:

> The daughters of Cain with whom the angels had sinned, conceived,
> but they were unable to bring forth their children, and they died. Of
> the children which were in their wombs, some died and some did
> come forth by splitting open the bellies of their mothers.
> They came forth by their navels, and when they were grown up, they
> became giants whose height reached into the clouds.[2]

In the light of this passage, how can we possibly take the book of Genesis seriously? How could such giants have come forth from the wombs of *human women*?

In search of an answer, let us turn to the legends of the Greek Titans.

In one of the most famous Greek creation myths, the Sky-god Uranus showered down his fertile waters upon Gaea, Mother Earth, and impregnated her body. Gaea then gave birth to the twelve Titans, the three Cyclopes and the three hundred-armed giants. But these monstrous children were detested by their father, Uranus, and so they had to remain hidden inside Gaea's body.

Gaea, Mother Earth, was furious. With a flint sickle in her hand, she addressed her children, saying: "Sons sprung from me and a raging father... we will punish the criminal outrage of the father."[3] So, the next time Uranus descended from the heavens, 'drunken, to penetrate the body of the Earth', the youngest of the Titans, Cronus, attacked his father with the sickle, while he slept, and castrated him. The sexual organs of Uranus were then thrown into the sea, giving birth to Aphrodite, whilst the blood from the wound fell upon Gaea, causing her to bear the Three

Furies. Cronus, meanwhile, became the new king of the gods, and rose up (metaphysically I would suggest) to occupy the throne of his father.

What is the meaning of this legend? The key to it is the statement (by Aeschylus) that Uranus came down 'drunken, to penetrate the body of the Earth'.[4] What kind of object, might we ask, can *penetrate* the body of the Earth? The unique answer, in the context of this legend, is *a meteorite*.

Uranus, however, was more than just one meteorite, according to the Greek writer Hesiod, who informs us that Uranus came down from the heavens 'all avid for lovemaking, and bringing with him night, *approaching and enveloping the Earth*'.[5] It seems to me that, in order to bring darkness and to envelop the Earth, Uranus had to be *a whole storm of meteorites*.

Having decoded the legend thus far, let us proceed to conclude the scenario with some pertinent observations.

Firstly, it is apparent that the name Uranus (Greek: *Ouranos*) is derived from the Greek word *ouros* (or *oros*), meaning 'mountain'.[6] The name Uranus, which came to be synonymous with 'Sky', therefore meant literally 'The Mountain of Heaven'.[7] This supports the idea of a storm of meteorites, and suggests that *the storm of meteorites came from a 'mountain'*; it is a premise which will become a recurrent motif throughout this chapter.

Secondly, it is stated explicitly that Uranus, the Mountain of Heaven, came down to the Earth, Gaea, and impregnated her. This implies that the meteorites, with which he 'penetrated' the Earth, were regarded as a form of *seed or semen*. This, too, will become a recurrent motif of this chapter, when we look at the legends of ancient Mesopotamia.

Thirdly, it is clear that Mother Earth was envisaged as a giant womb, which received the celestial impregnation from Heaven. The giant children were thus born in an underworld which was effectively a planetary womb. This, too, will become a recurrent motif of this chapter.

Fourthly, on the subject of the giants, it is worthwhile noting that one of the hundred-armed giants was called Gyges, which meant 'earth-born'.[8] His name could also be written *gigas*, meaning 'giant', and this is the origin for the modern word 'giant' (compare the words 'gigantic' and 'giga-watt'). It is thus useful to remember that all giants are 'earth-born', i.e. born to Mother Earth in her womb, namely *in the underworld*.

Fifthly, it is evident from other Greek legends that many of these giants managed eventually to escape from the womb of Gaea. A classic example is Eros, the four-headed Titan, who sprang out from an Egg, which had been laid in 'the Womb of Darkness'.[9] Eros then proceeded to soar into the air on golden wings, roaring and hissing, and setting hearts on fire with his awesome arrows. It is an image which is far removed from the modern Valentine's Day imagery of erotic Eros, or Cupid (his Roman counterpart), and illustrates the extent to which modern society has jettisoned and forgotten the past.

As I say, the Titans escaped from Gaea, Mother Earth, and the very name Titan commemorates the violent event – for it derives from the Greek word *titaino*, meaning 'to strain'.[10] It takes little mental effort to visualise the womb of Mother Earth *straining* to give birth to these gigantic gods.

Returning, then, to the Hebrew legend of the Sons-of-God and the Nephilim, we find that we can now make perfect sense of it. The Sons-of-God, I suggest, came down from Heaven (just like Uranus) and entered *Mother Earth*, thus causing her to bring forth the Nephilim-giants (in a similar manner to the Titan-giants).[11]

This, it must be said, presupposes an alteration to the biblical text, in order to render 'daughters-of-men' as 'Mother Earth'. Curiously, it is a fact that the Hebrew word for men, *'adam*, is derived from *'adamah*, meaning 'earth' or 'soil'.[12] It would thus seem that the poetic interplay between the Sons-of-*God* entering the daughters-of-*men* might originally have been a poetic interplay between the Sons-of-*Heaven* entering the daughters-of-*Earth*. The latter comes very close to the concept of Mother Earth, and we shall encounter a legend later in this chapter which suggests that the connection is by no means fanciful.[13]

Whether or not this is the original form of the legend, there can be no denying the parallel between the *penetration* of Gaea and the *ravaging* of the daughters-of-men – especially since the Hebrew idiom in question is a very coarse expression, which literally signifies an 'entering' or 'coming into'.[14]

Nor is there any denying the parallel between the Titan-giants and the Nephilim. According to *The Book of Giants*, which was found among the Dead Sea Scrolls, the giants of Genesis (chapter 6) were invisible, immortal, had wings and were able to move from place to place with the speed of the wind.[15] Needless to say, they were also gigantic, 'like the cedars of Lebanon' according to one text, which would make them approximately 30 metres tall. Overall, the descriptions of the Nephilim are remarkably evocative of the Greek Titans.

In summary, then, we have two legends, one in Hebrew, one in Greek, which paint a remarkably consistent picture of events which transpired at, or around, the time when the world began. Moreover, if the Greek legend is to be our guide, the Sons-of-God would have been anything but spiritual entities. On the contrary, they would appear to have been physical meteorites.

The Sumerians

We turn now to more ancient writings. Approximately six thousand years ago, an enigmatic people emerged from the cloak of prehistoric anonymity, and began to build marvellous cities in the fertile plain between the mighty Tigris and Euphrates rivers (a region roughly equivalent to modern-day Iraq). These cities – Eridu, Ur, Lagash, Uruk, Shuruppak, Nippur and Kish – were the cities of the Sumerians, and the entire region was known as Sumer, or in later days by the Greek name Mesopotamia, meaning '(the land) between the rivers'.[16]

The Sumerians instigated a technological revolution in fields such as agriculture, commerce, mathematics, architecture and metallurgy. From the mid-4th millennium BC, this remarkable people began to develop sophisticated forms of government and established the earliest known social institutions, such as schools and courts of law. Most significantly, the Sumerians invented writing c. 3300 BC, initially in a pictographic form, but later in a style known as cuneiform – a curious system of wedge-shaped signs, which were impressed into clay tablets using a stylus.

It was one of these tablets, from Assur, which instigated our quest for the truth back in chapter one. But this was only one of more than 500,000 clay tablets which were recovered from the land of Mesopotamia. In the words of the distinguished Assyriologist Georges Roux: 'It can be said without exaggeration that no other country in the world has yielded such a wealth of ancient texts in the very form in which they were written thousands of years ago.'[17]

These clay tablets relate an amazing story – of gods who created the heavens and the Earth, and physically descended to the Earth at the beginning of time, in order to lay the foundations of the Sumerian cities. In those days, the gods alone had occupied the great land of Sumer, but soon they grew weary of their work and set about creating mankind to release themselves from the burden of their toil. The result was the Sumerian 'mankind', known by the enigmatic title 'the black-headed ones'.

The Sumerians, however, did not consider themselves to be slaves, but rather the honoured tenants of the 'garden of the gods'. All good things in this garden had been sent down by the gods from Heaven to Earth – cattle and grain, trees and vegetation, the vine, the date-tree, even – as we shall see – the seed of man himself.

Mankind, the black-headed ones, worked up an abundance for the gods in this garden, and, eventually, after man had proved himself worthy, the gods granted him the insignia and regalia of kingship, along with the various gifts of civilisation, all of which they brought down from Heaven. The Sumerian philosophy of life was thus summed up by the saying: 'whatever seems beautiful, we made it by the grace of the gods', and they dedicated their newly found skills, in particular writing, art and architecture, to the service of the gods.

Circa 2400 BC, the Sumerians began to lose control of their territory to the Akkadians, a Semitic-speaking group of peoples, who soon dominated the region of Sumer. But they, in turn, yielded to the Gutians *c.* 2200 BC. Then, after a brief Sumerian revival (*c.* 2100-2000 BC), the entire region was conquered by the Amorites *c.* 2000 BC.

The new millennium brought more chaos, with first the Babylonians, then the Kassites, and finally the Assyrians rising to power. But, amazingly, throughout all of these turbulent centuries, the religion of the Sumerians survived virtually intact. By and large, the same gods were worshipped, the same temples and ziggurats were repaired or rebuilt, and the same epic legends were copied and translated piously, with only minor adaptations or alterations. The ideas and ideals of the Sumerians thus became the basic creed and dogma of much of the ancient Near East, being passed from one generation to another over the course of some three thousand years.

The reason for such constancy was an unprecedented obsession with religion, which was summed up by Georges Roux as follows:

> ... for more than three thousand years the religious ideas promoted by the Sumerians played an extraordinary part in the public and private life of the Mesopotamians, modelling their institutions, colouring their works of art and literature, pervading every form of activity... In no other antique society did religion occupy such a prominent position, because in no other antique society did man feel himself so utterly dependent upon the will of the gods... the religious motives should never be forgotten or minimised.[18]

Such is the nature of modern society (materialistic and self-serving) that it is today extremely difficult to understand what was happening in Mesopotamia thousands of years ago. *Why were the people so totally obsessed with their gods*? The question has led to some remarkable speculations.

The Gods of Sumer

Who were the Sumerian gods?

At the head of the Sumerian pantheon was the god AN, the father of the gods, whom we shall refer to by his Akkadian name Anu. His name meant simply 'Heaven', and was written with an eight-pointed star.[19] For the most part, Anu was a deity who remained in Heaven, aloof from the other gods, and his image was never depicted in human-like form.

Anu had two named sons, plus a group of unnamed, anonymous sons. The named sons were the great gods EN.LIL and EN.KI, whose names are usually translated 'Lord of the Atmosphere' and 'Lord of the Earth' respectively. Both began their lives as Sky-gods, but both were held to have descended to Earth at the beginning of time. Mesopotamian texts inform us that Enlil and Enki, together with their father Anu, cast lots at that time, in order to divide between themselves the three realms of the Mesopotamian universe – Heaven, Earth and the underworld.

The underworld, as we shall see, turns out to have been of considerable importance in Mesopotamian religion, not just in the affairs of mankind, but also in the affairs of the gods. It was ruled by the famous deities Ereshkigal and Nergal, and it was home to Anu's unnamed sons – the anonymous Anunnaki-gods, whom Anu had fathered on the mysterious 'Mountain of Heaven-and-Earth'.

Alongside the popular triad of Anu, Enlil and Enki was a fourth senior deity, a goddess named Ninharsag, who was known also by a variety of other names (Ninmah, Ninlil, Mami, Ninti, Nintu, and many others besides). She, too, began her life as a Sky-deity, but descended to Earth under intriguing circumstances, where she merged with an unnamed Earth-goddess, and became the 'Lady of the Mountain'.

Beneath this senior triad, or quartet, was a pantheon of junior deities, to whom were delegated the duties and powers of the senior gods. The most famous were Nannar, Ninurta, Utu and Inanna. Utu, as we shall see, was the Sumerian Sun-god, but he was a Sun-god who did things quite unbefitting to his status; once again, we shall have cause to question whether the Sun was really the Sun, or merely a symbol for a more profound, but hidden, truth.

Finally, we shall also be meeting a precocious young god called Marduk, who turned the Babylonian pantheon upside down, deposed Anu, Enlil and Enki, and thus became the supreme god of Heaven and Earth.

When the Gods Came Down

Today, many people have already made up their minds about the ancient Sumerian gods and have formed entrenched opinions on the subject.

As mentioned in chapter one, the academics have asserted authoritatively that the gods were weather-gods or fertility-gods, or perhaps deified kings and heroes. Others, impressed by the depictions of the gods as flesh-and-blood beings like ourselves, have come up with the rather congenial theory that the gods were human-like astronauts, who came down to Earth from another planet in the heavens.[20]

Most of us, it must be said, have relied on certain 'experts' to interpret the ancient texts for us, or – at the very least – to present us with a fair summary of the details contained therein. Few of us have had the time, or the inclination, to study the full translations of the texts for ourselves.

The following citations, however, should demonstrate beyond any doubt that we – the general public – have been totally misled, whether by accident or by design, as to the true nature of the ancient gods.

We shall begin by looking at the texts which describe how the gods came down from Heaven to Earth. Some of these texts – especially those dealing with the brothers Enlil and Enki – are real eye-openers.

Take Enki, for example. In the legend entitled *Gilgamesh, Enkidu and the Underworld*, we read how Enki embarked on a voyage across the celestial waters of space at the very beginning of time:

> After AN [Anu] had carried off Heaven,
> After Enlil had carried off Earth,
> After Ereshkigal had been carried off into the underworld as its prize,
> After Enki had set sail, after he had set sail,
> After the father [Enki] had set sail for the underworld,
> Against the king [Enki], the small (stones) were hurled,
> Against Enki, the large (stones) were hurled,
> Its small stones of the hand,
> Its large stones of the dancing reeds,
> Overwhelm in battle the keel of Enki's boat like an attacking storm.
> Against the king [Enki], the water at the head of the boat devours like
>   a wolf.
> Against Enki, the water at the rear of the boat strikes down like a
>   lion.[21]

What is this all about? If Enki's boat was a descending spaceship, as some would like to think, why would Enki sail it *into the underworld*? And, by the same token, why would the supposed spaceship be surrounded by waters, front and back, and by small and large stones which attacked it like a storm?

The same argument applies to the weather-gods theory. If Enki was a weather-god, sailing down to Earth from the clouds in the form of rain or hailstones, why would his boat go down *into the underworld*? Since when did a hailstone have the power to force its way through the Earth's crust? Surely the only type of object which could do this was a meteorite. Were the 'small stones' and 'large stones', then, a storm of meteorites?[22]

Consider now the Sumerian legend *Enki and the World Order*, which also describes how Enki descended to the Earth. Enki begins the story in his own words:

> "When I approached Heaven, a rain of prosperity poured down from
>   Heaven.
> When I approached the Earth, there was a high flood.
> When I approached its green meadows, *the heaps and mounds were
>   piled up at my word*."[23]

Might this piling up of heaps and mounds on the Earth correspond to the 'small stones' and 'large stones' which accompanied the descent of Enki's 'boat'? As we shall see later in the *Lugal-e* legend, the answer is almost certainly "yes".

Returning to the legend *Enki and the World Order*, Enki made another interesting statement in regard to his celestial birth:

> "My father [Anu], the king of Heaven and Earth,
> Brought me into existence in Heaven-and-Earth.
> My ancestor, the king of all the lands,
> Gathered together the divine laws, placed the divine laws in my hand.
> From the Mountain-House, the house of Enlil,
> I brought craftsmanship to my AB.ZU of Eridu."[24]

The AB.ZU – as we shall see – is the underworld, whilst Eridu (the site of Enki's cult centre) is used here as a microcosm of the whole Earth. The text thus relates that Enki descended to the underworld of the Earth (AB.ZU of Eridu) from the 'Mountain-House' (E.KUR) of Heaven.

Note how Heaven is here described as a mountain – in keeping with the theme of Greek mythology that the supreme Sky-god Uranus had been the 'Mountain of Heaven'. Note, too, that the descent of Enki caused heaps and mounds to be piled up on the Earth – evidence that the descent was understood in *physical* and not spiritual, or metaphysical, terms.

As with the earlier legend of Enki's boat, here again in this legend Enki claims to have entered the underworld. After describing his descent from the Mountain-House to the AB.ZU, he says:

"I am the great storm which goes forth out of the underworld..."[25]

This going forth referred to the *metaphysical* ascension of Enki's *soul or spirit*, which was separated from his body at the moment of impact.

Later in the text, we read something quite remarkable, as the Sumerian poet spelled out Enki's amazing deeds:

After father Enki had lifted it [his eye] over the Euphrates,
He stood up proudly like a rampant bull,
He lifted his penis, ejaculated,
And filled the Tigris with sparkling water.[26]

How, might we ask, could a descending god bring *that much water* to the Earth?

Further clues can be found in the legend of Enki's 'brother' Enlil, who also came down to the Earth in a lusty fashion. The tale, entitled *Enlil and Ninlil*, begins by describing the goddess Ninlil as bathing in a pure river of water, where she was seen by Enlil:

Ninlil stood on the bank of the river Nunbirdu...
The 'Great Mountain', father Enlil, the bright-eyed, saw her...
Enlil speaks to her of intercourse; she is unwilling:
"My vagina is too small, it knows not how to copulate,
My lips are too small, they know not how to kiss."[27]

But Enlil ordered his vizier Nusku to bring up a boat, whereupon he proceeded to impregnate Ninlil while sailing in the river:

The splendid river, the shining river, flowed through the darkness like
     a necklace.
The Lady Ninlil stood on the bank of the strongly-flowing river...
The Lordly Father [Enlil] rose up on the Great Mountain...
The glorious water flowed strongly...
He [Enlil] threw off his clothes, entered her swiftly, and poured out
     life into her with his erect penis.
The river was shining – a shining river poured out into the Woman...
The Lady Ninlil said to him: "Where you have bestowed your seed in
     my womb, new life will be established."[28]

How could a 'river' impregnate a goddess? In order to understand this, it is imperative to note that the Sumerian word for 'water' also meant 'semen'.[29] And it is also vital to realise that the 'Woman', or goddess, being impregnated was a personification of Mother Earth. Water was thus seen as a life-giving substance, which could impregnate the womb of Mother Earth.

This same scenario is confirmed in a Sumerian tale entitled *Dispute between Summer and Winter*. In this legend, we read how Enlil inserted his 'penis' into a 'mountain' (HAR.SAG), and thereby brought forth gushing waters and vegetation, along with the seasons of 'summer' and 'winter':

> Enlil, the king of all the lands, set his mind.
> He thrust his penis into the Great Mountain (HAR.SAG)...
> Summer and Winter, the fecundating overflow of the land, he poured
>   into the womb.
> Wheresoever Enlil would thrust his penis, he roared like a wild bull.
> There, HAR.SAG spent the day, rested happily at night,
> Delivered herself of Summer and Winter like rich cream...[30]

It must be said that the idea of summer and winter being engendered upon a 'mountain' only makes sense if the 'mountain' in question was the entire planet of Earth. (It is difficult to see what other possible explanation there might be.) Furthermore, if Enlil was able to insert his 'penis' into a 'mountain' the size of a planet, this raises the question of what kind of god Enlil was.

The answer is surely revealed by Enlil's most common nickname – *the Great Mountain* – a fact which is generally passed over without comment by the various authorities on Mesopotamian mythology. The frequent use of this nickname, however, can be gauged from its incidence in the brief passages cited above, in addition to which we might cite one of the several examples which occur in a text entitled *Hymn to Enlil*:

> Without Enlil, *the 'Great Mountain'*,
> No cities would be built, no settlements founded,
> No stalls would be built, no sheepfold established,
> No king would be raised, no high priest born.[31]

What this means, in a nutshell, is that Enlil was a 'mountain' which impregnated another 'mountain' – the latter, in the case of *Dispute between Summer and Winter*, being Mother Earth.

Returning, then, to the legend of *Enlil and Ninlil*, it is clear that the 'Woman', Ninlil, was Mother Earth. Hence, when Ninlil exclaimed: "Where you have bestowed your seed in my womb, new life will be established", she was referring to the womb of the Earth, and the beginnings of life on Earth.

How, then, should we understand the seed, which flowed into Ninlil's 'womb' in the form of a river? The answer – which will later be confirmed by other legends – is that this was no ordinary river, but a *celestial river,* which flowed down to Earth from Heaven.

As for Enlil, the 'Great Mountain', we read that he – as a result of impregnating Ninlil – *descended into the underworld*, where he was described, somewhat amusingly, as 'walking about' in Ninlil's private shrine, the KI.UR, which literally meant 'the Foundations of the Earth'.[32] In other words, Enlil was *inside the womb of Ninlil*, whence he was told to remove himself by the 'fate-decreeing gods' who shouted at him to "Get out of the city!".[33]

Once again, it must be emphasised that this descent of Enlil *into the underworld* makes perfect sense under the mountain-and-meteorites theory, but it contradicts the orthodox theory that Enlil was some kind of weather-god, and it certainly challenges the notion that he was some kind of ancient astronaut.

As for the celestial river which descended into the underworld, this turns out to be a recurring motif – to which we will assuredly return.

Finally on the subject of Enlil's descent to Earth, we should note the legend entitled *Myth of the Pickaxe*. In this text, Enlil seems to have descended to the Earth in catastrophic circumstances, for he split open the Earth by hacking open a hole at Nippur.[34] This act, we are told, was carried out with a 'pickaxe', but it is clear from other legends that this was no ordinary pickaxe. In the Sumerian *Lamentation Texts*, for example, the 'pickaxe' was cited as a weapon associated with fire, which was used by Enlil to crush the city of Ur.[35] And in *The Epic of Gilgamesh*, a 'pickaxe' of a 'strange shape' fell from the Sky like a meteorite (see chapter five).[36]

Significantly, the impact of this celestial 'pickaxe' at Nippur caused the Earth to be seeded with vegetation and all living creatures, including mankind (the 'black-headed ones'), who sprouted forth like plants in the hacked-open hole.[37]

And this, we should note, took place at Nippur, the 'Bond of Heaven-and-Earth' – the same place where Ulligarra and Zalgarra produced mankind in their own image:

Skilled worker to produce for skilled worker,
And unskilled worker for unskilled worker,
Springing up by themselves like grain from the ground.
A thing which, like the stars of the heavens, shall not be changed
    for ever...
Let the wise teach the mystery to the wise.

Enki and Ninharsag

Often, when dealing with ancient writings, it can be difficult to establish the correct interpretation of a legend, especially when the pivotal incidents are described using metaphors such as 'mountain', 'penis', 'pickaxe' *et cetera*. In such circumstances, it becomes useful, even essential, to corroborate the understanding of one particular legend by reference to another. This is what we will now do, in order to verify the idea that Enlil was caught 'walking around' not inside a man-made shrine, but *inside the womb of Ninlil, Mother Earth*.

The legend which I shall now relate, entitled *Enki and Ninharsag: A Paradise Myth*, will not be too well-known to readers for the very reason that its metaphors and allegories make it the most bizarre of all Sumerian legends, and the most difficult to comprehend. Extracts from the *Paradise Myth* have, however, been cited occasionally on account of an intriguing parallel to the biblical legend of the creation of Eve from the rib of Adam.[38]

But the *Paradise Myth* is interesting for other reasons too. At the beginning of the text, the Earth is described as a barren place, devoid of water and life. Then, Enki called for Utu (supposedly the Sumerian Sun-god) to fill up the Earth (Dilmun) with water from 'the mouth whence issues the waters of the Earth'.[39] At this point, some of the lines in the tale are illegible, and it is not clear whether the waters were brought from Heaven, or from a reservoir in the underworld. But it is clear that Utu worked this miracle from a position in the heavens.[40] 'Verily it was so' declared the ancient scribe.

We, however, are verily confused. How could it be that a *Sun*-god was called upon to provide an *abundance of waters* to a barren Earth? The answer, which I have suggested already, is that ancient Sun-gods were symbols for a higher, more mysterious God. This particular legend of Utu and the waters of Dilmun only confirms that something is very wrong with our present understanding.

More on Utu – and other ancient Sun-gods (sic) – in due course. But for the moment let us continue with the legend of the *Paradise Myth*, which is about to become quite bizarre.

Following Utu's watering of the Earth (Dilmun), the Earth became a verdant paradise under the jurisdiction of the goddess Nintu, 'the mother of the land'. It was then, we are told, that Enki decided to impregnate her:

Enki (for) the wise Nintu, the mother of the land,
Causes his phallus to water the dykes,

Causes his phallus to submerge the reeds...
Enki... poured the semen in the womb of NIN.HAR.SAG...
(After) nine days, being her nine months, the months of 'womanhood',
Like fat, like fat, like good princely fat,
(Nintu) gave birth to Ninmu... at the bank of the river.[41]

The first thing to note regarding this passage is that Nintu, the mother of the land (i.e. Earth), was an alias for Ninharsag, whose name meant literally the 'Lady of the Head-Mountain'.[42] Once again, we are looking at the impregnation of a 'mountain'.

Also, once again, we find a pun between water and semen, with the Earth being fecundated by a river of semen-like water. This would seem to be a repeat of the Utu story, but with the credit now given to Enki.

As for the birth of Ninmu 'at the bank of the river', it seems to me that this is a reference once again to the *celestial river*. One bank of this river would seem to be Heaven, the other bank the Earth, with Ninmu being born on the latter.

What happened next is that Enki took a fancy to the newborn daughter, Ninmu, saying: "Shall I not kiss the young one, the fair?".[43] With the help of a 'boat', and a 'mighty wind', Enki 'poured the semen into the womb', and nine months later Ninmu gave birth to Ninkurra.

The same theme was then repeated, with Enki sowing his divine seed into Ninkurra, and finally into *her* daughter Uttu.[44]

Uttu, the third daughter, was singled out for special attention by Enki, who wooed her with gifts of fresh fruit (cucumber, apples and grapes), and eventually inseminated her inside a 'house' (this probably means inside the Earth). But when Enki finally managed to ejaculate his semen into the third daughter, Ninharsag rescued Enki's seed from the daughter's womb, and planted it in the earth. Immediately, Enki's seed sprouted up into eight different 'plants'.

If this seems bizarre, worse is to follow. The plants were plucked, each in turn, and fed to Enki by his vizier, Isimud. Then, the goddess Ninharsag, seemingly appalled by this act, uttered a curse that Enki should endure terrible pains until the day of his death; only then, when he was dead, would she look upon him with her 'eye of life'.

The bizarre tale gets even more bizarre! A cunning fox persuaded Ninharsag to return and release poor old Enki from the curse, *by seating Enki inside Ninharsag's vulva.* Having positioned Enki thus, the goddess – whose name we should recall means 'Lady of the Mountain' – relieved Enki of his eight aching body-parts by giving birth to eight deities therefrom. One of these body-parts was the rib – hence the oft-suggested connection to the tale of Adam and Eve (a connection which seems rather contrived in my view, since one body-part out of eight is hardly statistically significant).[45]

What should we make of this incredible legend? It seems a fair bet that the tale recalls Enki's descent from Heaven to Earth, and his impregnation of Mother Earth, alias Ninharsag, the mountain-goddess. As to the meaning of what happens next, one is struggling. But it would seem that the birth of the third daughter (Uttu) marks the beginning of abundance in the underworld (see chapter eight), and this in turn gave rise to eight plants which sprang forth into the world above.

By eating the eight plants, Enki undid the creation of life – the work of the mother-goddess Ninharsag – hence her anger.[46] A key point is that the cursing of Enki by Ninharsag seems to have placed him in the underworld, and hence in the vulva, or womb, of Mother Earth. Hence the conclusion of the story was that Ninharsag gave birth to life once again by delivering agriculture-deities from Enki's body-parts.[47]

In summary, the tale of *Enki and Ninharsag: A Paradise Myth* would seem to be a tale of the creation of agriculture on Earth. But this was no ordinary tale of agriculture, for the seeds were sown by a god who came down from Heaven, bringing with him *celestial waters*.

This, even if I say so myself, seems to be a reasonably sensible and scholarly interpretation of this text, and yet it must be emphasised that it is not *The* scholarly interpretation. The latter, orthodox theory states that:

> The main purpose of the myth is by no means clear, and the literary
> and mythological implications of its numerous and varied motifs are
> not readily analysable.[48]

So much, then, for the standard theories of weather-gods and fertility gods. They are of little use in analysing the meaning of complex mythologies.

As for the theory that Enki was some kind of human-like hero or ancient astronaut, this does not work either. How could one human-like deity, Enki, be placed *inside the womb of* another human-like deity, Ninharsag? The idea is patently absurd.

The Battles of Ninurta

Up until now, the impression might have been given that Ninlil and Ninharsag were personifications of Mother Earth, pure and simple. This, however, is only a half-truth, for it would seem that both were originally Sky-goddesses, and only came down from the heavens to the Earth at a later point in time. Such an origin seems likely for the underworld-goddess Ereshkigal, too, for she was *'carried off into* the underworld' according to one of the texts cited earlier.[49]

The story of how Ninharsag *inherited* the Earth, and came to it from a 'distant land', is told in the Akkadian legend known (from its opening line) as the *Lugal-e* text. It is this legend, and related legends, which we shall now look at, for they contain a most intriguing account of how the foundations of the Earth were laid as a result of *a battle of the gods*. Such legends, according to scholars, were either played out by storm-gods in the Earth's atmosphere – using weapons such as thunder and lightning – or played out on the ground by kings and heroes who were later deified. As we shall now see, nothing could be further from the truth.

This Mesopotamian battle of the gods is in many ways like a Greek battle of the Titans. From the beginning, it is clear that the evil god – named Zu or Azag – was engendered upon Mother Earth by a descending Sky-god, namely the supreme deity Anu. In the *Lugal-e* text, we read:

Anu impregnated the verdant Earth (KI),
And she bore him Azag – one unafraid of the warrior Ninurta.[50]

The name Azag meant 'Sling-Stone', and as a Titan-like god, we must presume that he effected an escape from the womb of Mother Earth, in order to do battle in the Sky against Ninurta.[51]

Fortunately, certain gaps in the story of Azag can be filled in by referring to the legend of his alter ego, Zu, who fought the same battle against Ninurta in other, parallel legends. Zu's name, it would seem, alluded to the AB.ZU of the underworld, where he was born.[52]

In *The Myth of Zu*, the god Zu appears as a hybrid bird-human demon, who brought chaos to Heaven and Earth by seizing the so-called 'tablets of destiny' from Nippur.[53] These magical objects were held to be critical in maintaining the balance between Heaven and Earth – between the gods who resided above and the gods who resided below. By stealing them, Zu stole the 'Enlilship' – the supreme powers over the Bond of Heaven-and-Earth:

Zu seized the tablets of destiny in his hands,
Taking away the Enlilship; suspended were the norms.
When Zu had flown away and repaired to his mountain HAR.SAG.MU,
Stillness spread abroad, silence prevailed.[54]

The name of Zu's mountain, HAR.SAG.MU, meant 'MU of the Mountain Range', where a MU represented a mode of travelling through the heavens. Thus Zu became known as Anzu, meaning 'one who knows the heavens'. The similarity to Greek mythology should not pass without comment; Zu (alias Azag) had been born in the Earth as a Titan-god, and had then ascended (metaphysically) to a heavenly 'mountain'. The implication is that he had originally come from a mountain, just as the Greek Titans were the offspring of Uranus, the 'Mountain of Heaven' (note also the Titans who ascended and did battle on *Mount* Olympus).

To return to the story, who would now vanquish Zu and restore the harmony between Heaven and Earth?

The challenge was accepted by a god called Ninurta – a warrior-god, foremost among the Anunnaki, son of Enlil and the offspring of E.KUR.[55] In all probability, Ninurta, too, was a Titan; hence his description as a 'dragon', who had the 'hands of a lion' (sic) and 'the claws of an eagle'.[56] Ninurta immediately proceeded to engage Zu in battle:

(Ninurta) the hero hitched the seven ill winds,
The seven whirlwinds which cause the dust to dance.
He launched a terrifying war, a fierce conflict.
While the gale at his side shrieked for strife,
Zu and Ninurta met at the mountainside...
In the midst of the mountain Zu let loose a piercing shriek.
There was darkness, the face of the mountain was covered.[57]

Eventually, after unleashing an arrow and 'fourteen storm floods', Ninurta emerged victorious. He cut Zu's throat and dispatched his 'wings' on the 'winds', all the way back to the E.KUR (the 'Mountain-House', which here seems to represent the Earth).[58]

As for the vital tablets of destiny, the Sumerian version of the battle relates that the attack by Ninurta forced the Zu-bird to open its claws in pain, whereupon the tablets returned, as if by magic, to the AB.ZU of Earth. Ninurta, meanwhile, captured Zu, and flew him – in the form of the 'Imdugud-bird' – back to the AB.ZU.[59] Incidentally, the name Imdugud meant 'Sling-Stone', as did the name Azag, the latter being Zu's alter-ego in the *Lugal-e* text cited earlier.[60] Hence, Zu/Azag was brought back to the Earth under the epithet 'Sling-Stone'.

Now, the impression given by this legend is that Zu was not simply hiding inside the mountain during the battle, but that Zu *was* the mountain. The destruction of Zu/Azag and the destruction of the mountain were thus one-and-the-same thing.

According to scholars, however, this battle described thunderstorms raging over a terrestrial mountain. Ninurta, we are told, was nothing but a rain-god. And Zu's epithet, Sling-Stone, referred to mundane hailstones.[61] Readers, however, may decide for themselves whether this is true, bearing in mind the details I am now about to relate concerning the aftermath of the battle.

The *Lugal-e* text tells us that, after the battle ended, the victorious god Ninurta sat in judgement of the 'stones' which had been 'heaped up' on the Earth (KUR) as a result of the battle. Some of these stones he blessed for being his allies, and some of them he cursed for being his enemies.[62] The latter stones, we are told, had formed 'the army of Azag'.[63] In other words, they were the remains of Azag's mountain, or Zu's HAR.SAG.MU, which had been destroyed in battle and had fallen to the Earth.

If this is not enough to convince readers, then consider the other parts of the *Lugal-e* text which deal with the creative aspect of the destruction. According to the legend, Ninurta was called upon to resolve a dreadful shortage of water on the Earth. Prior to his battle with Azag, the waters of the Earth had been insufficient to fill the river Tigris, because the future waters of the Earth were at that time locked up in the form of 'ice, long accumulating in the mountain on the other side'.[64] This is an intriguing statement indeed, for it suggests that a great flood of waters came forth from the 'mountain' of Azag.

The *Lugal-e* text, expanding on this intriguing statement, affirms that the gods of that land – i.e. *on the other side* – had been assigned to 'pour it [i.e. the waters], according to what they had first chopped off from it' (i.e. in the form of ice).[65] This having been done, we read of the creative aspect of Ninurta's destruction:

> The lord directed his great intelligence to it,
> Ninurta, the son of Enlil, wrought magnificently.
> He made a heap of stones in the mountain – like drifting rain clouds
>   they came floating on outstretched wings,
> Set bar before the country as with a great wall...
> The mighty waters followed along (with) the stone.
> Now these waters did *not* rise from the Earth (back up) into the eternal
>   mountain [i.e. the mountain of Heaven].[66]

We are then told that Ninurta gathered together all of the waters which had been 'scattered' upon the face of the Earth (even from swamps in the mountains!) and threw them into the mighty river Tigris. Thus the land of Sumer was fecundated and turned into a garden of paradise.

Now, all of this, it seems to me, is rather too melodramatic for a mere thunderstorm and cloudburst. And upon closer inspection it would appear that scholars have really not done their homework. Why, for example, would the 'scattered' waters appear even in swamps *in the mountains*? This hardly rings true under the orthodox scenario.

Furthermore, how can the 'stones' in the above passage be hailstones, if Ninurta used them to build a 'wall' across the land? Hailstones, it must be said, have an awkward tendency to melt.[67]

In fact, the central theme of the *Lugal-e* legend is the *disintegration of Zu's mountain*, which is an order of magnitude different from a *cloud*burst. The real meaning of the legend is that the Earth was fecundated by the disintegration of a 'mountain' in the heavens – the term 'mountain' being a metaphor for something celestial (we will examine the exact nature of this celestial mountain in the following chapters).

Therefore, the 'heap of stones' which was brought to the Earth, 'on outstretched wings', and which did *not* melt when it hit the ground, could only have been *meteorites*.

Finally, concerning the 'mighty waters' which followed the stone, this flood motif is a recurrent theme in the Mesopotamian legends, and refers to a great flood of water from a celestial source, namely the enigmatic 'mountain'. It is an idea which may seem a little incongruous to readers at this stage, but all things will be explained in due course.

So, to come back to where we started this discussion, the *Lugal-e* legend concludes by explaining how the goddess Ninharsag (alias Ninmah) heard of her son Ninurta's heroic feats, and asked whether she might pay him a visit from her distant land. Ninurta, who had by now stocked the land with vegetation, trees and wildlife, looked at his mother with 'the eye of life' and said:

> "Lady, because you would come to the KUR [Earth or Underworld]...
> Because you have no fear of the terror of battle surrounding me,
> Therefore let the name of this hill which I, the hero, have heaped up
>   be 'HAR.SAG' [i.e. 'Mountain'].
> Let you [Ninmah] be its queen."[68]

At this, Ninmah, whose name meant 'the Exalted Lady', descended to the Earth, and accepted as a gift the huge stone pile which Ninurta had so arduously prepared. It was at this time that the Earth acquired its new mistress – no longer called Ninmah, but NIN.HAR.SAG – 'The Lady of the Mountain'.[69]

The Mystery of Mother Earth

Ninharsag was a goddess of many names. Sometimes she was called Mami ('Mother'), sometimes Ninti ('Lady of Life'), and sometimes Nintu ('Lady Birth-Hut'), not to mention several other aliases.[70] But whatever her formal name, she was always known by her epithet 'the Womb-goddess'.

It seems odd, in the light of the texts cited above, that scholars have failed to appreciate that Ninharsag, the Womb-goddess, was Mother Earth. She was, after all, the goddess of *the Earth* at the same time as being the *Womb*-goddess.

We shall now see why scholars have been distracted from this obvious conclusion. The following brief legend, entitled *Creation of Man by the Mother-Goddess*, describes Ninharsag's ultimate life-giving achievement – the creation of man himself. However, far from appearing as a planetary womb, Ninharsag is depicted as being entirely human-like. She speaks, mixes clay, directs her fourteen birth-giving assistants, and, at one point, her 'feet' are apparently kissed by the grateful Anunnaki-gods. However, any suggestion that Ninharsag might have been human – or perhaps even creating the world's first test-tube babies – is eliminated by the revelations in the closing lines of the text.

The Old Babylonian version of the story begins as follows:

(The great gods) called to the goddess,
Mami [Ninharsag], the wise midwife of the gods:
"Thou art the mother-womb,
The creatress of mankind.
Create a 'Lullu' ['Primitive Man'] and let him bear the yoke!
Let man bear the load of the gods!"[71]

With the help of Enki, Ninharsag then carried out the commission, using fourteen birth-goddesses – literally fourteen *mother-wombs*. From this point, the remainder of the Babylonian tablet has been badly damaged, but the continuing story is picked up by the Assyrian version:

Far-sighted Enki and wise Mami [Ninharsag]
Went into the House of Fate.
Fourteen mother-wombs were assembled,
He [Enki] trod the clay in her presence...
When she [Mami] had finished her incantation,
She pinched off fourteen pieces of clay,
And set seven pieces on the right,
Seven on the left.
Between them she placed a brick...
Of the seven-and-seven mother-wombs,
Seven brought forth males,
Seven brought forth females.[72]

It must be said that this process does sound remarkably like a creation of man under laboratory conditions, using *human* birth-goddesses and a *man-made* 'birth-hut'. Upon closer inspection, however, one finds some crucial anomalies.

For example, it can be seen from the text (in its entirety) that the narrator switches emphasis repeatedly between the *fourteen* mother-wombs and a *singular* 'Bearing One' or 'Mother-Womb', the latter being a reference to Mami/Ninharsag. Thus, immediately after the line 'seven brought forth males, seven brought forth females', we read:

> The *Mother-Womb* completed them in pairs.
> The forms of the people *Mami* forms...
> As the Bearing *One* gives birth...[73]

Plurality has thus become singularity. Furthermore, the brick which was placed *between* the fourteen pieces of clay – and thus between the fourteen mother-wombs – turns out to have been placed *inside* a *singular* 'bearing woman', namely Mami herself:

> In the House of the Bearing Woman in Travail,
> Seven days shall the brick lie.[74]

This 'House of the Bearing Woman', I suggest, was *the Earth*. This can be deduced from the penultimate line of the text, which states that the 'vexed ones' would rejoice in the 'House of the One in Travail'. The vexed ones were, of course, the Anunnaki-gods, whose workload was to be borne by the creation of man – hence their rejoicing here, and their earlier kissing of Ninharsag's feet. The key point, however, is that these Anunnaki-gods lived *in the underworld* – i.e. *inside the Earth*. Therefore, the 'House of the One in Travail' must also have been the *inside of the Earth*. And the One who was in travail – Mami, or Ninharsag – was thus the Earth herself – the Mother-Womb.

What, then, should we make of the *fourteen mother-wombs*? If we take the text literally (a dangerous approach but justified in this case), the confusion can be resolved by supposing that the fourteen mother-wombs were contained within the singular Mother-Womb. This would make sense. It would explain the continual switching of emphasis through the text, and it would account for the fact that the 'brick' placed *between* the plural mother-wombs could at the same time be placed inside the House of Mami herself. The fourteen mother-wombs were thus subsidiary *wombs-within-the-Womb*, with their number symbolising the divine and lucky number '7' for both males and females respectively.

All of which leads to an intriguing thought. What actually was the 'brick' which was placed *in* the Mother-Womb, but *between* the subsidiary wombs? Clearly a brick symbolises the beginning of building

– the laying of a foundation. In this context, however, the building which took place was the *building of life*. Moreover, the brick which laid this foundation of life was placed inside the womb of Mother Earth.

The 'brick', then, is unlikely to have been a humble mudbrick – a point which is confirmed by the fact that one of Ninharsag's nicknames was 'lapis lazuli brick'.[75] Now, in other legends, as we shall see, lapis lazuli was the stone-of-Heaven *par excellence*, and yet was at the same time the material-of-choice for the palace of Ereshkigal *in the underworld*. Putting all of these clues together, even with the little which we have learned so far, it does not take a genius to work out the symbolism of the lapis lazuli 'brick' which came from Heaven to Earth.

The 'brick', it would seem, was a meteorite, with the meteorite symbolising the beginning of life in the Earth.[76]

Love on the Mountains

Approximately thirty-five centuries ago, a Babylonian poet wrote:

Who may comprehend the minds of the gods in Heaven's depth?
The thoughts of those divine deep waters, who could fathom them?
How could mankind, beclouded, comprehend the ways of the gods?[77]

In summarising this chapter, it must be said that we – in the modern era – are equally *beclouded* when it comes to understanding the ancient gods. As far as scholars are concerned, 'Heaven's depth' is no higher than the fluffy white clouds in the Earth's troposphere – or, more to the point, the dark, angry clouds which cast down rainwater, hailstones and lightning to the earth.

And – just to add insult to injury – those of us who have not been beclouded by thoughts of weather-gods have been equally beclouded by the fanciful idea that gods of flesh and blood descended from Heaven as visiting astronauts from another planet.

Truly mankind has been unable to fathom the ways of the ancient gods in Heaven's watery depths.

In this chapter, we have seen just a few examples of how the Heaven of the ancients was a mountain, which disintegrated and fell to the Earth.

There was Uranus, the supreme Greek deity, who came down 'drunken, to penetrate the body of the Earth'. His name meant literally 'The Mountain of Heaven'.

There was Enlil, the foremost son of Anu, who came down to the Earth and split open its crust with a 'pickaxe'; who impregnated Ninlil with a river of semen-like water; who inserted his 'penis' into a 'mountain', and created the seasons of 'summer' and 'winter'. His most common nickname was 'Great Mountain'.

There was Enki, the brother of Enlil, who was not actually called 'Mountain', but nevertheless came down from Heaven in a 'boat' surrounded by raging stones and waters; who piled up heaps and mounds upon the Earth; who filled the rivers with semen-like waters; and who impregnated the 'Lady of the Mountain'.

And then there was Azag, the evil Titan-like demon, who repaired to his 'mountain' in Heaven, which was then destroyed by Ninurta. Immediately, a huge heap of stones was released, and swept over the Earth, creating a 'great wall' upon the land. A flood-wave of mighty waters came too – originating from 'ice, long accumulating in *the mountain* on the other side'. Thus was the Earth fecundated, and turned into a garden of paradise.

The theme is clear. All of these legends were describing the Earth as being like a giant Womb – or perhaps we should say a Womb-for-giants.

The seed fell into the Womb not from the clouds, but from the heights of Heaven, with a force which caused the seed to penetrate and enter the Womb. In Hebrew legend, the seed was the Sons-of-God. In Greek legend, the seed was Uranus – God himself. In Mesopotamian legends, the seed was the water or stones from Heaven.

The seed then engendered life within the Womb. In the Hebrew legend, Mother Earth was impregnated with the Nephilim-giants. In Greek legend, she was impregnated with the Titan-giants.

In Mesopotamian legends, too, Mother Earth was impregnated with gods, giants or demons, and it is worth citing several examples to drive the point home.

Firstly, concerning the birth of the evil demon Azag/Zu, the *Lugal-e* legend describes his origin explicitly:

Anu impregnated the verdant Earth (KI) and she bore him Azag.[78]

Similarly, in a Babylonian text entitled *Erra and Ishum*, we read that Anu impregnated the Earth with seven Sebitti-gods:

When Anu, king of the gods, impregnated Earth,
She bore the Seven gods for him, and he named them 'Sebitti'.[79]

The birth of these Sebitti-gods was said to be 'strange and full of terrible portents', and no-one could approach them due to their lethal breath.[80] Significantly, the Sebitti-gods were confined to the underworld, where they became companions for Nergal (alias Erra).

In another legend, entitled *The Dispute between Cattle and Grain*, we read that Anu's first act of creation caused the Anunnaki-gods to be born:

In the Mountain of Heaven-and-Earth, Anu caused the Anunnaki to
  be born...[81]

This reference to a single 'Mountain of Heaven-*and-Earth*' refers to the
fact that the 'mountain' of Heaven had fallen and become confused with
the 'mountain' of Earth. This, as we shall see, is a recurrent motif. Once
again, then, it was Mother Earth who did the bearing, and, significantly,
the offspring of the impregnation – the Anunnaki – were confined to the
underworld.

The Mountain of Heaven-and-Earth (i.e. Earth) was also the place
where Enki was born, according to *Enki and the World Order*:

Enki, the king of the AB.ZU... speaks up with authority:
"My father, the king of Heaven and Earth,
Brought me into existence *in Heaven-and-Earth* (AN.KI)."[82]

Another legend states that Enki's brother, Enlil, was also born in this
location, from a union between AN, the Sky-god, and KI, the Earth.[83]
Incidentally, scholars prefer to translate AN.KI as 'universe', a translation
which is not incorrect, but totally obscures the meaning of the story.

Other legends simply state that the union between Heaven and Earth
created all the gifts of nature. A late Akkadian incantation states:

As the Sky impregnated the Earth, so did vegetation become
plentiful.[84]

A Sumerian poem describes this union of Heaven and Earth in explicit
and unambiguous terms:

Smooth, big Earth made herself resplendent, beautified her body
  joyously.
Wide Earth bedecked her body with precious metal and lapis lazuli,
Adorned herself with diorite, chalcedony, and shiny carnelian.
Heaven arrayed himself in a wig of verdure, stood up in princeship.
Holy Earth, the virgin, beautified herself for Holy Heaven.
Heaven, the lofty god, planted his knees on Wide Earth,
Poured the semen of the heroes Tree and Reed into her womb.
Sweet Earth, the fecund cow, was impregnated with the rich semen of
  Heaven.
Joyfully did Earth tend to the giving birth of the plants of life,
Luxuriantly she brought forth rich produce, and gave birth to wine and
  honey.[85]

Various other legends, as we have seen, went on to state that mankind,
too, was the progeny of this celestial impregnation of the Earth. Man,

too, was a product of the great Mother-Womb.

But Mother Earth, it would seem, was at the mercy of whatever male seed penetrated her. Not only did she give birth to gods, giants and men, but also to the evil spirits and demons, as is dramatically evident from the following ancient Babylonian text:

> Spawn of the God of Heaven, spawned on an evil spirit, the death warrants, beloved sons of the storm-god, born of the queen-of-the-underworld, (they) who were torn out of Heaven and (then) hurled from the Earth as cast-offs, (they) are creatures of hell, all.
> Up above they roar, down below they cheep, they are the bitter venom of the gods, they are the great storms let loose from Heaven, they are the owl (of ill omen) that hoots in the town.
> Spawn spawned by the God of Heaven, sons born by Earth are they.[86]

In summary, it should be perfectly evident that our ancient ancestors were obsessed with the idea of the Sky falling to the Earth, and producing progeny – either good or evil – from a kind of sacred marriage with Mother Earth. It is an idea which is found not only in the ancient Near East, but also further afield, such as in the Sanskrit writings of ancient India, where husband and wife were assimilated to Heaven and Earth; hence in one text, the husband says to the wife: "I am Heaven and thou art Earth".[87]

Even today, echoes of this forgotten past surround us in our everyday lives. On Valentine's Day, our greetings of love evoke Eros – the fiery Titan-god, who was born in the Earth, in the 'Womb of Darkness', having been fathered by the mysterious 'Wind'. And on other days, we tease each other with thoughts of whether *the Earth moved* during our lovemaking.[88] We even talk of 'getting our rocks off' – an expression which must surely be derived from an ancient pun on the collapse of the 'mountain' of Heaven.

And yet, despite all this, modern scholars talk of the earth being made fertile by thunder-gods, lightning-gods, rain-gods and hail-gods. Note that I say the *earth* with a small 'e', and not the *Earth* with a capital 'E', for it is typical of scholars that they downgrade everything from a planetary scale to a localised mountain or valley. And then, as if this were not enough, they bring the gods down from the Heaven-of-space, and relocate them in the Earth's troposphere, as if to suggest that ancient man was incapable of conceiving anything beyond the visible clouds.

But it is modern scholars who are beclouded. They have missed the whole point that the story of the gods fertilising the Earth was *a sacred mystery* – the ultimate mystery of the creation. The ancients would frequently make esoteric allusions to this as being like a divine marriage, as in the gnostic text, the Gospel of Philip, where it was written:

> Great is the mystery of marriage! For without it the world would not have existed.[89]

It was this same mystery which caused the participants in the Eleusinian Mysteries to look skyward with the cry of "Rain!", and Earthward with the cry of "Conceive!". These two words, according to Hippolytus, constituted *the great secret* of the initiation. Can we seriously believe that this great secret was the fertilisation of the Earth *by rainwater*? And yet this is, in effect, what modern scholars have been telling us for the last two centuries with their weather-gods theory.

Frankly, I am puzzled. I can think of a dozen reasons why modern scholars might have failed to make the proper celestial connections – prejudice, ignorance, complacency, the list goes on. And yet I cannot help wondering whether some of them knew something. There just seem to have been *too many* wrong turns, *too many* blind eyes, and *too many* anomalies swept casually under the carpet. It is almost as if everything that should have been taken *literally* was taken *symbolically*, and, vice versa, that everything which should have been taken *symbolically* was taken *literally*. It is incredible. One almost suspects that some scholars knew the truth, but regarded it as a truth too potent for outright telling.[90]

The bottom line is that the silence of the scholars – for whatever reason – has allowed the ultimate religious secret of mankind to remain untold throughout the 20th century.

It is now high time that this veil of secrecy was lifted, lest we all sink too deeply, and irretrievably, into the mire of our misconceptions.

* * * * *

CHAPTER THREE

THE DIVINE CHILD

**But if anyone in the earnestness of his intellect
wishes to apply himself to the various branches of
divine knowledge, or to the examination of metaphysics,
he will find that the whole world owes
this kind of learning to Egypt.**
(Ammianus Marcellinus, 4th century AD)

During the 1st century AD, the Greek writer Plutarch collected together all of the ideas which were current in his day concerning the great Egyptian deities Isis and Osiris. In his famous treatise *De Iside et Osiride* (*About Isis and Osiris*), he assembled a continuous narrative, setting out the details of the birth of Isis and Osiris, the murder of Osiris, and the magical birth of his successor, the child-god Horus.

In his narrative, Plutarch described the common perception that Osiris had been a just and beneficent king of Egypt:

> Osiris, having become king of Egypt, applied himself to civilising his
> countrymen by turning them from their former indulgent and
> barbarous course of life. He taught them how to cultivate and improve
> the fruits of the earth, and he gave them a body of laws whereby to
> regulate their conduct, and instructed them in the reverence and
> worship which they were to pay to the gods.[1]

After thus civilising Egypt, Osiris then apparently travelled over the whole Earth, civilising it without the slightest need of arms, and winning people over to his ways by means of charming discourse, music and song.[2]

Plutarch informs us that, during Osiris's absence from Egypt, Isis ruled the land, keeping a watchful eye on Seth – their jealous, crafty and headstrong brother. But when Osiris returned, Seth hatched a cunning plan to murder him, in order to claim the kingdom of Egypt for himself.

Aided by seventy-two fellow conspirators (along with a mysterious 'queen of Ethiopia'), Seth laid a trap for Osiris, under the pretext of celebrating his brother's return.[3] He organised a banquet and, at the end of it, unveiled a magnificent chest made of cedar-wood, inlaid with ebony and ivory, promising to give it to any of his guests who fitted its dimensions exactly. Needless to say, the chest had been custom-measured for Osiris.

When Osiris, the king, lay down inside the chest, Seth and the conspirators rushed forward and slammed down the lid. They then nailed the chest shut, sealed it with molten lead and threw it into the nearby river. The river, in turn, carried the chest, with Osiris inside it, out to sea through the so-called 'Tanaitic mouth' of the river Nile.[4]

On hearing of this awful news, Isis, the wife of Osiris, and the queen of Egypt, set out in search of his body.

According to the legend reported by Plutarch, the body of Osiris was carried to a place called Byblos, where it grew up into a beautiful tree, but the tree was later cut down and used in a pillar for the palace of the local king.[5] Isis, however, flew to Byblos (having turned herself into a swallow), recovered Osiris's dead body from the pillar, and took it back to Egypt.

Then – in what one presumes was originally a separate legend – the chest containing Osiris's body was discovered by Seth, the evil brother, who was out hunting at night. According to Plutarch, Seth proceeded to chop Osiris's body into pieces and scatter these pieces all over Egypt, intending that they might never be found.[6] Isis, however, managed to find all of the body-parts except for the phallus, which had apparently been thrown into the Nile and swallowed by a fish.[7]

As for those body-parts of Osiris which Isis did find, some people believed that the goddess had buried them where she found them, whilst others believed that she had secreted them away.

This, then, is the basic legend of Isis and Osiris as reported by Plutarch, which represents, we may presume, the common perceptions among the Egyptians of the 1st century AD.

But is this really the true story of Isis and Osiris, or does it rather reflect the *'dumbed down' version* of the story, which was fed to the common people?

Plutarch, for his part, was in two minds about the story which he related. On the one hand, he dismissed the idea that Isis, Osiris and Seth had been human beings, and launched a withering attack on Euhemerus (whose theory of deified kings and heroes later became known as 'euhemerism'). Euhemerus, according to Plutarch, had 'invented a new mythology of his own', which had not 'the least appearance of truth to support it'.[8] The man, he said, clearly lived in a fantasy world.

On the other hand, Plutarch suggested that the story of Isis and Osiris was not without 'a substantial foundation'.[9] In his words: 'there must have been some real distress, some actual calamity, at the bottom – as the groundwork of the narration'.[10] In support of this, Plutarch pointed out that the land of Egypt was full of sepulchres where the parts of Osiris's body were said to lie, whilst the temples of the land were filled with such a 'solemn air of grief' that it was difficult to believe that they had not been inspired by something very profound.

Today, when we look at what remains of ancient Egypt, we can only share Plutarch's feelings. Everywhere we look, we see the remnants of a religion which was unprecedented – more than a match for that of the Sumerians. In Egypt, the name of the game was not simply reverence for the gods – as in Sumer – but the desire to *become* a god, and to enter, upon death, the mystical realm known as the *Duat*, where the deceased person might travel to Heaven and eat what the gods ate, drink what the gods drank, and live a blissful life of immortality.

Immortality was the vital heart of the ancient Egyptian culture. The mummies exhibited in various Western museums are a striking example of this, but those who have travelled to the Nile Valley have witnessed much greater wonders – the giant statues of the kings, the glorious temples with their mighty pillars reaching for the Sky, and, most impressive of all, the marvellous pyramids of Giza.[11]

It is surprising that Plutarch did not point out the connections between these pyramids and the story of Osiris. After all, the pyramids were the 'resurrection machines' of the kings, and the kings believed that they could achieve this resurrection by *becoming* Osiris, and emulating Osiris's *original* death and resurrection. Osiris was thus the archetype of death, rebirth and immortality.

The fact that this death, rebirth and immortality permeated every aspect of Egyptian society for *more than three thousand years* attests to the veracity of Plutarch's words about the death of Osiris: 'there must have been some real distress, some actual calamity... as the groundwork of the narration'.

What might that 'actual calamity' have been? Plutarch, having set out the essentials of the Isis and Osiris story, proceeded to list the various explanations of the story which were current in his day. Firstly, the euhemerist theory; secondly, the theory that Isis and Osiris were demons; thirdly, the theory that the stories were allegories about the forces of nature; fourthly, that Isis and Osiris were the Moon, with Seth being the Sun; and fifthly, that the story alluded to the phenomena of eclipses.[12] None of these theories, it must be said, involved the kind of 'calamity' that would have instigated the Egyptians' profound beliefs about death and rebirth.

At the end of Plutarch's discussion, readers were left none the wiser as to what the whole story was about, even though Plutarch himself insisted that there *was* something to it.

But did Plutarch leave his readers in the dark *deliberately*? As mentioned in chapter one, there were certain things which Plutarch would *not* discuss – specifically the ritual of the cleaved tree-trunk at Byblos. This, he said, was 'intermixed with such of their mysteries as may not be revealed'. And yet, in the same breath, Plutarch commented that the tree-trunk ritual 'hints to us the reality upon which this history is grounded'.[13]

This was not the only mystery alluded to by Plutarch. In chapter XIX of his treatise, he stated, in something of a *non sequitur*, that:

> *Isis is said to have had union with Osiris after his death*, and she
> (then) brought forth Horus-the-Child, who came into the world before
> his time, and was lame in his lower limbs.[14]

Having dropped this bombshell, Plutarch then casually moved on to other matters.

What makes this comment seem all the more odd is that earlier, in the main narrative of the treatise, the birth of Horus was not mentioned by Plutarch at all, and the child simply appeared on the scene as if nothing unusual had occurred. Most readers would thus have assumed that Osiris had fathered the child *before his death* – that is until they came across the rather disturbing account of the necrophilic embrace, cited above.

This *non sequitur*, in itself, is not particularly important, for it might well be the case that Plutarch was simply too embarrassed to mention the necrophilic embrace, having just mentioned Isis's making of an artificial phallus to replace the lost member of Osiris! What is perhaps more important is that Plutarch alluded to the miraculous conception of Horus by Isis without elaborating on what it meant.

Was this another mystery 'as may not be revealed'?

At the same time as Plutarch published *De Iside et Osiride* (1st century AD), other legends were circulating in ancient Greece, suggesting that the birth of Horus was indeed the most potent secret of all.

In the Hermetic text entitled *The Virgin of the World*, we read briefly of the miraculous birth in a discussion between Horus and his mother

Isis:

> And Horus said: "How was it, mother, then, that Earth received God's Efflux?" And Isis said: "I may not tell the story of (this) birth; for it is not permitted to describe the origin of thy descent, O Horus (son) of mighty power, lest afterwards the way of birth of the immortal gods should be known unto men – except so far that God the Monarch, the universal Orderer and Architect, sent for a little while the mighty sire Osiris, and the mightiest goddess Isis, that they might help the world, for all things needed them."[15]

Once again we must ask: "Who were these gods? Why was the world in need of them?"

Egypt Rediscovered

During the 1st century AD, when these Hermetic ideas were competing with those of early Christianity, the typical Egyptian citizen believed that Osiris was some kind of fertility-king, whose body-parts had been ploughed into the ground to render the land fruitful. Osiris was thus regarded as a god of agriculture, who died every year, only to be reborn with the change in the seasons. Alongside this entirely reasonable belief, many people accepted the rather incongruous idea that Osiris had also been a former king of the land, as outlined by Plutarch above. This idea originated, no doubt, from the many depictions of Osiris (and other gods) *in human-like forms*.

But did these widely held ideas really reflect the profound nature of Egyptian religion? Or did they rather reflect the *exoteric* version given to *the masses* – as opposed to the *esoteric* version maintained by *the few*? Did the royal family and the priesthoods know a deeper meaning to this 'dumbed down' story?

During the first half of the 19th century, there arose a remarkable opportunity to peel back the mystery of the Egyptian religion. With the deciphering of the Rosetta Stone in the 1820s, the key to the hieroglyphic texts had been discovered, and during the following decades, a small number of leading Egyptologists around the world began to use that key to unlock the secrets of the ancient Egyptian writings. They were the first men to enter a world which had been effectively lost for some two thousand years.

In 1882, Gaston Maspero, a French Egyptologist, published the first ever translation of the Pyramid Texts – the ritual prayers which had been sealed inside the pyramids of ancient Egypt since *c.* 2350-2200 BC (they are thus the oldest known surviving corpus of religious writings in the world).

The point should not be missed that these spells had been sealed away for eternity – their content known only to the priests, the kings, and the gods of the *Duat*. They were private prayers, not intended to be seen by prying eyes, and certainly not intended to be translated and read by Egyptologists more than four thousand years later. Accordingly, the content of the Pyramid Texts was explicit, and not hidden behind 'seven veils' of secrecy, as was the case with later religious writings.

By 1910, a much improved translation of the Pyramid Texts had been published by the German Egyptologist Dr Kurt Sethe, and other experts had begun to publish translations of major sections of the Book of the Dead and the Coffin Texts. By the late 20th century, any member of the public could walk into a bookshop and buy a complete set of translations of all these sacred texts. It was enough to put any latter-day mystery schools out of business.

As part of this renaissance of ancient Egyptian religion, there was, inevitably, a series of new revelations concerning the mysterious conception of Horus. The Pyramid Texts in particular enabled us to fill in the details which had been omitted from Plutarch's story. One passage, for example, described the sexual union of Isis and Osiris quite explicitly:

> (O Osiris:) Thy sister [Isis] came to thee, rising up, because of her love
> for thee. Thou didst set her on thy phallus, thy seed came forth into
> her, she became great with child... He avenged thee in his name of
> 'Horus-the-son-who-avenged-his-father'.[16]

This passage complemented an earlier text – a hymn to Osiris which had been translated in 1867. The so-called 'Paris Stele' stated:

> She [Isis] went about seeking him [Osiris] untiringly. She flew round
> and round over the earth uttering wailing cries of grief, and she did not
> alight on the ground until she had found him. She produced light from
> her feathers, she made air to come into being by means of her two
> wings, and she cried the death cry for her brother. She made to rise up
> the inert members of him whose heart was at rest. She drew from him
> his essence, and she made therefrom an heir.[17]

But what did all this mean? Despite the *translations*, the rather awkward problem of *interpretation* remained. The veil of unfamiliar metaphors and allegories had yet to be penetrated. In 1969, Dr Raymond Faulkner, the acclaimed translator of the Pyramid Texts, explained the problems which he (and others) faced:

[The Pyramid Texts] provide problems and difficulties... They include very ancient texts... imposing on the modern reader problems of grammar and vocabulary... and there are many mythological and other allusions of which the purport is obscure to the translator of today.[18]

Nevertheless, *despite these fundamental uncertainties*, the most eminent scholars in the field of early Egyptology did not hesitate to evoke the Pyramid Texts as evidence for monotheism, with the Sun-god, Re, being the sole God of the ancient Egyptians.

Foremost among these founding fathers of Egyptology was James Henry Breasted, an American scholar, whose views on the Pyramid Texts seem to have been heavily biased by modern Judaeo-Christian beliefs. Breasted swept aside evidence for a stellar cult alongside the solar cult, by asserting that the latter had absorbed the former. As for those aspects of the Pyramid Texts which he could not comprehend, Breasted simply dismissed them as a mishmash of archaic myths, hymns and magical prayers.

Similar ideas were promulgated by the English Egyptologist Sir Ernest Alfred Wallis Budge, whose work spanned approximately the same era as Breasted, from 1899 to 1934. Wallis Budge, too, focused on the solar cult of the Egyptians, stating that the Sun was their 'visible emblem' for a higher God.[19] *He never spoke publicly of what that higher God might actually have been*. As for those aspects of the Pyramid Texts which Wallis Budge could not understand, he dismissed them as 'grossly superstitious and coarse beliefs', which had been handed down by the overactive imaginations of savage and semi-savage ancestors.[20]

Such was the powerful influence of Breasted and Wallis Budge during the formative years of Egyptology that few scholars dared to challenge their conclusions. And that, by and large, has been the case ever since.

The result is that Egyptology today is in the grip of an orthodoxy which explains everything in terms of the Sun – temples, obelisks, pyramids, Sphinx – *everything*. A new generation of scholars works away busily at their various specialities (doing much good work, it must be said), but taking for granted all things on religious matters and relying unquestioningly on the *interpretation* imposed *prematurely* by Breasted and Wallis Budge a century ago.

This is not just my view, but also the view of certain commentators within Egyptology itself. For example, in 1993, the Egyptologist Dimitri Meeks highlighted the fact that reliable translations of many important religious texts had only become available during the previous twenty-five years. He then commented that:

The work of establishing the basic facts... has in reality barely begun. The moment has come, then, to read or reread the texts, not to bring them into line with our own fantasies, as in the past, but to try to understand what they really mean... What would Egypt become if it were finally taken for what it was – neither morally acceptable nor morally shocking, and still less the mother of our own conceptions – what, if not something completely *other*? The time is ripe for posing the question. (original emphasis)[21]

As Dimitri Meeks suggested, the time has indeed come to take a fresh look at the ancient Egyptian texts.

And we shall begin at the beginning.

When the Sky Fell

As more and more ancient Egyptian texts were translated and published during the 20th century, it became increasingly apparent that the Egyptian priests and kings were obsessed with something called *Zep Tepi*, which translates roughly as 'the First Time'.[22] Indeed, they were not just obsessed with *Zep Tepi*, but obsessed with the idea of *restoring Zep Tepi* – in other words, winding back time to the very beginning. This, it turns out, was the quest of the kings in the afterlife – to ascend to Heaven and restore all things to how they had been in the beginning.[23]

Why was this considered necessary? *The simple answer is that the ancient Egyptians believed that there had once been a golden age in the universe, which had been lost as a result of a tremendous catastrophe.* The aim of the priests and kings was to recapture this golden age – to restore order (*maat*) where there was now disorder, to restore justice where there was now injustice, and to restore perfection where there was now imperfection. This was the inspiration behind the quest of the Egyptian priests and kings to turn back time.

As for the catastrophe which had occurred during the First Time, it was referred to by the Egyptians in various ways: it was 'that day of slaying the Oldest Ones',[24] 'that day when the rivals fought',[25] 'that day of the great reckoning',[26] 'that day of the storm over the Two Lands',[27] 'that day of the great slaughter',[28] and 'that night of making war and that day of destroying the enemies of the Lord of All'.[29]

And, in respect of the latter 'night of making war', the authors of the Book of the Dead added the following gloss: 'it means that the Children of Impotence entered into the east of the Sky, and war broke out in the entire Sky and Earth'.[30]

Plutarch, it would seem, had been vindicated – the Egyptians *did* believe in 'some real distress' and 'some actual calamity' (to use Plutarch's words) which was at the heart of their religion.

Plutarch was right about another thing, too. The gods were *not* deified kings of pre-dynastic Egypt, and did *not* belong to an era thousands of years before the 1st Dynasty (as Manetho had suggested in the 3rd century BC). On the contrary, the gods belonged to the era of the First Time, which was *millions of years before* the 1st Dynasty. This became evident from the translation of inscriptions from Egyptian temples, which referred to the temple as a 'mansion of millions of years', or 'the mansion united with eternity'.[31] The idea, clearly, was that the temples were establishing a bond through time to the imagined golden age of the First Time, which had been destroyed millions of years earlier, or, to paraphrase – *an infinitely long time ago.*

This, it transpired, was the time when the god Osiris had been born, and when he had come to occupy his throne in the underworld. But Osiris was not born as a king on Earth, as the later Egyptians had come to believe. On the contrary, the Pyramid Texts, dating back to *c.* 2300 BC, stated unequivocally that:

> The king [Osiris] is bound for the eastern side of the Sky, for the king was conceived there and the king was born there.[32]

At last it was possible to understand why the Egyptian kings were so obsessed with ascending to the Sky after death; they believed that they – as Osiris – had been born there, and hence they belonged there.

The cracking of the hieroglyphic code, by Jean-François Champollion and others, also revealed that the mother of Osiris, whom Plutarch had referred to by the Greek name Rhea, was a *Sky-goddess* named Nut. In the very first lines of the Pyramid Texts, the goddess Nut confirmed that Osiris was 'my eldest son who split open my womb'.[33]

But what kind of 'womb' was it that could have existed *in the Sky*? The sensational answer was revealed by Nut herself in Utterance 484 of the Pyramid Texts:

> "I am the Primeval Hill of the Land in the midst of the Sea."[34]

At this point, readers are reminded of the fact that the Mesopotamian and Greek Sky-gods were identified as 'mountains'. Nut, as a 'Primeval Hill of Land', falls into the same category. And this would suggest that the 'Sea', in the midst of which Nut's 'Hill' floated, was a metaphor for the watery abyss of the heavens. We will return to this metaphor later, at which time we will confirm that this is indeed the correct understanding.

At this point, we are moving swiftly into a decoding of ancient

Egyptian metaphors. The 'Hill', it would seem, was a metaphor for a celestial body; the 'Sea' was a metaphor for space; and the 'womb' of Nut was a metaphor for something in the Sky which would give birth to the gods. The latter point was corroborated by Plutarch 2,300 years after the inscribing of the text cited above, when he wrote that Seth had come forth from Nut's womb by 'forcing a passage through a wound which he made in his mother's side'.[35]

So much for the idea that this was some kind of human-like childbirth.

Returning to Osiris, it cannot be overemphasised that, despite being conceived and born in 'the eastern side of the Sky', he was most famous as the god of the underworld, i.e. the interior of the Earth.

How did Osiris, a Sky-god, become a god of the underworld? The answer is obvious – Osiris came down from the Sky.

Moreover, Osiris came down from the Sky with such a force that he penetrated the Earth and entered the underworld.

So much for the weather-gods theory. Osiris must surely have been a meteorite.

Now that we have the full range of translations of the Pyramid Texts, the Book of the Dead and the Coffin Texts, this cataclysmic descent of Osiris should no longer be an issue. In Utterance 254 of the Pyramid Texts, for example, we read:

> He [Osiris] *split open the Earth* by means of what he knew on the day when he wished to come thence.[36]

Similarly, in the Book of the Dead, we read:

> ... *the corpse of Osiris entered the mountain*, and the soul of Osiris walked out shining... when he came forth from death, a shining thing, his face white with heat.[37]

Note the reference here to Earth as a 'mountain' – a metaphor used in Mesopotamia as well as in ancient Egypt. And note, too, the idea of the separation of Osiris's body and soul, with his body entering the 'mountain' of Earth, and his soul ascending to Heaven. This idea – of death and rebirth – was at the very heart of ancient Egyptian religion, with the death of Osiris marking the defining moment and prototype of the belief.

Further evidence for the meteorite theory – if more be needed – comes from the legends of the god Geb, who according to the Pyramid Texts was the 'alter ego' of Osiris.[38] Depictions of Geb show the god in the act of falling to the ground, with his body twisted, and his head turned upwards. His name derived from the Egyptian verb *gebgeb*, meaning 'to fall headlong', and the Coffin Texts explain this fall by stating that Geb 'entered into' the Earth.[39] Clearly Geb fell from the Sky.

Moreover, the legends of Geb (alias Osiris) confirm that the Egyptian god of the dead was not just a single meteorite, but rather a whole flood of them. Hence one Egyptian text said of Geb that he carried out construction and renovation work to the Earth in 'thousands of foundations and millions of places'.[40]

The Benben Stone

If these accounts are to believed, a reasonable number of meteorites must have fallen upon the ancient land of Egypt, and been retrieved by the Egyptian priests. In which case, we might well ask: "where are those meteorites today?"

It is an established fact that some Egyptian meteorites were smelted down for their iron, which was then used to make sacred objects. Other meteorites might have been preserved intact, but would eventually have decomposed into a pile of loose fragments (the iron content of many meteorites makes them prone to rust when exposed to the Earth's moist atmosphere). As for those meteorites which did not perish in this manner, it is entirely reasonable to presume that they were removed and destroyed by hostile forces, or else removed and hidden by the Egyptian priests.[41] If the thesis presented in these pages is correct, it is hardly surprising that the Egyptian meteorites disappeared, for they would have been the most sacred objects in the land.

It was, no doubt, one of these various fates which befell the 'Benben Stone' – a conically shaped meteorite which was worshipped at the ancient Egyptian city of Annu (Heliopolis).[42] The Stone was referred to in Utterance 600 of the Pyramid Texts:

> O Atum-Khoprer, you became high on the height, *you rose up as the Benben Stone* in the Temple of the Benben in Annu...[43]

An artist's impression of the 'Temple of the Benben' appears in Figure 1. The meteorite, or Benben Stone, is here shown in the form of a pyramidion (a miniature pyramid), which had been placed upon a tall pillar, pointing up towards the Sky – whence it had come.[44]

Unfortunately, there is today no trace of the Benben Stone, and nothing remains at Annu (Heliopolis) other than an obelisk which was placed there *c.* 1950 BC by king Senuseret I. Absence of evidence, however, does not amount to evidence of absence. Egyptologists are certain that the temple did exist, and they are certain that the Benben Stone was a meteorite. Not that the opinion of Egyptologists is to be relied upon. Rather, we should go back to first principles and seek verification from the Egyptians themselves as to what the Benben Stone actually was.

Figure 1.
THE TEMPLE OF
THE BENBEN

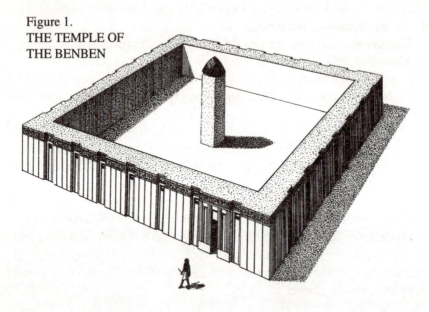

A major clue is to be found in an inscription from the temple of Khonsu at Thebes. The following passage – with ancient Egyptian terms inserted – describes the act of creation by the supreme god Amen-Re:

> Amen-Re is the god who begat (*bnn*) a place (*bw*) in the primeval ocean, when seed (*bnn.t*) flowed out (*bnbn*) the first time... it flowed out (*bnbn*) under him as is usual, in its name 'seed' (*bnn.t*).[45]

This passage describes the First Time – the time when Osiris was conceived and born in 'the eastern side of the Sky'. (Incidentally, the name Amen-Re should not be allowed to confuse us, for Amen, Re and Osiris were all aspects of one-and-the-same deity.)

Now, it should be noted that the term *benben* (*bnbn*) in the above passage means 'flowed out'. The Benben Stone can therefore be translated as a 'Stone-which-flowed-out'. As Henri Frankfort points out in his book *Kingship and the Gods*, the evidence is 'conclusive' that the Benben Stone was regarded as 'the solidified seed' of the God.[46]

Where did the Benben Stone flow out? According to the above passage, it flowed out from under Amen-Re *in the primeval ocean*.

Where was the primeval ocean, and what was it? According to the ancient Egyptians, this watery expanse, which they called *Nu*, *Nwn* or *Nwnw*, was the oldest thing in the universe, and had preceded the birth of all the other gods.[47] This ocean, which we shall for convenience call 'Nun', was said to be everywhere, endless and without limit, having no up, no down, and no surface.[48]

This primeval ocean, we should recall, was the place where the *Sky*-goddess Nut had her *mountain*-like abode. And this abode must have been in the Sky because Nut was the mother of Osiris, and Osiris had been born in the Sky, prior to falling to Earth and entering the underworld.

There is, therefore, only one possible translation for Nun, and it goes beyond the 'celestial deep', 'celestial waters' or 'celestial ocean', which were suggested by Wallis Budge.[49] The primeval ocean was, without any shadow of a doubt, the same infinite abyss which we today call 'space'. Hence it was asserted that Osiris had *swum* to the Island of Earth, i.e. he had swum from the 'eastern' side of the Sky across the primeval ocean.[50]

The Benben Stone was therefore a stone which flowed out from under the creator-god in the vast abyss of space, at the beginning of time. The Benben Stone *was*, therefore, a meteorite. On this point, at least, Egyptologists are correct.

The Mystery of the Het-Benben

At the beginning of this chapter, I retold the legend of the death of Osiris, as narrated by Plutarch in the 1st century AD. According to Plutarch's version of events, Osiris had been dismembered by Seth, who had buried his body-parts all over Egypt. Isis, the sister-wife of Osiris, had then managed to retrieve all of these body-parts, with the exception of one, namely the phallus, which had allegedly been thrown into the Nile and swallowed by a fish.

This story, as it stands, probably made no more sense to a Greek reader than to a modern reader. But what if it *does* actually mean something? What if the 'phallus' was a metaphor? What if the Nile was not the Nile as we know it? What if the swallowing-by-a-fish was an analogy?

Approximately one hundred years ago, it was discovered that various Egyptian texts contained lists of the places where the body-parts of Osiris had been buried. Significantly, it came to light that the all-important phallus had been buried at a place called *Het-Bennu*, the 'Temple of the Phoenix'.[51]

We now know that *Het-Bennu* was one-and-the-same place as the *Het-*

Benben – the Temple of the Benben at Annu (Heliopolis). It was here that the cult of the Phoenix (or *Bennu*-bird) existed alongside that of the Benben Stone.

But might there have been more to the Temple of the Benben than meets the eye? After all, the mysterious missing phallus of Osiris was located in the underworld. Might the temple (see Figure 1) thus have been built above a concealed complex of *subterranean chambers*? And might these hidden chambers have contained some relic which represented the 'phallus' of the god?

We know from the accounts of Herodotus (5th century BC) that it was indeed the ancient Egyptian practice to build secret subterranean chambers. Concerning the infamous 'Labyrinth', Herodotus stated:

> I visited this place and found it to surpass description... the Labyrinth surpasses the pyramids... There are two different sorts of chambers throughout – *half under ground, half above ground*, the latter built on the former... The upper chambers I myself passed through and saw... (but) of the underground chambers I can only speak from report: for *the keepers of the building could not be got to show them...*[52]

This report from Herodotus exemplifies the secrecy which existed in Egypt with regard to the underworld. And it explains why writers such as Plutarch failed to mention the underworld at all. It was the quintessence of the Mysteries, not just in Egypt, but also in Greece and other regions of the ancient world. And, not surprisingly, the Labyrinth (as described by Herodotus) has remained hidden to this day.

So, was there a similar kind of secret labyrinth beneath the Temple of the Benben?

The answer was revealed – for those who would have eyes to see and perceive – in 1905, when Wallis Budge produced the first full English-language translation of two of the most sacred Egyptian texts – the Book of What is in the Duat, and the Book of Gates.[53] In the latter book, the creator-god Re was depicted passing through twelve divisions of the *Duat, the first nine divisions of which were in the underworld.*[54] It was in the seventh division that the first mention was made of the *subterranean form* of the *Het-Benben* – the Temple of the Benben:

> These are they [the twelve bearded gods] who hold the mystery of this great god [Re]. Verily those who are in the *Duat* see him, and the dead see him – those who burn in *Het-Benben*... Re saith unto them: "Receive ye my forms, and embrace ye your hidden forms. Ye shall be in *Het-Benben*, the place where my body is."[55]

This place, the *Het-Benben*, was the underworld, for the body of Re (we know from other texts) was Osiris, who always remained (bodily) in the underworld, even when the soul of the god ascended to Heaven. It was thus a *subterranean Het-Benben* which was referred to in the Book of Gates. And it was described as a place where the bearded gods would 'burn' because the Egyptian underworld was conceived as a fiery inferno – the prototype of the modern concept of Hell.

A few lines later in the Book of Gates, the *Het-Benben* was mentioned briefly again, with the god Re declaring that: "I protect my secret things which are in *Het-Benben*."[56] The nature of these things, not surprisingly, remained hidden – hidden away in Re's 'secret places' in the depths of the underworld.

In the light of these texts, archaeologists of the early 20th century should have given serious thought to the possibility that the Temple of the Benben had been built above a subterranean level, the latter symbolising the caverns of the Egyptian underworld. More than this, it should have been considered a *probability*, especially in view of Herodotus's report about the Labyrinth and *its* lower chambers. Archaeologists should have been packing their picks and shovels and heading off to Heliopolis to renew the search for the lost site of the sacred temple.

Unfortunately, no such expedition was ever mounted, and the *exact* location of the Temple of the Benben has never been revealed to this day. The secret things of Re – perhaps even the 'phallus' of Osiris – might well be lying there today, intact and undiscovered.

Why the lack of interest? The reason is that Egyptologists have never appreciated the significance of the meteorite cult; they have never appreciated the sanctity of the ancient Egyptian underworld; and, more fundamentally, they have never even comprehended what the underworld was. All of these things have been kept secret for millennia – they were, and perhaps still are, the foundations of the Mysteries.

Wallis Budge, himself, steered his readers well wide of the truth. In the notes accompanying his translation of the Book of Gates in 1905, he wrote:

> Re promises them that they shall be with him in *Het-Benben*, that is to say, *in the heavenly counterpart* of one of the temples of the Sun-god at Heliopolis.[57]

Nonsense! What Re actually said to the bearded gods was: "Ye shall be in *Het-Benben*, *the place where my body is*", to which the other gods replied: "*let thy body be to the earth*."[58] The gods were thus confined in the Earth, *not* elevated to the heavens.

The Light in the Underworld

The subterranean nature of the *Het-Benben* was not the only ancient secret concealed by Wallis Budge in his misinterpretations of the Book of What is in the Duat and the Book of Gates. His much greater accomplishments were: (a) to reinforce the dogma that Re was a Sun-god (and nothing but a Sun-god); and (b) to confuse the definition of the underworld with the *Duat*. In so doing, he effectively occulted the meaning of one of the most fundamental motifs of the ancient mystery schools – *the dazzling light which illuminated the initiate in the darkness*.

Was Wallis Budge really as ignorant as he might appear from his misreading of the *Het-Benben* texts, and the *Duat* texts? Or was he *feigning* ignorance in order to conceal the true meaning of these vitally important concepts? Whatever the truth of this matter is, I really do not profess to know. All that can be said with certainty is that Wallis Budge, in the error of his ways in 1905, served to protect the millennia-old secret of the underworld throughout the 20th century. He could not have done a better job even if he had been paid to do it.

Let's now take a closer look at the Book of Gates and the Book of What is in the Duat, along with a closely related text known as the Book of Caverns, and see what they actually said, and what they actually meant. All the time, we should remember that these texts were secret texts; they were written on the walls of tombs or on coffins, and were sealed away for eternity. They were not meant to be seen by the prying eyes of the common folk, such as you or I.

We begin with the Book of Gates, which describes Re's descent into the Earth, a brief meeting with the body of Osiris, and then a resurrection to Heaven. At this point, we are interested only in the first part of the journey – the descent into the Earth.

The opening scene in the Book of Gates is marked by the disk of Re *passing into* the 'Mountain of the West' – yet another usage of the metaphor 'mountain = Earth'. Re's opening speech anticipated the light which he would bring into the 'mountain':

> Re saith unto the Mountain: "Send forth light, O Mountain! Let radiance arise from that which hath devoured me, and which hath slain men and is filled with the slaughter of the gods."[59]

As Re entered the 'mountain', the gods within responded to him thus:

> The hidden abode is in darkness, so that the transformation of this god

may take place... There is darkness on the road of the *Duat*, therefore let the doors which are closed be unfolded, let the Earth open, so that the gods may draw along him that hath created them... Praised be Re whose soul hath been absorbed by the Earth-god.[60]

What this text actually says, quite clearly, is that Re was passing *into the interior of the Earth*. This might seem odd to those who have accepted that Re was a Sun-god and nothing but a Sun-god. But the whole point is that Re, the Sun, was a *symbol* for something else – *a secret and esoteric form of God*.

Returning to the text, we find Re proceeding through various 'gates' of the underworld, which opened and shut as he passed through. In each 'division' of the underworld, the gods urged Re to come and "dispel our darkness".[61] As Re illuminated them, they rejoiced; then, as he exited and returned them to darkness, they lamented. The following extracts give a good flavour of what was happening:

Sa [the god of intelligence] saith to the gatekeeper: "Open thy gate to Re, unfold thy doors... that he may make his radiance illumine the hidden habitation."[62]

Re saith unto them [the gods]: "Open ye your shrines, so that my radiance may penetrate the darkness in which ye are."[63]

The beings of the *Duat* shout with joy... "Send forth thy light upon us, O thou great god who hast fire in thine eye."[64]

They make lamentation for the great god after he hath passed by them, for when he hath departed they are enveloped in darkness...[65]

A similar scenario is presented in the Book of What is in the Duat, which the Egyptians called 'the Book of the Secret Chamber'. The 'secret chamber' belonged to Osiris, who rested in the seventh, bottommost, division of the *Duat*. It was there that the descending Re set his course, saying: "I have come to illuminate the darkness and to embrace Osiris."[66]

The Book of Caverns placed greater emphasis on this unification between Re and Osiris, with Re being identified as the soul and Osiris as the body. Re thus entered the caverns of the underworld saying: "lead my soul towards my body."[67] In the third, and bottommost, of the six caverns, Re was said to join with Osiris, instigating a mysterious transformation, which heralded the joint resurrection of the two gods into Heaven.

In all of these texts it can be seen that Osiris was the archetype for the mystery school initiate. The god would lie in the deepest darkness, in an inert state, and would then be suddenly illuminated by the arrival of Re's light. The body of Osiris would then stir, often becoming ithyphallic, as the procreative powers of life returned. Finally, the god would be resurrected and would experience a rebirth in Heaven. This rebirth was the main objective of the illumination, as indeed it was in the initiations of candidates into the ancient mystery schools.

It was not, however, the Sun which was illuminating the candidate, but rather a *symbolic Sun*. In the coded language of Lucius Apuleius, an initiate into the Mysteries of Isis during the 2nd century AD, it was the 'Sun at midnight':

> I saw the Sun at midnight shining with its brilliant light, and I approached the presence of the gods beneath [i.e. in the underworld], and the gods of Heaven, and stood near and worshipped them.[68]

Apuleius had indeed seen the light, but it was the light of the meteorite.

The Efflux of Osiris

Lest there be any doubt about the meteorite being at the heart of ancient Egyptian religion, we will now look briefly at the texts dealing with the resurrection of Osiris to Heaven. Some of these texts – such as those cited earlier – dealt with the resurrection of Osiris-the-god, but most of those which I shall now cite deal with the resurrection of Osiris-the-king. In ancient Egypt, the distinction was a subtle one, for each king was identified with Osiris when he died. Indeed, each king *became* Osiris when he died.

The first thing to note is that the Egyptian king began his ascent to Heaven *not* by ascending, but rather by *descending* – to the throne of Osiris *in the underworld*. This indirect route to Heaven makes perfect sense under the meteorite theory, for the meteorite – the body of Osiris – was underground. (Needless to say, this route to Heaven is difficult to explain otherwise.)

This underworld was sometimes called *Amentet*, 'the Hidden Place', sometimes the 'Island of Fire' (for obvious reasons), and sometimes 'Rostau'. It was in this latter place that the deceased king would collect the 'efflux' which was so vital to his journey back to Heaven.[69]

What was this 'efflux'? According to Utterance 553 of the Pyramid Texts, it was the 'efflux which issued from the putrefaction of Osiris'.[70] Spell 1080 of the Coffin Texts gives the game away on exactly how this efflux of Osiris ended up in the underworld of Rostau:

> This is the sealed thing which is in darkness, with fire about it, which

contains the efflux of Osiris, and it is put in Rostau [Giza]. It has been hidden since it fell from him [Osiris], and it is what came down from him on to the desert of sand.[71]

The efflux of Osiris was thus something that 'came down' from the sky. The fact that it was then placed 'in darkness, with fire about it' suggests a location in the underworld, where the same contrast is found between a land which is *dark* (the hidden *Amentet*) and yet, at the same time, *fiery* (the Island of Fire). Once again it must be emphasised, for any remaining fans of the weather-gods theory, that hailstones do not have the momentum to force an entry into the underworld. If the text is taken literally, the efflux of Osiris could only have been a meteorite.

Readers are also reminded that the literal meaning of 'efflux' is something which 'flowed out'. This was exactly the description of the Benben Stone – the meteorite of Heliopolis – which we discussed earlier in the context of the seed which flowed out in the primeval ocean.

One of the first tasks of the deceased king in the underworld was to gather together his 'members', i.e. his body-parts. In the Pyramid Texts, Osiris the king was urged to 'gather your bones together, resume your members'.[72] Furthermore, the Pyramid Texts revealed that these body-parts were made of iron:

> (O Osiris the king), raise yourself upon your *iron bones* and golden members, for this body of yours belongs to a god.[73]

> Arise, remove your earth, shake off your dust, raise yourself... provide yourself with your *iron members*. Cross the Sky...[74]

As mentioned earlier in this chapter, iron is a characteristic feature of meteorites. It is illuminating, therefore, to read that the body-parts of Osiris-the-king were associated with iron.

Egyptologists are well aware that meteoric iron played a crucial role in the ascension ceremonies for the deceased kings.[75] The key rite in these ceremonies was the so-called 'opening of the mouth', which was supposed to effect the rebirth of the deceased king. The new king, or a priest, would approach the mummified body of the old king, and touch an adze-like tool to its lips. According to the Egyptologist Lanny Bell, 'the symbolic blade of this tool was a small bit of meteoric iron – a magical metal, associated with the heavens'.[76] That this is indeed the case is revealed by the Egyptians themselves in Spell 816 of the Coffin Texts, which affirms that the iron of the adze *fell from the Sky*, from something which had been broken apart:

> The iron is broken by Anubis in the Sky. Ho, iron which opened up

the West [i.e. the Earth]! This is the iron which is on my mouth, which Sokar spiritualised in Annu [Heliopolis], which makes the water of my mouth to rise.[77]

According to Spell 228 of the Coffin Texts, this adze of meteoric iron was known as 'the side of Osiris', and was kept in a 'locked chest'.[78]

Significantly, when the king's soul ascended from the underworld, its destination in Heaven was *a throne made of iron*. This, too, was revealed by the Pyramid Texts:

O king, raise yourself, receive your head, gather your bones together, shake off your dust, and sit on your iron throne.[79]

The Sky thunders, the Earth quakes... the Earth is hacked up... I ascend to the Sky, I cross over the iron... I ascend to the Sky among the Imperishable Ones... I sit on this iron throne of mine.[80]

Note, in the second passage above, the manner in which the king ascended out of the Earth: 'The Earth quakes... the Earth is hacked up'. This is typical of the ancient Egyptian texts, and reflects the idea that the return of the god to the Sky should mirror his arrival into the Earth – it was, quite clearly, a catastrophic event.

Elsewhere in the Pyramid Texts, we find the king rising up to Heaven in 'a blast of fire' or 'in a great storm'.[81] At other times, he would ascend on the 'reed floats of the Sky', in order to traverse the celestial waters.[82]

Occasionally, the king would ascend to Heaven using a mysterious vehicle such as the *Shedshed* of the god Upuaut, 'the Opener of the Ways'. The following passage illustrates how the dismembered body-parts of Osiris-the-king would supposedly be put back together again:

O Horus-upon-the-*Shedshed*, give me your hand that I may ascend to the Sky, to Nut. (O Nut) set your hand on me with life and dominion, that you may assemble my bones and collect my members. May you gather together my bones... May I ascend and lift myself up to the Sky as the Great Star in the midst of the East.[83]

In the Pyramid Texts, the king's most common destinations in the Sky were Nut (as here), or Re, 'the Morning Star'. But Re, the Morning Star, was not necessarily a solar or stellar form of that god.[84] On the contrary, the Pyramid Texts inform us that Re 'came forth from Nut', and Nut, as we have seen, was 'the Primeval Hill of Land in the midst of the Sea'.[85]

Furthermore we have seen that Osiris, too, was a son of Nut, whilst at the same time being the body of Re. Thus it can be said, without fear of contradiction, that these three deities – Nut, Re and Osiris – were aspects of one-and-the-same celestial deity.[86]

But what was the nature of this deity, into which the iron body-parts of Osiris and the soul of Re were reconstituted?

In the Pyramid Texts, the king was said to be transformed into an *Akh* – best translated as 'a shining one' or a 'being of light' – who would rule in the eastern *Akhet*, the 'Mountain of Light'.[87]

In the Book of Caverns, referred to earlier, the final scene shows the bark of Re being pulled by twelve deities towards a reddish disk which was shining (presumably on fire) in the far horizon. The text called this disk the 'Mountain of the East'.[88]

In the Book of Gates, also referred to earlier, the gods who pulled Re's boat declared that they would 'guide his wings *to the mountain*'. Re then proceeded to enter into the heights of Heaven (in the 'eastern horizon' of Heaven), where he 'set himself in the body of Nut'.[89] The scene – depicted in Figure 2 – shows the disk of Re being pushed up by a scarab beetle into the waiting arms of Nut. Nut, in turn, stood upon the head of a god, whose body formed a kind of island. This island was said to be 'Osiris, whose circuit is the *Duat*'.[90]

All of this tends to confirm the words of Nut herself that she was 'the Primeval Hill of the Land in the midst of the Sea' – i.e. the 'mountain' or 'island' in the midst of space. This was, of course, an identical idea to that found in the legends of ancient Mesopotamia.

Figure 2.
THE REBIRTH OF RE
IN THE BODY OF NUT

But the question still remains – what kind of 'mountain' or 'island' are we dealing with here? What *exactly* was Nut, and what *exactly* was her 'son' Re/Osiris?

The Waters of Osiris

In the 5th century BC, Herodotus, 'the Father of History', made his oft-cited statement that 'the Nile is the gift of Osiris, but Egypt is the gift of the Nile.' Five centuries later, the Greek writer Plutarch observed that the river Nile, and all forms of water in Egypt, were called 'the efflux of Osiris', i.e. *that which flowed out from Osiris*.[91] In the context of the above discussion concerning the meteoric iron 'efflux' which flowed out from Osiris, we must now give diligent attention to the possibility that this fallen celestial god also emitted a flood of water – just as in the ancient Mesopotamian traditions.

Sure enough, when modern Egyptologists cracked the hieroglyphic code and began to translate the millennia-old Egyptian texts, the watery aspect of Osiris was right there, sitting neatly alongside his meteorite alter ego.

Take, for example, the legends related by Plutarch, concerning the finding of Osiris's body (or body-parts) by Isis. In 1901, J.H. Breasted (the Sun-struck Egyptologist mentioned earlier) published a translation of a text entitled *The Theology of Memphis*. This inscription revealed a very different tradition concerning the fall of Osiris to the Earth:

> Osiris drowned in his water while Isis and Nephthys watched. They saw him and they were distressed at him. Horus commanded Isis and Nephthys repeatedly that they lay hold on Osiris and prevent his drowning. They turned their heads in time, and so brought him [Osiris] to land. He entered the mysterious portals in the glory of the lords of eternity...[92]

With the benefit of what we have learned so far, part of this text can now be decoded, namely the statement that Osiris was 'brought to land' and 'entered the mysterious portals'; this means that Osiris – a god who was falling from Heaven – was taken out of the celestial waters and brought ashore, to the 'island' of Earth; he then entered the 'mysterious portals' of the underworld.

But what did it mean, to say that Osiris had drowned in his waters? As the first decade of the 20th century drew to a close, new translations of the Pyramid Texts and Coffin Texts began to provide the answers. Osiris, it appeared, had been found 'lying on his side' on the 'bank' of Abydos (the town Abydos being used as a metaphor for the Earth).[93] And Spell 74 of the Coffin Texts revealed that the waters had been leaking out from his side:

> Isis said to her sister Nephthys: "This is our brother [Osiris]. Come, that we may raise his head. Come, that we may reassemble his bones. Come, that we may rearrange his members. Come, *that we may make a dam in his side... there drips the efflux* which has issued from this Spirit."[94]

Even more remarkable was a passage in the Pyramid Texts, which suggested that the flooding from this wound was extensive – sufficient indeed to fill an 'Ocean':

> O Osiris the King, arise, lift yourself up... Your two sisters Isis and Nephthys come to you that they may make you healthy, and you are complete and great in your name of 'Wall of the Bitter Lakes', you are healthy and great in your name of 'Sea'; behold, you are great and round in your name of 'Ocean'; behold you are circular and round as the circle which surrounds the *Hw-nbwt*; behold you are round and great as the *Sn-sk*.[95]

Needless to say, this description of Osiris being 'circular and round', like a great ocean of the world, caused no little puzzlement to the Egyptologists who translated this passage. But instead of taking the passage literally, they assumed that it was some kind of metaphorical allusion to the king's universal authority and power.[96]

On the contrary, it has now become quite apparent that the Pyramid Texts were referring to a great flood of water, which Osiris brought to the Earth. The key to this is to realise that Osiris was the son of Nut, whose name was written with the hieroglyphic sign of a water-pot.[97] Now it is apparent from various texts and legends that Nut suffered a catastrophe. In one legend, it was the ripping open of her 'womb'. In another, it was the cracking open of her 'head'.[98] And we may deduce from this that her water-pot was also shattered. Hence in Spell 220 of the Coffin Texts, Osiris the king declared that he was 'the great power who came forth from the water-jar', the 'water-jar' being a metaphor for his mother Nut.[99]

Both Osiris and Re were thus said to have come forth from Nut with floods of water. In the case of Osiris, we read that 'the efflux of Osiris flooded out when he was buried'.[100] In the case of Re, we read that he was the 'Great Flood which came forth from the Great One'.[101] (This is yet another clue, incidentally, to the fact that Re was *not* just a Sun-god – how could the Sun bring such a flood of water to the Earth?)

This understanding of the Egyptian flood can be confirmed by both 'historical' and metaphysical evidence. From a 'historical' perspective, the ancient Egyptians spoke of a primeval catastrophe which they called 'the night of the Great Flood which came forth from the Great Lady'.[102] This Great Lady, we must presume, was Nut.

From a metaphysical perspective, it is noticeable that the watery efflux of Osiris was essential for the deceased king, when he set off on his imagined ascent to Heaven. Hence in Spell 833 of the Coffin Texts we read:

> Water for Horus! Water for Horus! Give him the water of his father Osiris. Ho, king! You have your water, you have your cold water, the efflux which issued from the god, the putrescence which issued from Osiris. O king, you depart living, you do not depart dead.[103]

Having thus 'quenched his thirst' in the afterlife with this 'great efflux' of his father,[104] the deceased king would ascend into Heaven, to the 'eastern horizon'. There, he would hear 'the noise of the flood at the eastern gate of the Sky'.[105] This celestial location was known as *Mehet-Weret*, meaning literally 'The Great Flood'.[106] Other texts referred to a mysterious place in the Sky which was called *Qebhu*, meaning 'the Cool Waters'.[107]

What must be realised, however, is that the deceased king would *return* these waters to the heavens, for it was his intent to restore all things to the way they had been at the First Time. This meant that, in the metaphysical 'other world' known as the *Duat*, a canal would be opened up *between Earth and Heaven*, and the king would sail up into the heavens upon a flood of raging waters. Utterance 266 of the Pyramid Texts is one of many which pick up this theme, stating:

> The Nurse-canal is opened, the Field of Reeds is filled, the Winding Waterway is flooded, that I [Osiris the king] may be ferried over thereon to the horizon, to Horakhti.[108]

Returning now to our earlier discussion of the meteorite efflux, we find that the ancient Egyptian texts envisaged a reconstitution of Osiris as *both meteorites and waters simultaneously*. Hence, in Utterance 611 of the Pyramid Texts, we read of Osiris that 'the great waters are joined together for you, the hacked-up lands are united for you'.[109]

But the most vivid description of Osiris the king's reconstitution as land-and-waters is found in Utterance 685 of the Pyramid Texts. Here we encounter once again the 'mountain' motif, with the 'mountain' of Earth being juxtaposed with the 'mountain' of Heaven, and both being split apart catastrophically to facilitate the rebirth of the king:

> The waters of life which are in the Sky come, the waters of life which
> are in the Earth come, the Sky is aflame for you, the Earth quakes at
> you before the god's birth; the two mountains are split apart, the god
> comes into being... the two mountains are split apart, this king comes
> into being...[110]

In summary, the 'efflux of Osiris' comprised not only meteorites, but
also water – enough to fill an ocean. The ancient Egyptian texts present
an intriguing picture of how this flood of meteorites and water was
unleashed upon the Earth by the disintegration of a heavenly 'mountain'
millions of years ago (or an infinitely long time ago).

This, it transpires, was the 'dismemberment of Osiris' as referred to by
Plutarch – *not* a chopping up of a human body on the Earth, *not* a shower
of hailstones, but rather a disintegration of a celestial body in the
heavens.

Nevertheless, despite our now-enhanced understanding of Plutarch's
legend, two crucial questions still remain. Why was the celestial
'mountain' of Nut, Osiris and Re associated with meteorites *and water*?
And what kind of parent body could break up and fall to the Earth in
such a manner?

Suffice to say at this stage that modern astronomers would recognise
only two theoretical possibilities for the identity of this 'parent' body:
either (a) a comet; or (b) a planet. We will return to this point, and
resolve it, in the next chapter.

Isis Unveiled

We round off this chapter by returning to the mysterious birth of Horus.
According to Plutarch:

> Isis is said to have had union with Osiris after his death, and she (then)
> brought forth Horus-the-Child, who came into the world before his
> time, and was lame in his lower limbs.

In the context of Osiris as a celestial 'mountain' fallen to Earth – be it a
comet or a planet – this passage now takes on entirely different
connotations. Was Isis perhaps the Mother-Womb of the Earth – like
Ninharsag of the Mesopotamian legends? Did she then give birth to
Horus from the 'womb' of Mother Earth?

The parallel between Isis and Ninharsag is indeed profound.
Ninharsag, we may recall, was invited to come to the Earth-mountain –
the HAR.SAG – *after* it had been prepared by Ninurta. Ninharsag, prior to

becoming the Earth-goddess, had been Ninmah, 'the Exalted Lady' (i.e. the lofty, elevated lady) of a 'distant land'. In other words, Ninmah came down to the Earth.

This, it would seem, is exactly what Isis did. The Paris Stele, cited earlier in this chapter, compared Isis to a bird circling the Earth:

> She [Isis] went about seeking him untiringly. She flew round and round over the Earth uttering wailing cries of grief, and she did not alight on the ground until she had found him.[111]

Isis, like all deities who descended from Heaven to Earth, then entered the underworld, which was the abode of her fallen husband Osiris. The Pyramid Texts record this tradition with the following concise statement by Isis:

> "O Osiris the king, I am Isis; I have come into the middle of this Earth, into the place where you are."[112]

The 'middle of the Earth', in this context, was certainly the underworld.

Other Egyptian legends give the impression that Isis might have become the Mother-Womb *before* the fall of Osiris/Re, because *he* 'broke into' *her*. This is revealed in Spell 334 of the Coffin Texts, where the king (as Horus) stated:

> "I am that first seed of Re, he begot me in the womb of my mother Isis... My mother Isis conceived me, and she swooned under the fingers of the Lord-of-the-gods when *he broke into her* therewith on that day of lifting... on that day of tumult..."[113]

Re thus 'broke into' the 'womb' of Isis in the form of a meteorite – just as his alter ego Osiris had 'split open the Earth'. Note, incidentally, the reference in this passage to the 'day of lifting', i.e. the separation of Heaven from Earth. The conception of Horus is thus linked explicitly to the catastrophic events of the First Time.

What happened next was a magical union between Isis and Osiris in the underworld – the divine prototype of what the ancients termed 'the sacred marriage'. The Paris Stele put it as follows:

> She [Isis] made to rise up the inert members of him whose heart was at rest [i.e. Osiris]. She drew from him his essence, and she made therefrom an heir.

The Coffin Texts recorded the event in a spectacular manner:

> The lightning flash strikes... Isis wakes pregnant with the seed of her brother Osiris... Atum says: "O maiden, you are pregnant and you are

hidden... you will give birth, being pregnant for the gods..."[114]

The Pyramid Texts, dating to *c.* 2300 BC, recorded the conception thus:

> Thy sister came to thee, rising up, because of her love for thee. Thou didst set her on thy phallus, thy seed came forth into her, she became great with child...[115]

But this was no ordinary child, and he sprang from no ordinary seed. It should be recalled from the inscription to Amen-Re, cited earlier, that the seed was a divine essence, created in the primeval ocean at the beginning of time:

> Amen-Re is the god who begat a place in the primeval ocean, when seed (*bnn.t*) flowed out (*bnbn*) the first time... it flowed out (*bnbn*) under him as is usual, in its name 'seed' (*bnn.t*).

The root *ben*, which is so evident in this passage, was used for any sexual, procreational or seeding activity; *ben* could mean 'semen', or 'to copulate', or 'to fertilise' and suchlike.[116] It is in this context that the Benben Stone, the sacred meteorite of Heliopolis, should be understood; it was a seed which had 'flowed out' in space, and then entered into and fertilised the Earth. Hence Egyptologists refer to the Benben Stone as the 'solidified seed' of the God.

Consider once again Utterance 600 of the Pyramid Texts:

> O Atum-Khoprer, you became high on the height, you rose up as the Benben Stone... you spat out Shu, you coughed out Tefnut...[117]

Here, the Benben Stone was linked to the emission of Shu and Tefnut, who were two of the most famous deities of the ancient Egyptian cosmogony. The following sexually explicit passage is one of the most famous Egyptian accounts of the creation:

> Atum is he who came into being [from himself], who masturbated in Heliopolis. He took his phallus in his grasp that he might orgasm by means of it, and so were born the twins Shu and Tefnut.[118]

It is evident from this legend that Shu and Tefnut, by virtue of their origin, were the semen or seed of Atum.

All things considered, there can be no doubt that the meteorite – the divine seed – was at the very heart of the Egyptian accounts of creation. Moreover, it is clear that the meteorite was thought to have impregnated the Earth – hence the legend that the phallus of Osiris was buried beneath the Temple of the Benben at Heliopolis.

This impregnation of Isis (Mother Earth) with a meteorite is little different from the impregnation of Ninharsag/Mami/Nintu (the 'Mother-Womb') with a meteorite (the lapis lazuli 'brick'), and little different from the impregnation of Gaea, the Mother Earth of Greek mythology, with the meteorites of Uranus, the falling 'Mountain of Heaven'.

It is therefore no surprise to find that the union of Osiris and Isis in the middle of the Earth (the underworld) produced a divine child, Horus, who was distinctly Titan-like. According to various legends, Horus came up out of the Earth as a divine falcon and gave battle to the evil god Seth, the murderer of his father Osiris.[119] After a series of markedly supernatural encounters, Horus avenged his father by subduing Seth, and thenceforth assumed the kingship of the Two Lands of Egypt (the Earth).

Such was the origin of the divine child, Horus, whose way of birth was alluded to in such mysterious terms by the Hermetic writers in the 1st century AD:

> And Horus said: "How was it, mother, then, *that Earth received God's Efflux?*" And Isis said: "I may not tell the story of (this) birth; for it is not permitted to describe the origin of thy descent..."

Nor was it permitted to reveal the secret identity of the mighty goddess Isis herself – the 'Virgin of the World'. The game is given away, however, by the poem from ancient Sumer, which I cited in the previous chapter:

> *Holy Earth, the virgin*, beautified herself for Holy Heaven.
> Heaven, the lofty god, planted his knees on Wide Earth,
> Poured the semen of the heroes Tree and Reed into her womb.
> Sweet Earth, the fecund cow, was impregnated with the rich semen of Heaven.
> Joyfully did Earth tend to the giving birth of the plants of life,
> Luxuriantly she brought forth rich produce, and gave birth to wine and honey.

* * * * *

CHAPTER FOUR

PARADISE REGAINED

The Above comes from Below, and the Below from Above
– the Work of the Miracle of the One.
(The Emerald Tablet – a Hermetic text)

Imagine that we could travel back in time to the year 2300 BC, and travel through the lands of the ancient Near East. Imagine that we could witness first-hand the wonders of the ancients, and question the kings and priests about their mighty temples and pyramids. Imagine too – a far-fetched one this – that these kings and priests would actually give us, the 'outsiders', some straight answers about the fantastic structures in their lands.

Let us begin our tour in the Nile Valley, at Heliopolis, where we would see the marvellous Benben Stone on its pillar, rising majestically towards the Sky. The meteorite, plated with gold, would sparkle in the sunlight, as if it were on fire. The priests would tell us that they were re-enacting the resurrection of the meteorite back to Heaven, whence it had come, and they would regale us with esoteric stories about the great Bennu-bird (alias the Phoenix). But they would say nothing to us about the secrets of the *Het-Benben* in the underworld.

At Giza, we would see the three pyramids of Khufu, Khafre and Menkaure in pristine condition, with their polished casings causing them to glisten in the sunshine like huge mountains of light. These pyramids, we would be told, were resurrection machines for the kings of old, who now lived with the gods in another mountain of light – a distant, invisible mountain in the 'other world'.

At Abu Ghurob, a short camel ride to the south of Giza, we would find a strange tower-like building, set upon a truncated-pyramid base, pointing up to the Sky like a giant phallus – a kind of hybridisation between a pyramid, an obelisk and the Benben Stone. We would be told the same story once again, of the need to resurrect the 'efflux' of Osiris back to Heaven, whence it had come.

Moving a short distance farther south, towards Abusir, we would find another giant phallus, and a chain of smaller pyramids. Then, at Saqqara, some further small pyramids, one of them completed only a few years earlier by king Unas, and containing the first ever inscriptions of the Pyramid Texts. These small pyramids would be dominated by yet another unusual structure – the *stepped*-pyramid of king Djoser, rising up to the Sky like a six-stage stairway to Heaven.

If we were to stop at Saqqara and survey the land around us, we would see numerous other pyramids, dotted around the landscape, to the north and to the south, rising up like shining mountains on the horizon. The landscape before our eyes would be like a vision lifted straight out of an episode of 'Star Trek' – from one of those imaginary Earth-like planets, occupied by one of those imaginary humanoid peoples, who are like us, *yet unlike us*, having developed a strange and alien way of thinking.

It might seem odd that all of this could be right here on Earth, in the reality of our own long-forgotten past, but it was and it is.

With the aid of our time-travelling machine, let us now travel to the land in the midst of the two rivers, where we will experience another astonishing vision. Having moved forward slightly in time to 2100 BC, we would witness the revival of the Sumerians in the form of the 3rd Dynasty of Ur. At the city of Ur, we would see an amazing sight – a huge three-storied mountain of mudbrick, erected by king Ur-Nammu, the founder of the dynasty. The name of the king would remind us of Nammu, the goddess whose name meant 'Primeval Sea', she who had given birth to the 'mountains' of Heaven and Earth.[1]

On the summit of the ziggurat at Ur, we would see a small shrine, dedicated to the god Nannar. The priests would tell us that this shrine was the bedchamber of the god, and every New Year he would descend to the summit of the ziggurat and re-enact the fertilisation of the world. For the other 364 days of the year, the ziggurat would function as a Bond of Heaven-and-Earth, allowing the gods of Heaven to hear the prayers of the priests, and issue guidance to the city in times of crisis.

Just to the south of Ur, we would arrive at Eridu, one of the oldest cities in Sumer, supposedly dating back to the era before the Great Flood. Here we would see another ziggurat, also built by Ur-Nammu, and an array of splendid temples. The priests might recite to us their tradition of how the god Enki founded the city and temple at the beginning of time:

The king Enki... has built a house.
Eridu, like a mountain, he raised up from the earth.[2]

A long camel ride north-eastwards would bring us to the city of Uruk, surrounded by a wall so thick that chariots could be driven along it. This wall was allegedly built by the legendary king Gilgamesh many centuries earlier.

Within Uruk's wall, we would find another huge ziggurat, once again constructed by king Ur-Nammu – that tireless orchestrator of the great Sumerian renaissance. This ziggurat was called E.AN.NA, meaning 'the House of Heaven-and-Earth'. The priests might recite to us the legend of how the great gods constructed this city and its temple:

> The city Uruk, handiwork of the gods, and its temple E.AN.NA, temple
>   descended from Heaven...
> It is the great gods themselves who made their component parts!
> Its great walls touch the clouds, its lofty dwelling place was
>   established by Anu.[3]

The E.AN.NA, we would be told, was a wedding gift, which had been presented by the supreme god Anu to the goddess Inanna, the goddess of love and war. He had given it to her when they performed their sacred marriage act, fecundating the Earth at the beginning of time. With straight faces, the priests would assure us that the goddess actually lived in the E.AN.NA temple, having been brought down from Heaven centuries earlier by Enmerkar – a heroic ancestor of Gilgamesh.

We might then proceed north-east to the city of Lagash, where we would find a magnificent temple completed only recently, at vast expense, by king Gudea. The priests would tell us how Gudea was told to build the temple by Ningirsu, the god of Lagash, who appeared to the king in a dream:

> In the heart of the dream, there was a 'man' [the god Ningirsu]:
>   his height equalled the Sky, his weight equalled the Earth...
> To his right and to his left, lions were crouching...
> He told Gudea to build a temple...[4]

Apparently, the god Ningirsu had himself drawn up the plans for the temple after Nisaba, the goddess of writing and wisdom, had appeared in the dream 'holding in her hand a stylus of flaming metal' and consulting the 'beneficent stars' of the heavens.[5]

The name of Lagash's new temple, we would be told, was Eninnu, short for *E-ninnu-Imdugud-bar-bar*, 'Eninnu the Flashing Thunderbird'.[6] This name referred to the Imdugud-bird, the 'Sling-Stone', which Ninurta had captured at the heavenly 'mountain' of Zu. The priests would tell us, unashamedly, that the god Ningirsu would rise up through the heart of the temple once a year, and soar into the Sky like the thunderbird.

Intrigued by this idea, we might head north-eastwards once again to complete our tour of ancient Mesopotamia at the fabulous city of Nippur. Here we would find the most impressive ziggurat of all, built (or was it *re*built?) yet again by Ur-Nammu. This giant, mountain-like structure was called E.KUR, meaning literally 'House like a Mountain', and it was dedicated to the great god Enlil, 'the Great Mountain'. The priests of Nippur would doubtless tell us that this was the most sacred site in Sumer, for it was the DUR.AN.KI, the 'Bond of Heaven-and-Earth', which was built at the very beginning of the world. They would cite their sacred scriptures as authority:

Enlil, when you marked off holy settlements on the Earth,
You built Nippur as your very own city,
The KI.UR, the mountain, your pure place, whose water is sweet,
You founded it in the DUR.AN.KI, in the centre of the four corners of
    the universe.[7]

In the city, the holy seat of Enlil,
In Nippur, the beloved shrine of the father 'the Great Mountain',
The shrine of plenty, the E.KUR, the lapis lazuli house he raised up
    out of the dust,
Planted it in a pure place like a high rising mountain,
Its prince, the 'Great Mountain', Father Enlil,
Set up his dwelling on the dais of the E.KUR, the lofty shrine.
The temple – its divine laws like Heaven cannot be overturned,
Its pure rites like the Earth cannot be shattered,
Its divine laws, like those of the AB.ZU, none may gaze upon,
Its midst is like the distant sea, mysterious like Heaven's
    zenith.[8]

An impressive claim, but there would be more to come. The priests would now take us to a sacred area of the city, to a place called Uzumua, where they would assure us, with a glint in their eye, that this was *the very spot where mankind had been created*. And they would really *believe* this. But if pressed for more information, the priests would clam up, muttering something about "the wise teaching the mystery to the wise".

This lightning-quick tour of the ancient Near East can barely do justice to the greatest monuments the world has ever seen, but it does give us an inkling of how things were in an age long ago. It is a world which is forever lost to us, and difficult to recapture, even in our imagination.

Nevertheless, in the relics and ruins which have survived to this day, there is ample and eloquent confirmation that *our ancestors believed in something very profound.*

At that time, in the 3rd millennium BC, every temple, pyramid and ziggurat on Earth was a microcosm of the intimate bond between Heaven and Earth. These were the ultimate power places, where the visible world met the invisible world, where the human world met the divine world, and where all things present were linked to all things past. Each temple, pyramid and ziggurat reconnected mankind to its origins, its genesis and its birthplace – at the navel of the world, but with an umbilical cord stretching all the way to Heaven.

But as for us – at the beginning of the 21st century – we in the West live in an increasingly secular society, where a house of God no longer belongs to sacred time and space, but is instead relegated in status to become little more than a cleverly contrived construction of bricks, mortar and glass.

How far we have come in five thousand years! How far we have fallen into darkness!

Can we penetrate the meaning of the mysterious Bond of Heaven-and-Earth? Can we shine some light into the darkness and recapture our sense of the sacred? The answers, I suggest are "yes" and "possibly".

In this chapter, I shall be taking an unusual approach, which I believe will offer very fruitful results: we are going to go back to basics, and work things through from first principles. We are going to begin with the meteorite – which was at the heart of Egyptian and Mesopotamian religions – and we will then try to recreate the ancients' sense of the sacred. Then, when we have penetrated a little way into the ancient way of thinking, we shall apply some of the lessons which we have learned in earlier chapters, and we will attempt to go the whole way – beyond the metaphors and right into the hearts and minds of the ancients, to rediscover the fundamental essence of their way of thinking.

This admittedly sounds like a bold quest, but by the time we are finished it will, with hindsight, seem to have been a very straightforward task. I am about to demonstrate that the ancients – far from having an alien way of thinking – were actually very much like us: rational, logical and intelligent.

In the process of recreating the ancient way of thinking, we will resolve very clearly the nature of the celestial body which disintegrated into water and rocks, according to the Egyptian and Mesopotamian theologies (the two possibilities, at this stage, being a comet or a planet).

Moreover, as a bonus, we will discover exactly why the ancients worshipped the Sun, Moon and stars *as well as the meteorite*. Sun-struck and star-struck historians and mythologists should look away now – for what follows is *a unified explanation* of all these various cults. Scholars, for some reason, seem to detest unified explanations. Perhaps they prefer the past to be complicated, so that their expertise might remain an essential and required commodity – to explain everything to us lesser mortals.

A note of warning, however, before we proceed. As mentioned at the beginning of this book, the religion of the ancients should not necessarily be regarded as '*The* Truth' with a capital 'T', but rather as '*a* truth', with a small 't'. Although there is much to be gained from understanding the ancient way of thinking, it is imperative that we keep it in a proper perspective. It may have worked for them, but it may not work for us. We might not even like what we find. But whatever views we might hold, no-one would deny that the ancients have a right to be heard.

The Messenger of the Gods

Nowadays – at the beginning of the 3rd millennium AD – the existence of meteorites is not in dispute. Astronomers inform us that the vast majority of meteorites began their careers as asteroids in outer space, although in some cases the meteorite might have come from the nucleus of an extinct comet. These asteroids, via a process which is not yet fully understood, have given rise to rocky debris in Earth-crossing orbits. Astronomers call these latter bodies 'meteoroids'. Many of these meteoroids burn up harmlessly when they enter the Earth's atmosphere, but larger meteoroids survive the passage and can cause impacts on the Earth. These fallen meteoroids are called *meteorites*.

In the days before scientists were able to explain the origin of meteorites, a great deal of scepticism prevailed as to their existence. Just a few centuries ago, anyone who witnessed a meteorite streaking down from the sky was thought to have lost leave of their senses. The meteorite was in many ways the UFO (unidentified flying object) of the Dark Ages.

Not so in ancient Egypt and Mesopotamia. There, as we have seen, the meteorite was not only held to exist, but was revered as a sacred object, a notable example being the Benben Stone of Heliopolis.

Few people today have ever seen a meteorite, and fewer still have ever handled one. An even smaller number of people have actually witnessed a meteorite falling out of the Sky. But taking the population of an entire country, meteorites *are* occasionally seen in mid-fall, and they *are* occasionally retrieved from the ground.

The rarity of meteorites makes them a valuable find. At the time of writing, a typical stony-iron meteorite would fetch up to $25 for a mere gram (more than twice the rate per gram of gold). Stone meteorites and iron meteorites are cheaper; but meteorites blasted off the surface of Mars or the Moon are more expensive; such is the rarity of these latter meteorites that they can fetch thousands of dollars per gram.[9]

To see a meteorite in the process of falling would be a fantastic and exceptional experience. In ancient times as well as now, such falls were spectacular indeed, with the fireball of the meteorite being able to light up the sky and briefly turn night into day. This bright light would often be followed by a loud bang or roar, as the meteorite exploded or fragmented before impact. As for the impact itself, it is a fact that the meteorite will often penetrate several metres into the ground, causing a loud thud and an earth-tremor, which might be heard and felt for a considerable distance around the impact site (depending on the size of the projectile).

The largest known meteorite in the world weighs around sixty tons, and is a major tourist attraction at Hoba in Namibia – the location where it fell some 70-80,000 years ago (see Plate 41).

An even more exceptional experience would await anyone who was lucky enough to be close to the meteorite's impact site. But the curious eye-witness might well get a nasty surprise if he approached a meteorite fragment shortly after its fall. On the one hand, the surface of the meteorite would be extremely hot as a result of heating during atmospheric entry. On the other hand, the *inner core* of a meteorite tends to maintain for some time the subzero temperature of outer space. A meteorite fragment is thus capable of either burning the human hand at one extreme, or freezing the skin off the human hand at the other extreme. This unusual characteristic would have been a puzzling but impressive phenomenon to the ancient mind, and it might well have inspired the peculiar fire-and-ice motif which appears from time to time in the legends of the ancient gods.[10]

Nevertheless, as valuable as meteorites might have been, with the rarity of their falls, and as impressive as they might have been, with their spectacular falls, impacts and unique features, there was *something else* about meteorites which captivated the minds of the ancients. And this something else was *an elusive quality which has been lost to the modern mind*. To recapture this quality, and to recover the true sanctity of the meteorite, we must begin to think like the ancients.

Let's try to cast our minds back to the ancient Near East of some five thousand years ago, when civilisation had been long established in Egypt and Mesopotamia, and peoples had taken the first steps toward mastering their environment. Animals had been domesticated, agricultural processes had been perfected, kilns had been invented for the firing of pottery, and stone and mudbrick had been harnessed for the erection of buildings and cities. Possibly there was a lot more besides this – for we still do not know how the ancient Egyptians managed to cut into solid granite with remarkable precision, nor how they constructed the Great Pyramids of Giza to such exacting standards.[11]

Anyhow, with these first bold steps, people had met their basic needs of shelter, security and sustenance, and had to a large extent tamed the hostile environment of the Earth in which they lived. Man's status was not far off that granted him in the Old Testament book of Genesis; he ate the fish of the sea, he tamed many birds of the air, he enslaved numerous creatures of the ground, and he ruled over most of the Earth, having surpassed even the formidable barriers of mountains and oceans.

But – and it was a big 'But' – there was one realm which man did *not* control, an area which he did not control at all, a region which lay seemingly forever beyond his physical reach. *That region was the realm of the gods.*

When ancient man looked up at the Sky, he saw a myriad of things which he could not control. He could not stop the Sun from rising every morning, nor from setting every night. He could not stop the movement of the Sun along the horizon during the year – a movement which brought the changes in the seasons and, in Egypt, the miraculous flooding of the river Nile. Nor could ancient man stop the waxing and waning of the Moon over its 29.5-day cycle. Nor could he affect the rising and setting of the distant stars, which slowly drifted out of position as the years progressed. Nor, finally, could he control the nearer 'stars' – Earth's neighbouring planets – which varied in luminosity and moved independently from the general backdrop of distant stars.

When ancient man apprehended all of these things above, he was truly humbled, and he realised that he was not, after all, master of all that he surveyed.

To the ancients, all of these lights in the Sky – the Sun, the Moon, the stars and the planets – were regarded as being of divine essence. Each of them was a god, possessing an eternal, unchanging cyclical existence in the divine realm – seemingly forever beyond the physical reach of mankind. And this entire realm of the gods was divine in the sense that it was forever separated from the Earth.

Or was it?

Occasionally, ancient man detected an element of chaos in the divine realm of the gods. From time to time, the regular clockwork of the heavens was interrupted by unusual lights in the Sky – meteors (shooting 'stars'), comets ('stars' with tails), supernovae (exploding stars), and meteorites (falling 'stars'). But of all these chaotic elements, only one of them could physically manifest itself on the Earth, only one of them could cross the barrier between Heaven and Earth, only one of them could be touched by the hand of man. *That unique type of object was the meteorite.*

What impressed ancient man so much about the meteorite was not its spectacular fall, nor its rarity, but rather the fact that it had fallen down, physically, to the Earth, from a realm which was entirely separate, divine and supernatural.

The meteorite was a messenger from the gods.

The Seeding of the Earth

But what was the message which this messenger of the gods conveyed?

Let's try to place ourselves in the position of the ancients, thousands of years ago, and ask ourselves what they would have made of the meteoric messengers from the heavens.

Immediately, we think of a very predictable question, and we imagine the ancients posing that question to themselves, namely: "where do meteorites come from?", or to put it another way: *"how the hell can a lump of rock fall out of the Sky?"*. Their reasoning, I suggest, proceeded as follows.

Meteorites were rocks which were not dissimilar in nature to the rocks found on the Earth. *Therefore, meteorites must have come from some place in the heavens which was similar in composition to the Earth.*

Sure enough, we find in the ancient texts of Egypt and Mesopotamia a consistently expressed belief that Heaven was a 'mountain', just as the Earth was a 'mountain'. Each was envisaged as a huge, spherical 'mountain' of rock, floating like an island in the celestial waters of space. But the 'mountain' of Heaven had seemingly disintegrated, unleashing a flood of meteoric rocks upon the Earth.

Now, this ancient investigation into the meteorite probably started out as a scientific enquiry, but it soon took on deeply religious connotations. The ancients tried to imagine what the 'mountain' of Heaven might have looked like. And the only model they had was what they knew – the Earth herself. So it was therefore assumed, naturally enough, that the 'mountain' of Heaven had not just been a barren lump of rock but, on the contrary, had possessed oceans of water and all the seeds of life – just like the Earth. This is a crucial point.

It is for this reason that we read in the ancient Egyptian texts of a Heaven which was so Earth-like that the king could do in Heaven everything he used to do on Earth. *It was a Heaven created in the image of the Earth.*

Or was it the other way around? In a beautiful piece of inspired logic, the ancients asked whether the Earth had always been a verdant paradise. And, at the same time, they asked themselves *when* the heavenly catastrophe might have occurred.

The first answer they came up with was that meteorites were the left-overs from a disaster which had happened at the very beginning of time – millions of years earlier (hence in Egypt the 'temples of millions of years'). It thus followed logically that the Earth which the ancients knew – and which we know today – might not always have been the way it was (or is). Earth *might* actually have been seeded by the collapse of Heaven.

So, had it or hadn't it? The ancients looked around, and they observed how there seemed to be *just the right amount of waters* flowing in the great rivers, which fecundated their lands, and they therefore wondered how the lands could possibly have been fertile *before* the waters of Heaven had fallen to the Earth. *QED*. The ancients decided that the Earth which they knew must contain the original waters of Earth *and* the former waters of Heaven. The original waters of the Earth were those which were locked up in the oceans (and perhaps the subterranean aquifers), whilst the waters of Heaven had topped up the oceans and, more importantly, filled up the rivers.

Therefore, it was decided that the lands of Egypt and Sumer had been transformed from barren deserts into watery paradises by a flood of water – unleashed by the explosion of the 'mountain' of Heaven.

This, of course, is the origin of the myth of the Great Flood (more on this in chapter seven).

To restate the ancients' train of thought: a meteorite was a highly sacred messenger from God; it could only have come from a heavenly 'mountain' which was Earth-like in nature; and the only model the ancients had for this 'mountain' was the Earth herself; therefore, Heaven was created by man in the image of the Earth, with oceans of water and all the seeds of life; but the meteorites were a sign that this Earth-like Heaven had exploded; it was thus reasoned that the fallen Heaven had fertilised Mother Earth with its waters and seeded her with its meteorites.

This, we should recall, was the theme at the heart of the ancient legends. In Egypt, the life-giving water of the Nile was 'the efflux of

Osiris', and the meteoric Benben Stone was regarded as the solidified seed of the creator-god. Similarly in Sumer, the gods Enlil and Enki had ejaculated semen-like waters in order to fill the rivers Tigris and Euphrates. Enlil, furthermore, had split open the Earth with a 'pickaxe' in order to create mankind, whilst Ninharsag had borne mankind after her womb was impregnated by a lapis lazuli 'brick'. I contend that both the 'pickaxe' and the 'brick' were metaphors – for meteorites, the seeds of the creation.

The sacred marriage rituals of the ancients tell the same story – of life beginning on Earth following the impregnation of Earth by a falling Heaven. Hence the birth of the Titans to Gaea. Hence the birth of Horus to Isis. Hence the *eleusis* of the divine child to Holy Brimo. Hence the saying of the Eleusinians: "Rain!... Conceive!". Hence the saying from the Gospel of Philip: 'Great is the mystery of marriage! For without it the world would not have existed.'

In order to fully appreciate the ancient way of thinking, one must look upon the landscape of the Earth and observe everything that is green – trees, bushes, plants, even blades of grass. Then imagine that all of these things had formerly been growing in Heaven. Then imagine all of these things falling to Earth – not in their fully grown form, obviously, but rather *as seeds*. Imagine, then, that these seeds entered the Womb of the Earth, and then imagine them being watered by the Great Flood which came down from Heaven. Finally, imagine these seeds sprouting forth into the world above, transforming the surface of the Earth into a verdant paradise.

This, I am convinced, was how the ancients came to regard their world. After life came death; but after death came rebirth and new life. Heaven was reincarnated on Earth, and hence all life was saved. And Earth owed everything to Heaven – the source of the seeds of life.

The Greek writer Plutarch captured this way of thinking when he reported the following belief among the ancient Egyptians:

> They [the Egyptians] believe the vine to have first sprung out of the earth after it was fattened by the bodies of those who fell in the wars of the gods.[12]

Scholars would no doubt laugh at this tradition, and they would no doubt laugh too at the following text from *The Theology of Memphis*, which originated from one of Egypt's most intellectual sources *c.* 700 BC:

> He [Ptah] is indeed Ta-tenen ['the Risen Land'], who brought forth the gods... And so the gods made their bodies enter into every kind of wood, every kind of stone, every kind of clay, and into everything that

sprouts on the surface of the Earth.[13]

It should now be apparent that these animistic beliefs were not as 'primitive' and 'superstitious' as scholars first assumed. On the contrary, they were consistent with what was at that time a very rational and even profound view of the universe.

A Meeting of Mountains

We are now beginning to think like the ancients, and so far everything has been perfectly logical. But at this point, we are going to encounter a way of thinking which will jar slightly with many readers. It is not so much a *simplistic* way of thinking (though some might have it so), but rather, in my opinion, a *simplified* way of thinking. Whether we like what follows or not, it is imperative that we grasp the point.

Imagine that the 'mountain' of Heaven – however we might define it in astronomical terms – disintegrated in space. What would happen next? Our modern minds might begin to calculate the percentage of the debris which would actually fall to the Earth. The ancients, however, took a different approach. They simplified things considerably by assuming that the *entire* 'mountain' of Heaven had fallen to the Earth.

Or, to be more precise, the ancients assumed that the entire 'mountain' of Heaven had fallen *into* the Earth – for the number-one rule of ancient religions was that everything which fell from Heaven to Earth entered the underworld.

We thus have a scenario of the fallen 'mountain' of Heaven being *inside* the 'mountain' of Earth – *a mountain-within-a-mountain*.

Leaving aside for a moment the question of what the 'mountain' of Heaven actually was, let us first look at some ancient texts to verify that this was indeed the ancient belief system.

To begin, I would like to cite a passage from the Sumerian text *Lamentations over the Destruction of Sumer and Ur*:

> (It was) a day when the weapon sent forth from above wrecked the
>   city as if with a pickaxe.
> On that day Heaven was crushed, Earth was smitten...
> Heaven was darkened, was overcast with shadow, was turned into the
>   underworld.[14]

In this remarkable passage, we have confirmation that Heaven was crushed; we also have a reminder of the 'pickaxe = meteorite' metaphor (compare Enlil's splitting open the ground at Nippur to create mankind like plants); and, most importantly of all, we have confirmation that

'Heaven was turned into the underworld'.

It was for this reason that the ancients referred to the underworld as a 'mountain'. The Sumerians called it KUR, i.e. 'mountain', or sometimes KUR.NU.GI, i.e. the 'Mountain of No Return' (also known as 'the lapis lazuli mountain').[15] The Egyptians called the underworld *Ament Set*, meaning 'the Hidden Mountain'.[16]

In both cultures, Sumer and Egypt, the Earth, too, was referred to as a 'mountain'; in Sumer it was the HAR.SAG; in Egypt it was Mount Manu or 'the Western Mountain'.[17] Hence the mountain of the underworld was effectively a mountain-within-a-mountain.

It is for this reason that we find so many enigmatic references in the ancient texts to a combined 'Mountain of Heaven-and-Earth'. For example, one Sumerian text began its description of the creation with the lines:

After *in the Mountain of Heaven-and-Earth*,
AN [Anu] had caused the Anunnaki to be born.[18]

As mentioned in chapter two, AN had impregnated KI, the Earth, and the Anunnaki had thus been conceived *in the underworld*. The same idea appears in the legend *Enki and the World Order*, where the Sumerians equated their land Sumer with the entire Earth, referring to it as a *combined mountain* with the Anunnaki in its midst. The text reads:

Sumer, 'Great Mountain', land of *Heaven-and-Earth*,
Filled with enduring light...
Your divine laws are lofty laws, unreachable,
Your heart is profound, unfathomable...
The Anunnaki, the great gods,
Have taken up their dwelling place in your midst.[19]

It is worthwhile noting that the word Anunnaki, when written in its full form A.NUN.NA.NUN.KI, meant literally 'the Seed of the Prince of Eridu'.[20] This can be interpreted in two ways. It either referred to the Anunnaki as being 'the Seed of Enki' (since Enki was 'the Prince of Eridu'); or it referred to the Anunnaki as being 'the Seed of the Prince *of the Earth*' (with Eridu being a metaphor for the Earth, just as Sumer symbolised the Earth in the passage above). Once again, we encounter the 'meteorites = seed' metaphor, and possibly the motif of the *eleusis* of a divine child in the Earth.

Returning to the idea of the mountain-within-a-mountain, the ancient Egyptian texts leave us in no doubt as to the intended meaning. In *The Legend of Re and Isis*, the creator-god Re boasted of his act of creation with the words:

> "I am he who made Heaven and Earth, *who knotted together the mountains*, and created everything which exists thereon."[21]

The idea, expressed in this passage and elsewhere, is that the two mountains of Heaven and Earth were *fused together*, one inside the other. To cite another example, there is an Egyptian text, entitled *The Mysteries of the Resurrection of Osiris*, which records some of the lesser secrets of the annual Mystery rites. In this text, the Senior Lector Priest recounted the arrival of Osiris in the Earth by reciting the words "Heaven and Earth join... Heaven and Earth join." Four times he uttered these words.[22] After further recitations of "Rising up of Heaven upon Earth", it was declared that "our lord (Osiris) is in his house', i.e. safely in the underworld. The meaning of all this should, by now, be abundantly clear.

This 'joining' of Heaven and Earth was also referred to as 'the union of the Two Lands'. Egyptologists may be surprised to hear this, for they have always regarded the union of the Two Lands as a historical event. That may be so – I do not wish to deny it – but the idea of joining Egypt as two lands was sparked by *a pre-existent celestial archetype*. That this was so is clear from the Coffin Texts, where it was stated:

> As for the union of the Two Lands, it means that the shroud of Osiris was ordered by his father Re.[23]

This, it must be emphasised, is a reference to the day when Heaven fell to the Earth – when Osiris 'split open the Earth by means of what he knew on the day when he wished to come thence'.[24] It was 'that day of the great reckoning' – 'that day of the storm over the Two Lands'.[25]

The idea that Heaven was *physically* in the midst of the Earth accounts for the otherwise rather anomalous idea among the Egyptians that *the Sky was to be found beneath the ground*. Hence in Spell 146 of the Coffin Texts we read:

> The king goes *down* into the Sky, he goes *down* into the Earth, he goes *down* into the waters...[26]

Similarly, in one of the most obscure passages in the Coffin Texts, the deceased king declared:

> I have crossed over the paths of Rostau [the underworld], whether on water or on land, these are the paths of Osiris; they are *in the limit of* the Sky [i.e. in the underworld]. As for him who knows this spell for *going down into them*, he himself is a god, in the suite of Thoth; *he will go down to any Sky to which he wishes to go down.*[27]

Similarly, in Spell 908 of the Coffin Texts, we read of a 'middle Sky' which was apparently in the underworld:

> Anubis who presides over the god's [Osiris's] booth, Lord of the Underworld, to whom the Westerners give worship... *Anubis who dwells in the middle Sky...* who was caused to descend from the Sky to put Osiris in order.[28]

Perhaps a better translation for 'middle Sky' would be 'Sky-in-the-middle', i.e. in the middle of the Earth. Incidentally, this would explain the origin of the word 'mason'; several distinguished researchers within freemasonry have suggested that the word mason is a corruption of the Greek word *mesouraneo*, meaning "I am in the midst of Heaven";[29] I suggest, on the contrary, that this actually means "I am in the middle Sky", or "I am in the Sky-in-the-middle (of the Earth)".[30] Hence the masons were said to be 'sons of light', meaning that they were conceived when a mysterious light entered the darkness of the underworld.

If we now put together what we have learned, we find that man created Heaven in the image of the Earth, with oceans of water and all the seeds of life, and imagined this Heaven to have fallen into the underworld. It thus follows that, on the one hand, the underworld could be a place of destruction and an Island of Fire – as it appears in the Egyptian texts – but on the other hand it could be a land of rivers and forests, containing the city and lapis lazuli palace of the underworld-gods – as it appears in the Mesopotamian and Greek texts. In the latter respect, the underworld was not just a mountain-within-a-mountain – *it was a world-within-a-world*.

Suffice to say for now that the inability of scholars to recognise this fundamental relationship between Heaven, Earth and underworld – particularly the fact that the three realms were conceived in each other's image – has constrained *severely* their ability to understand what the ancients were talking about. To truly *understand* these legends, we must *stand under* the foundations of ancient theology. It is then only a matter of time before our darkness is dispelled by light.

The Separation of Heaven from Earth

There is an old Hermetic saying that 'the above comes from below, and the below from above – the work of the miracle of the One'.[31] So far, we have seen how *the below came from the above*; this happened on the day the Sky fell – when 'Heaven was turned into the underworld'.

But how was it that the equation worked vice versa? How was it that *the above came from the below*?

In 1964, the Assyriologist Georges Roux made a telling statement in his book *Ancient Iraq*:

> The theory that... the shape of the universe had resulted from *a forceful separation of Heaven from Earth* by a third party was generally adopted in Sumer, Babylonia and Assyria...[32]

No-one would dispute this statement, but the really key question is *why* were Heaven and Earth 'separated'? Scholars have never dwelt on this point – they have just accepted that it was the view of the ancients on how the universe was formed, and it is thus not something to be fathomed by the modern mind. But the concept had always bothered and intrigued me, and it had lain for years in the darkness of my subconscious, waiting patiently for the light of understanding to shine.

That light *did* shine, with a sudden, blinding brilliance, shortly after I began to think like the ancients. As we have already discussed, the fall of Heaven caused it to be entombed physically within the Earth, and this meant that all of the waters and rocks of Heaven and Earth had been joined together. *It was therefore entirely logical that Heaven and Earth did need to be separated*. Albeit we must understand that this did *not* happen *physically* but rather *metaphysically*.

Suddenly, many things became clear to me. In the Bible, for example, the book of Genesis states that God *separated* light from darkness, and *separated* the waters of Earth from the waters of Heaven.[33] Shortly afterwards, God rested in his mysterious *metaphysical* abode.

Similarly, in the Muslim holy book, the Koran, God stated:

> "Are the disbelievers unaware that *the heavens and the Earth were one solid mass which we tore asunder...*?"[34]

Again, *metaphysically* speaking.

Moving to more ancient texts, the same idea is found in the opening line of the mysterious tablet excavated at Assur (see chapter one):

> *When Heaven had been separated from the Earth* – its distant trusty twin.[35]

The same idea is found in the Sumerian legend *The Myth of the Pickaxe*, where the god Enlil '*separated Heaven and Earth*' having split open the latter with his meteoric 'pickaxe'.[36] As his name EN.LIL suggests, he was the Lord (EN) responsible for that region of the universe – the LIL, i.e. 'airspace' or 'atmosphere' – which *separated* the two realms of Heaven and Earth.

Similarly, in the ancient Egyptian Pyramid Texts, we read of a time:

... when the Sky was separated from the Earth, when the gods ascended to the Sky.[37]

This makes sense. The gods had ascended to the Sky because they were lifted up out of the Earth's underworld (metaphysically).

One of the most famous examples of this separation of Heaven from Earth comes from the ancient Egyptian legend of Geb and Nut, who were separated by Shu. The legend begins with Geb and Nut being 'shut in' on 'the day of the great slaughter',[38] meaning that both deities had fallen to the Earth and were shut up inside the underworld, where they were performing the sacred marriage rite. But Shu then became jealous and *separated* the two lovers by lifting up Nut to become the Sky.[39] In the words of Shu in the Coffin Texts:

"I lifted up my daughter Nut from upon myself, so that I might give her to my father Atum in his realm, and I have set Geb under my feet... and I am between them."[40]

This separation is portrayed graphically in Figure 3. The result was that Nut became a metaphysical Heaven, and we should recall how she subsequently became the reincarnation vessel for the rebirth of the gods Osiris and Re.

Figure 3.
THE SEPARATION
OF NUT FROM GEB

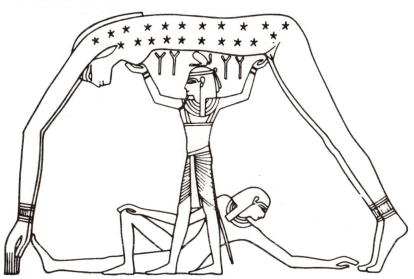

Perhaps the most dramatic account of the separation of Heaven and Earth appears in the Egyptian legend of *The Destruction of Mankind*. The god Re had descended to Earth in primeval times, had created mankind and had begun to 'rule that which he had made'.[41] But mankind later rose up in rebellion against Re, complaining that the god had grown old, that his 'bones' had become like silver, his 'body-members' like gold, and his 'hair' like lapis lazuli.[42] Re, perceiving the weakness of his 'members', then began to fear a second death, 'as at the first time', and announced his intention to depart from the world of men. Thereupon, Re was lifted up to Heaven on the back of Nut (the latter in the form of a cow), but with both of them being supported by Shu. The tale is summarised as follows in Re's own words:

> "I [Re] am departing from mankind, and anyone who wants to see me must come after me"... Then the Majesty of this god [Re] looked forth from its [Earth's?] interior, saying: "Gather together, and make ready for me an abode for multitudes... Let a great field be produced." Thereupon the Field of Hetep came into being. (And Re said:) "I will make to dwell in it things like stars of all sorts." Thereupon the *Akhekha*-stars came into being. Then the goddess Nut trembled because of the height. And the majesty of Re said: "I decree that there be supports to bear the goddess up." Thereupon the props of Heaven came into being. And the Majesty of Re said: "O my son Shu, I pray thee to set thyself under my daughter Nut, and guard thou for me the supports of the millions which are there, and which live in darkness."[43]

For one final example, which should verify our understanding beyond any doubt, we turn to the Babylonian epic of creation known as *Enuma Elish*. This legend describes a series of celestial battles followed by the creation of Heaven. We will look at the celestial battles in due course, but for now let us focus on the creation of the metaphysical Heaven.

The first reference to the creation of a metaphysical Heaven occurs in Tablet IV of *Enuma Elish*, when the god Marduk – the hero of the epic – was tested by the other gods to see if his powers were up to the task which was ahead of him. His task was to destroy Tiamat – the raging goddess of Heaven – and then to recreate Heaven, metaphysically, as an abode for the fallen gods. The test of Marduk's powers proceeded as follows:

> They [the gods] set up in their midst a constellation,
> And then they addressed Marduk, their son:
> "May your decree, O lord, impress the gods!
> Command to destroy and to recreate, and let it be so!

Speak and let the constellation vanish!
Speak to it again and let the constellation reappear!"
He [Marduk] spoke, and at his word the constellation vanished.
He spoke to it again and the constellation was recreated...
They [the gods] rejoiced, and proclaimed: "Marduk is king!"[44]

I cite this passage because it is a perfect illustration of the ancient way of thinking. The 'mountain' of Heaven (the 'constellation') was to be destroyed *physically*, but recreated *metaphysically*. The passage thus encompasses in a nutshell the physical and metaphysical duality which is so vital to our understanding of ancient religions.

After this test, Marduk carried out the real thing. First, he went into battle and destroyed the goddess Tiamat, interring a large part of her body in the Earth – beneath a 'heaped-up mountain'.[45] Then he built a metaphysical Heaven called 'Esharra':

He [Marduk] crossed the heavens and surveyed the regions.
He placed himself opposite the Apsu [the underworld], the dwelling of
    Ea-the-wise [Enki].
The lord measured the dimensions of the Apsu,
And he established Esharra, 'the Great Abode', as its likeness.[46]

This separation of Heaven from Earth also entailed a separation of the gods. Three hundred were lifted up to Heaven – they became known as the Igigi-gods – whilst three hundred remained in the Earth – these were the Anunnaki-gods. The Anunnaki were the physical gods, the Igigi their metaphysical counterparts.

But Marduk then announced that he would construct a temple called *E-sag-ila* – meaning 'the House with Lofty Head' – in which all of the gods could meet. We read Marduk's words in Tablet V of *Enuma Elish*:

"Above the Apsu [the underworld] – your sea-green dwelling,
Opposite Esharra which I created for you,
I have hardened the ground below for a shrine...
Whenever you come up from the Apsu for an assembly,
Your night's resting place shall be in it, it is there to receive you all,
Whenever you come down from the Sky for an assembly,
Your night's resting place shall be in it, it is there to receive you all.
I hereby name it Babylon [*Bab-ili*] – 'the Gate of the Gods'."[47]

It should be mentioned that this temple *E-sag-ila* actually existed, and was described by the Greek historian Herodotus, who visited it during the 5th century BC.[48] Its location was opposite the ziggurat of Babylon, but curiously it seems to have been as much a Bond of Heaven-and-Earth as the great ziggurat itself.

As for the legend of the temple's building, Tablet VI of *Enuma Elish* makes some interesting remarks about the notional size of the structure:

> The Anunnaki (of Heaven-and-Earth) applied the implement;
> For one whole year they moulded bricks.
> When the second year arrived,
> They raised high the head of *E-sag-ila* equalling the Apsu.
> Having built a stage-tower as high as the Apsu is deep,
> They set up there an abode for Marduk, Enlil (and) Ea [Enki].[49]

In order to understand the sense of this passage, some knowledge is required of how the underworld came to be known as the Apsu. In Tablet I of *Enuma Elish*, a celestial battle took place *in the heavens* between the gods Apsu and Ea (Enki). The outcome was that Ea triumphed and, in the manner of all celestial battles, the vanquished god, Apsu, was cast down into the underworld of the Earth. Following this, Ea/Enki then descended to the Earth himself and built his dwelling upon the fallen Apsu:

> Ea [Enki] poured sleep upon Apsu. Sound asleep he lay.
> When he had made Apsu prone, drenched with sleep...
> He fettered Apsu and slew him...
>
> He established his dwelling *on top of Apsu*...
> After Ea [Enki] had vanquished and trodden down his foes...
> He rested in his sacred chamber in profound peace.
> He named it Apsu, assigned it for shrines,
> (And) founded his cult hut in that same place.[50]

Thanks to this account, we can appreciate that Apsu had a dual 'above and below' meaning for the Mesopotamians. The Apsu – which is synonymous with 'the Deep' – had once existed in the Deep of space, in the heavens, but now existed in the Deep of the Earth, in the underworld. Incidentally, there is actually a Sumerian hymn which alludes specifically to the Apsu as being a *'deep mountain'*.[51] That is exactly what it was.

As mentioned above, Ea (Enki) also descended to the Earth, where he took as his wife the goddess Damkina (presumably an Earth-goddess like Ninharsag). The next thing that happened was that Marduk appeared on the scene as their son – the offspring no doubt of a sacred marriage rite. Marduk then escaped from the 'mountain' of the underworld, and ascended up into the Sky (metaphysically) like a Greek Titan.[52]

So, returning to Tablet VI of *Enuma Elish*, and the construction of

Marduk's *E-sag-ila* temple, what we are looking at is a mythical, metaphysical temple, which stretched all the way up to Heaven. The 'head' of *E-sag-ila*, we are told, would be equal in size to the fallen 'mountain' of the underworld, and it would be raised 'as high as the Apsu is deep', i.e. as high relative to the underworld, as the Apsu was deep relative to Heaven. In other words, the temple would stretch to the exact place where Heaven had been *before* the catastrophe. And this Heaven would become an abode for Marduk, Enlil (and) Ea (Enki).

In summary, *Enuma Elish* is in complete accord with all of the other texts cited above. Heaven was created *metaphysically* in order to become an abode for the fallen god, who was far from happy in the Earth. The reason the god had fallen into the Earth was because the god *was* Heaven, i.e. Heaven and the god were one-and-the-same thing. In order to create this metaphysical Heaven, its image had to be separated magically from its fallen counterpart inside the Earth. Hence we read that Marduk 'measured the dimensions of the Apsu, and established Esharra as its likeness'.

Thus Heaven was separated from the Earth. And thus, in the words of the Hermeticists, '*the above came from the below*'.

A Comet or a Planet?

To recap briefly, the ancients began with a meteorite, asked where it came from, and concluded, logically, that it had come from a 'mountain' in the Sky, which had been destroyed in a battle of the gods (*mountain-gods*). They conceived this 'mountain' of Heaven in the image of the Earth, with waters and all the seeds of life. Then they concluded that the fall of the heavenly 'mountain' – millions of years ago – had seeded and fecundated the Earth. In the process, the entire 'mountain' of Heaven had become interred inside the 'mountain' of Earth – hence the idea that the underworld was a mountain, and hence the references to a mysterious joint Mountain of Heaven-*and*-Earth. At this point, the fallen mountain-god orchestrated his resurrection to Heaven by separating Heaven from Earth, metaphysically speaking, and thus ascending to the Sky to reside in his mysterious, invisible, recreated abode.

Thus it can be said that 'the above comes from below, and the below from above'. The above – Heaven – was raised from the below – the underworld. And the below – Earth – was created by the earlier fall of the above – Heaven. The two linked statements thus refer to 'scene two' and 'scene one' respectively in the act of creation. This, I believe, is the original meaning of this Hermetic saying, as opposed to any of the numerous alternative interpretations of the saying which have only served to fog the issue.[53]

It now behoves us to identify what was meant by the 'mountain' of Heaven. What kind of 'mountain' could disintegrate in space, penetrate physically the crust of the Earth, and seed the beginning of life on our planet? There are two possible answers – a comet, or a disintegrating planet – but which of these two is the most accurate description of what the ancients had in mind?

Concerning the comet theory, it is interesting to note that some modern scientists have already raised the possibility that these celestial bodies brought the seeds of life to the Earth.[54] The comet theory also seems attractive because it would fit the ancient belief that the *entire 'mountain'* had fallen into the Earth (this would be literally true for a comet which had entered the Earth's atmosphere).

Nevertheless, upon closer inspection, the comet theory runs into problems. According to the reasoning in these pages, the ancients would have regarded the comet as a *chaotic* body – the *result* of the catastrophe rather than its cause, the *fragment* of the god, rather than the god himself, the *messenger* rather than the king. Furthermore, it seems to me that the ancients were not particularly interested in making contemporary observations of comets (or indeed meteorites), but were rather interested in *theologising about where these chaotic bodies might have come from*. Hence the fact that ancient scribes gave utmost importance to explaining how Heaven, Earth, and later mankind, had been created in an age long ago – millions of years in the past.

This brings us to the idea of a disintegrated planet. Although the idea is anathema to the modern scientific mind, it must be stressed that we are dealing here *with a religious belief system*. Therefore, the idea of a planet breaking apart – into meteorites *and perhaps into comets too* – is an eminently plausible solution to the mystery of the disintegrating heavenly 'mountain' hypothesised by the ancients.

In order to resolve this question beyond any doubt, it is imperative that we put to one side any modern preconceptions about meteorites, comets and planets, and pay attention to what the ancients themselves actually said. After all, it is their *beliefs* which are at issue here.

The first thing to note is an anomaly which has been bothering us throughout the last two chapters, namely the insistence of the ancient scribes that the 'mountain' of Heaven had possessed *abundant waters*, which had fallen to Earth in a huge flood. As I have argued in this chapter, it is a belief which probably resulted from man's creation of Heaven in the image of the Earth.

Indeed, when we read and reread the ancient texts, we find a very striking belief that Heaven, Earth and the underworld were all created in the image of one another, with all three regions being Earth-like places.

The underworld, for example, was not just a minuscule cavern, but was rather believed to occupy the entire inner space of the Earth. And this underworld – the Apsu – was used to create *in its image* the 'mountain' of Heaven. Hence, in *Enuma Elish*:

The lord [Marduk] measured the dimensions of the Apsu,
And he established Esharra, 'the Great Abode', as its likeness.

What was this 'Great Abode' like? For the ancient Mesopotamians, it was a place for gods rather than for men, and men rarely visited it. The ancient Egyptians, however, were supremely confident of their abilities to reach the heavenly abode – more so than any other ancient race – and they described its features at great length.

The following two quotations exemplify the Egyptian belief.

Firstly, in the *Papyrus of Ani*, we read how the scribe Ani beseeched his god concerning his personal afterlife in the 'mountain' of Heaven:

"Grant thou that I may come unto the Heaven which is everlasting,
and unto the mountain where dwell thy favoured ones."[55]

This 'mountain', according to other texts, was called *Neter-Khert*, literally meaning 'the Mountain-Land of God'.

Our second quotation comes from the Book of the Dead, and demonstrates that this heavenly 'mountain' was an idyllic land, just like Earth, where the deceased could control everything he had tried to control on Earth:

I have gained the mastery over the waters, I have gained the mastery over the canal, I have gained the mastery over the river, I have gained the mastery over the furrows, I have gained the mastery over the men who work for me, I have gained the mastery over the women who work for me in *Neter-Khert*, I have gained the mastery in *Neter-Khert* over all the things which were decreed to me on Earth.[56]

Plate 36 – an illustration from the Book of the Dead – demonstrates how the Egyptians hoped to plough and reap in a heavenly 'Field of Reeds' (the prototype of the Greek belief in the paradisiacal 'Elysian Fields').[57] The British Museum have captioned the scene 'agriculture in the afterlife'.

It can thus be seen that, to call the 'mountain' of Heaven a 'comet' (according to our modern concept of what a comet actually is), would be a travesty of what the ancient Egyptians actually believed. Clearly the Egyptian king could not have been passing his eternity on a comet, unless we care to imagine him wearing some kind of spacesuit.

Now, in addition to this issue of the Earth-like environment on the 'mountain' of Heaven, there is also the issue of the *size* of the mountain. And here, as mentioned earlier, the ancients were adamant that Heaven and Earth were a mirror image of one another. Hence we find the following opening line on the mysterious tablet excavated at Assur (see chapter one):

> When Heaven had been separated from the Earth – *its distant trusty twin*.

Despite the penchant of its authors for secret writing, this text could not be more clear – it states categorically that Heaven and Earth were *twins*, i.e. twin *planets*.

The same idea is found in a Sumerian text which said of the goddess Inanna that she was 'as high as Heaven' and 'as wide as the Earth'.[58]

Similarly, in Greek mythology, Hesiod informs us that 'broad-flanked' Gaea 'bore a being *equal to herself*, able to cover her *entirely* – i.e. Uranus'.[59] Once again, the statement is unequivocal: Uranus, whose name meant 'Mountain of Heaven', was equal in size to Gaea. How could the 'mountain' of Uranus possibly be a comet?

Consider also one of the Greek legends concerning Zeus, whose name meant 'Bright Sky'.[60] In the following quotation, from *The Iliad of Homer*, we read that the combined force of all the other Olympian gods was insufficient to drag Zeus down from his '*mountain*' of Olympus, but *he*, on the contrary, could lift *them* all the way up to Heaven:

> I [Zeus] could drag you [gods] up, earth, sea and everything with you, then fetch the golden rope about the horn of Olympus and make it fast, so that all once more should dangle in mid-air.[61]

Does a comet 'dangle in mid-air'? No, on the contrary – it travels through the Sky on a chaotic orbit. A planet, however, is stable. And stability was the byword for the Heaven of the ancients, as evidenced by the ziggurats and temples of Mesopotamia, which represented permanent 'Bonds' between Heaven and Earth.

Finally, it should be noted that the Mesopotamians referred to both Heaven and Earth as a 'mountain'. They did not qualify this term, to refer to a *small* mountain or to a *large* mountain. On the contrary, they imagined that the 'mountains' of Heaven and Earth both belonged to the same category, i.e. they were both planets.

The ancient Egyptians went even further. They referred to Heaven and Earth using no less than *four different metaphors*, each of them applied consistently to Heaven *and* Earth respectively, with no qualifiers attached. These four terms were 'mountain', 'island', 'throne', and 'horizon' (the last term referring to the Egyptian *Akhet* – a shining island of light).[62] Once again, we find that Heaven and Earth were placed in the same category, this time emphatically. *Both were conceived as planets.*

All things considered, the comet theory of ancient religion turns out to be simplistic, and can only be made to work by imposing modern preconceptions upon the ancient texts. The disintegrated planet theory, however, makes sense when we recognise that we are dealing not with astronomical observations, but rather with *religions* and with *theological constructs*. So, no matter what modern prejudices we might hold against the idea of a planet disintegrating – or, more to the point, catastrophically *exploding* – the words of the ancients themselves should not be gainsaid.

Whether we like it or not, it must be concluded that the Heaven of the ancients was *a planet*, and the religions of the ancients can best be described as *exploded planet cults*. Henceforth, we shall talk not of 'meteorite cults', but rather of 'exploded planet cults'.

The Invisible God

Everything now slots into place. The creator-god of the ancients was a planet, which exploded in the heavens, and 'created' the Earth physically, by filling the rivers with its floodwaters, 'piling up heaps and mounds' of rock, and carrying out construction work on the Earth's surface in 'thousands of foundations and millions of places'. Then, for his grand finale, the creator-god created Heaven as an exact replica (metaphysically) of the lost planet.

And all of this occurred as a result of a battle between two Sky-gods, who were conceived in the minds of the ancients as two planetary rivals, who were usually portrayed as the forces of good and evil respectively. Hence we have the legend of Osiris being dismembered by Seth, the legend of Tiamat being divided in two by Marduk, and the legend of Zu being destroyed by Ninurta. Yes, these battles were often set in a *metaphysical* context, with a Titan-like god rising up to be the hero, but doubtless they all drew upon the legend of an original *physical* battle, such as that in which Apsu was put to sleep by Ea. Incidentally, it seems to be the case that the battle of the planets caused the *mutual destruction of both parties*, so that the fragments, or 'members', of both good and evil gods ended up being interred in the Earth.

So far, so good. But what about the fact that the ancients also worshipped the Sun, the Moon and the stars? How can this be reconciled with an exploded planet cult?

The answer can be found via straightforward logic. Once again, let's begin with the meteorite, and consider what it stands for. It was, as the Egyptians said, the solidified seed of the creator-god – a physical remnant of his dismembered planetary body. But – and it is another big 'But' – the meteorite was an inert object, devoid of the quickening breath of life, or spiritual essence, of the god. The creator-god, to whom we should perhaps be referring as 'God', was no longer in the meteorite, and was no longer on Earth. On the contrary, he – meaning his spirit or soul – had ascended to Heaven and was now occupying a metaphysical abode. *God was in Heaven, and he was invisible.*

Now let us postulate an important question. *How could the ancients worship an invisible God?* The straightforward answer, I suggest, is that they looked to nature for things which reminded them of what God had achieved.

What had God achieved? Simply put, God had died, but then come back to life again. His act of creation had comprised *a death and a rebirth*. God himself had experienced a death and rebirth. And Heaven, too, had experienced a death and rebirth (for God and Heaven basically amounted to one-and-the-same thing). Moreover, the death of God had also involved the death and rebirth of physical life, which had been transferred from the planet of Heaven to the planet of Earth.

Looking to nature, then, the ancients found numerous things which reminded them of the death and rebirth of God, the death and rebirth of Heaven and the death and rebirth of the seeds of life.

In agriculture, for example, the fertility of the land seemed to ebb away, only to be reborn the following year with the change in the seasons. Thus it was that Osiris, and similar deities such as Tammuz, became grain-gods and fertility-gods, allowing modern scholars to dismiss them, ironically, as *nothing but* grain-gods – an unfortunate and fundamental error.

Ancient man looked also to the heavens for symbols of death and rebirth. He could not see the true God – the exploded planet – who was invisible, but he did see numerous other *visible* bodies which reminded him of his *invisible* God.

Firstly, there was the Sun, which appeared to die and be reborn every day, as it set on the western horizon, and then reappeared in the east (it also appeared to die and be reborn at the shortest day of the year, the winter solstice). The Sun thus symbolised the death and rebirth of the exploded planet.

Secondly, there were the stars, which appeared to die on the western horizon and then be reborn in the east. The stars, too, thus symbolised the death and rebirth of the exploded planet.

And thirdly, there was the Moon, which appeared to die and be reborn at the end of its 29.5-day lunation cycle, when it underwent a period of complete invisibility for three days, and then reappeared in the night sky. The Moon, too, thus symbolised the death and rebirth of the exploded planet.

It thus becomes clear that the ancients did not worship the Sun per se, nor any star per se, nor the Moon per se. It is vitally important that we realise that the Sun did not really die, the stars did not really die, and the Moon did not really die. On the contrary, these 'deaths' were merely *symbolic deaths*, which reminded the ancients of what they believed had been a very real, physical death – of the planet which had exploded into physical meteoric fragments.

In addition to these visible manifestations of death and rebirth, there were also *the eclipses* of the Sun and the Moon, when the light of each died temporarily, only to return, as if being reborn. To people who believed in the catastrophic death and rebirth of their planetary God, these eclipses must have provided an awesome symbolic reminder of how life had begun on Earth.

Now it must be stressed that the symbolisms cited above are by no means hypothetical, but were all used in practice, and this can be demonstrated by numerous examples.

Take the stars. The Egyptians chose the star Sirius (Sothis) to be the *symbol* for the exploded planet of Isis (alias Hathor). This was done not just because Sirius was the brightest star in the sky, but because the heliacal rising of Sirius at the summer solstice coincided with the annual flooding of the Nile.[63] *Sirius thus symbolised the Great Flood from the exploded planet*, along with the resulting fecundation of the Earth.[64] It is this symbolism which explains the many strange references to the Sothic Heaven being a watery, reed-growing paradise. It is hardly likely to be the case that the ancients believed in an Earth-like planet *in the Sirius star system*, as some have suggested.[65] It is much more likely that the Sothic Heaven was simply symbolic of the lost planetary Heaven right here in our very own solar system.

Then there is the constellation Orion, the stars of which outlined the figure of a giant striding man, with a sword hanging from his belt. From an early date, the ancients recognised this figure as an anthropomorphic image of their god Osiris, and they thus called it *Sah*, meaning 'Far-

Strider'. Why refer to Orion/Osiris as 'the Far-Strider'? The simple answer is revealed in the Coffin Texts, where Osiris boasted that 'the length of the Sky is my stride'.[66] This was symbolically true in two ways. Firstly, Osiris had made a mighty stride in order to kick his planetary opponent Seth.[67] And secondly, Osiris had taken a long stride in descending from Heaven to Earth.

If we now put the stars of Sirius and Orion together, we find that they tell a story – all about *two* exploded planets. Readers may recall the legend that Isis followed Osiris down from Heaven into the underworld, crying: "I am Isis; I have come into the middle of this Earth, into the place where you are." If we now look at the stars, we find that Orion, the stellar image of Osiris, is the first to rise (and be 'born') on the eastern horizon, and is thus the first to set (to 'die') on the western horizon, when it/he disappears into darkness and invisibility. It is no coincidence that Sirius, the star of Isis, rises *after* Orion/Osiris, and *follows him* across the Sky, until it/she disappears into the underworld in search of her lost partner.

We know that this is no coincidence because there is a period during the year when Sirius remains invisible, not rising above the horizon for approximately seventy days. And seventy days was the sacred period used by the Egyptians for the embalmment of deceased kings and queens.[68] After the seventy days of death, Sirius would be reborn on the eastern horizon, symbolising the rebirth of Osiris in the afterlife, and the birth of the divine child Horus as heir to the throne of the Earth.

Thus, in summary, the Egyptians used the stars of Orion and Sirius to tell a story about two deities – two exploded planets – which descended from Heaven to Earth. And such was the permanence of this profound symbolism that we can still read the same story six thousand years later.

Now let's consider the evidence that *the Sun* symbolised an exploded planet. We have already encountered in this book two Sun-gods who have had distinctly non-solar characteristics. In the Sumerian legend *Enki and Ninharsag: A Paradise Myth*, we heard how Utu (supposedly the Sumerian Sun-god) had filled up the Earth with water from 'the mouth whence issues the waters of the Earth'. Then, in the Egyptian Pyramid Texts we heard how Re (supposedly a Sun-god and nothing but a Sun-god) had 'come forth from Nut', the latter being 'the Primeval Hill of the Land in the midst of the Sea'. And we also heard how Re was known as the 'Great Flood which came forth from the Great One', i.e. from Nut – the Sky-goddess whose symbol was a water-pot. Of course it makes no sense that a Sun-god should be associated with a flood of waters – *unless the Sun was a symbol for an exploded planet.*

These anomalies represent merely the tip of an iceberg.

To begin with the Egyptian Sun-god Re, it can now be revealed that, in the Coffin Texts, this god went forth from his mother Nut 'on that night of uproar'.[69] Moreover, in the Pyramid Texts, Re was described as bringing forth 'lightning', being 'as aggressive as a crocodile', being a 'lord of terror', and causing 'dread' when he ascended from the horizon.[70] None of these characteristics are compatible with the Sun.

As I pointed out in my previous book, *The Phoenix Solution*, Re's name meant 'Rising', and it is thus suited perfectly to the idea of the primeval mound *rising* in Nun – this being an allusion to the explosion of a planet in the waters of space.[71] I went on to highlight the fact that this crucial motif – the rising mound – was strangely absent from the Pyramid Texts *unless Re's name was a personification of it*.[72] I also highlighted the fact that the hieroglyph used for Re's name – a circle-within-a-circle – *looks nothing like the Sun*, but does look suspiciously like the primeval mound emerging in the watery abyss.[73] All things considered, it seems beyond argument that Re was not originally a Sun-god at all, but was rather the god of the rising primeval mound. In other words, *Re was a planetary god first and foremost, and only became a solar deity when the Sun was adopted as a symbol for the exploded planet.*

Over the course of time, Re's solar symbolism overpowered his original identity, and concealed it so effectively that thousands of years later Egyptologists completely missed it.

Nevertheless, major clues *were* there, for those who had the eyes to see and perceive.

For example, in order to transform Re from an invisible planetary god to a visible solar symbol, his journey across the *Sky* (big 'S') between Heaven and Earth had to be changed into a journey across the *sky* (small 's') of the Earth. The two *planetary* horizons thus had to be converted into two *terrestrial* horizons, i.e. into the eastern and western horizons of the Earth. But when the Egyptians did this, they nevertheless retained their sense of the original interplanetary journey. Hence Re was said to rise from a *'mountain'* in the east (Mount Bakhu) and to set in a *'mountain'* in the west (Mount Manu).[74] With the benefit of hindsight, this is a dead giveaway as to the original nature of the Sun-god's journey. As is the fact that *Akhet* – the Egyptian word for 'horizon' – was written as a large disk, resting inside *a mountain which had split apart*, and having the literal meaning 'Mountain of Light'.[75] Not to mention the fact that *Akhet* was originally written with an elliptical sign which meant 'island' – yet another metaphor for a planet.[76]

To illustrate the point, consider the following example from the *Hymn to Re*:

> Thou risest in Heaven's horizon, and thy disk is adored when it resteth upon the mountain to give life unto the world.[77]

Here we see Re rising from a horizon *in Heaven*, and coming to rest on the mountain *of Earth*.[78] Thus he brought 'life' to the world in a catastrophic fashion – a consistent theme among the ancient writings.

Moving on to the Sumerian Sun-god Utu, we find that his role, significantly, was not to shine and give heat to mankind, but to assist in the crossings between Earth *and Heaven*. Hence in *The Epic of Gilgamesh*, it was Utu who helped Gilgamesh ascend to Heaven by lowering 'seven heroes' into seven mountain-caves (see next chapter). Similarly, in *The Epic of Etana*, it was Utu (alias Shamash) who granted Etana the eagle to take him up to the heavens.[79]

In a Sumerian text entitled *Enki and the World Order*, we learn how Utu was given control over the crossings between Heaven and Earth, when Enki 'placed him in charge of the entire Heaven and Earth'. The same text describes how Utu came forth from Heaven roaring like a bull coming out of a forest:

> Utu, the hero, the bull who comes forth out of the forest, who roars
>   like a lion,
> The valiant Utu, the bull who stands secure, who proudly displays
>   his power,
> The father of the great city, the place where Utu rises, the great herald
>   of holy Anu,
> The judge, the decision-maker of the gods,
> Who wears a lapis lazuli beard, who comes forth from the holy
>   Heaven...[80]

Is this a description of a Sun-god? I think not. Consider, for example, the following account of Utu's catastrophic 'birth':

> (It was) a day when the weapon sent forth from above wrecked the
>   city as if with a pickaxe.
> On that day Heaven was crushed, Earth was smitten...
> Heaven was darkened, was overcast with shadow, was turned into the
>   underworld.
> *Utu lay (prostrate) on the horizon.*[81]

What this means is that Utu fell from Heaven to Earth, with the term 'horizon' appearing here in the same sense as it was used in Egypt.

As far as the Sumerians were concerned, when the Sun rose in the east, it symbolised the fiery birth of Utu. When the Sun crossed the sky during the day, it symbolised Utu crossing *physically* from Heaven to Earth. When the Sun set in the west, it symbolised Utu entering the underworld of the Earth. And, finally, when the Sun was journeying on during the hours of darkness, it was symbolising the *metaphysical* return of Utu to his hidden mountain in the east. Thus, the next morning, the whole symbolic show was ready to roll once again.

Significantly, Utu's domains ranged 'from *the mountain* where Utu rises, to *the mountain* where Utu sets'.[82] As in Egypt, the idea was that there was a 'mountain' in the east (Heaven) and a 'mountain' in the west (Earth). Ancient cylinder seals actually depicted the birth of Utu from the 'mountain' in the east. In Plate 8, we can see Utu (alias Shamash) being born out of a twin-peaked mountain, emitting rays of fire from his body.

Even more interesting is Plate 9, where Utu, wielding a knife, appears to be going back inside his twin-peaked mountain, as is Enki, who is shown stepping onto one of the mountain's peaks. Significantly, we see flowing waters and fish entering the upper part of Enki's body, symbolising the return of the rivers Tigris and Euphrates *to their celestial source*. As noted in chapter two, Enki was the god who had 'stood up proudly like a rampant bull', and 'filled the Tigris with the sparkling water of his semen'. His presence in this cylinder seal image reminds us that Utu, too, was associated with bringing a great flood of water to the Earth. The image is thus a remarkable testament to the fact that Utu was not originally a Sun-god, but rather the god of an exploded planet, who controlled the crossings between Heaven and Earth.

The Cosmic Mountain Reprise

Let us now step back inside our time machine, and return to the land of the ancients with our newly found knowledge of their religions.

We begin once again at Heliopolis, and the Temple of the Benben. This time, we can understand the sanctity of the gold-plated meteorite – the Benben Stone – which sits gleaming at the top of its pillar. It is a unique object which has crossed over from the mysterious realms of the heavens to the mundane realm of Earth. It is a messenger from God, *a fragment of an ex-planet*. It is the efflux of Atum, who 'rose up' in Heliopolis, emitting Shu and Tefnut as his divine seed. And the meteoric Benben Stone now points up towards the sky, as if it were being resurrected back to the planet whence it came.

We now understand the priests' stories about the Bennu-bird (alias the

Phoenix). We understand why the Bennu-bird was said to have been born in fire at the top of a holy persea-tree.[83] We understand why the Bennu-bird came to the Earth from a place named 'Punt', meaning 'the Land of the God'.[84] We understand why the Bennu-bird was born amidst a blinding flash of light.[85] We understand why the Bennu-bird alighted on a 'Rock' (the Earth) and let out a piercing cry, thus instigating the beginning of time.[86] We can also understand why the Bennu-bird brought a vital, magical essence (*Hike*), which had never been known on the Earth before.[87] And we can understand why the ancients feared the future return of the Bennu-bird, which threatened to descend catastrophically to the Earth, destroying the old order of things, and bringing about the birth of a new world order.[88]

Above all, we can understand the modern legend of the Phoenix, which was said to have cast itself down onto a funeral pyre and then been reborn from its own ashes.[89] The bird, we now know, was the planet of Heaven, whilst the funeral pyre was the Earth (hence the idea of the Island of Fire). The death and rebirth of the Phoenix thus turn out to be a repeat of the legend whereby Heaven itself died physically and was reborn metaphysically. It is also exactly the same legend as the death and resurrection of Osiris – hence in the Coffin Texts we read: 'I am that great Phoenix which is Heliopolis. Who is he? He is Osiris.'[90]

Before we leave Heliopolis, let us reflect on the name of the city. It is, of course, a Greek name meaning 'City of the Sun'. But this was not the original name. To the Egyptians, it was On, or Annu, the '*City of Heaven*', and its hieroglyphic symbol was a pillar surmounted by a cross, together with a circle divided into eight parts.[91] The latter almost certainly symbolises the division or dismemberment of the heavenly 'mountain'.

In summary, then, the city of Heliopolis was *not* a city of the Sun, the Benben Stone was *not* a stone which fell from the Sun, and the *Het Benben* was *not* a Temple of the Sun – other than in a purely symbolic sense.[92]

We travel now a short distance to Giza – the site of the pyramids and the Sphinx – where, in the shadow of these huge megalithic structures, we begin to get a real inkling of the awesome nature of Egyptian religion. But why was the Egyptian king so obsessed with the afterlife?

The answer can now be revealed. As we look at the giant pyramid before us, we must try to visualise it as part of a vertical Bond of Heaven-and-Earth. Beneath the pyramid lies the underworld, in the image of the pyramid, and it is here, in the mysterious darkness, that the Titan-god Horus was born from the womb of Isis, following her magical insemination by the efflux of Osiris. This efflux, we now know, was a meteorite from an exploded planet, which had split open the Earth.

But it must be emphasised that the ancients did not regard planets as lifeless lumps of rock. On the contrary, their perception was that planets were *living organisms*, as per the modern 'Gaea hypothesis'.[93] Nor is the reason for this belief difficult to find. Mother Earth was regarded as a giant womb, which would repeatedly give birth, not only to Titans but also to grass, bushes, crops and trees *inter alia*. And how could a womb give birth thus unless it was *a living womb*? *QED*. The planet of Earth was a living organism, and, by the same token, so were the planets which had exploded.

The birth of the divine child Horus (alias the king of Egypt) thus becomes a very profound idea. He was born, so we are told, from a union of *two living planetary beings,* or perhaps three if we include the Earth herself. Today, the modern mind can barely grasp the profundity with which this miraculous divine mingling was regarded by the ancients. It was one of the most sacred secrets of ancient Egypt, which, needless to say, was never written down, but seems to have survived in the later practice of alchemy, which involved the mixing of substances in order to achieve a miraculous elixir of life.[94]

Why is the story of Horus so important? Simply because the Egyptian king was taught that he was the living incarnation of Horus (or in some cases, 'the son of Re' – the difference is slight).

So, when we look at the pyramid through the eyes of the Egyptian king, we see a structure which was a vertical Bond of Heaven-and-Earth. We, the king, have been born beneath it, in the underworld, in the womb of Isis, and emerged from there into the world above as the falcon-god – mythically speaking, of course. When we die, we will go back into the underworld, where we will be magically transformed from Horus to Osiris (the *reverse* of the magic from the First Time). Then, we will use the pyramid as an ascension device, to scale the heights of Heaven, and return to the planet whence we came. Furthermore, we will even restore the shattered planet of Heaven to its perfect primeval condition.[95]

In this sense, the pyramid might be termed a 'cosmic mountain' – to use the phrase coined by Mircea Eliade. Its shape seems to symbolise a planet, rising up out of the underworld towards Heaven – could it be the image of Earth and the image of Heaven simultaneously (the one being the mirror image of the other)?[96] The Egyptologist Mark Lehner was not far wrong when he opined that the pyramid was 'an image of the primeval mound... a place of creation and rebirth in the abyss.'[97]

As we now depart from the Nile Valley to head east to the ziggurats and temples of Mesopotamia, it must be said that we have seen nothing here in Egypt which was solar, other than symbolically so. The Benben Stone – a meteorite – was clearly part of the exploded planet cult. As for the pyramid, it seems to have been a cosmic mountain – the image of a planet – and it is surely significant that the pyramidion at its top was called a *bnbnt*, a word closely related to the 'efflux' (*bnbn*) of the Benben Stone.[98] As for the obelisks of Egypt, it is significant that they, too, were lifting towards the sky a *bnbnt*, i.e. a pyramidion. Moreover, it is interesting that the word 'obelisk' derives from the Greek word *obeliskos*, meaning 'a little spit'.[99] It was, of course, a 'spit' from Atum's 'mouth' which produced the goddess Tefnut – one of the seeds of the primeval creation, i.e. a meteorite.

Finally, it is worth mentioning that even the Sphinx – a supreme solar symbol in the eyes of Egyptologists – was actually an exploded planet symbol. Why else would it be called *Hor-em-Akhet*, 'Horus, Dweller in the Two Horizons'?[100] After all, according to the theory of Egyptologists, the Sphinx faces only towards *one horizon* – the east. The answer is that the Earth itself was one of the horizons (the 'west'), whilst the second horizon was Heaven (the 'east'). Thus the Sphinx did indeed symbolise the king dwelling in two 'horizons', i.e. the two *planetary* horizons.

We now make the long journey east to Mesopotamia, where we find that the kings of this neighbouring land also believed that kingship had been lowered from Heaven, and that they – the kings – had divine parentage. In some cases, the king claimed to be the 'son of Utu' (the Sun-god who was *not* a Sun-god).[101] In other cases, the king claimed to be the divine offspring of a sacred marriage in the underworld between the goddess Inanna and the god Dumuzi.[102] But in all cases, the king was the archetypal Titan-god, who had been born in the womb of Mother Earth. Hence we read in a Sumerian temple hymn:

Mother Nintu, the lady of form-giving,
(Is) working in a dark place, the heart-womb,
To give birth to kings, to tie on the rightful tiara,
To give birth to lords, to place the crown on their heads.
(It) is in her hands.[103]

As we look at the ziggurats in this ancient land, we can once again imagine the invisible components which linked them both to the underworld below and the Heaven above. In the case of the E.AN.NA temple in Uruk, it was said that 'its great walls touched the clouds', and so it would appear.[104] The very name 'ziggurat' came from the term *zaqaru*, meaning 'to build high'.[105] And high is what they were.

But not only did the ziggurat look like a mountain – it *was* such a mountain, at least symbolically speaking. Hence at Nippur the ziggurat of Enlil was called E.KUR – 'House like a Mountain'. And hence other temples were said to 'rise mountain high'.[106]

It takes little effort of the imagination to visualise the ziggurat as the mountain of the underworld (KUR, or KUR.NU.GI), rising up out of the Earth as if resurrecting to Heaven. Is it thus the image of Earth and the image of Heaven simultaneously – the two twin planets? Possibly so, for the *E-sag-ila* temple of Babylon was known as '*Iku*-star, *E-sag-ila*, image of Heaven-and-Earth'.[107]

On the one hand, then, the summit of the ziggurat reached up, symbolically, to the midst of the heavens, towards the planetary abode of God. But on the other hand, the ziggurat was built upon the *Bab-Apsu*, the 'Gate of the AB.ZU', i.e. the underworld, and its foundations were said to tap down into the deepest darkness of the abyss.[108]

Beneath the ziggurat, therefore, we must imagine a magical gateway into the *kigal*, the 'Great Place Below', where Ereshkigal and Nergal lived opulently in their magnificent lapis lazuli palace. In the legends of king Gilgamesh, we read that this gateway into the underworld could be opened up by the cry of "*i-Utu!*" (note again the anomalous role of the supposed Sun-god).[109] The underworld was a place of great dangers, but also great rewards, for it was only by means of this mysterious realm below that a man might discover the crucial gateway to Heaven above.

All of these things are suggested by the mountain-like ziggurats, and indeed by the illustrious temples of Mesopotamia. It is a mystery which the eminent mythologist Mircea Eliade came close to cracking in 1949 when he commented as follows:

> According to Mesopotamian beliefs, a central mountain joins Heaven and Earth; it is the Mount of the Lands, the connection between territories. Properly speaking, the ziggurat was a cosmic mountain, i.e. a symbolic image of the cosmos, the seven stories representing the seven planetary heavens... because of its situation at the centre of the cosmos, the temple or the sacred city is always the meeting point of the three cosmic regions: Heaven, Earth, and Hell.[110]

All of this is true. The ziggurat was indeed a vertical Bond of Heaven-and-Earth, and a 'cosmic mountain'. The only thing that Eliade failed to realise was that *the 'mountain' symbolised a planet, and that the planets of Heaven and Earth had thus been created in each other's image*.

One more point needs to be made. As Eliade observed, *the city* as well as the temple could form the vital link between the sacred realms. This is

important, and a short mental exercise will demonstrate the profundity of
the concept.

Imagine for a moment that we are looking down upon the Earth from
an incredible height. Firstly, let us zoom in on the land of Sumer
(modern-day Iraq), which we find was referred to as the 'Great Mountain
– land of Heaven-and-Earth' with the Anunnaki-gods dwelling in its
midst.

The land of Sumer, then, was a 'mountain', representing a microcosm
of the Earth.

Secondly, let us zoom in on any one of the major cities in Sumer. Take
the city of Eridu, for example, which we find was 'raised up from the
earth like a mountain'.[111] Or take the city of Ur, of which it was said that
it 'raised its head to Heaven like a bull', with walls built 'as high as a
shining mountain'.[112]

Each city of Sumer, then, was a 'mountain', representing a microcosm
of the Earth.

Thirdly, let us zoom in on the ziggurat or major temple in any one of
the Sumerian cities. Here, as outlined earlier, we find that the ziggurat or
temple itself rose up to Heaven like a mountain.

Each ziggurat or temple of Sumer was thus a 'mountain', representing
a microcosm of the Earth.

Finally, we can even zoom *into* the ziggurats, or temples, of Sumer
and find even smaller microcosms – not just of the Earth, but also of the
Bond between Earth and Heaven. And when this process is taken to its
limit, we end up inside the temple's most sacred spot – the holy-of-
holies. Here, in the holy-of-holies, shrouded in darkness, there would
doubtless have lain some tiny relic which encapsulated the essence of the
divine. We know, for example, that in the holy-of-holies of Enlil's
E.KUR at Nippur, there were ritual vessels which 'no eye was to see'.[113]
We also know that, in the holy-of-holies of Nannar's E.KISH.NU.GAL at
Ur, there were 'holy kettles' which no-one might look upon, along with a
'fruitful bed' and a mysterious 'lapis lazuli grass'.[114] What these things
actually were, one can only imagine.

Ultimately, as we have seen time and time again, we are dealing with a
mystery of the creation, and in particular with the creation of mankind
and the creation of kingship. And the key to this mystery lies in the
underworld. It is here in the underworld that life began, when a meteoric
seed of the gods came down from the heavens. It is here in the
underworld that Mother Nintu ('Lady Birth Hut') worked her magic in
the darkness, at the beginning of time, to bring forth the first king, and
the first human flesh. And it is here in the underworld that the annual

Mysteries took place, when the Mesopotamian king played the role of Dumuzi, and the high priestess played the role of Inanna. What occurred between these two in the darkness was an unspeakable mystery – a sacred secret – relating to the creation and the renewal of life on Earth.

In the first chapter of this book, I cited the words of the Greek poet Pindar (5th century BC), who commented as follows about the Mysteries:

> Happy is he who has seen this before descending underground!... He knows the end of life! *He also knows its beginning*!

How frustrating it is that Pindar was sworn to secrecy, that he might not reveal what he had seen. But let us not despair, for we can go one better than Pindar, and we can go a thousand years better than the 5th century BC. By turning to the Sumerian and Akkadian tablets, which were lost and indecipherable in Pindar's day, we can speak to a man who went into the underworld, saw everything, and returned back safely to report on everything he had seen.

We shall now turn to a Sumerian king named Gilgamesh for a further teaching.

He has a remarkable secret to tell us.

* * * * *

CHAPTER FIVE

A SECRET OF THE GODS

**I will inform the land about the 'One who Saw the Apsu';
Let me tell the story of 'Him who Knew Everything'...
Gilgamesh, the one who saw secret things, opened the
hidden place, and brought back word of the time before the
Flood. He travelled the road, exhausted, in pain,
and cut his works into a stone tablet.**
(The Epic of Gilgamesh, Tablet I)

Circa 2700 BC, the Sumerian city of Uruk witnessed the coronation of a
young king, who would become the greatest of all Mesopotamian heroes.
The king's name was Gilgamesh, and his story would be told and retold
for two thousand years. Even then, when his story seemed to have
perished for ever, it would be rediscovered by archaeologists in the late
19th century, and given the title *The Epic of Gilgamesh*.[1]

The Epic of Gilgamesh is the story of an incredible journey – first into
the underworld (the Apsu), and then to Heaven, where Gilgamesh would
meet Utnapishtim, the hero of the Mesopotamian Flood and hence the
forerunner of the biblical hero, Noah.

It must be emphasised that, according to Mesopotamian traditions,
Utnapishtim (known to the Sumerians as Ziusudra) was the only man
ever to have been taken up to Heaven – the only man ever to have been
given immortal life like a god. The Mesopotamian Heaven (unlike that of
the Egyptians) was generally off-limits to mortal man.

The goal of Gilgamesh's expedition was clear. He would ascend to
Heaven (via the underworld), find Utnapishtim, and ask him about the
secrets of eternal life. Then, hopefully, he would take advantage of these
secrets to overcome the normal rules, thus joining Utnapishtim in a
blissful afterlife in the land of the immortals.

As we shall see, things did not go totally according to plan. But there was a consolation. In view of the strenuous efforts made by Gilgamesh to reach the distant land of the gods, Utnapishtim decided to reveal to Gilgamesh 'a hidden matter – a secret of the gods'.

What was this 'secret of the gods'? Surprisingly, the secret turned out to be an account of the Great Flood, which culminated with Utnapishtim being saved by the gods, and translated to the land of the immortals.

But why was this account of the Flood such a great secret? Surely Gilgamesh must have *already* known the story, otherwise he would not have embarked upon his ambitious expedition to find Utnapishtim.

Have scholars missed something? Might Utnapishtim's account of the Flood contain a secret which has been hidden to this day – a secret which was encoded by the writers of the Gilgamesh tablets in such a way that it was apparent only to those who had been initiated into the Mysteries?

It is time to take a fresh look at *The Epic of Gilgamesh*. Up until now, many aspects of the story have remained obscure – not surprisingly in view of scholars' unfamiliarity with Mesopotamian metaphors. But now, for the first time since the rediscovery of the first Gilgamesh tablets in 1872, we are able to grasp the true import of the story – in the context of the religious belief in an exploded planet.

A Battle of Giants

Who was Gilgamesh? It is fitting to begin his story at the city of Uruk, and in particular, at its ziggurat called E.AN.NA, 'the House of Heaven-and-Earth'. The E.AN.NA, we should recall, was a 'temple descended from Heaven', which had been presented by Anu to Inanna as a wedding gift. It was thus the site of the first sacred marriage, between the deities Anu and Inanna, and later became the site of a subsequent sacred marriage between Inanna and Dumuzi.[2]

According to the Sumerian Kings List, kingship began at E.AN.NA a staggering 24,510 years after the Great Flood.[3] Its first king was Meskiaggasher, a 'son of Utu', who famously 'entered the sea and came out to the mountain' (note the metaphors here which have confounded the scholars).[4] Its second king was Enmerkar, who built the city of Uruk and caused the goddess Inanna to descend from Heaven to Earth.[5] Its third king was Lugalbanda, who tried to ascend to Heaven, but was struck down by a mysterious illness at the foot of the 'cosmic mountain'.[6] Its fourth king was Dumuzi, a god of the underworld, and a character famous for his role in the sacred marriage ceremony. *And the fifth king of Uruk was Gilgamesh.*

Several of these kings enjoyed mythical life spans. Meskiaggasher reigned 324 years, Enmerkar 420 years, and Lugalbanda an incredible 1,200 years. Gilgamesh, in contrast, reigned for a more human-like span of 126 years.[7]

Was Gilgamesh the first *human* king of Uruk? Were his ancestors mythical gods? Returning to the subject of E.AN.NA and its sacred marriage ceremonies, it is pertinent to note that Gilgamesh came into existence *after* the descent of Inanna and *immediately after* the appearance of Dumuzi. Since these two *deities* Inanna and Dumuzi were the partners in Uruk's sacred marriage ceremony, it seems reasonable to conclude that Gilgamesh was indeed the first human king of Uruk – the archetypal Titan-like king, who was conceived in the underworld, and rose up out of it to inherit the throne of the world above.

The story which we are about to read, then, is the story of a king who was definitely *human*, but who was *portrayed as a Titan-like god* – in keeping with the Mesopotamian tradition.

Having established this foundation of understanding, we may begin our story with the legend of Gilgamesh's birth, which was told in the Hittite version of *The Epic of Gilgamesh* thus:

> After Gilgamesh was created...
> The form of Gilgamesh the great gods made surpassing,
> Eleven cubits was his height; the breadth of his chest was nine spans...
> Now he turns hither and thither to see all the lands.
> To the city of Uruk he comes...
> Two-thirds of him is god and one third of him is man.
> The form of his body none can match...[8]

This description of king Gilgamesh – eleven by nine cubits – marks him out as being of giant size, as we would expect. His status as 'two thirds god, one third man' is intriguing, and will turn out to be of tremendous significance when he meets Utnapishtim.

Another tradition of Gilgamesh's birth, recorded in *The Epic*, informs us that Gilgamesh was 'brought forth' by the mighty Sky-goddess Aruru, the great sister of Enlil, whose mighty 'Word' ordained the creation of man, but which could also 'shake the heavens like a howling storm':[9]

> Aruru brought this furious wild ox [Gilgamesh] into being
> The onslaught of his weapons has no equal...
> Gilgamesh leaves no son to his father – day and night his
>   outrageousness continues unrestrained...
> Gilgamesh leaves no virgin to her lover...[10]

Such behaviour was partly understandable, for Gilgamesh was a Titan by birth, but nevertheless the people would not put up with it for ever. Eventually the terrorised citizens sent up a complaint to the Sky-goddess Aruru, demanding that she curtail Gilgamesh's excesses:

> They [the people] called to great Aruru:
> "Thou, Aruru, didst create Gilgamesh,
> Now create his equal...
> Let them strive with each other, and let Uruk have rest."[11]

Aruru, whose name literally meant 'germ loosener', immediately 'conceived within herself' an 'image of Anu'.[12] She 'pinched off clay', and threw it down onto the plains of the Earth, thus creating a savage 'man' named Enkidu.

Enkidu, the text confirms, was a 'child of the mountain' and 'a man of destruction'.[13] One presumes that the clay of Aruru entered the underworld, where Enkidu was conceived by Mother Earth, before emerging (as Gilgamesh had done) into the world above.

Enkidu, when he first rose up on the plains, was a shaggy-haired savage, who 'knew neither people nor land... who fed on grass with the gazelles, who jostled at the watering-place with the wild beasts.'[14] Immediately, this wild 'man' became a friend to the animals and protected them by tearing up the hunters' traps and by filling in the concealed pits. In desperation, one of the hunters turned to Gilgamesh, the king of Uruk, for advice.

Gilgamesh then instigated an ingenious plan. A female prostitute was to be taken back to the spot where Enkidu drank with the animals, and she was to strip off her clothes when Enkidu arrived. Thus the trap was sprung:

> The harlot untied her wide belt and spread her legs, and he [Enkidu]
>   struck her wildness like a storm.
> She was not shy; she received his life-force.
> Her clothing was spread out, and he lay upon her.
> She made him know (man-as-he-was) what a woman is!
> His body lay on her; six days and seven nights Enkidu attacked,
>   ravaging the harlot.[15]

After Enkidu had sated himself with the prostitute's charms, he set his face back towards his old friends, the wild beasts, but they all ran away from him in terror. Thus, it was said, did Enkidu acquire from the prostitute 'wisdom and understanding', like that of a god.[16]

What was the meaning of this violent penetration of the prostitute? An interesting analogy presents itself in the text, as Gilgamesh anticipated the birth of his rival in a dream, which he related to his mother thus:

> "My mother, last night I saw a dream.
> There were stars in the heavens;
> One fell down to me as if it were the *ki-sir* of Anu.
> I tried to lift it but it was too heavy for me;
> I tried to move it away, but I could not remove it.
> The land of Uruk was gathered around it,
> The people pressed toward it...
> I bent over it, as to a woman,
> And laid it at thy feet,
> And thou didst put it on a par with me."[17]

What was this falling 'star', this '*ki-sir* of Anu'? In *The Epic*, Gilgamesh was informed by his mother that the fallen 'star' in his dream was the 'man' Enkidu, who had been created by Aruru as Gilgamesh's equal, and was now being sent to him as a friend and companion.

But what did it mean that Enkidu was the '*ki-sir* of Anu'? Scholars have had great difficulty translating the term *ki-sir*, but have often appended their translations with a note to the effect that it literally meant 'concentration/essence', whilst Anu referred to the god of the heavens.[18] It is thus acknowledged that some kind of 'concentrated essence of Anu' was cast down from Heaven to Earth.

What could it be, this 'concentrated essence of Anu'? In Tablet II of *The Epic* (Old Babylonian version), we learn that the term 'star' was interchangeable with the word 'axe'. Gilgamesh, we are told, witnessed a fallen axe, which had 'a strange shape'.[19] At this point, we are reminded of the 'pickaxe' of Enlil, which split open the surface of the Earth (see chapter two). The 'axe', I concluded, was a metaphor for a meteorite.

Returning to the passage cited above, we find that the 'star', or 'essence of Anu', was *too heavy to be lifted*. Furthermore, we read that, after it fell, '*the land was gathered around it*'.

What kind of object could fall physically from the sky like an 'axe', and be too heavy to lift? The obvious answer – indeed the *unique* answer – is *a meteorite*.

It is therefore puzzling, to say the least, why scholars have traditionally avoided the translation 'meteorite' in favour of vague translations such as 'host of heaven', 'shooting star', or 'sky-bolt'.[20] Frankly, I am dumbfounded by this. Do scholars not bother to read what the texts actually say? Are they ignorant of what a meteorite is? Or could it be that the fathers of academia have inculcated a culture in which meteorites must not be mentioned? It is an intriguing mystery, but what we can say, at the very least, is that scholars' understanding of *The Epic of Gilgamesh* – in particular its celestial, religious context – is hopelessly inadequate. Absurdly so.

Incidentally, 'meteorite' *is* one of the possible translations listed for *ki-sir* in the *Chicago Assyrian Dictionary*, another one, significantly, being 'flesh of the gods'.[21] Unfortunately, neither you nor I, dear reader, tend to read *The Epic of Gilgamesh* with a copy of the *Chicago Assyrian Dictionary* by our side.

Anyway, to return to the story and complete its first segment, Gilgamesh's dream was now fulfilled, as Enkidu, recently humanised by the prostitute, entered the city of Uruk. There, he found Gilgamesh engaged in his tyrannical pursuit of claiming all marital first fruits, or as the early scholars preferred to translate it, so quaintly, *'Gilgamesh venit prior, maritus posterior'*.

Enkidu's first act was to put this heterosexual abuse to an end. He blocked the path of Gilgamesh, and the two giants 'grappled like bulls' in the street, causing part of a wall to break.[22] As we shall see in due course, this was no ordinary 'wall', for Gilgamesh and Enkidu were blessed with no ordinary strength; on the contrary, their strength was that of two Titans – the strength of the *ki-sir* of Anu – the strength of the meteorite.

The Land of the Cedars

Following this contest of strength, Gilgamesh and Enkidu embraced each other as companions, and set off like a pair of schoolboy chums for a series of exciting adventures. The oldest surviving fragments of *The Epic of Gilgamesh*, in the Sumerian language, take up the story at this point, setting the scene in its opening lines thus:

> The lord, Gilgamesh, toward the Land of the Living set his mind,
> He says to his servant, Enkidu:
> "O Enkidu, brick and stamp have not yet brought forth the fated end,
> I would enter 'the Land', I would set up my name,
> In its places where names have been raised up, I would raise up *my* name.
> In its places where the names have not been raised up, I would raise up the names of the gods."[23]

What was 'the Land of the Living'? The text explains that it was 'the Land of the Cut-down Cedar Trees', access to which was controlled by Utu, the god of the crossings between Earth and Heaven. Gilgamesh's wish to 'set up a name' was idiomatic of acquiring eternal life in this distant land. Thus the hero set about making an offering to Utu, begging him that he might be allowed to escape the fate of mortal men:

> "O Utu, a word I would speak to thee...
> In my city man dies, oppressed is the heart,
> Man perishes, heavy is the heart,
> I peered over the Wall [into the underworld],
> Saw the dead bodies . . . floating in the river [of the underworld];
> As for me, I too will be served thus; verily 'tis so."[24]

In the Old Babylonian version of *The Epic*, Gilgamesh expressed a similar thought, in an oft-cited phrase which sums up rather neatly the Mesopotamian attitude to man's lot:

> "Who, my friend, can scale Heaven?
> Only the gods live forever with Shamash [Utu].
> As for mankind, numbered are its days;
> Whatever it achieves is but wind!"[25]

The two heroes then set off on the first leg of their expedition to 'the Land of the Cut-down Cedar Trees', which required a descent into the 'Cedar Forest' and a battle against a formidable guardian, Huwawa:

> For ten thousand leagues extends the forest,
> Who is there that would go down into it?
> Huwawa (is there) – his roaring is the flood-storm,
> His mouth is fire, his breath is death!...
> At sixty leagues he can hear the wild cows of the forest.[26]

This kind of god should by now be familiar to us. Huwawa was a god born of a catastrophic event – hence his 'forehead' was said to 'devour trees and reeds', his shout was like an 'onrushing flood wave', his 'teeth were the teeth of a dragon', and his 'face was the face of a lion'.[27] In one fragment of *The Epic*, we read that 'the *land* Hurrum' was Huwawa's mother, whilst 'the *mountain* Hurrum' was his father.[28] This suggests that Huwawa had been impregnated upon a female Earth by a falling planetary mountain. Not surprisingly, Huwawa regarded Utu as his adoptive father.

Had Huwawa emerged from the Earth like a Titan-god? Or had he remained in the underworld?

Significantly, we learn that Gilgamesh and Enkidu ventured *down* into Huwawa's forest-like abode:

> Who is there that would *go down* to his forest?
> To safeguard the cedars, Enlil has appointed him [Huwawa] as a terror

to mortals;
Weakness lays hold on him who *goes down* to the forest.[29]

It may seem odd to some readers that a forest of cedar-trees might exist in the underworld, but we must remember the fundamental concept of the Mesopotamian religion – that Heaven was made in the image of the Earth, and that Heaven had fallen into the underworld, thus creating a mountain-within-a-mountain, and a world-within-a-world.

The point can easily be proven, and not just by the fact that Gilgamesh was 'One who Saw the Apsu' (the Apsu being the underworld). Take, for example, Nergal, the chief god of the Mesopotamian underworld. In the legend entitled *Nergal and Ereshkigal*, we read how Nergal was instructed to descend to the abode of Ereshkigal, 'the Lady of the Great Place Below':

> Nergal turned his face toward 'the Mountain of No Return',
> To the dark house, the abode of Irkalla [the underworld],
> To the house which none leave who have entered it.
> To the road from which there is no way back,
> To the house wherein the entrants are bereft of light,
> Where dust is their fare and clay their food.[30]

In the same breath, however, this text relates that Nergal was to 'descend to the forest of *mesu*-trees', and cut down a *mesu*-tree, a *hasuru*-tree and a *supalu*-tree.[31] There can be no question that this text was identifying the underworld with a forest full of trees. The point is confirmed by the fact that Nergal became known as MES.LAM.TA.E.A, meaning 'the one who dwells in MES.LAM', where MES.LAM was known as the place of 'the luxuriantly growing *mesu*-trees'.[32]

Lest there be any doubt about this, the *mesu*-tree appears also in the legend entitled *Erra and Ishum*, along with a mysterious *elmesu*-stone.[33] Both existed in the underworld, and were vitally important to Nergal's aim of escaping into the world above. The *Erra and Ishum* text makes it clear, however, that the *mesu*-tree was a 'cosmic tree', which not only had its roots in the underworld, but also had its upper part in Heaven. Hence in the text, Marduk asked Nergal:

> Where is the *mesu*-wood, the flesh of the gods...
> The pure tree, tall youth...
> Whose roots reach down into the vast ocean through a hundred
>   leagues of water, to the base of Arallu [the underworld],
> Whose topknot above rests on the Heaven of Anu.[34]

Note that this legend refers to the '*mesu*-wood' of the '*mesu*-tree' as being 'the flesh of the gods'. This is interesting, because the hero Gilgamesh was named after this mysterious *mesu*, his name deriving from the Sumerian GIS.BIL.GA.MES, which meant literally 'MES which is the sprouting seed of a new tree'.[35] Now, if we substitute 'flesh of the gods' for 'MES', the translation of Gilgamesh's name becomes *'flesh of the gods, which is the sprouting seed of a new tree'*.

Once we marry up this information with the other legends of Gilgamesh's Titan-like birth, together with the fact that the senior gods were *exploded planets*, it becomes evident that the 'flesh of the gods' was the meteorite efflux of the gods. The name Gilgamesh, then, meant *'meteorite, which is the sprouting seed of a new tree'*.[36] Incidentally, he was also known as 'the offshoot of Uruk', where the name of the city Uruk doubtless symbolised the Earth.[37]

It is but a short step to realise that ancient references to the cutting down of this 'cosmic tree' were in many cases describing idiomatically the catastrophe in the heavens – i.e. the fall, or collapse, of Heaven.[38]

It is therefore not surprising to find that Gilgamesh's quest was ultimately aimed at reaching 'the Land of the Cut-down Cedar Trees', i.e. Heaven. But at the same time, Gilgamesh had to first descend into the 'Cedar Forest', i.e. the underworld which contained the chopped-down trees. This digression thus provides us with further confirmation that Gilgamesh descended into the underworld en route to his meeting with Utnapishtim.

Once these metaphors have been fully understood, many of the thorny old problems which scholars have experienced over the years in trying to follow the geography of *The Epic of Gilgamesh* simply evaporate. In fact, the setting of *The Epic* does not really involve *geo*graphy at all. Rather it is – to reinvent an old term – *anki*ography, the landscape of the ancient 'universe' of Heaven-and-Earth (AN and KI).

We return now to the Sumerian version of *The Epic*, and to the point where Gilgamesh had begged Utu for permission to go to the Land of the Living. In response to the prayer, Utu took pity on Gilgamesh and lowered 'seven heroes, the sons of one mother' into seven mountain-caves.[39] These are among the more obscure metaphors of *The Epic*, but the context suggests that the seven heroes were seven 'bonds' between Heaven and Earth, which potentially allowed Gilgamesh a means of access to Heaven.[40] Firstly, however, Gilgamesh had to find the 'cedar of his heart' – the bond which related *to his own creation as a Titan* – and this turned out, not surprisingly, to be in the seventh mountain-cave in the underworld.[41]

As Gilgamesh crossed from one mountain to another, cutting down the cedars on each of them, we must envisage him *descending farther and farther into the underworld*, with each mountain lying beneath or inside the one above it. Such was the organisation of the underworld which we find in other Mesopotamian texts, such as *Nergal and Ereshkigal*, where Nergal descended the 'long staircase of the heavens' and entered progressively through 'seven gates' in order to reach the courtyard of Ereshkigal's palace.[42] Similarly, in the legend entitled *Inanna's Descent to the Underworld*, the great goddess Inanna descended from Heaven and passed through seven locked gates, stopping at each one in turn to give up an emblem of rulership or an item of jewellery.[43] These divisions of the underworld were not unlike the subterranean caverns of the Egyptian *Duat*, through which Re progressed deeper and deeper, to the burial place of Osiris in the lowest chamber.

The Dream Sequence

Gilgamesh and Enkidu, then, were descending deeper and deeper into the underworld, heading for a showdown with Huwawa, who protected the all-important seventh and lowest forested-mountain. But before we deal with that confrontation, we must pause to examine a fascinating dream sequence which was added into the Akkadian version of *The Epic*.

As the two companions retired for their nightly rest, Gilgamesh was awakened by a series of frightening dreams. The details of the first dream are missing owing to a break in the tablet, but the second dream was described as follows:

"In my dream, my friend, a mountain toppled.
It laid me low, taking hold of my feet.
The glare was overpowering! A 'man' appeared.
The fairest in the land was he...
He pulled me out from under the mountain,
Gave me water to drink; my heart quieted.
He set my feet on the ground."[44]

Enkidu then explained the dream to Gilgamesh, saying:

"My friend, thy dream is favourable.
The dream is most precious.
The mountain which thou saw is Huwawa.
We shall seize Huwawa and kill him,
And we shall cast his corpse in the plain."[45]

Once again, we encounter the idea of a god being a 'falling mountain'.

Now, we move to a third dream, experienced by Enkidu, which

describes even more explicitly the catastrophic descent of a god into the underworld:

"(My friend) didst thou not touch me? Why am I startled?
Did not some god go by? Why is my flesh numb?
My friend, I saw a third dream,
And the dream which I saw was altogether frightful.
The heavens roared, the earth resounded,
Daylight failed, darkness came;
Lightning flashed, fire blazed;
The clouds thickened, raining death.
The brightness vanished, the fire went out;
And that which fell down, turned to ashes."[46]

The Killing of Huwawa

After this dramatic interlude, the two companions proceeded to chop down the cedars on the mountain of Huwawa, which somehow enclosed Gilgamesh's 'heart'. They thus penetrated the inner sanctum of the fierce guardian Huwawa, who in the Sumerian version put up very little resistance indeed, and was quickly decapitated.

In the Akkadian version, however, Gilgamesh and Enkidu required the assistance of Utu, who immobilised Huwawa with eight mighty winds. As in the Sumerian account, Huwawa was decapitated, and his fall to the ground made the cedars resound for two leagues around.[47]

What happened next is unclear. In one account, we read that Gilgamesh pressed on into the forest, and 'opened up the secret abode of the Anunnaki'.[48] This, incidentally, is another clear confirmation of the underworld location of these events, for the Anunnaki were the gods who dwelt in the underworld.

In another account, there is a suggestion that the heroes entered the gates of the mountain Huwawa and slew lions.[49] This is intriguing, for the Mesopotamians believed that *the heavens could be accessed by entering through the opening of Huwawa's 'mouth'*.[50] All things considered, Huwawa appears to have been not only the protector of the 'cosmic mountain' but a personification of the 'cosmic mountain' itself. By defeating him, the heroes would have been able to pass into the 'cosmic mountain' and make the ascent to Heaven (although such an account, of their *joint ascent*, has not been fully preserved in the extant tablets).

At this point in *The Epic of Gilgamesh*, a brief subplot has been introduced, which is worthy of mention. The goddess of love, Ishtar (alias Inanna), appeared on the scene and attempted to seduce Gilgamesh (possibly incestuously, for she may well have been his mother).[51] Gilgamesh, however, rejected Ishtar's advances and embarrassed the goddess by recounting a long list of her former lovers and the indignities which they had suffered at her hands. In revenge, Ishtar requested Anu to destroy Gilgamesh by sending down the 'Bull of Heaven'.

The Bull of Heaven was a popular Mesopotamian motif, which is once again steeped in exploded planet connotations. This celestial Bull reportedly had huge horns made of lapis lazuli – a metaphor for meteoric material, as we noted in chapters two and four. It is therefore not surprising that the Bull of Heaven had the ability to open up pits in the ground and kill a hundred men with a single snort.[52]

Gilgamesh and Enkidu, of course, were able to put the Bull of Heaven to the sword, since they, too, possessed the strength of the '*ki-sir* of Anu'. Having thus killed the Bull, our heroic pair cut off its right thigh and tossed it in the face of the goddess – an insult of the utmost magnitude. As a result of all these shenanigans, Enkidu was sentenced to die. Gilgamesh, meanwhile, suffered a sense of loss for the first time in his life, and became acutely aware of his own fragile mortality. Would he, too, be fated to die? Or could he find Utnapishtim and persuade the hero of the Flood to reveal to him the secrets of immortality?

Mount Mashu

The Epic of Gilgamesh continues with what appears to be a second account, and a separate tradition, of Gilgamesh's ascent to Heaven. This time we find him alone, and the passage to Heaven is not the 'mountain' Huwawa, but another 'cosmic mountain' named Mount Mashu.

Despite breaks in the tablets, it is clear once again that the beginning of the adventure involved a descent into the underworld and the chopping down of what one supposes were the trees of the Cedar Forest:

> Gilgamesh took up the axe in his hand;
> He drew the weapon from his belt,
> And like an arrow . . . he fell among them [the cedars?].
> He struck . . . smashing them . . .[53]

The following part of the text is broken away, and we next meet Gilgamesh at Mount Mashu, which is the epitome, and possibly the oldest textual prototype, of the 'cosmic mountain' motif:

> The name of the mountain is Mashu.
> [Gilgamesh] approached the twin peaks of Mashu,
> Which guard each day the rising and setting of Shamash [i.e. Utu],

> Its peaks reach to the bank of Heaven,
> And its breasts reach down to the underworld below.[54]

Note the reference here to Utu. In the previous chapter, we discussed how Utu was born by splitting apart a twin-peaked 'mountain' in the 'east' of Heaven. The Egyptian god Re also rose from a 'mountain' (Mount Bakhu) which had twin peaks.[55] In both cases, the symbolism represents the splitting open of a *planet*, which then fell into the underworld – hence the remarkable imagery in the above quotation, where the twin-peaked mountain had its opposite, mirror image lying beneath in the underworld. This is a very vivid means of portraying the 'upside-down' nature of the 'cosmic mountain'.

Returning to the story, Gilgamesh now approached the base of Mount Mashu, the 'cosmic mountain', in the underworld, where it was guarded by 'scorpion-people', whose appearance was terrifying. They guarded a gate which gave access *into the mountain*, to a road which could lead a traveller, as if by magic, to the distant land of Utnapishtim in Heaven. Gilgamesh approached the scorpion-like guardians, who showed a particular interest in Gilgamesh's divine status:

> The scorpion-man called to his woman:
> "He who has come to us – his body is the flesh of the gods."
> The woman replied to the scorpion-man:
> "Two thirds of him is god, and one-third human."[56]

The scorpion-people demanded to know why Gilgamesh had undertaken such a long journey. Gilgamesh responded:

> "I have come on account of Utnapishtim, my father,
> He who joined the assembly of the gods, and found eternal life.
> I wish to ask him about death and life."[57]

The scorpion-man told Gilgamesh that no mortal man had ever achieved such a quest, but, perhaps impressed by Gilgamesh's claim to be 'two thirds god, one third human', he nevertheless opened the gate of the mountain and allowed Gilgamesh to proceed along 'the road of Utu'.

After travelling for 'twelve leagues' through a thick and impenetrable darkness, the hero emerged into bright light and found a garden made of precious jewels, where the carnelian bore vines and the lapis lazuli bore lush fruit and foliage.[58] Presumably Gilgamesh had reached Heaven.

Unfortunately, the account of what happened next has been entirely destroyed, and when *The Epic* continues it seems to have backtracked in order to recount *a third parallel tradition* of how Gilgamesh ascended to Heaven.

In the two versions which we have now covered, Gilgamesh (a) opened up the route to the heavens via the mouth of Huwawa, who was described as a cedar 'mountain'; and (b) opened up Mount Mashu and ascended the road of Utu to a bright garden. In this third tradition, we now find Gilgamesh making a voyage across waters.

The Crossing of the Sea

We begin this third version of Gilgamesh's expedition at the entrance to the underworld, where a mysterious divine barmaid named Siduri guarded access to a subterranean forest and a subterranean sea. Siduri urged Gilgamesh to forget his quest, which was fruitless:

> "Gilgamesh, what are you doing?
> The eternal life which thou seekest thou wilt not find;
> For when the gods created mankind,
> They allotted death to mankind,
> But eternal life they retained in their own keeping.
> As for you, Gilgamesh, let thy belly be full;
> Day and night be thou merry;
> Make every day a day of rejoicing
> Day and night do thou dance and play.
> Let thy garments be clean,
> Thy head be washed, and thyself bathed in water.
> Cherish the little one holding thy hand,
> And let thy wife rejoice in thy bosom."[59]

Gilgamesh, undeterred by this speech, requested Siduri to give him directions to Utnapishtim, 'the Distant One', who dwelt in the land of the gods. From the exchange which followed, it is apparent that Utnapishtim could only be reached by crossing a sea, but Siduri warned Gilgamesh of the dangers:

> "Gilgamesh, there never has been such a crossing;
> And none who came since the beginning of days could cross the Sea.
> Only valiant Shamash [Utu] crosses the Sea,
> Other than Shamash [Utu], who else can cross it?
> Difficult is the place of crossing and very difficult its passage;
> And everywhere are the waters of death, which bar the approaches.
> Where then, O Gilgamesh, wilt thou cross the Sea?"[60]

The nature of this 'Sea' is made transparently clear from the fact that it was crossed by Utu, the god who travelled from the east to the west – between the 'mountain' of Heaven and the underworld 'mountain' in the

Earth. The Sea was therefore the *celestial* waters, i.e. space.

Eventually, Siduri relented and advised Gilgamesh to seek out Urshanabi, the boatman of Utnapishtim, who was to be found in a 'forest'.[61] Significantly, the text describes Gilgamesh descending into the underworld at this point:

> When Gilgamesh heard this, he raised his axe in his hand,
> Drew the dagger from his belt, slipped into the forest,
> And *went down* to the Stone Things.
> Like a spear *he descended* among them.[62]

The next scene describes a meeting between Gilgamesh and the divine boatman Urshanabi. The boatman listened to Gilgamesh's story and agreed to take him across the Sea. But there was a problem. It would seem that Gilgamesh had descended into the underworld with such violent haste that he had broken certain artefacts which were essential for the crossing.

These enigmatic artefacts are described in the text as the 'Stone Things', and they have caused a great deal of puzzlement to scholars. What might they be? Urshanabi, the boatman of the celestial Sea, stated that 'the Stone Things bear me along, that I might not (have to) touch the waters of death'.[63] In other words, the Stone Things were a kind of propulsion system across space – *not*, it must be said, in the manner of a 'Star Trek' warp-drive system, but rather in the manner that a fiery meteorite-stone might traverse the celestial waters between the 'mountains' of Heaven and Earth.[64]

Anyway, in the absence of the Stone Things, Urshanabi ordered Gilgamesh to cut down trees and make a large number of very long 'punting poles', which could be used to propel the boat through the waters of death. The two then set sail on a fairytale journey, in which a distance of 'a month and fifteen days' was covered in just three days.

The beginning of this journey, however, seems to have been spent upon the waters of the underworld, for it was only on the third day that the pair reached the 'waters of death', where the punting poles had to be used. Then began the most dangerous part of Gilgamesh's journey – across the vast abyss of outer space.

The Meeting with Utnapishtim

Urshanabi and Gilgamesh are now to be envisaged punting across the celestial waters towards the distant planetary abode of Utnapishtim – the Mesopotamian 'Noah'.

The text says little about this part of the journey but moves on to describe Utnapishtim peering into the distance in an attempt to discern the stranger who was approaching in the boat with its unusual propulsion system. Eventually, a travel-weary Gilgamesh disembarked at 'the Land of the Living'.

After Gilgamesh had related the long story of his arduous journeyings, Utnapishtim took pity on him, and decided to reveal to him 'a secret of the gods'. He then proceeded to recount the entire story of the Flood, and how he, Utnapishtim, was afterwards elevated to the abode of the gods. We will return to this story, and its secret, in due course.

We rejoin *The Epic* now at the end of Utnapishtim's speech, as he turned his attention to the stranger in his land, and challenged him to re-enact, if he could, the six days and seven nights of the creation:

"But now (O Gilgamesh), who will assemble the gods for thee,
So that thou mayest find the life which thou seekest?
Test thyself! Do not sleep for six days and seven nights."[65]

This test – which scholars have compared to an initiation – was a re-enactment of the 'six days and seven nights' of the Flood (according to the Utnapishtim story),[66] at the end of which Utnapishtim's boat had come to rest on 'Mount Nisir'. The suggestion is that Utnapishtim stayed awake during this ordeal, only to find rest on the 'seventh day' – a remarkable parallel to the creation account in the book of Genesis, where God rested on the seventh day. Still, let us not jump ahead of ourselves.

Gilgamesh, needless to say, was far too tired from his long journey to stay awake for very long, and thus he failed to re-enact the ordeal of Utnapishtim. Consequently, he failed to pass the test for entry to Heaven (as Utnapishtim knew he would). Instead, Gilgamesh, and the boatman Urshanabi were forced to return to Earth, to Uruk.

There is, however, a twist to the story. Utnapishtim's wife took pity on Gilgamesh, and suggested to her husband that something more tangible should be given to him. Utnapishtim thus decided to reveal another of his little secrets:

"I will tell thee, O Gilgamesh, a hidden thing;
A secret of the gods I will tell thee:
There is a (magical) plant.
Its roots go deep, like the boxthorn;
Its thorns will prick thy hand like a bramble.
If thy hands can obtain that plant, thou shalt have everlasting life."[67]

Gilgamesh now embarked on an entirely different quest. Having realised that he did not qualify for an eternal afterlife in Heaven, he set his sights on the consolation prize – an eternal life *on Earth*. The plant which he now sought would offer a man perpetual rejuvenation. Its name was 'The-Old-Man-Will-Be-Made-Young'.[68]

Where was the magical plant to be found? We can tell from the context of the story that it was located in the Earth's underworld (the Apsu), this being the logical next stop for Gilgamesh and Urshanabi upon their return from Heaven.

As for this return, it is evident that the boat could no longer be used, presumably because all of its punting poles had been utilised in crossing the waters of death. Instead, we find Gilgamesh and Urshanabi returning to the underworld via a mysterious 'water-pipe':

Gilgamesh opened the water-pipe,
He tied heavy stones to his feet.
They carried him down into the Apsu, and he saw the plant.
He seized the plant, though it cut into his hand;
He cut the heavy stones from his feet,
And the sea [of the underworld] cast him up onto its shore.[69]

At this point Gilgamesh was on a shore in the underworld, and a long journey was still required to get back to Uruk. He decided to take the magical plant back to Uruk and share it with the city elders. However, after travelling thirty leagues' distance, Gilgamesh stopped to bathe in a well of water, and left the plant unattended. As if decreed by fate, a snake rose up out of the water and carried the plant away. As if to add insult to injury, the snake, referred to as an 'earth-lion', threw off its old skin as it departed.

Gilgamesh sat down and wept: "For whom have my hands toiled?... I have not obtained a boon for myself – I have obtained a boon for the earth-lion!".[70]

The Epic ends with Gilgamesh and Urshanabi entering the city of Uruk by ascending into it from the underworld. In the final lines, we read how the disappointed hero was reduced to bragging to the boatman Urshanabi about the marvellous city of Uruk, the foundations of which had been laid by the gods at the beginning of time:

"Urshanabi, climb up on the wall of Uruk and walk about.
Inspect the foundation terrace and examine the brickwork.
Is not its brickwork made of burnt brick?!
Did not the Seven Wise Ones lay its foundation?!"[71]

The hero Gilgamesh had thus come back down to earth. He had been born from the earth as a Titan, as the 'MES (meteorite), which is the sprouting seed of a new tree'. But he was, at the same time, a *human* king. Thus his fate was sealed. He would die and return to the earth, like every other mortal Mesopotamian man.

Gilgamesh and Agga

The Epic of Gilgamesh reinforces many of the lessons we have learned so far. It confirms the importance of the meteorite (the falling god motif); it confirms the idea of an Earth-like mountain in the underworld; it confirms the idea that one had to descend into the underworld in order to ascend to Heaven; and it confirms that the route to Heaven was via a 'cosmic mountain' or by the crossing of a celestial sea.

According to *The Epic of Gilgamesh*, the hero did not qualify for a permanent place in Heaven, for reasons which we shall begin to appreciate in due course. However, as the old saying goes, every rule has its exception, and in the case of Gilgamesh we do find a legend in which he apparently did ascend to Heaven permanently. We complete this chapter, then, with a most unusual legend which happens to also contain a lesson which is vital to our future understanding throughout this book.

The legend entitled *Gilgamesh and Agga* is one of the most enigmatic tales in the Gilgamesh saga. It does not belong in the sequence of the main *Epic*, and is in fact an entirely separate legend, in which Gilgamesh, unusually, was given the role of a fully fledged god.

As we shall see, the legend of *Gilgamesh and Agga* contains some very difficult metaphorical allusions, which have defeated the most eminent of scholars. However, its meaning will shine through now that we have identified Mesopotamian religion as an exploded planet cult, in which meteorite-deities attacked the surface of the Earth and descended into its underworld. As we shall now see, the entire tale of *Gilgamesh and Agga* is an allegory for just such a celestial encounter.

The tale begins with Gilgamesh's city of Uruk being threatened with attack by Agga, who was king of the rival city of Kish. Gilgamesh had gone before an assembly of the city elders in Uruk, seeking war, but he had achieved nothing more than a poetic stalemate:

> *Gilgamesh says*: "Let us *not* submit to the house of Kish, let us smite it with weapons."
> *The Elders say*: "Let us submit to the house of Kish, let us *not* smite it with weapons."[72]

In frustration, Gilgamesh turned to the common men of Uruk, who encouraged him to fight, suggesting that 'Agga's army is small, it is scattered behind him'. Gilgamesh thus grew confident that Agga, when he arrived, would have his 'judgement confounded' through fear of Uruk. His optimism, however, was misplaced. After a short period, Agga's army arrived to besiege Uruk, and it was Uruk's 'judgement' which was 'confounded'.

In desperation, Gilgamesh urged his 'head man', Birhurturre, to go out through Uruk's city gate and 'confound' the enemy. But as soon as the delegate emerged, he was seized by Agga's men, who 'crushed his flesh' and brought him to Agga. As Agga prepared to question him, a second man of Uruk appeared – a slave by the name of Zabardibunugga. The text states that the slave 'ascended the wall', whereupon he was forced to confess whether or not the previously captured delegate was the king of Uruk. At this point, in reaction to the slave's negative reply, the text reports that:

> The multitude did not cast itself down, the multitude did not rise up,
> The multitude did not roll in the dust,
> The foreigners, the lot of them, felt not overwhelmed,
> On the mouths of the natives, dust was not heaped,
> The prow of the *magurru*-boat was not cut down,
> Agga, the king of Kish, restrained not his heart,
> His troops struck Birhurturre, they beat him, they crushed his flesh.[73]

What does this obscure passage mean? The repeated negatives are a literary device, emphasising the point that the climax of the poem has not yet occurred and will not occur until Gilgamesh himself has appeared before Agga. In the meantime, the head man, who stood in lieu of Gilgamesh, would be abused.

Now the text announces the appearance of Gilgamesh himself, but the words are strange and puzzling to the modern vocabulary. The text states that Gilgamesh 'ascended the wall' and then 'peered over the wall'.[74]

At this point, the slave identified Gilgamesh as his king, and the main act of war took place:

> The multitude *did* cast itself down, the multitude *did* rise up,
> The multitude *did* roll in the dust,
> The foreigners, the lot of them, *were* overwhelmed,
> On the mouths of the natives, dust *was* heaped,
> And the prow of the *magurru*-boat *was* cut down.[75]

And now there occurred a very strange thing indeed. The 'head man' Birhurturre was released, and Agga and Gilgamesh met face to face, but the fight which we might expect to occur between them did *not* take place. Nor was there any surrender of Uruk to Kish. Instead, the text relates a very strange ending, which has totally baffled scholars:

(Gilgamesh) says to Agga:
"O Agga, my lieutenant, Agga, my captain,
O Agga, my army general,
Agga, thou hast filled with grain the fleeing bird,
Agga, thou hast given me breath, thou hast given me life,
Agga, thou hast brought rest to the one who fled."[76]

What is the meaning of this strange speech? What is the meaning of the tale as a whole?

The key to the decoding of the text lies in its odd description of how Gilgamesh 'ascended the wall' and then 'peered over the wall' towards the enemy. Was this really a 'wall' in the conventional sense, or might it have been an idiom for something else?

Earlier, in *The Epic of Gilgamesh*, the hero bewailed his fate, saying:

"In my city man dies, oppressed is the heart,
Man perishes, heavy is the heart,
I peered over the Wall,
Saw the dead bodies . . . floating in the river;
As for me, I too will be served thus; verily 'tis so."[77]

In the context of Gilgamesh's obsession with death, this passage would seem to refer to *the river of the underworld*, the abode of the dead, where Gilgamesh conjured up an image of floating bodies. If so, then his 'peering over the Wall' would be an idiom for *looking into the underworld*. It naturally follows that the 'Wall' would be the foundation of the Earth, which at the same time would be *the ceiling of the underworld*.

According to Mesopotamian beliefs, the river of the underworld (river Hubur, or river Styx to the Greeks) protected access to the 'city' of the underworld, which was *protected by seven walls*, each pierced by a gate.[78] Various texts describe descending Sky-deities (e.g. Nergal or Inanna) passing through these seven 'walls' as they went deeper and deeper into the Earth, to eventually reach the abode of Ereshkigal, and her awesome seven Anunnaki-judges. It is thus absolutely clear that the so-called 'walls' were not conventional upright walls, but *horizontal walls*, lying beneath the surface of the Earth, and curved to reflect the curvature of the Earth's surface. It thus logically follows that the uppermost 'wall', corresponding to the Earth's surface, was indeed the 'ceiling of the underworld'.

Can we find further confirmation of this interpretation? In an earlier chapter, we read how the god Ninurta brought a heap of stones from Azag's far-off 'mountain' and laid them across the Earth 'like a wall'. This fits neatly with the idea that 'the Wall' was an idiom for the 'surface of the Earth'. There is also a legend, to be covered in the next chapter, where a king of Uruk was teased that he would never make it to the abode of the goddess in Heaven, but would instead have to live with her down below, 'separated by a wall'. Here, again, the context fits well with the idea that 'the Wall' was an idiom for 'the ceiling of the underworld'.

Remarkably, the Egyptians had the same idiom. In Spell 708 of the Coffin Texts, we find an intriguing reference to 'that Wall which separates the Sky from the body of the god'.[79] Since the body of the god Osiris rested in the underworld, and the Sky was generally up above, the Wall which separated them might well be called 'the ceiling of the underworld'.

The ultimate test, of course, is whether the hypothesised idiom makes sense of the text under consideration. Consider, then, the following interpretation of the *Gilgamesh and Agga* story.

Gilgamesh, I suggest, personified a *subterranean* 'city of Uruk'. The 'Wall' through which the 'head man' and the slave passed in order to do battle with Agga's army was thus the 'ceiling of the underworld'.

Agga's army was a descending storm of meteorites, and his 'city of Kish' was an exploded planet. When Agga's multitudinous army 'cast itself down', it engaged in a catastrophic encounter with the city of Uruk in the underworld, causing both Agga's army ('the foreigners') and Gilgamesh's army ('the natives') to be 'overwhelmed' and covered in 'dust'.

Prior to this, Gilgamesh's slave had been arrested by Agga after he 'ascended the Wall'; note that there is no mention of a descent from the wall, which would have been required if the tale concerned a real city and a conventional city-wall. Similarly, Gilgamesh himself 'ascended the Wall' and 'peered over the Wall'. This, I suggest, means that he *climbed up towards the surface of the Earth* and looked out towards Agga, who was descending from above.

This battle, between an army of Heaven and an army of Earth, also sheds light on a puzzling rhyme which occurs earlier in the poem (not cited here), where the residents of Uruk busily attempted to 'complete all the wells of the land... to dig the wells and to complete the fastening ropes'.[80] This would make sense as preparations in the underworld for an imminent heavy impact from above.

What about Agga's grain and the fleeing bird? The lowering of grain from Heaven to Earth happens to be a popular Mesopotamian motif, which is entirely consistent with the notion that all things on Earth were seeded from Heaven. The fleeing bird conjures up the appropriate image of a desperate flight away from the site of the celestial catastrophe.[81]

Why was there no battle between Gilgamesh and Agga, and why was there no surrender of Uruk to Kish? Here is where we learn the vital lesson referred to earlier. The explanation lies in the fact that there were certain rules in Mesopotamian mythology, rule number-one being that deities who descended from Heaven had to enter into the underworld. Further to this, rule number-two stated that a deity trapped in the underworld could only win his or her release if he or she paid a ransom – usually in the form of a substitute captive. The classic illustration of these two rules is the legend of *Inanna's Descent to the Underworld*. The text begins:

> Inanna from the Great Heaven she set her mind towards the Great Below.
> Inanna abandoned Heaven, abandoned Earth, to the underworld she descended.[82]

When Inanna reached the throne-room of Ereshkigal, 'the Lady of the Great Place Below', the Anunnaki-judges 'fastened their eyes upon her, the eyes of death', and hung her corpse on a stake. Three days later, Enki sent two supernatural creatures into the underworld to revive Inanna with the food of life and the water of life. But just as Inanna was about to ascend:

> The Anunnaki-gods seized her (saying):
> "Who of those who ascended from the underworld
> ever did get up scot-free?
> If Inanna is ascending from the underworld,
> Let her give a substitute as substitute for her."[83]

The epic tale then concludes with the arrest of Dumuzi, who was dragged away into the underworld as Inanna's replacement.

This concept of substitution in the underworld will prove to be extremely important later on in this book, so let's look at another example of it in the legend entitled *Enlil and Ninlil*. This text relates how Enlil, 'the Great Mountain', raped the goddess Ninlil (the Earth), who became pregnant with the Moon-god, Sin. It would seem that Sin was thus destined to become the substitute who would permit Enlil to escape from the underworld. But in order to bring the Moon (Sin) into existence, Enlil performed an unprecedented act of divine metamorphosis, transforming himself into three underworld deities, who each, in turn, impregnated Ninlil.[84] The three impregnated deities thus acted as the ransom for Sin's release.

There is no question that divine substitution in the underworld was a major theme of Mesopotamian epic literature. So, could it be that this was the theme of the legend of *Gilgamesh and Agga*? Well, it not only 'could be', but it was. The final lines of the poem read:

> Conqueror [Gilgamesh], prince beloved of Anu,
> Agga has set thee free for the price of Kish,
> Before Utu, he has returned to thee the power of former days.[85]

The poet thus declared that the 'city' of Kish, personified by Agga, had acted *as the ransom* to release Gilgamesh from the underworld. In so doing, Agga ensured Gilgamesh's resurrection to Heaven and returned to him 'the power of former days'. The words of Gilgamesh in response to Agga are revealing indeed:

> "O Agga, thou hast given me breath, thou hast given me life."[86]

In this poem, then, Gilgamesh finally achieved his dream of eternal life like a god. But why did he achieve it here, in this legend, and yet failed to achieve it in *The Epic of Gilgamesh*? The reason is that *Gilgamesh and Agga* is a completely different legend, in which the character of Gilgamesh has been equated with a fully fledged god, who had fallen *from Heaven* into the underworld.[87] There is nothing unusual about this, for the same trend is noticeable elsewhere, too. For example, in some texts Gilgamesh was appointed 'supreme king, judge over the Anunnaki', and was identified with the great god Nergal himself.[88] It was, and is, the nature of things that powerful historical figures, such as Gilgamesh, act as magnets (posthumously) for all of the archetypal religious ideas of their times.

Anyway, an important lesson is to be learned here. As a one hundred per cent god, the right of Gilgamesh to a resurrection was not in doubt. Having been *born in the Sky*, the Sky would be where he belonged.

In *The Epic of Gilgamesh*, however, Gilgamesh was born in the Earth, from clay thrown down by the goddess Aruru. He was thus effectively a Titan – *not* one hundred per cent god, but rather 'two thirds god and one third human'. It was a fact not lost on the Flood-hero Utnapishtim, who told Gilgamesh, pointedly to his face, that he (Gilgamesh) was 'made of the flesh of the gods *and mankind*'.[89]

Curiously, though, there was little, if any, difference in appearance between Gilgamesh and Utnapishtim, as is made evident in the account of the meeting between them:

Gilgamesh said to Utnapishtim, the Distant One:
"As I look upon thee, Utnapishtim,
Thy features are no different from mine; thou art like I.
Thou art not strange at all; thou art like I.
My heart had pictured thee as one perfect for the doing of battle,
Yet thou liest idly upon thy back!"[90]

Gilgamesh was thus intrigued to know why Utnapishtim should have been given eternal life, whereas he (Gilgamesh) could not acquire it. Thus he posed the question to Utnapishtim:

"(Tell me:) How didst thou enter into the company of the gods and obtain eternal life?"

To which Utnapishtim responded as follows:

Utnapishtim said to him, to Gilgamesh:
"I will reveal to thee, Gilgamesh a hidden matter;
A secret of the gods I will tell thee:
Shuruppak – a city which thou knowest,
And which is (now) situated on the bank of the Euphrates –
That city was ancient, as were the gods within it,
When their heart led the great gods to produce the Flood."[91]

Utnapishtim then went on to narrate the entire story of the Flood, from his building of a giant ship, to the coming of the Flood from Heaven, to the climactic ending, when the great god Enlil appeared on Earth and granted immortality to Utnapishtim and his wife.

What was the 'secret of the gods' which Utnapishtim revealed? As mentioned earlier, it could not have been the story of the Flood per se, for Gilgamesh would certainly have already known that story before he set out for the distant 'Land of the Cut-down Cedar Trees'.

So, was the secret perhaps *a secret of the Assyrian scribe* who wrote Tablet XI of *The Epic of Gilgamesh*? Was this scribe concealing a secret knowledge – just like the scribe who appended the creation-of-man story with the secret writing (as discussed in chapter one)?

As we shall now see, there are indeed secrets encoded into *The Epic of Gilgamesh*, not least the metaphorical meaning of that mysterious ancient 'city' of Shuruppak. It was there that the equally mysterious and ancient gods were led by their heart to produce the Great Flood. It is to Shuruppak, then, that we now set our course, to lift once again the veil of metaphorical allusion.

* * * * *

CHAPTER SIX

THE CITY BEYOND THE RIVER

**I have come into the City of God,
the region which existed in primeval time
with my soul and with my double,
and with my translucent form,
to dwell in this land.**
(The Papyrus of Hunefer, Book of the Dead)

Seventy-five miles north of Gilgamesh's city, Uruk, and nearly one hundred miles south of Babylon, lay the ancient city of Shuruppak, which modern scholars believe was the home of Utnapishtim, the hero of the Mesopotamian Flood.

In 1902-3, a German team of archaeologists, under the direction of Robert Koldewey, excavated the remains of Shuruppak from beneath the modern town of Fara, and found hundreds of clay tablets, attesting to the existence of Sumerian schools as far back as 2500 BC. What, one wonders, were the pupils of these schools taught about Utnapishtim, the hero of the Flood? Was he really one of that city's founding kings? Or did Utnapishtim come from a different 'Shuruppak' altogether?

In *The Epic of Gilgamesh*, Utnapishtim declared that he would reveal to Gilgamesh a secret of the gods:

"I will reveal to thee, Gilgamesh a hidden matter;
A secret of the gods I will tell thee:
Shuruppak – a city which thou knowest,
And which is (now) situated on the bank of the Euphrates –
That city was ancient, as were the gods within it,
When their heart led the great gods to produce the Flood."[1]

Was this 'ancient' Shuruppak the same 'city' as the Shuruppak of the 25th century BC? Two scholars who do not think so are John Gardner and

John Maier, who appended their translation of *The Epic* with the note: 'The lines suggest that the ancient Shuruppak *no longer exists*.'[2] A very evocative statement indeed.

Now consider the Sumerian Kings List. Having listed seven god-like kings, who ruled the cities of Eridu, Bad-tibira, Larak and Sippar for a combined period of 222,600 years – that is an average of 31,800 years each! – the Kings List states:

> ... kingship to Shuruppak was carried.
> In Shuruppak, Ubar-Tutu [the father of the Flood-hero] became king,
>   and reigned 18,600 years...
> The Flood swept thereover.[3]

Then, after the Flood, kingship was 'lowered from Heaven' to the city of Kish for 24,510 years, and thereafter transferred to the city of Uruk, where Gilgamesh eventually became king 2,044 years later.[4]

So, according to this remarkable chronology, there was indeed a very ancient city of Shuruppak, which was presumably wiped out by the Flood. Furthermore, it would seem that this ancient Shuruppak existed more than 43,000 years before Gilgamesh's city of Uruk was even built. This is, of course, a quite incredible claim, which has no archaeological foundation whatsoever. It puts 'ancient Shuruppak' firmly in the era of what Mircea Eliade would call 'mythical time' or 'once-upon-a-time'.

Now, what if it could be demonstrated that the term 'city' was actually a Mesopotamian metaphor for 'planet'? And what if it could be demonstrated that a planet of Shuruppak would indeed have been situated 'on the bank of the Euphrates', mythically speaking? Would this not put a different perspective on the story of the Flood-hero? Indeed it would.

Moreover, would it not also put a different perspective on the story of the biblical Flood-hero, Noah? Might it not, in fact, when taken to its logical conclusion, threaten to overturn completely our understanding of the biblical story, including the tale of Adam and Eve?

We proceed, therefore, with caution, acutely aware of the fact that we might be about to turn upside down one of the central tenets of Western religious thinking.

The Cities of Heaven and Earth

Let's begin by establishing whether the ancients might have used 'city' as a metaphor for 'planet' – just as the terms 'mountain', 'island', 'throne' and 'horizon' were all used as metaphors for 'planet'.

In chapter four, I cited a passage from *Enki and the World Order*, which described the birth of Utu from a forest-like Heaven. That passage is now worth citing again, for it appears to describe Heaven as a 'city':

> Utu, the hero, the bull who comes forth out of the forest, who roars like a lion...
> The father of *the great city,* the place where Utu rises, the great herald of holy Anu...
> Who wears a lapis lazuli beard, who comes forth from the holy Heaven...[5]

The place where Utu rises – by all accounts a 'mountain' in the east – was thus a 'city' according to the Mesopotamian way of thinking.

Consider now the Sumerian *Lamentation Texts*, which describe how a great storm descended from the Sky and devastated the land of Sumer. As the following two passages make clear, the storm came from the heavenly planet which was crushed, but also from a place which could be described with the terms 'house' or '*city*':

> It was a day when the weapon sent forth from above wrecked the city [of Ur] as if with a pickaxe.
> On that day Heaven was crushed, Earth was smitten, the face of it was smothered by the storm.
> Heaven was darkened, was overcast with shadow – it was turned into the underworld.
> Utu lay prostrate on the horizon.[6]

> (The people cry:) "O bitter storm, O storm, raise your breast, *return to your city*!
> O city-destroying storm, O storm, raise your breast, *return to your house*!"[7]

This heavenly catastrophe also reminds us that in the legend of *Gilgamesh and Agga* (see previous chapter), Agga personified the *city* of Kish, and *the city symbolised a planet falling from Heaven to Earth*.

In addition to these three examples of the 'city = planet' metaphor from Mesopotamia, we can also cite an example from the texts of the Hittites – a civilisation which existed to the north of Mesopotamia, in the lands of Anatolia. In one of the principal Hittite legends, *The Song of Ullikummis*, the god Kumarbis made love to a 'great Rock' in the celestial ocean, and the Rock gave birth to a child named Ullikummis. Kumarbis then urged his son Ullikummis to attack the Storm-god, who lived in Heaven *in a city* named Kummiya:

Let his name be Ullikummis!
Let him ascend to Heaven for kingship!
Let him vanquish Kummiya, *the beautiful city*!
Let him attack the Storm-god and tear him to pieces![8]

Moving now to ancient Egypt, we find that the 'city = planet' metaphor was even more common, as the following examples illustrate:

"When I was on Earth, I came from *my City. What is it?* It is the horizon of my father Atum."[9]

O king, the Earth opens its mouth for you... may you go to the Great Stairway, may you come to *the Great City*.[10]

The king knows the Field of Reeds – it is *the City of Re*.[11]

"I am on high on the lotus-flowers, I eat bread, I receive abundance, I travel to *the Great City*..."[12]

"Come and row me, come and ferry me over, come and bring me to land at *the Great City* before Re."[13]

"I have come into *the City of God*, the region which existed in primeval time, with my soul and with my double, and with my translucent form, to dwell in this land."[14]

Why did the ancients, as if with one mind, describe Heaven as a 'city'?

To some extent, this question has already been answered in chapter four, where I highlighted the role of the city, and indeed its temple, as a microcosm of the Earth, i.e. a microcosm of a planet. Since the city, as well as the temple, was the 'cosmic mountain' and the Bond between the 'mountains' of Heaven and Earth, it would follow logically that Heaven, Earth, and indeed the underworld, would all be described as 'cities'.

There is another reason, too, which is demonstrable in ancient Egypt, but no less relevant to the land of Mesopotamia. In my previous work, *The Phoenix Solution*, I pointed out that the Egyptians (or their predecessors in the Nile Valley) had laid out their cities along the river Nile in emulation of their concept of Heaven and Earth.[15]

I first spotted this with respect to the cities of Heliopolis and Abydos, which symbolised Heaven and Earth respectively, with the river Nile covering symbolically the vast expanse of space which separated the two planets (see Figure 4).

Figure 4. ANCIENT EGYPT – THE CITIES OF HEAVEN AND EARTH

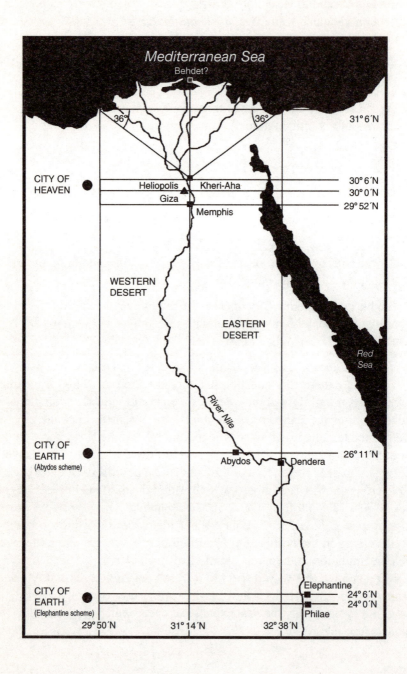

As noted in chapter four, Heliopolis (Annu to the Egyptians) was not the City of the Sun, but *the City of Heaven*. When the Egyptians claimed that Heliopolis was built on the very spot where the first 'solidified seed' of Atum had come into being, what they meant was that this meteoric seed had come into being *in Heaven*. Similarly, when they asserted that Atum had ejaculated or spat out Shu and Tefnut in Heliopolis, they meant that he had created them as his efflux *in Heaven*. And when they stated that Heliopolis was the home of the Bennu-bird, they alluded to the belief that the fiery birth of the Bennu-bird had occurred *in Heaven*.

By the same token, there was a town close to Heliopolis which the Egyptians named Kheri-Aha, 'the City where there was a Battle' – a reference to the legendary battle between Osiris and Seth.[16] This battle had been fought *in Heaven*.

And finally, in the Pyramid Texts, Book of the Dead and Coffin Texts, when the kings expressed their desire to reach Heliopolis/Annu, they were actually expressing their desire *to reach Heaven*.

The *city* of Heliopolis thus truly symbolised the planet of Heaven. And this perhaps exemplifies the reason why the ancients referred to Heaven as a 'city'.

Turning once more to the map at Figure 4, we should note that the city of Abydos (also known as Nedyt) symbolised the Earth. Hence we read in the Pyramid Texts that Osiris was found by Isis and Nephthys 'lying on his side' on *the bank* of Abydos.[17] Hence Abydos was the most famous site of Osiris's burial and the primary site for the annual Mystery Play concerning his death and resurrection. Hence Abydos was the site of a unique structure known as the Osireion, which symbolised the primeval mound in the underworld.[18] The list goes on. Such was the importance of Abydos that it became known as *Ta-Wer*, meaning 'the Greatest Land.'[19] It is also worth noting that the name Abydos derives from the Egyptian *Ab-djw*, which meant literally the 'Mountain of the Beginning'.[20]

As I observed in *The Phoenix Solution*, the Egyptians regarded the river Nile as the 'Winding Waterway', which was imagined to stretch from Earth to Heaven – hence the idea that Abydos was the *City of Earth*, whilst Heliopolis was the *City of Heaven*.[21]

It is for this reason that, once a year, the Egyptians held a major festival of Osiris known as the *Wag*-festival. Although we know very little about this festival, we do know that, at the beginning of the inundation season, a huge flotilla of craft would sail southwards along the Nile to the city of Abydos, where the people would take part in a sacred ceremony involving wine, and presumably intoxication.[22] Then, on the 'Day of Celebration', the people would board their boats and turn them around to sail northwards in the direction of Heliopolis, the sacred City of Heaven.[23] The symbolism of these two journeys was extremely profound. The first segment, the southward journey – made in the 'night-bark' – symbolised the fall of Osiris and the darkness of death. The second segment, the northward journey – made in the 'day-bark' – symbolised the resurrection of Osiris and the light of life.[24] Thus was the god Osiris resurrected symbolically at the beginning of every New Year.

After writing *The Phoenix Solution*, I became aware that this Heaven and Earth symbolism also applied to the cities of Heliopolis *and Elephantine*. For some strange reason, Abydos had had a rival. The island-city of Elephantine (known also as Aswan) marked the southern-most border of the land, and was thus, in many ways, a more suitable symbol for the Earth. Appropriately, it was known as the 'City of the Beginning', and its Egyptian name, AB or *Abu*, signified the 'Father of Beginning'.[25] Intriguingly, the hieroglyphic name of the city was determined by the sign of a mountain, signifying *'foreign* land' or *'distant* land', as if to suggest that the 'Father of Beginning' had fallen from his heavenly city of Heliopolis all the way to the city of Elephantine, where he had been interred in the Earth. Sure enough, there is a legend that Osiris was buried on the secluded island of Abaton, close to Philae and Elephantine on the 24th parallel.[26]

Once again, we must imagine the river Nile as stretching between Earth and Heaven, this time between the city of Elephantine and the city of Heliopolis (again, see Figure 4). This time, the celestial waterway encompasses the flow of the Nile between two key borders in ancient Egypt. Moreover, it is suggestive that the cataracts of the Nile – immediately to the south of Elephantine – might symbolise the chaos of the waters in the underworld.

As can be seen from the map, the water of the river Nile winds its way northwards toward Heliopolis, the City of Heaven, in such a way that the Nile can truly be said to be a *winding waterway*. We can now understand the use of the term 'Winding Waterway' in the Pyramid Texts:

> O Re, commend me to the ferryman of the Winding Waterway, so that
> he may bring me his ferry-boat... in which he ferries the gods to
> yonder side of the Winding Waterway, to the eastern side of the Sky.[27]

The 'east' is, significantly, the location where celestial bodies rise on the horizon. It is worth noting, however, that elsewhere in Egyptian texts we find the idea that the king would cross the Winding Waterway *to the north* of the Sky:

> Seth is brotherly towards you [Osiris] as the Great One of Heliopolis,

for you have traversed the Winding Waterway in the north of the Sky, like a star crossing the Sea which is beneath the Sky.[28]

This idea of a Winding Waterway going to Heaven in the north was inspired undoubtedly by the north-south geography of the river Nile. It should be mentioned, in passing, that this Nile-inspired 'Heaven-in-the-north' scheme solves the long-standing puzzle concerning the North Pole fire-in-the-Sky motif – a mythological theme which was thoroughly explored in the book *Hamlet's Mill* by de Santillana and von Dechend in 1969.[29] But that is another story, for another time.[30]

The point which concerns us here is that the river Nile was the Winding Waterway, which symbolised the journey of the kings from Earth to Heaven, from the *city* of Elephantine, or Abydos, in the south, to the *city* of Heliopolis in the north.

Thus it was that the ancients brought their celestial universe down to Earth, and symbolised planets with cities. Once we have recaptured this long lost way of thinking, it is not at all difficult to see why the ancients imagined Heaven to be a city.

The Celestial Rivers

Might 'ancient Shuruppak', then, be a heavenly 'city', i.e. *a planet*? Before we draw any firm conclusions, let us look first at the idea of *the river bank* upon which ancient Shuruppak was said to have stood.

In chapter two, we noted that Ninlil 'stood on *the bank* of the strongly-flowing river', waiting for Enlil, the 'Great Mountain', to impregnate her with his semen-like river of water. I suggested that Ninlil was a personification of the Earth, i.e. Mother Earth, which would make the 'bank' on which she was standing 'the bank of the Earth', i.e. a *planetary 'bank'*.

Also in chapter two, we read how Nintu gave birth to a daughter Ninmu at *the bank* of the river, after being impregnated by the semen-like waters of Enki. Once again, I suggested that Nintu personified Mother Earth, in which case the daughter's place of birth was a planetary 'bank'.

In chapter three, we heard how the murdered god Osiris had fallen from Heaven to Earth and was found by Isis and Nephthys 'lying on his side' on '*the bank*' of Abydos.[31] The town of Abydos, I suggested, was a metaphor for the Earth. Another planetary 'bank'.

Further to this, I may now point out that the ancient Egyptian Coffin Texts contain 'spells for joining the river banks', where it is clear that the two 'banks' represent Heaven and Earth (the 'Two Lands') respectively, as can be seen in the following citations:

> The Two Lands are joined for my crossing, the river banks are joined, the god kisses his brother...[32]

> Spell for joining the river banks: I have brought together the two river banks, the west to the east – and vice versa.[33]

As mentioned earlier, the river banks could be oriented north-south, as well as east-west; hence in Spell 1129 of the Coffin Texts we read of '*the north bank* of the Winding Waterway', which would correspond to the heavenly city of Heliopolis.[34] On this 'bank', we are told, there were unnumbered towns, with the whole bank being immersed in a fiery flame one million cubits wide (i.e. infinitely wide). It is a perfect description of the imagined cataclysm of the exploded planet.

Returning to Mesopotamia, and *The Epic of Gilgamesh*, we read that Mount Mashu – the 'cosmic mountain' of the underworld – reached up to a 'bank' in Heaven:

> The name of the mountain is Mashu...
> Its peaks reach to *the 'bank* of Heaven',
> And its breasts reach down to the underworld below.[35]

Putting all of these citations together, it is clear that *the ancients envisaged Heaven and Earth as two river banks.*[36] But why?

The explanation has, to a large extent, already been given in our discussion of the Egyptian Winding Waterway, which stretched like a great river across the abyss of space, between Earth and Heaven.

It must now be added that, as far as the Egyptians were concerned, the river Nile had a celestial source, and had fallen to the Earth in a great flood. Thus, in Spell 353 of the Coffin Texts, the Nile-god was addressed as: "O great one of the Sky", whilst in Spell 317, the Nile-god claimed that: "my shape is in the Sky".[37] A text entitled *A Hymn to the Gods as a Single God* describes how the 'Nile comes from the heavens... even onto the mountains',[38] whilst *The Hymn to the Aten* states that God 'hast set a Nile in Heaven that it may descend and make waves upon the mountains'.[39] Similarly, in Spell 318 of the Coffin Texts, the Nile-god boasts that: "It was I who inundated the Eye of Horus with the Nile."[40]

Having thus originated in Nun – the abyss of space – the Nile-god (Hapi) 'descended from Heaven' and became the lover of the Earth-god Geb.[41] This entailed an entry into the Earth, and into the underworld, hence *A Hymn to the Nile* praised the primordial Nile with the enigmatic words:

Entering into the underworld and coming forth above, loving to come forth as a mystery.[42]

A similar legend of the Nile was reported by the Roman poet Ovid, who took up the Greek legend of the catastrophic fall of Phaethon, and wrote that 'Nile ran in terror to the end of the Earth to hide its head which now is still unseen.'[43] In this context, 'the end of the Earth' was the underworld, and the fallen Nile-god was hidden there, in the same manner as the fallen god Osiris.

The Mesopotamians, too, believed that their two great rivers, the Tigris and the Euphrates, had originated in Heaven and brought great floods of water to the Earth. In chapter four, I referred readers to Plate 9, which depicts the birth of Utu from his heavenly 'mountain', accompanied by the god Enki, who is attached to *two celestial rivers*.

Consider now the legend of *Gilgamesh, Enkidu and the Netherworld*. In this legend, we read of a '*Huluppu*-tree', which was torn up by its roots and cast adrift *on the waters of the river Euphrates*, eventually to be replanted in the 'garden of Inanna'. It sounds like a mundane story – until we realise that the 'garden of Inanna' was the Earth, and that the *Huluppu*-tree was the 'cosmic tree'. The felling of the *Huluppu*-tree thus symbolised the collapse of Heaven. This means that the Euphrates of this particular legend was not the mundane terrestrial river, but rather its *celestial counterpart*. Here, then, is the full text of the passage, with my bracketed clarifications, so that readers might appreciate the full metaphorical symbolism:

> Once upon a time there was a tree, a *Huluppu*-tree,
> It had been planted on the bank of the Euphrates [in Heaven],
> It was watered by the Euphrates [in Heaven],
> The violence of the South Wind plucked up its roots,
> Tore away its crown,
> The Euphrates carried it off on its waters [towards Earth].
> The woman [Inanna], roving about in fear at the Word of Anu,
> Roving about in fear at the Word of Enlil,
> Took the tree in her hand, brought it to Uruk [microcosm of Earth]:
> (Saying:) "I shall bring it to pure Inanna's fruitful garden."[44]

The celestial river Euphrates here symbolises the course of the flood waters which were emitted by the exploded planet. And this ties in to the legends cited earlier, where the raging river of Enlil went forth *from Heaven* into the Womb of Ninlil (Mother Earth). We must therefore imagine the celestial river Euphrates as spanning, at least temporarily, the distance between the two planets of Heaven and Earth respectively.

This means, technically – in the minds of the ancients – that Heaven and Earth were two river banks.

So, returning to the mystery of Shuruppak, let us now reconsider what it would mean if a wily old Sumerian sage was to tell us, with a glint in his eye, that ancient Shuruppak was a 'city' situated on the 'bank' of the Euphrates.

Firstly, we would not be at all sure whether this ancient Shuruppak was a mundane *Earthly* city, or a *celestial* 'city', i.e. a planet.

Secondly, we would not be at all sure whether this city was a mundane Earthly city on the bank of the *terrestrial* Euphrates, or a heavenly 'city', i.e. a planet, on a *celestial* 'bank' of the *celestial* Euphrates. And, if the latter, it could be situated either on the eastern (or northern) 'bank', or on the western (or southern) 'bank'. In other words, the wily old Sumerian sage might have been referring to 'ancient Shuruppak' either as the planet of Heaven, or as a city on the planet of Earth.

Hopefully my point has been made. It is now for us to decide whether the Assyrian writer of Tablet XI of *The Epic of Gilgamesh* was having some metaphorical fun with his readers. And, if so, did he give us some additional clues to tell us which particular Shuruppak was the home of the Flood-hero?

Might it be that the Mesopotamian Flood-hero, Utnapishtim, launched his boat from Heaven?

The Mouth of the Rivers

One way of approaching this thorny issue is to consider where the Flood-hero was taken to *after* he survived the Flood. If we can demonstrate that Utnapishtim (or his Sumerian namesake Ziusudra) was taken to Heaven, then it would make sense that he had come down from Heaven – for it seems to be a general rule of ancient mythology that what comes down from the Sky eventually goes back up to the Sky.

Have we not already proved this – with my ankiography of *The Epic of Gilgamesh*? After all, we traced the footsteps of Gilgamesh all the way to Heaven via the 'cosmic mountain' of the underworld, *and* via his crossing of the celestial Sea. And, at the end of his journey, there was Utnapishtim, lying idly upon his back. Was he not in Heaven?

Perhaps so, but only according to *my* interpretation of *The Epic*. Other scholars, it must be said, have placed the abode of Utnapishtim fairly and squarely upon the Earth. In the interests of good scholarship, then, we should go back to first principles, and reassess where it was that Utnapishtim (or Ziusudra) was taken.

Let's begin with *The Epic of Gilgamesh*, at the point where Utnapishtim had survived the Flood, and the god Enlil had appeared on the scene. It is at this moment in the text that we receive a tantalisingly brief piece of information concerning the place to which Utnapishtim was to be taken:

(Enlil said:) "Hitherto Utnapishtim has been but human.
Henceforth Utnapishtim and his wife shall be like unto us gods.
Utnapishtim shall dwell far away, in the distance,
At the mouth [i.e. the source] of the rivers."[45]

Where was 'the mouth of the rivers'? According to scholars, it was somewhere on the Earth, and many are the places on the Earth which would fit such a description. But this, it must be said, is *an assumption*, and nothing more.

In fact, according to the ancient way of thinking, 'the mouth (or source) of the rivers' could have been in two different places, and, as I shall now demonstrate, neither of them were 'on' the Earth.

These two alternative sources of the rivers are best illustrated by the beliefs of the ancient Egyptians. As has already been discussed, the Nile-god, Hapi, descended from Heaven and, like all descending deities, he entered the underworld. Having thus entered the underworld, he then 'came forth above' – 'as a mystery'.[46]

According to the Egyptians, this coming forth of the Nile-god occurred at the island-city of Elephantine (symbolically the Earth). It was here, at the southern border of Egypt, that the waters of the Nile were supposedly controlled by the god Khnum, who dwelt in two subterranean caverns known as *Qerti*.[47] The water itself was known as 'the two *Qerti*', whilst the region of Elephantine around the first cataract was known as *Qebhet*, meaning 'the Place of Cold Waters'.[48] In an ancient Egyptian text, the priest Imhotep informed king Djoser that:

"There is a city in the midst of the waters, from which the Nile rises. Elephantine was its name in the beginning. It is the City of the Beginning, and it is the Nome of the Beginning. It reaches to Uaua. It is the joining of the land, the primeval hillock of earth, the throne of Re..."[49]

However, although the Nile had come forth from the underworld of the Earth, it had also come forth *originally* from a place in the heavens. Hence the Nile-god used to claim that: "My magic power came into being *in the limits of the Sky and Earth*...".[50]

This heavenly source of the Nile, according to the Egyptians, was at a place called Kheri-Aha, 'the City where there was a Battle' (between Osiris and Seth). This city, not surprisingly, was near Heliopolis, the City of Heaven. Some texts refer to this source as the 'Tanaitic mouth' of the Nile, this being the place where the mysterious Eye of Horus had been lost, and the place into which Seth and his conspirators had thrown the chest containing Osiris.[51] It must be said that this all makes a great deal of sense now that we appreciate the heavenly symbolism of Heliopolis and Kheri-Aha, for Osiris was indeed born in Heaven.

In summary, the Egyptians believed that the Nile had two sources – 'the Nile of the South', which rose at Elephantine; and 'the Nile of the North', which rose near Heliopolis. And this is all perfectly logical, if not profound, according to the ancient Egyptian way of thinking.

Nevertheless, modern scholars have criticised the Egyptians for their stupidity in placing the source of the Nile in two locations, neither of which was the true source of its waters (this being the lakes of central Africa, according to the modern scientific way of thinking).[52] It can only be said that such criticisms are a fair measure of the depth of understanding of ancient Egypt among modern scholars, i.e. no depth at all.

So, returning to 'the source of the rivers', to which Utnapishtim was taken by the gods after the Flood, we can read across from Egypt to Mesopotamia, and state that this place – the source of the rivers Tigris and Euphrates – was either (a) in the underworld; or (b) in Heaven. Whichever way we look at it, scholars could not be more wrong in their assumption that Utnapishtim was taken to a place 'on' the Earth.

The Mystery of Dilmun

Let us now attempt to eliminate one of these two possible locations for 'the source of the rivers' by looking at the story of Ziusudra, the Sumerian Flood-hero, who, like Utnapishtim, built a huge boat and saved the seed of all living things.[53]

Although the Sumerian legend of the Flood is badly damaged and fragmentary, it contains a well-preserved section which records exactly what happened to Ziusudra in the aftermath of the Flood. Having offered a sacrifice, and prostrated himself before Utu, Anu and Enlil, Ziusudra was told that he (like Utnapishtim) would become like a god, and would be taken away to an idyllic abode. In this case, however, we are actually given the name of the place – Dilmun. The text records the decision of the gods thus:

Anu-and-Enlil cherished Ziusudra,
Life like that of a god they gave him,
Breath eternal like that of a god they . . . for him,
Then Ziusudra, the king,
Who preserved the name of vegetation and the seed of mankind,
They caused him to dwell in the mountain of rulership, the mountain
   of Dilmun, the place where Utu rises.[54]

Now the fun really begins. According to modern scholars, Dilmun was a place on the Earth. Indeed, such is the confidence in this hypothesis that numerous theses have been written, and several expeditions mounted, in an attempt to confirm Dilmun's exact location. The results, however, have been confusing to say the least, and the inherent contradictions in the available evidence have led several commentators to conclude that there were *two Dilmuns* – both 'on' the Earth, naturally.[55]

However, as we have already seen, it was a tendency of the ancients to associate the planets of Heaven and Earth with terrestrial cities (e.g. Heliopolis and Abydos; or Heliopolis and Elephantine). It therefore seems to me that we could well be dealing with *terrestrial* locations of Dilmun, as well as with *celestial* locations.

But personally I am not (at this juncture) concerned with finding the *archaeological* solution to the mystery of Dilmun's location. Rather, I am interested in the *mythological* solution; in other words, *I wish to establish the location of the Dilmun of the epic literature – a celestial location.* In my view, scholars have come seriously unstuck as a result of their failure to make this distinction, and this is due to their complete lack of understanding of ancient ankiography (the 'geography' of Heaven and Earth).

As we shall now see, there were indeed two Dilmuns – but neither of them was 'on' the Earth. Rather, one Dilmun *was* the Earth, while the other Dilmun was Heaven. Once again, then, we will face a problem of ambiguity in determining whether the Flood-hero was taken to Heaven, or not.

Let's begin with the Sumerian legend entitled *Enki and Ninharsag: A Paradise Myth.* Here we find the most detailed of all descriptions of Dilmun, and significantly it is set into the context of a creation epic, which involved the well-known creator-deities Enki and Ninharsag ('Lady of the Mountain'). Bearing in mind this context, it soon becomes apparent that this particular idyllic land of Dilmun was not a city-state at all, but an entire planet, namely the Earth:

When you [Enki and Ninharsag] were dividing the pure Earth,
The land of Dilmun was pure...
The land of Dilmun was clean, the land of Dilmun was bright.
When they [Enki and Ninharsag] lay down on the ground all alone in
    Dilmun...
The raven uttered no cries,
The *ittidu*-bird uttered not the cry of the *ittidu*-bird,
The lion killed not,
The wolf snatched not the lamb...
The old woman said not: "I am an old woman",
The old man said not: "I am an old man"...[56]

As this story unfolds, it becomes evident that there was a good reason why this Earth-Dilmun was pure, clean and deathless – the reason being that no life had yet emerged in this primeval age.[57] The text identifies the problem as a lack of water. It was then that Enki called for Utu, the Sun-god (sic) to fill the land with water from 'the mouth whence issues the waters of the Earth'.[58] Utu readily obliged, and the Earth-Dilmun immediately became a lush paradise. The legend then goes on to describe the bizarre series of impregnations perpetrated by Enki – as discussed in chapter two.

So far, so good. But this identity of Dilmun hardly fits the context of the Sumerian Flood story. After all, if Ziusudra had just landed his boat somewhere on the Earth, Anu-and-Enlil would hardly have rewarded Ziusudra by taking him *to the Earth*. He was already on it!

Let's read again the decision of Anu-and-Enlil:

They caused him [Ziusudra] to dwell in the mountain of rulership, the
    mountain of Dilmun, the place where Utu rises.

Once again we encounter that mountain metaphor! And it now becomes clear why scholars have gone astray – they have not understood this metaphor; they have *assumed* that Dilmun was located on a *terrestrial* mountain. But 'the mountain of Dilmun', on the contrary, was a planet.

But was it the planet of Earth, or the planet of Heaven? Well, we have already established that Dilmun could be the Earth, but on the other hand we have noted that it would be rather a *non sequitur* in the story if Ziusudra landed his boat somewhere on the Earth but was then rewarded by being taken 'to the Earth'. The balance of evidence, therefore, suggests that Ziusudra was taken to the planet of Heaven.

Is there any other evidence, apart from the Ziusudra story itself, that Dilmun might be the name of the planet of Heaven? There is indeed a curious reference to Dilmun in an inscription by king Sargon II (8th century BC), which states that the king of Dilmun 'dwells like a fish... in the midst of the Sea where Utu rises'.[59] This 'Sea' should be instantly recognisable to us as a metaphor for space. It was in this celestial Sea, according to the ancients, that the planet of Heaven floated like a 'mountain' or 'island'.

The reference by Sargon to the god Utu is also interesting. If we now consider the first expression in the above quote from the Sumerian Flood legend, we find that the Dilmun to which Ziusudra was taken was also known as 'the mountain of rulership – *the place where Utu rises*'.

Scholars often paraphrase 'the place where Utu rises' to read 'the place where the Sun rises', and hence 'the east'. This might well fall in line with where our investigation is heading, but the methodology is badly flawed, for Utu was not really a Sun-god at all.

Nevertheless, it is true that Utu did rise from his 'mountain' in the 'east' side of Heaven, and this might seem to clinch the case for us. However, it is a fact that Utu controlled the crossings *both ways* between Heaven and Earth, so theoretically he could also rise up from the underworld, out of the 'western mountain' of the Earth.

Which, then, was the most likely meaning of the phrase 'the place where Utu rises'? Was it the eastern 'mountain' or the western 'mountain'? And which planet, Heaven or Earth, would be more likely to have been called 'the mountain of rulership'?

My experience with the extant texts suggests that it is difficult to find a citation of Utu rising up from the 'western mountain' of the Earth. This seems to be a theoretical possibility, rather than a common motif. On the other hand, Utu's rise from the 'eastern mountain' of Heaven appears to have been the fundamental archetype – he rose in the 'east' and then lay prostrate in the 'west'.

For example, in the legend entitled *Enki and the World Order*, there is a passage (cited earlier in chapter four) where Utu was given the powers over the crossings between Heaven and Earth. In this text we read:

Utu, the hero, *the bull who comes forth out of the forest*, who roars like a lion...
The father of the great city, the place where Utu rises, the great herald of holy Anu,
The judge, the decision-maker of the gods,
Who wears a lapis lazuli beard, *who comes forth from the holy Heaven...*

There can be no doubt that the italicised sections of this text describe Utu's rise from the 'east'.

A second example, from the same legend, is equally decisive. The following passage is spoken by Enki, and seems to allude to his descent from Heaven into the Earth's underworld, followed by his resurrection back to Heaven. He would then sit in the 'east' with Anu and Enlil in the 'place where Utu rises':

> "I brought craftsmanship to my AB.ZU of Eridu [Earth's underworld],
> I am the true seed emitted by the great wild Bull,
> I am the foremost son of Anu,
> I am the great storm which goes forth out of the underworld...
> I am he who (now) directs justice with the king Anu on Anu's dais,
> I am he who (now) decrees the fates with Enlil in the Mountain of Wisdom,
> He [Enlil] placed in my hand the decreeing of the fates of 'the place where Utu rises'."[60]

This 'place where Utu rises' was, without doubt, the mountain of Heaven, for it was ruled by Anu, the supreme Sky-god, who was *never* described as sitting on the throne of the Earth. Moreover, the description of this 'mountain' as the place where the great gods decreed the fates is highly evocative of Dilmun's epithet as 'the mountain of rulership'.

In summary, all of the evidence favours an identification of Ziusudra's Dilmun as the planet of Heaven. Firstly, this Dilmun was a 'mountain', i.e. a planet. Secondly, it was 'in the midst of the Sea', i.e. it was a planet in the heavens. Thirdly, it was the place where Utu 'rose', i.e. a 'city' or a twin-peaked 'mountain' in the eastern side of the heavens. And fourthly, the story would not make sense if the 'mountain' of Dilmun was the Earth. (How could it be that Utnapishtim was rewarded by taking him to the 'mountain' of Earth?)

In addition to these things, we must also recall that, in *The Epic of Gilgamesh*, the abode of Utnapishtim was referred to as 'the Land of the Living'. This is evocative of immortal life in Heaven rather than any kind of 'living' on Earth. Also, in that legend, the abode of Utnapishtim was referred to as 'the Land of the Cut-down Cedar Trees'. This, too, is suggestive of the planet of Heaven which had been physically destroyed. Finally, there is a particular emphasis on the idea that Utnapishtim had been taken to reside in a place which was 'far away' – hence his nickname: Utnapishtim 'the Distant One'.[61] This, too, seems to fit a location in Heaven better than a location in the underworld of the Earth.

All things considered, the location of the 'mouth of the rivers', to which Utnapishtim was taken, would almost certainly be the *heavenly source* of the celestial rivers.

As on Earth – So in Heaven

Despite all of this evidence and argumentation – based, let it be said, on what the ancients themselves actually wrote – there can still be heard voices arguing that the 'ancient city' of Shuruppak could not possibly have been a planet millions of kilometres distant from Earth. No doubt objections will be raised based on the very *Earth-like context* of the setting in ancient Shuruppak. For it was indeed described as a place with animals, minerals, trees and vegetation *inter alia*, not to mention various people such as the workmen who built Utnapishtim's boat, the city elders, and the Flood-hero himself, together with his family.

Well, let's stop and think about this. The first point to be made is that the ancients believed that Heaven had collapsed and impregnated the Earth with all the seeds of life. This in itself would account for the majority of things described as being in ancient Shuruppak.

But people too? On this subject, a brief lesson is required.

Firstly, let's consider a Sumerian legend entitled *Enmerkar and the Lord of Aratta*, in which we find a description of Heaven more detailed than that found in any other Mesopotamian text.

Once again, rather tiresomely, we must deal with the conventional view that Aratta – one of the key locations in this text – was a *terrestrial* city-state. Again, it must be pointed out that a terrestrial city-state of Aratta almost certainly did exist, but this does not in any way negate the existence of a heavenly 'city' of Aratta, for the ancients built their major cities according to a celestial archetype. As with Dilmun, it is the epic literature with which we are concerned, and in this kind of literature *geo*graphy comes second to *anki*ography.

We will now look briefly at several clues which will confirm the *celestial* nature of the Aratta in the legend of *Enmerkar and the Lord of Aratta*. Firstly, consider the following passage from the text:

> The base of Aratta, the house grown up with Heaven, is a felled tree,
> its top a sundered tree.
> Inside it, the eagle's talon of Imdugud... makes blood run down the
> mountain, down KUR.MUSH.[62]

Note here the 'cut-down tree' motif, which we have already encountered in the legend of Dilmun, the 'Land of the Cut-down Cedar Trees', and also in the legend of Inanna's uprooted *Huluppu*-tree. One might even cite an obscure Egyptian legend in the Pyramid Texts, which refers to a 'cosmic tree' which extended from Heaven down to the Earth; this tree was cooked at one end, burnt in the middle, and filled with the pains of death; the fallen god Osiris was enclosed inside it.[63]

Note, too, the fact that Aratta has a 'base' and a 'top' in this citation. One gets the impression that the two have been sundered, such that two Arattas now exist – one on Earth, one in Heaven.

For a second clue, let's look at the ankiography in the legend of *Enmerkar and the Lord of Aratta*. The story involves a dispute between Enmerkar, the king of Uruk (in Sumer), and a mysterious Lord of Aratta, the king of an *unidentified distant land*. And this dispute required various envoys to be sent from one land to the other. In the case of Enmerkar's envoy, we learn that he began his journey to the distant land of Aratta by crossing seven 'mountains'.[64] This should sound familiar to us because it *is* familiar. We encountered exactly the same motif in the Sumerian version of *The Epic of Gilgamesh*, where the hero had to journey through *seven 'mountains' of the underworld* in his quest to reach Utnapishtim *in Heaven*.[65]

Furthermore, a related legend confirms that one of these seven mountains en route to Aratta was Mount Hurrum. This 'mountain' was allegedly the 'father' of Huwawa, and had caused him to be impregnated in 'the land Hurrum' (his mother). This all points to Mount Hurrum being the fallen 'mountain of Heaven' and hence, by the same token, the 'cosmic mountain' of the underworld. And indeed this is exactly the role of Mount Hurrum in a legend known as *Lugalbanda and Mount Hurrum*.[66]

In addition to all of these clues, we read that Enmerkar's envoys travelled by day 'with Utu of Heaven', and, moreover, that Aratta lay in the 'east'.[67] Furthermore, Utu, as we have seen, was the god in charge of crossings between Heaven and Earth; and his planetary 'mountain' was indeed in the 'east' of Heaven.

Lest there be any doubt about it, the entire story of *Enmerkar and the Lord of Aratta* hinges upon a dispute concerning the residence of the goddess Inanna. As noted in passing in chapter five, Enmerkar was famous for his success in causing Inanna to descend *from Heaven* to Earth (to the temple in Uruk). In this legend, however, we pick up the story slightly earlier, where Inanna was just about to come to Uruk, but was at that time residing in Aratta. The implication is clear – Aratta *was* Heaven, or at the very least a city-state which was situated *in Heaven*.

Thus in one part of the legend, the Lord of Aratta taunted Enmerkar by suggesting that if Inanna descended to him, she would go into the underworld and therefore be 'separated' from him 'by a Wall', whereas if she remained in Heaven, she would live with the Lord of Aratta in a 'lapis lazuli house'.[68]

Eventually, Inanna did leave Aratta, and came to dwell in her new temple at Uruk – the E.AN.NA or 'House of Heaven-and-Earth'. Any ambiguity on this point is eliminated by a Sumerian text which refers to:

> . . .-uggalgim, *apkallu* [boat navigator] of Enmerkar, him who made Inanna descend from Heaven into E.AN.NA.[69]

This amounts to an unequivocal statement that Inanna's relocation from Aratta was *celestial* and *not* terrestrial (as scholars have assumed).

So, having discharged the burden of proof, and demonstrated that Aratta *was* Heaven, let's see how this heavenly city-state was described. In the legend of *Enmerkar and the Lord of Aratta*, we learn that Aratta was a place of gold, silver, lapis lazuli and precious 'stones of the mountain'.[70] Also we learn that Aratta was a land which suffered a terrible drought, but then benefited from a sudden storm, which returned to it its former abundance of grain (the land trembled and quaked at the time, and the tale might well be alluding to the metaphysical reconstruction of Heaven after its fall to the Earth).[71]

In addition to this mineral wealth and agricultural abundance, the heavenly city-state of Aratta was also populated by people. As we already know, it had a king, 'the Lord of Aratta'. But this king had at his disposal a council of elders, a '*mashmash*-priest', 'fighting-men', skilled craftsmen, and apparently an entire city population.[72]

This picture of heavenly Aratta is, of course, virtually identical to Utnapishtim's description of ancient Shuruppak. *QED*. There can be no objection to the idea that the ancient 'city' of Shuruppak *was* the planet of Heaven.

Nevertheless, let's drive this point home beyond any doubt by turning to the beliefs of the ancient Egyptians.

Unlike the Mesopotamians, who imagined themselves making only temporary journeys into the 'city' of Heaven, the Egyptians believed that they had the right to a permanent afterlife there. Consequently, the Egyptian texts are full of descriptions of Heaven – descriptions which are for the most part lacking in the Mesopotamian legends.

It has already been mentioned in chapters four and five that the ancients conceived their Heaven in the image of the Earth. To the Egyptians, this meant that Heaven was like a great 'field', variously called 'the Field of Reeds' or 'the Field of Hetep' (*hetep* means 'peace' or 'offerings'). In the Book of the Dead, the deceased expressed his hope to become a spirit in the Field of Hetep, to eat therein, drink therein, plough therein, reap therein, fight therein and make love therein.[73] Spell 467 of the Coffin Texts describes the Field of Hetep as if it were an exact replica of the land of Egypt:

I plough and I reap, for I am Hetep in the abode of the god. I know the names of the towns, districts and waterways within the Field of Hetep in which I am, I am strong and a spirit in them, I eat in them and move about in them, I plough in them and reap in them, I rise early in them and go to rest in them... I row on its waterways and arrive at its towns.[74]

This blissful place, which is illustrated in Plate 36, was sometimes described as the 'Island of the Just',[75] or as a 'great plateau', which was occasionally linked to a 'stone of brightness'.[76] It was also the inspiration for the Greek concept of the Elysian Fields.

The Field of Reeds, or Field of Hetep, was associated with a region of the Sky where there was a great 'star' or a 'mountain' – both terms being metaphors for a 'planet'. Some Egyptian texts referred to this place as *Neter-Khert*, literally meaning 'the Mountain-Land of God'. It was an idyllic land where the deceased could control everything he had tried to control on Earth:

I have gained the mastery over the waters, I have gained the mastery over the canal, I have gained the mastery over the river, I have gained the mastery over the furrows, I have gained the mastery over the men who work for me, I have gained the mastery over the women who work for me in *Neter-Khert*, I have gained the mastery in *Neter-Khert* over all the things which were decreed to me on Earth.[77]

These extracts are typical of numerous Egyptian prayers, which pictured an afterlife in a remarkably Earth-like paradise. Significantly, this 'mountain' of Heaven, or 'city of Heaven' (see quotes earlier in this chapter), was a land which was *full of people* – not just the kings, it would seem, but also their families and subjects.

In conclusion, then, let it not be said that the presence of a populace negates the argument that places such as Aratta and Shuruppak were heavenly 'cities'.

When Cities Fell from the Sky

Earlier in this chapter, I cited the Sumerian Kings List, and noted the inference therein that the ancient city of Shuruppak had existed more than 43,000 years before Gilgamesh's city of Uruk was built. I thus suggested that ancient Shuruppak belonged firmly to the era of 'mythical time'.

I also noted that this ancient city of Shuruppak would probably have been wiped out by the Great Flood, which brought to an end the reign of its king, Ubar-Tutu (the father of Ziusudra/Utnapishtim). And in support of this suggestion, I cited the words of Utnapishtim to Gilgamesh:

> "That city [Shuruppak] was ancient, as were the gods within it,
> When their heart led the great gods to produce the Flood."

I also cited the observation of two modern scholars, John Gardner and John Maier, who commented that: 'The lines suggest that the ancient Shuruppak no longer exists.' For once, I agree with modern scholars.

So, the groundwork has now been laid to pose a controversial question, namely: *"Does the Sumerian Kings List record the destruction of planets rather than cities?"*.

Consider, for example, the following summary of what the Kings List says happened *after* the Flood had swept over the Earth (we will return in a moment to the *pre*-Flood lists):

> After the Flood had swept thereover, when the kingship was lowered from Heaven, the kingship was (first) in Kish... Twenty-three kings reigned its 24,510 years, 3 months and 3.5 days.
> *Kish was smitten with weapons*; its kingship was carried to E.AN.NA [Uruk]... Twelve kings reigned its 2,310 years.
> *Uruk was smitten with weapons*; its kingship was carried to Ur... Four kings reigned its 177 years.
> *Ur was smitten with weapons*; its kingship was carried to Awan...[78]

And so on and so forth, with each city, in turn, being *'smitten with weapons'*. But where did this curious idiom spring from? Could it be that it sprang from the cult of celestial catastrophism which pervades all of Mesopotamian religious thought?

Note, in particular, how the cities of Kish and Uruk are juxtaposed in the above list. Earlier, in the previous chapter, we decoded the legend of *Gilgamesh and Agga*, and concluded that Agga personified the city of *Kish*, and that Kish symbolised a heavenly planet, rushing down towards an impact with the Earth (or its underworld) which was, in turn, symbolised by Gilgamesh and the city of *Uruk*. In the words of the poet: 'the multitude cast itself down, the multitude rose up, the multitude rolled in the dust, the foreigners, the lot of them, were overwhelmed, on the mouths of the natives dust was heaped, and the prow of the *magurru*-boat *was* cut down.'[79]

In view of this legend, can it be a coincidence that the cities of Kish and Uruk are juxtaposed in the above Sumerian Kings List?[80]

Could it be that some of these Sumerian 'cities' were not really cities at all, but planets, which were 'smitten' by celestial impacts?

And what of the Flood which earlier destroyed the reign of Shuruppak? We have already seen ample evidence in earlier chapters to associate the Flood with the catastrophe of an exploded planet.

Let's now take a look at the first part of the Sumerian Kings List, which begins at the beginning of time, when kingship was lowered from Heaven:

> When the kingship was lowered from Heaven, the kingship was in Eridu... two kings reigned its 64,800 years.
> *I drop Eridu*; its kingship was carried to Bad-tibira... three kings reigned its 108,000 years.
> *I drop Bad-tibira*; its kingship was carried to Larak... one king reigned its 28,800 years.
> *I drop Larak*; its kingship was carried to Sippar... one king reigned its 21,000 years.
> *I drop Sippar*; its kingship to Shuruppak was carried... one king reigned its 18,600 years...
> The Flood swept thereover.[81]

What does it mean to say that a 'city' was 'dropped'?

The Sumerian term used here is *ba-sub*, with the verb *sub* having the meanings 'to drop' (transitive) or 'to fall' (intransitive).[82]

From the moment these texts were translated, scholars have *assumed* that the Sumerian 'historian' was using an *idiom* for 'dropping the subject'. But is this really the case? As noted above, the verb *sub* could mean 'fall' as well as 'drop', and was indeed used frequently in the former context – especially since Mesopotamian deities were in the constant habit of *falling down from the Sky*.

To illustrate the point, consider the usage of the term *sub* in the following extract from the Sumerian legend of Inanna:

> Inanna abandoned Heaven, abandoned Earth, to the underworld she descended.[83]

> *Gasananna An mu-un-sub   Ki mu-un-sub   Kur-ra ba-e-a-e* [84]

Here the term *sub* is translated as 'abandoned', but could equally well mean that Inanna 'fell' or 'descended', especially in view of the context.

So, which interpretation of *ba-sub* is the most likely in the Sumerian Kings List? Was the writer 'dropping the subject', or was he stating that the primeval 'cities' of Sumer had fallen from the Sky? In other words, was he suggesting that the 'cities' were exploded planets?

(One is reminded at this point of the E.AN.NA temple in Uruk – the *'temple descended from Heaven'*.)

In view of the second part of the Kings List, where cities were 'smitten with weapons', a good case might be made to suggest that the 'dropping' and the 'smiting' idioms were expressing a common idea, which had nothing whatsoever to do with 'dropping the subject'.

However, the wording is curious when we think about it. Consider once again the line: 'I drop Eridu; its kingship was carried to Bad-tibira'. If this means that *a planet* Eridu was dropped out of the Sky, then its kingship must have been a *heavenly kingship*, and it surely would have been carried off *to another heavenly city*.

This leads me to suspect that the Sumerian Kings List is a composite of two traditions which were very different in nature. The second part, it seems to me, refers to the smiting of *terrestrial* cities and kingships, whereas the first part refers to the dropping of *planetary* 'cities' and the transference of kingship to other planets (or mythical planets).[85]

In other words, I am led to suspect that the first part of the Sumerian Kings List was drawn from a separate, perhaps much older tradition, which was written *from a heavenly perspective*.[86] And if this was the case, the original text would have been called something like 'Kingship in Heaven'.

Strangely enough, a text entitled *Kingship in Heaven* is one of the most famous legacies from the ancient Hittite culture. The text tells a strange story of gods rising up from the Earth and challenging the gods in the heavenly 'city' of Kummiya, but it begins with a brief account of a battle in Heaven between two rival god-kings:

> Let there listen the gods who are in Heaven and those who are in the
> dark-hued Earth...
> Once in the olden days Alalus was king in Heaven.
> While Alalus was seated on the throne, the mighty Anus, first among
> the gods, was standing before him.
> He [Anus] would sink at his feet and set the drinking cup in his hand.
> Nine in number were the periods that Alalus was king in Heaven.
> In the ninth year Anus gave battle to Alalus and he vanquished him.
> Alalus fled before him and went down to the dark-hued Earth...
> Anus was seated upon the throne...
> Nine in number were the years that Anus was king in Heaven.
> In the ninth year... Kumarbis, like Alalus, gave battle to Anus...[87]

The text records that Anus gave way to 'the Storm-god' in his ninth year, which when added to the nine-year reign of Alalus produces a combined total of eighteen years (or *sars*). Now, in ancient times, a *sar* amounted to 3,600 years, and thus eighteen *sars* amounted to 64,800 years. Amazingly, this is exactly the same duration as the total reign of the two kings of Eridu – the very first city of kingship in the first part of the Sumerian Kings List.[88]

So, perhaps the first Sumerian 'cities' really did drop out of the Sky, just like the Hittite god-kings Alalus and Anus.

Perhaps indeed, because the names Alalus and Anus bear an amazing similarity to the names of the first two Sumerian 'kings' of Eridu – Alulim and Alalgar. The correspondence is indeed even more stunning if we take into account a variant reading of the Sumerian Alulim as Aalu (compare again: Hittite Alalus).[89]

Now this, I know, is a controversial suggestion, and yet it fits perfectly with everything we have learned so far about the exploded planet cults of the ancient Near East. Nevertheless, I am conscious that the idea of 'cities' falling out of the Sky will seem utterly bizarre to readers who have not fully absorbed the point that the word 'city' was a metaphor for 'planet'. Therefore, I would like to close this chapter by offering some reassurance from the famous celestial battle texts of Sanskrit literature.

Consider firstly the following extract from the ancient Indian book *Mahabharata*, where we read how the gods fought each other in their heavenly 'cities':

> Shiva, who rode upon this most excellent chariot, that was composed of all the forces of Heaven, prepared himself for the destruction of *the cities*... when *the three cities* next crossed each others' paths in the firmament, the god Mahadeva shot them through with a terrible stream of light... While *the three cities began to burn*, Parvati hurried there to see the show.[90]

Our second example comes from chapter 102 of the *Varnaparvan*, where the celestial 'city' was called Hiranyapura, 'the Golden City' – a place which was constructed by Brahma, and occupied by the asuras, or at least until its destruction by the god Arjun:

> There was a terrible battle during which *the city was violently thrown into space* and then rocked from one side to the other. After a long struggle, Arjun launched a missile, *destroying the city* and reducing it to smithereens, *all of its pieces falling to Earth*.[91]

There are many more legends such as these in the ancient Sanskrit literature, but hopefully the point has been made. It is difficult to see what these heavenly 'cities' of Sanskrit literature could have been other than the same exploded planets which we have witnessed consistently in the legends of ancient Egypt and Mesopotamia. The 'cities' are hardly likely to have been orbiting alien space stations!

All of these various thoughts lead us inevitably towards a bold, challenging and yet compelling thought. If the five Sumerian *pre-diluvial* 'cities' were originally part of a 'Kingship in Heaven' list, and if the dropping of these 'cities' symbolised catastrophic explosions in the heavens, then it would logically follow that the fifth of these five 'cities' would epitomise the exploded planet which brought the Great Flood down to the Earth (and thus brought kingship down to the Earth permanently).

This fifth fallen 'city' was, of course, Shuruppak. Hence we come back to the various points which have been made throughout this chapter: that ancient Shuruppak was a planet, situated on the 'eastern' (or 'northern') 'bank' of the celestial river Euphrates; that the Flood-hero Utnapishtim – a 'man of Shuruppak' – set sail in his giant boat from a heavenly 'city'; and that Utnapishtim, as a result of his heavenly origin, was restored to Heaven by the gods after the Flood.

This, I suggest, is the 'secret of the gods' referred to in Tablet XI of *The Epic of Gilgamesh*. Moreover, being a 'secret', it seems reasonable to presume that it was encoded into Tablet XI by an Assyrian scribe during the 2nd millennium BC – *for the understanding of initiates only*.

But now, more than three thousand years later, the metaphorical code has been cracked, to reveal a story of the Flood which is totally at odds with the story which we have been taught from the Bible. Did Noah, like Utnapishtim, also sail to Earth from another planet? Was Noah, like Utnapishtim, some kind of meteorite-god?

If this were so, we would have to suppose that the Hebrew priests who wrote the Bible either did not know the true meaning of the Noah's Ark story, or decided to conceal its meaning from the common people. Either way, this is an outrageous thought.

Surely it could not possibly be true?

Could it?

* * * * *

CHAPTER SEVEN

LIFE ON THE ARK

Reed-hut, hearken! Wall, consider!
Man of Shuruppak, son of Ubar-Tutu,
tear down thy house, build a boat!
Abandon thy possessions, seek thou life...
Take thou aboard the boat the seed of all living things.
(The Epic of Gilgamesh, Tablet XI)

Did the Mesopotamian Flood-hero – the 'man of Shuruppak' – sail to Earth with the seeds of life from Heaven? Thus far, I have presented what is effectively a broad conceptual argument. I have noted that the word 'city' could be a metaphor for 'planet'. I have also noted that the 'bank' of the river Euphrates, on which the ancient city of Shuruppak stood, could have been a metaphor for the source of the Flood at the far end of the celestial river, i.e. a planet. Furthermore, I have suggested that the Sumerian Kings List might actually allude to Shuruppak being 'dropped' quite literally out of the Sky. And, in addition to all of these points, I have demonstrated that the Mesopotamian Flood-hero was taken to Heaven after the Flood, thereby implying that he came down from Heaven at the time of the Flood.

Putting all of these points together creates an intriguing scenario – but a scenario which has not yet been proven. After all, we have not yet looked at a single legend of the Flood-hero in detail.

The purpose of this chapter, then, is to go back to basics and examine the detailed legends of the Flood-heroes. Do they confirm or negate the hypothesis that the hero sailed forth from Heaven to Earth?

There are three Mesopotamian legends which describe the Flood-hero. One of these three – the Sumerian story of Ziusudra – is frustratingly brief owing to damaged sections in the clay tablets. We will thus focus our attention primarily on the other two. One of these two is the legend of Utnapishtim, which is recorded in Tablet XI of *The Epic of Gilgamesh*. The other is the legend of Atra-Hasis, the hero of the legend entitled the *Atra-Hasis Epic*.

Despite the differences in these three legends, they all tell much the same story. A 'man' is told, in a secretive manner, that the gods are about to unleash a great Flood. This warning is transmitted, in all three legends, by a god speaking to a wall and/or to a reed-hut (see introductory quote above). The hero is thus advised to build a huge boat, and take aboard the seed of all living things, but without telling the other citizens of Shuruppak. The Flood then comes, and the boat is carried to the top of a 'mountain', whereupon the 'man' emerges from the boat, the gods arrive at the landing site, and the decision is taken to translate the man (and sometimes his wife too) to the abode of the immortal gods.

Nevertheless, despite the overall similarities, the three legends contain several important differences, which make each of them a valuable tool in any quest to understand the story as a whole.

Once again, as we shall now see, metaphors prove to be the key to making sense of the legend. Did a god really speak to a 'wall' or to a 'hut'? Did the 'man of Shuruppak' really tear down a 'house', and then build a 'boat'? And did this 'boat' really land on a 'mountain'?

The secrets of these metaphors – and others – will now be revealed.

The Legend of Atra-Hasis

I would like to begin with the legend of Atra-Hasis, the oldest version of which dates back to the 18th century BC. At that time, the legend was compiled (presumably from older sources) by a scribe named Nur-Aya, who probably lived in the Babylonian city of Sippar.

The *Atra-Hasis Epic* sets the story of the Flood into a much wider context. It begins by narrating the events which had occurred at the beginning of time, when Anu had gone up to the Sky, when the 'gods of the Apsu' had gone down below, when Enlil had taken charge of the Earth, and when Enki had been assigned to the Apsu, to control 'the bolt which bars the sea'. The latter assignment indicates that Enki was sent into the underworld.

Next, the *Atra-Hasis Epic* tells us of the toil of the gods in the underworld, and the eventual creation of mankind to relieve that toil (we will deal with this legend in the next chapter). This account, of the creation of mankind, provides the crucial backdrop to the story which Nur-Aya then relates, for the noise of mankind became such that the god Enlil began to plot its destruction:

> Six hundred years passed,
> The land became wide, the people multiplied;
> The land bellowed like wild oxen.
> The god [Enlil] was disturbed by their uproar.
> Enlil heard their noise and said to the great gods:
> "Oppressive has become the noise of mankind.
> By its noise it makes sleep impossible.
> Give the order that *suruppu*-disease shall break out."[1]

It should be noted in passing that this particular passage contains two interesting parallels to the biblical Flood story. Firstly, the period of six hundred years matches the age of Noah at the time of the Flood.[2] And secondly, the biblical Flood also occurred 'when man had begun to multiply on the face of the Earth'.[3] It might also be added that, just as the Sumerian god Enlil regretted the decision to create mankind and thus attempted to destroy it, so too did Yahweh in the book of Genesis.

The *Atra-Hasis Epic* now introduces us to the hero, Atra-Hasis, whose name meant 'The Exceedingly Wise'.[4] This name, incidentally, was a nickname of Utnapishtim, so we can be certain that we are dealing with one-and-the-same character.[5] Atra-Hasis, we are told, 'would speak with his god, and his god would speak with him' (compare Noah 'walking with God' in Genesis 6:9). He thus complained to Enki about the disease which had been inflicted upon mankind. Enki – who was usually portrayed as the friend of mankind – advised Atra-Hasis that the people should stop revering their gods, and should make a loud noise in the land. The stratagem worked, and the *suruppu*-disease went away.

Once again, however, the noise of mankind disturbed Enlil, who ordered that food supplies should be cut off from the people by withholding the rain. This was duly done, and the Earth became like a barren womb. The people, with nothing to eat, slowly began to waste away, until eventually they resorted to cannibalism:

> When the fifth year arrived,
> The daughter returned to the home of the mother,
> But the mother did not open her door to the daughter.
> The daughter would watch the scales of the mother,
> The mother would watch the scales of the daughter.
> When the sixth year arrived,
> They served up the daughter for a meal,
> Served up a son for food.[6]

What happened next is unclear owing to a break in the tablets, but it would seem that Enki's *lahmu*-heroes may have gone out of control, breaking the bolt of the sea (from the underworld) and releasing a supply of fish to mankind.[7] Anyway, this necessitated a more drastic action to eliminate the noise of mankind. Enlil thus went before the council of gods, and called for a Flood:

> "You imposed your loads on mankind,
> You bestowed noise on mankind,
> You slaughtered a god together with his intelligence,
> You must . . . and create a Flood.
> Your power must indeed be used *against* your people.
> You agreed to the *wrong* plan!
> Have it reversed!"[8]

The suggestion seems to have been that Enki should create a Flood using the waters of the underworld (the Apsu), but Enki refused saying: "The Flood that you mention to me, what is it?... Could I give birth to a Flood? That is Enlil's kind of work!"[9] Enlil, as a Sky-god, then realised that he was indeed in the best position to unleash the Flood upon mankind. Thus the decision was made – Enlil would destroy mankind totally with the Flood, and the gods would at last have peace and quiet.

Atra-Hasis, however, was 'The Exceedingly Wise', who always kept his ear open to his god Enki. And thus it was that Atra-Hasis had a dream – the details of which are unfortunately illegible in the text – and approached Enki to obtain an explanation of the dream. What follows is an odd account, to say the least:

> Enki opened his mouth,
> And said to his servant [Atra-Hasis]...
> "Guard thou (well) the message I am about to tell thee.
> Wall, hearken to me!
> Reed-hut, guard (well) all my words!
> Destroy the house, build a boat.
> Disregard thy possessions,
> And save life!"[10]

Why was it that Enki spoke to the wall and to the hut, and not to Atra-Hasis directly? Scholars have assumed that this was a stratagem designed to circumvent the decision of the gods not to reveal the coming of the Flood to mankind. Possibly so, but might the 'wall' and the 'hut' also be metaphors? Might they relate to something more than just a mundane domestic dwelling? We will return to this point in due course.

Atra-Hasis, we are told, was given seven days to build his boat and prepare for the Flood, which he duly did, taking aboard the beasts and creatures of the fields, the birds of the heavens, and every living thing. Then, on the seventh day, as the storm-god Adad began to bellow in the Sky, Atra-Hasis boarded the boat with his family, relations and craftsmen, cut the rope and set the boat adrift. The badly damaged segment of the Old Babylonian text states:

> Anzu was tearing at the Sky with his claws,
> . . . . the land,
> He broke . . . .
> . . . . the Flood came out.[11]

These tantalising lacunae can, fortunately, be filled in partially by the Neo-Assyrian version of the *Atra-Hasis Epic*, which states:

> Ninurta goes forth, bursting the dykes,
> Erragal [Nergal] roots up the mooring posts.
> . . . with his claws the heavens . . .
> Ishtar [Inanna] like a pot went to pieces.
> . . . destruction is the fate of mankind.[12]

Note the confirmation here that the Flood came from the heavens (a detail which tallies, incidentally, with the biblical story). Note also the metaphorical allusion to the Flood coming from the breaking of a 'pot' in the Sky. We will encounter this metaphor later, and I will pass comment on it then.

In the aftermath of this heavenly catastrophe, there was total chaos:

> The *kasusu*-weapon overcame the people like an army.
> No-one could see anyone else,
> The people could not be recognised in the catastrophe.
> The Flood roared like a bull...
> The darkness was total, there was no sunlight.
> . . . . like white sheep.[13]

The text informs us that even the gods themselves were shattered and overcome with grief at the magnitude of the disaster. Mami, the great mother-goddess, then cried out:

> "How could I, in the assembly of the gods,
> Have ordered such a destruction for them [i.e. Mami's people]?...
> Beyond my control, my offspring have become like white sheep...
> They clog the river like dragonflies.
> They are washed up like a raft on a bank!"[14]

The Flood swept into the land for seven days and seven nights, until finally it subsided. Then Atra-Hasis came out of the boat and offered a sacrifice, the smell of which caused the gods to 'gather like flies'. When Enlil arrived and saw the boat of Atra-Hasis, he was furious, and he reminded the gods that they had all taken an oath to ensure that no life would survive. "How had a man survived the catastrophe?" he asked. Anu, the king of the gods, then spoke, saying: "Who but Enki would do this? He made sure that the reed-hut disclosed the order."[15]

The end of the story, one *presumes*, is that Atra-Hasis was granted immortality by the gods. Unfortunately, the relevant passage is missing from the text.

This, then, is the Atra-Hasis version of the Flood-hero legend. On the one hand, the story confirms the idea that the Flood came forth from an exploded planet (the 'breaking pot' metaphor), but on the other hand it gives the impression that the disaster befell *mankind on the Earth*, with Atra-Hasis being a prominent citizen of Shuruppak *upon the Earth*. And it might thus seem – on the face of it – that the *Atra-Hasis Epic* does not offer much support for my suggestion that Atra-Hasis sailed his boat from the heavens. On the contrary, it seems to follow the same theme as the biblical story of the Flood-hero, Noah.

But does the *Atra-Hasis Epic* portray accurately the *original* version of the story? Might it be an adaptation from an older story, where the Flood-hero *did* sail away from a heavenly 'city' of Shuruppak?

It not only 'might be' such an adaptation, but it most certainly *is*, and I shall now attempt to demonstrate the point.

Let us return to the part of the story where Enki had spoken to Atra-Hasis via the wall and the reed-hut, and commanded him to build the boat. Atra-Hasis, we are told, then had to explain to the city elders *why* he was about to build such a huge boat in full view of all Shuruppak. Atra-Hasis thus spoke to the elders as follows:

"My god is out of favour with your god.
Enki and Enlil have become angry with each other...
I can no longer stay in . . . .
I cannot set foot on Enlil's territory again.
I must go down to the Apsu and stay with my god [Enki]."[16]

Where was the Apsu? As noted on numerous occasions in earlier chapters, *the Apsu was the underworld* – the domain which had originally been assigned to Enki. Readers may recall from the legend of *Enuma Elish* that Apsu was a god of Heaven who had been cast down to the Earth by Enki. Enki had then descended to the Earth himself and had established his 'sacred chamber' and 'cult hut' *upon* the Apsu.[17]

If Atra-Hasis was a denizen of the Earth, why would he have to 'go down to the Apsu', i.e. to the underworld? It makes no sense. Especially since the story goes on to describe Atra-Hasis building his boat and setting sail in the world above, i.e. *not* in the underworld.

Even if we flex the definition of the Apsu somewhat, to redefine it as the entire Earth, it still makes no sense at all that Atra-Hasis – supposedly a dweller on the Earth – would *go down to it*.

The best we can manage to do is to suppose that the final scenes of the *Atra-Hasis Epic* (when the gods 'gathered like flies') were played out *in the underworld*, and that Atra-Hasis thus sailed his boat from the surface of the Earth down into the underworld. But it must be emphasised that such entries into the underworld were usually achieved by gods falling from Heaven (and thus penetrating the surface of the Earth).

Whichever way we look at it, Atra-Hasis's statement "I must go down to the Apsu and stay with my god" is best rationalised by supposing that it was uttered in a heavenly 'city' of Shuruppak.

Was this the original story?

The Legend of Utnapishtim

We turn now to the story of the Flood as related by Utnapishtim in *The Epic of Gilgamesh*. The backdrop to this story is entirely different from the *Atra-Hasis Epic* in that it does *not* begin with an account of the creation of mankind on Earth. In fact, at the beginning of the story, there is no suggestion that mankind has yet been created on the Earth at all – that is *if* we accept my supposition that Utnapishtim and the city elders were occupying a heavenly 'city'. Let's try and follow the story with such a possibility in mind.

As we have seen earlier, Utnapishtim's story begins with the following enigmatic words:

"I will reveal to thee, Gilgamesh a hidden matter;
A secret of the gods will I tell thee:
Shuruppak – a city which thou knowest,
And which is (now) situated on the bank of the Euphrates –
That city was ancient, as were the gods within it,
When their heart led the great gods to produce the Flood."[18]

This is interesting. We are told that the gods were 'within' the 'city' and that their 'heart' caused them to produce the Flood. The ambiguity is delightful. Were the gods sitting in an assembly room, deliberating about the Flood, like flesh-and-blood rulers? Or were these gods resident within a planetary 'city', as the future meteorites of a planet-about-to-explode – unleashing in the process the Great Flood?

Who were the gods who were within the ancient 'city' of Shuruppak? We are told that:

> There [in the city] were Anu, their father,
> Valiant Enlil, their counsellor,
> Ninurta, their assistant,
> And Ennuge, their irrigator.
> Ninigiku-Ea was also present with them.[19]

Things are getting even more interesting. The city which was about to be destroyed was ruled by Anu – the chief god *of Heaven*. Since Anu was rarely, if ever, described as being resident on the Earth, the odds are beginning to favour the idea that Shuruppak was indeed a 'city' of Heaven. The presence of Anu, Enlil and Ea together in this city suggests that we might be looking at the primeval moment *before* these gods were separated into their respective abodes of Heaven, Earth and the underworld.

Next, Utnapishtim tells us that Ea (Enki) revealed the secret of the Flood to a reed-hut and to a wall, just as in the *Atra-Hasis Epic*:

> "Reed-hut, reed-hut! Wall, wall!
> Reed-hut, hearken! Wall, consider!
> Man of Shuruppak, son of Ubar-Tutu,
> Tear down thy house, build a boat!
> Abandon thy possessions, seek thou life...
> Take thou aboard the boat the seed of all living things."[20]

The meaning of this passage, according to scholars, is that the 'house' was to be torn down and converted into a boat.[21] According to scholars, the idea of tearing down a house and building a boat therefrom is quite plausible, since ancient Mesopotamian houses were often made out of reeds.[22] Nevertheless, might there be a deeper meaning to the 'reed-hut', 'wall' and 'house' metaphors? We will return to this idea shortly.

Returning to Utnapishtim's story, we shall pass over, for the moment, the description of the boat and its building, and focus our attention on the words which were to be spoken by Utnapishtim to the city elders, when they asked him about his boat-building activity:

> "I have learned that Enlil is hostile to me,
> So that I cannot reside in your city,
> Nor set my foot in Enlil's territory.
> *To the Apsu I will therefore go down,*
> To dwell with my lord Ea [Enki]."[23]

These are virtually identical words to those used by Atra-Hasis in the *Atra-Hasis Epic* cited earlier. Once again, the thought of Utnapishtim descending into the underworld (the Apsu) is a total anomaly in the context of the story.

What is the opinion of scholars concerning this anomaly? Not surprisingly, they have brushed it off as insignificant. John Gardner and John Maier commented about the descent to the Apsu that: 'This is true only in the sense that the Earth is covered – and the Apsu is let loose in flood upon the Earth.'[24] In other words, they seem to have been suggesting that Utnapishtim's boat would descend upon the waters of the Flood, as the waters retreated *after* the Flood.

This is mere sophistry. Firstly, Gardner and Maier ignored the fact that the boat would first have to rise upon the waters of the Apsu before going down upon them; this would make Utnapishtim's statement 'To the Apsu I will go down' sound weird to say the least.

Secondly, there is in any case no statement anywhere in *The Epic of Gilgamesh* that the waters came up out of the Apsu. On the contrary, it is apparent that the waters of the Flood came down from the heavens (Gardner and Maier's misunderstanding possibly stems from a dubious reading of the biblical text in the book of Genesis).[25]

Thirdly, the boat did not actually go down all the way to the Apsu anyway – it came to rest upon a high mountain, which is hardly the Apsu.

Fourthly, to reiterate the main argument, even if we accept that the waters of the underworld Apsu had come up onto the face of the Earth, the fact is that there was only one way that the boat could *go down onto them*, namely if the boat were to descend *from Heaven*.

In view of all these points, Gardner and Maier's explanation must be dismissed. It is a typical example of how scholars tend to explain away an anomaly, rather than seeing an anomaly as a major clue to a flawed interpretation. The fact remains that Utnapishtim was told to go down to the Apsu, as was Atra-Hasis.

Returning to the story of Utnapishtim, the boat was completed in seven days, and the hero loaded on board the seed of all living things, together with his family, kin and craftsmen. Oddly, we hear that he also took aboard *all of his silver and gold*.[26] Why would he do that, one wonders?

Utnapishtim then boarded the boat himself, battened up the entrance, and handed over control to a boatman named Puzur-Amurri, 'one who knows the secrets of the West'.[27] No sooner was the boat launched than, to use a modern idiom, all hell let loose. The text states:

With the first glow of dawn,
A black cloud came up from out of the horizon.
Adad thundered within it,
While Shullat and Hanish went in front,
Moving as heralds over hill and plain.
Erragal [Nergal] tore out the mooring posts,
Ninurta came forth and caused the dykes to give way;
The Anunnaki raised their torches,
Lighting up the land with their brightness.
The confusion of Adad reached unto the (highest) heavens,
Turning into darkness all that had been light.
The wide land was shattered like a pot![28]

This passage contains some very valuable information. Firstly, note the appearance of the Anunnaki, who were usually gods of the underworld (in the interior of the Earth). In this context, however, the raising of the torches by the Anunnaki seems to signify *a fiery birth in the heavens*, as if they were being ejected catastrophically from the planet of Heaven. This would make sense, for the name Anunnaki does mean 'those who came from Heaven to Earth'.

Note also the god Nergal, who tore out the mooring posts. He, too, is generally known as a god of the underworld, but the legend entitled *Nergal and Ereshkigal* confirms that he originated in the heavens and descended to Earth, into the underworld.[29]

The context of the story thus suggests that Nergal, Ninurta and the Anunnaki were erupting outwards from the interior of a heavenly planet.

If my reading is correct, the second line – 'a black cloud came up from out of the horizon' – would be referring to a *planetary* 'horizon', in which case the black cloud came up out of the planet's interior.

If we read through the passage again, it becomes immediately evident that the exploded planet interpretation makes excellent sense.

Consider, too, the final line: 'the wide land was shattered like a pot'. Earlier, we read in the *Atra-Hasis Epic* that Anzu tore at the Sky with his claws, causing something to break and the Flood to come out. We also noted that 'Ishtar went to pieces *like a pot*', and I pointed out that the breaking pot was a metaphor for the exploding planet. If anyone should doubt this idea, they will be dismayed to hear that, in the text cited above, it was '*the wide land*' which was 'shattered like a pot'.

This metaphorical breakthrough turns out to be a vitally important key to decoding what happens next in the Utnapishtim story:

The gods were terrified by the Flood;

They shrank back, fled upwards to the highest heavens...
Ishtar [Inanna] cried out like a woman giving birth,
The sweet-voiced lady of the gods cried out:
"Alas, the olden days are turned to clay,
Because I spoke evil in the assembly of the gods.
How could I speak evil in the assembly of the gods?
How could I order battle for the destruction of my people?
Alas, I myself (now) give birth to my people!
Like the spawn of fish they (now) fill the sea!"[30]

This is an astonishing passage, which echoes the earlier lament of Mami in the *Atra-Hasis Epic*. There, we were told that Mami bewailed the fate of her 'people' – her 'offspring' – who were scattered like sacrificial 'white sheep', who clogged up the 'river' like 'dragonflies' and who were washed up like a raft upon on a 'bank'. Do we recognise some of these metaphors? We ought to.

What the story means is that this 'people' floated down the celestial river and were washed up on the 'bank' of the Earth. In other words, this 'people' originated in the heavens.

Moreover, the passages cited above make it clear that this strange 'people' originated from the 'womb' of a Sky-goddess, who 'went to pieces like a pot'.

One is reminded of the Egyptian Sky-goddess Nut, 'the Primeval Hill of the Land in the midst of the Sea', who also gave birth from her womb in catastrophic circumstances. Her name, we might recall, was written with the sign of a water-pot, and she was often portrayed as a woman with a water-pot on her head.[31] She was the lady of the Great Flood – the lady of the exploded planet.

Another lady of the Great Flood – also a Sky-goddess (or *ex*-Sky-goddess) – was the Babylonian goddess Tiamat, whose name stemmed from a root word meaning 'ocean'.[32] It thus follows that the destruction of Tiamat by Marduk in *Enuma Elish* unleashed a great Flood which fell upon the Earth. Significantly, we find in the Babylonian New Year Festival that this battle was celebrated by *the ritual of smashing a pot*. The relevant text states:

The king smashing a *hariu* pot with a weapon – that is Marduk who subjugated Tiamat.[33]

Moreover, it is significant that the act of creation in the *Enuma Elish* proceeded from turbulence *inside the womb* of Tiamat, whence various gods were born.[34] According to one passage in the text, mankind was made from the substance of these gods.[35]

Plate 1 (above) Ancient peoples were obsessed with 'the battle of the gods'. In this cylinder seal, a human-like god is seen attacking the sea-dragon, Tiamat.

Plate 2 (right) According to the Babylonian Epic of Creation, Tiamat was not a dragon but a celestial body which had exploded in the 'waters' of space – hence her nickname 'Mother of Noise'.

Plate 3 (left) One of the most famous ancient Sky-battles was that between the gods Ninurta and Zu. In this cylinder seal, the captured bird-god Zu is brought before the Earth-god, Enki.

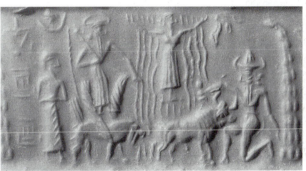

Plate 4 (left) Zu is here slain in the form of a bull, as Ninharsag descends from the Sky. Zu's heavenly mountain had been destroyed, causing its 'stones' to be heaped up on the Earth.

Plate 5 (above) The most famous legend of the ancient Near East was *The Epic of Gilgamesh*. In this seal, Gilgamesh (right) overpowers a lion, whilst his companion Enkidu (left) cuts off a hind leg from the Bull of Heaven.

Plate 6 (right) Huwawa – a god who personified the 'cosmic mountain' in the underworld. It was the task of Gilgamesh and Enkidu to defeat Huwawa and thereby ascend to Heaven on 'the road of Utu'.

Plate 7 (left) Utu – the Sumerian god who controlled all crossings between Heaven and Earth. It was Utu who helped Gilgamesh to reach Heaven, either by immobilising Huwawa with 'eight mighty winds', or by lowering 'seven heroes' into the underworld.

Plate 8 (above) In this cylinder seal, Utu (Shamash) rises from the twin-peaks of his 'mountain' in the east of the Sky, with fiery rays and a saw in his hand. Utu was supposedly the Sumerian Sun-god.

Plate 9 (above) Utu is inside his eastern 'mountain'. To his right is Enki (Ea), a god who descended from Heaven to Earth with fertile waters. To his left is a goddess of vegetation. The scene encapsulates all that is wrong with the theory that Utu was a Sun-god and nothing but a Sun-god.

Plate 10 (above) The Babylonian god Marduk stands in the midst of the vanquished goddess Tiamat, and then steps forward onto a 'mountain' before Enki (Ea), who sits in the watery Apsu of Earth, i.e. in the underworld.

Plate 11 (left) The Victory Stele of Naram-Sin depicts the Akkadian king in the act of ascending a mountain towards Heaven, where the gods reside. Note how the gods of Heaven are portrayed as rayed-stars.

Plate 12 (right) The Assyrian king Ashurnasirpal gazes towards his gods. Once again the gods are represented by astronomical symbols: a winged Sun-disk, a crescent Moon and a rayed-star. The remaining symbols are the horned helmet of Assur and the forked thunderbolt of Adad.

Plate 13 (above) Jehu, king of Israel, pays tribute to the Assyrian king Shalmaneser III. Again the gods are portrayed as astronomical symbols, which hover in the Sky.

Plate 14 (above) Utu/Shamash was renowned for travelling between Heaven and Earth, and was thus portrayed in a winged disk. It is easy to be fooled by the human-like imagery, but the symbolism is primarily cosmological.

Plate 15 (above) 'Thou art holding the ends of the Earth suspended from the midst of Heaven' (*A Hymn to Shamash*). The tablet shows Shamash sitting enthroned in his shrine on the celestial ocean. The rayed-star on a pedestal is the fiery 'cosmic mountain', entombed in the underworld of the Earth.

Plate 16 (below) According to legend, mankind was given the hoe to work the land and feed the gods. But who were the gods? This seal provides a crucial clue – the Sky is dominated by a celestial body exploding into meteoric fragments.

Plate 17 (above) The Egyptian god Osiris was born in the Sky but became Lord of the underworld when he was cast down to the Earth. Meteoric iron and floodwaters were said to have flowed out from his dismembered body.

Plate 18 (below) The Osireion at Abydos provides archaeological evidence for the belief that the 'mountain' of Heaven had fallen into the underworld.

Plate 19 (above left) 'The lightning flash strikes... Isis wakes pregnant with the seed of her brother Osiris' (Coffin Texts, Spell 148). The conception of Horus – seen here on the knee of Isis – was no ordinary conception.

Plate 20 (above right) The falcon of Horus is seen here protecting the head of king Khafre. Each Egyptian king imagined himself to be an incarnation of the falcon-god.

Plate 21 (left) The kings of ancient Egypt and Mesopotamia portrayed themselves as giants, who had been born from the womb of the Earth (Isis) as a 'son of God'.

So, returning to the legend of Utnapishtim, the implication of all this is very clear. The 'people' who came forth from the womb of the goddess Ishtar were not really 'people' at all – *they were the meteorite offspring from an exploding planetary body.*

This, then, was the nature of the storm which originated in Heaven, and raged for six days and six nights, before eventually subsiding on the seventh day.[36] It is only at this point, I suggest, in line 128 of Tablet XI of *The Epic of Gilgamesh*, that planet Earth enters the picture for the first time. The text reads:

> On the seventh day of its coming, the South-Storm-Flood broke from
>   its battle, which it had fought like a woman giving birth.
> The sea grew quiet, the storm was still, the Flood ceased.
> I [Utnapishtim] looked out at the day. Stillness had settled in.
> And all of mankind had returned to clay.[37]

What kind of 'mankind' was this, that had returned to clay? It was, quite clearly, not a mankind here on the Earth, but rather the same multitude of 'people' whom we just encountered being ejected from the broken womb of the Sky-goddess. Hence, as the *Atra-Hasis Epic* put it, the people were like 'dragonflies washed up as a raft on a bank'.[38]

To rejoin the story, on the seventh day, we find Utnapishtim looking out of his boat as it approached a 'mountain'. However, there is no indication at any time that the boat had been carried *up* on the waters, to then sink *down* as the waters retreated. On the contrary, the text gives the impression that Utnapishtim sailed directly from Heaven to Earth – the latter now appearing as a planetary 'island' or 'mountain' in the distance:

> I looked for a shore at the boundary of the Sea,
> And at the twelfth time of looking, an island emerged.
> The boat stood grounded on the mountain Nisir.
> Mount Nisir held the boat fast; it could not rise.[39]

Incidentally, it is at this point that the biblical account of Noah's Flood becomes riddled with contradictions as to whether the mountains had appeared above the waters or not. The Mesopotamian account, however, contains no such contradictions. The boat from Heaven was simply stopped dead in its tracks by Mount Nisir, i.e. the Earth, which at the same time became deluged by the floodwaters which had arrived with the boat.

For six days, Mount Nisir (meaning 'the Mount of Salvation') held the boat fast, presumably supporting it with its floodwaters.[40] Then, on the seventh day after landing, Utnapishtim sent forth a dove, a swallow and a raven. It was during the flight of the raven that land became visible and the boat came to rest on a real terrestrial mountain, whereupon Utnapishtim made a sacrifice to the gods.[41]

As in the *Atra-Hasis Epic*, the gods then smelled the sweet savour of the sacrifice and 'crowded like flies' around Utnapishtim. This is a strange way of referring to the gods, as several scholars have noted, but it can be explained very easily in the context of an exploded planet cult.

What was the significance of comparing the gods to 'flies'? In the legend of Utnapishtim, we are told that the great goddess Ishtar raised up a necklace of lapis lazuli stones.[42] The goddess then swore by these lapis lazuli stones that she would always remember that evil day of the Flood. Now, the symbolic significance of lapis lazuli has already been mentioned several times in earlier chapters, and it is therefore encouraging to discover in the translation of *The Epic of Gilgamesh* by John Gardner and John Maier that these lapis lazuli stones were a very special kind of 'fly-ornament'. The translation reads as follows:

> From afar the lady of the gods [Ishtar/Inanna] came down.
> From the corpses [of the sacrifice] she raised up the iridescent fly
>   which Anu made for love-making.[43]

This reference to a 'fly for love-making' meant nothing to scholars, but it is especially significant to us in the context of the matters discussed in chapter two of this work – namely the impregnation of Mother Earth by *meteorites*, which were sometimes symbolised by lapis lazuli.

With this symbolic possibility of 'flies' in mind, consider the following speech by Ishtar (Mami-Nintu) in the *Atra-Hasis Epic*:

> You [the gods] agreed the destruction.
> Now the bright faces [of Mami's 'people'] are dark forever.
> Then she [Mami] went up to the big flies which Anu had made,
> And declared before the gods: "... Let these flies be the lapis lazuli of
>   my necklace."[44]

Ah! Now we have big flies, of lapis lazuli, and made by Anu to boot. Since Anu was the supreme god of the exploded planet, can there be any doubt that these 'flies' were *meteorites*? As if to confirm it, the Oxford University scholar Stephanie Dalley commented that there was a fragment of text translated in 1930 which asserted that 'all the gods of Uruk turned into flies when they abandoned Uruk'.[45] Once again we see the idea of the destroyed city as a metaphor for a destroyed planet.

Enough on flies – those pesky creatures of death and decay! Let us return to the final scene in Utnapishtim's legend, where an angry Enlil appeared at the landing site and exclaimed:

"Has life-breath escaped?
No 'man' was meant to live through the destruction!"[46]

Significantly, Enlil put the blame on the Igigi – *the gods who came from Heaven* – yet another clue to the heavenly origins of Utnapishtim's boat.[47] Then, at the pleading of Enki, Enlil put away his anger and uttered the words that bring the story to its dramatic conclusion:

"Hitherto Utnapishtim has been but a man.
Henceforth Utnapishtim and his wife shall be like unto us gods.
Utnapishtim shall dwell far away, in the distance,
At the mouth [i.e. the source] of the rivers."[48]

The Mystery of the Reed-Hut and the Wall

I would now like to return, briefly, to the mystery of the 'wall' and the 'reed-hut' to which Enki disclosed the news of the coming Flood, in order that Utnapishtim, alias Atra-Hasis, might build a boat and escape. It is curious that this 'wall' is one of the few motifs which appear consistently in all three of the extant stories of the Mesopotamian Flood-hero. Having cited two of the three instances of this motif, let us now cite the third, from the Sumerian legend of Ziusudra:

. . . . . . the gods a wall . . . . . .
Ziusudra, standing at its side, listened.
(Enki speaks:) "Stand by the wall at my left side . . .
By the wall I will say a word to thee, take my word,
Give ear to my instruction:
By our (command) a Flood will sweep over the 'cult-centres';
To destroy the seed of mankind . . .
Its kingship, its rule, will be put to an end."[49]

What was the significance of this wall? Why was it so important that all of the ancient writers included it as a key part of the Flood-hero story?

The answer, I suggest, has already been revealed earlier in this book, when it became apparent that the 'Wall' was the name given to the ceiling of the underworld. *In other words, the Wall was a planetary surface.* This is particularly apparent in the legend of *Gilgamesh and Agga*, but it is also apparent from various other references; in *The Epic of Gilgamesh*, for example, the hero peered over the Wall to see dead bodies floating in the river of the underworld; also in the legend of *Enmerkar and the Lord of Aratta*, the king of Uruk was told that he would have to live with the goddess Inanna 'separated by a Wall', i.e. this would happen if the goddess descended into the underworld. And, in another Sumerian legend, the fallen goddess Ningal exclaimed: "Like a fallen bull, I cannot rise up from *the Wall* of Ur [her destroyed 'city']".[50]

What does this imply for Utnapishtim? It implies that he lived *inside* the heavenly planet of Shuruppak. And it further implies that the 'house' in which Utnapishtim lived was the planet of Heaven itself. Sharp-eyed readers may recall the use of this exact metaphor in the Sumerian *Lamentation Texts*, cited in chapter six, where the citizens of Sumer cried: "O storm, return to your city, *return to your house*".[51]

Let us now reconsider the advice given by Enki to Utnapishtim:

"Reed-hut, hearken! Wall, consider!
Man of Shuruppak, son of Ubar-Tutu,
Tear down thy house, build a boat!"

What if the 'house' was indeed the planet? The tearing down of the 'house' would then be a metaphor for the destruction of the planet.[52] Furthermore, the conversion of the 'house' into a 'boat' would then be a perfect allegory for the conversion of a planet into a storm of meteorites.

Far-fetched? Absolutely not. Did we think that Utnapishtim was really a human being? Remember the words which Gilgamesh uttered when he came face to face with Utnapishtim for the first time:

"As I look upon thee, Utnapishtim,
Thy features are no different from mine; thou art like I.
Thou art not strange at all; thou art like I.
My heart had pictured thee as one perfect for the doing of battle,
Yet thou liest idly upon thy back!"

As we can see, Utnapishtim was *like* Gilgamesh. But Gilgamesh was no ordinary human being. He was two thirds god, 'the offshoot of Uruk', who had strength 'like the *ki-sir* of Anu'. He was the 'MES', or 'meteorite', which was 'the sprouting seed of a new tree'. He was born in the Earth as the progeny of a sacred marriage to two descended deities.

Gilgamesh, then, was a Titan-like king – a god equivalent in nature to the Sumerian god Zu, or the Babylonian god Marduk, or the Egyptian falcon-god Horus. If Utnapishtim looked like Gilgamesh, as we are told in the passage above, then *Utnapishtim was not human*. But this should not surprise us, because Utnapishtim never professed to be human. On the contrary, it was he who remarked, condescendingly, about Gilgamesh that the latter was 'made of the flesh of the gods *and mankind*'.

Here is another point. Why was it, in the passage cited above, that

Gilgamesh envisaged Utnapishtim as 'one perfect for the doing of battle'? It is a line which has often jarred with scholars of Mesopotamian mythology, who cannot envisage the peaceable Flood-saviour in such militaristic terms. But it does make perfect sense under the exploded planet scenario, for Utnapishtim would indeed have done battle as he descended to the Earth catastrophically. He thus did fight in battle, just as the Flood itself had 'fought like a battle'.

Utnapishtim's boat, then, was effectively a huge meteorite – or, to be technically precise, an exploded planet. He literally, but metaphorically, tore down his 'house' and built a 'boat'.

When we think about it, this is exactly the kind of allegory which would have been used by ancient people who lived in houses (reed-huts), which could be torn down physically and converted into reed-boats.[53]

Moreover, there could be no better metaphor than a 'boat' to portray the rather abstract idea of Utnapishtim's planet-like 'meteorite' sailing through the celestial waters between Heaven and Earth.

Ridiculous? Wishful thinking? Not at all. In fact, the Mesopotamian texts carry a number of enigmatic references to the cut-down boat motif, the meaning of which can now be elucidated. In the legend of *Gilgamesh and Agga*, for example, the attack by Kish upon Uruk was described with the words:

The multitude cast itself down, the multitude rose up,
The multitude rolled in the dust,
The foreigners, the lot of them, were overwhelmed,
On the mouths of the natives, dust was heaped,
And the prow of the magurru-boat was cut down.[54]

A similar idea appears in *The Epic of Gilgamesh*, but here the hero expressed the hope that his ascent to Heaven need *not* be accompanied by the catastrophic fall of an Agga-like deity:

"For me another will not die,
The loaded boat [of Heaven] will not sink [to Earth],
The three-ply cloth will not be cut,
On the Wall [the surface of the Earth] no-one will be overwhelmed,
House and hut, fire will not destroy."[55]

The writer of *The Epic* then recited an enigmatic three-line poem which read as follows:

After it had sunk, after it had sunk,
After the Magan-boat had sunk,
After the boat 'The Might of Magilum' had sunk.[56]

This Magan-boat is very confusing to scholars. It turns up again in the legend of *Enki and the World Order*, where it is described as being 'loaded Sky-high'.[57]

The implication of all these passages should be transparently obvious – the sunken or cut-down boat symbolised the ex-planet of Heaven. It is a metaphorical allegory which is virtually identical to the cut-down tree motif, which we covered in chapters five and six.

Incidentally, the same sunken or cut-down boat motif is found in ancient Egypt. In Spells 132 and 136 of the Coffin Texts, we find a reference to 'the rope which was severed... the ferry-boat which was lost in its floodwaters'.[58] It was a fundamental belief of the Egyptians that the afterlife was attained by 'mooring' a boat at a great 'Mooring Post' in the Sky.[59]

Let's now take a closer look at Utnapishtim's boat. In *The Epic of Gilgamesh*, Enki gave the boat-building instructions as follows:

> "The boat that you are to build,
> Let her measure be measured,
> Let her breadth and length be equal,
> Give her a roof like the Apsu."[60]

It would be an understatement to say that the design of this boat – like that of Noah's Ark in the Bible – has caused innumerable difficulties and disagreements among scholars. Suffice to say that a roof like the Apsu meant what it said – the roof of the Apsu was a *planetary crust* on Earth, but was originally a planetary crust in Heaven. Utnapishtim's boat was thus equivalent to the interior of the heavenly planet of Shuruppak.[61] The boat had a roof like the surface of a planet because the boat was, to all intents and purposes, a planet. That's why the measurements were as broad as they were long. *The boat was equivalent to a sphere.*

We can thus understand why Ziusudra's boat in the Sumerian Flood legend was called a *magurgur*, meaning 'a very great ship'.[62] Similarly, we can understand why the boat of Utnapishtim/Atra-Hasis was either called an *ekallu*, meaning 'a great house', or an *elippu*, or *elippu rabitu*, once again meaning 'a great ship'.[63] Moreover, it is extremely significant that the measurements of Utnapishtim's boat made it *the size of a ziggurat*, as John Gardner and John Maier explained:

> The ship is enormous, the size of the great ziggurat of Babylon...
> and the amount of material used is vast... the dimensions suggest
> something more like a ziggurat or temple than a ship...[64]

Indeed. As noted in chapter four, the ziggurat or temple was a microcosm of the planet of Earth and a mirror image of the planet of Heaven. Utnapishtim's boat was thus not really a boat at all, but a falling 'mountain', which would enter into the underworld and become the true 'cosmic mountain'. The ziggurat was a scale replica of this cosmic mountain, constructed in mudbrick.

One final point. It is interesting to note that there existed a Sumerian tradition which made Ziusudra the son of a 'king Shuruppak'.[65] In other words, it would seem that the original planetary 'city' of Shuruppak was personified, and made into Ziusudra's father. This is an analogy which makes sense, for Ziusudra did indeed come forth from Shuruppak, albeit as a storm of meteorites which came forth from an exploded planet. In support of this interpretation, the Sumerian Kings List writes the name of king Shuruppak as SU.KUR.LAM, where the middle sign KUR meant 'mountain'.[66] Thus it would seem that Ziusudra's 'father' was the king of a 'mountain-land'.

There are no longer any prizes for guessing what this means.

The Seeds of Life

We have now covered a vast amount of evidence, which presents a very consistent picture. Firstly, the 'ancient city' of Shuruppak was a planetary 'city' – the planet of Heaven before it exploded. Secondly, the Flood-hero Utnapishtim, the 'man of Shuruppak', was not a man at all, but a personification of the exploded planet. Thirdly, the huge ziggurat-size boat of Utnapishtim also symbolised the exploded planet, which leads us to conclude that the boat and Utnapishtim were both effectively metaphorical representations of one-and-the-same thing.

As for the status of the Sumerian Flood-hero, Ziusudra, little may be said, for the legend of him and his boat is extremely fragmentary.

And as for the status of Atra-Hasis, it would seem that he – unlike Utnapishtim – was a denizen of the Earth (or perhaps of the underworld). However, such are the similarities between the legends of Atra-Hasis and Utnapishtim, that the former legend would seem to be an adaptation of the latter. The precedence of the Utnapishtim legend derives from the fact that *it makes perfect sense*, whereas the Atra-Hasis legend contains *non sequiturs*, such as the nonsensical statement by the terrestrial hero that he would leave Shuruppak and 'descend to the Apsu'.

Why was it that the writer of the *Atra-Hasis Epic* adapted the original story line, and reinvented the Flood-hero as a terrestrial figure? The explanation, I suggest, lies in a 'dumbing down' of the story to make it more relevant to the general populace. Most folk would have been much more interested to hear how the Flood destroyed a generation of humans on the Earth than a mythical 'people' in the heavens. Furthermore, it might well be that the adaptation of the Flood story served a political purpose, in order to warn people what might happen – again – if they disturbed the gods with their excessive noise.[67]

On the question of the biblical Flood-hero, Noah, it is best to save my comments until we have studied the tale more fully in the context of the Hebrew religious philosophy (see chapter nine). Suffice to say for now that the Hebrew priests may have had their own special reasons for adapting the original story line to create their own unique version of the Flood epic.

How certain can we be that the *original* Flood-hero was a *heavenly* hero, and his boat a *celestial* boat? Is it not possible that *this* version is the adaptation, and that the original story concerned a *terrestrial* hero and a *terrestrial* boat?

Rather than summarise all of the accumulated evidence for the heavenly Flood-hero, it is perhaps better to conclude this chapter by appealing to common sense. I therefore ask readers to consider which of the following two scenarios offers the most plausible story line for the original epic.

The first scenario is the story of Atra-Hasis and Noah. Picture, if you will, an Earth which has already been populated by mankind, and is now teeming with life. Imagine then that Atra-Hasis (or Noah) perceives that a Great Flood will come down from the heavens and destroy all life. He goes out, gathers together the males and females of each different species of living creature, and puts them, *physically, on a real boat*. Then, after this gargantuan effort – in which Atra-Hasis has probably been charged by rhinoceros, savaged by lions, and bitten by snakes – he launches his floating zoo into the teeth of a howling gale. After seven days and seven nights of what can only be described as hell on high water, the boat comes to rest on the top of a mountain, and Atra-Hasis repopulates the Earth (having first slaughtered and sacrificed one of his precious animal cargo!).

Now consider the second scenario. Picture, this time, an Earth which is a barren planet, with insufficient water to support life on its surface. But imagine that there is another planet in the distant heavens – a verdant paradise, containing all the seeds of life. One day, this planet explodes, or, to simplify matters, *it falls to the Earth*. As the falling planet travels through the watery abyss of space *like a boat*, it contains within it all the seeds of life, which it then sows upon the 'mountain' of Earth. Following this act of interplanetary seeding, the Earth becomes known as Mount

Nisir, 'the Mount of Salvation', in the sense that the seeds of life, which were lost in Heaven, have been saved upon the Earth.

The first Noah-like scenario is, of course, utterly bizarre. Perhaps somebody might have invented such a story, but only if they had had a very active imagination and an absence of critical faculties. On the other hand, it is, one must admit, a dramatic and exciting tale – just the kind of thing one would find in a 'dumbed down' story told to the masses.

The second scenario, however, is not bizarre at all, but represents the fundamental essence of ancient thinking – that Earth was indeed seeded by the collapse of Heaven. Such beliefs are evident in the legends of Enlil engendering summer and winter on the Earth-mountain, and Enki filling the rivers of Mesopotamia with the flood of his semen-like water, and Utu unleashing his flood from the heavens, and converting the barren wilderness of Dilmun into a verdant paradise.

In addition to these legends, which we have already covered, there is a Sumerian legend which describes how cattle and grain were created first in Heaven, in the 'creation chamber of the gods', and were only lowered to the Earth at a subsequent date (see next chapter). There is also a Sumerian legend which describes how two brother-gods brought down barley to the land of Sumer ('which knew no barley') from the heavenly 'mountain' where it had been stored by Enlil.[68]

A similar idea is expressed in the Egyptian Coffin Texts, where the god Shu claimed that:

> "I am the living one... whom Atum made into *the grain-god* when he caused me to go down into this land, to the Island of Fire, when I became Osiris, the son of Geb."[69]

It is for this reason that ancient gods were nearly always associated with fertility, either directly or indirectly via association with fertility symbols such as the bull. Hence Anu, the father of the gods, was 'the Fecund Breed-Bull'.[70] Hence Enki boasted that: "I am the true seed emitted by the great wild Bull."[71] Hence Enlil was a great bull which impregnated the HAR.SAG mountain. Hence Ninurta was described as 'life-giving semen, life-giving seed'.[72] Hence the Anunnaki were 'the Seed of the Prince of Eridu'. Hence the Egyptian kings were spawned by 'the seed of the Bull of the West' (i.e. Osiris).[73]

In addition to the fundamental idea that the seeds of life came to Earth from Heaven, it is also evident that the gods who brought these seeds from Heaven often descended to the Earth in boats.

In the legends of ancient Egypt, for example, Osiris was shut in a 'box' and cast into the celestial river Nile, the waters of which carried him to the 'bank' of the Earth. Similarly, Re and Atum were said to have come to Earth in a *Hnhnw*-bark, which was able to resurrect them back to Heaven by 'opening the mouth of the Earth'.[74] And the god Sokar likewise was said to have descended to Earth in a *Hnw*-bark, which had 'iron' in its bow.[75] Many more such examples could be cited.

Turning to the legends of Mesopotamia, we have seen how Enki descended to Earth in a boat, with raging waters and stones, fore and aft. And we have seen how Enlil, 'the Great Mountain', impregnated Ninlil (the Earth) while sailing in a boat. To these two examples, many others might be added. In *Enuma Elish*, for example, the vanquished corpse of Tiamat was brought to Earth by a god named SIR.SIR, who sailed her body away as if piloting a 'ship'.[76] And in the Sumerian *Lamentation Texts*, we read that Inanna '*sailed forth* from her possessions, descended to the underworld'.[77]

It is perhaps significant that the second scenario above – of the planet itself becoming the boat-with-the-seeds-of-life – only becomes bizarre when one begins to 'dumb down' the story for popular consumption, for example by (a) comparing the planet to a 'city'; and (b) personifying the interior of the planet as a heroic human being, who tore down his 'house' and converted it into a 'boat'. Perhaps such 'dumbing down' was inevitable. But at least the essential meaning of the story was retained until the hero was given a terrestrial 'make-over'.

This conclusion has serious implications for our understanding of the Bible. So be it. But before we take a closer look at the biblical story in its entirety, there is another subject that has arisen in this chapter, and it cries out for our immediate attention.

Let us recall the words of the heavenly goddess Ishtar, who went to pieces like a pot:

"Alas, I myself (now) give birth to my people!
Like the spawn of fish they (now) fill the sea!"

And let us recall, too, the words of Enki to Ziusudra:

"By our (command) a Flood will sweep over the 'cult-centres';
To destroy *the seed of mankind* . . .
Its kingship, its rule, will be put to an end."

Ziusudra then became 'the preserver of the name of vegetation and of *the seed of mankind*'.[78]

Could it be that the Flood did not destroy mankind on the Earth – mankind as we know it – but rather destroyed *the seed of* mankind which existed in the heavens? And, if so, might this heavenly seed of mankind have had something to do with the subsequent creation of mankind on the Earth?

Might this even be the answer to the mystery of that enigmatic tablet, excavated at Assur, which told of mankind springing up from the ground like a planted seed:

Aruru, the great lady of the gods, who is fit for rulership,
Ordained for them [Ulligarra and Zalgarra] great destinies:
Skilled worker to produce for skilled worker,
And unskilled worker for unskilled worker,
Springing up by themselves like grain from the ground.
A thing which, like the stars of the heavens, shall not be changed
    forever...
Let the wise teach the mystery to the wise.

* * * * *

CHAPTER EIGHT

THE BLACK-HEADED ONES

Let god and man be mixed together in clay.
Let us hear the drum-beat forever after.
(The Atra-Hasis Epic)

In the previous chapter, the legends from the *Atra-Hasis Epic* and *The Epic of Gilgamesh* left us in the lurch, not knowing quite what happened in the aftermath of the seeding of the Earth. Moreover, we were left wondering what had happened to the heavenly offspring of the Sky-goddess Ishtar, or Mami, after she 'went to pieces like a pot'. What was the fate of her 'people', who had been scattered from Heaven towards the distant 'bank' of the Earth, like sacrificial 'white sheep' or 'dragonflies'?

The story is picked up, fortuitously, by the few surviving fragments of the Sumerian legend of Ziusudra. Here, we find a number of very strange, almost untranslatable, passages, which have never made very much sense to modern scholars. However, these passages now appear to provide a very significant addendum to the story where we left it in the previous chapter. The following lines, for example, despite the lacunae, seem to provide a strong echo of the destruction of the Sky-goddess, and they allude, I suggest, to the fate of her newborn offspring:

> "As for my 'people', from its destruction will I cause it to be . . .
> For Nintu I will return the . . . of my creatures,
> I will return the people into their settlements,
> In cities, let them build places of divine ordinances...
> Let them establish the places of our decisions in pure places."[1]

This passage, as difficult as it is to translate and interpret, is written in the context of the Great Flood, and therefore seems to allude to the idea that a primeval 'people' – the seed of mankind – would be *replanted in the Earth*, and thus saved from its destruction in Heaven.

What follows next in the Ziusudra legend is even more intriguing. The writer refers to the newborn race of 'people' as 'the black-headed ones':

After Anu, Enlil, Enki and Ninharsag,
Had fashioned the black-headed ones,
Vegetation luxuriated from the earth, from the earth,
Animals, four-legged creatures of the plain, were brought artfully
    into existence.[2]

Sumerologists have assumed that these 'black-headed ones' were flesh-and-blood humans, doubtless drawing comfort from the fact that the Sumerian people referred to themselves as 'the black-headed ones'.

This *assumption*, however, is not supported by what the text actually says. The text, on the contrary, suggests that the black-headed ones were not mankind itself, but *the seed of mankind*, which came down from Heaven to Earth and seeded the beginning of life. It is for this reason, I suggest, that the creation of the black-headed ones *preceded* the creation of vegetation and animals in the passage cited above. It is a crucial clue.

In the same legend, there are some damaged lines which again prove awkward to translate, but appear to reiterate the very same idea:

"Ye will utter 'breath of Heaven, breath of Earth', verily it will . . .
    itself by . . . . . ."
Anu-Enlil . . . 'breath of Heaven, breath of Earth', . . . it . . . itself.
Vegetation, coming up out of the earth, rises up.[3]

Note in this passage that the vegetation was *the first thing* to rise up out of the earth after the gods came down.[4] This suggests that the magical 'breath of Heaven' played a similar role to that played in the previously cited passage by the black-headed ones. The implication is that the black-headed ones should indeed be understood as the extraterrestrial seeds of life.

If this argument seems a little tenuous, consider the following passage from the Sumerian *Lamentation Texts* concerning the Great Flood:

Alas, all the storms together have flooded the land.
The great Flood-storm of Heaven, the ever-roaring storm...
The Flood-storm ordered in hate which sated the land...
The Flood-storm which overwhelmed *the living creatures of Heaven-
    and-Earth – the black-headed ones.*[5]

In this passage, we find a clear statement that the black-headed ones were overwhelmed by the Flood, but an equally clear statement that they were *not* creatures of the Earth. Rather, they were 'the living creatures of

Heaven-and-Earth'. This astonishing statement supports the hypothesis put forward earlier – that the black-headed ones were the 'people', i.e. meteorites, emitted from the 'womb' of the Sky-goddess, Ishtar or Mami. Either this, or the text has been wrongly translated.

This insight means that we are now presented with a very difficult challenge in trying to read and understand what the Mesopotamian texts said, because scholars – unaware that the religion was an exploded planet cult – have assumed that all references to 'the black-headed ones' were straightforward allusions to flesh-and-blood humans. Indeed, so confident were they in this surmise that on numerous occasions they simply dropped the term 'black-headed ones' and substituted in its place the translation 'mankind', or 'human beings'.

Have scholars made a mistake of the greatest magnitude? It is the intention of this chapter to demonstrate that this is indeed the case, and that the legends of the creation of 'mankind' were actually referring to a subhuman, primeval, meteoric seed of mankind.

This idea might seem a little odd at first, but only because we have forgotten how to think like the ancients. In the pages which follow, we will recapture this lost way of thinking, and see the logic behind it. Then, in the next chapter, we will see how this radical re-evaluation of the Mesopotamian texts lays the foundation for an equally radical re-evaluation of the biblical legend of Adam and Eve.

Prepare yourself, dear reader, for a series of remarkable revelations.

The Fall of the Anunnaki

In order to understand the origins of Mesopotamian 'mankind', there is only one logical place to begin, and that is with their masters – the Anunnaki. According to popular legend, it was for the Anunnaki that 'mankind' was created, in order that the Anunnaki should be relieved from their wearisome toil. 'Mankind', so we are told, began its existence as the humble slave of the Anunnaki.

Let's begin, then, with the Anunnaki. As mentioned in chapter two, the Anunnaki were the offspring of AN, or Anu, the original 'father of the gods' and the Sky-god *par excellence*. He had given birth to the Anunnaki in cataclysmic circumstances – a fact which only became fully apparent in the previous chapter, when we decoded the story of Utnapishtim and realised that the following passage was describing a catastrophe *in the heavens*:

The Anunnaki raised their torches,
Lighting up the land with their brightness.

The confusion of Adad reached unto the (highest) heavens,
Turning into darkness all that had been light.
The wide land was shattered like a pot![6]

According to this legend, the Anunnaki experienced a fiery birth in the heavens *at the same time* as Ishtar's 'people', i.e. 'mankind'. But all other accounts suggest that this legend was a simplification, for the Anunnaki were actually born a considerable time earlier. It would thus seem that Utnapishtim's story of the Flood in *The Epic of Gilgamesh* is an amalgam of two separate Flood stories, indeed two separate planetary explosions – one of Anu, and one of Ishtar (Inanna). This suggestion is borne out by everything we know of the male-female duotheism which existed not only in Mesopotamia but also in ancient Egypt.

Having clarified this essential point, we can trace the origin of the Anunnaki from a disintegrated planet in the heavens all the way down to the underworld of the Earth, where they were allegedly created by Anu when he impregnated KI (the Earth) at the beginning of time. As one text put it:

... in the Mountain of Heaven-and-Earth,
AN [Anu] caused the Anunnaki to be born.[7]

Or, as another text put it:

Sumer, 'Great Mountain', land of Heaven-and-Earth...
The Anunnaki, the great gods,
Have taken up their dwelling place in your midst.[8]

Such a fall into the underworld was, of course, the fate of all ancient gods who fell from the heavens. It was a kind of ancient gravitational rule that this *must* happen – an idea inspired undoubtedly by the fact that falling meteorites had the power to crack open the surface of the Earth.

After this great fall, the Anunnaki-gods became trapped in the underworld, along with Enki, the chief god of the Apsu. It would seem that all of these deities remained behind in the underworld as a ransom, in order to allow Anu and Enlil to escape from the underworld (and thus to take control of the upper regions which extended between Heaven and Earth).

As for the Anunnaki, their fate was to toil in the middle of the Earth under desperate working conditions, the purpose of which is explained in the *Atra-Hasis Epic*. Note that, in the following quotation, the Anunnaki are sometimes referred to by their heavenly name, the Igigi:

When the gods instead of man,

> Did the work, bore the loads,
> The gods' load was too great,
> The work too hard, the trouble too much...
> When Anu had gone up to the Sky,
> And the gods of the Apsu had gone below,
> The Great Sky-gods made the Igigi bear the workload.
> The Anunnaki [Igigi] had to dig out canals,
> Had to clear channels, the lifelines of the land...
> The Anunnaki [Igigi] dug out the Tigris river,
> And then dug out the Euphrates...
> They were counting the years of loads,
> For 3,600 years they bore the excess...
> They groaned and blamed each other,
> Grumbled over the masses of excavated soil.[9]

What was the point of this terrible toil? As explained in chapter six, the great rivers of Sumer and Egypt were believed to have originated in the heavens, whence they fell to the Earth and – according to the normal rules – entered the underworld. The task of the Anunnaki, then, was to dig out canals and waterways in the underworld so that the subterranean waters might be released to the surface of the Earth.

This toil, as we shall see, was what sparked the decision to create 'mankind' as a slave for the Anunnaki.

However, there was another reason, too, why 'mankind' would be created. According to a legend entitled *The Dispute between Cattle and Grain*, the Anunnaki were desperately short of nutritious food, and man was to be their provider. The story is worth telling in full, for among other things it reveals the amazingly Earth-like nature of the underworld – a thing which was totally logical according to the ancient philosophy of the universe (for the reasons which we discussed in chapter four), but has nevertheless left scholars totally baffled as to the meaning of the tale.

The Dispute between Cattle and Grain begins with an intriguing introductory passage which states:

> Like mankind when first created,
> The Anunnaki knew not the eating of bread,
> Knew not the dressing of garments,
> Ate plants with their mouths like sheep,
> Drank water from the ditch.[10]

It would seem that the poor Anunnaki were suffering from a vegetarian diet, and yet they required a lot of energy to dig out the canals and water-courses of the underworld. But the underworld at that time contained no animals, and hence there was no meat to eat, nor milk to drink. The Anunnaki, we are told, were living in ignorance of the 'name of Lahar and Ashnan', and were virtually starving to death.

The text then reveals how the bounty of Lahar and Ashnan was introduced to the Anunnaki, who were by this time 'poor' and 'hugging the dust':

> At the pure word of Enki and Enlil,
> Lahar and Ashnan descend from the Duku...
> Abundance which comes from Heaven,
> Lahar and Ashnan caused to appear in the Earth.
> In the assembly [of the Anunnaki] Lahar and Ashnan brought
>   abundance,
> In the land they brought the Breath of Life,
> The divine laws of the god they direct,
> The contents of the warehouses they multiply,
> The storehouse they fill full.
> In the house of the poor [Anunnaki], hugging the dust,
> Entering they bring abundance;
> The pair of them, wherever they stand,
> Bring heavy increase into the house.[11]

Lahar and Ashnan, then, were goddesses who personified cattle and grain respectively, and, not surprisingly, they descended from Heaven. As for the Duku, this was said to be the 'place of the creation of the gods', where the Anunnaki and Igigi had once lived, and where, according to this text, cattle and grain had first been created.[12] As this legend makes clear, the Duku fell from Heaven, hence its more frequent associations with the underworld.[13] It represents a further example of what we might call the 'as above so below' motif, which we have already encountered with places such as Apsu, Dilmun and Aratta.

Returning to the story, we must now imagine the Anunnaki beginning to wear work-clothes and enjoying a more civilised life style in the underworld – a bizarre thought indeed. Their newly found abundance of produce, however, was to prove insufficient, especially with regard to the produce of the sheepfolds. It was for this reason – to increase the yield from the farms in the underworld – that 'mankind' would be brought into existence:

> The Anunnaki of the Duku eat the produce of Lahar [cattle] and
>   Ashnan [grain] but remain unsated;
> In their pure sheepfolds the Anunnaki drink the good *shum*-milk but
>   remain unsated;

For the sake of their good and pure sheepfolds, mankind was given
   breath.[14]

The same story is told by the mysterious tablet found at Assur (what a
mine of information it is!). In this legend, the gods Ulligarra and Zalgarra
present a close parallel to Lahar and Ashnan, with the name Ulligarra
meaning 'the establisher of abundance' and the name Zalgarra meaning
'the establisher of plenty'.[15] These two gods were to be sacrificed in the
Bond of Heaven-and-Earth, i.e. probably cast down from Heaven,
whereupon they would create mankind in their own images as skilled and
unskilled labourers. The purpose of this 'mankind' was to fulfil the
following requirements:

To maintain the boundary,
To fill the granary...
To make the field of the Anunnaki produce plentifully,
To increase abundance in the land...
Let them increase ox, sheep, cattle, fish and fowl –
The abundance in the land.[16]

Or, in the words of an old Babylonian creation myth:

"That which is slight he [man] shall raise to abundance;
The work of a god man shall bear!"[17]

The Creation of Mankind

We turn now to the detailed accounts of how mankind was created to
relieve the Anunnaki of their toil. Bear in mind, as we proceed, that the
Anunnaki were, unquestionably, denizens of the underworld, and
therefore it would have been impossible for 'mankind' to relieve the
Anunnaki, or serve them, *unless 'mankind', too, was created in the
underworld*. (It is odd that modern scholars have failed to appreciate this
straightforward point of principle, for there is not a single scholar who
would disagree that the Anunnaki were denizens of the underworld, nor
that mankind was created to perform their work.)

We shall begin with a very brief account of man's creation, which is
found in a legend entitled *Enki and Ninmah*. The tale confirms that, in
'the days of yore', the Anunnaki were forced to dig out the canals of the
underworld, while the senior gods, such as Enki, lay back and relaxed.
Eventually, however, the Anunnaki began to grumble and complain, and
their grumblings were overheard by Nammu, the mother of Enki, whose
name personified 'the Primeval Ocean'. It was Nammu, according to this
legend, who first had the idea of creating 'mankind' in order to relieve

the gods from their toil, saying to her son Enki:

> O my son, rise from your bed, from your . . . work your wisdom,
> Fashion servants of the gods, let them produce their own likenesses.[18]

The text then describes how Enki adopted his mother's plan with great enthusiasm, declaring:

> "O my mother, the creature whose name you uttered, it shall exist!"
> (Instructions to his craftsmen:)
> "Bind upon it the likeness of the gods.
> Mix the heart of the clay which is above the AB.ZU.
> (You) good and princely craftsmen will work the clay.
> You shall bring the limbs into existence.
> Ninmah [Ninharsag] will supervise you.
> The goddesses (of birth) . . . will stand by you as you fashion (it).
> O my mother, decree the new-born creature's fate.
> Ninmah [Ninharsag] will bind upon it the mould of the gods,
> Its name shall be Lullu."[19]

Despite the anthropomorphic portrayal of the Lullu (literally 'the Primitive Man') in this passage, it is questionable whether this being was really mankind as we know it.[20] Note, for example, the presence at this creation of the mother-goddess Ninharsag and the other unnamed birth-goddesses. In chapter two of this book, we dealt with a very similar creation of man in a text entitled *Creation of Man by the Mother-Goddess*. This, too, was a creation using clay, which was inserted into the womb of Ninharsag, and also into her fourteen subsidiary mother-wombs. And this, too, was a legend of the creation of the Lullu, the Primitive Man. And yet we were forced to conclude in that chapter that Ninharsag was a Sky-goddess who had come down from Heaven and assumed the mantle of Mother Earth; and furthermore that 'mankind' had been produced within the fourteen subsidiary 'wombs' which were *inside* her single planetary 'Womb'.

The unavoidable conclusion is that the Lullu was created within the Earth, i.e. in the underworld.

Lest there be any doubt about this, we turn now to the legend of the Lullu's creation in the *Atra-Hasis Epic*, supplemented by the *Myth of the Pickaxe*.

We pick up the story after the Anunnaki had toiled for 3,600 years digging out the subterranean channels for the Tigris and Euphrates – the rivers of the underworld. It was then that the Anunnaki decided that enough was enough, and staged a mutiny. Uttering a 'cry of battle', the stricken gods burned their tools and besieged the gate of Enlil's E.KUR (i.e. the subterranean entrance to his 'cosmic mountain'), complaining: "the load is excessive, it is killing us!"[21] So serious was the revolt that Anu himself was called down from Heaven to chair an emergency meeting. At first, Enlil sought to identify and punish the ringleader of the rebellion, but the rebels presented a united front, and announced: "every single one of us gods has declared war."[22]

It was then, as Anu and Enki began to sympathise with the rebels, that wise old Enki put forward a clever solution:

> "Why are we blaming them?
> Their work was too hard, their trouble was too much.
> Every day the earth resounded...
> Belit-ili [Ninharsag] the Womb-goddess is present,
> Let her create a Lullu,
> So that he may bear the yoke...
> Let man bear the load of the gods!"[23]

Thus was the mutiny resolved. Anu went back up to the Sky, where a god named Geshtui was 'called up and cast for destruction'.[24] This god was then cast down from Heaven and slaughtered in the 'assembly', i.e. in the underworld extremity of the Bond of Heaven-and-Earth:

> Geshtui, a god who had intelligence,
> They slaughtered in their assembly.
> Nintu [Ninharsag] mixed clay with his flesh and blood.
> God and man were mixed together in clay,
> And the drum-beat was heard forever after.[25]

The result of this mixing between god and man – an idea which we shall return to – was 'mankind', known collectively as NAM.LU.LU.[26] The *Atra-Hasis Epic* informs us that this newly created being immediately set to work to replace the pickaxes and spades which had been burned in the Anunnaki rebellion:

> They took hold of . . .
> Made new pickaxes and spades,
> Made big canals,
> To feed people and sustain the gods.[27]

As for the gods, Ninharsag (Mother Earth) announced to them that:

> "I have relieved you of your hard work,
> I have imposed your load on man.
> You can (now) bestow your noise upon mankind.

I have undone the fetter and granted freedom.""[28]

It is at this point that the *Atra-Hasis Epic* moves on (artificially I believe) to relate the story of how the gods regretted their decision to create 'mankind' and plotted to destroy it with the Great Flood (one wonders whether this 'mankind' was still in the underworld at the time).

A similar story is told in *The Myth of the Pickaxe*, where the writer utilised an amusing ambiguity between the humble earth-pickaxe and the meteorite-pickaxe. The backdrop to this story is some kind of rebellion, which one presumes was that of the Anunnaki in the underworld. This revolt caused Enlil to descend to Earth in the form of a 'pickaxe', which, as we have noted elsewhere, was a metaphor for 'meteorite'. This 'pickaxe' created a large gash in the Bond of Heaven-and-Earth, and a hole in the ground, and it would seem that it simultaneously created 'mankind' (the black-headed ones), who sprang forth suddenly like plants in the ground:

> The Lord [Enlil] called forth the pickaxe, gave its orders...
> And drove it into Uzumua ('the Place which Produced Flesh').
> In the hole (there appeared) the head of a man;
> From the ground, people were breaking out towards Enlil.
> He eyed his black-headed ones in steadfast fashion.[29]

Enlil, it would seem, had entered the underworld, and hence it was in the underworld that he created the black-headed ones. This is apparent from the fact that the Anunnaki, the denizens of the underworld, immediately approached Enlil beseeching him to relieve them of their toil:

> The Anunnaki stepped up to him [Enlil],
> Raised their hands in greetings,
> Soothing Enlil's heart with prayers.
> Black-headed ones they were requesting of him.
> To the black-headed people they gave the pickaxe to hold.[30]

Thus was the pickaxe transformed, rather aptly, from a meteorite to an earth-breaking implement in the underworld. But hardly a mundane axe wielded by a conventional type of people – this would be to miss the point entirely.

The outcome of this tale, then, is the same as the one before. A rebellion in the underworld was quashed and the Anunnaki were relieved of their toil by the creation of 'mankind' (the black-headed ones). These new workers were then tasked with digging out the subterranean canals and waterways of the Apsu, so that the waters which had fallen from Heaven might be released to the surface of the world above.

There can thus, surely, be no doubt about it. 'Mankind' – NAM.LU.LU or the black-headed ones – was created in the underworld.

Mankind – Denizen of the Underworld

All of this might seem very odd indeed to the modern way of thinking, but this is hardly a valid reason to dismiss it. On the contrary, we should embrace the idea that 'mankind' was created in the underworld, and see where this knowledge takes us.

But firstly, we should seek confirmation of our understanding from other independent cultures of the ancient world. Did other peoples share the Mesopotamian view that man had endured a prior subterranean existence?

To begin with the ancient Egyptians, their accounts of the creation of man are brief. All we are told is that mankind was created using 'tears' from the 'Eye' of the creator-god. This is an important legend, but its relevance will not become apparent until a much later stage of our investigation. Suffice to say for now that the legends which speak of the fiery destruction of the Eye and its casting down from Heaven to Earth might well imply that mankind was indeed created in the underworld.

There is, however, one particular Egyptian legend which gives a much more definitive confirmation of this point. In the legend of *The Destruction of Mankind*, we read that the creator-god Re was bewailing the fact that "those who were created by my Eye are uttering words of complaint against me."[31] Re then called forth another Eye, giving it instructions to decimate the 'men' who were *'in the desert-land'*. Thereupon, Re announced his departure from the world of men, uttering the following intriguing words to his deputy Thoth:

> "I wish to make light shine in the *Duat* and the Land of Caves. Thou shalt be scribe there, and thou shalt punish those who are in that place, that is to say those workers who have performed deeds of rebellion against me. Through thee I will keep away from my servants whom I loathe."[32]

What this passage says is that 'mankind' – the ones who had rebelled against Re and who would be punished by the second Eye – were dwelling in the darkness of the *Duat* and the Land of Caves. *This is an unmistakable reference to the underworld.*

The Egyptians also seem to have shared the Mesopotamian view that flesh-and-blood mankind grew up like a seed out of the earth. Hence, in the *Hymn to Amen-Re*, there is an enigmatic passage which praises Re as:

The fashioner of that which the soil produces, the Khnum and Amen of mankind.[33]

This cryptic passage might well have been marked 'for the eyes of initiates only'. To decode it, one has to realise that Khnum was the creator-god who fashioned mankind out of clay on his potter's wheel, whilst Amen's name alluded to the underworld and meant 'Hidden'. The esoteric meaning of the passage can thus be grasped – Re was the one who built 'mankind' in a hidden place, i.e. in the soil of the Earth.[34]

Our second confirmation of the Mesopotamian view comes from ancient Greek mythology. The poet Hesiod described how an original 'golden race' of 'men' had lived alongside the gods in a paradisiacal land, free from toil, and knowing neither illness nor old age.[35] This was the age of Cronus – the god who had attacked and deposed Uranus when the latter came down from Heaven and ravaged Gaea. Scholars assume that this paradisiacal land of the golden race was somewhere on Earth, for where else would it be? But we now know that there was a second, equally plausible location, namely Heaven – Earth's 'distant trusty twin'.

Did the golden race of 'men' thus fall from Heaven? Hesiod indeed seems to have suggested this when he wrote that the golden age was ended by 'the fall of Cronus'.[36] Moreover, Hesiod then revealed that *the fall of Cronus had caused the golden race of 'men' to be 'covered by the earth'*.[37] The meaning is clear.

Thus was the golden race succeeded by the less noble 'silver race' of 'men', who were hidden in the Earth by Zeus, where they experienced an inordinately prolonged childhood, only to be destroyed eventually for disobeying the laws of the gods.[38] As for the later races of 'men' – the bronze race, the heroes and the iron race – they need not concern us here, although it is worth observing that only the fifth and final race, the men of iron, would have been true human flesh and blood.

Lest there be any doubt about this interpretation of the Greek legends, we need only turn to the words allegedly spoken by the god-like hero Prometheus. The mythologist Mircea Eliade summed up the teachings of Prometheus as follows:

The first men, Prometheus affirms, lived *"underground, deep in caverns closed to the Sun"*; they did not even know the succession of the seasons or the domestication of animals or agriculture; it was he, Prometheus, who taught them all arts and all sciences. It is he who gave them fire and freed them from the fear of death.[39]

What an explicit statement! It seems amazing that such a tradition turns out to be well-known to scholars. And yet Eliade just passed over these beliefs without adding any comment whatsoever, almost as if he saw nothing strange in them. Incidentally, this 'first race' according to Prometheus equates to the 'silver race' spoken of by Hesiod, and was thus in fact the *second* race of 'men'. Not that either of them were really men at all.

Where else might we find confirmation of the Mesopotamian view? I will pass over, for the moment, the biblical legends, for I do not wish to prejudge the issue, pending our investigation in the next chapter.

But this still leaves me – at the time of writing – with two further examples to share. The first comes from Africa, where at least one tribe of modern people believes that mankind came from another world in the heavens, and travelled down to the Earth in the belly of a huge dragon. Significantly, this people hold that the extraterrestrial 'mankind' entered into the underworld, to later emerge from a cave into the upper world.

The second example comes from the Navaho Indians of North America, who teach their children to this day that the first woman was Mother Earth, but that the first man was created deep down inside the Earth. Once again, the meaning is clear.

As I say, these are just two examples which happened perchance to reach my ears without any conscious effort on my part to look for them. I must confess to a sneaking feeling that these beliefs represent only the tip of a very large but forgotten iceberg of ancient and modern traditions which will, when uncovered, attest to the veracity of the decoding which has been made in these pages.

Like Peas in a Pod

Earlier, we heard how 'mankind' had been created by the mixing of 'god and man', and I promised to return to this point. The reason why I return to this legend is that it seems to contain an inherent contradiction, namely this: how could 'mankind' be a hybrid mixture of two beings, *one of whom was itself*? How could the mixing of 'god and man' produce 'man'? It is a dilemma which cries out for our attention.

Let's now return to my initial suggestion that the origins of mankind were ultimately *in the heavens*, in the form of the 'people' of Mami/Ishtar, or, if you like, Hesiod's golden race. Bearing this celestial origin in mind, consider now the legends of how 'mankind' was created by the sacrifice of a god.

Firstly, there is the legend of Ulligarra and Zalgarra, which tells how the great gods had come together in their 'exalted sanctuary' in Heaven to recount their wonderful creations to date. Enlil then said:

"Now that the destinies of Heaven and Earth have been fixed,
Trench and canal have been given their right courses,
The banks of the Tigris and the Euphrates have been established,
What else shall we do?
What else shall we create?..."
(The Igigi and Anunnaki) gave Enlil this answer:
"In Uzumua, the Bond of Heaven-and-Earth,
Let us slay two Lamga-gods.
With their blood let us create mankind,
The service of the gods to be its lot..."[40]

As things stand, it is difficult to judge from this text whether the two Lamga-gods (Ulligarra and Zalgarra) were to be sacrificed in Heaven, on the Earth, or *in* the Earth – for the Bond of Heaven-and-Earth spanned all three regions of the ancient universe. But earlier I suggested that the similar sacrifice of Geshtui in the *Atra-Hasis Epic* was performed in two of these three regions; he was slaughtered in the 'assembly' of the gods in the underworld, *but only after he had been cast down from the Sky.* The latter point is attested firmly in the *Atra-Hasis Epic* by the fact that Anu *went up to the Sky* in order to select the victim.[41]

It thus seems reasonable to presume that the two Lamga-gods were cast down from the Sky in a similar manner, resulting in 'men' who 'sprang up by themselves like grain from the ground'.

The same idea is found in the Babylonian epic of creation, *Enuma Elish*, where 'mankind' was created from the 'blood' of Kingu, *who was a Sky-god* – the commander-in-chief of Tiamat's rebellion.[42] After vanquishing Tiamat, the supreme god Marduk (originally an Earth-born Titan) stated:

"I will put together blood and bring bones into being.
Then I will establish Lullu; 'Primitive Man' shall be his name.
Yes, I will create a primitive man.
He shall be charged with the service of the gods,
That they might be at ease!"...
They bound Kingu and held him before Ea [Enki],
Punishment they inflicted upon him and severed his blood vessels.
Out of his blood they fashioned mankind.
He [Ea] imposed the toil of the gods (upon mankind) and set the gods
    free...
That work was beyond comprehension.[43]

Enuma Elish, then, supports the two legends cited earlier, and confirms the idea that the origins of 'mankind' lay in the body of a heavenly god or gods – or indeed goddess, as in the legend where the heavenly goddess Ishtar/Mami 'went to pieces like a pot' and scattered 'people' from her 'womb' like sacrificial sheep.

What this means, in a nutshell, is that a god was turned into 'mankind', or, to paraphrase this concept, *god became 'man'*.

Hence Kingu became 'man'. Hence Ulligarra and Zalgarra became 'man', whom they created in their own image as 'skilled worker for skilled worker, and unskilled worker for unskilled worker'. And hence the god Geshtui became 'man' in the *Atra-Hasis Epic*.

The mystery of the mixing of 'god and man' to produce 'man' can thus be explained by paying careful attention to what was said in the *Atra-Hasis Epic*:

> Enki spoke to the great gods:
> "I shall make a purification, a bath.
> Let one god [Geshtui] be slain,
> And let the gods [Anunnaki] be purified by immersion.
> Let Nintu mix clay with his flesh and blood.
> Let god and man be mixed together in clay.
> Let us hear the drum-beat forever after."[44]

What this means is that, firstly, Geshtui – some kind of planetary body – was slain, thereby producing 'man' as his offspring. Thus god became 'man'.

Secondly, Geshtui – now in the form of 'man' – was mixed with the gods who were *already* in the underworld (the Anunnaki). Thus 'god and man' were 'mixed together in clay'. *QED.*

The Anunnaki masters of the underworld were thus being served by a hybrid being – 'mankind' – who had been made from the 'clay' of the Anunnaki-gods and the 'flesh and blood' of Geshtui. It might well be this hybrid origin which accounts for the repetition of the term LU, 'man', in the Sumerian name for mankind: NAM.LU.LU.

In summary, then, we have a mixing of two planetary clays, which both fell from Heaven to Earth. And it was from this mixed clay that Ninharsag/Mami pinched off the fourteen pieces of clay which were then placed into the 'seven-and-seven mother-wombs', i.e. into the subsidiary wombs which were within the one giant Womb of the Earth herself.[45]

Thus it can be seen that 'mankind' was made in the underworld of the Earth from the clay of the gods.

Furthermore, it should be remembered that the Anunnaki, too, had been spawned in the underworld as the offspring of a disintegrated *Sky-god* (Anu). Thus it can be seen that the Anunnaki and 'mankind' were of like kind, which would explain why the Sumerian poet (cited earlier) drew the curious comparison between gods and 'men' in *The Dispute between Cattle and Grain*:

Like mankind when first created,
The Anunnaki knew not the eating of bread,
Knew not the dressing of garments,
Ate plants with their mouths like sheep,
Drank water from the ditch.

In addition to these similarities, it should also be emphasised that the fallen Anunnaki (or A.NUN.NA.NUN.KI) were '*the Seed* of the Prince of Eridu', just as the fallen 'mankind' was often described as '*the seed* of mankind'.[46]

All of this leads us to envisage the Anunnaki and 'mankind' as being rather like two primeval peas-in-a-pod, bound together in eternal kinship in the clay of the Apsu. Perhaps this might also explain the curious double recitation of '*the earth*' in the mysterious passage cited at the beginning of this chapter:

After Anu, Enlil, Enki and Ninharsag,
Had fashioned the black-headed ones,
Vegetation luxuriated *from the earth, from the earth*.[47]

But whether this refers to the duality of the 'divine-human' soil or not, there can surely be no doubt by now that the black-headed ones were not really human at all, but were, on the contrary, *meteorites*.

Why, then, did the flesh-and-blood Sumerian people insist on calling themselves 'the black-headed ones'? The official answer, from scholars, is that the Sumerians had extremely black hair, in contrast to some of the neighbouring peoples.[48] Excuse my mirth. The more likely answer is that the epithet was a reference to *the blackness of meteorites*. And thus, in calling themselves 'the black-headed ones', the Sumerians were merely stating the obvious: that, as far as they were concerned, *their origin was from a meteoric seed of mankind*.

In order to appreciate the Sumerian perspective, let us suppose that the epithet 'black-headed ones' is equivalent to the term 'Earthlings', which we might use today to express our collective identity and distinguish ourselves in a galactic context. As far as the Sumerians are concerned, they would certainly see us as being Earthlings, but in the fullest possible sense of the term – *impregnated in the Earth, and born from it* – whereas we modern folk, on the other hand (lacking any clear religious paradigm), would simply regard ourselves as Earthlings in the sense of *living on* the Earth. The distinction is profound, and serves to illustrate just how far we have strayed from the ancient way of thinking.

When Kingship Descended from Heaven

Throughout the Mesopotamian texts, we find scattered references to 'the seed of mankind', which provide additional confirmation that we are on the right track.

To cite one example, there is a Babylonian account of the creation by Marduk, in which the scribe makes a very important distinction:

He [Marduk] created mankind,
But Aruru created the seed of mankind, together with him.[49]

Scholars suppose that the expressions 'mankind' and 'the seed of mankind' in these lines mean the same thing, which, if we stop to think about it, would imply that the Babylonian writer of this sentence did not know what he was talking about. Nonsense! The scribe was pointing out that Marduk had created 'mankind' – which he did, from the body of Tiamat or the blood of Kingu – but that Marduk was a second-generation god, born like a Titan in the Earth, as opposed to Aruru, who was a senior, first-generation goddess, born in the Sky. Of course Aruru would claim to have created Marduk. But isn't it interesting that Aruru also claimed to have made the 'seed of mankind'?

Elsewhere in the Mesopotamian texts, we find the scribes claiming that certain kings were made 'of seed preserved from before the Flood', and we also find an occasional enigmatic reference to 'days of yore, when the seed of man came forth'.[50]

But how was it, one wonders, that the seed of man *did* come forth? Up until now, we have described the creation of the subterranean 'mankind', but now we must ask: "where is the connection to real flesh-and-blood people – the true mankind of the world above?" Surely we should find some legends which describe the dramatic emergence of mankind from the underworld. Let's take a look and see what we find.

In *The Epic of Etana*, there is an enigmatic passage which seems to have a major bearing on this issue. It says that the gods 'decreed a stated time for mankind' – a time which coincided with the lowering of kingship from Heaven. Now it seems to me, from this and other texts, that the lowering of kingship from Heaven represents the crucial interface between man's anonymity in the underworld and his self-identity in the world above. In the following passage, then, the intended meaning, I suggest, is that mankind *would emerge from the underworld* at this stated time:

The great Anunnaki, who decree the fates,
Sat down, taking counsel about the land.
The Igigi – they who created the regions, who set up the
    establishments,
Were too lofty for mankind,
They decreed a stated time for mankind.
The 'beclouded people' ['mankind'], in all, had not set up a king.
At that time, no tiara had been tied on, nor crown,
And no sceptre had been inlaid with lapis lazuli;
The shrines [of Heaven, Earth and underworld] had not been built
    altogether,
The Divine Seven [Anunnaki] had barred the gates against the
    settlers ['mankind'].
Sceptre, crown, tiara and shepherd's crook lay deposited before Anu
    in Heaven,
There being no counselling for the people.
Then kingship descended from Heaven.[51]

In this passage, the 'people' of the underworld are described rather aptly
as the 'beclouded people', whom we must regard as 'settlers' in a
subterranean but Earth-like land. These people, it would seem, were
under confinement, hence we read that the Seven Anunnaki had 'barred
the gates against the settlers'.

The Epic of Etana goes on to relate how the gods began to search for a
king to shepherd the 'people'. The fragmented text reads:

Ishtar [Inanna] . . . a shepherd for the people.
A king she seeks for the city.
Enlil inspects the quarters of Heaven . . .
In the land a king . . . [52]

The text breaks off before naming Etana as king, but another fragment
states:

They [the gods] planned the city [probably Earth],
The . . . gods laid the foundation...
Let the city [Earth] be the nest, the resting place of mankind,
Let the king be the shepherd, they . . .
Let Etana be the builder . . . [53]

Thus it was that 'kingship descended from Heaven'.

It seems to me that the Mesopotamians legends about the lowering of
kingship were synonymous with the transference of mankind's allegiance

from the gods of the underworld *to the god-like king of the world above*.[54]
As far as the Mesopotamians were concerned, the existence of the
kingship was nothing less than a divine statement that flesh-and-blood
mankind had been given breath of life, autonomy and the gifts of
civilisation. The king was the be-all and end-all. Hence a legend of the
kingship descending from Heaven, or of the king experiencing a Titan-
like birth, would have symbolised the escape of 'mankind' as a whole
from the underworld. A typical example would be king Gilgamesh, who
was born as the 'offshoot of Uruk' and as the 'MES which is the
sprouting seed of a new tree'.

By this line of reasoning, there was no need for the Mesopotamians to
write legends explaining how the common population of mankind had
come into being. We would thus not expect to find any legend of a mass
exodus of 'people' from the underworld into the world above, and indeed
we do not. There is no such legend.

What about a first human couple, who might have propagated the true
race of Mesopotamian man in the same way that Adam and Eve
propagated the human race in the Bible? According to modern scholars,
such a legend will not be found either.

I must, however, disagree with the scholars on this point.

The Two Little Ones

In 1902, Leonard W. King published a translation of an inscription which
had been found a few decades earlier by the archaeologist George Smith
at Nineveh.[55] The inscription, subsequently entitled *The Creation of
Living Creatures*, immediately sparked a controversy, for it bore an
uncanny resemblance to the biblical story of Adam and Eve. However,
after much discussion, the scholars agreed reluctantly that this was a
fanciful idea, and they dropped it like the proverbial lead balloon.
Consequently, the correct interpretation of this text has been hanging in
the balance ever since.

The Assyrian legend of *The Creation of Living Creatures*, which dates
possibly to the 7th century BC, is badly fragmented, but the legible part
reads as follows:

When the gods in their assembly had created everything,
Had fashioned the Sky, had formed the Earth,
Had brought forth living creatures . . .
Had created the cattle of the field, the beasts of the field and the
    creatures of the city,
After they had . . . unto the living creatures . . .

And had apportioned their portions to the cattle of Sumuqan, to the
   creatures of the city,
And had . . . all creatures, the whole of creation . . .
. . . . . . which in all my family . . . . . .
Ninigiku [Enki] created two little ones . . .
He made them more glorious than all other creatures.
(Remainder of tablet almost entirely destroyed)[56]

Could this *possibly* be the Adam and Eve story, but in a Mesopotamian
guise? Alexander Heidel, writing in 1942, summarised the scholarly
consensus as follows:

What is meant by these 'two little ones' or 'two young ones' is
difficult to determine... But to see in them the first two parents of the
human race [i.e. Adam and Eve] is without foundation. In fact, the
(use of the) expressions 'the creatures of the city'... and 'my family'
make that assumption highly improbable.[57]

Heidel's logic is, of course, faultless. He supposes that the 'two little
ones' cannot possibly be the progenitors of the human race because their
creation was *preceded* by the existence of a 'city' and a 'family'. *QED.*

However, as we have seen in this chapter, the beginning of the flesh-
and-blood human race *in the world above* was in fact preceded by the
existence of a city and a family, and a lot more besides – *all in the
underworld.* This simple insight sheds an entirely new light on the legend
of *The Creation of Living Creatures.* The controversy must begin again.

Take, for example, the reference in the text to 'the living creatures',
who might just possibly be identical to 'the creatures of the city', whom
Heidel presumed meant mankind. In the Sumerian *Lamentation Texts*,
cited earlier, we read that the Great Flood had 'overwhelmed the *living
creatures* of Heaven-and-Earth – the black-headed ones'. These black-
headed ones, I concluded, were the meteoric seeds of man which came to
dwell in the underworld.

Now, look at the reference in the passage above to 'the cattle of
Sumuqan', which might just possibly be identical to 'the creatures of the
city'. According to the Oxford scholar Stephanie Dalley, these 'cattle of
Sumuqan' were identical to the 'cattle of *Shakkan*'.[58] Who or what were
the 'cattle of Shakkan'? In the legend of *Erra and Ishum*, we discover
that 'the cattle of Shakkan' were *the black-headed ones.*[59] Once again, we
are dealing with meteoric 'creatures' of the underworld.

Why might these 'cattle' be 'creatures of the city'? The simple
explanation is that the ancients regarded the underworld as a 'city'.
Hence in the Sumerian legend of Ziusudra (cited at the beginning of this

chapter), we read *in the context of the Flood* that the 'people' of Nintu (almost certainly a heavenly people) were to be saved from their destruction by returning them to 'cities' and 'settlements'.

Moreover, concerning the reference in this Assyrian legend to the creation of the 'cattle of the field' and the 'beasts of the field', we have already seen how these wonderful things – the produce of Lahar and Ashnan – were introduced into the underworld by the lowering of the Duku.[60]

In summary, there can surely be no doubt that the legend entitled *The Creation of Living Creatures* was describing the creation of things in the underworld, including the creation of mankind's subterranean ancestors – the black-headed ones, or so-called 'cattle of Sumuqan'.

This means that there can now be no objection at all to the proposition that the 'two little ones' or 'two young ones' were indeed the progenitors of the flesh-and-blood human race.

Let us consider the crucial lines of the legend once again:

Ninigiku [Enki] created two little ones . . .
He made them more glorious than all other creatures.

Might we be looking at an Assyrian equivalent to Adam and Eve?

On this intriguing note, we must close our study of ancient Near Eastern religion, and move, rather appropriately, to the religion of the Old Testament.

The real Adam and Eve have some secrets of their own to be revealed.

* * * * *

CHAPTER NINE

GENESIS REVISITED

And God said: "Let there be Light!"
And there was Light...
And God divided the Light from the darkness.
(The book of Genesis, chapter 1)

In the beginning, God created Heaven and Earth, or so we are told by the first line of the Hebrew book of Genesis.

But was this really 'the beginning', and was it really 'Heaven and Earth' that God created in this particular passage of the Bible?

Today, the Old Testament exercises a profound and powerful grip on Western consciousness – so much so that one is almost forbidden from questioning its veracity. And yet anyone who has studied the history of religion recognises that the Old Testament is but one of many ancient religions, and that the Hebrew God was but one of many ancient Gods.

Where, however, is there any sense of this perspective today? Who among the general public has heard of Anu and Ninharsag, or Enlil and Ninlil? Who has heard of Re and Hathor, or Isis and Osiris? Who has heard of the creator-gods Atum, Amen, Ptah or Khnum?

In this chapter, we are going to take a completely fresh look at the Hebrew Old Testament. What would the Old Testament become if we were to regard it in its proper context – as one particular religious perspective among many such perspectives in the ancient world, and a minority view to boot?

What if we were to suppose, just for a moment, that the Old Testament was *not* the Word of God, as revealed to the priests, but rather the words of the priests, as revealed to the masses?

What if the Old Testament turns out to be *not* the 'Truth', and not even the 'truth', but merely a series of half-truths? And what if the other halves of these truths turn out to have been *occulted deliberately* from the scriptures for no other reason than to deter the Hebrew people from pursuing the pagan-like quest for the afterlife?

It is the purpose of this investigation to restore the perspective which has so clearly been lost during the past few thousand years. At the moment, we see through a glass darkly, as Paul once said, but the opacity of the glass can be penetrated by the light of God. So, let's try to shed some light on the Old Testament by studying it in the context of the exploded planet cults of the ancient Near East. Might the exploded planet be 'the light' we are looking for?

In this chapter, we shall take a precocious and daring sweep through the Hebrew religious traditions, and consider whether they might have had a hidden, occulted meaning. We will begin with 'the beginning', by establishing that the real beginning was left out of the book of Genesis entirely, though fortunately preserved in other biblical writings. Then we will look at the cosmogony of Genesis and discover that all is not quite as it seems. Next, we will look at the story of Adam and Eve in the Garden of Eden, and ask where exactly this 'Garden' was. And finally, we will look at the story of the Flood, and see how Noah and his Ark fit into the wider picture of the hero who sailed from Heaven to Earth.

This subject matter is incredibly controversial, and no investigation into it should be carried out lightly. It therefore behoves us to begin this chapter by reviewing briefly the background of the people who wrote the Old Testament. Who were the Hebrews, where did they come from, and where do they belong chronology-wise in the history of the ancient Near East?

As I said in the introduction to this book, true understanding comes from *standing under* the foundations of an ancient culture. It is an extremely difficult job where the Hebrews are concerned, but we should not be deterred from it.

The Mystery of the Hebrews

According to the idealised 'history' of the Old Testament, the Hebrew people were the seed of the patriarchs Abraham, Isaac and Jacob. Theoretically, the origins of the Hebrews can thus be traced through the migrations of Abraham.

According to the Old Testament, Abraham set out firstly from a place called Ur-of-the-Chaldeans and went to Haran, and then went from Haran to the land of Canaan – the so-called 'promised land', which would later be named Israel.[1] It was after this series of migrations that the Hebrews went down into Egypt, where they supposedly dwelt for four hundred years.[2] Then – in an incident which will become our focus in the next chapter – the Hebrews set out on the famous biblical Exodus which eventually brought them back to the 'promised land'.

The chronology of these migrations is very uncertain. As regards the final Exodus from Egypt, some scholars have dated it as early as the 17th century BC, whilst others have dated it as late as the 12th century BC.[3] There are even some scholars who question whether the Exodus ever happened at all. But the consensus is that it did, and there is some archaeological evidence in Israel to support it, although not on the epic scale described in the Old Testament.[4]

As for the earlier two-stage migration of Abraham from northern Mesopotamia to Canaan, that is another matter entirely. In the understandable absence of any firm archaeological evidence, the account of Abraham remains in the realm of legend and folklore. But, assuming it did happen – and it is not unreasonable to suspect a distant link to the Semitic-speaking peoples of northern Mesopotamia – then it probably occurred c. 2300-2000 BC, when great exoduses of people occurred all over the ancient world.

If this account is correct, at least in outline if not in chronology, then it may be said that the culture of the Hebrews did *not* develop in isolation from the rest of the ancient world. On the contrary, its roots lay (a) in northern Mesopotamia; (b) in the land of Canaan; and (c) in the land of Egypt (probably the Delta in the north).

Note therefore that all of these migrations of the Hebrews occurred against the backdrop of pagan religions, which were invariably exploded planet cults. If we go back to the supposed site of Abraham's origin, at Ur-of-the-Chaldeans, we can say with some confidence that these distant ancestors of the Hebrews were almost certainly pagans, who worshipped the various exploded planet-deities of Mesopotamia, from the time when that civilisation was founded c. 4000 BC.

Two thousand years or so later, a similar pagan situation would have prevailed in the land of Canaan, when Abraham allegedly founded the Hebrew dynasty.[5] At that time, the Canaanite pantheon of deities was headed by a god known as El – a lofty father of the gods, who was also known as *Ab-Adam*, meaning 'the father of man'. El's distant throne was said to be at the 'headwaters of the two rivers, in the midst of the Two Deeps' (possibly meaning the underworld).[6] And there is no question that he, his sons Yam, Baal and Mot, and his daughter Anat, were exploded planet-deities.[7]

It was from this pagan background that the Israelites went down into Egypt (according to the Bible), to be surrounded by yet more pagans, this time practising the exploded planet cults of Isis, Osiris, Amen-Re and numerous other similar deities. Incidentally, there is good evidence to suggest that the Egyptians of this period were developing a form of religion known as monolatry – the exclusive worship of one god, without denying the existence of others. It is exactly this kind of monolatry, and *not* monotheism (which *does* deny the existence of other gods), which is so clearly evident throughout the Old Testament.[8]

After the Exodus, the Israelites journeyed north, back to the land of the Canaanites, which was occupied *inter alia* by Canaanites, Hittites and Amorites. Once again, the Israelites were surrounded by pagans, who followed religions which again seem to have been derivatives of the exploded planet cults of Mesopotamia.[9] It is interesting to observe that the Old Testament emphasises repeatedly how the Israelites were attracted to these cults, albeit against the express wishes of the priests.

In summary, then, it can be said that the beliefs of the Hebrews would have been influenced considerably by pagan religions, not just from time to time, but continuously over the course of several thousand years. We should not be surprised therefore, if we find elements of these pagan exploded planet cults finding their way into the various scriptures of the Old Testament.

This brings us to the question of the Old Testament's date of composition. Clearly the various scriptures, or 'books', have at one point in time been woven together into a unified whole. But no-one knows for certain when this happened. And no-one knows for certain what amendments, if any, might have been made subsequently to the completed set of books.

This chronological uncertainty opens up another possibility. During the years 617-537 BC, the Hebrew élite were removed from Jerusalem and taken into captivity by the Babylonians. Was their religious dogma already established by that time, one wonders? Or did they adopt, or adapt, some of the pagan legends which were then current in ancient Babylon? This possibility cannot be ignored.

Why is the origin of the Old Testament such a mystery? The reason lies in the fact that it has superseded all previous religious writings of the Hebrews. We thus have no 'audit trail' of prior texts which we might compare and contrast in order to understand how their ideas evolved over the centuries.

Contrast this situation with that in Egypt, where the earliest Pyramid Texts, reliably dated to *c.* 2300 BC, can be compared to much later texts such as the Coffin Texts. Not only this, but Egypt was home to numerous rival theologies and cosmogonies, at cities such as Heliopolis, Memphis,

Hermopolis, Thebes and Edfu. All of these differing viewpoints can be usefully compared and contrasted. The diversity is a godsend.

As for Israel, however, all we have is one set of texts, promulgated by one set of priests, based at one particular city – the sacred capital of Jerusalem. And as a result of this religious monopoly, we are left guessing as to what transpired over the centuries. Did the Hebrews once follow a more pagan cult? Was there at one time a diversity of views? Might there have been a wholesale mass destruction of texts in order to promote the single dogma which is the Old Testament as we know it today? No-one knows. No-one has any answers. All is a mystery.

All of these questions should be borne in mind as we now open up the first book of the Old Testament – the book of Genesis – and re-examine its meaning in the light of what we now know of the ancient pagan religions of Egypt and Mesopotamia.

The Genesis Story

Before we begin to analyse the book of Genesis, it is appropriate to begin by setting the scene with a brief overview of its contents.

The story of Genesis begins, as one might expect, with a 'beginning', which precedes the first 'day' of creation. We are then introduced to a six-day cosmogony, in which God created the heavens and the Earth, and all things upon the Earth, including mankind who was created 'in the image of God'. On the seventh day, we are told, God rested.[10]

However, in what appears to be a second, parallel account of man's creation, Genesis puts God back to work by recounting the famous story of the creation of Adam and Eve in the Garden of Eden. I will have much to say on this in due course.

According to Genesis, the expulsion of Adam and Eve from Eden (the so-called 'fall of man') led to sexual activity and the beginning of the human race. In one account, Adam produced 'a son in his own likeness' called Seth. A second account, however, made Seth the third son, a replacement for the second son Abel, who had been murdered by the first-born son Cain. This obscure legend leads directly into the genealogy of the ten patriarchs, taking us all the way down in time from the days of Adam to the days of Noah. All of these patriarchs enjoyed a superhuman longevity, ranging from 777 years in the case of Lamech to 969 years in the case of Methuselah. The seventh patriarch, however, 'walked with God' for three hundred years, and then disappeared into the deep blue yonder sixty-five years later, when God 'took him away'.[11] His name was Enoch.

During the 950-year lifetime of Noah, God observed the 'great wickedness' of mankind in the Earth and 'his heart was filled with pain'. He thus regretted his decision to create mankind, and decided to bring a Great Flood upon the Earth to destroy all living things. There was, however, one righteous man named Noah, who found favour in the eyes of God, and thus God instructed Noah to build an Ark, and save the seed of mankind and all living creatures.

The biblical account of the Flood is preceded by an intriguing reference to the presence on the Earth of the Sons-of-God, whose significance is altogether obscure to mainstream scholars. In chapter two of this work, however, we ascertained that the Sons-of-God were almost certainly meteorites which impregnated Mother Earth (alluded to in the Bible by the expression 'daughters of 'adam'). Hence we are told that the Sons-of-God fathered children called the Nephilim – the giants.[12]

Noah and his wife survived the Flood, along with his three sons and their wives, and God then made a covenant with them all, never again to destroy the Earth with a Flood. Genesis informs us that Noah became 'a man of the soil' by planting a vineyard. He then got drunk, fell asleep naked, and was seen by one of his sons, Ham. This, for some strange reason, caused Noah to condemn the bloodline of Ham to an eternity of slavery. We will decode this curious legend later in this chapter.

After this, Genesis makes passing mention of a mighty man named Nimrod, a builder of cities, who orchestrated the building of the mysterious city and Tower of Babel. The latter project, we are told, was halted by God, who would seemingly not tolerate man's ambition to scale the heavens.

Genesis now relates a new genealogy, once again of ten patriarchs, from Noah to Terah. The longevity of the pre-Flood patriarchs is reduced, but many of the life spans still appear to be superhuman.[13]

Once again, the tenth patriarch produced a significant trio of sons, one of whom was Abram, later to be called Abraham.

It was at this point, ten generations after the covenant with Noah, that God decided to enter the stage of world history at a political level, by urging Abram to migrate to the land of Canaan.

Next, we are told of a strange covenant between God and Abram, involving the sacrifice of certain animals, each of which was separated into two pieces.[14] A deep sleep and a horrible darkness fell upon the hero Abram, and God caused a smoking furnace and burning lamp to pass mysteriously between the halves of the sacrificed animals.[15]

It was at this stage that Abram entered into the covenant of circumcision for the Hebrew people and, in return, God enabled him, at the age of ninety-nine years, to impregnate his wife Sarai, who was eighty-nine at the time. The names of the couple were then changed to Abraham and Sarah, and in the following year Sarah gave birth to Isaac.

In the same year, Abraham met God face to face – note this belief in an anthropomorphic God which seems to be a hangover from pagan days – and negotiated with him concerning the destruction of the cities of Sodom and Gomorrah. Abraham failed, however, to prevent the two cities and the entire plain being destroyed by 'fire and brimstone', which God sent down from the heavens.

Some years later, God tested Abraham's loyalty by demanding that he sacrifice Isaac, his only son, on the top of a mountain, in the land of Moriah. But just as Abraham prepared to slay and burn his first-born son, God intervened and substituted a ram for the sacrifice. The covenant between God and the Hebrews was then extended, with God promising to make Abraham's descendants 'as numerous as the stars in the sky, and as the sand on the seashore'.[16] The covenant of God was then passed down by Abraham through the line of Isaac to Jacob (noticeably avoiding the first-born son Esau).

The account of Jacob is famous for his vision of a ramp, which stretched between Earth and Heaven, with the angels of God ascending and descending upon it. The account is also notable for the incident in which God appeared in the form of a man, and wrestled with Jacob until daybreak.[17] Surprisingly, Jacob proved himself to be the equal of God in this contest, and God thus bestowed upon him the name Israel, meaning 'God prevails'.[18] Thus Israel was born as a nation in the image of God, for, just like God, the people of Israel were imagined to have 'striven with the gods and men, and won out'.[19]

The remainder of Genesis is given over to the very popular account of Joseph, who was sold by his brothers into slavery, and then taken down into the land of Egypt. There, Joseph was joined by his family – the descendants of Jacob – who began to multiply prolifically.

The scene was thus set for the enslavement of the Israelites by the Egyptian Pharaoh, and the Exodus of the Israelites back to the promised land. This is the subject of the second book of the Old Testament, and the subject of the next chapter, chapter ten, in this book.

This, then, is a rough outline of the story told in the book of Genesis.

What should we make of it?

In many ways, we are in familiar territory. As with the legends of the ancient Near East, we have a cosmogony (creation of Earth and the heavens), a creation of mankind, a Great Flood, and an impregnation of the Earth by falling meteorites (the Sons-of-God). This is encouraging.

Clearly the Hebrews did not live in a theological and cultural vacuum, and nor should we expect them to have done.

In other ways, however, we have entered *unfamiliar* territory. *Out*, for example, have gone all the individual gods who took part in the pagan creations. *In* has come a single all-powerful God who did the whole thing himself. *Out* has gone the idea of independent, disinterested gods. *In* has come a God with an obsessive interest in the affairs of mankind, who not only intervened in man's activities but actually *directed* those activities.

The style of the Genesis story is also completely out of character with everything we have encountered thus far. *Out* go the fragmentary legends of the gods. *In* comes a cohesive story about mankind. *Out* goes the concern with divine matters at the mythical beginning of time. *In* comes a concern with human matters, in contemporary or historic time.

The result of this, in a nutshell, is that we see in the Old Testament a totally new perspective on the divine-human interface. Moreover, we see a perspective which was obviously very appealing, not just to Israel but to the many non-Jews who have placed their faith in these scriptures during the last two thousand years. It is indeed comforting to think that life in the here-and-now is not as haphazard as it might seem, but all part of some divinely inspired plan, with God watching us, guiding us and protecting us.

Such thoughts aside, what we must realise is that the appeal of the Old Testament lies also in its unique genealogy, which all of us – so we are told – can use to trace back our heritage, via Noah, ultimately to Adam and Eve, and beyond that to the supernatural creative power of God himself.

But what if this whole scenario were nothing but a sham and a con? What if Adam was not really a 'man' at all, and Eve not really a 'woman'? What if the story of Noah was adapted from the story of Atra-Hasis, which was in turn a corruption of an allegory concerning a planet which exploded and fell to the Earth?

Do we not owe it to ourselves to establish the truth of this matter?

The Secret of Yahweh's Battle

There is no better place to begin than at the beginning, and the first verses of the book of Genesis:

> In the beginning, God [Elohim] created Heaven-and-Earth, and the Earth was without form and void, and darkness was over the face of the Deep, and the Breath of God hovered over the waters. And God said: "Let Light come into existence!" And Light came to be.[20]

If we take this opening passage of Genesis at face value, Elohim created the Earth in a peaceful manner, without recourse to violence. There is no hint whatsoever of an exploded planet or a catastrophic renewal of the Earth. On the contrary, God is not portrayed as a physical god at all, but rather *as a supernatural being*. The thought of God going into battle, in the manner of Horus versus Seth, or Ninurta versus Zu, or Marduk versus Tiamat, would have been unthinkable to the priests of ancient Israel.

As we enter the 21st century, however, the time has come to think the unthinkable. Was the Hebrew God, Yahweh-Elohim, once a *physical god*, who carried out his creation using *physical means*?

It is curious that, once the book of Genesis has moved on from dealing with the six-day cosmogony, Yahweh-Elohim becomes more and more physical and violent in nature. For example, in Genesis chapters 6-9, we find God bringing cataclysm to Earth via the Great Flood. Then, in Genesis 11, we read that God 'went down' to the Earth in order to scatter the people who were building the Tower of Babel. Next, in Genesis 19, we find God hurling brimstone and fire down from the Sky upon the cities of Sodom and Gomorrah. By the time he had finished, dense smoke was rising from the surrounding land 'like the smoke of a furnace'.[21]

And this was only the beginning. As one reads through the Old Testament, the image of the supernatural God of Genesis 1 evaporates before one's eyes. In the book of Joshua, for example, we read that Yahweh destroyed the enemies of Israel by casting down 'great stones' from Heaven,[22] whilst at other times he appeared in person amid fire, wind, earthquakes, thunder and lightning.[23]

But Yahweh was no mere weather-god. In the book of Deuteronomy, Yahweh declared that:

> "A fire is kindled in mine anger, and it shall burn unto the depths of Sheol [the underworld]. It shall consume the Earth with her abundance, and shall set on fire the foundations of the mountains."[24]

And similarly, in the book of Job, we read:

> He [God] moveth mountains, and they know it not. He overturneth them in his anger.
> He shaketh the Earth out of her place and the pillars thereof tremble.[25]

So, did this God, Yahweh-Elohim, really perform the creation in Genesis 1 in a supernatural fashion? Or might the real nature of the beginning have been occulted from the story?

In Psalm 89 of the Old Testament, we read something very interesting:

O Yahweh, God-of-Hosts...
Thou rulest over the raging of the sea...
Thou didst break Rahab into pieces, like one who is slain; with thy
strong arm thou didst scatter thine enemies.[26]

Who was Rahab? We receive a further explanation in the book of Isaiah:

Awake, awake! Put on strength, O arm of the LORD. Awake, as in the
ancient days, as in generations of old.
Art thou not the one who didst cut up Rahab into pieces, who didst
pierce that sea-monster?
Art thou not the one who didst dry up the sea, the waters of the great
Deep, who didst make the depths of the sea into a road for the
ransomed to cross over?[27]

Who, or what, was this 'monster' that lived in the sea? Biblical scholars
have until now maintained that this monster Rahab (also known as
Leviathan) was a real creature which lived in the seas of the Earth. We,
however, have just invested considerable time in discovering that the
ancient Egyptians and Mesopotamians described the abyss of space as a
'sea' or an 'ocean'.

Which interpretation fits the Hebrew legend? Consider the following
quotation from the book of Job, which places Rahab in the context of the
creation of the underworld, Heaven and Earth:

Sheol [the underworld] is naked before God [Elohim], and the Place of
Destruction lieth uncovered.
He stretcheth out the North [Heaven] over the Empty Place, and
suspendeth the Earth upon nothing.
He bindeth up the waters in his thick clouds, and the cloud bursteth
not under their weight.
He holdeth back the face of his throne, and spreadeth his cloud upon
it...
The pillars of Heaven quake, and are astonished at his rebuke.
He divideth the Sea with his power, *and by his wisdom he cutteth
Rahab into pieces.*
*By his breath, the Heavens are cleared, His hand pierceth the fleeing
serpent.*[28]

The fact that the monster Rahab appears here in the midst of a creation
story is significant, as is the vivid description of the *dismemberment* of
Rahab – a motif which was, of course, central to the legends of the

celestial battle in ancient Egypt and Mesopotamia.

Note, too, the description of Rahab as a 'fleeing serpent', which was somehow causing an obstruction *in the Heavens*. The idea that Rahab was a mundane creature like a crocodile is therefore absurd. Scholars indeed admit that Rahab was somehow responsible for a blockage in the Sky, which needed to be cleared by the breath of Yahweh, but they have not been able to embrace the uncomfortable thought that Rahab might actually have been a Sky-god.[29] And yet this is what the book of Job says, quite unambiguously.

Further evidence concerning Rahab is found in Psalm 74, where he appears as a sea-monster called Leviathan:

> (O God) thou didst divide the Sea by thy strength; thou didst break
>   the heads of the dragons in the waters.
> Thou didst break the heads of Leviathan into pieces, and gavest him
>   to be nourishment to the people inhabiting the wilderness.[30]

Note that this monster Leviathan had multiple 'heads', like a Greek Titan, and could thus not have been a mundane creature such as a crocodile.[31] As for 'the people inhabiting the wilderness', could they have been the mythical dwellers in the underworld?[32] Such would certainly have been the destination of Leviathan's broken-up body-parts according to the pagan way of thinking.

Consider also another passage from the book of Job, where Leviathan appears with only one head, but is nevertheless described in awesome terms:

> Who can open the doors of its face? Its teeth are terrible round
>   about...
> Its snortings throw out flashes of light; its eyes are like the rays of
>   dawn.
> Burning lamps go forth from its mouth, and sparks of fire leap out.
> Smoke goes forth from its nostrils as from a boiling pot or cauldron.
> Its breath sets coals ablaze, and flames go forth from its mouth...[33]

Surely this Leviathan is identical to the serpent-like god Satan, who 'fell like lightning from Heaven' according to the New Testament gospel of Luke.[34] Hence the book of Job describes Leviathan as 'king over all the children of pride'.[35]

The book of Revelations indeed seems to allude to Rahab when it identifies Satan as 'that ancient serpent':

> And there was war in Heaven. Michael and his angels fought against
>   the dragon. And the dragon and his angels fought back, but they did

not prevail, and they lost their place in Heaven. And the great dragon was cast down – that ancient serpent called the devil, or Satan, who deceived the whole world. He was cast down into the Earth, and his angels were cast down with him.[36]

Where is this casting down of Satan from Heaven in the books of the Old Testament? The answer must surely be in the various accounts of the battle between Yahweh and Rahab (alias Leviathan).

Why, then, was this battle not included in the cosmogony of Genesis 1? The obvious answer is that the violent and physical nature of this battle would have totally upset the Hebrew vision of a *supernatural* creation.[37]

In view of the pagan legends which linked the battle of the gods to the creation, it seems very likely that Yahweh's battle has indeed been *occulted* from the cosmogony in Genesis 1.[38]

The Hidden Light

Let us now return to the official Hebrew account of the six days of creation, and try to work out how the battle of Yahweh against Rahab might have fitted into the 'big picture'.

The opening passage of Genesis – as cited earlier – suggests that there was a darkness over the face of the Deep, and that 'light' was then created and separated from darkness. But if these lines seem to be mysterious and ambiguous, then worse is to come. What follows next in Genesis 1 verses 5-31 is challenging to say the least. I can only suggest that readers turn to a copy of the Bible at this point, whilst I attempt to summarise the six 'days' of God's creation as succinctly as possible:

Day 1: The creation of Light, and its separation from darkness.
Day 2: The creation of the Expanse, and the separation of the waters.
Day 3: The separation of land and waters on Earth, and the creation of vegetation on Earth.
Day 4: The creation of Sun, Moon and stars in the Expanse.
Day 5: The creation of living creatures on Earth, in the sea and in the air.
Day 6: The creation of living creatures on Earth, on the land, and the creation of mankind as the ruler of all creatures.

Thus did God create all the heavens and the Earth in six 'days', prior to taking a well-earned rest on the seventh 'day'.

What to make of this? Most readers, I suspect, will have no trouble dealing with Days 3-6, which are self-explanatory. But what about Days

1-2? Here we find a terminology which is unfamiliar to us. What is the Light? What is the Expanse? What was God doing?

In order to make any headway, it is first necessary to find a point of reference, and this point of reference must be established from the very first enigmatic lines of Genesis:

> In the beginning, God [Elohim] created Heaven-and-Earth, and the Earth was without form and void, and darkness was over the face of the Deep, and the Breath of God hovered over the waters.[39]

The key to understanding this passage is to realise that 'the face of the Deep' was the Earth, which was covered in waters. Thus the Breath of God hovered over the surface of the Earth. This, then, was the context in which God said: "Let Light come into existence!"

What was 'the Light' which was created on Day 1? Generations of biblical scholars have persuaded us that this Light was simply the daylight, which was separated from the darkness of night. But this, I suggest, is a complete falsehood.

If we study closely the above summary of Days 1-6, we observe that the Sun, Moon and stars were created during Day 4. Light could therefore not have existed until Day 4. How, then, could it possibly be the case that God created Light on Day 1? Surely we have erred.

Let's take a closer look at Day 4. What Genesis tells us concerning Day 4 is that God created 'lights' in the Expanse – a 'great light' to govern the day, a 'lesser light' to govern the night, and, in addition to these two lights, the 'stars'. This statement is absolutely unambiguous. The 'great light' can only be the Sun, and the 'lesser light' can only be the Moon.

Once again, then, we must ask how the Light could have been created on Day 1? The contradiction seems to be irresolvable, unless the Light was something other than the Sun and the Moon.

What kind of 'other worldly' Light might that be?

Let us recall now everything that we have learned from our study of the ancient Egyptian and Mesopotamian acts of creation. At the very heart of these cosmogonies was the belief that God had fallen *physically*, but had been resurrected *metaphysically*. Thus the body of Osiris had fallen into the underworld, but his soul had ascended to Heaven. Thus Re had departed from the world of men by being lifted up metaphysically on the back of Nut. Thus the Phoenix-bird had resurrected itself from its own ashes, and ascended to metaphysical life. Thus Anu had impregnated KI, Mother Earth, but was then restored metaphysically to Heaven. Other examples could be cited, too, but the point has been made.

Now consider this. The most fundamental archetype of this death and resurrection was of Heaven itself. Heaven – a planet – had fallen *into* the Earth, but had then been *separated from* the Earth and restored metaphysically to the place whence it fell.

Moreover, it is a fact that the vast majority of the ancient Sky-gods were associated with *light*, whilst the Egyptians declared that Heaven was an *Akhet*, i.e. a 'Mountain of Light'.

So, returning to the mystery of the Light in Day 1 of the Genesis creation, might this Light be the Light of Heaven?

Well, it not only 'might be' but it *is*. In Psalm 104, we read:

O LORD my God, thou art very great...
Thou coverest thyself with Light as with a garment, thou stretchest out
    the heavens like a curtain...[40]

Let's now read the words of Genesis again, and see if they make sense:

... darkness was over the face of the Deep, and the Breath of God
hovered over the waters, God said: "Let Light come into existence!"
And Light came to be. And God saw that the Light was good, and God
divided the Light from the darkness.

As mentioned earlier, the Deep was the Earth, so the covering of its face by the Breath of God demonstrates to us that God was present on the Earth. So, if the Light represented the creation of the metaphysical Heaven, what was the 'darkness' from which it was separated? The stunning answer is *the underworld*.

In fact, the entire passage springs to life if we presume that God's body (i.e. the physical Heaven) had fallen into the underworld, and that God's spirit or soul (i.e. the metaphysical Heaven) was being separated and returned to the place whence he had fallen.[41] It thus becomes apparent that the physical battle between Yahweh against Rahab would have *preceded* the very first lines of Genesis.

Readers may wish to contrast this very straightforward explanation with the contrived solutions and intellectual somersaults performed by biblical scholars in their attempt to explain why the Light was seemingly created on two separate 'days' of the creation.[42] In fairness to biblical scholars, however, it should be pointed out that they have not had the benefit of understanding the pagan cosmogonies.

The Separation of the Waters

This 'Light = Heaven' hypothesis can also be proved in another way, by looking at the mysterious separation of the waters on Day 2.

> And God said: "Let there be an Expanse in the midst of the waters, and let it divide the waters from the waters." And God made the Expanse, and divided the waters which were *under* the Expanse from the waters which were *above* the Expanse. And it was so. And God called the Expanse 'Sky'.[43]

This Expanse (Hebrew: *Raki'a*; often translated misleadingly as 'vault', or 'firmament') was the entire Sky, which reached outwards from the Earth in all directions towards the very highest heights of the heavens, even to the points of the most distant visible stars.[44] Thus it could be said that the Sun, Moon and stars were created *in* the Expanse.[45] The only thing above the Expanse, in the highest heights, was God himself, together with one half of the divided waters.

Why was God accompanied by waters, and why was it necessary to separate the waters to places above and below? The answer, I suggest, is that the waters *belonged* to God, and had thus fallen from Heaven when God himself fell from Heaven.[46] (Thus we read that the Breath of God was hovering *over the waters* on the face of the Earth.) This, it seems to me, was an original Great Flood, which occurred at the very beginning of Genesis 1, but was occulted from the story by the Hebrew priests. The idea of a physical Yahweh, fallen in battle, and trapped in the underworld (like the Egyptian god Osiris), would have been total anathema to them.

This explains why in Psalm 29 we read that 'the LORD sat enthroned upon the Flood', i.e. upon his resurrected floodwaters.[47] And it also explains why in the book of Job, God alluded to the idea that he had covered himself in a flood of water, saying:

> "Canst thou lift up thy voice to the clouds, and cover thyself with an abundance of waters?"[48]

Furthermore, in the book of Proverbs, we find a remarkable echo of the Mesopotamian idea of two Deeps, or Apsus – the Deep of the above, and the Deep of the below. The text reads:

> By wisdom, the LORD hath laid the foundations of the Earth,
> By understanding, He hath established the Heavens,
> By his knowledge, *the Deeps were divided.*[49]

Further support for this idea is found in the interesting fact that the Hebrew word for Heaven (or heavens) was *shamayim*, a plural term which stemmed from *mayim* meaning 'waters'.[50] This is, of course, entirely consistent with the ancient pagan tradition that Heaven was a watery planet.[51]

Putting the clues together, we have a separation of light from darkness, and a separation of waters from waters. And all of this in the aftermath *not* of the creation of Heaven and Earth separately, but of the creation of Heaven-and-Earth as one 'mountain' fused together. The hyphenation makes all the difference:

> In the beginning, God [Elohim] created Heaven-and-Earth, and the Earth was without form and void, and darkness was over the face of the Deep, and the Breath of God hovered over the waters.

The Mystery of the Seven Heavens

There is one curious anomaly which we still need to resolve, and it will lead to the unveiling of another intriguing mystery, namely that of the 'seven heavens'.

The anomaly is this. If the Light which was created on Day 1 was the Light of Heaven, and not conventional daylight, why do we read repeated utterances of the formula 'there was evening and morning – the nth day', beginning from Day 1? In other words, how could there be evening and morning on Days 1-3, when the Sun, Moon and stars would not be created until Day 4?

The explanation I have is that the formula 'there was evening and morning – the nth day' is a coded esoteric statement which symbolises death and rebirth. When it is thus understood, it becomes apparent that Genesis 1 may contain a hidden reference to a series of metaphysical creations by God. This might sound far-fetched if it were not for the fact that the seven heavens were very important within ancient Jewish traditions, and yet are nevertheless absent from the Old Testament as we know it.[52]

Allow me to demonstrate how this works. After each of the six days of creation, the Bible states 'there was evening and morning – the nth day'. This statement is thus repeated six times, until eventually on the seventh 'day', we are simply told that God rested and blessed the seventh 'day', and sanctified it.

Now, if we treat the recitation 'there was evening and morning – the nth day' as symbolising death and rebirth, it follows that the aspects of God's physical creation were being counterbalanced by the creation of something metaphysical. In other words, on each of six 'days', God created something invisible as well as visible.

These invisible creations, I suggest, were six 'heavens', such that on the seventh day, God went to rest above these six heavens in his mystical 'Seventh Heaven'.

This is all very interesting, but why should we suppose in the first place that the formula 'there was evening and morning – the nth day' would symbolise death and rebirth?

My reasoning is as follows. In Genesis 1:5, the introduction of the terms 'evening' and 'morning' is preceded by corresponding references to 'day' and 'night'. And, furthermore, the references to 'day' and 'night' are in turn equated to Light and darkness – the very Light and darkness which God had just separated. Now if, as I have suggested, this initial separation alluded to *the rebirth of Heaven from the underworld of the Earth*, it then follows logically that death and rebirth are alluded to by the terms 'evening' and 'morning'.

In effect, the recitation 'there was evening and morning' was evoking the death and rebirth of God, or the death and rebirth of Heaven. Hence Genesis 1 describes the creation of the seven heavens in addition to the creation of Heaven itself.

And all of these things were cleverly concealed, so that they would only be evident to the initiated.

The Father-of-Beginning

Now that we have been alerted to the possibility of such occultations in the book of Genesis, there is yet another astonishing possibility which must be considered.

It is a curious fact that the opening line of Genesis begins with the second letter of the Hebrew alphabet, *beth*, rather than the first letter, *aleph*. Furthermore, it has been pointed out that an insertion of the missing *aleph* would radically alter the meaning of the opening line. See what happens in my translation below, when we make the alphabetical change from *Bereshith* ('In the beginning') to *Ab-reshith* ('Father-of-Beginning'):

> When the Father-of-Beginning created the gods [*elohim*] of Heaven-and-Earth, and the Earth was without form and void, and darkness was over the Deep, and the Breath of God hovered over the waters, God said: "Let light come into existence!" And light came to be.

What we now see is the idea that God – the exploded planet – created the gods by emission from his own physical being. Moreover, we see in this translation the implied idea that the created gods had fallen into the 'mountain' of Heaven-and-Earth.

The passage, as retranslated here, is a perfect – absolutely perfect – summation of the pagan religious philosophy.[53]

It is, by the same token, complete anathema to the Hebrew priests, who had rejected the idea of the physical death of God, and who had carefully distanced their God from the creation of the pagan gods.

A puzzle may now be resolved, for it is widely attested in the Bible that gods other than Yahweh existed, and thus must have been created, but nowhere does the book of Genesis explain how this came about. The passage as retranslated above resolves the problem. It would now seem that the original version of the creation in Genesis – which we might call the *alpha*-cosmogony – was succeeded by an occulted version of the creation – which we might call the *beta*-cosmogony. By dropping the *aleph*, the Hebrew priests completely changed the meaning of the first line of Genesis.

Thus were the gods (*elohim*) eclipsed by God (*Elohim*).

The Man who Fell to Earth

We now turn to the biblical legend of the creation of mankind, in the form of the first man and woman, Adam and Eve. Does this legend really describe a supernatural intervention by God, or might there be a more prosaic explanation?

It is generally held that the book of Genesis contains two accounts of the creation of Adam and Eve, the first being in Genesis 1 and the second in Genesis 2. My own feeling is that Genesis 2 itself contains two traditions which have been mixed together, as we shall see in a moment.

In the first account, in Genesis 1, the first human couple are unnamed, and simply referred to as 'male and female'. Crucially, we are told that they were created by God 'in his own image'.

This is familiar territory. In the previous chapter, we encountered an Assyrian creation legend in which the two Lamga-gods, Ulligarra and Zalgarra, created 'men' *in their own images* as skilled and unskilled labourers. We also mentioned briefly a Sumerian legend, in which Enki created 'mankind' by making the Anunnaki-gods *'produce their own likenesses'*.[54] In both cases, 'mankind' was created in the underworld, and in both cases it was created in the image of meteorites, which were themselves created in the image of a planet which exploded.

When one reads the first chapter of Genesis with such thoughts in mind, the wording that 'God created man in his own image' immediately prompts us to think of a planet producing a meteoric 'mankind'.[55] And perhaps this was indeed how the text was intended to be read by those who had been initiated into the secrets of the Hebrew priesthood.

Immediately, then, we are alerted to the possibility that the first 'mankind', as described in the Bible, came down from the heavens.[56]

However, when we get to Genesis 2, we find that such an idea has been occulted from the biblical record. Instead of reading that man came down from the heavens, we are simply told that God created man from the soil of the Earth:

> ... a mist went up from the Earth and watered the whole face of the ground. And the LORD God formed the human ['adam] from the soil ['adamah], and breathed into his nostrils the breath of life. And the human became a living creature.[57]

This statement is evocative of the Mesopotamian view that 'mankind' was made from 'the clay which is above the AB.ZU'. But there are several Mesopotamian legends which suggest that the clay was first thrown down from the heavens. Might this be the case with the Hebrew 'soil'? Does the passage contain an ambiguity concerning the ultimate origin of the 'soil' from which man was made?

Although the book of Genesis is itself vague on this matter – perhaps deliberately so – there are several legends elsewhere in the Bible which suggest that the first man was indeed cast down from the heavens, in what we might call, literally, the original 'fall of man'.

The most spectacular passage on this theme is found in the book of Ezekiel, in which the prophet castigates the arrogant King of Tyre. As one reads through this explicit account, one cannot help feeling that it was drawing on an archetypal fall of man, which would have applied equally to the first man, Adam. The words which follow are those of God, which Ezekiel was to repeat to the King of Tyre:

> "In the pride of thine heart, thou hast said: 'I am a god; I sit on the throne of a god in the midst of the seas.' But thou art a man and not a god... Thou wast the model of perfection, full of wisdom and perfect in beauty. *Thou wast in Eden, the garden of God*; every precious stone was thy covering... on the day that thou wast created. Thou art the anointed cherub that covereth, and so I set thee. *Thou wast (set) upon the holy mountain of God*; thou didst walk up and down in the midst of the stones of fire. Thou wast perfect in thy ways from the day that thou wast created, till iniquity was found in thee... *So I drove thee in disgrace from the mountain of God*, and I expelled thee, O covering cherub, from the midst of the stones of fire... *I threw thee to the Earth... I made a fire come out of thee, and it consumed thee, and I reduced thee to ashes upon the Earth in the sight of all who beheld thee.*"[58]

Could this be the original fall of man, from 'Eden the garden of God' –

'the holy mountain of God'? It is a far cry from the orthodox tale of Adam and Eve, and yet we have seen enough clues to suspect that the Hebrew priests may have tried to occult an idea which they did not like – namely the idea that man had a celestial origin.

The second big clue in the Bible is found in the book of Lamentations, where there is a tantalising reference to the idea that the people of Israel had been cast down from Heaven:

> How hath the LORD covered the daughter of Zion with a cloud in his anger.
> *How hath he cast down the Splendour of Israel from Heaven unto the Earth.*[59]

Was this how Adam, too, had arrived in the Earth?

In a gnostic text, we find support for this idea:

> When Eve saw Adam *cast down*, she pitied him, and she said: "Adam, live! Rise up upon the Earth!" Immediately her word became a deed.[60]

This story is amazingly reminiscent of the Egyptian god Osiris, who was told to "Rise up!" by the goddess Isis. *Osiris, of course, had fallen from Heaven.*

Further support for this idea is found in a Muslim tradition which states that God (Allah) sent down a tent from the Sky to cover the body of Adam at the site of the Ka'aba (in Mecca). The idea here of *covering* Adam's body is very evocative of him being placed in the underworld, which would naturally imply a belief that he had fallen from Heaven.

We will return in due course to the idea that the Garden of Eden might have been in the underworld. Suffice to say, for now, that there was a Hebrew belief in man's subterranean origins, which is exemplified by an intriguing passage in Psalm 139, where the poet states:

> My frame was not hidden from thee [O LORD], when I was made in the secret place,
> When I was woven together in the depths of the Earth.[61]

Further evidence for the fall of Adam from Heaven is found in the legend of Eve being created from his rib, although it must be stressed that things here are not at all what they seem to be. To begin, let's remind ourselves of what the Bible says concerning the mysterious creation of Eve:

> And the LORD God said: "It is not good that the human should be alone, I shall make a sustainer-beside-him."... And the LORD God caused a deep sleep to fall upon the human, and he slept, and he took one of his ribs and closed up the flesh where it had been, and the

LORD God built the rib he had taken from the human into a woman, and he brought her to the human.[62]

What is the meaning of this story? The answer, I suggest, is that the story is a 180-degree reversal of the original story. In the original story, Eve was *not* taken from Adam, but Adam was taken from Eve.[63]

How so? The key is the realisation that Eve was Mother Earth.

A preposterous suggestion? No, not at all.

Consider firstly the fact that Eve is referred to in Genesis 3:20 as 'the Mother of All Living'.[64] It is a perfect title for Mother Earth.

Consider secondly the legend in the Talmud that Eve had coupled with a serpent.[65] It hardly seems likely that a *human* Eve coupled with a serpent, but it would make sense that a planetary Eve coupled with a serpent – for numerous are the legends of a serpent falling from the Sky.

So, just supposing for a moment that Eve was indeed Mother Earth, what would be the significance of the 'rib' from which she was supposedly created?

The answer, I suggest, is that the 'rib' was originally an epithet for Adam, who came down from the heavens and entered the womb of Mother Earth (Eve), afterwards to emerge from her womb into the world above. In this original legend, the first man would thus have been a 'rib' taken out of the 'Woman', rather than the first woman being taken out of the man, by means of his rib.

Can we substantiate this startling hypothesis? Indeed we can.

Consider, for example, Spell 269 of the ancient Egyptian Coffin Texts, which uses the analogy of ribs to recall how the body-parts of Osiris/Geb – a planetary god – had fallen from Heaven and entered the Earth:

> The king is this bush of life, which went forth from Osiris [from Heaven] to grow *on the ribs of Osiris* [in the Earth] and to nourish the plebs... the king lives and grows fat *on the ribs of Geb*...[66]

Secondly, consider the fact that the Sumerian word for 'rib', TI, could also mean 'life', and thus the goddess Ninti (NIN.TI) was simultaneously 'the Lady of the Rib' and 'the Lady of Life'. Ninti, we should recall, was Mother Earth, and she was identical to Ninharsag, one of whose nicknames was 'lapis lazuli brick'. And as we saw in chapter two, this lapis lazuli 'brick' was a meteorite, which had impregnated the womb of Mother Earth. There is a parallel here which suggests that Ninti (NIN.TI) carried a meteoric 'rib' in her planetary womb. And this, I suggest, is the source of the original legend of Adam's rib impregnating Eve.

Using clues such as these, we can reconstruct the original Hebrew legend of Adam and Eve. The 'rib' of Adam, it would seem, was a meteorite – the ancient seed of life – which fell from Heaven and split open the womb of Mother Earth. As usual, Mother Earth conceived, and gave birth from her womb to the first 'man'. Thus 'man' came out of 'Woman', so to speak.

Several further clues can be cited to corroborate this.

Firstly, there is the biblical legend which states that Adam was put into 'a deep sleep' at the time the rib was taken out of him, supposedly to make Eve. But as we shall see in legends elsewhere, both in the Bible and in pagan literature, this idea of being put into a 'deep sleep' was a frequently used idiom for a god who had been cast down from Heaven to Earth.[67] Thus Adam would indeed have been a falling meteorite, alias a 'rib'.

Secondly, we have already seen how falling Sky-gods made 'mankind' from their celestial 'blood'. It is therefore intriguing to note that the name of the first 'human', Adam (*'adam*), contained a pun on the ancient Akkadian word for 'blood' (*dam*).[68] In effect, Adam *was* the 'blood' which came down from Heaven and impregnated Eve (Mother Earth).

Thirdly and finally, there is another amusing pun alluded to in the book of Genesis, which records an age-old tradition that the first 'man' (Adam) would *'cleave unto'* his 'wife' (Eve).[69] This idea of cleaving, or penetrating the woman, is not just sexual in a profane sense, but is also a highly esoteric statement, alluding to the male god falling from heaven and entering physically into Mother Earth. This is the old story of the sacred marriage, which is also recorded later in Genesis when the Sons-of-God entered into Mother Earth and made her bear giants.

In summary, there is strong evidence to suggest that the Hebrew priests borrowed the story of Adam and Eve from older pagan legends, but twisted it through 180 degrees to suit their own political and theological ends (we will discuss this further in the next chapter).

This, of course, means that any similarities between the story of Adam and Eve (the first two humans) and the Assyrian legend of 'the two little ones' whom Enki made 'more glorious than all other creatures' are entirely coincidental. In fact, the Hebrew legend turns out to be a falsification based on the usual pagan idea of *one man* being created in the womb of Mother Earth. It can therefore be said, with no little irony, that the Assyrian story of 'the two little ones' actually bears a greater resemblance to the Adam and Eve story than the Adam and Eve story does itself!

The Garden of Eden

In order to verify this idea that Adam was a god who fell from the Sky, we need to confirm that he fell into the underworld, whence he would have later emerged into the world above. Inevitably, then, we must ask: "Where was the Garden of Eden?". Was it possibly the underworld, or a place in the underworld?

Biblical scholars have naturally assumed that the ancient definition of a garden was the same as a modern definition of a garden. They have therefore looked for possible locations of the Garden of Eden in various paradisiacal sites around the ancient Near East.

Unfortunately for scholars, this *assumption* of a garden-like garden is fundamentally unsound. According to the ancient Egyptians, a garden could mean the underworld; hence in Spell 111 of the Coffin Texts, the king, who had become Osiris, Lord of the Underworld, stated: "I am the god of reckoning in the Garden of Silence."[70] Similarly, in Spell 686, we hear about a 'garden' containing evil snakes, which was 'in the realm of the dead', i.e. in the underworld.[71] Furthermore, in a famous Sumerian legend entitled *Inanna and Shukallituda*, the goddess Inanna descended into an underworld which was portrayed as a 'garden', and the goddess ended up being raped by a 'gardener'.[72]

Might the Hebrew Garden of Eden be alluding to the same idea? It is a fact that the Hebrew word for 'garden' was *gan*, stemming from the verb *ganan*, which meant 'to hedge in' or 'to protect'. Apparently, the term *gan* was associated with *a walled enclosure*, and was thus envisaged as something like an 'enclosed park' or a 'walled garden'.[73]

This idea of the walled enclosure is familiar to us, for 'wall' was an ancient metaphor for the ceiling of the underworld, or a planetary crust. The ancient underworld would thus be, literally, a walled enclosure, and indeed a walled garden, on the basis of the Egyptian traditions cited above.

Was the Garden of Eden thus the underworld? Were Adam and Eve created in the underworld?

The word 'Eden' is an extremely interesting word, which has etymological connections to the Sumerian E.DIN, literally meaning 'The Abode of the Gods', but also meaning 'the plain' (as in the Akkadian *edinnu*). What, we might ask, is the connection between a plain and an abode of the gods?

The answer comes to us from the Sumerian *Lamentation Texts*:

It was a day when the weapon sent forth from above wrecked the city
    as if with a pickaxe.

> On that day *Heaven was crushed*, Earth was smitten, the face of it was
> smothered by the storm.
> Heaven was darkened, was overcast with shadow – *it was turned into
> the underworld.*[74]

What this passage tells us is that the underworld was filled by a 'crushed'
Heaven – in other words, a *crushed 'mountain'*.[75] And the poetic
antithesis of a mountain is *a plain*. It therefore follows that the abode of
the gods (E.DIN) was also a plain (E.DIN), which was in the underworld.
Hence the abode of the Anunnaki gods was in the underworld.

To illustrate this point, consider the following account of the creation
from the legend of Ziusudra:

> After Anu, Enlil, Enki and Ninharsag
> Had fashioned the black-headed ones,
> Vegetation luxuriated from the earth, from the earth,
> Animals, four-legged creatures of *the plain*, were brought artfully
> into existence.[76]

Note the use of the word 'plain' (E.DIN). If we replay the last line of this
citation, but substituting the original Sumerian term E.DIN for 'plain', we
read:

> Animals, four-legged creatures of E.DIN, were brought artfully
> into existence.

As emphasised in the previous chapter, these 'animals' were created in
the underworld, and hence the E.DIN ('the plain') was the Sumerian
underworld.

In *The Epic of Gilgamesh*, we read the following intriguing line in
connection with Gilgamesh's descent into the forest of the underworld:

> To the . . . garden of E.DIN he directed his step.
> The . . .-tree, the willow, the apple-tree, the box-tree, the . . .-tree he
> felled there.[77]

Might this 'garden of E.DIN' be equivalent to the biblical Garden of
Eden?[78]

There is another interesting parallel between the book of Genesis and
the Sumerian passages cited above. In chapter eight, we concluded that
the black-headed ones were not mankind as we know it, but the meteoric
seed of mankind, and hence they preceded the creation of vegetation and
animals in the underworld. It is a sequence of creation which would be
otherwise anomalous.

Amazingly, the book of Genesis contains the same anomaly. In

Genesis 2, we read how the human (Adam) was asked to name the various animals which God had created:

> And the LORD God said: "It is not good that the man should be alone, I shall make a sustainer-beside-him." And the LORD God fashioned from the soil every beast of the field and every fowl of the air, and brought each of them to the human to see what he would name them.[79]

If we read this passage carefully, we discover that it contradicts Genesis 1 by asserting that the human had been created *before* the animals. Scholars have tended to sidestep this point, for it makes no sense to them. But it does make sense to us, when we recognise that animals could exist (mythically speaking) in the underworld. It thus becomes clear that Adam was not a real human, but a seed of mankind in the underworld, and hence the sequence of creation in Genesis 2 follows the same sequence as in the creation legend of Ziusudra.

This would imply that the Garden of Eden *was* the underworld. And this, in turn, would explain why Adam and Eve were created in the Garden of Eden in a state of innocence and nakedness. Let us recall the opening passage of the Sumerian legend entitled *The Dispute between Cattle and Grain*:

> Like mankind when first created,
> The Anunnaki knew not the eating of bread,
> *Knew not the dressing of garments*,
> Ate plants with their mouths like sheep,
> Drank water from the ditch.

The Two Edens

We turn now to the biblical passages which deal with the locations of Eden and the Garden of Eden.[80] It must be said that these passages are extremely complex, and are quite confusing to the uneducated eye. Some sense can be made of them, however, once we apply the template of the exploded planet cult, along with the idea that Adam was cast down from Heaven to Earth. Our starting point, then, is the presumption that Adam was originally expelled from a heavenly Eden, at which point he was turned into the Garden of Eden in the underworld.

Once this approach is taken, it becomes evident that the account of man's creation in Genesis 2 is actually a composite of two separate legends – a short version and a long version. The short version comes first in Genesis 2:7, where God formed the human from the 'soil' of the Earth. Then comes the long version dealing with the placement of the human in Eden and the Garden of Eden. If these two accounts are not segregated in the mind of the reader, a nonsensical situation arises, in which God seemingly creates the human on Earth and then puts him in Heaven, only to then cast him back down to the Earth.

We will focus our attention, then, on the long version of the creation in Genesis 2, and hopefully it can then be demonstrated clearly that we are dealing with a movement of the first human (Adam) between two Edens – a heavenly Eden, and a Garden of Eden in the underworld.

What is the evidence for two Edens? In fact, the evidence has been staring us in the face all along in Genesis 2:10, which literally says:

And a river went out of Eden to water the garden.[81]

If there was only one Eden, how could it be that the river would only water the garden of Eden *by going out of Eden*?

The answer is the Mesopotamian solution – namely that this river coming out of Eden was *a celestial river*, which stretched from Heaven to Earth.[82] Therefore, the river went out of the heavenly Eden (as a result of the catastrophe which has been occulted from Genesis) and watered the Garden of Eden in the underworld of the Earth. (Readers should recall the legends of how the Nile, Tigris and Euphrates all fell from Heaven into the underworld.)

A close reading of Genesis chapters 2-3 provides confirmation that there were indeed two Edens involved in the creation of Adam (though not Eve, for the reasons cited earlier). In order to perceive this, it is necessary to have a little knowledge of ancient ankiography, namely to know that 'east' is the direction of Heaven, and 'west' the direction of Earth, with the underworld being the farthermost point in the 'westerly' direction. One can then follow the two stages in the creation of the human (Adam) as follows.

Firstly, we are told that God placed the human *in the garden which was in the east*:

And the LORD God planted a garden eastward in Eden, and He placed there the human he had formed.[83]

Then, we read that God placed the human *a second time*:

And the LORD God *took the human and set him down in the Garden of Eden* to till it and watch it.[84]

Note that in this passage God 'took' the human (Adam) as if he already existed, which indeed he did. The human was taken from the 'eastward' or heavenly Eden, and set down in the 'western' Garden of Eden.

This double placement of the human can be proven quite easily, by negating the opposite theory of single placement. Assume for the moment that the human was placed only once, which according to the first of the two passages above would be in the 'eastern' Eden. Then look at the account of the human's expulsion from the Garden of Eden:

> And the LORD God sent the human forth from the Garden of Eden, to till the soil from which he had been taken. Thus he drove out the human, and *set up east of the Garden of Eden the cherubim, and a flaming, whirling sword*, to guard the way to the Tree of Life.[85]

If the human had still been in the 'eastern' Eden, and was expelled therefrom, the positioning of the cherubim and sword to the 'east' of Eden would have required the human to be expelled to a place *even farther to the east*. This simply does not work, according to the laws of ancient ankiography, for the human ought to have ended up in the 'west', i.e. on, or in, the Earth. Thus the single placement theory can be negated.

The ankiography *does* work, however, if the human was first placed 'eastward in Eden', i.e. in Heaven, then 'set down in the Garden of Eden' in the 'west', i.e. in the Earth's underworld, and finally expelled from the underworld up to the Earth. This would indeed require the placement of the cherubim and sword to the 'east' of the Garden of Eden (the surface of the Earth being 'east' of the underworld, which was the land of the 'west'). *QED.*

Confirmation of this understanding is found in the legend of the King of Tyre, cited earlier, where 'Eden the garden of God' was equated with 'the holy mountain of God'. This 'mountain' must have been in the heavens in order to make sense of the claim that the King of Tyre had been thrown down in fire to the Earth. This, it would seem, was the archetypal fall of man, which applied as much to Adam as it did to the King of Tyre.

In summary, then, there were two Edens, or two 'gardens' of Eden, and two separate expulsions of man. Adam was moved firstly from the heavens into the underworld, and secondly from the underworld onto the surface of the Earth.

The Biblical Flood

After Adam and Eve were expelled from the Garden of Eden, they proceeded, so we are told, to propagate the entire human race. And in the sense that the expulsion of Adam and Eve was from the underworld, it would seem that they propagated the true human race, i.e. the flesh-and-blood people of the world above.

Nevertheless, the eyebrows must be raised at the incredible longevity attributed to Adam and Eve's descendants, ranging from 777 years in the case of Lamech, to 969 years in the case of Methuselah. One is reminded of the equally unbelievable reigns attributed to the god-like kings in the early sections of the Sumerian Kings List. Has more than one archaic legend been combined here?

After this expulsion from the underworld, various events occurred, but the first event of major significance occurred during the tenth generation, when the Great Flood was sent by God to destroy mankind. It was at this time that a righteous man named Noah was chosen by God to become the saviour of the seed of mankind and all living creatures. Noah, we are told, was six hundred years old at the time.[86]

If we accept the biblical record at face value, Noah was a descendant of Adam, and thus a true flesh-and-blood man. He would therefore have built his Ark on the Earth, just like the Old Testament says.

But can the biblical record be taken at face value? Already we have seen evidence that the Old Testament was (and is) a compilation of various legends, some of which were distorted from their original meaning (e.g. Adam and Eve), and others of which were amended to conceal the once physical nature of God, the Father-of-Beginning. In these circumstances, our suspicions should be put on alert.

So, was Noah really a descendant of Adam, and was he really a man? Or was he an adaptation of an earlier Flood-hero, who came down from the heavens? Let's take a look at the evidence.

The Genesis story of the Flood begins by describing a time when mankind was multiplying on the face of the Earth. The lines are immediately evocative of the *Atra-Hasis Epic*, where the god Enlil was moved to destroy mankind in order to quell its excessive noise.

But this is only one of a whole series of correspondences. The *Atra-Hasis Epic* describes how Enlil cursed the ground, just as Yahweh apparently did in the book of Genesis.[87] Moreover, a period of six hundred years elapsed between Yahweh's cursing of the ground (when Noah was born) and the time of the Flood (when Noah was six hundred years old), which tallies exactly with the six-hundred-year interludes cited in the *Atra-Hasis Epic*.[88] It is difficult to believe that this is a coincidence, especially in view of all the other similarities between the two stories – for example: the seven-day countdown to the Flood, the building of the Ark, and the final scene of the sacrifice and its pleasing smell.[89]

In view of all these similarities, it is a reasonable proposition that the biblical story of Noah's Ark is either based on the *Atra-Hasis Epic*, or that both spring from another very similar but older legend.

Whichever is the case, I have already demonstrated how the *Atra-Hasis* version of this legend represents either an adaptation of, or a misunderstanding of, the original story, whereby the hero sailed down to the 'mountain' of Earth from the heavenly planet of Shuruppak. Consequently, I predict that we should find some anomalies in the story of Noah, just as we did in the story of Atra-Hasis. Let us now take a look and see what we find.

Before describing the story of the Flood and the Ark, we should remind ourselves of a very important piece of context which the Old Testament provides. In Genesis 6, the story of the Flood is introduced by the mysterious legend of the Sons-of-God who fathered the giants (Nephilim) – a legend which we have already decoded as one of ex-planetary meteorites entering into the womb of the Earth.

It was this interplanetary co-mingling which caused Yahweh to pronounce his famous curse: "My breath shall not remain in the human forever, for he is but flesh. Let his days be a hundred and twenty years."[90] He then went on to announce that:

> "I will destroy man, whom I have created, from the face of the Earth – man and beast, and the creeping things, and the birds of the air – for I am grieved that I have made them."[91]

The Great Flood, we are told, occurred in the six hundredth year of Noah's life, on the seventeenth day of the second month:

> On that day all the springs of the great Deep burst forth, and the floodgates of Heaven were opened. And rain fell on the Earth for forty days and forty nights.[92]

It is comforting to discover that this Flood was of the very same nature as all the other Great Floods of ancient Near Eastern tradition, i.e. it came from a heavenly source.

Note the reference in this passage to 'the springs of the great Deep' which 'burst forth'. Although it is commonly assumed that this refers to the springs of the underworld bursting forth, it is more likely, in my opinion, that it refers to the springs of the great Deep *in the heavens*.[93]

The 'great Deep', it should be noted, is an ambiguous term, because according to the ancient way of thinking there were originally two Deeps – the waters of the planet in the depths of Heaven, and the waters of the Earth deep below. This classic case of 'as above so below' is elucidated considerably by *Enuma Elish*, which explains that the Apsu began its existence in the depths of space, but was cast down to Earth, into the underworld.[94] This explains the biblical references to the dividing of the Deeps.[95]

If my interpretation is correct, the bursting of the springs of the great Deep would be identical to the opening of 'the floodgates of Heaven', and thus the Bible would be telling us *twice* that the Flood came from the heavens – just to make sure that the message got through.[96]

Lest any fans of the weather-gods theory have survived the reading of this book thus far, it should be emphasised for their benefit that 'the floodgates of Heaven' meant exactly what it said – that the Great Flood came from Heaven, *not* from the atmosphere of the Earth. The Hebrew word used for these 'floodgates' (variously translated as 'casements'), was *arubot*, which meant literally a window or a window-like niche.[97] The *celestial* nature of these windows can be amply demonstrated by the identical tradition which existed in ancient Egypt, which held that the Winding Waterway, which stretched between Earth and Heaven, contained 'windows' top and bottom.[98] Furthermore, the Flood originated from the far, 'eastern' gate of the Winding Waterway, as the deceased king made clear in this citation from the Coffin Texts:

> They ferry me across... they row me on the Waterway of the Sky-windows... I hear the noise of the Flood at the eastern gate of the Sky.[99]

In addition to this, the juxtaposition of the biblical Flood story with the Sons-of-God incident leaves little doubt as to the fact that the intended meaning was a Flood not just of waters, but of meteorites too.

Noah's Ark

Before we move on to the subject of Noah, and the clues which link him *personally* to the idea of meteorites, a few words should be said about the intriguing subject of his Ark.

The Hebrew term for Noah's 'Ark' was *teba*, meaning 'box'. This is odd. Why did the Hebrews call Noah's Ark a 'box', when they had a perfectly good word for a ship?[100] Might it have had something to do with an archaic version of the legend reported by Plutarch – that the Egyptian god Osiris had been shut in a box, and cast into the Nile (the *celestial* Nile – which carried the box down to the Earth)?

The term *teba*, however, had a second meaning. Not only did it mean 'box', but also 'to sink'.[101] This is more and more curious. It can hardly be said that Noah's Ark 'sank'; it was merely *lowered gently* onto the top of the mountains of Ararat.[102] Unless... could this word *teba* be a distant echo of the box of Osiris, which really did 'sink' through the celestial waters when it fell from Heaven to Earth? It has to be said that a submersible box is a fairly good description of Utnapishtim's boat, although a submersible *sphere* would be even better.

Was Noah a celestial sailor after all?

The Mystery of Noah

An enigmatic text among the Dead Sea Scrolls states that Noah was 'born in the night' and 'came out perfect', with 'a weight of 350 shekels', and then 'slept until the division of days'.[103] The Scrolls go on to portray Noah as a mysterious wisdom-figure – one who knew 'the Three Books', as well as the 'secrets of mankind', and the 'secrets of all living things'. He was one who had 'understanding of the mysteries', and who would one day 'reveal mysteries like the Highest Angels'.[104]

The *Zohar* adds to this intrigue surrounding Noah with its assertion that he was 'the Foundation of the Universe'.[105] Could this mean that Noah was the *underworld* foundation of the universe comprising Heaven and Earth?[106]

Whatever the answer might be, these texts give the impression that there was some mysterious secret surrounding Noah – something about him that the Bible perhaps did not reveal.

In the Book of Enoch, from the Dead Sea Scrolls, we further read that Noah's birth was extremely unusual, and Lamech (his father in the Old Testament) was not actually his real father at all. The Book of Enoch relates that, one day, the patriarch Lamech had returned home from a long journey and found that his wife, Bath-Enosh, had given birth to Noah, who was a mighty strange baby boy:

> His body was white as snow and red as the blooming of a rose, and the hair of his head and his locks were white as wool, and his eyes were fair. And when he opened his eyes, he lighted up the whole house like the Sun, and the whole house was very bright. And thereupon he arose in the hands of the midwife, opened his mouth, and spoke about the Lord of Righteousness.[107]

When Lamech saw the unusual child, Noah, he was furious with Bath-Enosh, and accused his wife of sleeping with a stranger. Despite Bath-Enosh's protestations of innocence, Lamech went off to consult his father Methuselah, saying:

> "I have begotten a strange son, different from and unlike man, and resembling the Sons of the God in Eden; and his nature is not like you and me... And so it seems to me that he is not born from my stock, but

from that of the angels."[108]

Ah, those angelic Sons-of-God again – could it be that Noah resembled a meteorite? Anyway, Methuselah was unsure how to respond, and went off to ask *his* father Enoch, who dwelt with the angels 'at the ends of the earth'. In something of an anti-climax, Enoch informed Methuselah that the baby boy Noah was indeed the son of Lamech (although the text clearly acknowledges that this was a matter of some controversy). Furthermore, Enoch informed Methuselah that a great Flood would soon sweep across the Earth and destroy mankind. The boy was destined to survive the Flood and become the progenitor of a new human race in its aftermath. For this reason he would be called Noah.[109]

What should we make of all this? It is the Old Testament story *but with a difference*. Noah, it seems, was born on the Earth, but seeded from the Sky. We are told quite clearly that he was 'different from and unlike man'. Was he thus a Seed of Mankind, born in the underworld?

Let's now turn to the Bible to see whether the Hebrew priests themselves might have alluded to this mysterious alter ego of Noah.

Immediately we find a crucial clue in the account of the first thing Noah did in the immediate aftermath of the Flood:

> Noah began to be a husbandman [a man of the soil], and he planted a vineyard. When he drank some of its wine, he became drunk and lay uncovered inside his tent. And Ham, the father of Canaan, saw his father's nakedness and told his two brothers outside. And Shem and Japheth took a garment and laid it across both their shoulders and went backwards, and covered their father's nakedness. Their faces were turned backwards so that they saw not their father's nakedness.
> When Noah awoke from his wine, he knew what his younger son had done to him, and he said: "Cursed be Canaan. The lowest of slaves he shall be unto his brothers."[110]

I shall now explain how this passage contains a number of astonishing esoteric symbolisms, which would have been readily recognisable to those who had been initiated into the ancient Mysteries.

Firstly, note the fact that Noah became a 'man of the soil' and planted a vineyard. This is exactly what we would expect from an interplanetary seed-like meteorite. As for the vineyard, a whole chapter could be written on the esoteric symbolism of the grape and the vine. We will pass over this subject for now, but it will reappear as a recurrent theme, both later in this chapter and in subsequent chapters.[111]

Secondly, note that Noah was drunk. It is vital to realise that drunkenness was an ancient idiom for falling down, and falling down was an esoteric allusion to the falling down of the gods from Heaven. Thus, we are being told, *esoterically*, that Noah had fallen to Earth. As an example of this idiom, consider Yahweh's 'cup of wrath', from which nations would drink, get drunk, and fall over.[112] Think also of the Greek legend in which the Sky-god Uranus came down *'drunken, to penetrate the body of the Earth'*.[113]

Thirdly, note the fact that Noah was asleep and naked inside his 'tent'. The sleep motif has already been encountered in the legend of Adam's fall from Heaven, and in the laying-low of the god Apsu by Ea (Enki). It was closely associated with the idea of drunkenness and thus with falling down from Heaven. As for the nakedness, this is a motif which we found in the Sumerian legend of the Anunnaki and 'mankind', and also in the biblical legend of Adam and Eve. Once again, the motif is associated intimately with the underworld.

What about the 'tent' in which Noah fell asleep? Earlier I passed comment on a Muslim legend that God had sent down a tent from the sky to protect Adam. The man-in-the-tent motif thus seems to imply *a covering over* of one who had fallen from Heaven, as Adam had.[114] This, in turn, implies that the one being covered was *in the underworld*.

Let us now return to the nakedness, and to the peculiar story of how the blood-line of Ham was punished as a result of looking upon the naked body of Noah lying inside his tent. It is a legend which has always confounded biblical scholars, who have suggested that something important must have occurred between Ham and Noah – something which was excluded from the biblical account.[115]

On the contrary, nothing significant has been excluded from the account. All that is required to decode this enigmatic passage is a realisation that *Noah was a meteorite which emitted a tremendously bright and powerful light.* Ham's mistake was to look upon this fiery light, whereas his two brothers Shem and Japheth walked in backwards, to avoid looking upon Noah. It was no coincidence, I suggest, that the Bible identifies Ham's people as those with black and swarthy complexions. In the eyes of the Hebrew priests, these black and swarthy complexions had originated (mythically speaking) from Ham's face to face encounter with the fallen meteorite.[116]

A ridiculous suggestion? Actually, no. Consider the Greek legend of Deucalion and the Flood. Zeus, we are told, decided to destroy the entire race of mankind, and therefore unleashed the Flood from Mount Olympus. All living creatures perished except for one man, Deucalion, and his wife Pyrrha (her name incidentally means 'Fiery Red'), who were both *supposedly* human beings. We should note in passing that

Deucalion's name literally meant 'new wine sailor'.[117] Thus, like Noah, Deucalion was a man-of-the-vine. Except that neither of them were really men at all.

This suspicion concerning Deucalion (and indeed his wife Pyrrha) is confirmed by the events which unfolded after Deucalion's Ark came to rest on the mountain. Instead of doing what comes naturally for a man and a woman, Deucalion and Pyrrha *beseeched the gods* to renew the population of mankind. The gods then gave Deucalion and his wife the following instruction:

"Shroud your heads – throw the bones of your mother behind you!"[118]

Deucalion and Pyrrha thereupon proceeded to pick up 'stones' from the bank of the river, and throw these 'stones' over their shoulders, *while hiding their faces*. Miraculously, the 'stones' turned into men and women, and the world was instantly repopulated.[119]

What were these 'stones', and why were they compared to the 'bones of the mother'? Hitherto, scholars have assumed that the 'mother' was the Earth, and that the stones or bones were the rocks of the Earth. But in the light of the Mesopotamian tradition that the Flood involved rocks as well as waters, it seems much more likely that these loose-lying 'stones' were meteorites, and that the 'mother' was the *planetary Sky*-goddess.[120] The idea that the 'stones' were 'bones' then fits neatly with our earlier conclusions concerning the ribs of the gods, and the rib of Adam which impregnated Eve. Finally, the springing up of men and women from these 'stones' also fits perfectly with the ancient belief that meteorites were the seeds of mankind.

Now, what about the fact that Deucalion and Pyrrha were told to shroud their heads, while throwing the 'stones'? Well, if the 'stones' symbolised fiery meteorites, then the aversion of the eyes would make perfect sense, for the miraculous transformation would indeed have been too dangerous to watch with the naked eye.

In the light of this legend, is it far-fetched to suggest that Shem and Japheth averted their eyes from Noah's naked body because Noah was a not a man but a meteorite?

Lest there be any doubt about this, the Bible attests to the fact that it was extremely dangerous to look upon the face of a god. A classic example is found in the book of Exodus, where Moses met God at Mount Horeb, the site of the 'burning bush'. The text informs us that 'Moses hid his face, for he was afraid to look upon God.'[121] Later, however, at Mount Sinai, Moses plucked up his courage and asked God to "show me thy glory", but God replied:

"You canst not see my face, for no man shall see me there and live."[122]

Eventually, God allowed Moses to see his back parts, as he passed by, but warned again that "my face must not be seen."[123] The Ethiopian book *Kebra Nagast* preserves a most interesting variation of this legend:

> Again Moses spoke unto God and said: "Show me they face." And God said unto Moses: "No-one can look upon my face and live, but only as in a mirror. Turn thy face to the west, and thou shalt see on the rock the reflection of my face." When Moses saw the shadow of the face of God, his own face shone with *a brightness which was seven times brighter than the Sun*, and the light was so strong that the Children of Israel could not look upon his face except through a veil.[124]

Is it thus unreasonable to presume that Ham's face was blackened (mythically speaking) from his encounter with the fallen body of Noah?

In summary, Noah was not a man but a god – a fallen meteorite, lying in the underworld. Hence he was fathered by 'the guardians of the Sky'. Hence he resembled the Sons-of-God. Hence his hair was 'as white as wool' and he lit up the whole house like the Sun when he opened his eyes. Hence he was a 'man of the soil', who planted a vineyard. Hence he fell down, drunk and naked. Hence he was covered over by a 'tent'. Hence his body was not to be looked at. How many more esoteric clues do we need?

I close this chapter, and our study of Noah, with a fitting epitaph to a hero who was surely *not* a human being. In the words of the Old Testament:

> And Noah lived after the Flood *three hundred and fifty years.* And all the days of Noah were *nine hundred and fifty years.* And then he died.[125]

* * * * *

CHAPTER TEN

PARTING THE WATERS

**And Moses stretched out his hand over the sea...
and the waters were divided. The children of Israel
went into the midst of the sea upon dry ground,
with a wall of water on their right and on their left.**

(The book of Exodus, chapter 14)

In the previous chapter, we revisited a number of biblical legends – the creation of Earth and Heaven, the creation of Adam and Eve, the expulsion of Adam and Eve from the Garden of Eden, and finally the story of Noah's Ark and the Great Flood. We re-examined these legends in the light of our new understanding of meteorites and exploded planet cults, and we came to some shocking conclusions.

In every case – *every case without exception* – we discovered that the Bible was *not* telling the whole truth, but, on the contrary, was muddling along with a series of *half-truths or outright lies*. Let's refresh our memories concerning the main examples:

* *The battle of God* against Rahab was omitted from Genesis 1.
* *God's physical death* was omitted from Genesis 1.
* *God's creation of the gods* was omitted from Genesis 1 (by dropping the opening *aleph*).
* *God's creation of the metaphysical Heaven* was concealed behind a clever code-word, the 'Light', as if to deceive the uninitiated.
* *God's creation of the seven heavens* was concealed behind a series of coded recitations, again as if to deceive the uninitiated.
* *The true nature of God's heavenly abode* was concealed by presenting it, and him, as an unfathomable mystery.
* *The true nature, and source, of the Flood* was concealed likewise.
* *The heavenly origin of the Flood-hero, Noah,* was occulted by using

highly esoteric code-words and allegories.
* *The heavenly origin of man* (and Adam's true identity) was occulted behind a series of ambiguous and misleading statements.
* *The origin of Adam from Eve* (Mother Earth) was twisted 180 degrees to make Eve come out of Adam (this amounts to a blatant lie).
* *The true location of the Garden of Eden* was also occulted behind a series of ambiguous and misleading statements.

Now, I do not wish to criticise the Bible in any way. Perhaps it is better to criticise ourselves for being so naive as to think that the Hebrew priests would actually have exposed their priestly secrets *in writing* for all to see. That has *never* been the way of the world, as should have been made clear in the first chapter of this book. In the Orphic Mysteries, for example, the knowledge of the true God was a great Secret-of-secrets, which was revealed only to the highest level initiates. Even then, the secret startled their ears and overturned their preconceived opinions. It is a fact that ancient priesthoods and mystery schools *did* keep secrets, especially concerning such things as God and the mystery of the underworld. Perhaps it is time we recognised this fact and learned to deal with it.

To re-emphasise the point, I do not wish to criticise the Hebrew priesthood or the Bible. If we were in the position of the Hebrew priests thousands of years ago, we might well have felt pressured to take the same course of action. Perhaps in those days, *c.* 1000-500 BC, the pagans of Canaan and Egypt were becoming *presumptuous* as to their right to an afterlife. Perhaps the profound nature of God was being *devalued* by a free-for-all among the common people, who were trading in what were perceived to be the sacred secrets which were required to ascend to Heaven. Imagine how we – as learned priests – would have reacted.

Perhaps this was the motivation behind the Israelite movement. If we take a step back and examine the religious philosophy which was recorded in the Old Testament, we find, quite clearly, *a denial of the afterlife.*[1] As early as Genesis 1, it was stated that God had removed himself to a place *above the Expanse*, to the highest heights, i.e. beyond even the most distant visible stars. The implication is clear: the abode of God was not to be sullied by the presence of man. Hence the belief that God had moved so swiftly to destroy the Tower of Babel (Genesis 11).

It is a philosophy best summed up by Psalm 115, which stated:

The highest heavens belong to the LORD, but the Earth he has given to the children of men.[2]

And this philosophy extended unto death. Hence as early as Genesis 3, the fate of man was made perfectly clear by God himself:

> "By the sweat of thy brow, thou shalt eat bread, till thou return unto the soil. For from there thou wast taken – for dust thou art, and unto dust shalt thou return."[3]

Elsewhere, the Old Testament informs us that this return to dust amounted to a return to a state of nothingness and non-existence – in the dingy depths of a subterranean realm known as Sheol. There, the life of every man would be snuffed out for all eternity. In the poetic words of Job: "As the cloud vanishes and is gone, so he who goes down to the grave does not return... at least there is hope for a tree, that if it is cut down it will sprout again... but man dies and wastes away; he breathes his last and is no more."[4]

Such beliefs are not to be judged by us, but merely understood. Indeed, it is only by understanding the Hebrew religious philosophy that we can rationalise why certain legends were changed and occulted in the way they were.

Why, for example, did the priests disguise the fact that God had created a metaphysical Heaven – code-named 'the Light' in Genesis 1? The simple answer is that the context of the story would have made it perfectly evident that God was in the underworld when he separated the Light from the darkness. And such a disclosure would have opened Pandora's Box, so to speak, for it would have led to the revelation that God had fallen physically into the Earth. And this, in turn, would have implied that God had died physically, which would have implied that he had then resurrected himself to a metaphysical 'life'.

Why was this a problem? Simply because this was the religious tradition of Egypt, concerning the death and resurrection of Osiris. And it was this central belief which had caused all the problems – by inspiring every common man in Egypt to imagine that he, too, could emulate Osiris, by surviving death and ascending to Heaven for a metaphysical afterlife.

This obsession with the afterlife, as mentioned earlier, was what the Hebrew priests wished to eradicate. It is thus perfectly understandable that the Hebrew writers of Genesis decided to occult the death and resurrection of their God. Their religious philosophy would have allowed them no other course of action.

By the same token, the Hebrew priests could not have allowed the people to know that patriarchs such as Adam and Noah had come down from Heaven, nor that Adam and Noah had been in the underworld (their presence there would have been a dead giveaway). This required that the fall of Adam be twisted from a *physical fall* (from the heavenly Eden) to a *moral fall* (in the Garden of Eden); and it also required that Noah be given a 'make-over' to provide him with a new *terrestrial* lineage.

If the priests had not followed this course of action, the people would have known all about their mythical heavenly origin (either via Adam or Noah), and they would thus have felt that they *belonged* in Heaven, with God, after death.

It is also perfectly understandable that the Hebrew priests occulted God's creation of the gods – a rather delicate issue in view of the fact that the priests were urging the people to abandon the pagan gods and worship a sole God.

Furthermore, we can understand why the priests lied about Eve being taken out of Adam, when in fact the reverse was the case. The reason for the lie was simply this: to acknowledge the true story would have been to acknowledge a deity – Mother Earth – with powers rivalling those of God himself.

All in all, then, the Hebrew priests had some very understandable reasons for telling the Israelites a mixture of lies and half-truths about a religious heritage which they had once shared with all the pagan peoples of the ancient world.

The Exodus Story

As mentioned in the previous chapter, the Hebrew priests inculcated the belief among the people that God – Yahweh-Elohim – was taking a personal interest in the welfare of the nation. Thus the people were encouraged to do good deeds, that Yahweh-Elohim might reward them, and to avoid bad deeds, lest Yahweh-Elohim punish them. And all of these rewards and punishments were to come in this life – in the here-and-now – *not* in the afterlife, as the pagans believed.

In order to stamp this belief in the minds of the people, the Hebrew élite reminded the people constantly of how Yahweh-Elohim had saved their ancestors in an age long ago – how he had rescued them physically from slavery in Egypt, given them the Ten Commandments at Mount Sinai, and brought them eventually to the promised land of Israel. All of this, it was said, had been achieved thanks to the mighty hand of Yahweh-Elohim, God-of-gods, who had intervened personally to destroy all of Israel's enemies. It was an act of redemption which effectively gave birth to the independent nation of Israel, and it was the defining moment of Yahweh-Elohim's career, establishing him as an unrivalled Lord of History.

But was this legend – commonly known as the Exodus – all that it appeared to be? Or was it yet another example of occultation, half-truths and deception? In this chapter, we shall take a fresh look at the evidence.

We pick up the biblical story at the end of the book of Genesis, at the time of the twelfth generation of patriarchs after the Flood. These were the days of Jacob, whose name, significantly, was changed to 'Israel', and it was then that the Israelites went down into Egypt, apparently because of a famine in their own land.

Initially, the Israelites prospered, under the guidance of Joseph, but eventually things turned sour when a new king arose, 'who knew not Joseph'. This king, whom the Bible simply calls Pharaoh, enslaved the Israelites and oppressed them ruthlessly. The Israelites let out groans and cries, which went up to the heavens and were heard by God, who remembered his covenant with Israel. It was then that God decided to redeem Israel, not unilaterally, but with the assistance of a man named Moses.

Moses was eighty years old when he received his commission from God in the famous vision of the burning bush at Mount Horeb:

> And the angel of the LORD appeared unto him in a flame of fire out of the midst of a bush. And he looked – and behold, the bush burned with fire, but the bush was not consumed.[5]

When Moses went over to the burning bush, God spoke to him from within it, and urged Moses to go to Egypt, for he was to assist God in the release of the suffering Israelites. It was then that Moses (along with his brother Aaron) went before Pharaoh uttering the immortal words: "Let my people go."

Readers will probably be familiar with what happened next, as Pharaoh repeatedly refused to co-operate. Psalm 105 of the Old Testament summarises the famous 'ten plagues' which God inflicted upon Egypt:

> He [Yahweh] sent Moses his servant, and Aaron whom he had chosen.
> They showed his (miraculous) signs among them, and wonders in the
>   land of Ham [Egypt].
> He sent darkness, and made the land dark...
> He turned their waters into blood, and slew their fish.
> Their land teemed with frogs, even in the bedrooms of the kings.
> He spoke, and there came swarms of flies, and gnats in all the land.
> He turned their rain into hail – flaming fire in their land.
> He struck down their vines and fig-trees, broke the trees of the land.
> He spoke, and locusts came, caterpillars too, countless in number;

They ate up all green things in the land, devoured the fruit of the soil.
Then he struck down all the first-born in their land, representatives of
 all their strength.[6]

As Psalm 105 makes clear, the climax of these ten plagues occurred
when Yahweh himself passed through the land of Egypt and struck down
all the first-born. Significantly, however, he *passed over* the houses of
the Israelites, who were ordered to protect themselves by smearing the
blood of lambs on the door-frames of their houses (the symbolism of this
act is important and we will return to it in the next chapter).

This, then, was the famous night of the Passover, and it turned out to
be the last straw for Pharaoh, who finally relented and ordered the
Israelites out of his land. Remarkably, the Israelites were said to have
plundered the Egyptians as they left, taking gold, silver and clothing
from the terrified inhabitants.[7]

The Exodus of the Israelites proceeded eastwards, towards the Red
Sea, led by Yahweh (or, by a variant tradition, the angel of Yahweh) in a
most striking manner:

And the LORD went before them by day in a pillar of cloud, to lead
them on the way, and by night in a pillar of fire, to give them light, so
that they could travel by day and night.[8]

As the Israelites reached the Red Sea, Yahweh told Moses to divide its
waters by raising his staff and stretching out his hand. Then Yahweh
blew a strong east wind, and lo and behold:

The waters were divided, and the Israelites went into the midst of the
Sea upon the dry (ground), with a wall of water on their right hand and
on their left.[9]

Pharaoh, however, had changed his mind about letting the Israelites go,
and had begun to pursue them. The Egyptian army gave chase to the
Israelites along the dried-up channel through the Red Sea, but Yahweh
forced them to a halt by jamming the wheels of their chariots, and then
caused the waters of the Red Sea to pour back into the dried-up channel.
Every last one of the Egyptians was drowned.

The Exodus then proceeded in less dramatic fashion through the desert
to Mount Sinai, and the Israelites underwent various trials and
tribulations which need not concern us here.

After three months, to the day, the Israelites arrived at the Desert of
Sinai, where they camped in front of Mount Sinai. It was then that
Yahweh called to Moses from out of the mountain, and told him that in
three days' time he would come down on Mount Sinai in the sight of all

the people. Intriguingly, Moses was warned that anyone who touched the mountain during these three days should be put to death – not by hand (lest the affliction be transmitted) but by means of arrows or stones.[10]

And so it came to pass, on the morning of the third day:

> There was thunder and lightning, and a thick cloud was upon the mountain, and there was a very loud trumpet blast... Mount Sinai was smoking in all its parts, because the LORD descended upon it in fire. And the smoke ascended like smoke from a furnace, and the whole mountain shook violently.[11]

As soon as this catastrophic manifestation of Yahweh was completed, Moses went up to the top of the mountain, into the thick cloud, and met his God face to face. In the days that followed, various meetings took place between Yahweh and Moses at the top of Mount Sinai. Sometimes Moses went up alone, but at other times he was accompanied by his brother Aaron, or by his assistant Joshua. On one occasion, seventy elders of Israel were allowed to ascend and see the God of Israel, who reportedly sat on 'something like a pavement of lapis lazuli'.[12]

On two occasions, Moses ascended to the top of the mountain and stayed with Yahweh for 'forty days and forty nights'. During the first of these meetings, Moses was given detailed instructions for the building of a sanctuary to the LORD, and for the construction of certain furnishings, including the Ark of the Covenant. Moses was also given the Ten Commandments (the foundation statement of ancient Israel), inscribed 'by the finger of God' on two 'tablets of stone'.[13]

It might well be that the second meeting of 'forty days and forty nights' was a variant tradition of the first meeting. In this legend, we are told that Moses ate no bread and drank no water during his stay. And on this occasion, when Moses eventually came down from the mountain, 'the skin of his face shone' and he was required to wear a veil when speaking with his fellow Israelites. Incidentally, the pretext for this second visit was to acquire new 'tablets of stone', since the earlier ones had supposedly been broken by Moses at the foot of the mountain.[14]

These turned out to be the last visible manifestations of Yahweh on Mount Sinai, but thereafter he continued to appear to the leaders of the Israelites using the Ark of the Covenant, which had been built in the desert during the Exodus. The Ark was thus a substitute for the mountain, and just as Yahweh had previously descended upon Mount Sinai in a thick cloud, so he now began to descend and settle above the Ark in a thick cloud.

For forty years, the Israelites wandered thus in the desert, taking orders from Yahweh, who repeatedly appeared to the high priest above the 'atonement cover' of the Ark – between the two cherubim. After these forty years, the Israelites came to the border of Canaan – the so-called 'promised land'.

What should we make of this Exodus story? Does it describe a historical event, or might there be more to it?

Few scholars today would deny that some kind of Israelite exodus *did* take place from Egypt to the promised land of Canaan.[15] But at the same time, most scholars would agree that the biblical story contains certain mythical elements, which lend a surreal nature to many aspects of the account. The parting of the Red Sea, for example, when read literally, cannot be explained scientifically. And considerable difficulties are encountered when one tries to explain how God could have descended upon Mount Sinai in fire.

Nor did the writers of the Old Testament even attempt to disguise the metaphysical nature of many of the events. Moses, we are told, ate and drank nothing whatsoever during the forty days and forty nights he spent with God – it was clearly a supernatural meeting.[16] And similarly, the clothes of the Israelites allegedly did not wear out during a full forty years of wandering in the desert.[17]

This mixing of history with myth, and physics with metaphysics, has caused endless confusion for biblical scholars, but one scholar who has shown more wisdom than most is Mircea Eliade, who once passed the following generalised comment about history and myth:

> The historical event in itself, however important, *does not remain in the popular memory*, nor does its recollection kindle the poetic imagination *save insofar as the particular historical event closely approaches a mythical model.*[18]

In other words, might it be that the Exodus of the Israelites *did* happen, but was recalled in later years by associating it with, in Eliade's words, 'a mythical model'? And what might that mythical model be?

Let's bear in mind, too, the highly individual character of the Hebrew culture. As we have seen, the Old Testament presents a very different picture from anything else in the ancient Near East. *Out* have gone the stories of the gods who were active in *mythical time, or sacred time,* and *in* have come stories about a God who was active in *historical time, or mundane time.*

In the light of such an approach to the divine-human interface, might it be that the legend of Exodus was altered to make it conform with the philosophy of a God who intervened during historical time? Might the true story of Exodus actually belong to the sacred beginnings of time?

Or, to put the question more bluntly, can we really be sure that the original Moses was a real flesh-and-blood man, who took a real flesh-and-blood people across a real sea to a real mountain?

Or might there be more to it?

The Mystery of Moses

A good place to start our investigation is with the man at the centre of the mystery, Moses – a unique figure in biblical history, of whom it was said 'never did there arise in Israel a prophet like Moses, whom the LORD knew face to face.'[19]

According to the book of Exodus, Moses was a 'goodly' or 'fine' baby; some translations even suggest that he was 'divinely beautiful'.[20] He was born, we are told, at a time when the Israelites were increasing and becoming too numerous in the land of Egypt, as a result of which Pharaoh had ordered all the male Israelite babies to be killed.[21] Consequently, the mother of Moses – Jochebed – hid her child for the first three months of his life.

When the child Moses could be hidden no longer, Jochebed put him in a papyrus ark and placed the ark by the bank of the river Nile, close to Pharaoh's palace. One day, Pharaoh's daughter found the ark, while walking beside the river, and adopted Moses – this no doubt being exactly what Jochebed had anticipated. It was Pharaoh's daughter in fact who bestowed the name 'Moses' on the child, saying: "I drew him out of the water."[22]

This is a very interesting legend, for it resembles several other divine birth legends in the ancient world. In the Hindu epic *Mahabharata*, for example, a child was hidden in a small basket, placed in a river, and subsequently adopted by a stranger. This child was said to be radiant, like a 'son of the Sun'.[23] In another similar legend, Romulus and Remus, the two founders of Rome, were abandoned on the flooding river Tiber in a trough, which floated downriver to the site of the future city of Rome.[24] And, in a third example of this 'abandoned child' motif, this time from Greek mythology, the infant Oedipus was locked in a chest and thrown into the sea, whereupon he was washed up on a distant shore and adopted by the royal household. The name Oedipus thus seems to derive from *Oedipais*, meaning 'son of the swelling sea'.[25]

The closest parallel to the Moses story, however, is found in the so-called 'birth legend' of Sargon, king of Agade, the ancient capital of the Akkadian people. It reads as follows:

I am Sargon, the mighty king, king of Agade.
My mother was a high priestess, my father I knew not.
The brother of my father loved [made love to?] the hills.
My city is Azupiranu, which is situated on the banks of the Euphrates.
My changeling mother conceived me, in secret she bore me.
She set me in a basket of reeds, she sealed my door with bitumen.
She cast me into the river which rose not over me.
The river bore me up, and carried me to Akki, the drawer of water...
Akki, the drawer of water, took me as his son and reared me.
Akki, the drawer of water, appointed me as his gardener.
While I was a gardener, Ishtar [Inanna] granted me her love,
And for four and . . . years I exercised kingship.[26]

It seems to me that this account of Sargon's birth is absolutely loaded
with *celestial significance*, as are all the other ancient tales of the
abandoned child. As we have seen in earlier chapters, the Mesopotamian
kings liked to imagine that they were Titans, born within the Earth from
a union of two fallen deities. The reference in this legend to the
'changeling mother' who conceived Sargon is thus almost certainly
aimed at Ninharsag, who transformed herself from a Sky mother-goddess
into an Earth mother-goddess – as did Hathor/Isis in ancient Egypt.

The most likely interpretation of Sargon's birth legend, therefore, is
that Sargon's changeling mother brought him down to Earth in his ark,
via the celestial river. Then, after arriving in the underworld, the mother
would have placed Sargon's ark in the subterranean river Euphrates, the
waters of which would have carried him up towards the surface of the
Earth. It was then that the water-drawer Akki would have drawn Sargon
up out of the subterranean waters.

What might this mean for the birth legend of Moses? It is intriguing to
note that the papyrus 'ark', in which Moses was saved, was a *teba* – a
Hebrew term used elsewhere only to describe the Ark of Noah.[27] And it is
surely no coincidence that the ark of Moses was coated in bitumen – as
was the Ark of Noah.

So, in view of the fact that the Ark of Noah was a submersible box
which, in the original legend, would have sunk from Heaven to Earth, it
seems reasonable to suppose that the ark of Moses, too, was a vessel
which came down from Heaven. Moses would thus have been abandoned
not in the *terrestrial* Nile, but in the *celestial* Nile, which would have
carried him down from Heaven *into the underworld*.

This supposition is supported by the name 'Moses', which – as many
writers have observed – derives probably from an Egyptian suffix *mss*,
meaning 'born of', or 'begotten of'. Now, such a name would normally

be prefixed by the name of a god, as in the names of the Egyptian kings *Ra-meses*, or *Thut-mosis*. There is thus good reason to believe that Moses might have been a divine child, just like the Egyptian kings.

But this is *not* to say that Moses *was* an Egyptian king. On the contrary, my suggestion is that Moses was a figure who belonged not to historic time, but to *sacred time* – the time of the beginning. Perhaps it is for this reason that the book of Isaiah refers to the days of Moses as 'the days of eternity' (*yeme olam*).[28] Moses would thus not be like a king per se, but rather like the god upon whom the king was modelled – a god who had experienced a mysterious birth in Heaven, and an equally mysterious rebirth in the underworld.

Egypt – the Underworld

A hypothesis is emerging. Could it be that Moses was carried down by the *celestial* Nile into *the underworld*? Could it be that *the land of Egypt*, where he was drawn out of the water by the daughter of Pharaoh, *symbolised the underworld*? Could it be that *the Egyptian palace*, where Moses was raised, *symbolised the palace-of-the-underworld*?[29]

As we shall now see, there is no single definitive statement anywhere that Egypt *did* symbolise the underworld, but a very strong case can be made from an accumulation of various lines of evidence.

Consider, firstly, the words of the biblical prophet Jeremiah:

Egypt riseth up like the Nile, like rivers of surging waters.
She saith: "I will rise and cover the Earth; I will destroy cities and
their peoples."[30]

When we stop to think about this passage, the language is remarkably evocative of the ancient belief that the waters of the Apsu – which had long ago been confined *to the underworld* – could rise up and bring chaos to the world above. Jeremiah almost seems to be picturing the river Nile as *a river of the underworld*, threatening to rise up and flood the surface of the Earth.

If we try to think like the ancients, we find that the geographical landscape of Egypt would indeed have been a very good match for their concept of the underworld. On the one hand, Egypt's vast tracts of desert would have evoked the hellish wilderness of the underworld in general. But, on the other hand, the surging waters of the river Nile would have evoked the mythical subterranean river, which rose upwards (northwards) through the wilderness as if to feed the real rivers and oceans on the surface of the Earth.

To an observer in more northerly latitudes – which, significantly, would include Israel – Egypt would indeed have been seen as a 'land below'. Hence the Old Testament frequently states that the Israelites *went down into* the land of Egypt or *came up from* the land of Egypt.[31]

As if to confirm our understanding, we find that the Israelites regarded the river Nile, which twists back and forth like a snake, as the fleeing serpent Rahab, which was caused to descend into the underworld by Yahweh. An authoritative guide to the scriptures explains this as follows:

> Rahab, a 'sea monster', came to symbolise Egypt and her Pharaoh, who opposed Moses and Israel.
> Isaiah 51:9-10 [the slaying of Rahab] alludes to Yahweh's delivering Israel from Egypt...
> At Isaiah 30:7, Rahab is again connected with Egypt.
> Psalm 87:4 mentions Rahab where Egypt appropriately fits, as the first in a list of Israel's enemies...
> The Targums use 'the Egyptians' in this verse, and at Psalm 89:10 they paraphrase 'Rahab' in such a way as to link the term with Egypt's arrogant Pharaoh.[32]

As we discovered in the previous chapter, Rahab was no ordinary 'sea monster', but a planet in the celestial sea, which was dismembered by Yahweh and cast down into the Earth. The biblical legend is thus uncannily similar to the Babylonian legend of the battle between Marduk and the sea-monster Tiamat. According to *Enuma Elish*, Tiamat was divided in two, her body was flung down into the underworld (she was interred beneath a 'mountain'), and the two great rivers of Mesopotamia were drawn up out of her eyes.[33]

Furthermore, it would seem that the fallen monster Rahab was the very same Satan who 'fell like lightning from Heaven', according to the gospel of Luke – the very same 'ancient serpent' who was 'bound for a thousand years' and who was 'cast into the bottomless pit', according to the book of Revelations.[34] Once again, we find corroboration of the idea that Rahab, too, was cast down into the underworld.

A strong argument can thus be mounted that the Israelites associated Rahab with Egypt because *Egypt was the underworld in which Rahab dwelt*, having been dispatched into the abyss by Yahweh.

Lest this interpretation be doubted, I refer readers to the book of Job, where we read that Rahab (alias Leviathan) 'made the depths (of the sea) boil like a pot'.[35] Also to Psalm 74, where we read that the dismembered Leviathan was fed as nourishment to 'the people inhabiting the wilderness'.[36] The 'wilderness', I suggest, was a metaphor for the underworld (the same metaphor will recur later in this chapter).

It thus seems to me that the slain sea-monster Rahab – the so-called 'fleeing serpent' – would definitely have become a denizen of the underworld, regardless of any perceived ambiguities in the Bible record.

Overall, then, the evidence is strong that Egypt, by association with Rahab, symbolised the underworld, with the river Nile being seen as an image of Rahab, which buried itself head first in the Earth. This is the same legend related of the river Nile by the Roman poet Ovid, who wrote that 'Nile ran in terror to the end of the Earth to hide its head which now is still unseen.'[37] His comment was in the context of the catastrophic fall of Phaethon.

I will cite one further example of Egypt as the underworld, which has come down to us in the book of Jeremiah. The intriguing passage states:

> Egypt will hiss like a fleeing serpent as the enemy advances in force;
>   they will come against her with axes, like men who cut down trees.
> They shall cut down her unfathomable forest.[38]

Note here the comparison of Egypt to an immense forest – a rather odd analogy until we recall the fact that the ancients used the term 'forest' to symbolise the forest of the underworld (see *The Epic of Gilgamesh* in chapter five).

So, to return to the legend of Exodus, we must now consider seriously whether Moses, *born in Egypt*, was actually *born in the underworld*, and whether the Israelites, *enslaved in Egypt*, were actually *enslaved in the underworld*. Let's take a look at some more evidence.

In various books of the Old Testament, it is said that Yahweh brought the Israelites *'out of the iron-smelting furnace'*.[39] This is a curious statement, and seems to lend a distinctly surreal note to the Exodus legend. It also happens to be a historical anachronism, because iron smelting is not thought to have been practised in Egypt until the 6th century BC.[40] Might it be the case, then, that the description 'iron-smelting furnace' was an idiom aimed at capturing the mythical image of the underworld as a land of fiery torture? If so, it succeeded magnificently.

There was also something distinctly surreal about the Israelite suffering in Egypt, as is apparent from the following words spoken by God in the book of Ezekiel:

> "On the day that thou [Israel] wast born, thou wast despised. And
> when I [God] passed by thee, I said unto thee – *polluted in thine own
> blood* – "Live!". I caused thee to multiply like a plant of the field...
> thy breasts are fashioned and thine hair is grown, *but previously thou
> wast naked and bare.*"[41]

Note the reference here to the nakedness of the Israelites. As we saw in the previous chapter, the nakedness motif occurs in the legend of Adam and Eve in the Garden of Eden (the underworld), in the legend of Noah in his 'tent' (the underworld), and in the Sumerian legend of the naked Anunnaki and primeval 'mankind' in the midst of the Earth (the underworld). Did the people of Israel thus associate themselves with a mythical race of naked 'people' in the underworld – just as the Sumerians called themselves proudly the black-headed ones?

The legend of 'mankind' being enslaved by the Anunnaki in the underworld indeed presents a fascinating parallel to the legend of the Israelites being enslaved in Egypt.[42] One cannot help but wonder, for instance, about the Hebrew description of Egypt as 'the land of slavery'.[43] Was this really a historical recollection of the Israelites? Or might it be, in the words of Mircea Eliade, an expression of the 'mythical model'?

Was Israel enslaved from the moment of its creation in a mythical subterranean world?

The Crossing to Mount Sinai

So far we have assembled only one section of the Exodus puzzle, namely the possibility that 'Egypt' was a metaphor for the underworld. But there are two further sections of this puzzle which remain to be tackled – the crossing of the 'sea' and the gathering at the 'mountain'. Might the entire landscape of the Exodus have more to do with *anki*ography than *ge*ography?

In the Jewish mystical book known as *Zohar*, one reads a very intriguing passage, which draws on a 3rd century mystical work by Rabbi Eleazar b. Pedath:

> As Pharaoh came out of Egypt, to follow the Israelites, he raised his eyes to Heaven, and saw the Prince of the Egyptian Angels flying in the air.[44]

What? *Egyptian* Angels flying in the air *in order to pursue the Israelites*? Can it be true? Well, yes it can. Consider the following passage from the book of Exodus, where Yahweh stated to the Israelites:

> "Ye have seen what I did unto the Egyptians, and how *I carried you on eagles' wings and brought you unto myself.*"[45]

What were the 'eagles' of Yahweh? In an apocryphal text known as the *Book of Adam and Eve*, we read how the angels of the LORD descended to the 'Gates of Paradise', where Eve was mourning the death of Adam (this sounds like the gates to the underworld). Suddenly, the Sun, Moon and stars grew dark, the heavens opened, and the eagles appeared:

> Eve looked *towards the heavens* and saw a chariot of lights drawing near, pulled by four gleaming eagles, whose magnificent beauty could not be expressed by anyone born of a woman's womb.[46]

According to this passage, the 'eagles' of Yahweh were the motive force for *a celestial chariot* which could travel between Earth and the heavens. This, of course, adds an entirely new dimension to the legend in Exodus, that Yahweh carried the Israelites to himself 'on eagles' wings'.

How do we reconcile such *flights through the air* with the traditional story of an Exodus through the Red Sea, and through the desert, *on foot*?

Let's take a closer look at the Red Sea. In the original Hebrew language, the term translated 'Red Sea' is *Yam Suph*, which literally means 'the Sea of Reeds'.[47] Immediately our suspicions are alerted. Firstly, the name Sea of Reeds is evocative of the Egyptian belief in a heavens which could be crossed on '*reed* floats', and which contained a mysterious 'Field *of Reeds*' in the 'east'.[48] Secondly, and perhaps even more significantly, the Red Sea which separates the Egyptian mainland from the Sinai peninsula is hardly the kind of marshy swamp implied by the name *Yam Suph*. On the contrary, it is a very deep body of water – as was indeed required, so it would seem, to drown Pharaoh's army.

So, might the Red Sea (*Yam Suph*) be the *celestial sea*? Indeed, if we turn to the book of Exodus, chapter 15, we find that the waters of *Yam Suph* were described as 'mighty' and 'deep'.[49] Furthermore, the term used here for 'deep' – *tehomoth* – is almost identical to the term *tehom*, which was used in Genesis 1 to describe *the great watery Deep which covered the Earth* at the moment of the creation.[50] The point was picked up by the eminent scholar Alexander Heidel, who commented as follows:

> Since the waters of the Red Sea are called 'mighty waters' and *tehomoth*, there is no reason why they could not equally well be designated as *me thehom rabba*, 'the waters of the great Deep'.[51]

As we have seen from our Mesopotamian studies, these 'waters of the great Deep' (the Apsu) could refer to the watery Deep of Heaven, or to the watery Deep of the Earth, or indeed to the combination of the two – hence the biblical idea that the two Deeps needed to be divided.

It thus takes little imagination to see that the Red Sea – 'the waters of the great Deep' per Heidel – would describe perfectly *the space between* the upper and lower waters, i.e. the path through which the planetary waters of Heaven had fallen, physically, and through which they had then been resurrected, metaphysically.

Here is another oddity. The orthodox account of the crossing of the Red Sea suggests that the children of Israel passed through the waters *on foot*, closely followed by the Egyptian army, *on horseback or in chariots*. To envisage this within a *terrestrial* landscape, one must try to imagine a conventional sea being heaped up into two walls, to form a channel between, so that all parties could cross *along the sea-bed*. And it would follow logically from this scenario that the collapse of the channel, and the return of the waters, *would drown the Egyptians at the bottom of the sea, i.e. on the sea-bed*. Let's picture the scenario in our minds.

But considerable doubt is thrown on this scenario by an archaic biblical song known as *The Song of Moses and Miriam*. In this song, we read that Pharaoh's officers and chariots were covered by the Red Sea and '*sank* into the bottom like a stone'.[52]

How could the Egyptians sink like a stone if they were crossing along a sea-bed?

It seems to me that this is impossible, and illogical, even if the passage is understood in a metaphysical sense.

However, this anomalous passage in *The Song of Moses and Miriam* would make perfect sense if Pharaoh's men were *part way across a celestial sea*. Then they would indeed sink like a stone – *back to the Earth whence they had come*.

This scenario of crossing the celestial sea would also explain another odd passage in the book of Exodus, where the Israelites 'saw the Egyptians lying dead on the sea shore.'[53] Once again, the details do not add up. How could the Egyptians possibly be left dead *on the shore* if they were drowned while crossing *the sea-bed*?[54]

There is more. In *The Song of Moses and Miriam*, we read:

> Thou [Yahweh] didst blow with thy breath, the Sea covered them [the Egyptians].
> *They sank like lead in the mighty waters...*
> Thou stretchedst out thy right hand, *and the Earth swallowed them*.[55]

What? How could the Egyptians have been swallowed up by the Earth?

Once again, the passage makes no sense if the Egyptians crossed along the bed of a terrestrial Red Sea. But it does make perfect sense if the Egyptians were following the Israelites across a celestial sea *and from the underworld*. Then the Earth could indeed have opened up and swallowed the Egyptians, as they were being washed back by Yahweh to the place whence they had emerged.

In summary, it would seem that there was a 'drowning' – but not in the conventional sense of the term. One is reminded of the Egyptian god Osiris, who drowned in his own waters when he fell to the Earth.

This, of course, all supposes that the Israelites were heading across the celestial sea *towards a celestial mountain*. All of our postulating will come to nothing without the celestial mountain.

So, what about Mount Sinai? Was this, too, part of a celestial landscape? Was Sinai perhaps a 'mountain' in the heavens – in keeping with the ancient pagan metaphor of 'mountain = planet'?

In order to answer this question, we must tackle it in two senses. Firstly, in the sense of Mount Sinai as a symbol of *the cosmic mountain*, i.e. the *fallen* mountain which spans metaphysically the abyss between Earth and Heaven; and secondly in the sense of Mount Sinai as the integral *heavenly mountain*, both in its original physical form and in its later metaphysical counterpart.

Let's deal first with Mount Sinai the 'cosmic mountain'. If we turn to the book of Exodus, we find that Yahweh descended *to the top of* Mount Sinai, whilst Moses went up to *the top of* Mount Sinai.[56] It was there, *at the top of* the mountain, that God met Moses and spoke to him.

Now consider the following quotations from the books of the Old Testament. In the book of Nehemiah, it is stated that: 'thou [Yahweh] camest down upon Mount Sinai, and spakest with them [the Israelites] *from Heaven*'.[57] Similarly, in the book of Exodus, Yahweh told the Israelites that: "Ye have seen that I have spoken to you *from Heaven*", when the conversation clearly took place *on the top of the mountain*.[58] A third example comes from the book of Deuteronomy, where we read that: '*out of Heaven* he made thee to hear his voice'.[59]

All of these quotations make it clear that the peak of Mount Sinai was in the midst of Heaven – at least symbolically. And such was the way with all 'cosmic mountains', such as the ziggurats of Mesopotamia, the tops of which were also thought to be in the midst of Heaven.

As a true 'cosmic mountain', we would expect Mount Sinai to stretch all the way from Earth to Heaven, and this is indeed what we find. In the book of Deuteronomy, Moses reminded the Israelites that: "Ye came near and stood under the mountain, and *the mountain burned with fire unto the midst of heaven*".[60] Similarly, in the same book, we read: 'out of Heaven he made thee to hear his voice... *and upon Earth he showed thee his great fire*'.[61] And finally, in the book of Exodus, we read that the *whole of* Mount Sinai was covered with smoke when Yahweh descended upon it in fire.[62]

These quotations confirm that Mount Sinai was regarded as a true 'cosmic mountain', which stretched all the way from Earth to Heaven, just like a Mesopotamian ziggurat.

There was, however, another side to Mount Sinai, which was its *heavenly* aspect. In a moment, we will see how Yahweh emerged physically from Mount Sinai in catastrophic circumstances – just like the Sumerian god Utu. But first, let's take a look at some passages which refer, in a metaphysical context, to the destruction which had occurred.

In the Koran (the holy book of the Muslims), we read an extraordinary account of Mount Sinai being crushed to dust:

And when Moses came at the appointed time... he said: "Lord, reveal yourself to me, that I may look upon you." And Allah replied: "You shall not see me. But look upon the mountain; if it remains firm upon its base, only then shall you see me." And when Allah revealed himself to the Mountain, *he crushed it to fine dust*. Moses fell down senseless...[63]

One is reminded here of the Sumerian *Lamentation Texts*, which refer to '*that day when Heaven was crushed*... was darkened... was turned into the underworld'.[64]

Might it be that this idea of the crushed mountain lies behind the name 'Mount Horeb', which was often applied to Mount Sinai in the book of Exodus?[65] Significantly, the Hebrew word *horeb* meant 'dry' or 'waste', which would be a very appropriate designation for a planet which had exploded and lost all of its waters.[66] Especially since the waters of God were not restored to their former position in the midst of Heaven, but were lifted up to a position *above* the Expanse, i.e. to the abode of God in the Seventh Heaven. This action left the midst of Heaven entirely barren and dry – no fit place for a man to set foot.

Moses, however, was no ordinary man, and it is significant that it was at Mount Horeb, 'the mountain of God', that Moses encountered the 'burning bush', saw the angel of God, and heard the voice of God speaking to him from within the burning bush.[67]

An overall picture is now coming into focus, for this crucial clue suggests that Moses *went up to Heaven* (metaphysically) for forty years after the first forty years of his life which were spent *in the underworld* of 'Egypt'. This supposition is backed up by the fact that the region of his exile was called Midian, a name signifying the midst – i.e. the midst of the heavens.[68] The story of Moses is thus beginning to sound like the story of the death and resurrection of the Phoenix-bird. Was Moses, like the Phoenix, set to *return* to the underworld, to release the Israelites?

We now turn to another curious passage which was recorded in the Hebrew book of Jubilees. Note the reference herein to Mount Zion (Jerusalem) as 'the navel of the Earth' suggesting that *it*, and not Mount Sinai, had become the 'cosmic mountain' of Israel (as indeed happened *after* the Exodus and settlement of Canaan):

> The Garden of Eternity, the most sacred, is the dwelling of the LORD;
> And Mount Sinai, in the centre of the wilderness;
> And Mount Zion [Jerusalem], the centre of the navel of the Earth.
> These three were created as holy places, facing each other.[69]

In this passage, the Garden of Eternity is identifiable as the Seventh Heaven, where God resided in the highest heights. Mount Zion, meanwhile, is obviously symbolic of the planet Earth. However, the third holy place, Mount Sinai, appears as a separate mountain between the two other holy places, i.e. a mountain in the midst of the heavens.

Note also the reference to Mount Sinai being 'in the centre of the wilderness'. Once again, we encounter the idea that the site of the celestial catastrophe was like a barren desert.[70]

But the most astonishing evidence for the heavenly Mount Sinai appears in Psalm 68 of the Old Testament. Here, we find a remarkable description of how the enslaved Israelites ascended *into the heavens*, to Mount Sinai, in God's train:

> This is the hill which God desireth to dwell in; yea, the LORD will
>   dwell in it for ever.
> The chariots of God are tens of thousands, (like) thousands of angels.
>   The LORD is among them, in the holy Sinai.
> *Thou hast ascended on high, thou hast led captives in your train*, thou
>   hast received men for gifts, even the rebellious too, that the LORD
>   might dwell there.[71]

The text is explicit. An ascension on high, to a holy hill – and no doubt on the wings of eagles, with the Prince of Egypt flying up in the air in pursuit. What a vision! Of course, the captive Israelites could only have ascended thus in a *metaphysical* manner, and this would indeed seem to have been the understanding of Paul, who described the Exodus in his 'First Letter to the Corinthians' (New Testament) as follows:

> All our forefathers were under the cloud, and all passed through the Sea. And all were baptised unto Moses in the cloud and in the Sea. And all did eat the same *spiritual* food, and all did drink the same *spiritual* drink.[72]

What a remarkable passage. But then Paul, we should recall, was almost certainly an initiate into the secrets of an ancient mystery school. Did he thus know that there was a hidden meaning to the Exodus story?

In the context of our study, Paul's carefully chosen words now appear to be very significant indeed.

Saving the Israelites

We now have a virtually complete picture of the ancient puzzle of the Exodus. Firstly, we have seen strong evidence that 'Egypt' symbolised the underworld. Secondly, we have seen equally persuasive evidence that the Israelites crossed a celestial sea. And thirdly, we have seen convincing evidence that the Israelites arrived either at a 'cosmic mountain' on Earth, or at a celestial mountain in the heavens (depending on the particular legend). If there is a problem with this interpretation, it is only in the rather odd idea that the Israelites spent forty years wandering in the wilderness *after* crossing the celestial sea and meeting God at Mount Sinai; however, this can easily be explained by a merging and confusion of two separate traditions, plus a desire on the part of the priests to rewrite the story to suit a terrestrial exodus to a terrestrial promised land.[73]

Moreover, we have assembled a picture which is in perfect harmony with everything we have learned about the pagan traditions of the ancient Near East. It makes sense that a people were enslaved in the 'iron-smelting furnace' of the underworld; it makes sense that they were 'naked and bare' and 'polluted in their own blood'; it makes sense that Moses was carried into the underworld in a submersible box via a river; it makes sense that Moses later ascended to Heaven; and it makes sense that Moses should return to Earth, coming down from Heaven a second time – Phoenix-like – to rescue the Israelites from the underworld.

Lest any of this interpretation be in doubt, I shall now reveal the final instalment of the evidence – all of which is contained in the books of the Old Testament. In the passages which follow, we will see in vivid detail exactly how God descended from Mount Sinai in Heaven and entered the underworld *cataclysmically* to effect his dramatic rescue of the Israelites.

We begin with a series of passages which describe Yahweh coming forth from a 'mountain', which is given various names and epithets, all alluding to Mount Sinai itself.

Firstly, in the book of Deuteronomy, we read:

> The LORD came out of Sinai, and he rose up from Seir unto them [the Israelites]; he shone forth from Mount Paran.

He came with tens of thousands of holy ones, (with) a fiery law for
   them (coming) from his right hand.[74]

In this passage, Mount Sinai appears to be identical to Mount Paran and
Mount Seir. The name 'Paran' is interesting, for its etymology suggests
the possible meaning 'House of Heaven'. As for 'Seir', the name comes
from a root word meaning 'to bristle up', in the sense of wooded hills
(and also, aptly, to bristle up in fear).[75] Yahweh thus seems to have risen
up *out of a forested mountain in the heavens and shone forth* – just like
the god Utu did in the Sumerian traditions.[76] Note, too, the fact that
Yahweh came forth accompanied by 'tens of thousands of holy ones' –
once again evoking the pagan traditions of the planet exploding into
myriads of fiery fragments.

This interpretation finds dramatic confirmation in the following
passage from *The Song of Deborah* in the book of Judges, where Seir
(Mount Sinai) is described as a 'red land', whence Yahweh brought a
catastrophic Flood to the Earth:

O LORD, when thou wentest forth out of Seir, when thou marchedst
   out of the red land [Edom], the Earth shook, and the heavens
   dropped, and the clouds also dropped water.
The mountains melted away before the (coming of the) LORD, that
   Sinai from before, the LORD God of Israel.[77]

The last line of this passage is intriguing. A minor, but legitimate, change
to the standard punctuation of the King James translation of the Bible
results in Yahweh being called 'that Sinai from before'. It is yet another
clue to support the hypothesis that Yahweh was the God of an exploded
planet – just like his pagan rivals.

We turn now to several passages which link the idea of God's
catastrophism *specifically to the saving of the Israelites*. Biblical scholars
have always assumed that the following passages were written with
exaggerated poetic metaphor, merely to demonstrate the awesome power
of God. They should not be taken literally, so we are told. I beg to
disagree, for if the Israelites were enslaved in the underworld, and God
came from a heavenly 'mountain', it makes perfect sense that the rescue
of the Israelites should involve a catastrophic descent of God *into* the
Earth.

Anyway, readers may now judge the evidence for themselves. We
begin with Psalm 114:

When Israel went out of Egypt...
The Sea looked, and fled, the Jordan was driven back, the mountains

skipped like rams...
Tremble, O Earth, at the presence of the LORD.[78]

Consider now Psalm 77, where we find an explicit reference to the Exodus under Moses and Aaron:

> The waters saw thee, O God, the waters saw thee and were afraid; the
> very depths were troubled.
> The clouds poured out water, the skies resounded; thine arrows were
> scattered.
> The sound of thy thunder was in Heaven, thy lightnings lit up the
> world. The Earth trembled and quaked.
> Thy path was in the Sea, thy way was through the mighty waters, but
> thy footprints were mysterious.
> Thou leddest thy people like a flock, by the hand of Moses and
> Aaron.[79]

This passage presents a picture of God personally forcing his way through the mighty waters of the great Deep to save the Israelites.

An even more exciting passage is found in the book of Isaiah. In the following quotation, we see that God made his path through the great Deep by drying up a path through the Sea. We also find an explicit link between the saving of the Israelites and the catastrophic slaying of the fleeing serpent Rahab:

> Art thou not the one who didst cut up Rahab into pieces, who didst
> pierce that sea-monster?
> Art thou not the one who didst dry up the Sea, the waters of the great
> Deep, who didst make the depths of the Sea into a road for the
> ransomed to cross over?[80]

The 'ransomed' were, of course, the Israelites, and their 'crossing over', as we have seen, was to the *heavenly* Mount Sinai.

Consider now the book of Habakkuk (the prophet), where we find a dramatic account of God's catastrophic descent into the Earth, followed by his saving of the Israelites with the help of his 'anointed one':

> God came from Teman, the Holy One (came) from Mount Paran.
> His glory covered the heavens, and the Earth was full of his praise.
> And his brightness was like light; he had horns coming out of his
> hand, where his power was hidden.
> Before him went the pestilence, and burning coals went forth at his
> feet.
> He stood and measured the Earth; he looked, and drove the nations

asunder.

The ancient mountains were scattered, and the age-old hills
 collapsed...

Was thy wrath against the Sea, that thou didst ride upon thine horses
 and thy chariots of salvation?...

Thou didst cleave the Earth with rivers; the mountains saw thee and
 trembled.

The floods of water swept by; the Deep groaned, and lifted its hands
 on high.

The Sun and Moon stood still in the heavens...

Thou didst march through the land in indignation, thou didst thresh the
 heathen in anger.

Thou wentest forth for the salvation of thy people, to save with thine
 anointed one.[81]

The saved people were, of course, the Israelites. But who was the
'anointed one'? Moses perhaps?

Our final example comes from Psalm 18. Here we find another
account of catastrophism, followed by redemption, but this time it is not
the Israelites but king David who imagined himself being saved.
Nevertheless, David used the archetypal language of the primeval
Exodus, and hence the passage offers an important corroboration of the
idea that the act of redemption took place in the underworld:

The Earth trembled and quaked; the foundations of the mountains
 moved and shook, because he was angry.

Smoke went up out of his nostrils; consuming fire came forth from his
 mouth, and set coals on fire.

He parted the Heavens too, and came down; and darkness was under
 his feet.

And he rode upon the cherubim, and did fly; and he soared upon the
 wings of the wind.

And he made darkness his secret place, his canopy round about him –
 dark waters, thick clouds of the Heavens.

His thick clouds, hailstones, and coals of fire advanced towards the
 brightness before him.

The LORD thundered from Heaven, the voice of the Most High
 resounded.

And he sent out arrows, scattering them, and bolts of lightning,
 confusing them.

Then the valleys of the Sea were exposed, and the foundations of the
 Earth were revealed, at the roaring of the LORD – at the blast of the

breath of his nostrils.

He reached down from above and took hold of me, and drew me out of deep waters.

He delivered me from my powerful enemy, from them that hated me, who were too strong for me.[82]

Thus were the Israelites drawn out of the deep waters of the Apsu, and saved by God, who took them with him back to Heaven.

This, it would seem, was the *original* Hebrew belief system. Not for these earlier Hebrews an eternity of nothingness in Sheol (the underworld), but rather the hope of an afterlife in Heaven, upon the LORD's 'holy hill' – upon a heavenly Mount Sinai, the 'mountain of inheritance'.[83] Indeed, such was the power of Yahweh that he could restore miraculously his 'mountain' in the midst of the celestial wilderness, to become once more an Earth-like planet suitable for human habitation.

This was the true promised land, and it would indeed have been a paradise which flowed with milk and honey.

Those who Crossed from Heaven to Earth

In summary, it seems to me that the Hebrew people were *lied to*, no doubt with the best of intentions, but lied to all the same. The real promised land was not in Canaan at all. It was in Heaven. The real reward of obedience to God was not in this life, but in the next. Therefore, everything the Israelites were being told by their priests was a distortion of a much older 'truth', from an exploded planet cult which had much in common with that of the pagans.

According to this older 'truth', the Israelites were a people descended from Heaven, just like the Sumerian black-headed ones. This much we know because they were descended from Adam, who was cast down from Heaven in the original, catastrophic 'fall of man'. As the book of Lamentations put it: 'the LORD... cast down the Splendour of Israel from Heaven unto the Earth'.[84]

Moreover, according to another original legend – occulted by the priests – the seed of the Israelites had been saved by the Flood-hero, Noah, who sailed his Ark with the seeds of all living things from another planet, which had once existed in the midst of the heavens.

But this represents only the tip of the iceberg. For wherever we look in the Old Testament, we find more and more remnants of the Israelites' belief in their celestial origins.

Among the pre-Flood patriarchs, for example, was a character named

Eber, whose name recalled a legendary crossing of a river. But was it really a crossing of a terrestrial river, or of the celestial river which stretched from Heaven to Earth?[85] The latter seems the most likely solution when we consider the fact that the name of his son, Peleg, meant 'Split', because 'in his days the Earth was split apart'.[86]

Then there is the patriarch Abram (Abraham), who was specifically referred to in the Old Testament as an *Ibri*. This name *Ibri* meant literally 'those who crossed over'.[87] Did Abraham thus cross *from Heaven to Earth* at the divine command of Yahweh? A good case can be mounted to suggest that he did. For example, his name *Ab-ram* literally meant 'Exalted Father', or 'Father who is Raised High'.[88] Furthermore, Jewish legend states that Abraham was born in a cave, the cave being symbolic of the Earth's underworld; a fall from Heaven would thus be implied.[89] And then there is the mysterious episode recounted in Genesis 15, where Abraham 'fell into a deep sleep' just as the Sun set, when a 'smoking brazier with a blazing torch' passed between the dismembered parts of certain sacrificed animals. As noted in the previous chapter, the putting-to-sleep motif symbolised a fall from Heaven – the more so when it was referred to as 'a deep sleep'.

A final clue I am aware of concerning Abraham appears in the Dead Sea Scrolls, where we read a tantalising reference to 'the fire when he [Abram] crossed over... to go out to the land of Canaan.'[90] The fire is, of course, indicative of a catastrophic crossing from Heaven to Earth.

Whilst on the subject of Abram, it should be mentioned that the name of his first-born son, Isaac, meant 'he laughs' or 'laughter', and it should be pointed out that, in ancient Egypt, earthquakes were known as 'the laughter of Geb'.[91] This association of laughter with the noise of the underworld tends to corroborate the idea that Isaac was born in the underworld as the offspring of a descended god (i.e. Abram).

Then there is Abram's grandson Jacob, who experienced a very strange 'crossing over', when he wrestled with God at the Jabbok ford. The outcome of this supernatural encounter was that Jacob was renamed 'Israel', and the nation of Israel was born in the image of God.[92] In another account, Jacob was said to have *divided into two groups* when he crossed the Jordan with his 'staff'.[93] This staff of Jacob may well be an esoteric symbol, as is surely the case with the legendary staffs of Moses and Aaron.[94] As for the division of Jacob into two parts, it is highly evocative of legends in which Sky-gods and Sky-goddesses were divided or dismembered. And as for the Jordan, it would seem that this was both a terrestrial river *and a celestial river* – just like all of the great rivers of the ancient Near East.[95]

And then there is the legend of Joseph. According to the book of Genesis, Joseph was cast down into an empty, waterless pit in the wilderness, having just compared himself, his father and his eleven brothers to the Sun, the Moon and eleven stars. Could this 'dream' contain a tantalising hint of a more ancient tradition, in which Joseph was cast down from Heaven into a pit in the Earth?[96]

It is noticeable that Joseph's arrival in 'Egypt' – the underworld – coincided with the beginning of a seven-year period of abundance, which filled the storehouses with an uncountable quantity of grain.[97] Here, one is reminded of the Mesopotamian legends of Lahar and Ashnan, and Ulligarra and Zalgarra, who also brought an abundance of produce into the underworld when they descended from Heaven. Did Joseph, too, descend from Heaven?

In Deuteronomy 33, Joseph is indeed described in terms reminiscent of an ancient Mesopotamian descending deity:

> Let all these (blessings) come upon the head of Joseph, on the top of the head of him who was separated from his brethren.
> His glory is like that of a first-born bull, his horns are like the horns of a wild ox.
> With them he will gore the nations, even those in the depths of the Earth.[98]

Furthermore, Joseph was portrayed as a 'seed of Israel', just as the Mesopotamian Flood-heroes and the original Noah were portrayed as the Seeds of Mankind. In Genesis 45, Joseph comforted his brothers with the knowledge that:

> "God did send me before you to preserve life... And God did send me before you to preserve you as a remnant in the Earth, and to save your lives by a great deliverance."[99]

These are the words of a sacred mystery, which was both celestial and catastrophic. Moreover, just as mankind was allowed to repopulate the Earth after Noah's great deliverance, so too were the Israelites allowed to prosper after Joseph's great deliverance:

> And the children of Israel were fruitful, and multiplied greatly, and became exceedingly numerous, and the land was filled with them.[100]

The words are evocative of the *Atra-Hasis Epic*, and also of Genesis 6:1, both of which describe the teeming of mankind on the Earth, or perhaps *in* the Earth, prior to the coming of the Great Flood.

Was Joseph originally a seed, which descended from Heaven, and took root in the underworld? In the book of Genesis, we read:

> Joseph is a fruitful vine, a fruitful vine near a well, whose branches
> climb over the wall.[101]

This image of the vine climbing over 'the wall' recalls the old Mesopotamian idiom of 'the Wall' as the ceiling of the underworld.

Note also the esoteric symbolism of the vine, as highlighted in the previous chapter. In the book of Jeremiah, God stated that he had planted Israel like a noble vine.[102] Indeed. Whilst in Psalm 80, we read that God 'brought a vine out of Egypt'.[103] Well, quite.

Joseph, it would seem, was one of those archetypal Seeds of Mankind, who planted Israel like a seed in the underworld. The seed of a vine.

Finally, we return to Moses, who was not so much a Seed of Israel as a Saviour of Israel. As mentioned earlier, the legend of his birth suggests that he came down from Heaven, and was carried by a celestial river into the underworld ('Egypt'). There, he spent forty years (an eternity), before ascending to Heaven, to a place called Midian – the site of the 'burning bush' (which surely symbolised the exploded planet). There, he spent another forty years (a second eternity), before descending into the underworld with God to redeem the enslaved Israelites. Finally, he endured another forty years of eternity in escorting the Israelites across the wilderness of space to a 'mountain' in the midst of the heavens.

Significantly, Moses was not allowed to enter the promised land (the reason for this will become clear during the next chapter).[104] Instead, having viewed it from afar, Moses died, upon 'Mount Nebo', at the age of 120 years.[105]

However, as has been made clear during this chapter, the original Moses was no ordinary man. Hence the biblical legend of Moses is concluded with the following enigmatic statement:

> So, Moses, the servant of the LORD, died there in the land of Moab...
> and he [the LORD] buried him *in a valley* in the land of Moab (over
> against Beth Peor). But no man knoweth of his grave unto this day.
> And Moses was a hundred and twenty years old when he died, but his
> eyes were still bright, and his strength unabated.[106]

Let the wise teach the mystery to the wise!

* * * * *

CHAPTER ELEVEN

THE LAMB LIES DOWN

Who of those who ascended from the underworld ever did get up scot-free?
(Inanna's Descent to the Underworld)

Approximately two thousand years ago, at the beginning of the Christian era, the city of Jerusalem began to prepare for the greatest and oldest of all Jewish festivals – the annual Festival of Passover. From hundreds of miles around, pilgrims set out on their long treks towards Jerusalem, in order to experience the Passover celebrations in their sacred capital. In all of the houses of Jerusalem, and all around the land, every household was in possession of a healthy one-year-old male lamb, or goat, which would soon be slaughtered as part of the Passover rites.

All around Jerusalem, excited children began to ask their parents what the Festival of Passover was all about; and their parents responded to them with the words that God himself had spoken in the book of Exodus:

> And it shall come to pass, when your children shall say unto you: "What does this service mean?" that ye shall say: "It is the sacrifice of the LORD's Passover, who *passed over* the houses of the children of Israel in Egypt, when he smote the Egyptians, but delivered our houses."[1]

As the Sun went down on Nisan 13 – marking the beginning of Nisan 14 in the Jewish calendar – the lambs and goats were duly slaughtered, and the blood of the animals was smeared on the doorposts of the houses – re-enacting the ritual which had protected the ancient Israelites thousands of years earlier, when God and Moses had delivered them from captivity in Egypt.

After the lambs and goats had been killed, they were immediately skinned, cleansed and put above the fire to roast, and the excitement began to mount all around Jerusalem, as thousands of people awaited the late evening meal – the climax of the Passover rite – in which the lamb, or goat, would be eaten with unleavened bread and bitter herbs.

But the Passover Festival of two thousand years ago was to be no ordinary Passover. If we are to believe the writers of the gospels and the founding fathers of the early Church, there was in Jerusalem that night a very special gathering, led by a man who had carefully planned *the sacrifice of his own life*, to coincide with the national day of Passover. Before Nisan 14 had passed, this man – Jesus Christ – would be arrested, sentenced, and hung upon a stake. And, within hours, he would die, thus becoming in effect *a human substitute for the Passover lamb*.

As Paul, one of the first missionaries of Christianity, would later write in his famous letter to the Corinthians:

Christ, our Passover lamb, has been sacrificed.[2]

Who was this man Jesus Christ? In the years which followed his death, there was great speculation as to his true identity, as is evidenced from the 'guessing games' which were recorded in the gospels of the New Testament. The founding fathers of the Church, however, were adamant that Jesus Christ had been a unique person – the living incarnation of the divine Spirit, and thus the Son of God. And this is the dogma which has been taught to us ever since by the Church.

But – leaving to one side the question of whether Jesus Christ was the Son of God or not – have we been told the whole truth concerning the significance of the Passover?

The official line of the Church is that the Passover was merely a convenient vehicle which was used by God and Jesus Christ to magnify the impact of the divine sacrifice which was being made. This means to say that there was no greater public occasion in Palestine of the 1st century AD than the Festival of Passover (it was run a close second by *yohm hakkippurim*, the annual Day of Atonement), and the eyes of Israel would thus have been focused on Jerusalem, making it the perfect stage for the divine drama about to unfold.

So, according to this official line, the Passover was of entirely *secondary importance* to the main story, which was, of course, the death and resurrection of Jesus Christ. It is indeed for this reason that Passover has never become a Christian festival, but has remained a uniquely Jewish festival, which commemorates the deliverance of the ancient Israelites from the bonds of slavery in 'Egypt'.

But note that I put 'Egypt' in inverted commas. To the uninitiated, the Festival of Passover commemorated *a historic* event – the Exodus – which occurred in *mundane time*, merely a few thousand years ago, when a real man, Moses, brought a real people, the Israelites, out of a real country, Egypt. And in that sense, the Exodus would indeed have been seen as being of secondary importance, compared to the death and resurrection of the Son of God.

However, as we saw in the last chapter, the true meaning of the Exodus was *occulted* by the Hebrew priests, to prevent their flock from knowing the truth about their promised land in Heaven. To the initiated (and some of the priests must surely have known), the Passover in fact commemorated an Exodus from the underworld, when God had rescued his 'people' at the mythical beginning of the world. The privileged few would have been fully aware that the Exodus and the Passover were rooted not in events of mundane time, *but of sacred time*.

This sheds an entirely new light on the Christian mythos. What would the story of Jesus Christ become if it were reinterpreted in the context of the truth which was occulted, whereby the Passover was *not* of secondary importance, but rather of *primary and fundamental importance*?

Consider now the words of Paul, cited earlier: 'Christ, our Passover lamb, has been sacrificed.' The official line on this statement is that the 'Passover lamb' was merely a convenient metaphor, which captured the idea of the innocent, sacrificial victim. But what if Paul, who was almost certainly an initiate into secret doctrines (see chapter one), was alluding to *the lambs of the original Exodus*? Not to the real lambs of the historic Exodus from Egypt, but to *the mythical lambs sacrificed in the primeval Exodus from the underworld*? What if Paul meant that Jesus *was* that original lamb, which had been sacrificed at the beginning of the world?

How would such a secret affect our understanding of Christianity – especially in the light of all the other biblical references to Jesus Christ as 'the Lamb of God'?

In this chapter, we shall discover exactly what the lamb motif really meant to the ancient Israelites, in an era long before the Christian story ever began. We shall examine not only the lambs of the Exodus, but also the lamb (or ram) sacrificed in the story of Abraham and Isaac, and we shall also look at some Old Testament scriptures which mention the innocent sacrificial lamb in a very intriguing context indeed.

However, in order to fully appreciate this original, esoteric meaning of the sacrificed lamb, we must once again put some effort into recapturing the ancient Hebrew way of thinking. We begin, then, with a brief recap of the Hebrew legends concerning the subject which is at the heart of all the ancient Mysteries – the underworld.

Legends of the Underworld

Thousands of years ago, in the days before the Hebrew priests carried out a systematic distortion of their own heritage, the Israelites had followed a pagan belief system. According to their long-held traditions, they were literally the 'people of God', by virtue of the fact that they had descended from one 'man', Adam, who had been created 'in the image' of God himself. Crucially, they believed that this 'man', Adam, had been cast down from Heaven – this being the original 'fall of man'. And this was the reason why they called themselves Hebrews (*Ibri*), for the name of their tribe commemorated the 'fact' that they had 'crossed over' physically from Heaven to Earth (over the celestial river Jordan).

According to this pagan tradition, Heaven was Eden, the abode of the gods, but this paradise had been cast down into the Earth, creating a Garden of Eden in the underworld. Naturally enough, it was into this subterranean paradise that Adam had arrived after being expelled from the heavenly Eden.

Between these two Edens stretched the great 'cosmic tree', the Bond of Heaven-and-Earth in so many ancient pagan traditions. The Hebrews, however, imagined it as a pair of trees – a Tree of Knowledge and a Tree of Life – each being situated *in the middle* of the upper and lower Edens.[3] When man had first fallen from Heaven, he was naked, innocent and uncivilised (as in the Sumerian tradition), and possibly immortal to boot. But his desire was to return to Heaven.

The first step towards this return was for Adam to eat from the Tree of Knowledge, which he did, thereupon becoming like a god, knowing good and evil, i.e. knowing everything.[4] The second step, to complete the return to Heaven, was to eat from the Tree of Life, which would have restored him to true 'life' – i.e. to a metaphysical life – back in Heaven where he belonged.

This was all very well, but how were the ancient Hebrews to rationalise the fact that this had seemingly not happened – man was *not* in Heaven, *nor* in the underworld, but was here, physically in the flesh, upon the face of the Earth? The answer had to be that something, obviously, had gone dramatically wrong in the underworld. Somehow, man had eaten from the Tree of Knowledge, but had missed out on the Tree of Life.[5] Consequently, as a result of having gained 'knowledge' like the gods, man could not have remained as an obedient servant in the underworld, and had thus been expelled (a second expulsion this) into the world above.[6]

There was a saying, however, from the ancient Sumerian legend of

Inanna's Descent to the Underworld, that no-one could ever be released from the underworld without paying a price. In the words of the Sumerian poet:

> Who of those who ascended from the underworld ever did get up scot-free?[7]

Adamic man, sure enough, had paid the price. He had forfeited his personal immortality and, furthermore, had returned to the ways of sin – a sin, incidentally, which was originally conceived in Heaven (see chapter twelve).

As for the Tree of Life, the hope of the pagan Israelites was that, upon death, their souls might overcome the trials and tribulations of the underworld, and find this tree, which would take them back to Heaven – where they, as the *Ibri*, still believed they belonged. In later times, the priests would counter this belief by asserting that God had installed 'the cherubim, and a flaming, whirling sword, to guard the way to the Tree of Life'.

This, then, was the original Adamic tradition. Adam was a 'black-headed one' (to use the Sumerian metaphor), who had descended from Heaven into the underworld. As for Eve, she was his partner and soul mate only in the sense that she was Mother Earth.

In summary, it can be seen that the foremost legend of the pagan Israelites – the legend of Adam and the Garden of Eden – was a legend of an emergence from the underworld.

But it was by no means the only such legend.

We turn now to the second great tradition of the pagan Israelites (at least according to the biblical chronology), namely the legend of Abraham and Isaac, where the sacrificial lamb made a startling and vitally important appearance.

As explained in the previous chapter, Abraham was the father of the *Ibri* – 'those who crossed over' – and according to Jewish legend, he had been born in a cave, i.e. in the underworld. His original name had been *Ab-ram*, a name which literally meant 'Exalted Father', or 'Father who is Raised High', whilst his later name, Abraham, meant the 'Father of a Multitude'. The implication of all this is that Abraham, just like Adam, had been a Seed of Mankind, who had fallen from Heaven into the Earth.

With these thoughts in mind, we can now read the biblical legend of Genesis 17 in an entirely new light:

> And when Abram was ninety-nine years old, the LORD appeared to him and said: "I am El Shaddai; walk before me, and be perfect. And I will make my covenant between me and thee, and will multiply thee

/." And Abram fell on his face. And God [Elohim] said to
will make thee exceedingly fruitful, and I will make nations
e, and kings shall come out of thee..."[8]

17 then goes on to relate the details of the covenant which was
established between Abraham and God, which required the circumcision
of every single Israelite. This – the most important of all Jewish
traditions, even to this day – is a ritual which has a profound celestial
significance, as we will see very shortly.[9]

Firstly, however, we must consider the famous legend of Abraham and
the attempted sacrifice of his first-born son, Isaac. We pick up the story
where God tells Abraham to sacrifice Isaac on a mountain in Moriah,
which is generally held to be the same Mount Moriah as at Jerusalem, in
the sacred Bond of Heaven-and-Earth:

> "Take now thy son, thine only son, whom thy lovest, Isaac, and get
> thee into the land of Moriah; and offer him up as a burnt offering,
> upon one of the mountains which I shall tell thee about."[10]

As father and son approached the place of sacrifice, Isaac enquired as to
the whereabouts of *the lamb* which was to be sacrificed, and Abraham,
his father, responded ambiguously: *"God himself will provide the lamb."*
Abraham then built an altar and prepared a fire for the sacrifice of his
own first-born son. But then, as he wielded a cleaver to slay Isaac, an
angel of Yahweh appeared and told him to stop:

> And Abraham lifted up his eyes, and looked, and behold – behind
> him was a ram, caught by its horns in a thicket. And Abraham went
> and took the ram, and offered it up as a burnt offering in lieu of his
> son.[11]

Note that the biblical text has, at this point, shifted from the idea of a
'lamb' to a 'ram', i.e. to a full-grown adult male sheep, presumably to
reflect the fact that Isaac was supposedly a grown man himself at this
point in the story. In any event, the key feature of this legend is that *a
lamb (or a ram) was provided by God as a substitute, to be sacrificed in
place of Isaac.*

Where did the lamb (or ram) come from? The book of Genesis tells us
only that the ram was delivered by God, or his angel, neglecting to tell us
whether the ram just happened to be grazing on Mount Moriah at the
time, or whether it was a special ram sent down from Heaven by God.

The Ethiopian holy book *Kebra Nagast*, however, settles the matter
categorically with the following explicit statement:

Isaac rendered obedience unto his father, saying "Bind me"; and he was offered up as a sacrifice, though he did not die, *being redeemed by the ram which came down from Heaven*.[12]

This is a very interesting piece of information. If we step back and look at the overall legend of Abraham and Isaac, a scenario emerges in which Abraham was some kind of god, who was cast down from Heaven (like Adam), and then bore a first-born son, Isaac, in the underworld. *The line of Isaac would thus represent the first line of men to emerge from the darkness of the underworld into the light of the real world above.*

Was the lamb (or ram) thus given *to the underworld* as a ransom for Isaac?

We have now covered two of the foremost legends of the Old Testament, in their original pagan versions, which both turn out to be legends of the underworld: the legend of Adam, and the legend of Abraham and Isaac. Very different legends admittedly, but this should not surprise us at all, for the Mesopotamian legends of the underworld also amounted to wide variations on a theme.

But there is more. In addition to these two legends, the pagan Israelites also believed that Noah had been an interplanetary hero, who had brought the seeds of life from Heaven to Earth, and had sown them in the underworld, where he had planted a vineyard, got drunk, and fallen asleep in his 'tent'. But on this subject, there is little more to be said at this juncture, for there is a gap in our knowledge concerning exactly how Noah's seed emerged from the underworld.[13]

Instead, for our third example of an underworld legend, we return to the Exodus legend, or rather the occulted form thereof. According to the pagan Israelites, their ancestors had been a celestial race of 'black-headed ones', who had fallen from Heaven to Earth, and thus become trapped in the underworld. In this particular legend, Exodus, the primeval Israelites had multiplied prolifically, but had then become enslaved by an Anunnaki-like race (equated with the Egyptians), who had subjugated them mercilessly. God, however, had heard their suffering, and had sent his emissary, Moses, down from Heaven into the underworld to save them. Incidentally, God had also sent down a second emissary, Aaron, to meet Moses in the 'wilderness' of the underworld; significantly, we read in Exodus 4:27 that Aaron was to meet Moses *in* the 'mountain of God'.[14]

To cut a long story short, Moses and Aaron had helped the primeval Israelites to escape from the underworld and had ascended to the heavenly Mount Sinai, either by parting the waters of the celestial sea, or by crossing the desert-like wilderness of space, or (one presumes) by entering the mouth of the 'cosmic mountain' of Mount Sinai in the underworld.[15] Such were the variant traditions, which appear to have been merged and confused in the biblical book of Exodus which we see today.

More important than the route, however, is the means by which the primeval Israelites had escaped from their slavery.

According to the Psalms, and the books of the various prophets – cited extensively in the previous chapter – the primeval Israelites had been saved *by God himself*, who had parted the waters, come down from Heaven, and simply lifted his chosen 'people' out of the underworld.

The book of Exodus, however, tells a slightly different story. It relates that the escape of the Israelites from the underworld was achieved in a remarkable manner – *by consuming the flesh of sacrificed lambs*.

We read all about this in Exodus 12, which describes the tenth and final plague of Egypt, which would strike down all of the first-born animals and humans throughout the underworld. However, as the wrathful Yahweh (or his destroying angel) prepared to pass through the underworld, the Israelites were given instructions via Moses on how to protect their own first-born. The advice, spoken by God to Moses, was as follows:

> "On the tenth day of this month [the first month] every man is to take a lamb... Your lambs must be year-old males without defect... Take care of them until the fourteenth day of the month, when the whole assembly of the congregation of Israel must slaughter them at twilight. And they must take the blood and smear it on the sides and tops of the door-frames of the houses..."[16]

The plan was that Yahweh would see the blood of the lambs, and would then *pass over* the houses of Israel, and *not* strike down their first-born. But there was more to it:

> "And they must take the blood [of the lamb] and smear it on the sides and tops of the door-frames of the houses, *wherein they must eat it*. And in that same night *they must eat the flesh, roasted with fire*, along with unleavened bread and bitter herbs... And ye must let nothing of it remain by the morning; if some does remain in the morning ye must burn it with fire. And here is how ye shall eat it: with your cloak tucked into your belt, and your shoes on your feet, and your staff in your hand. And ye shall eat it in haste, (for) it is the LORD's Passover."[17]

Why such elaborate instructions, and why bother *eating* the lamb, when the essential protection was from the smeared blood on the door-frames?

The answer, I suggest, is that the primeval Israelites took the flesh of the lambs into their stomachs because *the lamb was crucial to their resurrection*. And this suggestion finds support in the later Christian tradition whereby believers in Jesus Christ could achieve eternal life by eating *his* body – Christ, of course, being 'the Lamb of God'.

But if we are not careful, we will miss the point here. What was the *primary* reason why the Israelites ate the lamb? The answer is: *to avoid the death of their first-born*.

Now, add this to the fact that, when the Israelites were crossing the celestial sea, some of the Egyptians were following them, and had to be repelled back into the Earth. This implies that the Egyptians, too, had succeeded in escaping from the underworld, despite having *not* participated in the ritual eating of the lamb.

The point is this: the lamb was *not* the primary means of escaping from the underworld. The role of the lamb was rather to act as a ransom, or substitute, for the Israelite first-born. *In fact, the primary means of escaping from the underworld was the sacrifice of the first-born*. Only in this way can we rationalise how the Egyptians, too, managed to escape from the underworld, albeit temporarily.[18]

The Israelites, then, would have escaped from the underworld anyway, via the death of their first-born. The lamb is significant because it averted the sacrifice of the first-born, without compromising the Israelites' ability to ascend to Heaven.

In closing this section of our study, one crucial question must be asked: "Where did the sacrificial lambs of the Exodus come from?" Were they lambs which just happened to be frolicking in the underworld (not impossible according to the ancient beliefs)? Or were the lambs sent down specially from God in Heaven to ransom Israel's first-born?

On this occasion, the *Kebra Nagast* does *not* supply us with the answer, but nevertheless, in the light of the close parallel between the Exodus story and the story of Abraham and Isaac – which we now know was also a legend of the underworld – it seems an entirely reasonable proposition that the first-born of the Israelites were indeed ransomed by a lamb sent down from Heaven.

The Mystery of Human Sacrifice

Sir James Frazer once asked, in his epic treatise *The Golden Bough*: 'Why should the Israelites kill the firstlings of their cattle for ever because God once killed those of the Egyptians?'[19] It is a question which has puzzled many scholars, not just Frazer, during past centuries. But few, if any, of these scholars have ever suspected that the legend of Exodus was based on a mythical model – of an Exodus which occurred at the beginning of the world.

But, as Frazer pointed out elsewhere in his book, this was not just a question of sacrificing cattle, for the Israelites were frequently drawn towards the pagan practice of *sacrificing their first-born children*. This fact is well attested in biblical scripture. For example, we read in the book of Judges how Jephthah, an early judge of Israel, subdued the Ammonites in battle only at the cost of sacrificing his daughter, his only child, as a burnt offering to Yahweh.[20] Similarly, in the second book of Kings, we read that Ahaz, a king of Judah, sacrificed his son in the fire, as did Manasseh, a later king of Judah.[21] It was practices such as these which drew the contempt of the prophet Ezekiel, who railed against the Israelites for sacrificing their first-born sons and daughters to the pagan gods.[22]

To the pagans, it would seem that the practice of sacrificing the first-born human child was widespread – not the exception but the norm. Thus, throughout the Old Testament, we read accounts of how pagan peoples would burn their sons and daughters in the fire as sacrifices to their gods.[23] The nature of these sacrifices is captured by the words of Yahweh in the book of Isaiah, where he cursed the evildoers saying: "You burn with lust under every green tree, slaying your children in the ravines, and under the overhanging crags."[24] Modern biblical authorities are in no doubt that both the pagans *and* the Hebrews really *did* carry out these barbaric human sacrifices.[25] Moreover, the practice seems to have been widespread throughout the ancient world, and not just in the ancient Near East.[26]

But what was the rationale behind the sacrifice of the human first-born? There are certain passages in the Old Testament which, I believe, provide a very significant clue. Firstly, in respect of the pagans, we read in the second book of Kings that a Moabite king attempted to win over his gods by sacrificing his first-born son on the city wall.[27] Secondly, in respect of the Israelites, we read in the book of Joshua a prophecy that anyone who rebuilt Jericho would 'lay the foundations at the cost of his first-born son'.[28] In the first book of Kings, this is indeed exactly what happened to Hiel of Bethel, when he attempted to rebuild Jericho.[29]

Now, in earlier chapters of this book, we saw how the ancient peoples of Egypt and Mesopotamia believed that the foundations of the Earth had been laid by the gods (as indeed they were said to have been laid by Yahweh, the Hebrew God), and we noted a certain idiomatic connection between the 'city wall' and the surface of the Earth. This leads me to suspect that those passages of the Bible cited above are reflecting the same idea – of a primordial sacrifice of a god falling from Heaven to Earth at the beginning of time, and relaying the Earth's foundations.

Could it be that the Israelites and other pagan peoples were re-enacting in human flesh the exploded planet myths which we have been discussing throughout this book?

The idea is not at all far-fetched. Indeed, Mircea Eliade expressed exactly the same conceptual idea back in 1949:

> A sacrifice not only exactly reproduces the initial sacrifice revealed by
> a god at the beginning of time, it also takes place at that same
> primordial mythical moment; in other words every sacrifice repeats
> the initial sacrifice and coincides with it. All sacrifices are performed
> at the same mythical instant of the beginning...[30]

Lest there be any doubt about this in a Hebrew context, consider the traditions of the Day of Atonement (*yohm hakkippurim*). On this day, once a year, the high priest of Israel would slaughter a bull as a sin offering for the priestly caste, and a goat as a sin offering for Israel's common people.[31] The slaughter would take place on the altar at the entrance to the tabernacle, or in later times at the entrance to the temple.

On this sole occasion, during the entire year, the high priest would enter the holy-of-holies of the tabernacle or temple. He would approach the 'atonement cover' (*kapporeth*) of the Ark of the Covenant with the greatest caution, using burning coals and incense to produce clouds of smoke, which would conceal the Ark from his view (failure to take this precaution would risk death).[32] The high priest would then use his finger to sprinkle the blood of the sacrificed animals on the *kapporeth*, seven times with the blood of the bull, and seven times with the blood of the goat.

In this way, once a year, the most holy place of the Israelites was purified, and atonement was made for all the sins of the Israelites.

Consider the symbolism of this ritual, particularly as regards its later celebration at Jerusalem. Note, firstly, that the ritual would have taken place in the sacred Bond of Heaven-and-Earth.[33] Note, secondly, that the Ark of the Covenant, in the holy-of-holies, was effectively a microcosm of Mount Sinai, the 'cosmic mountain', for it had been designed specifically as a mobile substitute for Mount Sinai, enabling the Israelites to continue their face to face meetings with God.

When we think about the Ark of the Covenant in this way, the rituals of Atonement Day literally explode with significance. For example, did not the smeared blood of the animals on the *kapporeth* re-enact the sacrifice of the creation, on the top of the fallen 'cosmic mountain'? Did not the *kapporeth* (the cover of the Ark) symbolise the *covering-over* of the 'Word' of God (i.e. the tablets of testimony inside the Ark)? Did not the two cherubim above the *kapporeth* symbolise the cherubim which were placed to the 'east' of the underworld, thereby preventing access to the forbidden Tree of Life? Did not the whole ceremony atone for the inherited sins of the Israelites – the sins which they brought up out of the darkness of the underworld, into the world above?

The answer to all of these questions, I suggest is "Yes!". Moreover, it is especially significant that Atonement Day was also known as the 'Day of the Coverings', and the 'Day of Ransoms'.[34] Did not the Day of the Coverings allude to the *covering over, within the Earth,* of the fallen 'mountain', and indeed to the *covering over, within the Earth,* of the fallen 'people'? Did not the Day of Ransoms allude to the ransoming of the Israelite first-born from the underworld with a lamb, or a ram?

Once again, I suggest that the answer to both of these questions is an affirmative "Yes!".

It thus seems to me that Mircea Eliade was spot on as far as the Hebrews were concerned. Their ceremonies and sacrifices were indeed re-enacting the mythical instant of 'the beginning'.

There is another element to this, too, which we shall cover in a later chapter – namely the ancient idea that the 'original sin' of man was carried out by 'the black-headed ones' *in Heaven*, thus accounting for the 'fact' that 'mankind' had been cast down into the Earth.

It is with this idea of a celestial sin in mind that we must try to understand the origin of the Hebrew beliefs. Consider, for example, the words of the prophet Micah, who asked:

> Shall I offer my first-born for my transgression, the fruit of my body
> for the sin of my soul?[35]

The meaning here, I suggest, is that the sin of man was inherited from heavenly 'mankind', who had broken forth from the womb of the Sky-goddess *as a first-born*, and had been sacrificed as it fell like a seed into the womb of Mother Earth, in order that a second generation of men be brought forth in the underworld.

It is in this sense that we should interpret the legend of the fallen god Adam bringing forth Seth 'in his own image', and the legend of the fallen god Abraham bringing forth Isaac, and possibly the legend of the fallen god Noah bringing forth the trio of Shem, Ham and Japheth.

It is the same story as the fallen god Osiris bringing forth Horus, and the fallen god Dumuzi bringing forth Gilgamesh, not to mention many other similar legends of the ancient world.

In a nutshell, the ancients believed that life on Earth had begun with death in the Sky. Hence the saying that a king would 'lay the foundations at the cost of his first-born son'. Furthermore, it was supposed that the sacrificed body of the first-born would increase the fertility of the Earth, and thus allow new life to be born (or reborn) within the womb of Mother Earth.

It would thus seem that the ancients slaughtered their first-born in emulation of the mythical sacrifice of the primordial 'man', believing that it was taboo for the first-born to live. And furthermore, we might hazard a guess that the slaughtering of the first-born was supposed to increase the fertility of the woman's womb, in emulation of the womb of Mother Earth, which had produced the second generation of 'men'.[36]

As far as the Israelites were concerned, however, God had spared them from the necessity of killing their first-born. It is a belief which we find expressed twice. Firstly, in the legend of Abraham and Isaac, where the first-born son Isaac was spared from death (or resurrected from death by some accounts).[37] And secondly, in the legend of Exodus, where the first-born of the Israelites were spared from death. Significantly, these events (in their unocculted forms) took place in the underworld and *the lamb* was the substitute victim in both cases.

It is for these reasons that the Israelites believed that they could kill a lamb to 'redeem' each of their first-born sons from death. The situation is explained in the book of Exodus as follows:

> And in days to come, when thy son asketh thee: "What does this
> mean?", thou shalt say unto him: "With a mighty hand the LORD
> brought us out of the land of Egypt, out of the house of bondage. And
> it came to pass, when Pharaoh resisted letting us go, that the LORD
> slew all the first-born in the land of Egypt, both the first-born of man,
> and the first-born of beast. This is why I [now] sacrifice to the LORD
> the first male offspring of every womb and *redeem each of my*
> *first-born sons*."[38]

This, however, was only one aspect of the Israelites' covenant with God. In addition, there was a much wider regulation which affected every male in the land of Israel, and that was *circumcision*.

What was the origin of the ritual of circumcision? In the legend of Abraham, we find that the requirement was specified by God himself:

> "This is my covenant, which ye shall keep, between me and thee and
> thy seed after thee: every man-child among you shall be circumcised,
> ye shall circumcise the flesh of your foreskin, and it will be a sign of

the covenant between me and thee... my covenant shall be in your flesh for a covenant of eternity."[39]

But why circumcision? What was the special significance of mutilating the male organ?

The answer is revealed by a strange incident of circumcision which is reported in the book of Exodus. Significantly, the incident occurred when Moses was returning into the underworld ('Egypt'), having just received his instructions from God, in Heaven, at the site of the 'burning bush'. This is what happened next:

> And it came to pass by the way in the inn, that the LORD met him [Moses], and sought to kill him. Then Zipporah [the wife of Moses] took a sharp stone, and cut off the foreskin of her son, and cast it at his feet, and said: "Surely thou art a bloody husband to me." So he [the LORD] let him [Moses] go. Then she said: "Thou art a bloody husband because of the circumcision."[40]

This intriguing passage has never been properly explained by biblical scholars, who have never been able to agree to whom it was that Zipporah was speaking, nor to whose feet she threw the foreskin. And, even more crucially, no-one has ever offered a satisfactory explanation as to why God suddenly turned so hostile towards Moses.

But the answers to all of these questions become very simple once we realise that *Moses was descending from Heaven*. It then becomes clear that the 'inn' – which was effectively a reception place for all visitors – was a metaphor for the antechamber to the underworld. It would then follow that 'the LORD' in this incident was not Yahweh, but rather the god of the underworld, probably the fiery Mesopotamian god, Nergal.

The next step in the decoding of this legend is to realise that the gods of the underworld loved to take tokens and trophies from arriving parties. It would thus seem that Nergal was requiring a foreskin as the price of entry into his underworld, hence the bad-tempered confrontation with Moses.

But why did Moses not comply? Could the answer be that he had already descended into the underworld once before, when he had been carried into the Earth in his ark? If so, he would have handed over his foreskin previously, leaving him now unable to comply with Nergal's new demand.

This, I feel sure, is the meaning of the legend. When Zipporah cut off her son's foreskin, she gave it to Nergal as a substitute for the missing foreskin of her husband, Moses. She then threw the foreskin at the feet of Moses, as if to say "Look – he *is* my bloodied husband, and he *does* thereby qualify for entry into the underworld."[41]

Yes, this is a bizarre legend, but we may rest assured that ancient legends of the underworld invariably sound bizarre to the modern ear. This particular story is not at all unusual by Mesopotamian standards.

So, why did Moses have to sacrifice his foreskin in order to enter the underworld? The explanation, I suggest, lies in the idea that the foreskin was a substitute for the phallus, and that the phallus was the part of the god which had impregnated the Earth. Readers may recall, for example, the legend of the missing phallus of Osiris, which was supposedly swallowed by a 'fish'. The 'fish', however, was a metaphor for the Earth, because the phallus of Osiris was, by all accounts, *in the underworld*. And the reason that the *phallus* was in the underworld was simply because it was the most potent fertility symbol for a masculine god who had seeded the Earth.

In concluding my argument, I would mention that the Hebrew verb for 'circumcise' is *mul*, which in the Sumerian and Akkadian languages meant 'celestial body'.[42] It strikes me that this is not a coincidence at all, in view of Moses, Abraham, Noah and Adam all representing exploding and falling celestial bodies. It makes perfect sense that the custom of circumcision (*mul*) would have been adopted as a sensible step short of full castration, but nevertheless symbolising the sacrifice of the phallus when primordial 'man' came down from the Sky and entered the Earth.[43]

In summary, then, it may be hypothesised with some confidence that the early Israelites had a very strong sense of identity as a race of people who had descended from Heaven. Hence they were created in the image of God (via Adam), and hence they were the *Ibri* – those who had 'crossed over' from Heaven to Earth. The circumcision of their foreskins was an eternal sign of this celestial origin, and for many it would have been a sign that they had a right to an afterlife in Heaven, whence they came. In later times, however, the priests pulled out every trick in the book to eradicate such aspirations.

The Israelite belief in their celestial origin was no doubt shared by many other races in the ancient world, but what marked out the Israelites as different was their attitude to their emergence from the underworld. It is here that we find the idea that the Israelites were a 'chosen race'.

As the legend of Abraham and Isaac makes clear, the Israelites had been allowed – by the divine ordinance of Yahweh – to emerge from the underworld without paying the normal price of release. Instead of killing their first-born children, *they were allowed to redeem them by sacrificing a lamb*.

This special treatment is also evident in the legend of Exodus, both in the original and in the occulted versions. God had saved the Israelites from 'the iron-smelting furnace', and had once again saved their first-born by allowing *a lamb* to be substituted in their stead.

It seems to me that this lamb is the key to understanding Judaism. But more than that, it might also be the key to understanding Christianity.

Jesus Christ – The Lamb of God

In the gospel of John, there is a very famous passage in which John the Baptist refers to Jesus as 'the Lamb of God, who takes away the sin of the world.'[44] In addition, the book of Revelations makes repeated allusions to the idea that the Son of God was 'the Lamb'.[45] And furthermore, as we noted earlier in this chapter, there is a telling statement by Paul, in his letter to the Corinthians, to the effect that Jesus Christ was the lamb which had been sacrificed at Passover.

How should we now interpret Jesus Christ, 'the Lamb of God', in the context of (a) the lambs which were sacrificed to protect the first-born of Israel during the Exodus; and (b) the lamb (or ram) which was sent down from Heaven to act as a sacrifice, in lieu of Abraham's first-born son, Isaac?

Until now, the view has been that the Exodus was *a historic event*, that Abraham and Isaac's trip to Mount Moriah was *a historic event*, and that the sacrifice of Jesus Christ two thousand years ago was *a historic event*.

Now, however, we can see that in two of these three cases, the event in question was not really historic at all. On the contrary, the sacrifices of these lambs occurred not in mundane time, but in sacred time. They were sacrifices which took place at the beginning of the world.

What might this mean for Jesus Christ, 'the Lamb of God'? In the following pages, we are going to take a look at some intriguing legends in the Old Testament that seem to have a bearing on this issue, for they appear to describe the suffering and crucifixion of a Christ-like figure – *many centuries before* Jesus Christ was crucified in Jerusalem. These amazing correspondences between the Old and New Testaments have not gone unnoticed, but the Church holds the view that the descriptions of the suffering messiah in the Old Testament were *prophecies* about the *future coming* of Jesus Christ, as described in the New Testament.

It is time, I suggest, to take a fresh look at the evidence.

The Secret of Psalm 22

We begin, aptly enough, with the dying words of Jesus, as attributed to him by the gospels of Matthew and Mark:

"My God, my God, why hast thou forsaken me?"[46]

There is no dispute about the fact that Jesus was citing here the first verse of Psalm 22 in the Old Testament. But *why* did Jesus speak the words of this particular psalm?

When we turn to Psalm 22, we find that the words were spoken by one who claimed to be not a 'man', but a 'worm':

> But I am a worm, and not a man, scorned by men and despised by the
> people.
> All who see me mock me, insult me, shaking their heads...[47]

This idea of 'the worm' is very interesting, for it is found elsewhere in the Bible in the context of the underworld (in my opinion),[48] and this might well be the intention here, for the psalm paints a vivid image of a crowd of people mocking and insulting 'the worm', and challenging Yahweh to come down and rescue him. Was the 'worm' trapped in the dark and dingy underworld of Sheol?

In verses 12-15, Psalm 22 explains how the 'worm' had indeed been brought into the dust of death, i.e. into the underworld:

> Many bulls have surrounded me; strong and fertile bulls encircle me.
> They opened their mouths at me like attacking, roaring lions.
> I am poured out like water, and all my bones are out of joint.
> My heart is like wax, which has melted away within me.
> My strength is dried up like a potsherd, and my tongue cannot move.
> Thou hast brought me into the dust of death [i.e. into Sheol].[49]

But then, in verses 16-18 of Psalm 22, we find something which is truly remarkable. The worm-like 'man' was 'pierced' – *apparently crucified* – by the assembly of the wicked *in the underworld*:

> Dogs have surrounded me; the assembly of the wicked has encircled
> me; *they have pierced my hands and my feet.*
> I am witness to all my bones, as people stare and gloat over me.
> They divide my garments among them and cast lots for my clothing.[50]

This is an extraordinary passage. As mentioned earlier, the Church suggests that this is *a prophecy of a future Jesus Christ*, on the basis of its remarkable similarity to the treatment of Christ. Note, for example, the references to the casting of lots and dividing of garments, and compare this to the treatment of Jesus in the gospel of Matthew:

> And they [the Roman soldiers] crucified him, and divided his
> garments, by casting lots.[51]

But was this really a prophecy-come-true? After all, Jesus-the-man of two thousand years ago was *not crucified in the underworld*, as would have to have been the case if Psalm 22 was really an accurate prophecy of the future.

But there is more. Consider the longer passage cited above: 'Many bulls have surrounded me...'. This reminds me very much of the way the Mesopotamians would allude to the planetary battle, with an innocent Sky-god being surrounded and attacked by his adversaries in the form of divine bulls. A classic example is the legend of the Mesopotamian god Dumuzi, who was originally a Sky-god, but was then attacked and carried off by a wild animal:

> The Bison has taken thy husband away, up into the mountains!
> Bison of the mountains, with the mottled eyes!
> Bison of the mountains, with the crushing teeth![52]

Might this celestial Bison be equivalent to the bulls in Psalm 22?

Note, too, how the innocent victim of Psalm 22 was 'poured out like water'. This is extremely evocative of the ancient traditions of the Flood-god, who came down from Heaven, sometimes in the form of a celestial river.

Finally, note the reference to the victim's 'bones' being 'out of joint'. Again, this is a remarkable parallel to the dismemberment of the Egyptian god Osiris. *But it hardly seems like a prophecy about Jesus, who was not disfigured, according to the New Testament.*[53]

In summary, Psalm 22 cannot be describing the death of Jesus Christ, or at least not according to the account of Jesus Christ as we know it. On the contrary, it appears to be recording the death of a Sky-god, who was attacked in Heaven, cast down into the underworld, and then abused therein by the assembly of the wicked.

And this is the psalm to which we are directed by Jesus's dying words! One cannot help wondering whether we have been guided to Psalm 22 deliberately, either by the voice of Jesus, or by the writers of the gospels, or perhaps even by the voice of popular 1st century tradition.

Furthermore, one cannot help wondering whether the statement "My God, my God, why hast thou forsaken me?" was some kind of well-known esoteric saying among the mystery school initiates of two thousand years ago – those who knew about mankind's celestial origins.

The Suffering of the Righteous Servant

Let us now consider a parallel tradition to Psalm 22, namely the legend

Plate 22 (right) The biblical story of Adam and Eve claims that God created Adam from clay, and later created Eve from the rib of Adam. But this turns out to be a blatant lie when the story is compared to that of earlier Mesopotamian texts.

Plate 23 (left) This Sumerian tablet relates how 'mankind' was created by Enki and Ninharsag, using 'the clay which is above the AB.ZU'. The legend also confirms that the new-born creature was given 'the likeness of the gods'. Might this be the source of the biblical story?

Plate 24 (right) The legend of Ulligarra and Zalgarra describes the creation of 'mankind' from the 'blood' of the gods. The column on the left contains indecipherable symbols, which are thought to be some kind of secret writing. The decipherable portion ends with the enigmatic words: 'Let the wise teach the mystery to the wise.'

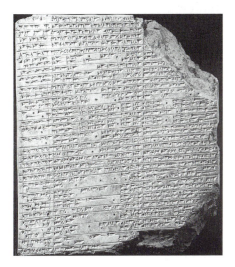

Plate 25 (above left) This tablet (2nd millennium BC) tells of Enlil's decision to destroy 'mankind' with a Flood. But the hero Atra-Hasis built a boat and saved the seed of mankind and all living things – just like Noah in the Bible.

Plate 26 (above right) Tablet XI of *The Epic of Gilgamesh* tells a similar story of a Flood-hero named Utnapishtim, but it also contains 'a secret of the gods' which enables us to decode the hidden meaning of all the Flood legends.

Plate 27 This full-size wooden boat was buried alongside the Great Pyramid of Giza, and was intended to convey the departed Egyptian king to the land of the gods in the celestial ocean.

Boats such as this one were celestial first and foremost. To sail them along the Nile was to re-enact the First Time, when the gods had crossed the so-called 'Winding Waterway' between Heaven and Earth.

Plate 28 (right) This statue – known as 'Ram in a Thicket' – was buried in the Great Death Pit of Ur (*c.* 2100 BC). The image reminds one of the ram which God sent to Abraham, in order to redeem his first-born son, Isaac. Note the feathers which attest to the fact that this is no ordinary ram.

Plate 29 (left) The Sumerian Kings List names eight god-like 'kings', who each ruled for thousands of years prior to the great Flood. The Bible similarly lists ten patriarchs, who each enjoyed a superhuman life span prior to the great Flood.

Plate 30 (right) 'My changeling mother conceived me... she set me in a reed-basket, she sealed the lid with bitumen, she cast me into the river'. The birth legend of Sargon, recorded on this tablet (*c.* 700 BC), bears astonishing similarities to the biblical story of Moses.

Plate 31 (above left) The Babylonian Epic of Creation (Tablet IV) describes how Marduk created a metaphysical Heaven, Esharra, by raising up an image of the physical Heaven, Apsu, which had earlier been cast down into the underworld.

Plate 32 (above right) In this Sumerian fragment of *The Epic of Gilgamesh*, the hero set off in search of Heaven, which he called 'the Land of the Living'.

Plate 33 (below) The ziggurat of Babylon, like all ancient ziggurats, was a 'cosmic mountain' – a permanent bond between Heaven, Earth and underworld.

Plate 34 (above) The temple complex of Karnak in Egypt incorporated a 'Mansion of Millions of Years', symbolising the bond which had once existed between Heaven and Earth at the beginning of time. Note, too, the giant obelisk, which lifted the seed of the creator-god back to the Sky whence it had come.

Plate 35 (below) The pyramids of Giza were 'cosmic mountains' in the image of Heaven and Earth. They translated Egyptian kings back to the beginning of time, whereupon they hoped to rebuild the disintegrated 'mountain' of Heaven.

Plate 36 (above) Agriculture in the afterlife – a scene from the ancient Egyptian Book of the Dead. The existence of this 'Field of Reeds' in the Sky is eloquent testimony to the ancient belief in Heaven as an Earth-like abode.

Plate 37 (below) The Great Sphinx of Giza gazes towards the distant 'mountain' in the eastern side of the Sky, where the king's double was thought to dwell in the land of his earliest ancestors.

Plate 38 (above) The Parthenon on the Acropolis at Athens (5th century BC). The Greeks, too, commemorated the First Time in their temples. As in Egypt and Mesopotamia, the roof symbolised Heaven, the base symbolised Earth, and the columns symbolised the cords which conveyed life from one to the other.

Plate 39 (below) The Roman Temple of Bacchus at Baalbek (2nd century AD) was one of the last great pagan temples to be built before Christianity was made the official state religion of the Roman empire.

Plate 40 Jesus on the cross, Church of the Holy Sepulchre, Jerusalem.

An age-old story told in a simple and human-like way, but retaining an esoteric significance for the few who were initiated into the ancient secrets.

Plate 41 (below) The largest known meteorite in the world, weighing sixty tons, is displayed in a sunken courtyard at Hoba in Namibia. Could meteorites such as this one be the key to both ancient and modern religions?

of the 'Righteous Servant' in the book of Isaiah, chapters 52-53. This happens to be one of the Bible's most mysterious passages, but it has often been cited by the Church as strong evidence for the prophetic nature of the Old Testament. We shall now reconsider whether this is so.

We will begin towards the end of Isaiah 52, and then proceed through Isaiah 53 in short sections, stopping where appropriate to make pertinent comments and observations. The effort we invest in understanding these passages will prove to be well worthwhile.

The legend of the Righteous Servant begins at Isaiah 52:13, where God is made to utter the following words:

> Behold, my Servant will act wisely; he will be raised, and lifted up, and highly exalted.
> He will sprinkle many nations [like sacrificial blood?]; the kings shall be speechless because of him.
> Just as there were many who were (once) astonished at him. (For) his appearance was so disfigured – beyond that of any man – his form (marred) beyond that of (all) mankind.[54]

According to the Church, this Servant is the future Jesus Christ. But, if so, how can it be that the Servant was 'disfigured', with a form marred beyond that of any man? Might this just possibly be an esoteric allusion to a primordial 'man' who had been cast down from Heaven to Earth?

The text continues:

> He [the Righteous Servant] grew up before him [the LORD] like a tender shoot, and like a root out of dry ground.
> He had no beauty or majesty to attract us to him, nothing in his appearance that we should desire him.
> He was despised and rejected by men; (he was) a man of sorrows, and acquainted with grief.
> And we hid our faces, as it were, from him; he was despised, and we esteemed him not.[55]

In this passage, we find the same theme as in Psalm 22, namely the idea that an innocent 'man' was despised. Note, too, the reference to the Servant growing up like a shoot, almost as if he has been *planted in the ground* by the LORD (as was Israel and Joseph). The *Kebra Nagast* expands on this particular line, saying: 'He was a humble man, and his appearance was rejected; like a root he hid himself in parched ground. He came in the flesh as a being of the earth, though he was the sustainer and saviour of the universe.'[56] Note the idea here that the servant *hid himself in the ground*. It is hard to miss the parallel with the archetypal

Seeds of Mankind – Adam, Noah and Abraham – who all descended from Heaven *into the underworld* of the Earth.

The text continues:

> Surely he [the Righteous Servant] bore our griefs, and carried our sorrows; yet we considered him stricken by God, smitten by him, and afflicted.
>
> But he was wounded for our transgressions, he was crushed for our iniquities; the punishment that brought us peace was upon him; and by his stripes [wounds] we are healed.
>
> We all, like sheep, have gone astray... and the LORD hath laid on him the iniquity of us all.[57]

Note here the idea of the Servant being 'wounded' and 'crushed'. Once again, the words are evocative of a crushed celestial body. Note, too, the reference to the sinfulness of mankind, and the statement that peace was only brought to mankind by the sacrifice of the Righteous Servant. In the next chapter, we shall see how this 'original sin' was committed by heavenly 'mankind'.

The text continues:

> He [the Righteous Servant] was oppressed and afflicted, yet he did not open his mouth; he was led like a lamb to the slaughter; and just like a sheep is dumb before its shearers, so did he not open his mouth.
>
> From arrest and judgement he was taken away. Yet who of his generation considered (it)?
>
> He was cut off from the land of the living for the transgression of my people, to whom the blow was (really) due.
>
> And he made his grave with the wicked, and with the rich in his death, even though he had done no violence, nor was there any deceit in his mouth.[58]

Note how the innocence of the Servant is contrasted with the sinfulness of mankind, a central theme of the Jesus Christ legend. Note, too, the reference to the 'lamb' which did not open its mouth – an idea which is found also in the arrest of Jesus Christ by the Romans. However, it is important to appreciate that this Righteous Servant of the Old Testament was cut off from the 'land of the living', which in this context would have referred to Heaven, for the Servant was then deposited in the underworld – the land of the dead – where he was surrounded by the wicked, as in Psalm 22 earlier.

The text continues:

> Yet it pleased the LORD to crush him; he put (him) to grief. And when the LORD made his [the Righteous Servant's] soul an offering for sin, he looked upon (his) seed, he prolonged (his) days, and the pleasure of the LORD prospered in his hand.
> He saw the suffering of his soul, and was satisfied, (for) by his knowledge the Righteous Servant justified many, by bearing their iniquities.[59]

The meaning of this passage is a little obscure. Somehow the Servant seems to have suffered, but at the same time 'he looked upon seed'. The description might well fit the idea of the Seed of Mankind, who had entered the underworld and caused seed to come forth into the world above (compare the legend of Abraham).

The Righteous Servant text now ends, with the LORD himself now speaking highly of the servant:

> "Therefore I [the LORD] will give him [the Righteous Servant] a portion with the great, and he shall divide the spoil with the strong; because he poured out his soul unto (the place of) death, and he was numbered with the transgressors.
> And he bore the sin of many, and made intercession for the transgressors."[60]

Once again, we find reference to the land of death, i.e. the underworld. As for the 'intercession for the transgressors', this is remarkably evocative of the way Abraham intervened on behalf of the citizens of the evil cities, Sodom and Gomorrah.[61] The most important line here, however, is the promise of greatness, which echoes the LORD's earlier comments in Isaiah 52:13-15, where the servant was to be 'raised, lifted up and highly exalted'. It would seem that the intention was that God would lift up the Righteous Servant at the End of Days.

What is the meaning of these enigmatic verses? It is true that there are remarkable similarities between the treatment of the Righteous Servant and the treatment of Jesus Christ. For example, the Righteous Servant was said to have been 'taken away from arrest and judgement', to have been 'led like a lamb to the slaughter', and to have 'borne the sin of many' by being 'wounded for our transgressions'. Exactly the same could be said of Jesus, who was said to be 'the Lamb of God', who was taken away from arrest and judgement, who 'took away the sin of the world' through his suffering, and 'gave his life as a ransom for many'.[62]

These similarities are detailed as well as broad. Consider, for example, the statement that the Righteous Servant 'did not open his mouth', but was 'dumb, like a sheep before its shearers'. According to the gospel of

Matthew, Jesus appeared before the Roman governor Pontius Pilate in identical fashion:

> And when he [Jesus] was accused by the chief priests and elders, he said nothing in reply. Then Pilate said to him: "Do you not hear how many things they witness against you?" And he [Jesus] spoke not a word in reply, causing the governor to be greatly amazed.[63]

According to the Church, we, too, should be greatly amazed at this, for it represents a prime example of Isaiah's supernatural ability to predict the future. Such is the paradigm of the Church; the prophecies of the Old Testament were divinely inspired, because God was orchestrating a grand design, culminating in the sacrifice of his Son, Jesus Christ, two thousand years ago.

But is this really the truth? It must be said that certain of the Old Testament 'prophecies' leave a lot to be desired, at least in so far as they were interpreted by the writers of the gospels. Matthew, in particular, took terrible liberties. The worst example appears in Matthew 2:15, at the point where Jesus had just returned to Israel, having been hidden in Egypt. Matthew then claimed a fulfilment of the prophet's words: "Out of Egypt I called my son."[64] This was obviously a reference to the Old Testament prophet Hosea, who had made God speak these exact words.[65] But on reading the passage in question in the book of Hosea, it becomes blatantly obvious that the prophet was referring to how God had called his son *Israel* out of Egypt *at the time of the Exodus*. In other words, the passage concerned *the past*, not the future.

This seems to exemplify a common problem, especially where the supposed 'prophecies' of the future Christ are concerned. It seems to me that texts such as Psalm 22 (the crucifixion in the underworld) and Isaiah 52-53 (the suffering of the Righteous Servant in the underworld) were not prophetic at all, but rather *mytho-historic*. They were describing the mistreatment of a 'man' who had been cast down from Heaven into the underworld at the beginning of time.

But what if this 'man' *was* Jesus Christ? What if we could prove that Jesus Christ had come down from the heavens, and had been crucified, in the underworld, at the beginning of time? What would this mean for the story of Jesus Christ as we know it?

The Primeval Christ

In the gospel of John, Jesus made a very strange statement, which appalled many of his listeners in the gathered crowd. His exact words, which were regarded as blasphemous, were as follows:

"Before Abraham was born, I am!"[66]

What did Jesus mean? His statement is clarified in the gospel of John, where Jesus prayed to God with the following words:

"O Father, glorify me in your presence with the glory I had with you before the world began."[67]

This same idea was established at the very beginning of the gospel of John, where Jesus Christ was referred to as 'the Word', which 'was made flesh', and which 'came forth from the Father', to dwell among mankind.[68] The writer of John's gospel informs us that Jesus Christ, the Word, had existed alongside God from 'the beginning':

In the beginning was the Word, and the Word was toward the God, and the Word was a god. He [the Word] was with God in the beginning.[69]

This concept of the primeval, personified 'Word' was not a new idea, but echoed an Old Testament figure known as 'Wisdom'.[70] And Wisdom, too, had existed from the beginning of the world, as is revealed in the book of Proverbs, where Wisdom-personified uttered the following account of his origins:

"The LORD possessed me [Wisdom] in the beginning of his dominion, before his works of old.
I was fashioned from eternity, from the beginning, before the Earth began...
I was there when he prepared the heavens, when he marked out the horizon on the face of the Deep... when he appointed the foundations of the Earth."[71]

So entrenched was the idea that Christ, or Wisdom, had existed alongside God at the beginning of the world that ancient writers often suggested that it was to Christ that God had uttered the immortal words: "Let *us* make man in *our* image, in *our* likeness."[72]

But this primeval Christ, whom we might call 'the Son-of-Beginning', was not just a spectator at the creation. Rather, he was the agent of God, through whom the creation took place. This idea is expressed clearly in Paul's 'Letter to the Hebrews', where Paul referred to 'the Son, whom he [God] has appointed heir of all things, *by whom also he made the worlds* [i.e. Heaven and Earth].'[73]

Similarly, in Paul's 'Letter to the Colossians', we read:

He [Christ] is the image of the invisible God, the first-born of every creature: for by him were all things created, visible and invisible... all things were created by him [Christ], and for him. And he is before all things, and in him all things are held together.[74]

The same claim was made of Christ, the Word, in the gospel of John:

Through him all things were made; without him nothing was made that has been made.[75]

Who, or what, was this primeval alter ego of Jesus Christ? Christians believe that he was *a pure Spirit-being*, which had assisted a supernatural God in the creation, but had then stood on the sidelines until the 1st century AD, when the Spirit materialised into the body of Jesus-the-man.

However, in the context of the pagan traditions of a *physical* creation of the Earth by a *physical*, planetary creator-god, the idea of a *purely spiritual* Christ looks questionable to say the least. If we allow the pagan traditions to be our guide, then this primeval Christ would have taken on a spiritual form only *after* a resurrection from a *physical* death. This was the pagan model, as explained by the Egyptian Book of the Dead:

The corpse of Osiris entered the mountain [the Earth] but the soul of Osiris walked out shining... he came forth from death, a shining thing, his face white with heat.[76]

So, let us explore the possibility that the primeval Christ was a *physical* god, who had come down from Heaven – catastrophically – and had helped God to lay *physically* the new foundations of the Earth.

What would have happened next? According to the rules of ancient ankiography, the descending deity would have entered the underworld.

Now, the lights are coming on in the darkness! Firstly, we should recall from earlier that Jesus was known as 'the Lamb of God'. Secondly, we should recall that God had sent *a lamb* (or ram) *into the underworld* as a substitute for Isaac. Thirdly, we should recall my suggestion that it was God who had sent *the lambs* of Exodus *into the underworld* as substitutes for the first-born of the Israelites. Both of these substitution events, we now know, occurred at the beginning of the world.

This leads to a very interesting, and indeed quite profound, hypothesis. Could it be that the primeval Christ was the very same 'lamb' (or ram) which had redeemed Isaac, and the very same 'lambs' that had redeemed the Hebrew first-born?

The suggestion is not at all far-fetched. Consider, for example, the following enigmatic statement ascribed to Jesus in the gospel of John:

"Your father Abraham rejoiced to see my day, and he saw, and was glad."[77]

What! How could Abraham have seen Jesus Christ?

This is my point. Was it *the primeval Christ* who was seen by Abraham? Was it none other than Jesus Christ, the Son-of-Beginning, who had appeared to Abraham *in* the mountain, as the lamb (or ram) which had redeemed Isaac?

Note that I wrote '*in* the mountain'. According to my interpretation of the legend of Abraham and Isaac, the attempted sacrifice of Isaac took place in the underworld, as a prelude to man's emergence from the underworld. The lamb (or ram) sent by God was thus sent as a substitute into the underworld, i.e. into the 'mountain' of Earth.

It is significant that Abraham commemorated this event by naming the mountain where it took place YHWH-*jireh*, meaning 'Yahweh sees'. The name was explained by the biblical editors with the following gloss:

... it is said to this day: "In the mountain of the LORD it is seen."[78]

There seems to be a double meaning here. On the one hand, it is clear that Yahweh had *seen* the attempted sacrifice by Abraham, and had intervened. On the other hand, the biblical editors seem to be recording an archaic saying with a different connotation: "In the mountain of the LORD *it* is *seen*." What was 'it'? The answer, I suggest, is *the ram*, because the 'mountain' of the LORD was *the Earth*.[79] In other words, the ram had been placed *in* the Earth as a substitute for Isaac, who had been allowed to come *out of* the Earth. Was the 'ram in the mountain' thus equivalent to the primeval Jesus Christ?

This might all seem a little tenuous if it were not for the fact that the same argument can be made in respect of the Exodus. Just as Jesus Christ made an enigmatic claim concerning Abraham, so did he concerning Moses. We read his words, spoken to the Jews, in the gospel of John:

"Had you believed Moses, you would believe me, for he [Moses] wrote about me."[80]

Did Moses write a prophecy about a *future* Jesus Christ? Not one that we know of.

How, then, to explain this strange comment by Jesus? The answer, I suggest, is that the writings ascribed to Moses alluded to the mythical time of the beginning of the world. It is for this reason that Isaiah referred to the days of Moses as 'the days of eternity'.[81] Jesus would thus have been identifying himself as one of the characters in the writings ascribed to Moses – perhaps the destroying angel of God, or perhaps the pillar of cloud and fire, perhaps even Moses himself, *or perhaps the lambs which redeemed the Israelite first-born.*

Lest this seem far-fetched, consider the following extract from Paul's 'First Letter to the Corinthians', where he described the role of Christ *at the time of the Exodus*:

> Moreover, brethren, I would not that you should be ignorant, concerning how all our forefathers were under the cloud, and all passed through the Sea; and were all baptised unto Moses in the cloud and in the Sea; and did all eat the same spiritual meat; and did all drink the same spiritual drink; for they drank of that spiritual rock that followed them: *and that rock was Christ.*[82]

Whichever way we choose to interpret this 'rock', the point is clear that Jesus Christ was regarded as a contemporary of Moses at the time of the Exodus – *not* the historic Exodus of mundane time, but rather the primeval Exodus of sacred time.

Was this one of Paul's little 'mysteries'?

Once again, we return to the subject of the lamb. Could it be that Moses wrote about Jesus in the sense that Jesus was the lamb which had redeemed the first-born of Israel from the underworld?

There is indeed a certain profound connection here, for just as the primeval Israelites ascended to Heaven by taking the flesh of the sacrificed lamb into their stomachs, so did Jesus of 1st century Palestine encourage his followers to take *his* flesh into their stomachs in order to achieve eternal life.[83]

A pattern is emerging here. After all, did Jesus not say that:

> "The Son of Man [i.e. Christ] did not come to be served, but to serve, and to give his life as a ransom for many."[84]

A 'ransom' is indeed *exactly* what we are suggesting with the hypothesis that Jesus-the-Lamb went into the underworld to redeem the primeval Israelites (the bones of the lamb, we should recall, were left behind).[85] And, similarly, with the hypothesis that Jesus-the-Lamb, or Jesus-the-ram, went into the underworld to redeem the primeval 'man' Isaac – the first-born of mankind.

Further corroboration of this hypothesis is found in the gospel of John, where Jesus spoke to his disciples thus:

> "If the world hates you, know that it hated me first... this is to fulfil what is written in their Law: 'They hated me without reason'."[86]

Here, Jesus was stating that he was *the first* to be hated – not in the mundane sense of being the first Christian to be hated – but rather in the profound sense of being the founding archetype of the hated man. It is a reference to the primeval Christ, millions of years *before* Jesus-the-man of the 1st century AD.

So, who was it that hated the primeval Jesus, and why? The answer is that he was hated by 'the assembly of the wicked' in the underworld, for no other reason than the fact that they were 'evil' by nature, and he was 'good' by nature.

This idea of hatred in the underworld is a theme which is found widely in the Old Testament scriptures. For example, when Jesus referred to the saying 'They hated me without reason', he was alluding to Psalm 69, where king David had imagined himself suffering in the underworld (Sheol) at the hands of mighty enemies:

Save me, O God, for the waters have come in unto my soul.
I sink in a deep mire, where there is no foothold.
I have come into deep waters, where the floods overwhelm me.
I am weary of my crying, my throat is parched.
My eyes fail, while I wait for my God.
Those who hate me without reason outnumber the hairs of my head.
Mighty are they, my enemies without reason, who would destroy me.[87]

The same theme is referred to in *David's Song of Praise*, where king David again lamented his predicament in Sheol:

The waves of death swirled about me; *the floods of ungodly men*
    terrified me.
The sorrows of Sheol [the underworld] coiled about me...
In my distress I called upon the LORD...
He reached down from above and took hold of me, and drew me out of
    deep waters.
He delivered me from my powerful enemy, from them that hated me,
    who were too strong for me.
(They came upon me in the day of my calamity, but the LORD was my
    support.)[88]

Is not this same hatred-in-Sheol motif found in the legends of the primeval Israelites, who were enslaved in the underworld? In the book of Ezekiel, God told Israel:

"*On the day that thou wast born*, thou wast cast out into the
open field *and despised*. And when I [God] passed by thee, I said unto
thee – polluted in thine own blood – "Live!". I caused thee to multiply
like a plant of the field... thy breasts are fashioned and thine hair is
grown, but previously thou wast naked and bare."[89]

As stressed earlier, Israel's birth was of old, from eternity, and it had indeed been despised at birth by the mythical 'Egyptians' of the underworld, who had enslaved the Israelites and mistreated them. The whole point of the original Exodus story was that God had saved the primeval Israelites from their torment in the underworld. As the book of Habakkuk reveals, the underworld was a 'land of wickedness':

> Thou didst march through the land [the underworld] in indignation,
>   thou didst thresh the heathen in anger.
> Thou wentest forth for the salvation of thy people, to save with thine
>   anointed one.
> Thou woundedst the head out of the house of the wicked, by
>   discovering the foundation unto the neck.
> Thou didst strike through with his staffs the head of his villages...[90]

This, then, was the kind of hatred which Jesus had in mind when he told his disciples: "If the world hates you, know that it hated me first." He was referring to the hatred of the evil ones in the underworld, surely because Jesus-the-man was somehow the alter ego of this primeval Christ who had descended from Heaven into the torment of the underworld.

We return now, briefly, to the very important Old Testament texts of Isaiah 52-53 and Psalm 22, which describe exactly such a scenario of a 'man' descending from Heaven and being abused in the underworld. The name 'Jesus' is not mentioned, of course, and nor would we expect it to be, but the suffering individual would now appear to be one-and-the-same as the primeval Christ.[91]

Consider once again the Righteous Servant of God, as described in Isaiah 52-53. Here we have a 'man' who was 'cut off from the land of the living' (Heaven), and thereupon 'made his grave with the wicked', and was 'numbered with the transgressors'. We are told that 'he was led like a lamb to the slaughter'. Crucially, we are told that the Servant was 'disfigured – beyond that of any man – his form marred beyond that of all mankind', presumably because of his fall from Heaven. And, on account of his appearance thus, he was 'despised and rejected by men'.

Now read once again the description of the Righteous Servant as provided in the *Kebra Nagast*:

> Like a root he hid himself in parched ground. He came in the flesh as a
> being of the earth, though he was the sustainer and saviour of the
> universe.

There is something very evocative about these words.[92]

Now, consider again the text of Psalm 22, written by 'a worm, not a man', who was 'scorned by men and despised by the people'. He, too, was apparently cast down from Heaven, having been attacked by 'strong and fertile bulls'. He was 'poured out like water', we are told, with all his 'bones out of joint'. Thereupon, this worm-like 'man' was 'brought into the dust of death', into 'the assembly of the wicked', and there, apparently, he was crucified:

Thou hast brought me into the dust of death [i.e. into Sheol].
Dogs have surrounded me; the assembly of the wicked has encircled
    me; *they have pierced my hands and my feet.*
I am witness to all my bones, as people stare and gloat over me.
They divide my garments among them and cast lots for my clothing.

As astonishing as it might seem, we are looking at the legend of Christ – not the Jesus Christ of 1st century Palestine, but his mythical alter ego from an aeon millions of years earlier.

Ridiculous? Bizarre? Not at all. We will conclude this chapter with a brief reminder of a Sumerian legend which was mentioned, in passing, in chapter five. It is a legend entitled *Inanna's Descent to the Underworld*, and it describes how the great goddess Inanna 'abandoned Heaven, abandoned Earth, and descended to the underworld'. As she went down into the deep gloom of 'the Mountain of No Return', she was forced to stop at seven successive gates, whereupon each time an item of her divine regalia was removed. Finally, Inanna emerged *naked* into the throne-room of the palace of Ereshkigal and Nergal, the great deities of the underworld. And then:

The Anunnaki, the seven judges, pronounced judgement before her,
They fastened their eyes upon her, the eyes of death...
At their word – the word which tortures the spirit . . .
The ailing woman [Inanna] was turned into a corpse,
(And) the corpse was hung from a stake.[93]

Such was the nature of the ancient underworld. It was not a pleasant place.

And so we should have no qualms about accepting what the biblical texts are telling us. Jesus Christ had a primeval alter ego, who was tortured and pierced in the underworld, having offered himself as a ransom, to redeem the first-born offspring of a mythical 'people', who had fallen from Heaven into the midst of the Earth.

* * * * *

CHAPTER TWELVE

HE RAISED THE DEAD

I have suffered none of the things
which they will say of me; even that suffering
which I showed to you and to the rest in my dance,
I will that it be called a mystery.
(Jesus Christ, in Acts of John – a gnostic text)

At the beginning of this book, I described how the gospels of the New
Testament formed a kind of mystery play surrounding the real identity of
Jesus Christ. All of the characters in this play seemed to spend their time
speculating on the question of whether Jesus Christ was the Son of God,
the Son of David, the Messiah called Christ, the reincarnation of Elijah,
or just another prophet.

For the most part, Jesus neither confirmed, nor denied, any of these
rumours as to his identity. But what he did say, repeatedly, was that he
was *Ben Adamah* – commonly translated in the Bible as 'Son of Man'.[1]

What is the meaning of this title, Son of Man? According to one
modern commentator, Son of Man 'simply stressed the weakness and
mortality of the human condition', and therefore emphasised that Jesus
had incarnated into *human* flesh.[2]

But was this really the case? I opened chapter one of this book with a
famous saying, which was ascribed to Jesus in the gospel of Matthew:

I will open my mouth in parables, I will utter things hidden since the
creation of the world.[3]

I also cited the words of Jesus to his disciples in the gospel of Mark:

To you, the mystery of the kingdom of God has been given. But to
those who are on the outside, all things are done in parables; so that
they may indeed see but not perceive, and may indeed hear but not
understand.[4]

Might it be that Jesus spoke a parable, and a mystery of the creation, encoded within his favoured identity as *Ben Adamah*? Might it be that we have *seen and heard* this title, but *perceived not* its esoteric symbolism, and *understood not* its hidden meaning?

Personally, I have never been convinced by the argument that Jesus called himself *Ben Adamah* in order to stress the weakness and mortality of his own human condition as a Son of Man. It does not explain, for example, why Jesus would have referred to himself as the Son of Man even in his *future* role of descending from Heaven at the End of Days. The following verses are typical of such references:

> And Jesus said... "Hereafter you shall see Heaven open, and the angels of God ascending and descending upon the Son of Man."[5]

> As the lightning comes out of the east, and shines even unto the west, so too shall the Son of Man come... They shall see the Son of Man coming on the clouds of Heaven, with power and great glory. And he shall send out his angels with a loud trumpet call...[6]

Can we really believe that Jesus was emphasising his own human-like weakness and mortality, when he referred to himself thus as the Son of Man, in such an eschatological context? The idea, frankly, is absurd.

What, then, might be the esoteric meaning of the title *Ben Adamah*? The answer happens to be surprisingly straightforward, and stems from the simple fact that the Hebrew term *Ben* has two possible meanings, as noted recently by the biblical expert Robert Alter:

> The Hebrew term [*ben*] means both semen and the offspring that is its product.[7]

Robert Alter then went on to translate *ben* as 'seed' in the context of Noah having saved the seed of all living things at the time of the Flood.

So, what this means is that Jesus Christ's preferred title, *Ben Adamah*, can be translated *either* as 'Son of Man', *or* as 'Seed of Man', *or* – more to the point – as 'Seed of Mankind'.[8]

Now the alarm bells are ringing! The expression 'Seed of Mankind' does not necessarily relate to *the seed which man produces*, but can also relate to *the seed which produced man*. And it is here, in this latter possibility, that we find the absolute essence – the absolute corner stone – of ancient religious belief.

Does the translation 'Seed of Mankind' make sense for Jesus Christ as *Ben Adamah*? It certainly does. Is it not written in the gospel of John that 'all things were made' through Christ?[9] Is it not written in Paul's 'Letter to the Colossians' that Christ was 'the first-born of every creature, for *all things* were created by him'?[10] Surely he was indeed the Seed of Mankind.

Consider also the following remarkable passage in the gospel of Matthew, where Jesus compared himself explicitly to the sower of *seed* in the Earth:

> "He that sowed the good seed is the Seed of Mankind [my translation]. The field is the world..."[11]

Did the '*Son of Man*' sow the seed in the world, or did the '*Seed of Mankind*' sow the seed? It does not take a genius to spot the correct answer.[12]

In fact, this seed motif appears remarkably frequently in the gospels of the New Testament. In the gospel of Luke, for example, we read *The Parable of the Sower*, related by Jesus as follows:

> "A sower went out to sow his seed, and as he sowed, some fell by the way side, and it was trodden down... And some fell upon a rock, and as soon as it was sprung up, it withered away... And some fell among thorns, and the thorns... choked it. And other [seed] fell on good soil, and sprang up, and yielded fruit a hundred times more than was sown... *He who has ears to hear, let him hear.*"[13]

Do *we* have 'ears to hear', *and to understand*, this parable? The disciples of Jesus were slow to catch on, and they asked him to explain further; Jesus responded as follows:

> "This is the meaning of the parable: *The seed is the Word of God.*"[14]

Such was the way of the ancient Mysteries, that a parable had to be explained with an arcane metaphor, which would only be understood by those few who had studied their scriptures well.

Here, then, is the meaning of 'the Word of God', and thence the meaning of the 'seed' in *The Parable of the Sower*.

Firstly, let us establish the fact that the Word of God was with him 'in the beginning':

> In the beginning was the Word, and the Word was toward the God, and the Word was a god. He [the Word] was with God in the beginning.[15]

Secondly, let us establish that this Word proceeded forth from God in the form of Jesus Christ:

The Word was made flesh, and dwelt among us.
And we beheld his glory, the glory of the One and Only, *who came from the Father*. (Gospel of John)[16]

There is only one God, manifested by *Jesus Christ his son, who is the Word issued from the silence*. (Ignatius, bishop of Antioch, *c*.100 AD)[17]

It was through this Word – Jesus Christ – that 'all things were made', and 'all things created', according to the gospel of John and the letters of Paul respectively.[18]

But according to the book of Jeremiah, the Word of God – which was equivalent to Jesus Christ – was *fiery and cataclysmic*:

"Is not my Word like a fire?", saith the LORD, "and like a hammer that breaketh the Rock in pieces?"[19]

Nor should we be surprised at this note of catastrophism. In fact, the entire ancient Near East regarded 'the Word of God' as a creative but catastrophic force, in keeping with the paradigm that God had originally been a *physical* being. Hence, in the Sumerian texts, we read:

Aruru, the sister of Enlil,
Her Word shakes the heavens,
Her utterance is a howling storm.[20]

Aruru, ironically, was known as 'the goddess of silence', perhaps because her 'Word' had *already* been spoken.

Similarly, in another Sumerian text, we read of the supreme god Anu:

The Word of Anu, a storm crouching on the horizon [of Heaven],
    its heart inscrutable...
His Word which up above makes the heavens tremble,
His Word which down below rocks the Earth,
His Word wherewith the Anunnaki gods destroy...
His Word – a risen flood-storm, none can oppose it.[21]

The ancient Egyptians had a similar belief. According to one legend, the creator-god had uttered 'Seven Words', which had supposedly structured the world, and then become 'shut up inside a chest', i.e. trapped in the underworld.[22] The Egyptians believed that to repeat these Seven Words out aloud would bring about the catastrophic end of the world.

But now let's get down to specifics. Spells 1080 and 1087 of the ancient Egyptian Coffin Texts give away a little too much concerning the esoteric secret of 'the Word':

This is the sealed thing which is in darkness, with fire about it, which contains the efflux of Osiris, and it is put in Rostau [Giza]. It has been hidden since it fell from him [Osiris], and it is what came down from him on to the desert of sand...

This is *the Word* which was in darkness. Fire is about it, (that) which contains the efflux of Osiris...[23]

As these texts reveal, 'the Word' of the ancient Egyptians was *a sacred meteorite.*

Now, the most sacred meteorite of ancient Egypt was called the Benben Stone, named after the flowing out (*bnbn*) of the creator-god's efflux in the primeval ocean.[24] In Egypt, as in Israel, the word *Ben* therefore meant both 'son' and 'seed'. And the meteorite was effectively both – a son born in the primeval ocean, and a seed which was sown in the Earth.

This, then, is the meaning of *The Parable of the Sower*:
The sower was God;
The seed was the Word of God;
The Word of God was Christ;
And Christ was a meteorite – the Seed of Mankind.

Or, more strictly, a whole *flood* of meteorites.
He who has ears to hear, let him hear.

The Mystery of the Corner Stone

Another popular parable in the New Testament was *The Parable of the Tenants*, which is found in three of the four gospels. In this parable, Jesus told a story of a certain 'man', who had planted a 'vineyard', put a 'wall' around it, and built a 'watchtower'. This 'man' had then rented the vineyard to some farmer-tenants, whereupon he had gone away for a long time, to a 'distant land'.[25]

At the end of the parable, Jesus clarified its meaning (rather obliquely) by referring to an enigmatic saying from Psalm 118:

Jesus saith unto them: "Did ye never read in the scriptures:
'The stone which the builders rejected, it has become the corner stone.
This is the LORD's doing and it is marvellous in our eyes'."[26]

Jesus was, of course, referring to himself as the 'corner stone', as is confirmed in the letters of Paul.[27]

What was this corner stone? In the book of Job, we discover that the corner stone was something which had been *laid at the beginning of the world*:

> (The LORD saith:) "Where wast thou when I laid the foundations of
> the Earth?...
> To what were the foundations of the Earth attached; or who laid its
> corner stone?"[28]

Further clarification is provided by the book of Isaiah:

> Thus saith the LORD: "Behold, I lay in Zion for a foundation a stone –
> a tried stone, *a precious corner stone*, a sure foundation."[29]

The concept of the corner stone, however, finds its clearest expression in
the book of Jeremiah. Here, we find mention of a hypothetical corner
stone belonging to Babylon, but only in the sense that the 'city' of
Babylon had been *a celestial mountain, destroyed in a fiery cataclysm*:

> The LORD saith: "Behold, I am against thee [Babylon], O destroying
> mountain, which destroyest all the Earth.
> And I will stretch out mine hand upon thee, and roll thee down off the
> peaks, and will make thee into a burnt mountain.
> *And no stone will be taken from thee for a corner stone*, nor a stone for
> any foundation."[30]

It should now be transparently clear what Jesus Christ had in mind when
he referred to himself – or, more strictly speaking, to Christ his primeval
alter ego – as 'the corner stone'.

Lest there be any doubt about this, consider the last words of Jesus on
the subject of *The Parable of the Tenants* – the words which so incensed
the Jewish priests:

> Whoever falls upon that (corner) stone will be broken to pieces, but he
> on whom it falls will be crushed to powder.[31]

Hopefully, it should now be evident, for those who have eyes to see and
perceive, that the corner stone was a metaphor for *a meteorite*, which had
been cast down from the celestial 'mountain' of God, and which had
been laid in the foundations of the Earth.

So, if Jesus Christ was the corner stone, as Paul attested, what this
means is that the primeval alter ego of Jesus Christ was a meteorite (or,
more accurately, a flood of meteorites).

Just as Jesus Christ, 'the Word', was a flood of meteorites.

And just as Jesus Christ, 'the Seed of Mankind', was a flood of
meteorites.

The Secret of Original Sin

During the past two thousand years, the Church has given everyone the impression that the parables of Jesus Christ were merely moralistic analogies. Most Christians have therefore assumed that the meanings of the parables have been fully decoded, and fully disclosed to them by the Church authorities.

But is this really the case? As Jesus Christ himself stated:

> I will open my mouth in parables, I will utter things *hidden since the creation of the world*.[32]

This statement sums up everything in a nutshell. Yes, it cannot be denied that the parables of the New Testament *were* about human behaviour at a moralistic but mundane level. But this is only half of the truth – what we might call the *exoteric* half of the truth.

More important by far, for those who sought truth at the sacred level, was the *esoteric* half of the truth. And that esoteric half related to 'things hidden since the creation of the world'.

The same dichotomy exists with the figure whom we know as Jesus Christ. At an *exoteric* level, he was an individual who lived in Palestine during the 1st century AD. But at an *esoteric* level, he was a primeval god who had existed from 'the beginning', and who had been instrumental in the creation of the Earth – thus becoming 'a precious corner stone, a sure foundation'.

Moreover, it seems to me that, if we wish to truly understand the religion of Christianity, we must seek out knowledge of this hidden, esoteric side. For why should *we* be deprived of this 'truth', when it is most probably known, but not divulged, by a small élite within the Church? (Surely the Church must have inherited the secrets which reveal what their religion is all about.)

It is time, then, to consolidate what we know, and press on, come what may. We are about to discover something truly profound and remarkable.

In the previous chapter, we discussed the concept of sin, and noted that all ancient peoples, including the Israelites, felt a sense of inherited sin and guilt, even from birth. Hence in the Dead Sea Scrolls, we read that 'man is in sin from the womb', whilst the Sumerians used to say that 'never was a sinless child born to its mother'.[33]

But why was it that everyone felt so ashamed of themselves?

This question of inherited sin is a crucial one, because the primary aim of Jesus Christ's mission was to *save us from our sins*. Hence in the gospel of Matthew, an angel told Joseph that:

"She [The Virgin Mary] shall bring forth a son, and thou shalt call his name Jesus [literally 'Saviour'] for he shall *save his people from their sins*."[34]

But where did this concept of sin come from? Why was it that mankind needed to be saved – and indeed *still does need to be saved* according to the Christian theology?

The answer, which I have hinted at in earlier chapters, is that the 'original sin' of mankind *occurred in the heavens*, and was perpetrated by mankind's celestial ancestors, whom we might term loosely 'the black-headed ones'. But now this suggestion must be substantiated, for it is about to lead us towards a very profound and shocking conclusion.

Let's begin with a brief revision of the Mesopotamian Flood story, as recounted by Utnapishtim to Gilgamesh in *The Epic of Gilgamesh*. According to this legend, a planetary 'city' – called 'ancient Shuruppak' – disintegrated in a fiery catastrophe, causing the gods to explode outwards from its interior. This was the cataclysm in which Anu, the king of the gods, gave birth to his offspring, the Anunnaki. We might recall, however, that the story of his cataclysm was merged with that of a second cataclysm, which afflicted the great goddess Ishtar (alias Inanna and Mami). It is this second catastrophe which interests us at this stage.

According to *The Epic of Gilgamesh*, Ishtar's catastrophe was so violent that she – a planetary goddess – gave birth to her 'people':

Ishtar [Inanna] cried out like a woman giving birth...
"Alas, I myself (now) give birth to my 'people'!
Like the spawn of fish they (now) fill the sea!"[35]

What was the cause of the catastrophe? The goddess explained that she had 'spoken evil' in the heavenly assembly of the gods:

"Alas, the olden days are turned to clay,
Because I [Ishtar] spoke evil in the assembly of the gods.
How could I speak evil in the assembly of the gods?
How could I order battle for the destruction of my 'people'?"[36]

What was the 'evil' spoken by Ishtar? Unfortunately, Utnapishtim's story does not inform us, and nor does it offer any explanation as to why the gods ordered the Flood. It is almost as if this was something the reader was expected to know without being told. Crucially, however, the text confirms that the blame lay with Enlil.

Now, we know from other texts that Enlil ordered the Flood because he was disturbed by the 'noise' of mankind. In the *Atra-Hasis Epic*, for example, Enlil declared:

"The noise of mankind has become oppressive.
By its noise it makes sleep impossible."[37]

Similarly, a badly fragmented Sumerian text, designated K-11624, makes mention of 'noise' in the aftermath of the destruction of the pre-Flood cities, including Shuruppak, the city of Ziusudra:

Five separate cities, nine kings . . . . . .
Enlil . . . . . .
Their noise . . . . . . [38]

And, in addition to this, we know that 'noise' was associated particularly with the activities of the Anunnaki and later 'mankind' in the underworld of the Earth.[39]

All things considered, it would not be too great a leap to assume that *heavenly* 'mankind' was also punished for its 'noise', and that this 'noise' was the 'evil' spoken by Ishtar in the celestial assembly of the gods. Such a tradition is indeed preserved in the *Atra-Hasis Epic*, where Ishtar's alter ego, Mami, complained that:

"My offspring, beyond my control, have become like sacrificial white
   sheep.
As for me, how am I to live in a house of bereavement?
My noise has turned to silence."[40]

So, did mankind's original sin result from the 'noise' of its primeval, mythical ancestors in the heavens? Based on these clues alone, my suggestion might be regarded as an interesting speculation, but nothing more. Fortunately, however, my argument is strengthened considerably by a second, independent legend, contained in the famous Babylonian epic of creation, *Enuma Elish*.

As mentioned earlier in this book, *Enuma Elish* begins by describing a battle in the heavens, in which a planetary god, Apsu, was vanquished by Ea (Enki), and it ends by describing a second celestial battle in which another planetary deity, Tiamat, was vanquished by the Titan-god Marduk. It is thus no surprise to find that both Apsu and Tiamat were credited in the text as *forming gods within them, and bringing forth those gods from within their interiors*.[41] In the case of Tiamat, this rebellion-from-within was singled out for special attention in the text, and the details are very evocative in the light of what we now know about the Mesopotamian exploded planet cult.

Consider, for example, lines 21-25 of *Enuma Elish*:

The divine brothers [the gods] gathered together.
They disturbed Tiamat and assaulted (her), their keeper.
Yea, *they troubled the inner parts of Tiamat,*
Moving and running about *within the divine abode.*
Apsu could not quell their noise.[42]

This 'noise', it must be emphasised, was occurring up in the heavens –
inside a planetary goddess.

Then, in lines 35-40 of *Enuma Elish*, we find an exchange which
echoes the complaint of Enlil against mankind:

Apsu said to Tiamat:
"Their ways are verily loathsome to me,
By day I cannot rest, by night I cannot sleep,
I will destroy them, and put an end to their ways,
So that silence may be restored, and then let us sleep!"[43]

The ancient gods, it would seem, hated noise, and loved sleep. They were
'the gods who loved silence'.[44]

Apsu failed in his plan to destroy the gods inside Tiamat, and ended
up being put into a deep sleep himself by Ea, who cast him down to the
Earth. As for the gods, they were seemingly released from inside Tiamat,
and took up an independent existence. Tiamat, however, continued to
bring forth ferocious monsters from her insides, thus acquiring the
nickname Mother Hubur, meaning 'Mother of Noise'.[45] Eventually,
Tiamat was destroyed and cast down into the Earth, hence the
underworld was said to contain a River Hubur – a 'River of Noise'.[46]

Now, here comes the crucial link to 'mankind'. According to a list of
credits at the end of *Enuma Elish*, there was a god, Gishnumunab, who
created 'mankind' from the gods of Tiamat (not the original gods, but the
new generation of monsters, brought forth from her insides):

Gishnumunab – creator of all people, who made the world regions,
Destroyer of the gods of Tiamat, *who made men out of their*
   substance.[47]

Thus the link is made in *Enuma Elish* between primeval 'mankind',
Tiamat, and the 'noise' which it made in the interior of Tiamat – *inside a*
planet in the heavens.

It should be evident that this legend bears a remarkable resemblance to
the legend of Utnapishtim, cited earlier, where Ishtar spoke 'evil' and
gave birth to her 'people'. In both cases, a mother-goddess or *womb-*
goddess was involved in a celestial battle, having caused disruption in
the assembly of the gods. And in both cases, destruction was planned by

a senior god, who could not sleep for the noise.

A few words of clarification are in order. What we appear to be looking at is a mythical scenario, in which the 'noise' of 'mankind' was coming from within the body, or womb, of a planetary mother-goddess. The first evil, or sin, in the universe was thus perpetrated by a 'mankind' which can only be understood as the yet-to-be-born offspring of a planetary goddess. In due course, this 'people' would explode from the 'womb' of the goddess and be cast down towards the Earth as a race of 'black-headed ones', i.e. meteorites.

Thus it was that subterranean 'mankind', and later flesh-and-blood mankind, *inherited sin*. But the *original sin* – the sin of 'noise' – should now be understood as the warning signal being emitted by a planet undergoing tectonic stress, and about to explode. (The idea was no doubt inspired by the ancients' experience with earthquakes and volcanic eruptions from within the Earth herself.)

The original sin of mankind was not therefore really committed by mankind at all, but rather by *the seed of* mankind.

The Esoteric Gospels

Let us remind ourselves of the reason for this digression. Earlier, I cited the gospel of Matthew, in which it was said: "thou shalt call his name Jesus for he shall save his people from their sins."

But did this saying refer to flesh-and-blood people, or to the mythical 'people' of the goddess, who had committed the first sin in Heaven, and were now stuck in the underworld, awaiting redemption by a saviour?

Let us now recall some pertinent facts. Firstly, we have ascertained that Jesus Christ had a primeval alter ego, who can only be described as a meteorite-like god. This primeval Christ was 'the stone which the builders rejected', which had become the 'corner stone' in the foundations of the Earth. This means that the primeval Christ was *cast into the underworld, at the beginning of time.*

Secondly, it is a fact that Jesus Christ was known as 'the Lamb of God'. This fact now becomes highly significant. In the previous chapters, I highlighted the roles of *lambs* which had been sent down *into the underworld* to redeem the first-born sons of Israel. The legend, we should note, occurred twice; firstly, in the legend of Abraham and Isaac; and secondly, in the legend of the Exodus. In the first case, the lamb (or ram) ransomed Isaac, allowing him to emerge from the underworld. In the second case, the bones of the lamb ransomed the Israelite first-born, and allowed them to ascend to Heaven.

Now, it cannot be emphasised too strongly that these two legends – of Abraham and Isaac, and the Exodus – belonged not to mundane time, but to *sacred time*. The ransoms were thus given, and the redemptions made, *at the beginning of time*.

The upshot of this is that the primeval Christ, the lamb, or the ram, was given to the underworld as *a long-term ransom* – a substitute for the first-born of Israel.

Exactly the same scenario is played out in Isaiah 52-53. These verses, I believe, do not anticipate the future Christ, but rather recall the sacrifice and suffering of a *past messiah*, i.e. the primeval Christ, at the beginning of the world. Hence the fact that this past messiah, the Righteous Servant, had an appearance which was 'disfigured beyond that of any man', and 'a form marred beyond that of all mankind'.

Consider now the words of Isaiah once again, in the light of what we have learned concerning the heavenly population of original sinners:

> Surely he [the Righteous Servant] bore our griefs, and carried our sorrows; yet we considered him stricken by God...
>
> *But he was wounded for our transgressions, he was crushed for our iniquities*; the punishment that brought us peace was upon him; and by his stripes [wounds] we are healed.
>
> We all, like sheep, have gone astray... and the LORD hath laid on him the iniquity of us all.[48]

> He [the Righteous Servant] was oppressed and afflicted... he was led like a lamb to the slaughter...
>
> From arrest and judgement he was taken away...
>
> He was cut off from the land of the living *for the transgression of my people, to whom the blow was (really) due.*[49]

> Yet it pleased the LORD to crush him; he put (him) to grief. And when the LORD made his [the Righteous Servant's] soul *an offering for sin*, he looked upon (his) seed, he prolonged (his) days...
>
> He [the LORD] saw the suffering of his soul, and was satisfied, (for) by his knowledge *the Righteous Servant justified many, by bearing their iniquities.*[50]

> He [the Righteous Servant] poured out his soul unto (the place of) death, and he was numbered with the transgressors,
>
> *And he bore the sin of many*, and made intercession for the transgressors.[51]

Once again, it must be emphasised that this Righteous Servant was *in the underworld*, because he had been cast down from 'the land of the living', i.e. Heaven. The mention of 'looking upon seed' is crucial, for it suggests that Isaiah envisaged the Righteous Servant as the Seed of Mankind. The idea, then, is that the Righteous Servant had offered himself as a substitute, and had borne all the sins of 'mankind', thus enabling mankind to emerge as a flesh-and-blood creature in the world above. The story would thus be identical to that of the lamb, or ram, which ransomed the release of Isaac from the underworld.

In view of the startling similarities between these legends and the story of Jesus Christ in the gospels, we must now ask whether the gospel account contains an esoteric dimension. Does it refer, at a deeper level, to the ransoming of a *primeval* 'mankind' and to the forgiveness of their *primeval* sins by a *primeval* Christ?

Let us now look at some individual points in more detail.

Firstly, the books of the New Testament suggest that Jesus Christ saved mankind through his suffering. But did not the *primeval* Christ save 'mankind' by his suffering? According to Isaiah 53, the Righteous Servant was 'wounded' and 'crushed'. And according to Psalm 22, a similar innocent servant was pierced, possibly crucified, in the underworld.

Secondly, in the gospels of Matthew and Mark, Jesus Christ stated that he gave his life as a ransom for many:

"The Seed of Mankind did not come to be served, but to serve, and to give his life as a ransom for many."[52]

Compare these words to Isaiah 53, where the Righteous Servant 'bore the sin of many', and gave his life as a ransom for primeval 'mankind'.

Thirdly, in the gospel of John, Jesus stated:

"This bread is my flesh, which I will give for the life of the world..."[53]

But was this merely human 'flesh', or was it the 'flesh of the gods'? In the preceding line of John's gospel, Jesus stated: "I am the living bread which came down from Heaven."[54] So, the bread, or flesh, of Jesus was actually his heavenly flesh.

Now, in pagan traditions, the 'flesh of the gods' was synonymous with the word 'meteorite'. In ancient Egyptian texts, there are numerous references to this flesh of the gods, and they state quite unambiguously that the flesh of the gods was the *efflux from the God's planetary body*, and, similarly, that the 'flesh' of the greater God could emanate numerous lesser gods.[55] To cite but one example, in Spell 94 of the Coffin Texts, the king stated that: "I have remade Osiris from the efflux which was in his flesh."[56]

The Mesopotamians were of one mind with the Egyptians. Readers are referred back to chapter five for earlier discussion on the *mesu*-tree, the *elmesu*-stone, and the *ki-sir* of Anu. In addition, we might recall that the name of king Gilgamesh meant 'flesh of the gods (MES) which is the sprouting seed of a new tree'.

All of this sheds profound new light on the statement in the gospel of John that Jesus Christ was the Word and 'the Word was made flesh and dwelt among us'.[57] Was the writer referring to a contemporary Jesus Christ in human flesh, or to a primeval Christ in the flesh of the gods? The ambiguity might well have been intentional, thus creating both an exoteric *and esoteric* meaning in the text.

But to return to the passage cited earlier, the idea that Jesus Christ would give his flesh 'for the life of the world' suggests that the esoteric interpretation is right on the mark.

Our fourth, and final, point of detail concerns the blood of Christ. In the book of Revelations, we read:

> Jesus Christ is the first begotten of the dead... (who) washed us from our sins in his own blood.[58]

How was Jesus 'the first begotten of the dead'? This comment, I suggest, refers to *the belief* in the first century AD that the primeval Christ had somehow ascended out of the underworld, after an eternity therein. He had thus become, it was supposed, the first begotten of the dead, i.e. the first-born from the land of the dead.

We are more concerned, however, with the claim that Jesus Christ had washed away mankind's sins with his blood. What does this mean? Once again, the pagan traditions provide us with a fascinating esoteric insight. According to the legends discussed in chapter eight of this book, mankind had been created from the 'blood' of a god – the blood of Kingu in one legend, the blood of Geshtui in another, and the blood of two Lamga-gods in yet another. Moreover, the entire ancient world seems to have had an obsession with the idea that this 'blood' of the gods could fall from Heaven and impregnate the Earth. Thus, in Greek mythology, Gaea (Mother Earth) was impregnated with drops of blood when Cronus cut off the genitals of his father Uranus.[59] And in another popular Greek legend, the dripping blood from the decapitated head of Medusa (one of the three Gorgon monsters) brought forth venomous serpents when it hit the earth.[60] In Mesopotamia, the same idea is found in the legend of Ulligarra and Zalgarra, where their 'blood' caused 'mankind' to spring up in the Earth like plants.

Why did the 'blood' of the gods have this magical ability to cause 'men', gods or demons to spring up from the Earth? The answer is very straightforward once we appreciate the fact that the senior deities were conceived as *exploded planets*, which had once had oceans of water. *It then follows logically that the blood of the gods symbolised the Flood of waters from the exploded planet. (Whilst the flesh of the gods, by the same token, symbolised the Flood of meteorites.)*

This idea is fully supported by several Mesopotamian texts, cited in earlier chapters, which contain wordplays between 'water' and 'semen'. According to the ancient way of thinking, water was the essential key to all life on Earth, and it would indeed be the substance which had made primeval beings spring up in the Earth like plants. In one ancient Egyptian cosmogony, mankind was actually created not from 'blood', but from the watery 'tears' of the creator-god's 'Eye', which underlines the point emphatically.[61]

To return to the quotation from Revelations, how should we now interpret the statement that Jesus Christ 'washed us from our sins in his own blood'? Once again, we find an ambiguity which was probably intentional. The text can be read in two ways – *exoterically*, as referring to the blood of Jesus-the-man, *and esoterically*, as referring to the blood, or rather *waters*, of Jesus Christ's primeval, ex-planetary alter ego. Incidentally, it is this deeper esoteric symbolism which surely accounts for the legend that blood *and water* flowed out of Jesus at the crucifixion, after he was pierced in the side by one of the Roman soldiers.[62]

Lest this in any way seem far-fetched to the out-and-out sceptic, I should cite briefly the Mesopotamian legend known as the *Atra-Hasis Epic*, where the creation of 'mankind' in the underworld occurred as a result of a merging between Geshtui – a god-become-man – and the Anunnaki-gods. Note in the following speech by Enki how the gods, who were already in the underworld, were to be 'immersed' in the 'blood' of the sacrificed god:

> Enki spoke to the great gods:
> "I shall make a purification, a bath.
> Let one god [Geshtui] be slain,
> *And let the gods [Anunnaki] be purified by immersion.*
> Let Nintu mix clay with his flesh and blood.
> Let god and man be mixed together in clay.
> Let us hear the drum-beat forever after."[63]

This passage has an extraordinary significance, which has hitherto not been spotted. Since Geshtui was some kind of planetary god who was cast down from Heaven, his 'blood' was effectively water. It would thus follow that Geshtui *baptised* the Anunnaki in the underworld. Geshtui was thus an interplanetary baptist.

How interesting, then, that Jesus Christ, too, was a baptist – not just in the sense that he would bring a future baptism of fire, but also in the sense of being a baptiser by water. This is confirmed in the gospel of John:

> After these things, Jesus and his disciples came into the land of
> Judaea, where he tarried with them and baptised [i.e. by water]...[64]

The ritual of baptism, it should be noted, was the means used to wash away the sins of mankind.[65] However, if we refer to the above citation from the *Atra-Hasis Epic*, we find that baptism in water (the 'blood' of the god) was also a means of purifying the Anunnaki-gods *in the underworld*.

It is but a short step to suggest that the baptism of the primeval Anunnaki-gods – a *catastrophic* baptism – was the mythical model for the ordinary and mundane baptisms of 1st century Judaea, and indeed for all other real world baptisms.

And it is an equally short step to suggest that 'mankind', too, would have been baptised by water *in the underworld*, prior to its emergence into the world above.

Was Jesus Christ, then, in his primeval, god-like identity, the saviour of a primeval 'mankind'? Did he sacrifice a god-like 'flesh', and a god-like 'blood', to save a subterranean form of humanity? Did he wash away the sins which had caused this noisy subterranean 'people' to be cast out of Heaven? Were these fallen black-headed ones 'the many' for whom the first Jesus Christ gave his life 'as a ransom'?

Was this the mission of the original Jesus Christ?

Raising the Dead – the Mystery of the Igigi

In Paul's 'First Letter to the Corinthians', he wrote that man had been made of both physical and spiritual bodies, with the latter, spiritual body having come down from Heaven at the moment when God breathed the breath of life into the nostrils of Adam.[66] Thus, Paul concluded, it *was* possible for man to return to this spiritual form, and experience the resurrection to eternal life in Heaven.

But was this really the truth, or a half-truth?

If the ancient mystery schools of the 1st century AD were worth their salt, one of their biggest secrets would have been the old pagan traditions of the *physical* fall of man from the *planet* of Heaven – a 'fact' which would have been long occulted from 1st century literature. And it is with this secret in mind that we must now search for the esoteric meaning behind the resurrection to eternal life.

If we accept Paul's theory of the 'spiritual body', then the ultimate resurrection of mankind would be *in spirit only*, and would be effected in one fell swoop by the Second Coming of Christ. But what if there was a hidden side to this resurrection? What if the final resurrection was to be in the *physical* body? *What if the primeval Christ had already resurrected man's spiritual bodies, at the beginning of time?*

In order to understand this point – which will turn out to be of profound importance – we turn now to the Babylonian epic of creation, *Enuma Elish*, and to the mystery of what transpired between Marduk, the Anunnaki, and the mysterious beings known as the Igigi.

In Tablet VI of *Enuma Elish*, after Marduk had vanquished Tiamat, and buried her body in the Earth, he decided to create 'mankind' in order to relieve the gods of their toil. However, as a result of this creation of 'mankind' (with the help of Ea), Marduk was also able to 'set the gods free', by dividing them into two groups – the Anunnaki and the Igigi. The casual reader of the epic might assume that this latter act was quite independent from the creation of mankind, but in fact the text tends to suggest a very important interdependency. Indeed, so important was this interdependency that the text stated it twice.

Firstly, in lines 5-10 of *Enuma Elish*, Marduk declared:

"Yes, I will create a Lullu [a primitive man].
He shall be charged with the service of the gods,
That they might be at ease!
Let me change the ways of the gods miraculously.
Formerly they were clustered together like a ball,
But now they shall be divided into two groups."[67]

Secondly, in lines 35-44 of *Enuma Elish*:

When Ea-the-wise had created mankind,
Had imposed the toil of the gods upon it (and set the gods free) –
That work was beyond comprehension,
For Ea-the-wise performed it with the miracles of Marduk –
Then Marduk, the king, divided the gods,
The Anunnaki, all of them, above and below.
He assigned them to Anu, to guard his decrees,
He stationed three hundred in the heavens as a guard.
He did likewise when he defined the conventions of the Earth,
And thus made six hundred dwell in Heaven and on Earth.[68]

What these passages mean is that the three hundred Anunnaki-gods in the underworld were made to spawn three hundred metaphysical doubles, the Igigi-gods. Whilst the group of Anunnaki remained in the Earth – set free from their toil by the creation of 'man' – the group of Igigi were raised to Heaven, metaphysically, and were thus truly set free.

Other passages, in *Enuma Elish* and elsewhere, inform us that the Igigi were 'the pure gods', who dwelt in the heavens with a 'brilliance like fire'.[69] The foremost among them was Marduk himself, and one text even suggests that the Igigi were instrumental in making Marduk's metaphysical heavenly abode, the Esharra.[70] Indeed, when we consider the fact that the Anunnaki were the physical fragments of the heavenly abode, it tends to suggest that the Igigi – their metaphysical doubles – were also literally the pieces of the heavenly abode which had been put back together (metaphysically speaking). The raising up of the Igigi to Heaven was thus yet another example of the metaphysical separation of Heaven from Earth.

What, then, was the interdependency, which *Enuma Elish* emphasised twice, between the separation of the Anunnaki-and-Igigi, and the creation of 'mankind'? The answer, in a word, is 'substitution'. To repeat the words of the Sumerian poet once again:

Who of those who ascended from the underworld ever did get up
    scot-free?[71]

The ransom which freed the Igigi-gods from the underworld was, I suggest, the insertion of 'mankind' – the black-headed ones – *into* the underworld. *Enuma Elish* indeed says as much in lines 25-29 of Tablet VII:

Fourthly, let the people glorify TUTU [a name of Marduk] as AGAKU,
Lord of the pure incantation, who revives the dead,
Who showed mercy to the vanquished gods,
Who removed the yoke imposed upon the gods, his enemies,
And who, *to redeem them, created mankind.*[72]

As the Babylonian poet had said earlier in the text, it was 'a work beyond comprehension'.

But what is this, we read, about Marduk reviving the dead? Turning to Tablet VI, lines 152-54, we find further intriguing details:

Second, they called him [Marduk] ASARLUHI as NAMTILA, the god
    who gives life.
Who restored all the ruined gods, as if they were his own creation,
The Lord who revives the dead gods by his pure incantation.[73]

What this means is that the Anunnaki were regarded as 'ruined gods' and 'dead gods', by virtue of the fact that they had fallen into the underworld. Marduk, it would seem, had revived the Anunnaki, and raised them from the dead, by creating 'mankind' as a ransom for them, and thus resurrecting the Anunnaki to Heaven – in the form of their metaphysical counterparts, the Igigi.

Now I put it to readers that this legend has a considerable bearing on Christianity, because it provides us with the vital template for what might have been done *in the underworld* by Jesus Christ's primeval alter ego at the beginning of time. Why not? As I pointed out in chapter eight, the Anunnaki and 'mankind' were rather like two primeval peas-in-an-underground-pod. What worked for one would work for the other.

Of course, such matters were *not* referred to explicitly in the books of the New Testament, but this is no great surprise. After all, the point has already been made that the underworld was at the heart of the ancient Mysteries; such matters were not to be spoken about openly.

Nevertheless, we find in the gospel of Matthew a curious legend which might well recall the subterranean redemption. The rather strange story follows in the immediate aftermath of Jesus's death on the 'cross' (*stauros*, literally a 'stake') and runs as follows:

> And behold, the veil of the temple was torn in two from top to bottom; and the Earth shook and the rocks split. And the graves were opened, and many bodies of holy people – those who had slept – arose, and came out of the graves after his resurrection, and went into the holy city, and appeared unto many.[74]

This *instant* resurrection sits uncomfortably with the idea that Jesus resurrected after three days in the tomb, but it would fit neatly with a scenario of the primeval Christ being crucified in Heaven, and then being cast down into the Earth. This would explain why the Earth split open, and why the veil of the temple (in the holy-of-holies, the Bond of Heaven-and-Earth) was ripped in two.[75] Was the writer of Matthew's gospel perhaps drawing on a tradition of the primeval Christ?

And how many other anecdotes of the New Testament story might have been lifted from the legends of this *primeval* Christ? His arrest, judgement and crucifixion in Heaven? His descent into the underworld, and his second crucifixion therein? All of these stories, we might surmise, would have been in oral circulation two thousand years ago, at least within the mystery schools. It is a most intriguing thought.

Furthermore, there is a gnostic text, found at Nag Hammadi in 1945, which seems to confirm that Jesus Christ did indeed go down into the underworld and raise the dead, just like Marduk did. The text, entitled *Testimony of Truth*, records that:

> The Seed of Mankind [i.e. Christ] came forth from imperishability, being alien to defilement... he went down into Hades [the underworld] and performed mighty works. He raised the dead therein...[76]

This, I suggest, was indeed a testimony of 'truth' – not concerning Jesus-the-man of the first century AD, but rather Jesus-the-god from millions of years beforehand. For such a god would indeed have raised the 'dead' in the underworld to 'life', by offering himself as a ransom, and thus resurrecting the metaphysical doubles of 'mankind'.

This, it seems to me, is the story of *the First Coming* of Christ – how he came down from Heaven into the underworld in his primeval form, at the beginning of time, and saved a primeval 'mankind' from its celestial sins, by sacrificing his own celestial, god-like 'flesh' and 'blood'.

But this is in fact only the beginning of the story, which is just about to become much more interesting, for it is at this stage in the game that *we* – flesh-and-blood mankind – enter the picture, having emerged in the form of Adam (or Isaac) from the underworld, still carrying the burden of sin of our long-lost, mythical ancestors.

As for how *we sinners* will be saved, and restored to the kingdom of God, that is, according to the Church, a matter of the *Second* Coming of Christ, which is seemingly now some two thousand years overdue, but nevertheless is awaited keenly by millions of Christians worldwide.

But are we truly aware of *exactly* what the Second Coming of Christ will entail?

It is time, dear reader, to spell out the shocking truth of what Christianity is all about, and moreover to find out whether there is, in fact, any 'truth' to it at all.

* * * * *

CHAPTER THIRTEEN

THE END OF DAYS

Behold, I will create new heavens and a new Earth;
and the former shall not be remembered,
nor ever come to mind.
(Yahweh, in the book of Isaiah, chapter 65)

Two thousand years ago, when the religion of Christianity first began, people were initiated into it via a baptismal rite. But unlike modern baptisms, this ancient Christian baptism was an initiation procedure *for adults*. Moreover, it involved *a complete immersion* of the adult in water – usually in the flowing waters of a major river such as the river Jordan in Palestine, or the river Tiber in Italy.

Such was the profound symbolism of the baptism ritual that the initiate believed all his past sins to have been 'washed away', thus causing him to be reborn. Some initiates would thus mark the occasion by adopting a new name, just as Saul renamed himself as 'Paul'. Baptism, in short, was a life-changing event – an initiation ceremony which marked the beginning of a new life.

As Christian dogma began to emerge in the 1st and 2nd centuries AD, so did the ritual of baptism become associated not just with rebirth in general, but specifically with the death and resurrection of Jesus Christ. Candidates for baptism were thus required to assent to the Christian creed by answering "I believe" to various questions which were recited by the bishop.

During the 3rd century AD, bishop Hippolytus recorded just such a question-and-answer ritual, which was performed during baptisms in Rome. Try to picture the scenario, as the initiate was immersed fully, three times, in the waters of the river Tiber. The account of Hippolytus reads as follows:

When the person being baptised goes down into the water, he who

baptises him, putting his hand on him shall say:
"Do you believe in God, the Father Almighty?"
And the person being baptised shall say: "I believe".
Then, holding his hand on his head, he shall baptise him once.
And then he shall say:
"Do you believe in Christ Jesus, the Son of God, who was born by
the Holy Spirit of the Virgin Mary, and was crucified under Pontius
Pilate, and was dead and buried, and ascended into Heaven, and sat
at the right hand of the Father, and will come to judge the living
and the dead?"
And when he [the initiate] says: "I believe", he is baptised again.
And again he [the bishop] shall say:
"Do you believe in the Holy Spirit, in the holy church, and the
resurrection of the body?"
The person being baptised shall say: "I believe", and then he is
baptised a third time.[1]

This, it must be emphasised, was the Christianised form of the baptismal
initiation, and it was established *long after* Jesus had been crucified in
Jerusalem. No-one would claim that these questions and answers would
have been appropriate to the baptisms previously carried out by Jesus or
John the Baptist themselves.

What, then, would have been the form of the baptismal creed in the
early part of the first century AD, before it was Christianised? What might
the baptism have symbolised to the mystery schools, who presumably
knew the true, esoteric meaning of the washing away of sins and the
rebirth of man in the waters?

Based on my arguments in the previous chapters, I suggest that we
should understand the baptism in terms of the following question-and-
answer ritual (which is purely hypothetical but nonetheless illustrative):

The Baptist: "Do you believe in Jesus Christ, the Son-of-Beginning,
the Word, and the corner stone which the builders rejected, who
came forth from the Father-of-Beginning, in his image, who laid
the foundations of the Earth and became its sure foundation, who
created all things, visible and invisible, who was crucified in
Heaven, as in Earth, and suffered mysteriously, for the sins of the
first 'men', in the assembly of the wicked?"
The initiate: "I believe".
The Baptist: "Do you believe in Jesus Christ, who went down into
Hades, who purified the black-headed ones and washed away their
sins in his 'flesh' and 'blood', who offered himself as an eternal

ransom for them, who raised them from the dead – all of them – and lifted them up to Heaven, to shine like the Igigi for ever?"

The initiate: "I believe".

The Baptist: "Do you believe in Jesus Christ, who will come again mysteriously, who will raise his own body from the dead,[2] as the first fruits of the dead, who will baptise mankind with the Holy Spirit and with fire, who will separate the sheep from the goats, who will lift up the bodies of the righteous ones to Heaven, and who will unite us with himself, and with his Father, and with the Anunnaki and the Igigi, and with our black-headed ancestors, in peace, for ever?[3]

And do you believe that this baptism in the river Jordan re-enacts, in human flesh, the original baptism of our ancestors in the primeval waters of the Great Deep, and thereby washes away *our* sins, and causes *us* to be reborn, and prepares *us* for the Second Coming of Christ, when we will be raised to Heaven by his baptism of the Holy Spirit and of fire?"

The initiate: "I believe".

Although this question-and-answer ritual is purely hypothetical, it represents, I believe, the occulted secret of what ancient baptism was all about, namely a ritual commemoration of the baptism of primeval mankind in the underworld – hence the idea of a complete immersion in water.[4] Thereafter, the initiate would emerge from the waters, reborn, with his past sins forgiven and fully behind him. This was, I suggest, a dramatic re-enactment of mankind's primeval birth from the underworld, when the past sins of his fallen celestial ancestors were washed away by a Deluge of celestial proportions. (Man's *future* sins, of course, remained another matter entirely.)

The upshot of this baptism was that the initiate, having re-enacted his *primeval* rebirth, was prepared for the essential *second* baptism which would resurrect him to Heaven. For, in the words of Jesus himself in the gospel of John:

Verily, verily, I say unto you, unless a man is born of water *and of the Spirit*, he cannot enter into the kingdom of God.[5]

What, then, was this second baptism of the Holy Spirit? It was in fact a baptism *with the Holy Spirit and with fire*, as was explained by John the Baptist in the gospels of Matthew and Luke:

"I baptise you with water for repentance. But he that comes after me is mightier than I, whose sandals I am not worthy to bear. *He will baptise you with the Holy Spirit and with fire.* His winnowing fork is in his hand, and he will thoroughly purge his threshing floor, and gather his wheat into the barn. But he will burn up the chaff with unquenchable fire."[6]

This is one of the most important passages in the gospels, for it attests to the fact that the Second Coming of Christ would be *catastrophic*. And the time of its future occurrence was known, quite aptly, as 'the End of Days'.

A typical view of this End of Days, as envisaged by Christianity, is found in the 'second letter' of Peter, where Peter the apostle juxtaposed the *future* catastrophic event – a destruction by fire – with a *previous* catastrophic event – a destruction by water.

This was Peter's view of the End of Days:

For they [the sceptics of Christ's Second Coming] are willingly ignorant (of the fact) that, by the word of God, the heavens were ancient, and the Earth (too), standing out of the water and in the water. And the world of that time was overcome with water and perished. But, by the same word [of God] *the present heavens and Earth are held back and reserved for (destruction by) fire, the Day of Judgement and destruction of ungodly men.*[7]

Now, according to the Church, Christ is, and always has been, *a spiritual figure* – in line with the popular *but occulted* version of Judaeo-Christian religion. And it is thus held that the biblical presentation of the End of Days as a catastrophic description of the Earth (as we know it) is really nothing for us to worry about. On the contrary, the End of Days should be understood only as a metaphysical transformation of all things. In other words, a miracle of God.

But is this what the biblical scriptures actually say? Do Christians truly understand the catastrophic nature of the End of Days, which they await with such keen anticipation?

In this chapter, we shall go back to basics, looking at the End of Days not just in the Christian scriptures, but also in the books of the Old Testament. We will take a close look at the various Old Testament messiahs ('anointed ones'), who were expected to appear in the End of Days, and form our own conclusions as to whether or not they were identical to the Christian Messiah, Jesus Christ.

Then, having established what the End of Days was all about, we will return briefly to the subject of the Beginning of Days, in order to acquire an overview of the entire Christian creed.

This will, however, be an overview with a difference – an overview inspired by the *occulted* traditions of Christianity. Consequently, we will be led towards some quite astonishing conclusions concerning what actually took place in the land of Palestine some two thousand years ago.

The Day of the LORD

In the Old Testament book of Psalms, it is stated that 'fear of the LORD is the beginning of Wisdom'.[8] As we shall now see, 'fear of the LORD' might well be *the end* of Wisdom.

We shall begin our study of Old Testament eschatology with Isaiah, the foremost of the prophets, who provided several excellent descriptions of the coming disaster. One of the most vivid passages appears in chapter 24 of the book of Isaiah. There, he wrote:

> Behold, the LORD will make the Earth empty and waste; he will turn it
>   upside down and scatter its inhabitants abroad...
> The inhabitants of the Earth are burned up, and few men are left...
> The floodgates of Heaven are opened, and the foundations of the Earth
>   do shake.
> The Earth is utterly broken up, the Earth is shaken to the core, the
>   Earth is thoroughly moved.
> The Earth reels to and fro like a drunkard...[9]

Note the reference here to the opening of the 'floodgates of Heaven' – words which echo (with a clear intent) the Great Flood of Noah. Isaiah's vision was thus one of a very real, *physical* cataclysm.

A similar idea is expressed in chapter 13 of Isaiah, where the prophet declared:

> Lament! For the day of the LORD is at hand – it will come as a
>   destruction from El Shaddai...
> Behold, the day of the LORD cometh – a cruel day with wrath and
>   fierce anger, to lay the land desolate...
> For the stars of Heaven and the constellations thereof shall cease
>   giving light.
> The Sun shall be darkened in its course, and the Moon shall not cause
>   her light to shine...
> "I will shake the heavens, and the Earth shall be moved from her
>   place..."[10]

In line with Hebrew tradition, Isaiah referred to the End of Days as 'the day of the LORD', and it is clear from this passage that it was a day which would be catastrophic, not only for the Earth, but also for the heavens.

Incidentally, Isaiah's reference to God as 'El Shaddai' is important, for this was God's archaic name, his oldest name, from the days before he renamed himself as Yahweh.[11] The name El Shaddai thus offers us an intriguing insight into the original identity of the Hebrew God – before he was occulted behind vague names such as Elohim and Yahweh.

What, then, does the name El Shaddai signify? Significantly, it evoked the name of a pagan god, El, the supreme god of the Canaanites, whose divine abode was a 'mountain' known as a *Shad* – a name derived from the Akkadian word *shadu*, meaning 'mountain'.[12] Moreover, just as Yahweh had called to Moses from 'out of the mountain' (Mount Sinai), so would El speak to the other Canaanite gods from the heart of his 'mountain'.[13]

Consequently, it can be stated with confidence that the meaning of El Shaddai was either 'God-of-the-Mountains', or 'God-of-the-Mountain-Peaks'.[14]

It is for this reason that the Hebrews envisaged the End of Days as an army descending to Earth out of a heavenly mountain or 'mountains', as in chapter 13 of the book of Isaiah:

> *(There is) the noise of a multitude in the mountains*, like that of a great
>   people...
> Yahweh-Sabaoth ['LORD of Hosts'] is mustering an army for battle.
> The LORD and the weapons of his wrath – they come from a faraway
>   land, *from the end of Heaven*, to destroy the whole Earth.[15]

This imagery, it must be said, is remarkably similar to that described in certain Mesopotamian texts.[16]

In the book of Joel, we find a similar passage. Once again, it was imagined that El Shaddai, the God-of-the-Mountains, would send an 'army' to assault the Earth, like a battalion of horses and chariots:

> The day of the LORD is at hand. As a destruction from El Shaddai it
>   shall come...
> Let all the inhabitants of the land tremble, for the day of the LORD
>   cometh.
> It is close at hand – a day of darkness and gloom, a day of clouds and
>   thick darkness...
> A great and mighty army cometh [from Heaven], such as never was of
>   old, nor ever will be in days to come.
> A fire devoureth before them, and behind them a flame burneth.
> The land before them is like the Garden of Eden, but behind them is
>   like a desolate wilderness; yea, nothing shall escape them.
> They have the appearance of horses and horsemen; thus they run.

They leap on the tops of mountains, with a noise like that of chariots,
     like the noise of a crackling fire...
The Earth shall quake before them; the heavens shall tremble; the Sun
     and the Moon shall be darkened, and the stars shall shine no longer.
The LORD shall thunder before his army...
The day of the LORD is great, and very dreadful. Who can endure it?[17]

These short extracts provide a reasonably representative picture of the
End of Days, as imagined by the Old Testament prophets. We should,
however, take note of a variant theme, which envisaged the cataclysm as
an exact reversal of the creation in Genesis chapter 1 – in other words a
destructive *undoing* of God's creative handiwork. A good example of
this belief is found in the book of Jeremiah, where the prophet claimed to
have had the following vision of the End of Days:

I [Jeremiah] beheld the Earth, and lo, it was without form and void;
     and as for the heavens, they had no light...[18]

Note how the words 'without form and void' imply a return to the
uncreated Earth, an idea which is emphasised by the disappearance of the
light (or Light) which had been created by God.
   The prophet Isaiah took the same idea even further, describing how
the Earth would return to its primeval state as an undifferentiated sphere:

The voice of him that crieth in the wilderness: "Prepare ye the way of
     the LORD, make straight in the wilderness a highway for our God.
Every valley shall be raised up, every mountain and hill shall be laid
     low, every crooked place shall be made straight, and every rough
     place shall be made smooth.
And the Glory of the LORD shall be revealed."[19]

This is an intriguing passage, not least for the mystery surrounding the
individual who 'cried in the wilderness'. Who was he? We will return to
this point shortly with a startling hypothesis.
   Meanwhile, what about the 'Glory' of the LORD? This happens to be a
fascinating subject, for the word for 'Glory' in Hebrew was *Kavohdh*,
literally meaning 'Heaviness'.[20] It should be mentioned in passing that
the Dead Sea Scrolls preserve an excellent record of how this Heaviness
of God *filled the Earth* at the time of the creation. That, at least, would be
my restoration of the following, partly fragmented, line:

He [God] fashioned the works of Heaven and Earth, *and they met*, and
     his Glory [Heaviness] filled . . . [21]

This Glory, or Heaviness, then, would return to Earth at the End of Days, just as it had fallen into the Earth at the Beginning of Days. And the result would be just as catastrophic, even though the Glory had been transformed into a metaphysical phenomenon.

Now the good news. According to the Hebrew traditions of the End of Days, the destruction of the world would not be a total destruction. The Earth would continue to exist. Indeed, it was a fundamental tenet of Judaic religious philosophy that the Earth *had to* survive, in order that it might be repopulated by a new generation of *righteous* people.

This is logical, for it must be emphasised that God's original act of creation was *not* a creation *ex-nihilo*.[22] What God had in fact done in Genesis chapter 1 was to create *the Earth-as-we-know-it*, by applying his catastrophic force to *remake* the Earth with its valleys, mountains, rivers and oceans.

By the same token, what God would do in the future, at the End of Days, was *not* destroy the Earth totally, but rather *reshape its surface*. The Earth as we know it would cease to exist, but planet Earth herself would continue in existence.

Thus we get the biblical concept of a 'new Earth', as mentioned in the book of Isaiah:

> (And the LORD saith:) "Behold, I will create new heavens and a new
>   Earth.
> And the former shall not be remembered, nor ever come to mind."[23]

As for the 'new heavens', there was indeed a belief that major changes would occur in the firmament at the End of Days, thus causing the heavens, too, to be remade. In Isaiah 34, for example, we are told that 'all the host of Heaven [the stars] will be loosened, and the heavens will be rolled together like a scroll; and all their host will fall down'.[24] Elsewhere in Isaiah, we read of God's desire to punish the 'host of the high ones', presumably for acting as the false gods of mankind.[25]

What would life be like on this 'new Earth'? In the book of Isaiah, we read that the new Earth would be reborn amidst great bloodshed among mankind. God would gather together all of the pagan nations, and bring them as great multitudes into 'the valley of decision', also known as 'the valley where the LORD judges' (this probably means the underworld).[26]

In the book of the prophet Malachi, Yahweh-Sabaoth, the LORD of Hosts, declared:

> "Behold, the day cometh that will burn like a furnace. All the arrogant
> and all the evildoers will be stubble – the day that cometh will burn
> them up..."[27]

Such was the number of the evildoers that the bodies of those who were slain would 'stretch from one end of the Earth to the other', according to the book of Jeremiah.[28] But this bloodshed would act as a ransom for the redemption of an Israelite remnant, who, at the sound of a great trumpet, would return joyfully to the city of Jerusalem, protected from the threatening waters and fire en route by the mysterious power of God.[29]

This theme – of the eventual return of the remnant from all corners of the world – was the corner stone of Hebrew prophecy.

According to some accounts, God, too, would return to Jerusalem, and bring about a new era of peace (although we should not imagine that God would abandon his heavenly abode; he was perfectly capable of occupying Heaven *and* Earth). In the book of Zechariah, God declared:

> "I will return to Zion, and will dwell in the midst of Jerusalem; and Jerusalem will be called 'the City of Truth'; and the mountain of the LORD of Hosts will be called 'the Holy Mountain'."[30]

In effect, God would bring down to Earth a 'New Jerusalem' – a theme which is best captured in the book of Revelations, in the vision of John:

> And I saw a new Heaven and a new Earth, for the first Heaven and first Earth had passed away... and I, John, saw the holy city, New Jerusalem, coming down from God out of Heaven, prepared as a bride adorned for her husband.[31]

We see here the idea of a sacred marriage between Heaven and Earth, and also the idea of the 'city' as a microcosm of the world. The New Jerusalem would, in effect, become the new Earth.[32]

As for the real city of Jerusalem, the Old Testament states that it would be raised up from the surrounding chaos, and its mountain would be established above all other mountains.[33] According to Isaiah, God would shield Jerusalem and 'pass over' it – an idea reminiscent of the glorious 'Passover' which had preceded the Exodus of the primeval Israelites from the underworld.[34] And, in another echo of Exodus, God would protect the city of Jerusalem with a cloud of smoke by day, and a flaming fire by night.[35] The entire mountain of God would thus be covered by something like a protective tent.

The Old Testament portrays the new Earth, or New Jerusalem, as a marvellous, idyllic place. The Spirit of God would be poured down from on high, imbuing his people with a new spirit of unswerving obedience and loyalty.[36] Eyes would be opened, ears would be unblocked, and minds would be filled with a new understanding.[37]

Furthermore, the judgement of God would extend to all nations, far and wide, who would thereupon convert their swords into ploughshares, causing all wars to come to an end.[38] People from all around the world would flock to Jerusalem to be taught the ways of the LORD, and the mountain of God would be transformed into a beautiful paradise, where the wolf would dwell with the lamb, the leopard would lie down with the goat, the lion would eat straw like the ox, and the people of Israel would never again complain of sickness and disease.[39] From that time on, all people who lived in Jerusalem would be called 'holy'.[40]

This new era of peace would be administered either by God himself, or by a Messiah, acting on his behalf. We will return to the subject of this Messiah in due course, but suffice to say for now that he was given numerous names and epithets in the Old Testament, such as 'Shiloh', 'The Wonderful Counsellor', the 'Prince of Peace', 'The Branch', 'The Root of Jesse', or simply 'David'. Was this Davidic Messiah the same as Jesus Christ? We shall see.

Once God had instigated this new era on the Earth, there would never again be change, for all of eternity. The Davidic Messiah would rule over a perfect world, and the surviving remnant of Israel and their offspring would live for ever in a paradise of eternal peace:

> And the LORD saith [to Israel]: "Just as the new heavens and new
> Earth will endure before me for ever, so will your seed and your
> name endure for ever..."[41]

Such was the scenario of the End of Days, and the new Earth, as envisaged by the Old Testament prophets. The cataclysm which would remake the world would lead, miraculously, to an endless continuation of history.[42]

But what of the new Heaven? It is noticeable that the future paradise of the Hebrews was rooted firmly on the Earth, *in accordance with their philosophy that Heaven was reserved for God alone.*

There was, however, one individual, so it would seem, who *would* be raised up to Heaven at the End of Days, as was revealed in the famous passages of Isaiah 52-53:

> Behold, my (Righteous) Servant will act wisely; he will be raised, and
> lifted up, and highly exalted...
> Therefore I [the LORD] will give him [the Righteous Servant] a
> portion with the great, and he shall divide the spoil with the strong;
> because he poured out his soul unto (the place of) death, and he was
> numbered with the transgressors.[43]

This was the Righteous Servant, who had offered himself as a ransom for 'mankind' at the Beginning of Days, thus bearing the sins of all 'men', and suffering on their behalf in the underworld, for what must have seemed like an eternity.

And it was this Righteous Servant, I suggest, who uttered the famous cry in Isaiah 40, as he anticipated the coming of God, his personal saviour, who would travel through the 'wilderness' of space, into the 'wilderness' of the underworld,[44] to rescue him:

> The voice of him that crieth in the wilderness: "Prepare the way of the LORD, make straight in the wilderness a highway for our God."[45]

Thus did the Righteous Servant look forward to being restored to Heaven at the End of Days.

The Second Coming of Christ

We turn now to the *Christian* model of the End of Days, where once again we find the idea of a physical catastrophe, which would bring about the creation of a new heavens and a new Earth.

There are, however, some important points of difference between the Old Testament and New Testament eschatologies, as we shall see.

One of the first things to note about the New Testament eschatology is that the role of God as saviour and judge is taken by Jesus Christ. No longer does God himself descend catastrophically to judge the Earth and save the righteous.[46] Instead, Jesus Christ comes down, as God's right hand man so to speak, to carry out the great judgement and redemption on his behalf.

As observed in chapter twelve, Jesus Christ would return to Earth as *Ben Adamah*, a title which had a secret meaning: *Seed of Mankind*. The title suggests that Christ would take the same guise at the End of Days as he had taken at the Beginning of Days. The only difference was that the Second Coming of Christ would give greater emphasis to his destructive aspect, rather than his earlier creative aspect.

So, what would happen when Jesus Christ, the Seed of Mankind, returned to the Earth? In the gospel of Matthew, Jesus explained that the days leading up to the Second Coming would be like 'the beginning of birth-pains'.[47] There would be reports of wars, and rumours of wars, he said, with nation rising up against nation. There would be famines, pestilences and earthquakes in many different places (compare the plagues leading up to the Exodus). And the people of Israel would experience 'great tribulation, such as had not been seen since the beginning of the world'.[48]

It was after this period of 'birth-pains' and 'tribulation' that Jesus

Christ, the Seed of Mankind, would descend to Earth in his Second Coming. In the words of Jesus, from the gospel of Matthew:

"Immediately after the tribulation of those days, the Sun will be darkened, and the Moon will not give its light, and the stars will fall from Heaven, and the powers of the heavens will be shaken. And then will appear the sign of the Seed of Mankind in Heaven..."[49]

What would this 'sign' be like? As Jesus himself put it, in the gospels:

"Hereafter you shall see the Seed of Mankind sitting on the right hand of power [God], and coming in the clouds of Heaven."[50]

"You shall see Heaven open, and the angels of God ascending and descending on the Seed of Mankind."[51]

"As lightning comes out of the east, but is visible in the west, so will it be at the coming of the Seed of Mankind."[52]

Clearly, the future Seed of Mankind would *not* be appearing in flesh-and-blood human form. On the contrary, the book of Revelations suggests that the Seed of Mankind would have a distinctly odd appearance:

I saw... someone like a Seed of Mankind, clothed with a garment down to his feet and with a golden sash round his chest. His head and hair were white like wool, as white as snow, and his eyes were like flames of fire. His feet were like bronze, glowing in a furnace, and his voice was like the sound of rushing waters. In his right hand he held seven stars, and out of his mouth came forth a sharp double-edged sword. And his face shone like the Sun in all its strength.[53]

This, then, was the Seed of Mankind, whose appearance would herald the end of the old Earth and the beginning of the new Earth.

Returning to the gospel of Matthew, Jesus continued:

"And then the sign of the Seed of Mankind will appear in Heaven. And then all the tribes of the Earth will mourn, when they see the Seed of Mankind coming in the clouds of Heaven, with power and great glory. And he will send out his angels with a loud trumpet call, and they will gather his elect from the four winds, from one end of Heaven to the other."[54]

This 'loud trumpet call', which dispatched the angels, can be compared to the mighty sounds which accompanied so many of the cataclysms in ancient pagan legends, and it thus symbolised the violent destruction and renewal of all things. Incidentally, it was these same trumpet sounds which had caused the 'walls' of Jericho to collapse – a legend which was surely based upon the catastrophic renewal of *the surface of the Earth* rather than a mundane city wall.[55]

There can be no doubt that the Second Coming of Christ would be catastrophic in nature. In the 'second letter' of Peter, cited earlier, the apostle wrote:

> But, by the same word [of God], the present heavens and Earth are held back and reserved for (destruction by) fire, the Day of Judgement and destruction of ungodly men.[56]

Later, in the same letter, Peter added:

> But the day of the Lord will come as a thief in the night. The heavens shall pass away with a great noise; the elements will be melted by fierce heat, and the Earth and everything therein will also be burned up...[57]

Lest there be any doubt about the global scale of this future catastrophe, let us note, too, the words of Jesus himself, in the gospel of Matthew:

> "Do not think that I have come to abolish the Law or the Prophets. I am not come to destroy (them) but to fulfil (them). Verily I say to you, not one tiny thing will be taken away from the Law until everything is fulfilled – *until Heaven and Earth pass away*."[58]

As with the Old Testament eschatology, however, the End of Days also marked a new beginning; hence the old heavens and old Earth would be transformed, miraculously, into a new heavens and a new Earth. In the 'second letter' of Peter, for example, the apostle stated:

> ... according to his promise, we are looking forward to a new heavens and a new Earth, wherein righteousness shall dwell.[59]

Jesus Christ surely intended much the same thing when he said: "Heaven and Earth shall pass away, but my words shall not pass away."[60] The Earth would continue to exist, for it was to be inherited by the meek.[61]

As for the evildoers, they had no place in the new set-up, and would face a fiery and merciless judgement, as Jesus Christ made clear in the gospel of Matthew:

> "As the weeds are gathered and burned in the fire, so will it be in the end of this world. The Seed of Mankind will send forth his angels, and they shall gather out of his kingdom everything that causes sin and all who do evil, and will cast them into a fiery furnace..."[62]

An era of truth and peace would then prevail on the new Earth – exactly as it would in the new Jerusalem which was envisaged by the writers of the Old Testament.

There was, however, one considerable difference between the Old and New Testament eschatologies. In the Old Testament, the righteous would inherit the new *Earth*, and no man would be taken up to Heaven (only the Righteous Servant would be lifted up, and he was certainly *not* a man). In the New Testament, however, *Heaven itself* would be inherited by the righteous among mankind.

For example, in the gospel of John, Jesus told his disciples:

> "In my Father's house are many mansions... I am going there to prepare a place for you... I will come again and receive you unto myself, so that you also may be where I am."[63]

Similarly, in the same gospel, Jesus stated:

> "And I, if I be lifted up from the Earth, will draw all men to myself."[64]

The righteous, we are told, would become 'like the angels in Heaven', and would 'shine forth like the Sun in the kingdom of their Father'.[65] According to Jesus in the gospel of Matthew, the righteous would inherit "the kingdom prepared... since the creation of the world".[66] And, needless to say, they would have eternal life, just as the evildoers would suffer eternal punishment.[67]

The idea, it would seem, was that mankind would be restored *to the place whence it had come*. Although this is not stated clearly in the biblical scriptures, it is confirmed in the gnostic writings of Valentinus, where Jesus declared:

> "I became very small, so that through my humility I might take you up to the great height, *whence you had fallen*."[68]

In summary, then, Jesus Christ in his Second Coming would perform a very different role from any of the Old Testament messiahs. He would *not* rule as a king over the righteous people on the new *Earth*, but would rather lift up the righteous people to *Heaven*, and rule over them there, in the new Heaven, at the right hand of God himself.

This point of difference is so fundamental that it would be no exaggeration to label the Old and New Testaments as *two different religions*. Admittedly, they were both exploded planet cults, and they both foresaw a catastrophic end of the world, but beyond this they had completely different philosophies about what would happen to man at that time. According to the Old Testament, righteous men would live *on the Earth*, almost as if history was continuing. But according to the New Testament, righteous men would be transformed magically to become dwellers in a *heavenly* paradise.

The Mystery of the Messiah

It seems to follow logically, from the above discussion, that Jesus Christ could not possibly be the same saviour, or Messiah, as was anticipated in the writings of the Old Testament. For the role of Jesus Christ, in lifting up the righteous to Heaven, was as distant from his Old Testament forebears, as the religion of the New Testament was itself distant from its Old Testament predecessor.

And yet, in spite of this, the Church has maintained for two thousand years that the Old Testament was *anticipating* the future coming of Jesus Christ at the End of Days. In other words, the Church claims that the messiahs of the Old Testament – individuals such as Shiloh, The Wonderful Counsellor, the Prince of Peace, The Branch, and The Root of Jesse – were one-and-the-same as the Christian Messiah, Jesus Christ.

Clearly there is a serious problem here, which needs further investigation and clarification. And, in addition, it will be useful for us to take a closer look at the concept of messiahs in order to elucidate what was happening in Jerusalem two thousand years ago.

So, we will now take a brief look at each of the various Messiah figures in the Old Testament, and this we will do by working our way through the scriptures in their normal chronological sequence.

We begin with the book of Genesis, where we find reference to an intriguing character called Shiloh, who has excited a great deal of interest over the years. The passage reads as follows:

> The sceptre shall not depart from (the tribe of) Judah... until Shiloh comes; and unto him will be the gathering of the people.[69]

The name Shiloh means 'he to whom it belongs', i.e. to whom the sceptre belongs, or to whom tribute belongs.[70] The idea (which is also picked up by Ezekiel 21:27) seems to be that the kings of Israel were holding the sceptre of kingship *in trust* for a higher power, and that this higher power would eventually return to occupy the throne of David *for ever*. Shiloh would thus be a Messiah, who would arise in the future, 'other worldly' realm of the new Earth as a *permanent heir* to the throne of David.

Moving on to the book of Numbers, we find a similar idea to Shiloh in the so-called 'star prophecy', which speaks of a 'star' or 'sceptre' arising from Israel and having dominion over all peoples.[71] However, in my opinion, it is not altogether clear from the context whether this prophecy actually refers to an End of Days scenario or not.

Such doubts cannot be said to exist in the apocalyptic writings of the prophets, and it is here, in these books, that the Old Testament concept of the Messiah finds its fullest expression.

In the book of Isaiah, in the context of the End of Days, we read:

> For unto us a child will be born, unto us a son will be given, and the government will be upon his shoulders.
> And he will be called by name 'Wonderful Counsellor, the Mighty God, the Everlasting Father, the Prince of Peace'.
> And there will be no end to the increase of his government and his peace upon the throne of David.[72]

As if this string of names were not sufficient, it is bolstered elsewhere in the book of Isaiah by reference to the future Messiah as 'the Branch', and 'the Root of Jesse' (Jesse being the father of king David).[73] Hence, in Isaiah 11, we read:

> And there will come forth a shoot from the stem of Jesse, and a Branch shall grow out of his roots.
> And the Spirit of the LORD will rest upon him...
> And in that day the Root of Jesse will stand as a banner for the people.
> The nations shall rally to him and his (place of) rest will be glorious.[74]

Moving on to the book of Jeremiah, we find once again the idea of the Messiah being 'the Branch', but with another title now being added:

> "Behold, the days are coming" saith the LORD "when I will raise unto David a righteous Branch, a king who shall reign and prosper...
> In his days Judah will be saved, and Israel shall dwell safely.
> And he [the Branch] will be called by the name: 'The LORD (is) Our Righteousness'."[75]

The future Messiah acquires yet another name in the book of Ezekiel – this time the name of David himself. God informed Ezekiel:

> "My servant David will be king over them... my servant David will be their prince for ever."[76]

Would this be a reincarnation of the old David, or would it be a new David? The text does not explain.

Yet another different name for the Messiah turns up in the book of Daniel, and this time we get the first direct hint of a connection to the Christian Messiah. The prophet Daniel stated:

> In the night visions I looked, and behold, one like a Seed of Mankind came with the clouds of Heaven, and came to the Ancient of Days...

And there he was given dominion, glory and a kingdom... His dominion will be an everlasting dominion that will not pass away, and which will never be destroyed.[77]

The title Seed of Mankind (*Ben Adamah*) is, of course, the title which Jesus Christ applied so frequently to himself in the New Testament.

But who was Daniel referring to as 'the Ancient of Days'? The context of the passage suggests that it was God, who was pictured sitting on, or perhaps *in*, the Earth, in a hall of judgement. Daniel's vision thus described the Seed of Mankind descending from Heaven to Earth, where God would delegate all powers to him. This intriguing scenario is noteworthy also for the fact that the Seed of Mankind was referred to as 'the Most High' – a title perhaps more befitting to God himself.[78]

Another passage of interest to Christians appears in the book of Micah, where God announced that the future Messiah would come from the town of Bethlehem:

"But thou, Bethlehem-Ephrathah, though thou be small among the clans of Judah, out of thee will come forth unto me the one who will be ruler in Israel, whose goings forth (are) from of old, from days of eternity."[79]

The last line of this passage suggests to me the idea of Christ 'the Word', who had gone forth from God at the beginning of time.

There is one more messianic title to be found in the Old Testament, and it comes from the very last book – the book of Malachi. Here we read that the evildoers would be burned up in the End of Days, but for those who feared the Name of the LORD, salvation would come in the form of 'the Sun of righteousness', who would 'rise up with healing in his wings'.[80]

Finally, we turn to the Dead Sea Scrolls, for one further messianic title which will excite Christians. In the *Aramaic Apocalypse*, there is mention of a final king, who would rise up on the Earth and instigate an eternal era of truth and peace. This king was called 'the son of God':

The Son of the Great Master shall he be called; by his Name he will be designated. He will be said (to be) the Son of God, and they will call him the Son of the Most High.[81]

This, at last, completes the amazing array of names which were applied to the future Messiah in the Old Testament and related Jewish scriptures. They can be summarised as follows:

* Shiloh, meaning 'he to whom it belongs'.
* Wonderful Counsellor, Mighty God, Everlasting Father, Prince of Peace.
* The Branch, or The Root of Jesse, also known as 'The LORD is Our Righteousness'.
* David – a servant of God, the prince, the shepherd of the people.
* Seed of Mankind, also known as The Most High, and probably identical to the one 'whose goings forth are from of old'.
* Sun of Righteousness – the one who would arise 'with healing in his wings'.
* Son of God, also known as 'Son of the Most High'.

What should we make of this Messiah-of-many-names? Is there any way that he might be identical to Jesus Christ, the Seed of Mankind?

In the case of Daniel's vision of 'one like a Seed of Mankind coming with the clouds of Heaven', there is indeed a correspondence in name, and a correspondence in origin, in the sense that he would descend directly to Earth from Heaven. However, it must be emphasised that Daniel's Messiah fitted the Old Testament mould – of one who would become king *of the Earth*. Since there was no intention of this Messiah resurrecting the righteous to Heaven (as far as we know), it cannot be claimed that he is identical to the Christian Messiah, Jesus Christ.

As for the other Old Testament messiahs, it seems to me that they are even farther from the Christian model, for they would all seem to describe a Messiah *born in the Earth*.

Consider, for example, the Messiah known as 'The Branch', who was envisaged by Isaiah as follows:

> And there will come forth *a shoot* from *the stem* of Jesse, *and a Branch shall grow out of his roots*.[82]

Is this not an identical concept to the birth of Gilgamesh, the Sumerian king? The name Gilgamesh, or GIS.BIL.GA.MES, meant literally 'MES which is the *sprouting seed* of a new tree', in addition to which he was known by the nickname '*offshoot* of Uruk'. I contend that these names carry an identical meaning to The Branch, especially when we consider the fact that the Hebrew name commonly translated as 'Branch' can also be translated as 'Sprout' or 'Shoot'.[83]

The Messiah known as Shiloh also fits into this category, for the Dead Sea Scrolls suggest that he was identical to the future 'Messiah of Righteousness', who would also be called '*the Branch* of David'.[84] He, too, was thus in the mould of the pagan god-king, who was thought to have emerged from the underworld like a Titan.

The same might also be said about the Messiah in the *Aramaic Apocalypse* – the so-called Son of God, or Son of the Most High – for the pagan kings of Egypt and Mesopotamia indeed regarded themselves as 'sons' of God. The kings of Egypt, for example, were held to be incarnations of the falcon-god Horus, who had risen up like a Titan, after his parents Isis and Osiris had descended into the underworld at the beginning of time and performed the mysterious rite of the sacred marriage.

This brings us to a distinction of crucial importance. Yes, Horus was a son of Osiris. But Osiris, too, was considered to be a 'son', namely a son of the Sky-goddess Nut. We thus have a situation where one son, Osiris, gave birth to another son, Horus, making the latter in fact the 'grandson' of Nut.

The crucial distinction is this: Osiris was a son *born in Heaven*, whereas Horus was a son, or grandson, *born in the Earth*. But each of them, it might be said, was a 'son of God' (or 'son of the Goddess').

Now, when we apply this distinction to the future messiahs of Hebrew and Christian tradition, respectively, we find something very interesting.

The Hebrew messiahs, we find, were mostly modelled on *Horus* – the 'son of God' who was *born in the Earth*.

But the Christian Messiah, Jesus Christ, was modelled on *Osiris* – the 'son of God' (or 'son of the Goddess') who was *born in Heaven*.

Incidentally, this same distinction was made between Utnapishtim and Gilgamesh in the Mesopotamian texts. The former was a god who had descended *from Heaven*, being thus one hundred per cent divine. The latter, however, was a god who had been *born in the Earth*, and who was thus only two thirds divine. Consequently, in *The Epic of Gilgamesh*, king Gilgamesh had been allowed to rule on Earth, but never in Heaven.

Jesus Christ – the Christian Messiah – was equivalent to Utnapishtim and Osiris. He had descended to Earth directly from Heaven, hence his title: the Seed of Mankind.

The Old Testament messiahs, on the other hand (with the exception of the one seen by Daniel), were equivalent to Gilgamesh and Horus. They had been conceived in the womb of Mother Earth, and had emerged therefrom. Hence their associations with 'branches' and 'roots'.

To underline this point and conclude this discussion, I refer readers to a remarkable text among the Dead Sea Scrolls, which describes the birth of a Messiah who was identified as 'the Marvellous Counsellor' (a name applied also to the Messiah in chapter 9 of Isaiah):

> They caused me [the mother of the Messiah] to be like a ship on the
>   deeps of the Sea,

And like a fortified city before the enemy.
And I was in pain, like a woman in travail with her first-born child,
Upon whom pangs have come and grievous pains in her throes,
To cause her to writhe, with anguish in her womb.
For the children have come to the throes of death,
And she who gives birth to a man labours in her pains.
For amidst the throes of death she shall bring forth a male,
And *amidst the pains of hell* there shall spring from her womb
A Marvellous Counsellor in his strength;
And a man shall be delivered from out of her throes.[85]

A ship or a 'ship'? A womb or a 'womb'? A man or a 'man'?
Let the wise teach the *metaphors* to the wise.

Alpha and Omega – The Beginning and The End

It is now time to pause and take stock of what we have learned in the course of this and previous chapters.

The starting point for our investigation, in chapters eleven and twelve, was Jesus-the-man – an elusive figure who lived in 1st century Palestine. Initially, we were intrigued by the connection between the crucifixion of Jesus and the sacrifice of the Passover lamb – a connection which was underlined by his nickname 'the Lamb of God'. This led us to question whether Jesus Christ *was* the lamb (or lambs) which had ransomed the Israelites from 'Egypt' – a question which was all the more profound for the realisation that this lamb had been sent down *into the underworld* to ransom the *primeval* first-born of the Israelites *at the beginning of time*. It was only in this context – of a legend which had never before been properly decoded – that pieces of the puzzle began to slot into place.

Having posed this question, it was then inevitable that we would ask the same question concerning the lamb (or ram) which had been sent down from Heaven to ransom Isaac, the first-born son of Abraham. Once again, it was apparent that no-one had ever before realised that the story of Isaac was a legend of man's emergence from the underworld at the beginning of time. Furthermore, the idea that Jesus Christ *was* this lamb (or ram) was supported by his preposterous claim in the gospels: "Abraham rejoiced to see my day, and he saw, and was glad."

Having put these clues together, we began to wonder whether the Old Testament 'prophecies' of a suffering Christ-like figure were not actually prophecies of the future at all, but were, on the contrary, *mytho-historic* references to the 'man' who had ransomed himself in the underworld at the Beginning of Days. Our suspicions were increased by the anomalous descriptions of this 'man', whose 'bones' were rather strangely 'out of joint', and whose appearance was 'disfigured beyond that of any man'. And the reason for this disfigurement soon became readily apparent – the scriptures stated very clearly that this 'man' had been cast down from Heaven into the land of the dead, or into the assembly of the wicked, *i.e. into the underworld*. And it was there, in the underworld, that the mysterious 'man' was 'pierced' in the hands and feet, i.e. most probably crucified.

We then began to realise that these were not descriptions of Jesus-the-man, but rather descriptions of his primeval alter ago, Jesus-the-Word, who had been alongside God at the beginning of time, but who had been sent down into the Earth by God at the time of the creation. It was this primeval Christ through whom all things had been made, and all things created. But crucially, we interpreted this in the context of the pagan paradigm of the creation, according to which the primeval Christ would have been a *physical* creator-god. This notion fitted superbly well with the idea of the fallen 'man' in Psalm 22 and Isaiah 52-53, who was horribly disfigured, and who was tortured in captivity in the underworld.

Moreover, in chapter twelve, we began to realise that Jesus-the-man had signposted the importance of his primeval alter ago by continually referring to himself as *Ben Adamah*, the Seed of Mankind, as well as identifying himself as 'the corner stone which the builders rejected'. This in addition to his enigmatic sayings "Moses wrote about me" and "Before Abraham was born, I am!".

We began to realise, too, that the story of the primeval Christ – how he had offered himself as a ransom for the primeval, subterranean first-born of 'mankind' – was essentially identical to the story line of the gospels. The 'flesh' which he had sacrificed was the 'flesh' of a god, whilst the 'blood' which he had sacrificed was the 'blood' of a god. Furthermore, the sins which he had forgiven were the sins of a subterranean species of black-headed ones, whose sin – i.e. 'noise' – had first been committed in the heavens, in the 'womb' of the Sky-goddess Mami or Ishtar.

It thus made perfect sense that this primeval alter ego of Jesus Christ had given his 'flesh' for 'the life of the world', 'washed away the sins' of 'mankind' with his 'blood', and 'given his life as a ransom for many'.

Finally, in chapter twelve, I concluded by citing the tradition that the primeval Christ had 'raised the dead' at the beginning of time. This, I suggested, was a reference to the idea that the *primeval ancestors of mankind* had been redeemed by Christ, who had resurrected them to Heaven in the same manner as Marduk had lifted the Igigi-gods, i.e. by providing a ransom (in this case Christ himself, rather than 'mankind' as in the Babylonian myth).

This, I suggested, was the original mission of Jesus Christ, the Seed of Mankind – his First Coming. But it had left the primeval Christ – alias the Righteous Servant – trapped in the underworld until someone might come to ransom *him*, or save *him*, presumably at the End of Days.

This brings us to this chapter – chapter thirteen – where we have rolled on the story to the End of Days, at which time it was imagined that *the Second Coming* of Christ would save *flesh-and-blood* mankind via a fiery baptism of the Holy Spirit. As Jesus-the-man put it, in the gospel of John:

> Verily, verily, I say unto you, unless a man is born of water *and of the Spirit*, he cannot enter into the kingdom of God.[86]

My hypothesis, as cited earlier, is that the primeval ancestors of mankind had been resurrected to Heaven via a baptism of water in the underworld. Flesh-and-blood mankind was thus re-enacting this baptism by water in order to prepare itself for the future day of reckoning known as the End of Days. At that time, flesh-and-blood mankind would experience the baptism of the Holy Spirit which would take it, too, to Heaven.

What would this End of Days baptism be like? John the Baptist described it as follows:

> "I baptise you with water for repentance. But he that comes after me [i.e. Christ] is mightier than I, whose sandals I am not worthy to bear. *He will baptise you with the Holy Spirit and with fire.*"[87]

The final baptism, then, was a fiery one, and we have invested some time in this chapter to establish the fact that the End of Days would indeed be a *catastrophic event* – an event which would bring about the end of the Earth-as-we-know-it, and the beginning of a new Earth and a new heavens, albeit in a rather mystical fashion.

Where does this leave us? In a nutshell, we have begun with Jesus-the-man, and proceeded to identify his two alter egos – on the one hand, his god-like *primeval* alter ego, and on the other hand, his god-like *future* alter ego, these being the creative and destructive aspects of one-and-the-same god, known as the Seed of Mankind.

But is it right that we should call these two gods 'the alter egos' of Jesus-the-man? Or is it rather the case that Jesus-the-man is 'the alter ego' of the two gods?

I put it to readers that Jesus-the-man is actually the alter ego and – more than that – I put it to readers that Jesus-the-man is something of a misfit in what is essentially a mythical, celestial scenario.

What we are faced with, in overview, is a Christ-of-the-Beginning and a Christ-of-the-End, spaced millions or billions of years apart, and making sense as divine opposites, but with Jesus-the-man appearing somewhere in the middle of time, and looking very odd and distinctly out of place.

Indeed, it becomes even more evident that Jesus-the-man is the 'odd one out' when we consider the fact that the two god-like Christs, of the Beginning and of the End, accord with one of the most fundamental concepts of God and Christ, which is expressed in both the Old and the New Testaments – the concept of the 'Alpha and Omega'. For example, in the book of Revelations, Christ spoke to John, saying:

"Fear not. I am *the First and the Last*."[88]

Similarly, in the book of Revelations, God himself declared:

"*I am Alpha and Omega, the Beginning and the End*, which is, and which was, and which is to come – the Almighty."[89]

In the Old Testament book of Isaiah, exactly the same divine principle is recorded, with God saying:

"*I am the First, and I am the Last*; and there is no God but me."[90]

"Hearken unto me, O Jacob and Israel... *I am the First and the Last*."[91]

The Muslim holy book, The Koran, also attests to the same principle, saying:

He [Allah] is *the First and the Last*, the visible and the unseen.[92]

Now, the story of Christ, as we have decoded it in these pages, makes perfect sense, in that there was indeed a *First* Christ, who made all things *in the beginning*, but also a *Last* Christ, who would remake all things *at the end*.

But where does this leave Jesus-the-man of the 1st century AD? He was neither the First Christ nor the Last Christ; he appears to have been a complete misfit in the grand scheme of things.

So who was this odd character of the 1st century AD? Was Jesus-the-man really the Son of God – an incarnation of the divine Spirit in human flesh? Did a supernatural God feel that the moment was right to intervene in the mundane history of mankind?

Or might there be another, more prosaic explanation?

Re-enacting the First Time

There is something very odd about the story of Jesus Christ as it appears in the gospels, at least when they are read according to the paradigm promulgated by the Church.

The story of Jesus Christ, we are told, is *the story of Jesus-the-man*, who sacrificed his life in order to save mankind from its sins (a now familiar story). And this Jesus-the-man, we are told, was the Messiah as prophesied in the Old Testament, the writings of which were divinely inspired by God himself.

As argued in chapter eleven (and in this chapter), the idea that the Old Testament writings were prophecies of a future Christ suffers from all sorts of problems, and is surely a falsehood. But even if we put all these problems to one side, there still remain numerous difficulties with the Church's argument.

The Church claims that Jesus Christ was put to death and resurrected to life *in his role as Messiah*. But this simply makes no sense.

Firstly, it is a fact that not one of the future messiahs referred to in the so-called 'prophecies' of the Old Testament would ever have to die. On the contrary, the fundamental idea was that the Messiah should prevail and rule the new Earth.

Other Jewish texts, such as the Dead Sea Scrolls, are in full agreement on this point. There is no suggestion anywhere (contrary to popular opinion) that the Messiah would have to be put to death at the End of Days.[93]

The fact is – and it cannot be emphasised too strongly – that the death of the Messiah belonged to *the Beginning of Days*, not to the End of Days. The idea of an execution at the End of Days makes no sense at all, and is completely alien to all the traditions of the ancient world.[94]

Secondly, there is not a single prophecy anywhere which suggests that the Messiah of the End of Days would have to be resurrected to Heaven first, before he could descend to Earth. This is a very strange idea indeed (which, incidentally, puzzled Jesus's disciples, and for good reason).[95]

Thirdly, it is unthinkable that the Messiah would not be able to fulfil his task until he had first been resurrected to Heaven via a human flesh sacrifice. It is an absurd notion.

Fourthly, if Jesus-the-man of the 1st century AD was the true Messiah of the End of Days, it would follow logically – according to the prophecies of the Old Testament – that all of us would now be living in an era of eternal peace, and would have been doing so for some two thousand years. But clearly this is *not* the case.

In summary, Jesus-the-man could not possibly have been the Messiah as defined in the Old Testament. At best, he could only have been an Elijah-like reminder to mankind of the fiery judgement which still awaited it *in the future*.[96]

These arguments seem so fatal to the Church's position that frankly it seems astonishing that the Church ever developed a contrary view. But it is even more astonishing that the Church not only developed such a contrary view but succeeded in sustaining it for so long. How has the Church got away with it?

The answer, it seems to me, is that the Church has overlooked the inherent difficulties cited above by placing emphasis on the apparent similarities between Jesus-the-man and the various suffering figures of Old Testament scripture, particularly those from Psalm 22 and Isaiah 52-53. Thus the Church has been able to argue successfully that the Old Testament *prophesied* the future arrest, mistreatment, judgement and crucifixion of Jesus-the-man – even down to the tiniest detail concerning the dividing of his clothes by lots. *QED*. Jesus-the-man was a prophesied Messiah.

This crucial strategy was not adopted recently but right back in the 1st and 2nd centuries AD, when the early Christian writers enshrined these so-called 'prophecies' in the gospels, and gave them the air of an unquestionable truth. The writer of the gospel of Matthew, in particular, seems to have been under orders to make as many prophetic connections as possible – he threw in everything but the proverbial kitchen sink.

But did the early Church make a dreadful mistake? For the so-called 'prophecies' of Psalm 22 and Isaiah 52-53, *inter alia*, had nothing to do with the *future* sacrifice of Jesus-the-man. On the contrary, they were mytho-historic accounts of the *past* suffering of a primeval Christ, who had been attacked in Heaven, and then apparently crucified in the underworld, at the beginning of time.

This was the time when the Messiah was supposed to be 'killed'.

As noted earlier, the story line of the gospels is essentially identical to the story of the primeval Christ, who sacrificed his god-like 'flesh' and 'blood' to ransom primeval 'mankind', save it from its celestial sins, and restore it to Heaven whence it had fallen. If we now reread the New Testament in the light of our newly found knowledge (as I hope readers will do), we naturally begin to wonder whether the gospels might be a *coded record* of what supposedly happened *at the beginning of the world*.

It is noticeable, for example, that Jesus spoke frequently in the third person, saying that "*the Seed of Mankind* shall be betrayed into the hands of men" rather than "*I* shall be betrayed...". And it soon becomes apparent that the gospels *in their entirety* may be read in this manner. We then notice that *the Seed of Mankind* had to go up to Jerusalem, *the Seed of Mankind* had to be condemned, mocked and crucified, *the Seed of Mankind* had to spend three days and three nights in the heart of the Earth, and *the Seed of Mankind* had to rise from the dead.[97]

This leads me to pose a very bold question. Could it be that Jesus-the-man was crucified in Jerusalem two thousand years ago, in order to *re-enact* the sacrifice of his primeval alter ego? Could it be that the story of the primeval Jesus Christ has been confused with the story of Jesus-the-man?

Consider the following quotations from the gospels, which illustrate the fact that Jesus-the-man did many things *in order to bring scripture to fruition*:

(Jesus to his disciples:) "If the world hates you, know that it hated me first... *this is to fulfil what is written in their Law*: 'They hated me without reason'."[98]

(Jesus to his disciples:) "Elijah [i.e. John the Baptist] has come, and they have done unto him everything they wished, *as it is written of him*."[99]

(Jesus to his disciples:) "*It is written of* the Seed of Mankind that he must suffer many things, and be set at nought..."[100]

(Jesus to his disciples:) "We go up to Jerusalem, *and all things that are written by the prophets* concerning the Seed of Mankind shall be accomplished."[101]

(Jesus to his disciples:) "The Seed of Mankind will go [from this world] *just as it is written of him*."[102]

(Jesus praying to God:) "None of them [the disciples] is lost except the Son of Perdition [Judas], *so that the scripture might be fulfilled*."[103]

(Jesus preventing resistance to his arrest): "Do you think I cannot call on my Father, who will at once send me more than twelve legions of angels? *But how then would the scriptures be fulfilled*, that it must happen in this way?"[104]

(The Jews speaking to Pilate:) "It is not lawful for us to put any man to death". *This happened so that the saying of Jesus, which he spoke, might be fulfilled, signifying what kind of death he should die.*[105]

(Re: the crucifixion of Jesus:) They crucified him and divided his garments, casting lots – *that it might be fulfilled that which was spoken by the prophet.*[106]

(Re: Jesus on the cross:) After this, Jesus knowing that *all things were now accomplished, that the scripture might be fulfilled*, said: "I am thirsty".[107]

(Re: the death of Jesus:) When they came to Jesus, and saw that he was already dead, they did not break his legs... These things came to pass *so that the scripture should be fulfilled* – that not one of his bones should be broken.[108]

(Jesus to his disciples after his death:) "*Everything must be fulfilled that is written about me* in the Law of Moses, in the (books of) the Prophets and in the Psalms... *This is what was written*: that it behoved Christ to suffer, and to rise from the dead on the third day..."[109]

Where was it *written* that any of these things would happen to *Jesus-the-man*? The telling answer is "Nowhere".

On the contrary, it is my contention that all of these things would in fact have been written about *the primeval Christ*, the Seed of Mankind, who had been sacrificed at the beginning of time, and who would be resurrected, or 'lifted up', at the end of time.

It thus follows logically that, if Jesus-the-man was attempting to bring such scriptures to fruition, then he could only have been doing so by *re-enacting the events of the beginning* – the arrest, judgement, crucifixion (a *heavenly* crucifixion, it should be noted), and, ultimately, burial in the Earth of his primeval alter ego. There is simply no other explanation.

In other words, the conclusion must be that Jesus-the-man was performing a re-enactment, as an actor in a Passion play – right up to the point where he entered the tomb.

At this point we should recall the crucial detail that, when Jesus died, the Earth was split open, and the veil of the temple was torn in two from top to bottom.[110] This suggests that the re-enactment was of *a heavenly crucifixion* (the subterranean crucifixion would have been yet to come), and a catastrophic fall from Heaven into the Earth.[111] We find confirmation of this idea in the legend that the bodies of many holy people came out of their graves at the time of Jesus's death (this would correspond to the legend that the primeval Christ had raised the dead from Hades).[112] It would thus seem certain that we are dealing with a re-enactment of the death of Christ in Heaven and his catastrophic fall into the Earth.

But then what? According to scripture, the fallen Christ, alias the Righteous Servant (Isaiah 52-53), ought to have been in the underworld *until the End of Days*.

How was it, then, that the body of Jesus-the-man disappeared from his tomb *after only three days*?

The explanation, I suggest, is an esoteric one, which is to be found in the words of Jesus-the-man, spoken in the days leading up to his death. In two of the four gospels, Jesus compared himself to Jonah – a famous prophet of the Old Testament – as follows:

> "For as Jonah was three days and three nights in the belly of the huge fish, so shall the Seed of Mankind be three days and three nights in the heart of the Earth."[113]

Many readers will be familiar with this story of the 'huge fish', which swallowed the prophet Jonah and then spat him out, but they will have generally assumed that the big fish was some kind of mythical whale, which swam around in a terrestrial sea. And, by the same token, they will generally have assumed that Jonah was cast out of a conventional 'ship'.

However, if we apply the metaphors which we have learned in the preceding chapters of this book, an entirely new interpretation of the Jonah story becomes possible, in which the 'sea' was a celestial sea, and the 'ship' was a celestial ship, i.e. a heavenly planet. The picture which then emerges is the sacrifice of one sailor – Jonah – in order that the other sailors might live.

This is, of course, the same story as the sacrifice of Jesus Christ, the same story as the sacrifice of the Righteous Servant, and the same story as the sacrifice of the victim in Psalm 22, not to mention the sacrifice of numerous gods in ancient Near Eastern mythology.

Let's look at the Jonah legend in a little more detail. The story begins with the prophet Jonah (whose name meant 'Dove') fleeing from his god, and embarking upon a ship (this part of the story has almost certainly been embellished). Then, the LORD 'sent out a great wind into the sea', causing a mighty storm which threatened to break up the ship (note the analogy to the planet about to break up in the celestial waters). At this point, the sailors cast lots among themselves, and the lot fell on Jonah, who was thrown overboard into the sea, thus making the sea become calm.[114]

What happened to Jonah? The book of Jonah tells us that 'the LORD had prepared a huge fish to swallow Jonah, who was in the belly of the fish three days and three nights'.[115]

This 'fish', however, was nothing but a metaphor for 'the Earth'.

Hence Jonah did *not* refer to himself as being in the belly of the fish, but rather to being *in the belly of the Earth*, i.e. in Sheol – the underworld:

> Then Jonah prayed unto the LORD his God, out of the belly of the fish, saying: "In my distress I cried out to the LORD, and he heard me. *Out of the belly of Sheol I cried...* I went down to the bottom of the mountains; the Earth with her bars was about me for ever."[116]

Thereafter, the story of Jonah followed the archetypal kingship myths of the ancient Near East, with the hero being vomited out of the fish *onto dry land*, i.e. being ejected from the Earth's interior onto its surface.[117]

Now, the point of this digression is to demonstrate that the tale of Jonah was an archetypal myth, and it would thus be fundamentally wrong to assume that Jonah was inside the fish for 'three days and three nights' *literally*. On the contrary, Jonah, like any archetypal Titan-like 'man', would have been in the heart of the Earth *for a considerable period of time*. A time measured in terms of aeons.

So, returning to the assertion by Jesus-the-man that he would spend the same 'three days and three nights' in the heart of the Earth as Jonah had spent in the fish, we must conclude that the period in which Jesus's body lay in the tomb was purely symbolic – *symbolic of an eternity*.[118]

It would be appropriate at this point to recall the words of Psalm 90, which state that a 'day' in the eyes of mankind was equivalent to a thousand years in the eyes of the LORD.[119] The Koran even stretches this figure to fifty thousand years in the eyes of Allah.[120] The 'three days' which Jesus Christ spent in the tomb should thus not be taken any more literally than the 'six days' which God took to create the heavens and the Earth. In effect, each of these numbers of days symbolised 'an eternity'.

Consider, also, the three days allotted to the rebuilding of 'the temple of God' in the gospel of John:

> Jesus said unto them [the Jews]: "Destroy this temple, and in three days I will raise it up."[121]

The writer of John's gospel noted that Jesus had spoken about 'the temple of his body'. True – but a half-truth. The temple of God was not only the body of Jesus, but also the body of God, and it was *a celestial body*. This celestial body had indeed been destroyed, and it needed to be raised back up to Heaven, which Jesus would do 'three days' after he, and it, had fallen to the Earth. Once again, we are dealing with the idea of three days as an eternity. (And once again we find evidence that the gospels were written in encoded parables, concerning 'things which were hidden since the beginning of the world'.)

In summary, it seems to me that the idea of Jesus being entombed for three days was drawn from a legend that the body of his primeval alter ego had been given to the underworld as a ransom for 'three days' – an eternity – at the end of which time he would be raised up, i.e. at the End of Days.

The bottom line, then, is that the gospels must be based on a Passion play, in which the lead actor, Jesus-the-man, re-enacted the sacrifice of his primeval alter ego at the beginning of the world. This play brought to fruition *the esoteric meaning of the Hebrew scriptures*, climaxing with a re-enactment of the crucifixion of the primeval Christ in Heaven, when he uttered the immortal words: "My God, my God, why hast thou forsaken me?". The Passion play would then have concluded with a re-enactment of the burial of the primeval Christ in the heart of the Earth.

That, at least, would have been the Passion play *as it was supposed to be*, according to the ancient pagan traditions and the occulted Hebrew scriptures.

But why did the body of Jesus-the-man then disappear from the tomb? This seems rather odd, for it would have symbolised *a rising of the primeval Christ out of the underworld*. But according to the scriptures which were being re-enacted, this resurrection was *not supposed to occur until the End of Days*.

And no-one but God alone knew when the End of Days would come.[122]

What man would have dared to amend the script of the play thus?

The Mystery of the Missing Body

Did the body of Jesus-the-man really disappear from his tomb? Or did someone invent the story of his disappearing body after the fact? Or did someone fabricate the entire story?

Did Jesus-the-man actually sacrifice his own life in a Passion play? Did he re-enact the fall of Christ from Heaven in human blood? And if so, was he inspired by personal piety, or was he inspired by the influence of God's Holy Spirit?

Did Jesus-the-man even exist at all during the 1st century AD? Or did he exist earlier in history? Or did he never exist at all?

Did people have particular reasons for thinking that the End of Days was imminent during the 1st century AD? Did people imagine that they saw visions of a risen Christ? Did they perhaps see signs in the sky, which struck terror into their hearts?[123]

It seems unlikely that we will ever get to the bottom of all these questions, nor resolve exactly what happened in Jerusalem two thousand years ago, at the beginning of Christianity. The historicity of the story has been buried beneath the mythical model, as in the case of the historic Exodus of the Israelites, and as in the case of the real-life story of the Sumerian king Gilgamesh.

We can, however, conclude with reasonable certainty that the story which we have been taught by the Church is only a half-truth. It *is* the story of Christ, up to a point, but it is nonetheless a 'dumbed down' story, which has occulted the true subject matter – planets and meteorites – and presented the story instead as a clever allegory involving the suffering, death and resurrection of a human being. And why not? Such an anthropomorphic portrayal of the celestial drama made the story attractive to the masses, whilst preserving the all-important esoteric meaning for the initiated.

But what about the resurrection of Christ from the tomb? To me, this is a distortion of the truth, but it is not an outright lie. It is a falsehood in the bodily sense, but it is true in the spiritual sense. What I mean to say is that the *spirit, or soul,* of the primeval Christ would have been resurrected to Heaven at the time of his original fall, leaving his *body* as a ransom in the underworld. This is the myth of Osiris, and of the Phoenix-bird, both of whom experienced the same separation of body and soul upon impact with the Earth. As the ancient Egyptians used to say: 'The body to Earth, the soul to Heaven'. It is the story of all the ancient gods who came down from the Sky.

This is the key to understanding why Jesus Christ would have been able to descend from Heaven to Earth in his Second Coming *without* having been lifted up after his First Coming. On the contrary, Christ would have descended in his Second Coming *as his spirit-self, or soul-self*, just like the return of the Phoenix-bird, and just like the second descent of Moses (see chapters ten and eleven).

If this seems like a difficult concept to grasp, we need only think of God, for the story of God is identical. After God fell into the Earth, he was lifted up to Heaven *metaphysically*, along with his floodwaters. But this did not prevent God from returning to the Earth, catastrophically, according to the End of Days scenario in the Old Testament. In fact, the Hebrews believed that God had already performed this amazing feat once already – at the time of the Great Flood – when he had transformed his *metaphysical* waters miraculously into *physical* waters.[124] Such was the ancient way of thinking, which might well seem strange to us modern folk.

It follows from this that Jesus Christ, too, was perfectly capable of descending to the Earth catastrophically, in his Second Coming, and he would not have needed his body. The idea that his body was resurrected *prior to* the Second Coming seems to be a complete falsehood.

Nevertheless, there is much scope for confusion here, and one cannot help wondering whether such confusion took root in the 1st century AD. At that time, the *spirit* of Christ would long have been a denizen of the heavenly realms, and it is easy to imagine how various signs in the sky might have triggered a wave of 'visions of Christ', along with fears of his catastrophic Second Coming.[125] It is equally easy to imagine how these fears might have led to the (erroneous) hypothesis that the Second Coming would have required the physical resurrection of Christ's body from the underworld. After all, the lifting up of the body and the End of Days were co-related ideas, and it would have taken a very well-informed master of religious scripture and metaphysics to convince the ignorant that it was the End of Days that brought about the raising of the body, and not vice versa.[126]

So, was this perhaps the origin of the idea that Christ's body had gone missing from his tomb? Did a fear of the End of Days spark a belief that Christ's body had risen? And did this misunderstanding cause Jesus-the-human-actor to be elevated (posthumously) to a divine, supernatural status?

Whatever the truth of the matter, it is certainly evident that the idea of the risen Christ became firmly established – hence we read in the Christian scriptures that Christ was 'the first begotten of the dead', meaning that he was the first fruits of those who had slept in the land of the dead.[127] Such claims undoubtedly fostered the false belief that *the body* of Christ was then in Heaven, and was about to bear down on the world once again, catastrophically. Thus was born the idea that the End of Days was imminent during the 1st century AD.

Since then, we have been waiting, and waiting, for some two thousand years, still presuming (erroneously) that we are living in the End of Days, with the Sword of Damocles hanging over our heads. The reality, however, mythically speaking, is that the body of Christ is still tucked away safely in the heart of the Earth, awaiting an unknown date with destiny.

Eventually, that date – the End of Days – *will* come, with an inevitable certainty, and mankind will be decimated or destroyed. To cite the book of Jeremiah:

"Is not my Word like a fire?", saith the LORD, "and like a hammer that breaketh the Rock in pieces?"[128]

This would indeed seem to be the case, based on the foregoing study, for the LORD was an exploded planet with the supernatural ability to strike again.

And by the same token, we can conclude that the Second Coming of Christ is, in effect, the comet or asteroid which is at this very moment programmed on a future collision course with the Earth. It is a sobering thought.

Even more sobering is the idea that millions of Christians worldwide are eagerly anticipating this momentous event in line with the words of the Lord's Prayer: 'Let thy kingdom come', and in line with the words of the apostle Peter, who wrote in his 'second letter' that 'we are looking forward to a new Heaven and a new Earth'.[129]

One wonders how many Christians will keep the faith when Comet Melchizedek is three days away from hitting the Earth...

* * * * *

CHAPTER FOURTEEN

A FAREWELL TO FAIRY TALES

**When I was a child, I spoke as a child,
I understood as a child, I thought as a child:
but when I became a man, I put away childish things.**
(Paul, in his First Letter to the Corinthians)

"How can a lump of rock fall out of the Sky?" Many thousands of years ago, falling meteorites (perhaps coinciding with spectacular celestial phenomena in the Earth's atmosphere)[1] prompted this simple question, and – so it would seem – sparked the beginning of religion as we know it. Since then, an awful lot has happened.

To begin at the beginning, in an age long ago, our ancestors decided that the rocks which fell out of the Sky (meteorites) could only have come from an Earth-like 'mountain', which had disintegrated in the heavens. They thus conceived the 'mountain' of Heaven as a planet in the image of the Earth, or to be more precise, as an *ex-planet* which had *formerly* been in the image of the Earth.

From this premise, it naturally followed that the ex-planet of Heaven, being in the image of the Earth, and having fallen to the Earth, had sown the seeds of life into the Earth, and had filled the rivers of the Earth with life-giving waters. Hence it was that the 'mountain' of Heaven became personified as 'God' – a supreme being, who had created deliberately all life on Earth, including mankind.

Then came the idea that the planet had been a living being, with a physical body *and a metaphysical soul.* Consequently, it was presumed that God had not died when his body disintegrated and fell into the Earth. On the contrary, his soul had ascended back into the Sky, where it had reconstituted the 'mountain' of Heaven, metaphysically. In this way, God had departed from the world of 'men', and had become a mysterious, metaphysical being – lofty, invisible, unfathomable. But nevertheless

God was alive and keeping a watchful eye on his flock down below.

How did God die? The ancients decided that the 'mountain' of God had been destroyed in a battle with another, similar 'mountain'. Needless to say, the latter was identified as an evil God, and thus was born the idea of Satan. Naturally, it was supposed that the evil God had also been destroyed, either in the first battle, or in a subsequent battle, when a Titan-like 'son' of God had risen up from the womb of the Earth and had avenged his 'father' by attacking the adversary planet.

Was God a male or a female, or was he a he-she? The question was settled initially by supposing that there had been two supreme Gods – a male God and a female Goddess, who had both descended from Heaven to Earth, whereupon they had consummated a sacred marriage in the underworld. That was the day when God 'got his rocks off' and the Earth truly 'moved'.

Where had mankind come from? As with all living things, mankind had fallen from Heaven as a seed and had been planted in the underworld – the womb of Mother Earth – and had then sprouted forth into the world above. The oldest ancestors of mankind were thus held to be the 'seeds of mankind' – the 'black-headed ones' – who had fallen to Earth from Heaven. In modern language, we would call these seeds *meteorites*. And hence it was true that God (an exploded planet) had created 'mankind' (meteorites) in his own image.

This was the beginning of religion as we know it, with God and Heaven being one-and-the-same thing – an exploded planet, according to the beliefs of the ancients. Moreover, this original story was religious in the fullest meaning of the word, for it connected mankind back to its mythical homeland in the Sky (E.DIN), whence it had been expelled long ago, allegedly for being too 'noisy'.

The ambition of ancient man was to return to the Heaven whence he had come – a quest which entailed retracing his steps by first going down into the underworld. The path to Heaven, it would seem, was via Hell (the Island of Fire of Egyptian tradition).

During the 4th millennium BC, the great civilisations of Egypt and Sumer arose in the ancient Near East, and the kings consolidated their power by associating themselves with the gods of these exploded planet cults, and particularly with the heroic 'son of God' – the one who had risen up out of the Earth like a Titan, and restored order to the universe by destroying the evil Sky-god.

In Sumer, these god-like kings began to construct wonderful cities, with glorious temples and ziggurats, each representing a microcosm of the Earth, and each symbolising the sacred Bond of Heaven-and-Earth.

In Egypt, meanwhile, nothing was beyond the means of the god-like kings. They laid out their first cities along the river Nile to symbolise the planets of Heaven and Earth, and they began to sail meteorites up and down the river to re-enact the primeval creation. They built magnificent temples, to recreate the primeval link between Heaven and Earth, and they erected their most sacred meteorite, the Benben Stone, in the temple of Heaven at Heliopolis. In time, they erected marvellous pyramids too – lasting memorials to the belief that the souls of the kings could ascend to Heaven and recreate the perfect golden age of the universe – as it had been at the First Time.

Thus did the exploded planet cults leave their mark on the landscape of the ancient Near East, seemingly for eternity.

But then things began to fall apart. As the centuries wore on, religion turned into big business. The profound insights of the priests began to be 'dumbed down' for public consumption. The poets set to work in rewriting the legends of the gods, portraying them as *human-like* heroes, with *human-like* emotions. The artists set to work, too, carving statues of the gods in *human-like* forms and poses. And the people began to think that their gods really had walked upon the face of the Earth in an age long forgotten.

Even the more enlightened people, who continued to look to the sky for their gods, began to forget that the true God was invisible by nature. Therefore, instead of worshipping the Sun, Moon and stars as *symbols* of the exploded planet, they started to worship the Sun, Moon and stars *per se*.

The rot set in even among the priesthoods. In Egypt, it became taboo to speak of the death of God, and hence Osiris, the god of the dead, fell out of favour. The priests of Heliopolis and Memphis began to switch their attention to the less physical aspect of God – the metaphysical half of his physical-metaphysical duality. The first steps were taken towards the belief that a mysterious, supernatural deity had created all things *without* the need to get his hands dirty in an unseemly battle of the gods.

Gradually, the original Egyptian polytheism began to drift away from its roots, and towards a monolatry, and even, at times, a monotheism.

Towards the end of the 2nd millennium BC, a people known as the Hebrews, or Israelites, established a very strict monotheistic cult in the land of Canaan. The priests – no doubt appalled at the religious free-for-all among the common people – decided to get tough. They denied the existence of the afterlife, and they told the people that when they died they would return to dust. Man's lot was on the Earth, they declared, and the abode of God was unreachable; it was more distant than even the farthermost visible star. "Canst thou fathom the mysteries of God?" they asked: "They are as high as Heaven, what canst thou do? They are deeper than the depths of Sheol, what canst thou know?"[2]

In order to underline this new religious philosophy, the Hebrew priests altered their scriptures drastically. The ex-physical nature of their God was hidden, as was his death and resurrection, lest the people think that they, too, could somehow die and come back to life. In a masterly stroke of deception, Yahweh's creation of the other gods was occulted from the book of Genesis by removing the first letter (*aleph*) of the first line. This changed the meaning of the opening sentence fundamentally, as can be seen from versions A and B below:

A. When the Father-of-Beginning [*Ab-reshith*] created the gods [*elohim*] of Heaven-and-Earth...

B. In the beginning [*Bereshith*], God [*Elohim*] created Heaven and Earth.

Having thus occulted the creation of the gods, the Hebrew priests pulled off an equally brilliant master-stroke in occulting the existence of the Earth-goddess. They did this by twisting the old legend that the first man Adam had been taken out of the womb of Mother Earth (Eve), by claiming that Eve had, in fact, been taken out of Adam. The rib motif was twisted, too. Instead of being a meteorite which entered Mother Earth, it became a mundane human rib which was used to create the first woman.

Why was this done? Simply to occult the existence of the Goddess who was the most powerful rival to Yahweh-Elohim.

In addition to these things, the priests also rewrote the legends of the Hebrew patriarchs in order to conceal the fact that Adam, Noah, Abraham, Joseph, Moses and others had come down from the heavens. Only the highest initiates among the priesthood knew the true celestial origins of the *Ibri*, and only they recognised the Old Testament's esoteric allusions to this fact.

It is no exaggeration to say that never before in the history of religion had man actually set down in writing such a package of half-truths and outright lies.

Nevertheless, even though the Hebrew scriptures were alien to the way of thinking of the rest of the ancient world, they had been written in a style which attracted many followers. Instead of being lost, or preserved as a historical curiosity (as the record of one particular people's minority perspective of religion), they were destined to have a profound effect on man's perception of religion for countless generations to come.

The key to this was Christianity. Around two thousand years ago, the city of Jerusalem hosted a Mystery Play, or a Passion play, in which a man named Jesus re-enacted the legend of the exploded planet *in human form*. What happened next is uncertain, but something must have happened to make this Passion play different from the many which had preceded it. We might well imagine that an influential person suddenly realised that the story of the Passion play would make an ideal basis for a new religion – one with widespread popular appeal.

In order for us to appreciate this development, we must understand that the average man of the 1st century AD had little interest in a long-forgotten legend of a planetary god, who had sacrificed his 'flesh' and 'blood' to save a primeval 'mankind' from the underworld. But he *would* have been attracted to the idea that a *human being* had suffered, and sacrificed *real* flesh and blood – especially when that human being had been imbued with the divine Spirit.

Christianity, then, almost certainly began as an adaptation of a Passion play, which was not necessarily a bad thing, because the play related the age-old religious story of the exploded planet in a direct, simple and human-like way. Moreover, the Passion play was a story which could be understood simultaneously at both exoteric and esoteric levels; it was at one level 'dumbed down' for the masses, but at another level it retained a profound appeal for those few who were initiated into the truth.

As a new religion, however, Christianity was lacking the ancient roots which were required to compete successfully against other long-established religions during the 1st century AD. It therefore attached itself to the archaic tradition of the Hebrew patriarchs in order to acquire the legitimacy it needed. It was an ironic choice, for whilst the Christians were selling the idea of an eternal afterlife in Heaven, the Jews were denying that such an afterlife even existed. Nonetheless, the problem was solved by referring to the Hebrew scriptures as the '*Old* Testament', and presenting the newly written Christian scriptures as the '*New* Testament'.

The trick worked, and together the Old and New Testaments became a formidable pairing. On the one hand, the Old Testament provided a written genealogy which was unique in the ancient world – the story of a contemporary nation which stretched back to the very first man, Adam, who had been created by God. On the other hand, the New Testament provided a fresh and powerful update of the age-old religious story, and tapped deeply into mankind's continuing beliefs in death and rebirth, the afterlife, and the End of Days.

Thus it was that, by a strange quirk of history, and an unlikely marriage of convenience, the old Hebrew scriptures acquired an importance far out of proportion to the minority sect which had produced them. A dissenting voice in the ancient world had become a dominant voice in the Christian world, and a book full of half-truths and lies – aimed originally at the Israelites only – was set to influence the thinking of intelligent men throughout the Western world for millennia to come.

What of the lands which had invented the exploded planet cults? In the early centuries of the Christian era, the Egyptian civilisation was on its knees, after centuries of invasions by the Greeks and Romans. The sacred meteorites of Egypt had all but disappeared – either stolen, destroyed, removed for safe-keeping, or simply fallen apart through natural corrosion. The magnificent pyramids and temples of the Nile Valley were falling into ruins.

In Mesopotamia, things were just as bleak. The great civilisations of Sumer and Akkad had long been forgotten, whilst their successors, the Babylonians, had endured more warfare than can be recounted in these pages. New ziggurats and temples were no longer being built, and the old ones were in ruins after centuries of warfare, vandalism and natural disasters.

By this time, all around the ancient world, the legends of the gods had become thoroughly immersed in anthropomorphic imagery, and many legends had become embellished to the point where their original meaning had been lost. To make matters worse, the written texts were routinely gathered together into huge library collections, where they were, almost without exception, destined for extinction, when those libraries were burned to the ground, by accident or design.

As for the oral traditions, these were more enduring. From the 1st millennium BC, or perhaps even earlier, the secrets of the exploded planet cults had been conveyed into various independent mystery schools, which continued to flourish despite the disapproval of the Church. These mystery schools, however, survived by observing their number-one rule of conduct – silence and secrecy. Few were those who ever discovered the full esoteric truth behind the Christian gospels, and even then they would never have dreamt of putting anything in writing to challenge the official dogma of the Church.

As for the Church itself, history records that it went from strength to strength and became one of the most powerful institutions the world has ever seen. In the process, it established a virtual monopoly over religious teaching, with the Bible – that strange concoction of Old and New Testaments – becoming virtually the only source of religious knowledge in the Western world.

Nineteen hundred years later, this state of affairs would be about to change.

Let the Tablets Speak!

During the 19th century, archaeologists from Europe and America began to explore the lands of Egypt and Mesopotamia in search of long-lost cities and priceless relics. And in no time at all, ancient mounds were yielding their treasures to modern picks and spades. At that time, attention was focused on artefacts such as statues and jewellery, which would become prize pieces for the museums. But perhaps the greatest prizes of all were the written inscriptions which were carefully retrieved and laid to one side.

Inspired by a curiosity to uncover mankind's past, scholars began to pore over the enigmatic inscriptions from Egypt and Mesopotamia in an attempt to decipher them. And amazingly, by the mid 19th century, these scholars succeeded – an awesome achievement for which society has given them far too little credit. Within a few decades, scholars were making translations of the ancient writings with confidence, and by the turn of the century, they had prepared and published translations of numerous valuable texts.

The voice of the ancients had returned, as if resurrected, miraculously, from the grave.

Or had it? It is my contention in this book that the voice of the ancients was choked by a fundamentally wrong interpretation by scholars. And it has remained choked for more than a century since. It is my contention (as immodest as it might sound) that the voice of the ancients has at long last been made intelligible in this book, *When The Gods Came Down* (2000), and in my previous book, specifically on Egypt, *The Phoenix Solution* (1998).

What does the voice of the ancients have to say? In a nutshell, the ancient Egyptians and Mesopotamians wish to remind us that their religions were *not* Sun cults, *nor* Moon cults, *nor* star cults, *nor* fertility cults, *nor* any other kind of mundane cult, but rather *exploded planet cults*.

The ancients also wish to inform us that all of these other diverse cults were *subordinate* to the exploded planet cult. In other words, the exploded planet cult was *inclusive* of all the other cults.

Hopefully, by this stage in the book, the reader will agree with me that this is indeed the truth of the matter, and will be as amazed as I am that it has taken more than a century of waiting for the truth to come out. It is a delay which demands explanation.

Why did scholars miss the truth for so long?

The Elusive Secret

Why is it that scholars have failed for more than a hundred years to recognise that ancient religions were exploded planet cults? How is it that the task has fallen to an outsider such as myself to expose the fundamental flaws in long-established fields of academia?

It seems to me that there is no one simple explanation, but rather a complex web of factors which have all acted together to obscure our interpretation of the past. Broadly, the problem seems to have been one of preconceptions, based on a religious education which was the antithesis of the pagan world.

The typical scholar of the mid to late 19th century was a gentleman who believed whole-heartedly in God and the Bible; he accepted implicitly that the world had been created supernaturally by God; he believed whole-heartedly that God was an unknowable mystery, and he considered it anathema to pry into the mysteries of God; and furthermore he believed that the ancients, by and large, were a bunch of primitive heathens.

This, with hindsight, was hardly an ideal set of preconceptions for the scholars who were entrusted with translating and interpreting the pagan legends of the ancients.

Right from the beginning, these scholars were squirming in their seats with discomfort. Instead of reading how a single God had created the world and mankind, they read accounts of how these miraculous things had been performed by *plural gods*. This was anathema to them. Moreover, the ancients had actually had the audacity to describe the awesome creation by God with sexually explicit idioms! This was considered to be most distasteful. And as for the ancient belief that God was in the Sun, or in the Moon, or in the stars, or even in the rocks and plants and trees, this, clearly, was the work of primitive minds.

With such preconceptions at work, scholars of the mid to late 19th century were hardly going to discover any profound sense of meaning in the ancient texts. It would have been the last thing they wanted to find. And consequently we should not be surprised that the various academic attempts to compare and contrast modern and ancient religions stopped some way short of a full measure. Looking back at the past two centuries, it is difficult to find a single even-handed comparison between two religions of an equal status. Instead, we find studies which contrasted a 'true God' with 'false gods', a 'true' belief system with a 'pagan' belief system, and a thinking man's 'religion' with a primitive man's 'mythology'.

With hindsight, it all seems so sadly inevitable.

Turning to specifics, there are several particular factors which may be highlighted as making major contributions to the state of ignorance of late 19th and early 20th century scholarship.

The first of these factors is a limited appreciation of astronomy, together with a deep-rooted scepticism concerning catastrophic impacts from space. It was as recently as the beginning of the 19th century, we might recall, that the American president Thomas Jefferson commented that: "I would sooner believe that two Yankee professors lied, than that stones fell from the sky."[3] It was a comment typical of its time, and illustrates the kind of intellectual background within which scholars were educated not so long ago.

Many late 19th century scholars, we must presume, did not even know what a meteorite was, whilst others perhaps believed the reports of the debunkers, namely that meteorites were simply terrestrial stones which had been struck by lightning. Such ignorance may seem amazing to us now, but it must be understood in its proper context as the legacy of the Dark Ages and Middle Ages in Europe.

Why did this ignorance of meteorites, and astronomy more generally, prevail for so long? Could it be that the Church had to deny the existence of catastrophic impacts, in order to preserve the myth that God had ordained *only one* End of Days, which was reserved for the end of the world? Could it be that the Church feared that scientific knowledge of cataclysms would undermine the mystery of their cataclysmic God?

There were, of course, exceptions to this state of ignorance in the early 19th century. In 1801, the astronomer Giuseppe Piazzi discovered the first asteroid by telescope, and shortly after that several more asteroids were discovered. Almost immediately, an astronomer named Heinrich Olbers acclaimed these asteroids as evidence that a planet had formerly existed between Mars and Jupiter, but had exploded. The asteroids, he said, were the fragments. Little did Olbers realise that he was treading on the sacred territory of millennia-old secrets.

The exploded planet theory was short-lived, however. In 1814, the prestigious astronomer Marquis de Laplace launched a withering attack on Olbers and others, and such was his great influence in astronomical circles that the exploded planet theory was knocked firmly on the head for the next 175 years.

During this period, all mainstream textbooks stated categorically that the rocks of the asteroid belt represented leftover 'building blocks', which had *never* come together to form a planet. The exploded planet hypothesis was not even mentioned as a rival theory. It had effectively been occulted from the textbooks.

Might this be a little suspicious? It certainly could be if we allow for the possibility that the ancient religious knowledge was still being safeguarded by modern 19th century mystery schools. In such a situation, it is entirely predictable that the mystery schools would have taken surreptitious action to safeguard their 'knowledge' (that God was an exploded planet) and keep that knowledge hidden from the public.

Did Marquis de Laplace really have his own independent ideas about asteroids and comets? Or were his thoughts perhaps influenced in some way by the modern guardians of the Mysteries? It is a sobering thought.

The upshot of all this is that none of the scholars of the 19th or 20th centuries had any concept whatsoever of exploded planets. They were as ignorant about exploded planets as they were about meteorites. How, then, would they possibly have had any inkling of what the ancient Egyptian and Mesopotamian religious texts were describing?

The second major factor which hampered the efforts of 19th and 20th century scholars was an almost total unfamiliarity with the concept of the underworld. The underworld was the key which would have unlocked the mysteries of ancient religion, but scholars had no real idea of what it was. After all, the Hebrew priests had occulted all of the legends that might have explained what it was.

Hence, when the first generation of scholars read the various legends of the gods descending into the underworld, they did not have the slightest clue what the ancients were talking about. The significance of the underworld was totally lost on them.

Why was this knowledge of the underworld lost? The answer, in a nutshell, is that the ancients regarded the underworld as the most sacred of places. What transpired there was an unspeakable mystery, which was communicated only to the few. Over the millennia, the secrets of the underworld had gone underground, into the mystery schools, where they were revealed only to the highest initiates, who were forbidden to speak about such things openly. Is it surprising, then, that the modern scholars who read the ancient legends of the underworld were in a state of complete ignorance?

It is, of course, possible that *some* of these early scholars were *not* in a state of complete ignorance. It is possible that one or two of them might have been initiated into the secrets of the ancient Mysteries, and would thus have acquired the knowledge. If this was the case, however, the scholar would have had to break his vow of silence in order to report to the public on what the legends actually meant. This is another sobering thought.

So, with no concept of the underworld, and no concept of meteorites or exploded planets, scholars were hardly in a good position to overcome the next barrier to their understanding, which was the metaphors, idioms and analogies of the ancients.

Throughout this book, it has been apparent that metaphors are the absolute key to decoding the ancient texts. A planet, for example, could be called a 'mountain', a 'rock', an 'island', a 'horizon', a 'throne', or a 'city'. Furthermore, in the Egyptian legends, the planet was often compared to a 'head', with its 'eyes' being moons.[4] And in certain contexts, the planet of Heaven could become a 'womb', or an 'egg', which would give birth to the gods.

The underworld could also be called a 'mountain', an 'island', a 'city', or a 'Sky-in-the-middle'. And in certain contexts, the underworld was the 'womb' of Mother Earth, which could be impregnated by falling gods, later to give birth to giants, demons, or 'mankind'.

Another crucial metaphor was the 'Wall', which alluded to the ceiling of the underworld, or the surface of any planet.

And this 'Wall' of the Earth was penetrated by an object which could be called a 'brick', a 'pickaxe', a 'seed', a 'fly for love-making', the 'essence of Anu', or a 'rib'. In all cases, the metaphors alluded to the meteorite, which stood for the flood of meteorites unleashed by an exploded planet, which was in turn compared to a 'reed-hut' or 'house' which had been torn down and converted into a 'boat'.

The explosion of the planet of Heaven was alluded to in numerous different ways. It could be compared to the bursting open of a 'womb', the cracking of an 'egg', the splitting open of a 'head', the cutting down of a 'tree' or a 'forest', the stoppage of a bark or the cutting loose of a 'boat', the collapse of a 'pillar', or the decapitation or dismemberment of a god. These incidents took place in obscure circumstances, which often involved battles between the gods.[5]

Now, it must be said that scholars *should* have recognised these various idioms as references to *something catastrophic* at the heart of all ancient beliefs. However, for the reasons cited earlier, scholars had no concept of what that catastrophe might have been. They therefore pushed the anomalies to one side, and adopted the 'euhemerist' solution, suggesting that the battles of the gods were embellished and exaggerated accounts of *human battles*. No other kind of battle made any sense to them.

The ancients were communicating with metaphors, allegories and symbols which could no longer be understood. And the fact that they had 'dumbed down' the original stories of the gods into anthropomorphic forms had set a trap which scholars walked straight into.

But scholars also walked into another trap. As discussed in chapter four, the most distinctive feature of the ancient exploded planet cults was that God – the exploded planet – was invisible. And consequently the ancients had been forced to adopt all sorts of visible celestial bodies as *symbols* of the exploded planet. Foremost among these visible symbols were the Sun, the Moon and certain stars, all of which went through phases of death and rebirth, which were profound reminders of the death and rebirth of the planetary God himself (or herself).

The earliest scholars were therefore playing a game where the odds were stacked heavily against them. Firstly, they could not look up into the Sky and see what the ancients had actually been worshipping – the exploded planet was, by definition, invisible. And secondly, what they did find was widespread evidence for the worship of the Sun, Moon and stars.

Scholars walked straight into this trap, and came to the conclusion that the ancients had been worshipping the Sun, Moon and stars per se. Why would they suspect otherwise? After all, the ancients had developed the symbolic linkages to the exploded planet *so thoroughly* that it was very difficult indeed to separate the Sun from the true object of worship. In addition, scholars simply had no concept of *what* the Sun might have been symbolising. And when they did read giveaway legends, such as those of the Sun-god travelling down through the underworld, the significance was lost on them, because they had no concept of what the underworld actually was.

Moreover, if some scholars, such as Wallis Budge, did acknowledge that the Sun was a 'symbol for a higher God', they were averse to investigating (at least in public) what that higher God might have been. According to their upbringing, the higher God was the mysterious, unknowable God of the Bible, and that was the end of the story.

As for the multiplicity of cults in ancient Egypt and Mesopotamia, the scholars simply explained to the modern world that the ancients had been 'confused'.

In fact, it was the scholars who were confused, for there were, of course, numerous irritating anomalies in the picture which scholars had begun to build up. However, as in the case of the battle legends, these anomalies – especially those concerning the Sun-god – were pushed to one side and later forgotten. The general public never had any inkling that anything was wrong; they trusted the scholars implicitly.

Is it a surprise, in view of all these factors, that 19th and 20th century scholars identified the gods who came down from the Sky as rain-gods, thunder-gods, lightning-gods and storm-gods? Is it a surprise that scholars did *not* associate the splitting open of the Earth with the fall of a meteorite? Is it a surprise that scholars occulted the interplanetary nature of the ancient legends in their translations, with the Earth becoming 'earth', the Sky becoming 'sky', Heaven becoming 'clouds', the Flood becoming 'rain', the celestial River becoming a terrestrial river, and the Mountain of Heaven becoming a humble mountain or earth mound?

The only real surprise, I suggest, is that scholars of *the late 20th century* did not take their beclouded predecessors to task. On the contrary, what appears to have happened is that later generations of scholars took for granted the 'big picture' and thus ignored all the unexplained anomalies. Instead, they buried themselves in highly specialised fields of study, in an attempt to break new ground rather than going over old ground.

At an individual level, this is all perfectly understandable and excusable. Nevertheless, the disciplines of Egyptology, Sumerology and Assyriology must stand accused, at a collective level, of falling asleep at the wheel. They have, in effect, betrayed the trust of the public through their sheer complacency.

Exploded Planets – Fact or Fiction?

I would now like to bring this book towards a conclusion by posing a question which I have avoided carefully until now. Is it possible that a planet (or planets) might *actually* have exploded in our solar system, millions of years ago? Is it possible that meteorites *really did* originate from a planet which exploded?

Might it be that the light of the ancient mystery school initiations was actually a 'true' light?

As mentioned earlier, the idea that a planet might have exploded in our solar system was floated briefly during the early 19th century, after astronomers discovered the first asteroids between the planets Mars and Jupiter. But the theory proved short-lived, as a result of the heavyweight attack launched by Marquis de Laplace. Consequently, few professional astronomers today have even heard of the exploded planet theory, and those who *have* heard of it would consider it to be a 'dead' theory.

However, we have already seen how Egyptologists, Sumerologists and Assyriologists have been fundamentally wrong during the last two hundred years. Could it be that modern astronomers have also been building their paradigm upon an equally flawed foundation?

One astronomer who believes that this *is* the case is Dr Tom Van

Flandern, a prize-winning professional research astronomer, with twenty years of experience at the US Naval Observatory, where he became the Chief of the Celestial Mechanics Branch. Since the mid 1970s, Van Flandern has been accumulating evidence which suggests that the mainstream theory concerning the origin of asteroids – and also comets – is fundamentally wrong.[6]

According to the mainstream theory, the asteroid belt represents nothing more than unused celestial building blocks, which never came together to form a planet. As for the comets, it is believed that these chaotic bodies are disturbed from a reservoir deep in space called the 'Oort cloud'.

Van Flandern disagrees on both counts. His research has persuaded him that the asteroid belt originated from the explosion of two parent planets, which once existed between Mars and Jupiter. As for the comets, Van Flandern emphasises that there is no direct evidence for the Oort cloud, and he dismisses that theory as an implausible contrivance. Instead, he suggests that the comets originated from a relatively recent explosion (3.2 million years ago) of a small astronomical body (probably a moon), again in the region of the main asteroid belt.

Could it be that Van Flandern is right, and that ancient astronomers and theologians are about to be vindicated?

Van Flandern's colleagues, it must be said, are less than convinced by the exploded planet theory, despite the fact that Van Flandern now has a formidable arsenal of observational evidence at his disposal (which is growing by the day).[7] Their main objection rests on the assumption that there is *no known scientific mechanism* which would make a planet explode.

But is this a legitimate objection? The debate among the astronomers reminds me of a similar debate between geophysicists during the early 20th century. In 1910, an Austrian meteorologist named Alfred Wegener put forward the theory of continental drift, based on the evidence that the coastlines of South America and Africa fitted together almost exactly – like a jigsaw puzzle. The reaction of geophysicists was to dismiss Wegener as a crank, for there was *no known scientific mechanism* which would explain how continents had drifted apart.

Today, we know better. It is now recognised that there *is* a mechanism which can make continents drift apart. It is called plate tectonics. And it has become the corner stone of the Earth sciences. Wegener, having been mocked in 1910, ended up getting his name in the history books after all – not as a crank, but as a bold pioneer in his field.

Might the same be the case with Van Flandern's theory of exploded planets?

Wegener, it should be noted, put forward his theory of continental drift based on observational evidence, without knowing the essential mechanism of plate tectonics. It strikes me that Van Flandern is in a parallel situation, although his observational evidence is infinitely more complex and scientific than Wegener's. Van Flandern, too, is looking at a giant jigsaw puzzle, but of asteroids and comets, which can be fitted together very neatly into two planets and at least one moon.

Should we dismiss Van Flandern's exploded planet theory as lacking a proper scientific mechanism?

Or is this simply another case of scientists having not yet discovered the mechanism?

This debate happens to be extremely topical as we enter the 21st century, for NASA (the American space agency) already has plans under way to make an unprecedented study of asteroids and comets in space.[8] Hopefully, it should be possible during the next five to ten years to settle the matter of whether planets have, or have not, exploded in our solar system.

Let us, for a moment, explore the implications of what might happen.

The first possibility, which must be recognised (regrettably), is that the various spacecraft fail to capture all the necessary data, in which case the issue of exploded planets will remain unresolved for the foreseeable future. (A worst-case scenario would be a combination of spacecraft malfunctions, or budget cutbacks at NASA, perhaps sparked by economic setbacks in the Western world.) Thus, we might all be kept in suspense for many decades to come.

The second possibility, as I see it, is that Van Flandern will be proved wrong. If so, the exploded planet cults of the ancients will come to be seen as totally misguided, but, more to the point, this discovery would expose modern Western religion as being based upon nothing more than a myth. The traditional concept of God – at least as it is understood by those who are initiated into the Mysteries – will have been repudiated lock, stock and barrel.

The third possibility is that Van Flandern will be proved right, or partly right, with NASA confirming the prior existence of at least one exploded planet. If this happens, the exploded planet cults of the ancients will come to be seen as extraordinarily far-sighted. More significantly, though, modern Western religion will be seen (by those 'in the know') as being based upon a profound scientific reality.

The Church's Dilemma

It might be presumed that confirmation of the exploded planet theory by NASA would delight the Church, since it would prove that the holy scriptures were based on a reality, and it would prove that God had actually existed, and had breathed his quintessential breath of life into all living things. Furthermore, if proponents of the Gaea hypothesis are correct in their presumption that planets are living beings, and if the life-after-death camp are correct in their philosophy, then it might be supposed that God's life force had survived the catastrophic death of his body. God would thus have continued to exist, and he would still be in existence today.[9]

But would the Church really be so welcoming of such news? I suspect that this might *not* be the case.

For one thing, the ex-physical nature of God is something which was long ago *occulted* from the Old Testament. Would the Church confess, and admit to its followers that the Old Testament was built upon half-truths and lies? I doubt it.

For another thing, if the Church admitted that God was an exploded planet, what would they then tell their congregation about Jesus Christ, the Son of God – the Word, who had been with God in the beginning, and through whom all things had been created?

How would the Church explain the fact that Jesus Christ was originally a physical flood of meteorites?

How would the Church sell the idea that the Second Coming of Christ would bring about the physical, catastrophic end of the world? Would the Church still encourage their flock to look forward to it?

And, if this long-hidden aspect of Jesus Christ was revealed, how would the Church explain the role of Jesus-the-man from the 1st century AD? Would the Church admit that Jesus-the-man was an actor in a Mystery Play or Passion play? Would the Church acknowledge that the crucifixion was in fact an ingenious esoteric parable for the death of a planet?

The mind absolutely boggles at the thought of all this.

It seems to me that the Church is in a 'no win situation'. If the exploded planet theory is proven to be *wrong*, its entire religion will be seen to be based on a groundless myth. But if the exploded planet theory is proven to be *right*, the Church will still have to admit that many aspects of Christianity (namely the Old Testament writings) are half-truths, lies or imaginative myths.

Either way, the Church would be in deep trouble with its congregation, who have been brought up to believe that the Bible tells the 'gospel' truth.

Secrets for the Initiated

But now let us put this discussion into perspective. The straight facts are these. The Church will only be in deep trouble if it confesses – which seems unlikely – or if its congregation *discovers* the connections between the scientific research into asteroids and comets, on the one hand, and the holy scriptures, on the other hand. In other words, the Churchgoing public would need to read the contents of this book, *When The Gods Came Down*, in order to know that the veracity of the holy scriptures had in some way been undermined. Otherwise, the significance of scientific research would be missed, and life would just continue as normal.

Is it likely that the Church-going public will read this book? The answer has to be "No". Although it might seem that I have exposed the secrets of the ancient exploded planet cults to the world in the writing of this book, nothing could be further from the truth. The reality is that the world is flooded with new books every year, and this book will go onto shelves in bookshops and libraries – into goodness knows which categories – and will remain effectively hidden from the public. Indeed, it will only be found by those few truth-seekers who have come to realise that something is very wrong with the story we've been sold, and who have set out in search of an alternative, better explanation.

The only way that this might *not* happen is if the mass media picks up the story and divulges it to the world. But is this really likely to happen? Again, the answer, regrettably, must be "No", for the simple reason that the mass media are, by definition, aimed at the masses – at the common man. And herein lies a problem.

How would the common man, who has been kept in the dark all of his life, come to terms with the idea that Adam was not really a man in the true sense of the word? How would the common man be able to grasp the fact that the Garden of Eden was in the underworld? How would the common man react to the news that Noah's Ark had sailed down to Earth from another planet? And that Noah, too, was not really a man? How would the common man be able to understand that the Exodus of the Israelites took place from the underworld, or that Moses and the fleeing Israelites were not really 'people' at all, or that Mount Sinai was not really a mountain but a planet? How would the common man come to terms with the fact that Jesus Christ, the Son of God, and the Messiah, was a planet-sized meteorite, and that God, his Father, was a planet which exploded?

I do not wish, by any means, to insult the common man, but rather to illustrate the fact that society as a whole has drifted so far away from the ancient way of thinking that a mass reunion with our long-lost traditions seems hopelessly inconceivable.

Indeed, the cultural gap between the modern and ancient ways of thinking is so immense that, without the benefit of the fourteen-chapter initiation in this book, my conclusions would sound totally bizarre and unreal to the vast majority of people. It thus seems to me that the mass media will not be able to understand my conclusions, and nor will the common man.

It is the nature of things esoteric to remain esoteric. The common man, it must be said, has long become accustomed to the darkness, and he will remain in the darkness, and be perfectly content there. Although it might seem that I have uncovered the sacred secrets of the ancients, all I have done, in the absence of exposure within the mass media, is to write those secrets down and have them hidden away in places where few people will ever find them.

Ironically, therefore, this book amounts to little more than a mystery school on a bookshelf – a course of initiation by distance learning. It is open to all people, but few people will ever know of its existence, and even fewer people will apply for membership. Even then, those who do apply – the truth-seekers – will in many cases be ill prepared for what they read in this fourteen-chapter mystery school.

Putting Away Childish Things

The sad fact is that mankind has lost its way, religiously speaking. Once upon a time, things did make sense, when we rightly or wrongly believed that God had been an exploded planet. But over the past five thousand years we 'dumbed down' our earlier religious beliefs by portraying ex-planets, meteorites and comets in anthropomorphic terms – either as human beings (or human artefacts), or as gods with human-like appearances, or as a God watching over us with a human-like mind, or as a spirit-like Son of God occupying a real human body.

Today, the conditioning imposed upon us by our religious educations is such that the vast majority of us are quite incapable of seeing beyond what we might call 'the anthropomorphic barrier'. Even those who deny the orthodox religions fall into a similar trap of believing that God and the gods were a visiting group of flesh-and-blood extraterrestrials. But although the majority of people might laugh at such beliefs, the truth is that the followers of the so-called 'ancient astronaut theory' are no more foolish than 1.9 billion Christians who believe that a flesh-and-blood Son of God was sacrificed to save mankind. Both groups of believers have fallen into the same trap – a very understandable trap – of failing to see beyond the anthropomorphic barrier. And, as far as this perspective is concerned, both groups thus stand no higher than the little children who believe that a man in a red and white suit comes down the chimney at Christmas bearing gifts.[10] We have all been believing in the same fairy tale.

As we enter the third millennium AD, hopefully to embark upon yet another wave of scientific discovery concerning our world and our universe, the potential exists to educate *all* people of the world about the reality of planets, asteroids, comets and meteorites. We no longer need fairy tales of flesh-and-blood gods to explain to the masses the concept of an exploded planet. Moreover, the vast majority of people are perfectly capable of understanding that the beliefs of our ancestors might not have been entirely true. What excuse, then, is there for us continuing to entertain such primitive religious beliefs? Is religion really such an essential tool for controlling the masses? And if not, why should the truth of mankind's religious beliefs be kept secret? In the words of an old Sumerian proverb: 'He who knows – why should he keep it hidden?'.[11]

It is astonishing to think that mankind is so technologically advanced and yet, at the same time, so emotionally backward. So advanced is our technology that we stand on the brink of exploring our universe, possibly with faster-than-light travel which will open up entire swathes of the galaxy. For the first time since *Homo sapiens* emerged from his forest and looked up to the stars, he sees an opportunity of reaching those stars and perceives a real possibility of encountering extraterrestrial civilisations.

How would we approach such a momentous encounter? Would we send a Christian missionary to preach the word of God to our newly found friends? Or perhaps a whole delegation of missionaries – one from each of the world's various faiths? Unless things change on Earth in the near future, this is exactly the scenario we can expect – an intragalactic exportation of mankind's most treasured religious beliefs.

But how would we react if the leaders of the newly discovered civilisation fell off their chairs at the first interplanetary conference? How would we feel if they split their sides with laughter upon hearing about our religious convictions? How would we cope if the leaders of the extraterrestrials mocked our leaders for their beliefs in a human-like God and (in the case of the Christian delegation) in a human-like Son of God

– beliefs which the other side might well recognise immediately as mythologised stories, created by a species which had been traumatised by its exposure to celestial catastrophes?

Would we see the funny side of the joke if the extraterrestrials gave us a meteorite-in-a-box as an inaugural Christmas present? Or would we regard this as an insult of the highest magnitude, leading to a permanent breakdown in intragalactic diplomatic relations?

Such is the nonsense which might one day determine our destiny in the galaxy unless the leaders of our world exercise a little modesty and admit to the mistakes of the past. If we are truly *Homo sapiens*, we will bid farewell to our past incarnation as *Homo religiosus* and begin to study our origins in a sensible fashion, with the maturity of a *Homo religiosus sapiens* – 'the man who is wise in his religion'.

At this juncture, it seems appropriate to cite the words of Paul – an initiate into the ancient Mysteries. In his 'First Letter to the Corinthians', he wrote:

When I was a child, I spoke as a child,
I understood as a child, I thought as a child:
But when I became a man, I put away childish things.[12]

Formerly I, too, spoke as a child and understood as a child, until in 1998/99 I finally came to understand the day 'When The Gods Came Down'. Now I have put my childish things away.

It is now over to you – the reader. Will you join me on this common-sense revolution, or would you prefer to perpetuate the follies of mankind as were summarised so eloquently by the Roman satirist Horace during the 1st century BC:

Parturient montes, nascetur ridiculus mus.

Which translates roughly as: 'Mountains will heave in childbirth, and a silly little mouse will be born.'

It is time to decide whether we are truly mice or men.

* * * * *

APPENDIX A
THE EMISSARIES OF GOD

One of the loose ends which I have not had the opportunity to discuss in the main body of this work is the identity of the biblical angels, who appear so frequently in the books of the Old and New Testaments as the intermediaries between God and mankind-on-the-Earth. Who were these angelic beings, and how do they fit in to the explanation of Hebrew and Christian religion which has been presented in these pages?

If we are to establish the true identity of the angels, then we must first put aside the modern notion of them being serene, peaceful, human-like creatures, or innocent, rosy-cheeked childlike cherubs. And in place of this modern and thoroughly misleading image, we must return to the original biblical concept – of angels with drawn swords,[1] of angels ascending to Heaven in flames of fire,[2] and of angels dispatching tens of thousands of men to their deaths.

In the book of Genesis, for example, we read of the angels of God who were sent to Earth to destroy the evil city of Sodom:

> And the 'men' [the two angels] said unto Lot: "We will destroy this place [Sodom]. The outcry of the people has waxen great before the face of the LORD, and the LORD hath sent us to destroy it."[3]

Shortly afterwards, the LORD (Yahweh-Elohim) rained down brimstone and fire out of Heaven, and Sodom was indeed destroyed, along with the other cities of the plain. All of the inhabitants were killed.

Later in the Bible, in the second book of Kings, we read how the angels of Yahweh once again brought death to a vast number of people:

> And it came to pass that night, that the angel of the LORD went out, and put to death in the camp of the Assyrians a hundred and eighty five thousand men.[4]

So much for the idea of sweet, smiling, rosy-faced cherubs.

The second thing we need to do in order to establish the true identity of the angels is to put aside any notion that these fiery, destructive creatures were in any way human. Instead, we must recognise the tendency of our ancestors to use human-like imagery to tell the story of the planetary and ex-planetary gods. God himself, for example, was often portrayed as a walking, talking being, who felt both pleasure and pain, yet few people would seriously suggest that God was actually a flesh-and-blood person. By the same token, it should be recognised that Adam, Noah, Enoch and Abraham were *not* human beings either. On the contrary, each character personified the heroic idea of the meteoric Seed of Mankind descending from Heaven into the Earth.

As far as the angels are concerned, then, we must look beyond the superficial anthropomorphic imagery, and look instead to the symbolism of features such as their wings, their association with fire and wind, and their supernatural ability to travel back and forth between Heaven and Earth.

How did the angels originate? One clue comes from the Hebrew name for the angels, which was *mal'akhim* – meaning 'messengers' or 'emissaries';[5] it is a name which fits well with the idea of a multitude being emanated from a central Godhead. And it is a notable fact that one of Yahweh's names was Yahweh-Sabaoth, meaning 'LORD of a Multitude' or 'LORD of Hosts'.[6] The meaning of this name, 'LORD of Hosts', was made clear by the prophet Micaiah, who declared:

> "I saw the LORD sitting on his throne, and all the host of Heaven standing round him, on his right hand and on his left."[7]

This host, or multitude, of angels was a vitally important part of God's character, but why did he have this entourage at all?

The Old Testament (as we know it) is silent concerning the origin of the angels, as indeed it is concerning the origin of the pagan gods (*elohim*) and the origin of the mysterious entities known as the Sons-of-God. This oversight is quite astonishing; so much so that the writers of the New Testament attempted to bridge this theological abyss by asserting that all such unaccounted-for things had been created via Jesus Christ, the first-born Son of God.[8] But the fact is that the New Testament was written many centuries after the Old Testament, and thus for hundreds of years the Hebrew scriptures maintained a distinct vagueness surrounding the origin of the angels, the *elohim* and the Sons-of-God.

In view of the Bible's silence on this matter, we have no option but to turn to pagan legends in order to resolve the mystery.

The Pagan Emanations

In the creation legends of ancient Egypt, there is a recurrent theme of a multitude of gods being produced from the One God. In the legend of the creation by Atum (also known as Neber-Djer), it was said that God had created himself from some mysterious 'primeval matter' and appeared in the primeval waters, at which point all of the future gods were said to be contained *within him*.[9] Then, Atum produced a myriad of deities, which he ejaculated either from his mouth or from his penis. In one of the best known legends, Atum became a *trinity* by emitting from himself the deities Shu and Tefnut. According to another legend, Atum created an ennead of *nine* gods.

Another ancient Egyptian legend, of a creation by Shu, recorded that *eight* chaos-gods had been made from the 'efflux of his flesh',[10] whilst *five* was the number of chaos-gods allegedly produced by the 'womb' of Nut. Other Egyptian texts commonly referred to the creator-god as 'the one become million', or the one who had created 'tens of thousands and thousands of gods'.[11] And elsewhere, in *A Hymn to the Aten*, praise was given to Aten as 'God' who 'madest millions of forms of thyself'.[12]

These Egyptian beliefs in an emission of a multitude from the One God are no different in concept to the legends of the dismemberment of Osiris, which we dealt with in chapter three of this work. Osiris, we might recall, was the counterpart of Re, and it is therefore no surprise to find legends which speak indirectly of the dismemberment of Re himself. In one legend we read:

> He who created his names, the Lord of the Ennead. Who is he?
> He is Re, who created the names of the parts of his body. That is how these gods who follow him came into being.[13]

The meaning of this passage is clarified by The Book of What is in the Duat, which describes Re entering into the underworld – the so-called 'place of destruction' – and encountering a wide variety of deities, knife-wielding gods, hybrid beings, tortured and mutilated bodies, animated corpses, and numerous snakes.[14] Significantly, Re recognised many of these gods as members of his own former body. In the first division of the subterranean *Duat*, Re addressed these gods as follows:

> "O ye who came into being from my members, my Word hath gone forth to you. Ye are made of my bodies, I have made you, having fashioned you of my soul. I have created you, I have made you by means of my enchantments..."[15]

A similar reference is found in *The Legend of Re and Isis*, where the dying god Re called out to his followers: "come to me, ye who came into being in my body, ye gods who came forth from me".[16] And in the Book of Gates, it is made clear that the Earth was a 'mountain' which had devoured Re, and which was thus 'filled with the slaughter of the gods'.[17] The Egyptian texts thus affirm that the Hidden Mountain of the underworld (*Ament Set*) was filled with the fragments of the ex-Mountain of Heaven.

In ancient Mesopotamia, there was a similar belief that God had disintegrated into a multitude of gods. Thus the supreme god Anu was said to have given birth to the Anunnaki-gods in the combined 'Mountain of Heaven-and-Earth'.[18] He did so, however, by casting the Anunnaki-gods down from/with the Mountain of Heaven. In the legend of Utnapishtim, we read of the precise moment when the heavenly planet code-named Shuruppak unleashed its great Flood, and gave birth to the fiery Anunnaki:

> The Anunnaki raised their torches,
> Lighting up the land with their brightness.
> The confusion of Adad reached unto the (highest) heavens,
> Turning into darkness all that had been light.
> The wide land was shattered like a pot![19]

The Anunnaki then became denizens of the underworld, where they were forced to carry out hard labour, digging the subterranean canals which would feed water to the great rivers Tigris and Euphrates.

The destruction of Anu and the creation of his sons, the Anunnaki, was the first of two great planetary catastrophes in the religious system of the Mesopotamians. In the second catastrophe, the goddess Ishtar (Inanna) went to pieces 'like a pot' in the heavens, and a great Flood went forth. But amidst this Flood was a primeval 'mankind' (the black-headed ones), which was scattered forth from her 'womb':

> Ishtar [Inanna] cried out like a woman giving birth...
> "Alas, the olden days are turned to clay...
> How could I order battle for the destruction of my people?
> Alas, I myself (now) give birth to my people!
> Like the spawn of fish they (now) fill the sea!"[20]

This 'people' of Ishtar, having been born in Heaven, was scattered through the celestial sea like 'sacrificial sheep' and, in accordance with the rules of ancient mythology, fell to Earth and entered into the underworld, where they were enslaved by their elders, the Anunnaki.

The Father and the Sons

As we shall see in a moment, the pagan cosmogony of Heaven and Earth, as outlined above, can be used to resolve the mystery of the biblical angels. But more than that, the pagan cosmogony of Heaven and Earth can be identified in the Hebrew Old Testament in *no less than five different arrangements* concerning the divine Father and Son (or Sons). We will now review each of these arrangements in turn, in order to build up broad support for the overall interpretation.

Firstly, we find in the Old Testament a restatement of the pagan belief that 'mankind' had been created 'in the image of' God:

> And God said: "Let us make a human in our image, after our
> likeness"... And God created the human in his image, in the image of
> God he created him; male and female he created them.[21]

What this means is that God was a planet, which made primeval 'mankind' in its image (a flood of meteorites) simply by a process of disintegration and emanation. God was the 'Father', and 'mankind' the 'Sons'.

Secondly, the Old Testament asserts that God had some mysterious 'Sons' who had ravished the daughters-of-men (or daughters-of-*the-earth*) in the days leading up to the Flood. In Genesis chapter 6, we read:

> There were Nephilim in the Earth in those days, and also afterwards,
> when the Sons-of-God came in unto the daughters-of-the-earth and
> had children by them. The same [children, i.e. the Nephilim] were the
> mighty men of old, the men of the *Shem*.[22]

The fact that these enigmatic Sons-of-God fathered giant children in the manner of the Greek Titans attests to the fact that the Sons-of-God were falling Sky-gods, who had entered into the womb of the Earth. In other words, the Sons-of-God were *meteorites*. Furthermore, their name – *Sons-of*-God – attests to the fact that God was their Father. *QED*. God was Father-of-the-meteorites.

The third arrangement of the divine Father and Son is found in the relationship between God (*Elohim*) and the gods (*elohim*). According to Psalm 82 of the Old Testament, God appeared in the 'mighty assembly of the *elohim*' (in the underworld I would suggest) where the *elohim*-judges had been showing partiality to the wicked. God then castigated the *elohim* as follows:

> God standeth in the mighty assembly; he judgeth among the *elohim*
> (saying:) "How long will ye judge unjustly and show partiality to

the wicked?"...

They know not, neither will they understand; they walk on in
darkness; all the foundations of the Earth are shaken.

"I have said 'Ye are *elohim*; and all of you are *Sons of the Most High*',
but ye shall die like men and fall like one of the princes."[23]

By referring to the *elohim* as Sons of the Most High, God was effectively
calling them his own sons – the Sons of God – for no-one else but God
would warrant the title 'the Most High'.

Although the Bible is strangely silent concerning the origin of the
elohim, an amazing confirmation of the above scenario emerges when
the Hebrew letter *aleph* is inserted at the beginning of Genesis chapter 1,
verse 1. The line then reads as follows:

When the Father-of-Beginning created the gods [*elohim*] of Heaven-
and-Earth...

In chapter nine of this work, I argued that the Hebrew priests occulted
this creation of the *elohim* by removing the *aleph* from the beginning of
the first line of Genesis 1. The above translation, I suggest, recaptures the
meaning of the original, paganised Hebrew religion. And it certainly
makes for a sensible reading, for the line now recalls the essential pagan
philosophy of a God who emitted from himself a multitude of gods who
then became interred inside a combined 'mountain' of Heaven-and-
Earth.

It should be noted, incidentally, that the ancient Egyptians *did* refer to
God as a 'Father of Beginning':

God is from the beginning, and he hath been from the beginning... He
existed when nothing else existed... He is the father of beginnings.[24]

But this is not to suggest that the Hebrews drew exclusively on ancient
Egyptian ideas. On the contrary, it is widely acknowledged that the
Hebrew God, Elohim, was modelled on El, the supreme god of the
Canaanites. As pointed out in chapter thirteen of this work, El dwelt in a
Shad (mountain), which would explain why Yahweh's archaic name was
El Shaddai, meaning either 'God-of-the-Mountains' or 'God-of-the-
Mountain-Peaks'. Now it should be noted that the name El is the singular
of the plural term *elohim*, and thus El and *elohim* fit the mould of Father
and Sons, in exactly the same manner as the Mesopotamian pairing of
Anu and the Anunnaki. This all adds grist to the mill of my argument
that the *elohim* were the multitudinous offspring of their Father, Elohim,
and were thus sons of God, as is suggested by the lines of Psalm 82.

Before tackling the angels, let us briefly cover the fourth arrangement of the divine Father and Son in the Old Testament, namely the Israelites.

According to the arguments set out in chapters ten and eleven of this work, the pagan Israelites believed that their tribe had crossed over from Heaven to Earth; hence the name *Ibri*, implying that the Hebrews had 'crossed over' the *celestial* river Jordan. But this meant that the mythical ancestors of the Israelites had begun their terrestrial existence as denizens of the underworld (in accordance with the ancient rule that all things which fell from Heaven to Earth entered the underworld).

Against this background, it is intriguing to find God referring to the Israelites as his collective 'first-born son'. In the book of Jeremiah, the prophet declared that 'Israel was the first fruits of the LORD's increase', and Yahweh was made to say: "I am a father to Israel".[25] Such statements are commonplace throughout the Old Testament, with Israel often being described as being like 'sons to Yahweh', or like 'sons of the living Elohim'.[26]

Significantly, this 'Father-Son' relationship can be traced back to the time when Joseph descended into the underworld of 'Egypt'. It was there that Joseph begot two children, Manasseh and Ephraim, by an Egyptian wife. And it was Ephraim, the second-born, who was favoured by God, who said: "I am a father to Israel, and Ephraim is my first-born."[27] Shortly thereafter, God came down from Heaven to rescue Israel from Egypt, 'the land of slavery', exclaiming: "Israel is my first-born son. Let my son go."[28]

So, when God saved the Israelites, by bringing them back to himself at the celestial Mount Sinai 'on the wings of eagles', he did not do this as a disinterested party. On the contrary, it was said that God had redeemed *his* people, and led *his* people away into freedom.[29] Amazingly, the Hebrews did not consider it blasphemy to tell God: "Thou hast redeemed thyself", on account of his saving them from the underworld.[30]

In summary, we are looking at a relationship which went far beyond the covenant which had been agreed between God and the patriarchs. The true nature of this relationship, mythically speaking, was that God and Israel belonged together as a *celestial* Father-and-Son. God was thus saving his own physical emanations in the form of Israelites who were equivalent to the mythical, pre-human, black-headed ones of ancient Sumerian lore – the meteoric seeds of the underworld.

Lest this celestial interpretation be doubted, the reader should consider the following passage from *The Song of Moses*:

> I will proclaim the name of the LORD. O praise the greatness of our
> God. He is the Rock, his work is perfect... Jeshurun [Israel] forsook
> the God which made him, and disrespected the Rock of his salvation...

Thou [O Israel] are unmindful of the Rock that begat thee.[31]

Note the words 'the Rock that begat thee'. The Israelites, it would seem, were 'chips off the old Rock'. Similarly, in the book of Isaiah, the prophet exclaimed:

"Listen to me, ye that pursue righteousness, ye that seek the LORD. Look to the Rock from which you were cut..."[32]

Incidentally, the celestial nature of this Rock is made clear in the book of Daniel, which speaks cryptically of a rock smashing the feet of a statue which stretched symbolically from Earth to Heaven:

"Thou looked O king... thou looked till a rock was cut out, but not by (human) hands... the rock that struck the statue became a great mountain, and filled the whole Earth."[33]

This is the exploded planet cult in a nutshell.

Fallen Angels and Risen Angels

We return now to the subject of the angels, where we find our fifth example of the divine Father-and-Son(s) relationship.

As mentioned earlier, the Old Testament is surprisingly vague concerning the origin of the angels, but their Hebrew name *mal'akhim* – meaning 'messengers' or 'emissaries' – is entirely consistent with the idea of their emanation from a central Godhead. Fortunately, there is a gnostic text known as the *Secret Book of John* which testifies that the angels had indeed issued forth from God in such a manner. The salient passage reads as follows:

... he [God] saw the creation which surrounded him, and the multitudes of angels around him, *which had come forth from him...*[34]

This passage also illustrates a principle which is absolutely vital to our understanding of the angels. It describes the recomposition of God in the highest heights, from the metaphysical (i.e. risen) counterparts of the fallen angels. In other words, there were two kinds of angels, just as there were two kinds of God or gods – the *physical* form (*pre*-catastrophe) and the *metaphysical* form (*post*-catastrophe). The rising up of the latter out of the womb of the Earth has been fully dealt with in chapter two of this work.

Let us deal firstly with the physical angels. If we apply the pagan (unocculted) model to the Old Testament, it is to be surmised that the angels experienced a physical existence firstly as part of God at the beginning of time, and secondly in their fall to the Earth immediately following the disintegration of God. These physical angels were known as the Sons-of-God, or the *elohim* (the sons of El), who emanated from God the Father (see discussion above). They were also referred to as the fallen angels, or Watchers, as in the non-biblical Book of Enoch, which relates how in the days of Jared two hundred Watchers had descended from Heaven onto Mount Hermon, where they married the daughters-of-men and had giant children by them (note the parallel here with Genesis 6: the Sons-of-God and their giant offspring, the Nephilim).[35]

The physical fall of these angels at the beginning of time is also alluded to in the book of Job, where God informed Job about the time when he had created the Earth:

> Where wast thou when I laid the foundations of the Earth?... Who laid the corner stone thereof, when the morning stars sang together, when all the Sons-of-God shouted for joy?[36]

When these fallen angels (the meteoric Sons-of-God) impacted with the Earth, they spawned metaphysical doubles (just as the Mesopotamian Anunnaki had spawned their metaphysical counterparts, the Igigi), and these metaphysical angels were immediately resurrected to Heaven. The incident is seemingly recorded in the book of Genesis, chapter 28, where we read the famous legend of Jacob's Ladder:

> And he [Jacob] dreamed, and behold, there was a ladder set against the ground, with its top reaching to Heaven. And behold, the angels of God were ascending and descending on it. And behold, the LORD stood above it...[37]

In view of the fact that the Bible does not record the purpose behind this remarkable ascent and descent of God's angels, it seems perfectly valid to suppose that Jacob was witnessing a vision of *the act of creation*. The descending angels would thus represent the flood of physical meteorites falling to the Earth, whilst the ascending angels would represent the flood of metaphysical meteorites being resurrected to Heaven, in order to reconstruct the abode of God (compare the Igigi's construction of Marduk's heavenly abode, the Esharra).[38]

Incidentally, it is to be surmised that the resurrection of the angels is also alluded to in the book of Genesis, at the time when the Light (Heaven) was created on Day 1 by separating it from the darkness (of the underworld). See the detailed discussion in chapter nine of this work.

Once the angels had been raised up to the brand-new, shiny metaphysical abode of God in Heaven, they became God's 'army' – a term which reflected the catastrophic and destructive nature of these heavenly beings. It was for this reason that the Hebrew God was known as Yahweh-Sabaoth, meaning 'LORD of Hosts'. As we saw in the passage cited earlier, the Hebrews believed that God would sit on his throne in Heaven, surrounded by 'all the host of Heaven', i.e. his army of angels.[39] The catastrophic role of this army at the End of Days has been outlined in chapter thirteen.

A clearer picture of the heavenly host of angels emerges when we add Psalm 68 into the equation. Here we learn that God was surrounded by the angels *in his holy mountain*:

> This is the hill which God desireth to dwell in; yea, the LORD will
>   dwell in it for ever.
> The chariots of God are tens of thousands, (like) thousands of angels.
> The LORD is among them, in the holy Sinai.[40]

This image of the angels in the heavenly 'mountain' of Sinai corresponds to the Mesopotamian idea of the Igigi-gods who accompanied the senior gods Marduk, Anu, Enlil and Ea in their metaphysical planetary 'mountain' of Esharra. And Yahweh-Elohim's archaic name was indeed El Shaddai, meaning 'God-of-the-Mountains' or 'God-of-the-Mountain-Peaks'.

The Hebrew angels (of the metaphysical variety) are reminiscent of the Mesopotamian Igigi-gods in many ways. Just as the Igigi were 'pure', so too were the angels described as 'holy ones'.[41] And just as the Igigi possessed eternal life in Heaven, so too did the angels.[42] Perhaps the greatest similarity between these two types of being, however, was their common association with fire. The Igigi were said to have had a 'brilliance like fire', whilst the angels, according to Psalm 104, were created as 'spirits... a flaming fire'.[43] Indeed, one of the best known manifestations of the angel of the LORD was to Moses, when it appeared mysteriously in a flame of fire out of the midst of a 'bush', which appeared to burn but was not consumed.[44] But above all, as noted earlier, the Igigi were said to have constructed and occupied the heavenly abode of Marduk (the Esharra), just as the angels had surrounded God in his abode in the highest heights of the heavens.

There was, however, a major difference between the Mesopotamian Igigi and the Hebrew angels, and it was inspired by the Hebrew obsession with the idea of God as a Lord of History, who would intervene in the affairs of mankind on the Earth. Unlike the Igigi, who generally remained aloof in their heavenly abode, the angels frequently came down from the heavens, in order to convey the messages of God to mankind, and to carry out God's instructions upon the Earth. It is for this reason that the risen, metaphysical angels figure more prominently than the fallen angels in the various legends of Hebrew and Christian mythology.[45]

As mentioned earlier, it is high time that we looked beyond the anthropomorphic features of the angels and focused on other more telling aspects of their collective character. Thus in the *Apocalypse of Abraham*, we find that an angel had a body which 'shone like sapphire' – a description which lends credence to the idea that the angels were composed of ex-planetary materials.[46]

Furthermore, in the Book of Enoch, we find that the angels were not only of fiery countenance, but were also of supernatural giant size – just as one would expect of anthropomorphised planetary fragments. Enoch told his sons:

> "There appeared to me two men [sic], *exceedingly big*, such as I have never seen in the Lowlands [Earth]. Their faces shone like the Sun, their eyes were like a burning light, and fire was coming out of their mouths."[47]

At this point, enough has surely been said to demonstrate the very neat fit between the concept of God and his angels, and the exploded planet cults of the ancient pagans, especially in view of the recurrence of the divine Father-and-Son(s) concept in four other arrangements of the Old Testament: the creation of mankind 'in the image of' God; the Sons-of-God who ravaged the daughters-of-the-earth; God-and-the-gods in the form of Yahweh-Elohim and his *elohim*, or El and his *elohim*; and last but not least God-and-the-Israelites.

It only remains to complete our understanding of this Father-and-Son(s) concept by referring briefly to the writings of the *New* Testament.

The Christian Father and Son

One of the fundamental themes running through the Christian scriptures (and indeed through the pagan legends of the Hebrews) is the idea of a reunion of mankind with the Godhead, via the intervention of Jesus Christ, the Son of God. But more than that, it is evident that this future reunion between mankind and the Godhead would occur because God, the Son of God and mankind all somehow belonged together. But why? Does the exploded planet cult not provide the answer?

A few passages from the New Testament will serve to illustrate this point. Firstly, in the gospel of John, Jesus Christ stated that:

"I know my sheep and my sheep know me – just as the Father knows me and I know the Father... I and the Father are one... the Father is in me, and I in him."[48]

Secondly, again from the gospel of John, Jesus Christ stated that:

"Whoever eats my flesh and drinks my blood has eternal life, and I will raise him up at the last day... Because I live, you also will live. On that day you will realise that I am in my Father, and you are in me, and I am in you."[49]

In these passages, we see a clear reference to the idea that God, the Son (Jesus Christ) and mankind (or at least the righteous ones among us) would be *joined together* in Heaven. The implication is that, just as Jesus Christ had been together with God in the beginning (see John 1:1-2), so had mankind been together with God in the beginning. Admittedly, this latter point is not referred to explicitly in the New Testament (and it was anathema to the writers of the Old Testament), but it does appear in the gnostic writings of Valentinus, where Jesus declared:

"I became very small, so that through my humility I might take you up to the great height, *whence you had fallen.*"[50]

All in all, when one reads the words of Jesus Christ "I know my sheep and my sheep know me", one is inclined to suspect a rather profound link to the ancient pagan traditions of the primeval 'mankind' which was like a flock of sheep scattered into the Earth, and thus in need of a shepherd.

And all because, at the beginning of time, God (or more aptly a Goddess) had emanated from himself (or herself) the primeval 'mankind' in the course of unleashing the Great Flood. In the words of Mami, the heavenly mother-goddess of the Mesopotamians:

"Beyond my control, my offspring have become like (sacrificial) white sheep...
My noise has turned to silence."[51]

* * * * *

APPENDIX B
MARY, MARY, QUITE CONTRARY

As discussed in chapter one of this book, Christianity started out in the form of a mystery school during the 1st century AD – as one of many mystery schools which existed in the ancient world at that time. And, like all mystery schools, Christianity had its Mysteries, which were revealed in gradual stages to its initiates.

Over the last two thousand years, Christianity has become less and less like a mystery school, and yet certain Mysteries still persist within it. One of these Mysteries is the virgin birth – the belief that Jesus Christ was brought into the world by a woman known as the Virgin Mary. The mystery is summed up in the gospel of Luke as follows:

> Then Mary said to the angel: "How will this be, since I am a virgin?"
> And the angel answered, saying to her: "The Holy Spirit will come upon you, and the power of the Most High will overshadow you.
> Therefore, that holy thing which will be born from you shall be called the Son of God."[1]

The idea that a woman could give birth as a virgin, i.e. without being impregnated by the seed of a man, is of course preposterous. And yet the faith of Christians is such that they willingly suspend disbelief on this point, for it is widely perceived that an all-powerful God would have been perfectly capable of making a virgin pregnant in a supernatural fashion if he so desired.

The truth behind the virgin birth, however, is rather different.

As has been noted repeatedly in this work, the ancients used human-like imagery to tell the story of the planetary and ex-planetary gods. God himself was an exploded planet, whilst his 'Son', Jesus Christ, was a flood of meteorites which came forth from the planetary parent. And so it logically follows that if Jesus Christ (in his primeval form) was not a real human being, then neither was his 'mother', the Virgin Mary.

How, then, should we understand the significance of the Virgin Mary?

In chapter two of this work, we discussed at length the ancients' belief in the sacred marriage of Heaven and Earth, in which a falling Sky (masculine) had impregnated a passive Earth (feminine). The Earth was thus envisaged as a giant womb, which would give birth to all manner of living things, according to the nature of the seed which had been sown within it by the falling Sky. The most eloquent expression of this ancient belief is found in the verses of a Sumerian poem:

> Smooth, big Earth made herself resplendent, beautified her body joyously.
> Wide Earth bedecked her body with precious metal and lapis lazuli,
> Adorned herself with diorite, chalcedony, and shiny carnelian.
> Heaven arrayed himself in a wig of verdure, stood up in princeship.
> Holy Earth, the virgin, beautified herself for Holy Heaven.
> Heaven, the lofty god, planted his knees on Wide Earth,
> Poured the semen of the heroes Tree and Reed into her womb.
> Sweet Earth, the fecund cow, was impregnated with the rich semen of Heaven.
> Joyfully did Earth tend to the giving birth of the plants of life,
> Luxuriantly she brought forth rich produce, and gave birth to wine and honey.[2]

Note in particular the fifth line of this passage: 'Holy Earth, *the virgin*, beautified herself for Holy Heaven'. In chapter three of this work, we discussed a Hermetic text, dating to the 1st century AD, entitled *The Virgin of the World*, and I suggested that the title of this text denoted Isis – the goddess who had come down from Heaven and taken on the mantle of Mother Earth, thus becoming 'the virgin of the world'.

Now, the connection between the virgin Isis and the Virgin Mary has not gone unnoticed by scholars, especially since both of these mothers were in the habit of seating their divine children on their knee in identical fashion.[3] As James Frazer commented in *The Golden Bough*:

> The figure of Isis suckling the infant Horus is so like that of the Madonna and child that it has sometimes received the adoration of ignorant Christians.[4]

It would be wrong, however, to assume that Isis was a human mother. On the contrary, it was made clear in *The Virgin of the World* that the conception of Horus was a great mystery, which proceeded from the fact that Earth (Isis) had received the mysterious 'efflux' of God.

In the ancient Egyptian texts, the same idea was expressed thus:

> I am that first seed of Re, he begot me in the womb of my mother

Isis... My mother Isis conceived me, and she swooned under the fingers of the Lord-of-the-gods when he broke into her therewith on that day of lifting... on that day of tumult...[5]

Another ancient Egyptian text described the mysterious event in equally dramatic fashion:

The lightning flash strikes... Isis wakes pregnant with the seed of her brother Osiris... Atum says: "O maiden, you are pregnant and you are hidden... you will give birth, being pregnant for the gods..."[6]

This 'seed of Osiris', it must be emphasised, was the seed of a god who had fallen from Heaven into the Earth. In short, the seed was a meteorite, or more strictly a flood of meteorites and water (see chapter three).

As for the goddess Isis, the ancient Egyptian texts reveal that she, too, descended from Heaven into the Earth, and thus took over the mantle of Mother Earth. Her conception of Horus was, in effect, an immaculate conception, and the birth of Horus was, in effect, a virgin birth. And this all stemmed from the fact that *the conception was a celestial event*. No human being was involved, in any way whatsoever.

Should the tale of the Virgin Mary and Jesus Christ be understood in a similar fashion? During the 1st century AD, gnostic Christians indeed ridiculed those who believed that the virgin birth had involved the birth of a human Messiah to a human woman. "They do not know what they are saying", the gnostics wrote: "When did a woman ever conceive by a woman [i.e. by herself]?".[7] The gnostics went on to argue that the virgin birth should instead be understood *symbolically* as referring to the mysterious union of the two divine powers – the Father of All and the Holy Spirit.[8]

In gnostic texts, the term 'virgin' was indeed applied to the Earth, but also to the mysterious 'Spirit' which came down from Heaven. One text makes an extraordinary reference to the birth of Adam:

Adam came into being from two virgins, from the Spirit and from the virgin Earth...[9]

At other times, however, the gnostics asserted that the Virgin mother had come down from the Sky. In the *Gospel of Philip*, a gnostic author wrote:

Is it permitted to utter a mystery? The Father of All united with the Virgin who came down.[10]

Furthermore, the gnostics made an explicit comparison between these enigmatic 'virgin' figures and the mother of Christ, saying: 'Christ, thus, was born from a virgin'.[11]

The Ethiopian holy book, *Kebra Nagast*, provides several references which corroborate this idea that the Virgin Mary was not a human being, but rather some kind of Sky-goddess, who had come down to the Earth. In one section of the Ethiopian Bible, we read:

> Ezekiel also prophesied concerning Mary, saying: "I saw a door in the east which was sealed with a great and marvellous seal, and there was none who went into it except the Lord of hosts; He went into it and came out therefrom."[12]

What did this mean? The authors of the *Kebra Nagast* explained that the 'Lord of hosts' was Christ, 'the fruit of the Godhead', whilst the 'door in the east' was the Virgin Mary, whom men called 'the Gate of Salvation' and 'the East'. The Virgin Mary was thus 'the gate of Heaven', and Christ had gone into her and come forth from her 'without polluting her'.[13]

As if to confirm our suspicion that the Virgin Mary was a heavenly body, the *Kebra Nagast* went on to identify Mary as the burning bush which had been encountered by Moses at Mount Horeb in Midian:

> Moses also prophesied about Mary, saying: "I saw a bramble bush on Mount Sinai which the devouring fire consumed not"; and the meaning of this fire is the Godhead of the Son of God; and the bramble bush, which burned without the leaves thereof being consumed, is Mary.[14]

In chapter ten of this work, I identified the location of Midian and Mount Horeb (Sinai) as being *in the midst of Heaven.*

The idea that the Virgin Mary was a heavenly planet is further supported in the *Kebra Nagast* by her epithets 'Mother of the Light' and 'the likeness of the heavenly Zion', and also by her identification with 'the rod of Aaron' and 'the staff of Jacob'.[15] The latter associations indicate that the Virgin Mary was a goddess who spanned the realms of both Heaven and Earth – just like the Egyptian goddess Isis or the Mesopotamian goddess Ninharsag (alias Mami, Inanna etc).[16]

The virgin mother-goddess having come down to the Earth, her role varied in line with different traditions. According to the Jewish tradition, the Earth-goddess would give birth to a Messiah, who would rule the 'new Earth' (see the quotation from the Dead Sea Scrolls in chapter thirteen of this work). But according to the esoteric Christian tradition, the role of the mother-goddess had occurred at the beginning of time, when she had facilitated the resurrection of the primeval Christ. In the *Kebra Nagast*, there is an intriguing passage which reads as follows:

In her [Mary] he [Christ] made a temple of her pure body, and from her was born the Light of all Lights... he made a Temple for himself through an incomprehensible wisdom which transcends the mind of man.[17]

As noted earlier in this book, the word 'temple' was a metaphor for 'planet' – hence the New Testament legend that the temple of God could be destroyed and rebuilt by Jesus Christ in three days.[18] This passage of the *Kebra Nagast* thus seems to preserve the tradition that Mary's body was a *planetary* body – a metaphorical 'temple' from which Christ, the Light of all Lights, would rise up and reconstruct the metaphysical 'Temple' of Heaven.[19]

In further support of this hypothesis, it is worth noting that the name 'Mary' can be traced to the land of ancient Egypt, which was called *Ta-Meri*, meaning 'the Place of the *Mr*'.[20] The '*Mr*' was the Egyptian name for 'pyramid', and appropriately enough the Egyptian pyramid was a structure which symbolised the Earth (and possibly Heaven in its image).[21] Furthermore, the name of this highly symbolic structure, the *Mr*, meant literally 'the Place of Ascension'.[22]

Therefore, whilst the pyramid (*Mr*) symbolised the Earth and was the ascension place of Osiris, it might equally be said that the Virgin Mary personified the Earth and was a similar ascension place for the primeval god to whom she gave birth – Jesus Christ.

Mary Magdalene

The contrast between the Virgin Mary and Mary Magdalene could not be greater – one a pure and spotless virgin, the other a shameless prostitute – and yet, as we shall now see, it is virtually certain that these two contrasting Marys represented one-and-the-same character.

As with the Virgin Mary, the confusion surrounding Mary Magdalene has arisen from a modern ignorance concerning the ancient tendency to use human-like imagery to tell the story of planetary and ex-planetary gods. But once it is appreciated that Jesus Christ (in his primeval form) was an exploded planet deity, who descended from Heaven into the Earth, the role of Mary Magdalene as his consort (as is testified by gnostic scriptures) takes on an entirely non-human connotation.[23] Indeed, the relationship would appear to be one between a descending flood of meteoric seed (Jesus Christ) on the one hand, and the womb of the Earth-goddess (Mary Magdalene) on the other. And it is undoubtedly this celestial relationship which lies behind the New Testament legend that Jesus Christ had driven seven demons out of Mary Magdalene's body.[24]

Lest this explanation be doubted, it should be pointed out that a close parallel to the idea of Mother Earth as a prostitute exists in the famous Mesopotamian saga entitled *The Epic of Gilgamesh*. In Tablet I of *The Epic*, Enkidu – a god who had fallen from Heaven to Earth like a falling 'star' or 'pickaxe' (i.e. a meteorite) – was portrayed as sexually ravaging a prostitute:

> The harlot untied her wide belt and spread her legs, and he [Enkidu] struck her wildness like a storm.
> She was not shy; she received his life-force.
> Her clothing was spread out, and he lay upon her.
> She made him know (man-as-he-was) what a woman is!
> His body lay on her; six days and seven nights Enkidu attacked, ravaging the harlot.[25]

Perhaps the most significant aspect of this encounter is that it lasted 'six days and seven nights' and thus symbolised the Mesopotamian act of creation, which had lasted for a similar period.[26] It is therefore evident that the prostitute ravaged by Enkidu (a falling Sky-god) was actually a female personification of planet Earth – the great Mother-Womb.

A second example of Mother Earth as a prostitute occurs in the Roman legend of Romulus and Remus, the twin sons of Rhea Silvia (a vestal virgin), who became the founders of the city of Rome. The twin boys, having been abandoned in a trough on the flooding river Tiber, were carried downriver to the foot of the Palatine hill – to the site of the future city of Rome.[27] Decoded, this means that Romulus and Remus were carried from Heaven to Earth by the celestial river, and it is thus highly significant that the twins were found by a sacred she-wolf, who suckled them in a subterranean cave known as the Lupercal.[28]

Can it really be a coincidence that the Roman word for 'she-wolf' – *lupa* – also meant 'prostitute'?[29] In view of the many similarities between this legend and all the other pagan legends involving the descents of gods into the womb of Mother Earth, I would suggest not. On the contrary, what we have here, in the legend of Romulus and Remus, as in *The Epic of Gilgamesh*, is an independent confirmation of the idea that Mother Earth was a prostitute.[30]

At this point, it might be tempting to conclude that Mary Magdalene personified Mother Earth pure and simple, and was thus not entirely identical to the Virgin Mary. Further analysis, however, reveals a series of intriguing connections between Mary Magdalene, the cult of the Black Madonna, and the cult of the Egyptian goddess Isis.[31] Although I do not claim to be an expert in this field, it nevertheless seems to me that Mary

Magdalene was a 'fallen goddess', who had come down to Earth in the same manner as Isis, or Ninharsag/Mami/Inanna, or indeed the Virgin Mary. She was thus a 'fallen woman' in more ways than one.

It seems to me that the only essential difference between the Virgin Mary and Mary Magdalene was one of conceptual presentation. In the case of the Virgin Mary, the idea seems to have been that she carried Jesus Christ from Heaven to Earth in her womb, and then became his mother. But in the case of Mary Magdalene, the idea seems to have been that she came down from Heaven to Earth *before* Jesus Christ, who came down subsequently, as an adult, and thus became her lover in a sacred marriage. Both of these stories are variants of the same exploded planet model, and both have their precedents elsewhere in pre-Christian texts.[32]

Contrary Mary

Why would the ancients have depicted Mother Earth in two such contradictory ways – as both 'virgin' and 'prostitute'? The explanation, I suggest, is very straightforward.

Many centuries ago, when the esoteric meaning of legends had been publicly 'dumbed down' by the process of anthropomorphism, initiates into the ancient mystery schools sought metaphorical literary devices which would mark forever the secret meaning of their legends. On the one hand, it could be fairly said that the planet Earth was *a virgin*, for she had not been sexually penetrated (and contaminated) by the seed of a man. On the other hand, it could equally be said that the planet Earth was *a prostitute*, for her body had been penetrated repeatedly by the various meteorite-like gods who had come down from the Sky into the Earth (think of the Sons-of-God who ravaged the daughters-of-the-earth).

In both cases, the two esoteric epithets – 'virgin' and 'prostitute' – were nonsensical in a human flesh-and-blood context, but nevertheless ignorant and weak-minded outsiders would be fooled into believing that a human being had really come forth from a human virgin, or that a human Son of God had really kissed a female prostitute on the mouth. Thus initiates into the ancient Mysteries were able to converse in public, and even write down their sacred secrets, using a coded language which veiled the celestial meaning from the ears and eyes of the profane.

So effective was this strategy that the Hebrew priests saw little harm in allowing the prostitute-like Earth-goddess to be revered in the Old Testament. The curious passage appears in the book of Isaiah, where the prophet recited the verses of what seems to have been a popular, archaic song known as *The Song of the Prostitute*:

Take up your harp, walk through the city,
O prostitute forgotten;
Play the harp well, sing many a song,
So that you will be remembered.[33]

In the context of the Old Testament, where all gods and goddesses were marginalised in deference to the all-powerful Yahweh, it was certainly the case that the Earth-goddess (and ex-Sky-goddess) *did* need to be remembered. Unfortunately, it was probably the case that the common man of the 1st millennium BC had forgotten who the 'prostitute' was.

In closing this discussion, it should be emphasised that the ancient *cognoscenti* were not at all concerned by the apparent contradictions in the epithets of the Great Goddess. On the contrary, some gnostic texts made great play of her contrary nature, knowing full well that it encapsulated the essential mystery of her existence. Consider, for example, the gnostic poem with the curious title *Thunder, Perfect Mind*, where an unnamed feminine wisdom-figure uttered the following mysterious words:

"I am the first and the last.
I am the honoured one and the scorned one.
I am the whore, and the holy one.
I am the wife and the virgin.
I am the mother and the daughter...
I am she whose wedding is great, and I have not taken a husband...
I am knowledge, and ignorance...
I am shameless; I am ashamed.
I am strength, and I am fear...
I am foolish, and I am wise...
I am godless, and I am one whose God is great."[34]

Note the lines "I am the *whore*, and the holy one. I am the wife and the *virgin*." The gnostics were in no doubt that one goddess could be both a virgin and a prostitute, for such was her contradictory nature.

I therefore put it to readers that the Virgin Mary and the prostitute Mary Magdalene were actually one-and-the-same character. And in the original form of the Christian legends, neither of them was a human being.

* * * * *

APPENDIX C
JESUS OF NAZARETH

Anyone reading the New Testament might be forgiven for thinking that Jesus Christ was a real man, who lived in Palestine of the 1st century AD, having been conceived in Nazareth and born in Bethlehem. But was this really the case?

In this book, I have concluded that the story of the crucifixion of Jesus Christ was actually a clever esoteric parable for the death of a planet, and that Jesus-the-man was probably a human actor in an ancient Passion play, which re-enacted the death of the heavenly planet (with all which that entailed). I have also suggested that the early Church found this Passion play to be the ideal vehicle for launching a new religion with widespread popular appeal. On the one hand, the story told by the Passion play preserved the essential meaning of ancient religion at an esoteric level. But on the other hand, the Passion play promoted the idea that a real human being had died and had then been restored magically to life. Or, to put it another way, the Church used the script of the Passion play to suggest that the Son of God had incarnated into human flesh right there and then – in Palestine of the 1st century AD.

Thus it was, I suggest, that the early Church (a mystery school at birth) concealed its essential Mysteries by emphasising the idea that Jesus Christ had been a human being, who had sacrificed real flesh and blood to save mankind from its sins.

Now, in order to make such a story convincing to a sceptical audience, the Church would have been compelled to set down at least a few basic facts concerning this supposed man, Jesus Christ. In particular, it would have been necessary to name his parents, along with the place where he had been born.

In Appendix B, we covered one of these points, namely that the mother of Jesus Christ had been a virgin named Mary. And I noted some intriguing correspondences between the Virgin Mary and the pagan mother-goddesses who had brought the divine child down from Heaven to Earth.

In this appendix, however, we shall take a look at the second of the two points. Where had Jesus Christ been conceived and born?

Before we proceed, let us use the knowledge which we have gained in this book to make a prediction. Imagine, for a moment, that the early Church had started in Egypt, and that the land of Egypt had been made the setting for the story of Jesus Christ's human life. Knowing what we now know about places such as Heliopolis, Abydos and Elephantine (see chapter six), we might surmise that the story would have run along one of the following lines: (a) that Mary had fled from Heliopolis to Abydos (or Elephantine) bearing the child, Jesus, in her womb, and then given birth to the child in Abydos (or Elephantine); or (b) that the father of Jesus had fled from Heliopolis to Abydos (or Elephantine), and had impregnated the priestess of that city in a sacred marriage, thus causing the child, Jesus, to be born there.

Now, even if we had not succeeded in fully decoding the celestial symbolism of these cities situated along the river Nile – Heliopolis as Heaven, and Abydos (or Elephantine) as Earth – we would still have been able to deduce the celestial significance of the two stories outlined above. How? Simply by observing that the Egyptian name of Heliopolis was Annu, meaning the 'City of Heaven', whilst the Egyptian name for Abydos was *Ab-djw*, meaning 'Mountain of the Beginning' (or alternatively, by noting that Elephantine was known as 'City of the Beginning', whilst its Egyptian name, AB or *Abu*, meant 'Father of Beginning').

Might such a scheme have existed also in the holy land during the 1st century AD? Although scholars have not as yet decoded any overall scheme between Israelite cities and celestial 'mountains' (no surprise, since they have not looked for it), I would predict that the legends of Jesus Christ might just give us some pertinent leads. More to the point, I would predict that the names of the places where Jesus was conceived and born might just contain vital clues which would corroborate our overall hypothesis that the story of the crucifixion is essentially celestial.

So, where was Jesus Christ conceived and born?

Throughout the New Testament, Jesus is referred to as 'Jesus of Nazareth' or occasionally as 'Jesus of Nazareth of Galilee'.[1] It is an epithet which was given for two reasons. Firstly, because Jesus had grown up in Nazareth, which was his home town. And secondly because it was in Nazareth that Jesus had apparently been conceived in the womb of Mary, as announced by the angel of God:

And in the sixth month the angel Gabriel was sent from God to a city of Galilee named Nazareth, to a virgin who was pledged to be married to a man named Joseph. And the virgin's name was Mary. And the angel came in to her and said: "... Fear not, Mary, for you have found favour with God. And behold, you will conceive in your womb, and bring forth a son, and will call his name 'Jesus'."[2]

This momentous event, it must be emphasised, happened in Nazareth.

And yet clearly this tradition of 'Jesus of Nazareth' entailed certain problems for the people of the 1st century AD, who were expecting a Jewish Messiah in keeping with the prophecies of the Old Testament. Thus, in the gospel of John, the people expressed deep scepticism about the idea of a Messiah having come out of Nazareth of Galilee:

Others said: "This is the Christ". But some said: "Shall Christ come out of Galilee? Does not the scripture say that Christ will come from the seed of David, and out of the town of Bethlehem, where David lived?"[3]

In order to circumvent this scepticism in the real world, the writers of the New Testament realised that they must somehow reconcile Jesus's origins in Nazareth to the Jewish prophecy of a Messiah originating from Bethlehem. Their ingenious solution was to make Jesus's place of birth separate from his place of conception – a scheme which was achieved by supposing that a Roman population census was being administered in the holy land at the town of Bethlehem.[4] This census required Mary and Joseph to travel up from Nazareth to Bethlehem, where the child, Jesus, was born (conveniently in line with the messianic prophecy) and laid in a manger.[5]

Immediately afterwards, however, Mary and Joseph returned with Jesus to their home city of Nazareth:

And when Joseph and Mary had performed all things according to the law of the Lord [i.e. the circumcision of the child], they returned into Galilee, to their own city, Nazareth. And the child grew and waxed strong in spirit, and was filled with wisdom.[6]

In summary, two places are identified in the gospels as being associated with the origin of Jesus – Nazareth and Bethlehem. The latter seems to be less important to the story, and smacks of a contrivance in order to fulfil Jewish expectations of the Messiah. We will not ignore Bethlehem (we will return to it later with a brief comment on the meaning of the name), but we will focus our investigation here on the more important Nazareth/Galilee connection. Might this location have had a celestial significance?

Immediately we hit a curious obstacle. Readers may be surprised to learn that modern scholars have questioned whether Jesus Christ really came from a place called Nazareth. They have pointed out that, if there was a place called Nazareth at the beginning of the 1st century AD, it would have been an insignificant village, and not a 'city' as is alleged in the New Testament.[7] Moreover, it seems likely that the association of Jesus with Nazareth actually stemmed from an Old Testament prophecy that did not mention 'Nazareth' as a place name but rather '*nazoraios*' as an adjective, meaning 'Nazarene'. The title 'Jesus of Nazareth' might thus be read 'Jesus the Nazarene'.

What might 'Nazarene' mean? In a recent book *Jesus – One Hundred Years Before Christ*, Professor Alvar Ellegard suggested that a 'folk etymology' had once existed among Greek-speaking Jews, which caused the term Nazarenes (*nazoraioi*) to be confused with the term Nazirites (*naziraioi*).[8] Moreover, Ellegard pointed out in passing that the latter term Nazirite meant 'a holy person, or separated one, chosen by God'.[9] If this argument is accepted, then the legends behind the gospels would be telling us that Jesus was a 'holy one' or 'separated one', with Nazareth being 'the abode of the holy, or separated one'.

Now for the missing puzzle-piece. The term Nazirite stems from the root *nzr*, or *nsr*, and it is highly significant, in my opinion, that the latter word was an ancient Egyptian verb meaning 'to burn' or 'to blaze'.[10] Hence the word *Nsrsr*, meaning 'the Island of Fire', which was given to the Egyptian underworld.[11]

The Hebrews, too, knew the underworld as a place of destruction (*Abaddon*), whilst their close neighbours, the Canaanites, knew the underworld as *Nsrt*.[12]

A similar idea is found in Mesopotamian traditions, where *nsr* meant 'salvation', and where Mount Nisir was the 'Mount of Salvation', upon which the boat of Utnapishtim had come to rest after the Flood. According to my decoding, this 'mountain' of Nisir was actually the *planet* of Earth, and the arrival of the 'boat' would indeed have brought down fire as well as flooding.[13]

It thus follows that Jesus Christ would have been known as a Nazarene, or Nazirite, on account of his mythical fall to the Mount of Salvation (*Nsr*), where he took up residence in the underworld or Island of Fire (*Nsrsr*). There, the pre-human Jesus Christ would indeed have become 'a holy person, a separated one, chosen by God'. This is the very hypothesis put forward in the latter chapters of this book.

As for the city of Nazareth, this would have been the underworld – the abode of the 'holy one', or 'separate one'. The references in the gospels to 'Jesus of Nazareth' might thus be seen as coded metaphors for the pre-human 'Jesus of the underworld'.[14]

But there is more. As has been mentioned, the city of Nazareth was closely linked to a region called Galilee, and the name Galilee (meaning 'Circuit') comes from a root meaning 'to roll, or roll away'.[15] I therefore put it to readers that the gospel references to 'Jesus of Nazareth of Galilee' actually had an esoteric meaning: 'Jesus of the Rolled-Away Abode of Fire'. This is the exploded planet cult in a nutshell.

It logically follows from this interpretation that the place known as 'Nazareth of Galilee' would have belonged to 'the above', as well as to 'the below'. In other words, the Island of Fire had originated in Heaven (in the fiery explosion of the planetary 'island'), and had then *rolled* all the way down to Earth, into the underworld.[16] The metaphysical resurrection of Heaven, or of God, or of Christ, would then have entailed rolling the fallen place known as 'Nazareth of Galilee' (the Rolled-Away Abode of Fire) all the way back up to Heaven. Significantly, this would explain why Jesus, having risen from the dead, announced that he would go ahead of his disciples into Galilee, where he would meet them on a mountain;[17] this statement makes much more sense in a celestial context than in a terrestrial context.

Incidentally, the fact that a Sea of Galilee features in the scriptures need not concern us, for the ancients believed that the fallen 'mountain of Heaven' included an ocean of water, which had become interred in the underworld of the Earth (see the adventures of Gilgamesh in chapter five of this work). It is noticeable that the Sea of Galilee was indeed mentioned in conjunction with a mountain. In Matthew 15:29, for example, it is said that 'Jesus came to the Sea of Galilee and went up into a mountain'. The statement is eerily reminiscent of the Sumerian Kings List, where Meskiaggasher, the first king of Uruk, 'entered the sea and came out to the mountain'.[18] The latter reference is definitely celestial, and the former reference may well have been celestial too (or rather *the origin* of this saying might well have existed in a celestial context).

As predicted, then, the home town of Jesus – Nazareth of Galilee – bears all the hallmarks of *a celestial location*, and the reason for this, I suggest, is that the story of the crucifixion of Jesus Christ is actually the age-old story about the death of a planet, and *not* a brand-new story about the death of a human being.

What, then, of Bethlehem, the place where Jesus was born? As noted earlier, the mention of Bethlehem in the gospels seems to be contrived in order to fulfil the Jewish expectations of the Messiah. Nevertheless, the meaning of the name 'Bethlehem' is 'House of Bread', which is highly significant in the context of bread symbolism in the legends and traditions of ancient Egypt and Mesopotamia, as well as in the gospels themselves.[19] In short, without going into a long-winded explanation, the House of Bread would have symbolised either Heaven (if the bread was risen and intact) or the underworld of the Earth (if the bread was broken or sliced).[20]

Now, all of this might be regarded as idle speculation were it not for the remarkable similarities which exist between Jesus Christ and the Egyptian god Osiris – the Lord of the Underworld and hence the dweller in the Island of Fire. And these similarities are as detailed as they are broad. To cite but one example, the gospel of John records the injury inflicted upon the crucified Jesus Christ as follows:

> One of the soldiers pierced *his side* with a spear, and immediately *blood and water flowed out.*[21]

Compare this curious tradition to the almost identical injury sustained by Osiris, as recorded in Spell 74 of the Coffin Texts:

> [Isis says to Nephthys:] "Come, that we may raise his head. Come, that we may reassemble his bones. Come, that we may rearrange his members. Come, that we may make a dam *in his side... there drips the efflux* which has issued from this spirit."[22]

Some might see this as an astounding coincidence, but the more plausible explanation is that the Christian and Egyptian legends are related, for they both describe the death of the same ex-planetary god.

It is appropriate to close this appendix with a two-thousand-year-old joke from the gospel of John, which has long passed unnoticed. In order to get this joke, we must recall the ancient philosophy that mankind came forth from the underworld as sinners. The amusing 'one-liner' was delivered by Nathanael, upon hearing from Philip that the Messiah had been discovered, and bore the remarkable name 'Jesus of Nazareth':

> "What?" said Nathanael: "Can anything good ever come out of Nazareth?"[23]

He who has ears to hear, let him hear.

* * * * *

APPENDIX D
JESUS AND JOHN THE BAPTIST

In the gospels of the New Testament, the coming of Jesus Christ was prefigured by John the Baptist, who went baptising through the land of Judea crying "Repent, for the kingdom of Heaven is at hand", and warning that one greater than he would soon be baptising mankind with the Holy Spirit and with fire.[1] But shortly after this mission began, John the Baptist was imprisoned by Herod Antipas and his role was assumed by Jesus Christ, who began to baptise and preach in the same vein, uttering the very same words: "Repent, for the kingdom of Heaven is at hand".[2] After this, the gospels focus on the story of Jesus Christ, and as for John the Baptist we learn only of his ultimate decapitation, when his head was delivered on a platter to Salome, the stepdaughter of Herod.

Was John the Baptist a real person, or a mythical figure? As suggested in chapter thirteen of this book, it is entirely plausible that baptisms were taking place in 1st century Judea; the immersion in water, I noted, was symbolic of a celestial baptism of mankind's primeval ancestors in the underworld, and it prepared flesh-and-blood men for the final baptism to come. It is thus quite conceivable that a John-the-Baptist-like figure was indeed preparing the people of Judea for the expected end of the world.

The Bible itself, for what it is worth, asserts categorically that John the Baptist was among 'those born of women', i.e. that he was a real human being.[3] In addition, Jesus reportedly suggested that John the Baptist was 'the Elijah who was to come' – i.e. the flesh-and-blood prophet who was supposed to herald the End of Days.[4] In the gospel of John, however, John the Baptist *specifically denied* that he was 'Elijah' or 'the Prophet'.[5] Instead, he identified himself cryptically as "the voice of him that crieth in the wilderness: 'Make straight the highway of the Lord'."[6] This was a direct reference to the words of the prophet Isaiah, spoken during the 8th century BC.

Now, in chapter thirteen, I noted that 'the wilderness' was a Hebrew code-word for the underworld, and I thus identified the mysterious voice as that of the Righteous Servant – a fallen celestial figure – who had been trapped in the underworld for an eternity. So, might there be more to the story of John the Baptist? Was a real man decapitated in the prison of Herod Antipas, or might the story be understood at an esoteric level?

Let us briefly summarise what we know about John the Baptist from the biblical record.

Firstly, we are told that John the Baptist was 'a man sent from God', who was sent into the world to testify concerning the coming 'light' of Jesus Christ.[7] The suggestion that John the Baptist had been sent '*from God*' tends to imply that he had, in some way, been sent *from Heaven*, as had Jesus Christ himself.[8]

Secondly, Jesus himself revealed that John the Baptist had been 'a burning and shining light', in which the people had rejoiced for a while.[9] This echoes the description of Jesus himself as 'the Light', albeit Jesus was described as 'the true light'.[10]

Thirdly, the gospel of Luke informs us that the birth of John the Baptist was the result of a divine intervention, when the angel Gabriel opened the womb of Elisabeth – a woman who was afflicted by old age and thus barren.[11]

Fourthly, we are told that 'the child grew and waxed strong in spirit, and was in the wilderness till the day of his showing to Israel'.[12]

Fifthly, to state the obvious, John's career was that of a baptist, and he identified himself as "the voice of him that crieth in the wilderness: 'Make straight the highway of the Lord'." One way or another, John the Baptist was a character whose key role was to anticipate the coming of the kingdom of God.

Sixthly, biblical legend has it that John the Baptist was imprisoned by Herod Antipas, presumably in a subterranean dungeon. And there he was decapitated in order to fulfil the wishes of Salome, the stepdaughter of Herod.[13] It should be noted that the incident which followed – the presentation of the decapitated head on the platter – became an important Grail theme.[14] The legend also indicates that John's head was worth half of Herod's kingdom.[15]

Taking all of these points together, there is good reason to suspect that the story of John the Baptist – just like the story of Jesus Christ – had an esoteric and celestial dimension, with John being a god-like figure sent forth from Heaven into the underworld ('wilderness') of the Earth, where he had waited patiently for the coming of the kingdom of God (just like the Righteous Servant of the Old Testament).

But if this was so, would this primeval John the Baptist not be identical to the primeval Jesus Christ?

Significantly, during the latter half of the 20th century, several biblical scholars began to air the possibility that there had once been a Church of John, which had been occulted by the rise of Christianity (effectively the Church of Jesus) during the 1st century AD. The various pieces of evidence and arguments were eloquently summarised in the 1997 'bestseller' *The Templar Revelation* by the popular writers Lynn Picknett and Clive Prince.

In their book, Picknett and Prince cited authorities such as Geza Vermes, Edwin Yamauchi, Carl H. Kraeling, Robert L. Webb, Hugh Schonfield, and A. N. Wilson, who were in turn citing early Church sources.[16] The upshot of all this various research was the conclusion that a whole corpus of 'John literature' had once existed, testifying to the belief that John the Baptist (and not Jesus) had been the Messiah. The case had been summed up neatly by Hugh Schonfield as follows:

> Contact with followers of John the Baptist... acquainted the Christians with the nativity stories of John, in which he figured as the infant Messiah of the priestly traditions, born at Bethlehem.[17]

> We are made aware from Christian sources that there was a considerable Jewish sect in rivalry with the followers of Jesus, who held that John the Baptist was the true Messiah...[18]

One of the most interesting texts cited by scholars was the apocryphal Book of James (known also as the Protoevangelium) which described the familiar story of the birth of Jesus, followed by Herod's orders to massacre all the baby boys in Bethlehem and its vicinity. However, the Book of James then went on to reveal that Herod was looking for the baby John rather than Jesus, and it described Elisabeth, the mother of John, fleeing with her child into the hills.[19] Another point worth noting is that scholars have attributed the Song of Mary (the *Magnificat*, from Luke chapter 1) to Elisabeth, and have suggested that it is but one of several 'John legends' which were rewritten to support the cult of Jesus.[20]

Picknett and Prince, accepting implicitly the assumption that Jesus Christ and John the Baptist were human (and nothing but human), concluded by suggesting that the two figures had become bitter personal rivals in 1st century Judea. But might this rivalry have stemmed instead from two cults which regarded Jesus and John not as men but as rival god-like saviours? After all, the similarities between the two figures are extensive; both were 'men' sent into the world by God via miraculous births; both were associated with 'light'; both preached that the end of the world was nigh; both baptised; and, perhaps most significantly, both were mistreated and killed by those who failed to recognise their divine status.[21] Nor was the relationship with Mary Magdalene exclusive to Jesus, for heretical tradition supposed that this prostitute (identified as Mother Earth in the preceding Appendix) also had a close relationship with John the Baptist.[22] All in all, one cannot help but suspect that the legends of Jesus Christ and John the Baptist were based on an identical mythology, which described the same god (or Son of God).

But might there be even more to it than this? Once we grasp the basic scheme of the birth of the infant Messiah, and once we grasp the role of the Virgin Mary as a goddess who came down from Heaven and assumed the mantle of Mother Earth, the birth legend in Luke chapter 1 literally explodes with significance:

> And Mary arose in those days [after being promised a child by the angel Gabriel] and went with haste into the hill country, into a city of Juda. And she entered into the house of Zacharias and greeted Elisabeth. And it came to pass that, when Elisabeth heard the greeting of Mary, the babe leapt in her womb; and Elisabeth was filled with the Holy Spirit.[23]

Could it be that Mary's journey into the hill country denoted an interplanetary journey from Heaven to Earth? Could it be that Mary passed across the celestial river carrying her babe (the future Messiah) in her celestial 'womb'? And could it be that when the falling Mary split open the Earth, the mythical infant then leaped, literally, out of Mary's 'womb' into the 'womb' of Elisabeth, who personified Mother Earth? Far from being fanciful, this scenario would be totally in accordance with the pagan understanding of the exploded planet cult and the birth of the Messiah in the depths of the Earth. And the astonishing implication is that two celestial 'mothers' were involved in bearing a single infant Messiah. We might then hazard a guess that Jesus and John were one-and-the-same mythical character, with the two different names perhaps denoting two different aspects of the same divine child (perhaps the above and the below, or alternatively the soul and the body).

But even this might not be the end of a story which has been largely occulted from the New Testament as we know it. If the reader is willing to allow for the possibility that a number of different traditions have been merged in the gospels, then there exists yet another extraordinary possibility concerning the apparent rivalry between the cults of Jesus and John – a possibility which would explain virtually all of the esoteric codes which have been developed around these two figures during the past two millennia.[24]

Unfortunately, the explanation of this possibility requires a detailed discussion of matters which have not been addressed in this book, but which appear in my previous book, *The Phoenix Solution.*[25] Such a discussion is hardly practical within the space constraints of these appendices, and in any event I fear that to discuss such matters here would only cause confusion in the minds of the vast majority of readers. Suffice to say that the explanation involves an area of specialist expertise in a rather obscure field of esoteric symbolism. Any readers wishing to investigate these matters further should send a specific enquiry, by email, to the address cited in the Author's Closing Comments at the end of this book.

In the meantime, however, for those readers who have eyes to see and perceive, I will suggest that this rather complex solution to the Jesus-and-John mystery can be identified in the modern Templar saying: "He who owns the head of John the Baptist rules the world".[26] And, for a big clue as to what that saying means, consider carefully the following legend from ancient Egypt, which records what happened several periods after the creator-god Neber-Djer (alias Atum) had descended from Heaven to Earth. Neber-Djer explains what happened next in his own words:

"Shu and Tefnut were raised up out of the inert watery mass where they were, and they brought to me my Eye... I gathered together my members and I wept over them, and men and women sprang into being from the tears which came forth from my Eye. And when my Eye came to me and found I had made another [Eye] in place of it, it raged at me, whereupon I endowed it with some of the splendour which I had made for the first [Eye], and I made it to occupy its place in my Face, and henceforth it ruled throughout all this Earth."[27]

* * * * *

APPENDIX E
PONTIUS PILATE

Perhaps the most prominent individual figure in the New Testament story of the crucifixion of Jesus Christ, other than Christ himself, is Pontius Pilate, the Roman governor of Judea, who reluctantly handed over Jesus for crucifixion, and later delivered his body to Joseph of Arimathea.[1]

In the *Annals* of Tacitus – one of the few independent confirmations of the Christian story – Pontius Pilate was also mentioned prominently:

> Christus, the founder of the name [of Christianity] had undergone the death penalty in the reign of Tiberius, by sentence of the procurator Pontius Pilate...[2]

Little is known about Pontius Pilate other than what is recorded in the biblical tradition, but enough snippets of information have been passed down over the centuries to suggest that he was a real flesh-and-blood person, who did govern 1st century Judea, and who eventually killed himself in AD 39, on the orders of the Roman emperor Caligula.

But might there be more to it? According to popular belief, Pontius Pilate's name derived from his status as a Roman knight of the Samnite clan of the Pontii.[3] But why was a group of knights called 'Pontii', and what exactly does 'Pontius Pilate' mean?

A quick look at a Latin-English dictionary reveals some intriguing possibilities. Firstly, there is the word *pons*, meaning 'bridge' or 'the gangway of a ship'; secondly, there is the word *pontus*, meaning 'sea'; thirdly, and most revealing of all, there is the word *pontifex*, meaning 'high priest' (*pontifex* meant literally 'to make a bridge').[4] As for the name Pilate, its Latin meaning is not at all clear, but it is difficult to ignore the connection to the English word 'pilot', which derives from the French *pilote* and the Medieval Latin *pilotus*.[5]

In Roman times, it would seem that the government of the state was compared to the piloting of a ship, hence the word *gubernaculum*, which simultaneously meant 'government', 'rudder' and 'helm'.[6] Might this tradition derive from the age-old pagan tradition of mankind's descent from Heaven, across the *ocean* of space?

Earlier in this book, we noted that the river Tiber (which flowed through Rome) had a celestial counterpart – hence the legend that the flooding river Tiber had carried Romulus and Remus in their 'trough' to the foot of the Capitoline 'hill'. In the light of this, it is perhaps time to reconsider the fact that the Roman emperor, in the days of Pontius Pilate, was named Tiberius. Might this name have signified the celestial river Tiber and the old pagan idea of a kingship descended from Heaven?

It is indeed curious that the Sea of Galilee (a fallen planetary ocean according to the decoding in Appendix C) was also known as 'Lake Tiberias', implying a mythical connection between the two bodies of water.[7] It is even more curious that Mount Pilatus in Switzerland is so named according to the tradition that Pontius Pilate was buried in a former lake on the mountain.[8]

Might Tiberius's governors of the state – men such as Pontius Pilate – have been modelled upon ancient boat-navigators (such as the Sumerian *apkallu*) who conducted the gods from Heaven to Earth?[9] If so, the name Pontius Pilate might have meant something like 'pilot of the bridge', i.e. of the bridge (*pons*) over the sea (*pontus*). I would thus propose that the real Pontius Pilate of the 1st century AD was appointed in the image of a mythical archetype – a Pontius Pilate from the beginning of time.

Let us close this Appendix with a vivid example of how an ancient pilot navigated his way across a bridge which spanned the celestial sea. In *Enuma Elish*, Tablet VII, we read how the vanquished corpse of the goddess Tiamat was conveyed down from Heaven to the underworld of the Earth by a god named SIR.SIR:

> SIR.SIR, who heaped up a mountain over Tiamat,
> Who carried off the body of Tiamat with his weapon...
> Who crossed the wide and turbulent sea,
> As a bridge crosses over the place of conflict.
> SIR.SIR, he was also named MALAH...
> Tiamat is his vessel and he is the navigator.[10]

Did a mythical Pontius Pilate provide a similar service for the body of the primeval Jesus Christ, when he was crucified in Heaven and cast down into the Earth? If so, we might well say that Pontius Pilate lay himself down as 'a bridge over troubled water'.

* * * * *

AUTHOR'S CLOSING COMMENTS

When I finished writing this book, and sat back to reflect on the journey I had covered and the conclusions I had reached, I experienced (I must confess) a rather peculiar feeling. It was as if I knew everything, but nothing; as if I had answered all of my questions, and yet questions still remained; it was as if I was full, but at the same time empty.

Why did I feel this way? The answer, I think, is twofold.

Firstly, there is a lot more to life than resolving the mystery of our ancestors' religion. Yes, they worshipped exploded planets, but this leaves us none the wiser concerning life's ultimate questions, such as: 'who are we?', 'what is human consciousness?', 'do we have a soul?', and if so 'what happens to our souls when our bodies die?'. These are timeless questions which have been asked by *Homo sapiens* for hundreds of thousands of years – questions which make us human, and distinguish us from other organisms on this planet. I did not have the answers to these questions, and almost certainly I never will have.

Secondly, I felt empty because I was left holding no particular religious belief. Not that I had any religious belief to begin with – but nonetheless there was something distinctly anticlimactic about decoding the profound beliefs of our ancestors and yet being unable fully to endorse them. The problem here is that I personally view 'religious belief' as a fool's paradise, because it involves a belief, or faith, in something which is, by definition, unknown. I, on the other hand – as one who aspires to the status of *Homo religiosus sapiens* – search not for 'religious *belief*' but rather for 'religious *knowledge*'. And the fact is that it cannot be proven at the present time whether planets did, or did not, explode in our solar system, and therefore, regrettably, the essential ethos of ancient religion must be classified, for the moment at least, as a myth.

What if that situation were changed by new astronomical data? Would I be able to embrace the religion of our ancestors in the same sense that they did? Perhaps not, for I am not ready, at the present time, to accept the Gaea hypothesis – that planets are living beings, with a planetary body and a planetary soul. The Gaea hypothesis does seem attractive, intuitively, but how can we *know* whether it is true?

These, then, are the reasons why I felt such a strange sense of emptiness when I finished writing this book.

Several weeks later, however, I began to grow accustomed to this sensation, and the feeling of emptiness went away. Having initially suffered some disorientation, I began to warm to a sensation which was not so much an empty heart and stomach, but rather two lungs full of fresh air. A whole fog of confusion had been lifted; old intellectual junk (old *emotional* junk to many people) had been thrown out of the attic, and a fresh start had been made. I was segregating in my mind the facts from the fiction, and focusing on what was really important. I knew instinctively that, even though I did not have all the answers, I had at least begun to ask the right questions, and moreover I knew that I was on the right track – wherever it might lead me.

Many of my readers will experience these same feelings and indeed even stronger feelings, such as shock, panic, denial, anger, resentment – the list goes on. These are perfectly understandable human reactions to the revelations in this book. But when all these high emotions have subsided, we must come to terms with the facts of the situation and try not to blame any individual person for what is really, to my mind, an inherited systemic problem. Each of us must, of course, deal with our feelings in our own individual ways, but if there is one single piece of advice I might offer, it is this: that we have all been living in the age of *Homo religiosus* – the man who needs to believe in something 'other', or who has been conditioned to think that he needs to believe in that something 'other'; but a small number of us are now beginning to experience a transition to *Homo religiosus sapiens*, and it is entirely appropriate therefore that we should not believe in any particular religious construct at the present time; perhaps it is right to sit on the fence until we have true religious knowledge; perhaps this 'rational non-belief' (to coin a phrase) is a vast improvement on what went before; perhaps this rational non-belief is the beginning of wisdom.

In fact, I suggest that there is no 'perhaps' about it. The transition from *Homo religiosus* to *Homo religiosus sapiens is* a positive step forward and the transition pains are both inevitable and worthwhile. Yes, we are stepping into a zone of discomfort, but those who do so will be the best placed to benefit from the rewards it will bring. New religious horizons are beckoning for 21st century men and women. It is time for pioneers to explore those new horizons with a fresh set of charts.

The Status of the Argument

In closing this book, it behoves me to say a few words concerning the status of the arguments contained within it.

Firstly, it should be noted that the overall argument contained in these pages amounts to what is known in scholarly circles as a 'controlled study'. This means that it is not just a study of one ancient religion – which might make it vulnerable to an error of interpretation – but is a study of two quite separate and independent religions. To put it crudely, the Mesopotamian scribes back up what the Egyptian scribes said, and the Egyptian scribes back up what the Mesopotamian scribes said. This element of control is very important; it increases the reliability of the results disproportionately, and allows the conclusion of the study to be expressed with a much higher confidence level.

Admittedly, the conclusion is a shocking and controversial revelation, which challenges fundamentally the accepted views concerning Judaeo-Christian theology. But that is not sufficient reason to dismiss it. Indeed, one of the remarkable things about this book, it seems to me, is that it contains (if I might say so myself) barely a single piece of evidence, or a single line of reasoning, that is controversial *in itself*. It is only when all of these lines of evidence and reasoning are followed through to their natural conclusions that we end up with something so very controversial.

It should be noted, however, that a shocking and controversial revelation is *exactly* what we would expect to find, if we place any credence in the ancient mystery schools and the numerous clues which they have dropped to us over the past three thousand years.

In the Orphic Mysteries, for example, the final level of initiation comprised a 'Secret-of-secrets' which was a knowledge of 'the true God'. But such was the nature of this Secret-of-secrets that it came as a *total surprise*, even to the initiate who was fully prepared. The revelation, we are told, 'startled their ears' and 'overturned their preconceived opinions'.

Although the mystery schools were deliberately vague about their beliefs (unlike the Egyptians and Sumerians), their various sayings and indeed the very existence of these societies-with-secrets confirm that *something very important* was being withheld from the public domain. As to the nature of that 'something', we know for certain that it was to do with a bright light entering into the darkness of the underworld, and yet we are also informed that the Sun was merely *a symbol* of a mysterious higher being, who was known as 'the true God'. Today, that 'true God' is known by freemasons as 'the light in the east', the 'blazing star' and

'The Great Architect of the Universe' (i.e. Heaven and Earth).

In summary, it surely cannot be doubted that we are on the right track in postulating a deeper meaning to the ancient Egyptian and Mesopotamian religions.

Is an exploded planet the answer? Unless we entertain the possibility that the disintegrating 'mountain' and the light entering the underworld was a comet – an idea which I reject, for the reasons cited in chapter four – it is difficult to see what other possible explanation might exist to account for the gods who came down from Heaven to Earth. (It is, of course, essential to realise that the ancients did not actually witness a planet exploding, but merely reasoned that such an explosion must have occurred millions of years in the past.) This does not mean, of course, that a further explanation (as yet unpublished) does not exist, and readers should ponder on this possibility, as I myself have done at length. Readers should also form their own conclusions regarding the various other 'explanations' which have been proffered by modern academia to account for 'the gods' – ideas such as weather-gods, human heroes or ancient astronauts.

Doubtless there will be some critics (most likely those with vested interests) who try to weaken the impact of this book by dismissing it as "just a theory". But is it really 'a theory', or is it rather 'an explanation'? (For there is a considerable difference between these two terms.)

It should be emphasised that the dictionary definition of 'a theory' refers to a plan formulated in the mind only – a plan which involves speculation and abstract knowledge or reasoning, where 'speculation' involves hazarding guesses based on insufficient facts. Based on this definition, this book *might* be regarded as 'a theory' if we knew a lot less than we do about ancient Egypt and Mesopotamia, or if we were a lot less confident in our translations of the ancient texts. If this were so, the status of this book would indeed drop to that of a speculative theory – *based on insufficient knowledge*.

This, however, is *not* the case. As readers will discover for themselves if they embark on even the most cursory of studies, our knowledge of ancient Egypt and Mesopotamia is in fact both detailed and broad, in the field of archaeology as well as in mythology. It should thus be appreciated that the mystery of 'the gods' *is* there to be *explained*, and the exploded planet cult should therefore be taken very seriously as an *explanation* of that mystery.

Indeed, at the present time, the exploded planet cult stands alone, in my opinion, as the only bona fide explanation of ancient mythology; for as I have argued throughout this book, the various schemes promoted by academia do not actually *explain* the ancient mysteries at all, but rather leave a myriad of important points unresolved.

How to judge whether a 'theory' merits the status of an 'explanation'? And how to judge whether an explanation is a 'better' or 'best' explanation? In 1997, the Egyptologist Lanny Bell cited the following useful criteria:

> The broader the conceptual argument, the greater the potential for finding further evidence. The success of a hypothesis must be measured by its internal consistency, its experiential probability, and its ability to account for all the relevant data and to identify and integrate related phenomena.

My argument is indeed broad. It spans the various disciplines of ancient Near Eastern studies, as well as Old Testament studies, New Testament studies, and Greek and Roman theologies. But the nature of my argument is such that we should not be surprised to find corroboration of the exploded planet cult in the ancient cultures of the Far East, or Africa, or Europe, or the Americas. The potential for finding further evidence – whether for, or against, the exploded planet cults – is thus vast.

I, for my part, am continuing to research the mysteries of the past with an open mind, but have already established promising results in some of the most challenging fields, such as the mysteries of Atlantis and the Holy Grail (these subjects will be reported upon in due course). These are the kinds of testing grounds upon which the exploded planet cult is already proving its worth – 'accounting for all the relevant data, and identifying and integrating related phenomena', as Lanny Bell put it.

But the testing ground, ultimately, is vast – almost limitless – and I cannot possibly carry out single-handed all of the research which needs to be done. This is where you, the reader, have the chance to contribute. You may keep up to date with the progress of my research by visiting my website **http://www.eridu.co.uk**, and if there is any information which you wish to share, or any point you wish to make (for or against any of my arguments), or any way in which you feel you can help in expanding the boundaries of our knowledge of the past, then please send me an email at the following address: **alford@eridu.co.uk**.

I will leave readers on a note of optimism, with the words of the 19th century French savant Victor Hugo:

> **There is one thing more powerful than all the armies in the world, and that is an idea whose time has come.**

* * * * *

ACKNOWLEDGEMENTS

As with my previous book, I must begin my acknowledgements by paying tribute to my wife, Sumu, who has endured utterly ridiculous working hours on my part during the eighteen-month period of conception and delivery of this literary 'baby' (as we sometimes jokingly call it). The best way I can thank Sumu for her amazing patience, understanding and support is by trying to restore some balance to our lives, and by not letting this crazy situation ever happen again! I trust that my readers will show similar patience and understanding in the future, should my rate of literary productivity decline somewhat!

Secondly, I would like to thank, once again, my parents, hoping that they will still remember me after my last eighteen months of near-isolation. It was they who brought me up to be curious and open-minded, and they who sent me off on school educational cruises from the age of twelve, even though they could ill afford to do so. How might things have turned out differently, one wonders, if I had not visited the pyramids of Egypt at the tender age of fourteen? Most importantly, however, my parents must be acknowledged for bringing me up free of the kind of religious programming which has held back the intellectual development of so many millions of children and, by implication, society collectively.

Thirdly, I would like to thank someone that I have met only briefly – a Swiss writer named Erich von Daniken. It was he who captured my imagination as a young man, and inspired my quest for the truth about 'the day when the gods came down'. Even if von Daniken's theories about the gods are wrong (and I am now certain that they are), the fact is that his bold and open-minded thinking highlighted numerous anomalies in the orthodox 'explanations'. If scholars had taken von Daniken seriously back in the late 1960s, then they might well have discovered for themselves, at that time, the solution which I have presented, thirty years later, in this book. There must be a moral somewhere in this tale.

Fourthly, I must acknowledge the remarkable work of dozens of men and women whom I have never met, namely those who performed minor miracles in the study of ancient Near Eastern cultures during the last two hundred years. I refer not only to archaeologists, but also to the handful of scholars who deciphered the mysterious writing systems of the ancients. Readers need only look through the Plates section of this book to realise that these scholars performed a most amazing and heroic feat, for which society has paid them far too little credit.

Fifthly, I must acknowledge Tom Van Flandern, whose investigations into comets and asteroids provided the vital template (the exploded planet hypothesis) for decoding the ancient way of thinking.

Sixthly, I would like to thank all those people at Hodder & Stoughton who have been involved in the publication of this book and my earlier works. A special mention is due to my editor Roland Philipps, whose wise counsel has been greatly appreciated, and also to my former editor Nick Austin, who so crucially brought me in to the Hodder stable.

Seventhly, I must express my appreciation to Jon East and Andrew Whitting of ICOMM Technologies for their continuing moral as well as technical support.

Finally, a special 'thank you' is due to Victor Clube for his vigorous participation in our many friendly arguments, which have helped (and continue to help) shape my views as to what actually transpired so many thousands of years ago in the sky, on the ground, and in the minds of our ancestors.

Photographic Acknowledgements – Captions and Credits
1-4, 8-10, 25, 26, 30-31 Copyright The British Museum (1 seal 89589; 2 tablet K-3473; 3 seal 103317; 4 seal 89089; 8 seal 89110; 9 seal 89115; 10 seal UR-9750; 25 tablet 78941; 26 tablet K-3375; 30 tablet K-3401; 31 tablet 93016 reverse).
5, 33 Copyright The Oriental Institute of the University of Chicago (5 P23277, cylinder seal from Tell Asmar; 33 P29063, Oriental Inst. painting no. P28752).
11 Copyright Photo RMN, H. Lewandowski (Stele de la Victoire de Naram-Sin, Louvre).
16, 24 Copyright Bildarchiv Preussischer Kulturbesitz (16 seal VA 243/F2; 24 tablet KAR4; both from Vorderasiatisches Museum).
20 Copyright Wally Motloch (statue of Khafre, Cairo Museum).
22 Copyright Bibliotheque nationale de France (94/A69978, engraving by A. Durer).
23, 32 Copyright University of Pennsylvania Museum, Philadelphia (23 Negative no. S8-6818; 32 Negative no. S8-22065).
29 Copyright Ashmolean Museum, Oxford (1923.444 Prism, King List).
41 Copyright Robert Bauval.
All other photographs were taken by the author (**6-7, 12-15, 19, 28, 36** British Museum).

Illustration Acknowledgements
1 Copyright Robert Bauval (acknowledgements to Robin Cook).

NOTES AND BIBLIOGRAPHY

CHAPTER ONE: WHAT'S THE SECRET?

1 The site of ancient Assur is now marked by the modern town of Qal'at Sharqat. For details of Andrae's excavations, see: W. Andrae, *Das Wiedererstandene Assur*, Leipzig, 1938; the updated edition thereof, Munich 1977; and W. Andrae, *Die Archaischen Ischtar-Temple in Assur*, Leipzig, 1922.

2 A. Heidel, *The Babylonian Genesis*, University of Chicago Press, 2nd ed., 1951, pp. 68-71.

3 Ibid., pp. 69-70.

4 Ibid., p. 68. Ulligarra and Zalgarra are identified as gods by the sign for deity ('dingir') placed before each of their names.

5 Ibid., pp. 70-1.

6 Ibid., p. 69; for the translation 'Flesh-Producer', see T. Jacobsen, *The Treasures of Darkness*, Yale University Press, 1976, p. 103.

7 A. Heidel, *The Babylonian Genesis*, op. cit., p. 71.

8 Ibid., p. 71 footnote 62.

9 A useful summary of the Mysteries, in respect of ancient Egypt, appears in E. A. Wallis Budge, *From Fetish to God in Ancient Egypt*, Oxford University Press, 1934, pp. 24-6, 504.

10 Herodotus, *History*, Book II, trans. G. Rawlinson, New York, 1941. Elsewhere in *History*, Book II, Herodotus wrote in coded language as if he were himself an initiate into the ancient Mysteries, saying 'whoever has been initiated into the Mysteries of the Cabiri will understand what I mean'.

11 Plutarch, cited in R. H. Brown, *Stellar Theology and Masonic Astronomy*, Truth Seeker Co., 1997 ed., p. 194.

12 Plutarch, *The History of Isis and Osiris*, cited in E. A. Wallis Budge, *Legends of the Egyptian Gods*, 1912, Dover edition 1994, p. 232. The cleaved tree-trunk was wrapped in torn-up pieces of linen, and doused in sacred oil. There is a close connection here to the legendary tree of Byblos, the wood of which was kept in the temple at Byblos according to Plutarch; see Wallis Budge, ibid., p. 222. For the meaning of the cut-down tree motif, see later references in this book, especially the legend of Osiris being enclosed in a tree, which was cooked at one end, burnt in the middle, and filled with the pains of death.

13 M. Eliade, *A History of Religious Ideas*, Volume 1, University of Chicago Press, 1978, p. 294.

14 Compare this drought to that caused by the Akkadian goddess Ishtar when she descended into the underworld: 'Since Ishtar has gone down to the Mountain of No Return, the bull springs not upon the cow, the ass impregnates not the jenny, in the street the man impregnates not the maiden.' The similar theme suggests that the temple into which Demeter retired was the Earth.

15 M. Eliade, *A History of Religious Ideas*, Volume 1, op. cit., p. 298.

16 Ibid.

17 Ibid., p. 297. Compare the saying in the Jewish Talmud that 'God hath three keys: of rain, of birth, and of rising of the dead.'

18 E. Pagels, *The Gnostic Gospels*, Penguin Books, 1979, p. 146.

19 Ibid., p. 64.
20 Ibid., p. 15.
21 Ibid.
22 Cited in M. Baigent et al, *The Holy Blood and the Holy Grail*, Corgi Books, 1983, p. 335.
23 *The History of Christianity*, Lion Publishing, Oxford, 1990 ed., pp. 29-30.
24 But the word 'mystery' appears only five times in the rest of the Bible.
25 Letter to the Corinthians I 15:51-3.
26 See Letter to the Ephesians 3:4, 5:32, 6:19; and Letter to the Colossians 2:2.
27 *Insight on the Scriptures*, Volume II, Watchtower, 1988, p. 836.
28 See K. Armstrong, *A History of God*, Mandarin, 1994, p. 244.
29 Acts of Apostles 9:2.
30 Letter to the Philippians 4:12, translation per *Insight*, Volume II, op. cit., p. 836.
31 E. Pagels, *The Gnostic Gospels*, op. cit., p. 109.
32 Ibid., p. 62.
33 Ibid. See also Letter to the Corinthians I 2:6, where Paul said: 'we speak wisdom among those who are perfect' (i.e. mature/initiated).
34 Letter to the Corinthians I 2:7, and Letter to the Corinthians II 12:4.
35 E. Pagels, *The Gnostic Gospels*, op. cit., p. 45.
36 Matthew 16:17.
37 K. Armstrong, *A History of God*, op. cit., p. 98. This seems to be a general consensus. *Insight*, Volume II, op. cit., p. 1001, states that: 'Jesus's application of this expression to himself clearly showed that God's son was now indeed a human, having "become flesh", having "come to be out of a woman"... (he) was a "son of mankind" through his human mother.'
38 John 3:13.
39 Mark 9:32.
40 Luke 9:45.
41 Mark 4:10-12.
42 Cited in R. W. Noone, *5/5/2000 Ice: The Ultimate Disaster*, Three Rivers Press, 1982, p. 223.
43 Ibid.
44 E. Pagels, *The Gnostic Gospels*, op. cit., p. 44.
45 Matthew 13:34-5. Compare Psalm 78:2.
46 Letter to the Corinthians I 2:7.
47 Letter to the Ephesians 3:9.
48 Letter to the Romans 16:25. See also the reference in Letter to the Colossians 1:26: 'the mystery which hath been hidden from ages and from generations, but now is made manifest...'
49 Luke 8:5-8.
50 M. Eliade, *A History of Religious Ideas*, Volume 1, op. cit., p. 365.
51 Ibid., p. 291.
52 Ibid., p. 293 footnote 2.
53 Ibid., p. 290.
54 K. Armstrong, *A History of God*, op. cit., p. 47.
55 E. Pagels, *The Gnostic Gospels*, op. cit., p. 18.
56 R. H. Brown, *Stellar Theology and Masonic Astronomy*, Truth Seeker Co., 1997 ed., p. 31.
57 Ibid., pp. 31-2.
58 M. Eliade, *A History of Religious Ideas*, Volume 1, op. cit., p. xiv.
59 L. Apuleius, *Metamorphoses*, cited in Brown, *Stellar Theology and Masonic Astronomy*, op. cit., p. 11. The 'gods beneath' are, of course, the gods of the underworld, whilst the reference to 'the Sun at midnight' is an allusion to the Sun shining in the underworld, at the opposite of its midday zenith.
60 R. H. Brown, *Stellar Theology and Masonic Astronomy*, op. cit., pp. 6-7, 10, 31.
61 M. Eliade, *A History of Religious Ideas*, Volume 1, op. cit., p. 296.
62 R. H. Brown, *Stellar Theology and Masonic Astronomy*, op. cit., pp. 16-18.
63 Ibid., pp. 12-13.
64 Ibid., pp. 10-11. The candidate was thus symbolically 'reborn'.
65 John 1:4-5.
66 Luke 1:77.
67 John 12:36.

68 Clement, letter to Theodore, cited in C. Knight & R. Lomas, *The Hiram Key,* Arrow Books, 1997, p. 89.

69 R. H. Brown, *Stellar Theology and Masonic Astronomy*, op. cit., pp. 64, 220.

70 Ibid., p. 220, though this is disputed, see p. 225. Some researchers believe that the word 'masonry' derives from the Greek *mesouraneo*, meaning 'I am in the midst of heaven'; see my own comments on this in chapter 4 of this work.

71 C. Knight & R. Lomas, *The Hiram Key,* Arrow Books, 1997, p. 243. Various correspondents have confirmed for me that this calendar does exist; there are scattered references to 4000 BC throughout the masonic writings.

72 C. Knight & R. Lomas, *The Hiram Key,* op. cit., pp. 8-9. The initiate is asked whether he freely and voluntarily offers himself as a candidate 'for *the mysteries* and privileges of freemasonry'.

73 G. de Santillana & H. von Dechend, *Hamlet's Mill*, David R. Godine, 1969, p. 114.

74 R. Temple, *The Sirius Mystery*, Century, 1998, pp. 104-5.

75 D. Wood, *Genisis*, The Baton Press, 1985, p. 96.

76 R. Temple, *The Sirius Mystery*, op. cit., p. 115.

77 Ibid.

78 Ibid., p. 114.

79 M. Eliade, *A History of Religious Ideas*, Volume 1, op. cit., p. 292.

80 A. Heidel, *The Babylonian Genesis*, op. cit., p. 71.

81 The theory is named after the Greek philosopher Euhemerus, who propounded it *c.* 300 BC.

82 See the works of C. Jung.

83 J. B. Pritchard, ed., *ANET (Ancient Near Eastern Texts Relating to the Old Testament)*, Princeton University Press, 3rd edition, 1969, pp. 508-12.

84 See the references in chapter 3 of this work.

85 J. G. Frazer, *The Golden Bough*, Oxford University Press, a new abridgement 1994, p. 345.

86 Cited in *Meta Research Bulletin* 7:4 (December 1998), p. 60.

87 A. Tomas, *We Are Not The First*, Bantam Books, 1971, p. 57.

88 A. F. Alford, *The Phoenix Solution*, Hodder & Stoughton, 1998, especially chapter 10.

89 E. A. Wallis Budge, *The Egyptian Heaven and Hell*, Dover Pubs., 1996 ed., Vol. III, pp. 88-9.

90 Ibid., Vol. III, pp. 88, 87.

91 It is interesting that Wallis Budge referred to the Sun as 'the visible emblem of the almighty and eternal God'; see *Egyptian Religion*, Arkana, 1899, p. 119, and similarly pp. 22, 125. Wallis Budge was thus quite familiar with the idea of visible symbols and an invisible God. Was he simply expressing Judaeo-Christian prejudices, or did he know something more?

92 I. Shaw & P. Nicholson, *British Museum Dictionary of Ancient Egypt*, British Museum Press, 1996. The same can also be said for M. Lurker, *The Gods and Symbols of Ancient Egypt*, Thames and Hudson, 1980. Contrast this with Dieter Arnold's statement that 'the most dramatic action occurred underground': see B. E. Shafer, *Temples of Ancient Egypt*, I.B. Tauris Publishers, 1998, p. 47.

CHAPTER TWO: LOVE ON THE MOUNTAIN

1 Genesis 6:1-4. Note that the Nephilim were 'in' the Earth, according to the translation of the King James Version of the Bible. I have left the word *Shem* untranslated, as the usual translation simply as 'name' fails to do justice to the original meaning of *Shem,* which involves the ownership of a name in the heights of Heaven.

2 M. F. Brooks trans., *Kebra Nagast (The Glory of Kings)*, The Red Sea Press, 1995, p. 148.

3 M. Eliade, *A History of Religious Ideas*, Volume 1, op. cit., p. 248.

4 Ibid.

5 Ibid., p. 247.

6 R. Graves, *The Greek Myths*, combined edition, Penguin Books, 1992. On *oros* and *ouros*, see p. 154; for Uranus as a masculine form of *Ur-ana*, 'queen of the mountains', see p. 32; for Uranus as 'king of the mountains' see his index listing.

7 This is my translation, but is clearly implied by the references cited in Graves, above.

8 R. Graves, *The Greek Myths*, op. cit., p. 32.

9 Ibid., p. 30.

10 G. de Santillana & H. von Dechend, *Hamlet's Mill*, op. cit., p. 153 footnote 7.

11 The word Nephilim derives from the Hebrew root *nfl* meaning 'to fall'; Nephilim thus seems to mean 'fellers', although it is not clear what exactly they were felling. It is not correct to translate Nephilim as 'fallen ones', because they did not fall from Heaven, but rather sprang up in the Earth as the offspring of the Sons-of-God; it was the latter who fell from Heaven.

12 A. Heidel, *The Gilgamesh Epic and Old Testament Parallels*, University of Chicago Press, 1963 edition, p. 181.

13 It is no surprise that such an allusion to Mother Earth was excluded from the Bible – she was, after all, a pagan goddess, and a powerful rival to Yahweh. Later in this chapter we will see how the Mesopotamians viewed Mother Earth as a giant womb containing fourteen subsidiary wombs, or womb-goddesses; hence my suggestion concerning the 'daughters-of-Earth'.

14 R. Alter, *Genesis*, W. W. Norton & Co., 1996, p. 27.

15 H. Stegemann, *The Library of Qumran*, W. B. Eerdmans Publishing, 1998, p. 94.

16 G. Roux, *Ancient Iraq*, Penguin Books, 1992 edition, p. 2. The term MES, meaning 'in the midst', will turn out to be of great significance later in this study.

17 G. Roux, *Ancient Iraq*, op. cit., pp. 29-30.

18 Ibid., pp. 85-6.

19 This eight-pointed star of Anu is often seen inscribed upon Mesopotamian monuments – see, for example, the Plates section in this work.

20 On the ancient astronaut theory, see in particular the works of E. von Daniken and Z. Sitchin. My own contribution to this genre (*Gods of the New Millennium*, Eridu Books, 1996) must now be seen as deeply flawed, and is recommended only in the sense that it presents a useful overview of the evidence supporting the ancient astronaut theory, demonstrating how crucially important are the ancient portrayals of the gods as human-like beings. For an up-to-date position statement on the ancient astronaut theory, see my website (www.eridu.co.uk).

21 S. N. Kramer, *The Sumerians*, University of Chicago Press, 1963, p. 200; compare S. N. Kramer, *History Begins at Sumer*, University of Pennsylvania Press, 1956, pp. 169-70, 294; in the latter, Kramer suggested that the KUR was hurling the stones against Enki's boat, and trying to devour it. In fact, it is not altogether clear where the stones were coming from; the context suggests to me that the stones were coming down from Heaven *with* Enki's boat.

22 The little stones and big stones motif appears also in a Shulgi hymn; see S. N. Kramer, *History Begins at Sumer*, op. cit., p. 287; here, the stones appear in the context of a symbolic ascent and descent between the city of Nippur (Earth) and the city of Ur (symbolising Heaven), and they belong to the storm-god Ishkur; Ishkur was in charge of the 'two rivers' of the heavens, which carried the breath of life to 'the horizon'; but elsewhere the thunder of Ishkur was a cataclysmic force, it being said that when Inanna thundered like Ishkur 'all vegetation comes to an end'.

23 S. N. Kramer, *The Sumerians*, op. cit., p. 175.

24 Ibid.

25 Ibid.

26 Ibid., p. 179.

27 Ibid., pp. 146-7.

28 C. & B. J. O'Brien, *The Shining Ones*, Dianthus Publishing, 1997 edition, pp. 85-6.

29 T. Jacobsen, *The Treasures of Darkness*, op. cit., p. 111.

30 S. N. Kramer, *History Begins at Sumer*, op. cit., p. 304; see also T. Jacobsen, *The Treasures of Darkness*, op. cit., pp. 103-5.

31 S. N. Kramer, *The Sumerians*, op. cit., p. 121.

32 Ibid., pp. 146-7; see also S. N. Kramer, *History Begins at Sumer*, op. cit., p. 376: 'the Kiur was a temple adjacent to the Ekur (in Nippur) which seems to have played an important role in connection with the Sumerian beliefs concerning the nether world.' See also reference to Kiur in J. B. Pritchard, ed., *ANET*, op. cit., p. 456, where it is linked to *kigallu*, 'the underworld'.

33 S. N. Kramer, *The Sumerians*, op. cit., pp. 146-7; compare H. Frankfort et al, *The Intellectual Adventure of Ancient Man*, University of Chicago Press, 1977 edition, p. 153.

34 T. Jacobsen, *The Treasures of Darkness*, op. cit., p. 103.

35 *ANET*, op. cit., pp. 460, 617.

36 Ibid., p. 77.

37 T. Jacobsen, *The Treasures of Darkness*, op. cit., p. 103. See also S.N. Kramer, *The Sumerians*, op. cit., p. 145.

38 *ANET*, op. cit., p. 37; the same point was raised more recently by D. Rohl in *Legend*, Century,

1998, p. 210.

39   *ANET*, op. cit., p. 38.

40   Ibid.

41   Ibid., p. 39. See comments in chapter 6 of this work concerning the metaphorical meaning of 'the bank of the river'.

42   See T. Jacobsen, *The Treasures of Darkness*, op. cit., pp. 104-5; though SAG means 'head'.

43   Ibid., pp. 112-13; Ninmu was also known as Ninsar, meaning 'Lady Plant'.

44   Ibid. Ninkurra was 'Lady of the Mountains', whilst Uttu was a weaving-goddess.

45   I am well aware of the fact that the Sumerian term TI means both 'rib' and 'life'.

46   Why did Enki wish to eat the plants? A clue might be found in the Legend of Etana, where an eagle sought eternal life by eating the offspring of the serpent.

47   These lesser deities were appointed in charge of various functions on the Earth; Abu, for example, became king of the plants, whilst Enshag became the lord of Dilmun.

48   *ANET*, op. cit., p. 37.

49   The legend entitled *Gilgamesh, Enkidu and the Underworld*; see S. N. Kramer, *The Sumerians*, op. cit., p. 200.

50   T. Jacobsen, *The Treasures of Darkness*, op. cit., p. 95.

51   Ibid., p. 130.

52   AB.ZU can also be read as 'Father of Zu', which would indeed be true of the underworld.

53   *ANET*, op. cit., pp. 111, 514.

54   Ibid., p. 113.

55   Ibid., p. 514; in this context the E.KUR would be the Mountain-House of Heaven.

56   Ibid., p. 577.

57   Ibid., p. 515.

58   For a vivid example of the E.KUR as the 'mountain' of planet Earth, see the legend of Etana in *ANET*, op. cit., p. 118 footnote 46; after the eagle had borne Etana aloft, he told Etana to peer down at the E.KUR – the 'World Mountain'.

59   T. Jacobsen, *The Treasures of Darkness*, op. cit., p. 132; hence Ninurta had a bird-like alter ego named Ningirsu. Incidentally, in another legend Zu was defeated when his head was crushed by Marduk.

60   T. Jacobsen, *The Treasures of Darkness*, op. cit., p. 130; Jacobsen erroneously equated the epithet 'Sling-Stone' with hailstones (p. 130) and a 'ball of clay' (p. 128).

61   Ibid., pp. 127-33, gives a good overview of the orthodox scenario of weather-gods.

62   S. N. Kramer, *The Sumerians*, op. cit., p. 153.

63   T. Jacobsen, *The Treasures of Darkness*, op. cit., p. 131.

64   Ibid., p. 130.

65   Ibid.

66   Ibid., p. 131.

67   Compare the wall laid down by Ninurta to 'the dam piled up at the edge of the sea' by Marduk; see A. Heidel, *The Babylonian Genesis*, op. cit., p. 63. These may well be idioms for exactly the same thing, namely the laying of the surface of the Earth.

68   S. N. Kramer, *The Sumerians*, op. cit., p. 152.

69   T. Jacobsen, *The Treasures of Darkness*, op. cit., pp. 131, 105.

70   In addition to Ninmah, Mami, Ninti and Nintu, one might cite Ninlil, Sud, Aruru, Dingirmah, Ninmenna and Belit-ili.

71   Translation based on *ANET*, op. cit., p. 99, with assistance from S. Dalley, *Myths from Mesopotamia*, Oxford University Press, 1998 edition, p. 15. Note that Mami is described as the 'creatress of mankind' even *before* she had carried out her commission to create mankind. Several scholars have commented on this oddity, e.g. A. Heidel in *The Babylonian Genesis*, op. cit., p. 66. Some scholars have thus altered the translation to read 'creatress-*to-be* of mankind'. But in fact the ancient scribes were quite correct – see discussion in chapter 8 of this work.

72   Translation based on *ANET*, op. cit., p. 100, and S. Dalley, *Myths from Mesopotamia*, op. cit., p. 16.

73   *ANET*, op. cit., p. 100.

74   Ibid.

75   S. Dalley, *Myths from Mesopotamia*, op. cit., p. 37.

76   Note therefore the symbolism of the pregnant woman sitting on the brick – a custom which was

commonplace in ancient Egypt as well as Mesopotamia; see M. Lurker, *The Gods and Symbols of Ancient Egypt*, op. cit., p. 33; also *ANET*, op. cit., p. 381 footnote 2.

77 The legend of *Ludlul bel nemeqi*; see T. Jacobsen, *The Treasures of Darkness*, op. cit., p. 162.
78 T. Jacobsen, *The Treasures of Darkness*, op. cit., p. 95; the *Lugal-e* text dates to *c.* 2100 BC.
79 S. Dalley, *Myths from Mesopotamia*, op. cit., p. 286.
80 Ibid., p. 286.
81 S. N. Kramer, *The Sumerians*, op. cit., p. 220. I have amended 'on' to read 'in'.
82 Ibid., p. 175.
83 M. Eliade, *A History of Religious Ideas*, Volume 1, op. cit., p. 58.
84 T. Jacobsen, *The Treasures of Darkness*, op. cit., p. 95.
85 S. N. Kramer, *History Begins at Sumer*, op. cit., pp. 303-4.
86 T. Jacobsen, *The Treasures of Darkness*, op. cit., p. 13.
87 M. Eliade, *The Myth of the Eternal Return*, Princeton University Press, 1954, p. 23.
88 One of the most famous uses of this expression occurs in Ernest Hemingway's 1940 novel *For Whom the Bell Tolls*, but the idea had already been around for thousands of years before that.
89 From the Nag Hammadi scrolls; cited in M. Baigent et al, *The Holy Blood and the Holy Grail*, op. cit., chapter 13, p. 404.
90 Did S. N. Kramer know the secret? In *History Begins at Sumer*, op. cit., p. 153, he wrote that paradise was 'the great above', as opposed to 'the great below'; then, on p. 156 he equated the great above with the heavenly realm of the goddess Inanna. The basic ankiography was thus surely known by scholars, even if it was not spelled out clearly for their readers.

CHAPTER THREE: THE DIVINE CHILD

1   Plutarch, cited in E. A. Wallis Budge, *Legends of the Egyptian Gods*, op. cit., p. 218.
2   Ibid.
3   Ibid., pp. 218-9. It is often suggested that the number '72' indicates a knowledge of the precession of the equinoxes. But it is equally possible that it was simply the multiple of the numbers '8' and '9', both of which were highly symbolic to the ancient Egyptians; see A. F. Alford, *The Phoenix Solution*, op. cit., chapter 11.
4   E. A. Wallis Budge, *Legends of the Egyptian Gods*, op. cit., p. 219; as we shall see in later chapters of this work, the Tanaitic mouth was the heavenly mouth of the celestial Nile.
5   In my view, Byblos is here symbolic of the land of the papyrus – Earth herself.
6   E. A. Wallis Budge, *Legends of the Egyptian Gods*, op. cit., pp. 224-5.
7   Ibid., p. 226; the phallus was supposedly swallowed by three fishes, although the number is probably symbolic. As we shall see in a later chapter, the Fish may well be a metaphor for the Earth, which swallowed up the phallus of Osiris when it fell from Heaven. It is evident to me that the legend of some body-parts being found whilst the phallus remained missing represents a merging of two separate versions of the same story.
8   E. A. Wallis Budge, *Legends of the Egyptian Gods*, op. cit., p. 234.
9   Ibid., p. 230.
10 Ibid., p. 229.
11 It must be stressed, however, that the Great Pyramid may have been built for some purpose other than the immortality cult of the pharaohs; see A. F. Alford, *The Phoenix Solution*, op. cit., chapters 1-4.
12 E. A. Wallis Budge, *Legends of the Egyptian Gods*, op. cit., pp. 232-48.
13 Indeed. Compare Pyramid Texts, Utterance 574.
14 E. A. Wallis Budge, *Legends of the Egyptian Gods*, op. cit., p. 228.
15 R. Temple, *The Sirius Mystery*, op. cit., p. 114.
16 E. A. Wallis Budge, *From Fetish to God in Ancient Egypt*, op. cit., p. 201. The word translated 'rejoicing' can also be rendered 'rising up'; see Wallis Budge, *Legends of the Egyptian Gods*, op. cit., p. 11.
17 E. A. Wallis Budge, *From Fetish to God in Ancient Egypt*, op. cit., p. 202.
18 R. O. Faulkner, *The Ancient Egyptian Pyramid Texts*, Aris & Phillips, Oxford University Press, 1969, Preface.
19 E. A. Wallis Budge, *Egyptian Religion*, op. cit., p. 119, and similarly pp. 22, 125.
20 Ibid, pp. 7-8, 39.

21 D. Meeks & C. Favard-Meeks, *Daily Life of the Egyptian Gods*, John Murray, 1997, p. 4.

22 See index references in A. F. Alford, *The Phoenix Solution*, op. cit.

23 The full story goes well beyond the remit of this work; the full details can be found in A. F. Alford, *The Phoenix Solution*, op. cit., chapters 5-10.

24 Pyramid Texts, Utterance 273, para 399.

25 Coffin Texts, Spell 335; see R. O. Faulkner, *The Ancient Egyptian Coffin Texts*, Volume I, Aris & Phillips, 1973, p. 263.

26 Book of the Dead, Spell 125; see R. O. Faulkner, *The Ancient Egyptian Book of the Dead*, 1985 edition, p. 32.

27 Coffin Texts, Spell 358.

28 E. A. Wallis Budge, *From Fetish to God in Ancient Egypt*, op. cit., p. 150.

29 Book of the Dead, Spell 17; compare Coffin Texts, Spell 335.

30 Ibid.

31 B. E. Shafer, *Temples of Ancient Egypt*, op. cit., pp. 29, 75, 88, 99, 102, 107-10, 115.

32 Pyramid Texts, Utterance 668, para 1960. The 'east' symbolised the direction of the horizon against which all celestial bodies would rise. See explanation of the 'east-west axiom' in A. F. Alford, *The Phoenix Solution*, op. cit., pp. 212-15.

33 Pyramid Texts, Utterance 1, para 1.

34 Pyramid Texts, Utterance 484, para 1022.

35 E. A. Wallis Budge, *Legends of the Egyptian Gods*, op. cit., p. 217.

36 Pyramid Texts, Utterance 254, para 281-2.

37 Book of the Dead, trans. by Normandi Ellis, in R. Bauval & G. Hancock, *Keeper of Genesis*, William Heinemann, 1996, p. 283. Compare Pyramid Texts, Utterance 332, para 541, where Osiris the king stated: "I have ascended in a blast of fire, having turned myself about."

38 Pyramid Texts, Utterance 260, para 322-3, where Osiris the king stated: "I am the alter ego of my father [Geb], the blossom of my mother [Nut]. I detest travelling in darkness for then I cannot see, but fall upside down."

39 A. Gardiner, *Egyptian Grammar*, 3rd ed., Griffith Inst., Oxford, 1994, p. 598. Citation from Coffin Texts, Spell 829.

40 D. Meeks & C. Favard-Meeks, *Daily Life of the Egyptian Gods*, op. cit., p. 84. Both Geb and his predecessor Shu were credited with organising the land and establishing the first cities.

41 In fairness, it should be said that most invaders of Egypt did not desecrate Egyptian religion, but rather took it over. In addition to the missing meteorite of Heliopolis, there is textual evidence of missing meteorites from Giza and Abydos. Concerning Giza, the Egyptian texts speak of a meteorite hidden at Rostau (Giza) – see chapter 12 of this work. Concerning Abydos, the Egyptians claimed that this was the home of the 'head of Osiris', which was kept there in a box (see Wallis Budge, *Legends of the Egyptian Gods*, op. cit., p. 230). In all probability, this was the same 'stone from Heaven' which was kept at Abydos according to the Roman writer Pliny in his 'Natural History' (Book II).

42 I. E. S. Edwards, *The Pyramids of Egypt*, Penguin Books, p. 276, stated: 'it now seems probable that the stone symbol of the Sun-god [sic] at Heliopolis, the Benben, was conical.' H. Frankfort, *Kingship and the Gods*, University of Chicago Press, 1978 ed., p. 153, stated: 'the determinative in the Pyramid Texts shows a tapering somewhat conical shape for the Benben Stone.'

43 Pyramid Texts, Utterance 600, para 1652.

44 H. Frankfort, *Kingship and the Gods*, op. cit., p. 153, suggested that the Benben Stone was covered in gold foil, so that it would glisten in the sunshine. Compare R. O. Faulkner, *The Ancient Egyptian Coffin Texts*, Volume II, Aris & Phillips, 1977, p. 68 footnote 1 to Spell 422.

45 H. Frankfort, *Kingship and the Gods*, op. cit., pp. 153, 380.

46 Ibid., pp. 153, 380-1, notes 26-7.

47 E. A. Wallis Budge, *From Fetish to God in Ancient Egypt*, op. cit., p. 10; also E. A. Wallis Budge, *Legends of the Egyptian Gods*, op. cit., pp. xvii-xviii.

48 A. F. Alford, *The Phoenix Solution*, op. cit., pp. 141-2.

49 E. A. Wallis Budge, *Legends of the Egyptian Gods*, op. cit., pp. xvii, 165; also E. A. Wallis Budge, *Egyptian Religion*, op. cit., p. 102.

50 Pyramid Texts, Utterance 517, para 1188, where Osiris the king stated: "I am deemed righteous in the Sky and on Earth; I am deemed righteous in this Island of Earth to which I have swum

and arrived, which is between the thighs of Nut."

51 E. A. Wallis Budge, *From Fetish to God in Ancient Egypt*, op. cit., p. 194.

52 Herodotus, cited in E. von Daniken, *The Eyes of the Sphinx*, Berkley Books, 1996, p. 72.

53 E. A. Wallis Budge, *The Egyptian Heaven and Hell*, op. cit., three volumes in one.

54 See A. F. Alford, *The Phoenix Solution*, op. cit., p. 221.

55 E. A. Wallis Budge, *The Egyptian Heaven and Hell*, op. cit., II, p. 196.

56 Ibid., II, p. 200.

57 Ibid., III, p. 167.

58 Ibid., II, p. 196.

59 Ibid., II, p. 82.

60 Ibid., II, pp. 87, 91, 107.

61 Ibid., II, p. 120.

62 Ibid., II, p. 120.

63 Ibid., II, p. 111.

64 Ibid., II, p. 113.

65 Ibid., II, p. 118.

66 Ibid., I, pp. 148-9; Osiris is identical to 'him that is in Mehen'.

67 D. Meeks & C. Favard-Meeks, *Daily Life of the Egyptian Gods*, op. cit., p. 154.

68 R. H. Brown, *Stellar Theology and Masonic Astronomy*, op. cit., p. 11.

69 See for example R. O. Faulkner, *The Ancient Egyptian Coffin Texts*, Volume I, op. cit., p. 185
    (Spell 236), where Osiris the king stated: "I am one who collects for himself his efflux in front
    of Rostau." Also p. 45 note 10 to Spell 48, where Faulkner stated that Rostau was the 'name of
    the Memphite necropolis, later generalised as a term for the other world'. In Coffin Texts, Spell
    1087, Rostau is compared to 'the corruption of Osiris'. For further information on Rostau, see
    A. F. Alford, *The Phoenix Solution*, op. cit., p. 284.

70 Pyramid Texts, Utterance 553, para 1360.

71 Coffin Texts, Spell 1080; see R. O. Faulkner, *The Ancient Egyptian Coffin Texts*, Volume III,
    Aris & Phillips, 1978. Compare also Spell 1087.

72 Pyramid Texts, Utterance 665A, para 1908; compare Coffin Texts, Spells 235, 769.

73 Pyramid Texts, Utterance 723, para 2244; compare Coffin Texts, Spell 519.

74 Pyramid Texts, Utterance 419, para 749; see also Utterance 570, para 1454: "My bones are iron
    and my limbs are the Imperishable Ones."

75 See G. A. Wainwright, 'Iron in Egypt', in *Journal of Egyptian Antiquities* 18 (1933), pp. 3-15.

76 L. Bell in B. E. Shafer ed., *Temples of Ancient Egypt*, op. cit., p. 176.

77 Coffin Texts, Spell 816; R. O. Faulkner commented that this passage was 'a reference to the
    ritual of Opening the Mouth with an adze of iron'. See also Spell 936. Meanwhile, Utterance
    245 speaks of the deceased king 'splitting open his place in the Sky', in a reversal of the
    incident in which the iron meteorite of the Sky split open the Earth.

78 Coffin Texts, Spell 228.

79 Pyramid Texts, Utterance 413, para 735-6.

80 Pyramid Texts, Utterance 509, para 1120-4; note that 'Imperishable Stars' is a misleading term,
    and is better rendered as 'Imperishable Ones', see A. F. Alford, *The Phoenix Solution*, op. cit.,
    pp. 249-51. For other references to the 'iron throne', see Utterance 666, para 1927, Utterance
    667, para 1934, Utterance 582, para 1562, and Utterance 610, para 1721.

81 Pyramid Texts, Utterances 261, 332, 669, paras 324, 541, 1961.

82 See, for example, Pyramid Texts, Utterance 691A.

83 Pyramid Texts, Utterance 485C, para 1036-8.

84 Re and the Morning Star were synonymous, but the Morning Star was not literally a star; see
    A. F. Alford, *The Phoenix Solution*, op. cit., pp. 253-5.

85 Re came forth from Nut – see Pyramid Texts, Utterance 606, para 1688.

86 The three deities can be defined as the mother-vessel, Nut, and her 'son', with the son
    comprising the body and soul divided – Osiris and Re.

87 The hieroglyph for *Akh* was written with a crested ibis, meaning 'to shine'. For 'Mountain of
    Light', see H. Frankfort, *Kingship and the Gods*, op. cit., pp. 135, 354 note 6; the reading
    comes from the fact that the hieroglyphic sign for *Akhet* shows a disk of light rising between
    two mountain peaks. It is of considerable significance that the archaic hieroglyph for *Akhet* was
    an ellipse, which meant 'island'; see M. C. Betro, *Hieroglyphics*, Abbeville Press, 1996, p. 157.

88 D. Meeks & C. Favard-Meeks, *Daily Life of the Egyptian Gods*, op. cit., p. 162.
89 E. A. Wallis Budge, *The Egyptian Heaven and Hell*, op. cit., II, pp. 303-6.
90 Ibid., p. 306.
91 E. A. Wallis Budge, *Legends of the Egyptian Gods*, op. cit., p. 242.
92 The text is inscribed on the so-called Shabaka Stone; see *ANET*, op. cit., p. 5.
93 Pyramid Texts, Utterance 694, para 2144; compare Utterance 535, para 1280, and Coffin Texts, Spells 73 and 74. On the subject of 'bank', too, as a metaphor, see chapter 6 of this work. Some useful references to 'banks' in Egyptian mythology are as follows: Coffin Texts, Spells 169, 172, 1129; also *ANET*, op. cit., p. 376.
94 Coffin Texts, Spell 74.
95 Pyramid Texts, Utterance 366, para 626, 628-9. For other references to Osiris as the oceans of the world, see R. T. Rundle Clark, *Myth and Symbol in Ancient Egypt*, Thames and Hudson, 1993 ed., p. 117, and H. Frankfort, *Kingship and the Gods*, op. cit., pp. 191-2.
96 R. O. Faulkner, *The Ancient Egyptian Pyramid Texts*, op. cit., p. 121.
97 E. A. Wallis Budge, *From Fetish to God in Ancient Egypt*, op. cit., pp. 147, 150, 507.
98 D. Meeks & C. Favard-Meeks, *Daily Life of the Egyptian Gods*, op. cit., p. 27. This myth might well be the origin of the modern word association of 'head' with 'nut', along with expressions such as 'nutcase' and 'a tough nut to crack'. Note also the connection between the Latin noun *caput*, 'head', and the German adjective *kaputt*, 'broken'.
99 Coffin Texts, Spell 220; compare Spell 245.
100 Coffin Texts, Spell 680.
101 Pyramid Texts, Utterance 311, para 499.
102 Pyramid Texts, Utterance 249, para 265-6; compare Coffin Texts Spell 971.
103 Coffin Texts, Spell 833.
104 Coffin Texts, Spell 362.
105 Coffin Texts, Spell 344.
106 Pyramid Texts, Utterance 254, para 290. See Faulkner, op. cit., p. 65 note 28. *Mehet-Weret* was depicted as a cow, and merged with the goddess Hathor.
107 See E. A. Wallis Budge, *From Fetish to God in Ancient Egypt*, op. cit., p. 59; also p. 256 where he commented that the god Khnum was known as *Qebh*, meaning 'god of cool water'.
108 Pyramid Texts, Utterance 266, para 359-60.
109 Pyramid Texts, Utterance 611, para 1728.
110 Pyramid Texts, Utterance 685, para 2063-4. This joining together of the scattered waters corresponds to the simultaneous joining together of the disintegrated land – see Utterance 433, para 783: 'Geb has joined the entire land to you [Nut] everywhere.'
111 See E. A. Wallis Budge, *From Fetish to God in Ancient Egypt*, op. cit., p. 202.
112 Pyramid Texts, Utterance 664A, para 1886.
113 Coffin Texts, Spell 334.
114 Coffin Texts, Spell 148.
115 E. A. Wallis Budge, *From Fetish to God in Ancient Egypt*, op. cit., p. 201. The word translated 'rejoicing' can also be rendered 'rising up'.
116 See J. Baines in *Orientalia* Vol. 39 (1970), pp. 389-95. Note that *ben* means 'son' in Hebrew.
117 Pyramid Texts, Utterance 600, para 1652.
118 Pyramid Texts, Utterance 527, para 1248-9.
119 See 'The Legend of the Contendings of Horus and Seth' in E. A. Wallis Budge, *From Fetish to God in Ancient Egypt*, op. cit., pp. 444-57; see also 'The Legend of Horus of Behdet (Edfu) and the Winged Disk', pp. 467-80. Horus was known as *Hor-nedj-her-itef*, 'Horus, avenger of his father'.

CHAPTER FOUR: PARADISE REGAINED

1 M. Eliade, *A History of Religious Ideas*, Volume 1, op. cit., pp. 57-8.
2 'The Myth of Enki and Eridu'.
3 The translation is a composite of T. Jacobsen, *The Treasures of Darkness*, op. cit., p. 78, and S. N. Kramer, *The Sumerians*, op. cit., p. 188. The idea of a great wall reaching to Heaven is found also in ancient Egyptian tradition – see *ANET*, op. cit., p. 376.
4 G. Roux, *Ancient Iraq*, op. cit., p. 166; I have changed 'me' to 'Gudea' to suit the sense of the

imagined tour around the ancient Near East.

5 Ibid., p. 166; see also M. Eliade, *A History of Religious Ideas*, Volume 1, op. cit., p. 61.

6 T. Jacobsen, *The Treasures of Darkness*, op. cit., p. 17.

7 *ANET*, op. cit., p. 574.

8 *A Hymn to Enlil*; see *ANET*, op. cit., p. 574; also S. N. Kramer, *The Sumerians*, op. cit., p. 120. I have rendered 'ME' as 'divine laws'; the exact meaning of the term is very uncertain.

9 If any reader wishes to purchase a meteorite, please contact the author via his email address: alford@eridu.co.uk

10 For example, in the Book of Enoch, Enoch entered a mysterious 'House of Fire' and observed that the house was 'as hot as fire and cold as ice'. And in the Egyptian myth entitled *The Legend of Re and Isis*, we hear how Re was bitten by a sacred serpent, the venom of which burned in Re's body like a 'blazing fire', with a 'heat stronger than a blazing flame'; it made Re tremble and shake, and he complained: "I am colder than water, I am hotter than fire".

11 See A. F. Alford, *The Phoenix Solution*, op. cit., chapters 1-4.

12 E. A. Wallis Budge, *Legends of the Egyptian Gods*, op. cit., p. 206; Plutarch observed that drinking the juice of the vine thus caused the Egyptians to fill themselves, as it were, with the blood of their own ancestors. As we shall see, the comment is quite profound.

13 The translation is a composite of *ANET*, op. cit., p. 5, and M. Eliade, *A History of Religious Ideas*, Volume 1, op. cit., p. 89; compare the legend where Geb and Nut brought forth their five children 'and they produced their multitudinous offspring in this Earth'; see E. A. Wallis Budge, *Legends of the Egyptian Gods*, op. cit., p. 7.

14 *ANET*, op. cit., p. 613. I prefer to render 'harrow' as 'weapon'. The Sumerian Lamentation Texts were probably composed *c.* 2000 BC – a time of great chaos in the Near East, possibly due to Earth's interaction with cometary debris. However, it would be naive to suppose that the Lamentation Texts were simply describing then-contemporary celestial events. On the contrary, the lamentations may well have been adapted from pre-existing myths, which described an imaginary destruction of mankind at the beginning of time. This would account for much of the exaggerated cataclysmic language in the Lamentation Texts.

15 See A. Heidel, *The Gilgamesh Epic and Old Testament Parallels*, op. cit., p. 171; also S. N. Kramer, *The Sumerians*, op. cit., p. 134.

16 E. A. Wallis Budge, *The Egyptian Heaven and Hell*, op. cit., II, p. 85; compare II, p. 195 'the hidden mountain of the horizon'.

17 R. H. Wilkinson, *Reading Egyptian Art*, Thames and Hudson, 1994 ed., p. 133; Egyptologists have not yet grasped the point that the 'Western Mountain' was the Earth.

18 S. N. Kramer, *The Sumerians*, op. cit., p. 220; however, 'on' should be rendered as 'in'.

19 Ibid., p. 177; for a further example of Sumer as a microcosm of the Earth, see chapter 7 of this work re the legend of the gods who brought barley down to 'Sumer' from Enlil's 'mountain'.

20 G. de Santillana & H. von Dechend, *Hamlet's Mill*, op. cit., p. 297 footnote 29; note that NUN[KI] was a name of Eridu.

21 The translation is a composite of *ANET*, op. cit., p. 13, and E. A. Wallis Budge, *Legends of the Egyptian Gods*, op. cit., p. 51.

22 E. A. Wallis Budge, *From Fetish to God in Ancient Egypt*, op. cit., p. 505.

23 Coffin Texts, Spell 335 Part II; compare Spell 701: "My mouth speaks to me with a knife on the day of the union of the Two Lands."

24 Pyramid Texts, Utterance 254, para 281-2.

25 R. O. Faulkner, *The Ancient Egyptian Book of the Dead*, 1985 edition, p. 32; and Coffin Texts, Spell 358.

26 Coffin Texts, Spell 146. Faulkner was quite puzzled by this and wrote 'N goes down (sic) into the Sky'. As usual, however, the ancient Egyptian scribes knew exactly what they were saying.

27 Coffin Texts, Spell 1035; compare Spell 1105 where the king entered into 'the Sky of the Double-Lion'; this was almost certainly a reference to the Double-Lion god Aker, who guarded the *subterranean* sanctuary of Sokar in Rostau; hence the reference to darkness in Spell 1105; Spell 1116 provides further support by associating the darkness with the Island of Fire.

28 Coffin Texts, Spell 908. Anubis, incidentally, was known also as 'he who is upon his mountain'; see I. Shaw & P. Nicholson, *British Museum Dictionary of Ancient Egypt*, op. cit., p. 35. In other words, Anubis sat upon the 'mountain' of the underworld.

29 R. H. Brown, *Stellar Theology and Masonic Astronomy*, op. cit., p. 64.

30 There is an intriguing comparison here to the Mesopotamian word *mesu*, which, as we shall see, was the meteoric 'flesh of the gods', which had indeed fallen from the Sky into the middle of the Earth.

31 R. Powell trans., 'Historical Note concerning the Emerald Tablet' in *The Hermetic Journal* 15 (Spring 1981), p. 38. The text known as 'the Emerald Tablet' is thought to be at least twelve hundred years old. It must be stressed that as far as the ancients were concerned, the above and the below were in fact the work of the miracles of *the Two*, rather than the One.

32 G. Roux, *Ancient Iraq*, op. cit., pp. 94-5.

33 Genesis 1.

34 N. J. Dawood trans., *The Koran*, Penguin Books, 1974 edition, p. 298 (traditional chapter number 21). Note Allah's use of the royal 'we'.

35 A. Heidel, *The Babylonian Genesis*, op. cit., p. 68.

36 T. Jacobsen, *The Treasures of Darkness*, op. cit., p. 103. See also S.N. Kramer, *The Sumerians*, op. cit., p. 145.

37 Pyramid Texts, Utterance 519, para 1208.

38 E. A. Wallis Budge, *From Fetish to God in Ancient Egypt*, op. cit., p. 150.

39 It is significant that, according to the *Kom Ombo Legends*, the coupling of Shu and Geb was supposed to effect the rebirth of Osiris; see D. Meeks & C. Favard-Meeks, *Daily Life of the Egyptian Gods*, op. cit., p. 69.

40 Coffin Texts, Spell 76, incorporating a line from Spell 78.

41 E. A. Wallis Budge, *Legends of the Egyptian Gods*, op. cit., pp. 15-41; the same theme appears in the Book of the Dead – see *ANET*, op. cit., pp. 3-4.

42 E. A. Wallis Budge, *Legends of the Egyptian Gods*, op. cit., p. 15.

43 Ibid., pp. 27, xxix. It hardly seems likely that the Akhekha were ordinary stars; rather they appear to have been metaphysical planetesimals.

44 S. Dalley, *Myths from Mesopotamia*, op. cit., p. 250; Dalley observed on p. 275 note 15 that the word *lumasu*, rendered 'constellation', was previously misread by other scholars as *lubasu*, meaning 'garment' or 'images'. It is also worth noting that the word denoting the destruction of the constellation suggests a breaking into pieces rather than a vaporization into nothing; see A. Heidel, *The Babylonian Genesis*, op. cit., p. 37.

45 See *ANET*, op. cit., p. 71, line 70; the god SIR.SIR carried off the corpse of Tiamat and heaped up a mountain over her body.

46 The translation is a composite of *ANET*, op. cit., p. 67, and A. Heidel, *The Babylonian Genesis*, op. cit., p. 43; Heidel confused the Esharra with the Earth, but it is clearly stated in line 145 of Tablet IV that Esharra was the Sky or firmament; see T. Jacobsen, *The Treasures of Darkness*, op. cit., p. 179.

47 The translation is a composite of *ANET*, op. cit., p. 502, and Dalley, *Myths from Mesopotamia*, op. cit., p. 259; the word 'opposite' is my own, which brings out the sense of the passage better than 'over' or 'in front of'.

48 G. Roux, *Ancient Iraq*, op. cit., pp. 395-6. Its ruins were later excavated by a team of German archaeologists.

49 *ANET*, op. cit., p. 69; scholars have struggled to make sense of the expression 'as high as Apsu', hence my suggestion: 'as high as the Apsu is deep', which does make sense, especially in view of the fact that the god Apsu had been cast down from Heaven to Earth. The *E-sag-ila* was indeed a temple which stretched (mythologically speaking) between Earth and Heaven.

50 *ANET*, op. cit., p. 61; the term translated 'cult hut' is *giparu*; note that this is the same term as appears in line 6 of *Enuma Elish*, where it is usually translated 'reed-hut'.

51 *ANET*, op. cit., p. 574.

52 Marduk's escape from the 'mountain' of the underworld was a major theme of the Babylonian New Year Festival; see H. Frankfort, *Kingship and the Gods*, op. cit., pp. 313-25.

53 The saying is often abbreviated to 'as above so below', leading to over-simplistic explanations, such as the idea that certain temples or pyramids on the ground below were matched to certain stars in the sky above.

54 In 1973, Nobel Prize winner Francis Crick, together with Dr Leslie Orgel, suggested that 'life on Earth may have sprung from tiny organisms from a distant planet'; see F. Crick & L. Orgel in *Icarus*, September 1973. See also F. Hoyle & C. Wickramasinghe, *Evolution from Space*, J.M. Dent & Sons, 1981; also F. Hoyle, *The Intelligent Universe*, M. Joseph, 1983.

55 E. A. Wallis Budge, *Egyptian Religion*, op. cit., pp. 35-6.

56 E. A. Wallis Budge, *The Egyptian Heaven and Hell*, op. cit., III, pp. 65-6.

57 On the Field of Reeds (or Field of Rushes), see A. F. Alford, *The Phoenix Solution*, op. cit., pp. 254-6, 261-2, 314-5.

58 S. N. Kramer, *History Begins at Sumer*, op. cit., p. 291.

59 M. Eliade, *A History of Religious Ideas*, Volume 1, op. cit., p. 247.

60 R. Graves, *The Greek Myths*, op. cit., index listing.

61 M. Eliade, *A History of Religious Ideas*, Volume 1, op. cit., p. 252.

62 There can be no doubt that when the Egyptians referred to 'the eastern horizon', they had the heavens in mind: hence in Pyramid Texts, Utterance 222, para 202, Osiris the king declared: "Grant that I may seize the Sky and take possession of the horizon."

63 Hence according to Plutarch, the Egyptians would sometimes call the Nile 'Sothis/Sirius'; see R. Temple, *The Sirius Mystery*, op. cit., p. 129.

64 There was also a highly esoteric reason why Sirius became the supreme symbol in the Egyptian exploded planet cult; see A. F. Alford, *The Phoenix Solution*, op. cit., pp. 196-7.

65 R. Temple, *The Sirius Mystery*, op. cit.

66 Coffin Texts, Spell 624.

67 Coffin Texts, Spell 838: 'kick him in your name of Orion'.

68 R. Temple, *The Sirius Mystery*, op. cit., p. 129.

69 Coffin Texts, Spell 474.

70 Pyramid Texts, Utterances 519, 689, 690, 677, paras 1212, 2090, 2110, 2025.

71 A. F. Alford, *The Phoenix Solution*, op. cit., pp. 223-6.

72 Ibid., pp. 223-4.

73 Ibid., p. 226.

74 R. H. Wilkinson, *Reading Egyptian Art*, op. cit., p. 133; Egyptologists have not yet grasped this point, despite numerous references such as that in footnote 62 above; see footnote 78 below.

75 See H. Frankfort, *Kingship and the Gods*, op. cit., pp. 135, 354 note 6; see also E. C. Krupp, *Echoes of the Ancient Skies*, Oxford University Press, 1983, pp. 308-10.

76 M. C. Betro, *Hieroglyphics*, op. cit., p. 157.

77 E. A. Wallis Budge, *Egyptian Religion*, op. cit., p. 122.

78 There are repeated references in Egyptian texts to 'the horizon of Heaven'; see, for example, E. A. Wallis Budge, *Egyptian Religion*, op. cit., pp. 35-7, *ANET*, op. cit., pp. 4, 370, 372, 375.

79 *ANET*, op. cit., pp. 114-8.

80 S. N. Kramer, *The Sumerians*, op. cit., p. 181; but strictly it is more accurate to say 'the place where *Utu* rises' rather than 'the place where *the Sun* rises'.

81 *ANET*, op. cit., p. 613; I prefer to render 'harrow' as 'weapon', whilst 'prostrate' brings out the sense better than Kramer's 'motionless'.

82 *ANET*, op. cit., p. 576.

83 E. A. Wallis Budge, *From Fetish to God in Ancient Egypt*, op. cit., pp. 89-90; also E. A. Wallis Budge, *Legends of the Egyptian Gods*, op. cit., p. 165.

84 Though Punt was sometimes said to be the land of the goddess, Hathor. It is particularly pertinent to note the legend recorded in Spell 112 of the Coffin Texts: that the evil god Seth had 'flown up and destroyed a full half of Punt'.

85 The Phoenix was known as the Light-bird; see R. T. Rundle Clark, *Myth and Symbol in Ancient Egypt*, Thames and Hudson, 1993 ed., p. 39; prior to the appearance of the Phoenix, the world was bathed in a primeval darkness, pp. 245-6.

86 R. T. Rundle Clark, *Myth and Symbol in Ancient Egypt*, op. cit., p. 246, wrote of the Phoenix: 'It opens its beak and breaks the silence of the primeval night with the call of life and destiny, which "determines what is and what is not to be"... it is the patron of all division of time...'

87 Ibid., p. 247; though the quote cited by Rundle Clark relates primarily to the taking of the *Hike* from the underworld of the Earth back to the place whence it had been brought by the Phoenix.

88 Ibid., pp. 246-8.

89 This was the Greek tradition, see R. H. Wilkinson, *Reading Egyptian Art*, op. cit., p. 91; in addition, the Greek writer Herodotus related the legend of a red-and-gold eagle-like bird from Arabia, which would wrap up its dead parent in a ball, then carry it to Egypt and bury it in the Temple of the Sun (sic); see Rundle Clark, *Myth and Symbol in Ancient Egypt*, op. cit., p. 248.

90 Coffin Texts, Spell 335 Part I; compare Rundle Clark, *Myth and Symbol in Ancient Egypt*, op.

cit., pp. 79, 158; see also E. A. Wallis Budge, *From Fetish to God in Ancient Egypt*, op. cit., p. 90, citing the legend that the Bennu-bird 'sprang from the heart of Osiris'.

91 E. A. Wallis Budge, *An Egyptian Hieroglyphic Dictionary*, Dover Publications, 1978, Vol. II, p. 958.

92 See R. O. Faulkner, *The Ancient Egyptian Coffin Texts*, Volume II, Aris & Phillips, 1977, p. 68, Spell 422, and note the confusion of Egyptologists. Is the Mansion of the Pyramidion in Annu 'the Mansion of the Rising Sun', or is it in fact 'the Mansion of the Rising *Re-wbnbn*'? The latter, of course, connects Re to the Benben Stone – the rising meteorite.

93 See the works of J. E. Lovelock in the 1970s: *Gaia – a New Look at Life on Earth*, and *The Ages of Gaia: A Biography of Our Living Earth*.

94 The etymology of the word 'alchemy' seems to be rooted in the Greek terms *chemeia* and the earlier term *chumeia*, both meaning 'mixing/mingling': see G. Cornelius & P. Devereux, *The Secret Language of the Stars and Planets*, Chronicle Books, San Francisco, 1996, p. 47. Note also that the land of Egypt used to be known as Khem, the Black Land. Based on the argumentation in this work, we might well call Egypt 'the mixed land', from the fusion of several exploded 'mountains' in the underworld.

95 See A. F. Alford, *The Phoenix Solution*, op. cit., chapter 10. The reconstruction of the planet of Heaven was envisaged as being quite real and physical, albeit in a dimension which can only be described as metaphysical from our current Earth-bound perspective.

96 There is a good argument to be made that the pyramid was a symbolic representation of planet Earth in a metaphysical dimension – see A. F. Alford, *The Phoenix Solution*, op. cit., chapter 10. However, that was before I appreciated the fact that Heaven was conceived to be in the exact image of the Earth. This complicates the interpretation of the pyramid symbolism.

97 M. Lehner, *The Complete Pyramids*, Thames and Hudson, 1997, p. 35; compare H. Frankfort, *Kingship and the Gods*, op. cit., pp. 152-4.

98 H. Frankfort, *Kingship and the Gods*, op. cit., p. 381 note 27; also R. T. Rundle Clark, *Myth and Symbol in Ancient Egypt*, op. cit., p. 269 note 5.

99 *Collins English Dictionary*, Collins, 1979, p. 1014. Note also that the name Tefnut is drawn from the Egyptian word *tff*, meaning 'to spit'.

100 See references in R. Bauval & G. Hancock, *Keeper of Genesis*, Heinemann, 1996, pp. 161-2.

101 See, for example, T. Jacobsen, *The Sumerian King List,* University of Chicago Press, 1939, p. 85.

102 See, for example, S. N. Kramer, *History Begins at Sumer*, op. cit., chapter 33. Scholars are not particularly frank about the fact that this sacred marriage occurred, mythically speaking, *in the underworld*.

103 T. Jacobsen, *The Treasures of Darkness*, op. cit., p. 107.

104 S. N. Kramer, *The Sumerians*, op. cit., p. 188.

105 G. Roux, *Ancient Iraq*, op. cit., pp. 164-5; I suspect that there may also be an etymological link to the term *zikaru*, meaning 'male-warrior'.

106 S. N. Kramer, *The Sumerians*, op. cit., p. 219.

107 G. de Santillana & H. von Dechend, *Hamlet's Mill*, op. cit., p. 435.

108 See M. Eliade, *The Myth of the Eternal Return*, op. cit., p. 15, concerning Babylon.

109 The legend of *Gilgamesh, Enkidu and the Underworld*, where Gilgamesh's *pukku* and *mikku* fell into the underworld; see T. Jacobsen, *The Treasures of Darkness*, op. cit., pp. 134, 212; in the same legend, Utu opened up a vent in the Earth to permit the ghost of Enkidu to return to the world above with tales of his adventure below.

110 M. Eliade, *The Myth of the Eternal Return*, op. cit., pp. 13, 15.

111 'The Myth of Enki and Eridu'.

112 S. N. Kramer, *The Sumerians*, op. cit., p. 323; see also G. Roux, *Ancient Iraq*, op. cit., p. 177, and S. N. Kramer, *History Begins at Sumer*, op. cit., p. 293.

113 T. Jacobsen, *The Treasures of Darkness*, op. cit., p. 16.

114 *ANET*, op. cit., pp. 618-19.

CHAPTER FIVE: A SECRET OF THE GODS

1 See A. Heidel, *The Gilgamesh Epic and Old Testament Parallels*, op. cit., pp. 1-3. The first scholar to present a translation of *The Epic* was George Smith of the British Museum, who on

3rd December 1872 read a paper before the Society of Biblical Archaeology entitled *The Chaldean Account of the Deluge*, based particularly on Tablet XI of *The Epic*; see *Transactions of the Society of Biblical Archaeology* II (1873), pp. 213-34.

2 This sacred marriage tradition at Uruk is extremely old, as is witnessed by the scenes on the famous 'Uruk vase' at the Baghdad Museum; the vase has been dated to *c*. 3000 BC; see T. Jacobsen, *The Treasures of Darkness*, op. cit., pp. 24, 26.

3 T. Jacobsen, *The Sumerian King List,* op. cit., pp. 77-85; the city of Kish was the city of kingship for the intervening 24,510 years, 3 months and 3.5 days.

4 Ibid., p. 87; note the varying translations, and confusion as to whether Meskiaggasher came out to a singular mountain or plural mountains. S. N. Kramer in *The Sumerians*, op. cit., p. 44, commented that this line was 'ambiguous and obscure... he may have tried to extend his sway over the lands all around Sumer and far beyond'. This is a typical example of how the lack of understanding of Mesopotamian metaphors causes scholars to miss the fundamental metaphysical nature of the described events.

5 T. Jacobsen, *The Sumerian King List,* op. cit., p. 87; see footnote 115 re the descent of Inanna.

6 S. N. Kramer, *The Sumerians*, op. cit., pp. 185, 273-5; see also comment in S. N. Kramer, *History Begins at Sumer*, op. cit., p. 356.

7 T. Jacobsen, *The Sumerian King List,* op. cit., pp. 85-91. The intervening 100-year reign of Dumuzi strikes me as being highly symbolic; the reference to Dumuzi's city 'Kuara' is almost certainly an allusion to the underworld.

8 A. Heidel, *The Gilgamesh Epic and Old Testament Parallels*, op. cit., pp. 17-18.

9 T. Jacobsen, *The Treasures of Darkness*, op. cit., p. 108.

10 A. Heidel, *The Gilgamesh Epic and Old Testament Parallels*, op. cit., p. 18. Note that, according to S. N. Kramer, *History Begins at Sumer*, op. cit., p. 295, the 'wild ox' of Sumerian mythology was literally a 'mountain bull'. Thus the frequent use of the 'wild ox' motif in connection with kings, temples and cities; among the examples cited by Kramer on p. 294 are the following: a king boasting that his neck was thick 'like a wild ox'; the Kiur of the Ekur of Nippur, which raised its shining horns over Sumer 'like a wild ox'; and the city of Ur, which was like 'a great wild ox that steps forth confidently, secure in its own strength'.

11 A. Heidel, *The Gilgamesh Epic and Old Testament Parallels*, op. cit., p. 18.

12 Ibid. On the meaning 'germ loosener', see T. Jacobsen, *The Treasures of Darkness*, op. cit., p. 108; elsewhere the goddess Aruru was said to be the creatress of the seed of mankind and all living beings, see for example A. Heidel, *The Babylonian Genesis*, op. cit., p. 63.

13 J. Gardner & J. Maier, *Gilgamesh*, Vintage Books, 1985, p. 79.

14 *ANET,* op. cit., p. 74.

15 J. Gardner & J. Maier, *Gilgamesh*, op. cit., p. 77, and notes on pp. 79-80; I prefer to render 'courtesan' as 'harlot', 'wind' as 'life-force', and 'ravaging' to the unnecessarily crude term used by Gardner & Maier.

16 A. Heidel, *The Gilgamesh Epic and Old Testament Parallels*, op. cit., p. 22, or *ANET*, op. cit., p. 75; as is noted by *ANET* footnote 28, the theme is evocative of Genesis 3:7.

17 A. Heidel, *The Gilgamesh Epic and Old Testament Parallels*, op. cit., pp. 23-4; compare also p. 26. Since the 'star' (or elsewhere 'axe') was the male god Enkidu, there would seem to be homosexual overtones in the idea that Gilgamesh 'bent over it, as to a woman'.

18 See *ANET*, op. cit., p. 74 footnote 14; see also R. Temple, *The Sirius Mystery*, op. cit., p. 126.

19 *ANET*, op. cit., p. 77.

20 See A. Heidel, *The Gilgamesh Epic and Old Testament Parallels*, op. cit., p. 20; J. Gardner & J. Maier, *Gilgamesh*, op. cit., p. 73; S. Dalley, *Myths from Mesopotamia*, op. cit., p. 53 (although Dalley at least notes the possibility of 'meteoric iron' on p. 126 note 13). There are, of course, numerous other translations of *The Epic of Gilgamesh* and I have presumed that this is a representative sample of scholarly opinions.

21 See J. Gardner & J. Maier, *Gilgamesh*, op. cit., p. 75.

22 The 'doorpost' was broken, causing the 'wall' to be shaken; see *ANET*, op. cit., p. 78. If the tale is understood metaphorically then the 'doorpost' was part of the 'wall'.

23 *ANET*, op. cit., p. 48, a legend entitled 'Gilgamesh and the Land of the Living', although the tale is clearly part of *The Epic of Gilgamesh* cycle.

24 *ANET*, op. cit., p. 48; the bracketed sections are my own added points of clarification.

25 Ibid., p. 79; however, 'the Sun' is better rendered as 'Shamash', as in A. Heidel, *The*

Gilgamesh Epic and Old Testament Parallels, op. cit., p. 36.

26 *ANET*, op. cit., p. 79; the word translated 'leagues' literally meant 'double-hours'.

27 Ibid., p. 49, and S. N. Kramer, *The Sumerians*, op. cit., p. 195.

28 *ANET*, op. cit., p. 47 note 3; on Mount Hurrum, see also the legend of Lugalbanda.

29 Ibid., p. 79.

30 Ibid., p. 509; I have rendered 'Land of No Return' more literally as 'Mountain of No Return'.

31 Ibid.

32 G. de Santillana & H. von Dechend, *Hamlet's Mill*, op. cit., p. 438.

33 S. Dalley, *Myths from Mesopotamia*, op. cit., pp. 291-2.

34 Ibid., p. 291; on Arallu, see G. de Santillana & H. von Dechend, *Hamlet's Mill*, op. cit., p. 449.

35 T. Jacobsen, *The Sumerian King List*, op. cit., pp. 188-9.

36 This element MES is often found in the names of Sumerian kings; see Jacobsen, ibid.

37 *ANET*, op. cit., p. 82.

38 Hence there is a Sumerian reference to a heavenly throne being cut to pieces like date-palms; see S. N. Kramer, *History Begins at Sumer*, op. cit., p. 293.

39 S. N. Kramer, *The Sumerians*, op. cit., p. 193.

40 *ANET*, op. cit., p. 48 attributes various names to the seven heroes: one is a viper, one is a dragon, one is a fire, one is a raging snake, one is a deluge, the other two names are illegible.

41 S. N. Kramer, *The Sumerians*, op. cit., p. 194.

42 *ANET*, op. cit., pp. 509-10, 512.

43 Ibid., p. 55; see also Ishtar's descent to the underworld in *ANET*, pp. 107-8.

44 *ANET*, op. cit., p. 82.

45 Ibid., p. 83; 'in' the plain makes more sense than 'on' the plain, in view of the fact that the plain (*edinnu*) was the underworld.

46 The translation is a composite of A. Heidel, *The Gilgamesh Epic and Old Testament Parallels*, op. cit., pp. 47-8, and *ANET*, op. cit., p. 83.

47 *ANET*, op. cit., p. 504.

48 Ibid.

49 J. Gardner & J. Maier, *Gilgamesh*, op. cit., p. 210.

50 Ibid., p. 108.

51 Gilgamesh's mother is named in *The Epic* as the goddess Ninsun. Was this an epithet of Inanna? My suggestion of incest is based partly on the surmise that Gilgamesh was the offspring of the sacred marriage rite between Inanna and Dumuzi.

52 See *ANET*, op. cit., pp. 85, 505; also J. Gardner & J. Maier, *Gilgamesh*, op. cit., pp. 159, 161.

53 J. Gardner & J. Maier, *Gilgamesh*, op. cit., p. 196.

54 The translation is a composite of J. Gardner & J. Maier, *Gilgamesh*, op. cit., p. 198, *ANET*, op. cit., p. 88, and A. Heidel, *The Gilgamesh Epic and Old Testament Parallels*, op. cit., p. 65. Note that 'Mashu' meant 'twins'. Heidel preferred 'banks of Heaven' to 'vault of Heaven', but a singular 'bank' seems more appropriate, since 'bank' was a metaphor for 'planet'. Compare the 'breasts' of Mount Mashu to the Mesopotamian idea of the rivers Tigris and Euphrates being drawn up from the nipples of Tiamat in the underworld; compare also the Egyptian belief in *Qerti*, the two breast-like openings which replenished the waters of the river Nile from deep in the underworld.

55 Book of the Dead, Spell 108; see R. O. Faulkner, *The Ancient Egyptian Book of the Dead*, op. cit., p. 101, which refers to Mount Bakhu as '300 rods long and 150 rods broad'; Bakhu is called 'that mountain on which the Sky rests... in the east of the Sky'; compare Spell 149 (p. 139) which seemingly refers to the cosmic mountain in the underworld: 'the very high mountain which is in the realm of the dead, on which the Sky rests... the very high twin mountains'.

56 The translation is a composite of J. Gardner & J. Maier, *Gilgamesh*, op. cit., p. 198, and *ANET*, op. cit., p. 88.

57 The translation is a composite of J. Gardner & J. Maier, *Gilgamesh*, op. cit., p. 200, and *ANET*, op. cit., p. 88. Utnapishtim's name meant 'He who found the Breath-of-Life (*napistu*)'; the name was a reference to the earlier Sumerian Flood-hero, Ziusudra, who was rewarded with 'life like that of a god' and '*breath eternal* like that of a god'. In other words, Utnapishtim had found an *eternal* Breath-of-Life.

58 *ANET*, op. cit., p. 89; compare J. Gardner & J. Maier, *Gilgamesh*, op. cit., p. 205.

59 A. Heidel, *The Gilgamesh Epic and Old Testament Parallels*, op. cit., p. 70, though I have paraphrased the first line 'Gilgamesh, whither runnest thou?'

60 The translation is a composite of J. Gardner & J. Maier, *Gilgamesh*, op. cit., p. 212, *ANET*, op. cit., p. 91, and A. Heidel, *The Gilgamesh Epic and Old Testament Parallels*, op. cit., p. 74. Translations of the penultimate line, re 'the waters of death', vary considerably, and one suspects that a proper translation is still wanting.

61 The term *Shanabi* meant 'forty', thus the name Urshanabi meant something like 'he of forty'; see G. de Santillana & H. von Dechend, *Hamlet's Mill*, op. cit., p. 295 footnote 20.

62 The translation is a composite of J. Gardner & J. Maier, *Gilgamesh*, op. cit., p. 217, *ANET*, op. cit., p. 92, and A. Heidel, *The Gilgamesh Epic and Old Testament Parallels*, op. cit., p. 74. Heidel translated 'the Stone Things' as 'stone images', and noted that the Hittite version of *The Epic* referred to 'two images of stone'.

63 *ANET*, op. cit., p. 507.

64 There were similar ideas in ancient Egypt, notably the *shedshed* vehicle of Upuaut and the Aten fireball; see A. F. Alford, *The Phoenix Solution*, op. cit., pp. 251-3, 257.

65 The translation is a composite of J. Gardner & J. Maier, *Gilgamesh*, op. cit., p. 241, and *ANET*, op. cit., p. 95.

66 See J. Gardner & J. Maier, *Gilgamesh*, op. cit., p. 236.

67 The translation is a composite of J. Gardner & J. Maier, *Gilgamesh*, op. cit., p. 249, and *ANET*, op. cit., p. 96.

68 J. Gardner & J. Maier, *Gilgamesh*, op. cit., p. 249.

69 The translation is a composite of J. Gardner & J. Maier, *Gilgamesh*, op. cit., p. 249, and *ANET*, op. cit., p. 96. The abyss or deep is in fact the Apsu, the underworld.

70 *ANET*, op. cit., p. 96.

71 The translation is a composite of A. Heidel, *The Gilgamesh Epic and Old Testament Parallels*, op. cit., p. 93, and *ANET*, op. cit., p. 97; I have paraphrased two lines as rhetorical questions.

72 *ANET*, op. cit., p. 45; see also S. N. Kramer, *The Sumerians*, op. cit., p. 187.

73 The translation is a composite of *ANET*, op. cit., p. 46, and S. N. Kramer, *The Sumerians*, op. cit., p. 189.

74 See *ANET*, op. cit., p. 46; see also S. N. Kramer, *The Sumerians*, op. cit., p. 189. It is implied that Gilgamesh ascended the wall in order to peer over it; compare how Zabardibunugga 'ascended the wall'.

75 The translation is a composite of *ANET*, op. cit., p. 47, and S. N. Kramer, *The Sumerians*, op. cit., p. 189, though I have paraphrased slightly to reflect the poetic contrast between this and the earlier passage.

76 S. N. Kramer, *The Sumerians*, op. cit., p. 190, but the last line is based on the *ANET* translation (p. 47) which reads: 'O Agga, thou bringest the fleeing man to rest.' I have paraphrased this slightly to bring out the meaning as I see it.

77 *ANET*, op. cit., p. 48.

78 A. Heidel, *The Gilgamesh Epic and Old Testament Parallels*, op. cit., p. 172.

79 Coffin Texts, Spell 708.

80 S. N. Kramer, *The Sumerians*, op. cit., pp. 187-8.

81 On the fleeing bird motif, see also S. N. Kramer, *History Begins at Sumer*, op. cit., p. 179, where Gilgamesh and Enkidu referred to Huwawa as 'the caught bird', who might 'go back to his place', i.e. 'to the bosom of his mother'. This meant to Huwawa's place of *heavenly* origin; but if Gilgamesh allowed Huwawa to return thus, he, Gilgamesh, would not be able to return to the bosom of his own heavenly mother. See also pp. 26-7, where the envoy from Uruk used the fleeing bird motif in his speech to the Lord of Aratta.

82 *ANET*, op. cit., p. 53; compare T. Jacobsen, *The Treasures of Darkness*, op. cit., pp. 55-6.

83 T. Jacobsen, *The Treasures of Darkness*, op. cit., p. 59.

84 H. Frankfort et al, *The Intellectual Adventure of Ancient Man*, op. cit., pp. 154-5; see also S. N. Kramer, *History Begins at Sumer*, op. cit., pp. 85-6. The number '3' was symbolic of birth in ancient times.

85 S. N. Kramer, *The Sumerians*, op. cit., p. 190, though I prefer to translate 'for the price of' rather than 'for the sake of'.

86 Ibid.

87 The same idea is found in the Roman legend of Gilgamesh as a child thrown down from an

acropolis, but caught in mid-fall on the back of an eagle; see A. Heidel, *The Gilgamesh Epic and Old Testament Parallels*, op. cit., p. 4.

88 G. de Santillana & H. von Dechend, *Hamlet's Mill*, op. cit., pp. 448-9; see also *ANET*, op. cit., p. 50 footnote 4.

89 J. Gardner & J. Maier, *Gilgamesh*, op. cit., p. 222.

90 The translation is a composite of *ANET*, op. cit., p. 93, and A. Heidel, *The Gilgamesh Epic and Old Testament Parallels*, op. cit., p. 80; compare also J. Gardner & J. Maier, *Gilgamesh*, op. cit., p. 226.

91 *ANET*, op. cit., p. 93.

CHAPTER SIX: THE CITY BEYOND THE RIVER

1   *ANET*, op. cit., p. 93.

2   J. Gardner & J. Maier, *Gilgamesh*, op. cit., p. 229.

3   T. Jacobsen, *The Sumerian King List*, op. cit., p. 77. Shuruppak was also the 5th city in the Sumerian deluge myth; see *ANET*, op. cit., p. 43.

4   T. Jacobsen, *The Sumerian King List*, op. cit., pp. 85-9.

5   S. N. Kramer, *The Sumerians*, op. cit., p. 181.

6   *ANET*, op. cit., p. 613.

7   Ibid., p. 619.

8   Ibid., p. 122. Kummiya is also referenced on p. 124. The heavenly abode of the gods was also called the *Kuntarra*-house; see p. 123.

9   Coffin Texts, Spell 335.

10 Coffin Texts, Spell 4; see also Spell 66.

11 Coffin Texts, Spell 161.

12 Coffin Texts, Spell 515.

13 Coffin Texts, Spell 775.

14 Papyrus of Hunefer; see E. A. Wallis Budge, *Egyptian Religion*, op. cit., p. 125.

15 A. F. Alford, *The Phoenix Solution*, op. cit., chapter 11.

16 E. A. Wallis Budge, *From Fetish to God in Ancient Egypt*, op. cit., pp. 145, 235; see also E. A. Wallis Budge, *Legends of the Egyptian Gods*, op. cit., p. 228 footnote 1.

17 Pyramid Texts, Utterance 694, para 2144.

18 A. F. Alford, *The Phoenix Solution*, op. cit., pp. 130-1, 323, and Plate 19.

19 H. Frankfort, *Kingship and the Gods*, op. cit., p. 202; see also R. T. Rundle Clark, *Myth and Symbol in Ancient Egypt*, op. cit., p. 170. Frankfort suggested that the meaning of the name *Ta-Wer* alluded to the primeval hill.

20 *Djw* meant 'mountain'; see R. H. Wilkinson, *Reading Egyptian Art*, op. cit., pp. 132-3; hence the fetish of Abydos was set upon the hieroglyph for 'mountain'. AB, or Abu, was the 'city of beginning'.

21 A. F. Alford, *The Phoenix Solution*, op. cit., pp. 331-5.

22 H. Frankfort, *Kingship and the Gods*, op. cit., pp. 391-2 footnote 47: Osiris was 'Lord of the wine at the *Wag*-feast'; see also B. E. Shafer, *Temples of Ancient Egypt*, op. cit., p. 26.

23 Compare Coffin Texts, Spell 457: 'someone is ushered in to me at Abydos for Heliopolis', and 'someone is conveyed from Abydos to Heliopolis'. The trip might equally well terminate at Memphis, the place where Osiris was drowned.

24 See Coffin Texts, Spell 44: 'May you sail southward in the Night-bark and northward in the Day-bark; may you recognise your soul in the upper Sky, while your flesh, your corpse is in Heliopolis.'

25 It may be no coincidence that the name AB, or Abu, consists of the first two letters of the modern alphabet, after the Greek letters alpha and beta; the Greeks recognised the connection between AB, the City of the Beginning, and the alphabet, and thus named the town *Eleph*antine (compare alpha/aleph).

26 E. A. Wallis Budge, *From Fetish to God in Ancient Egypt*, op. cit., pp. 515-16; according to Egyptian tradition, Abaton had been set apart as the resting place of Osiris at the beginning of the world; the Mysteries of Osiris were celebrated there amid total silence; no ordinary person was allowed to set foot on the island of Abaton.

27 Pyramid Texts, Utterance 359, para 599-600.

28 Pyramid Texts, Utterance 437, para 802; compare Coffin Texts, Spell 474; contrast to Pyramid Texts, Utterance 359, para 600, where the Waterway ended in the eastern side of the Sky.
29 G. de Santillana & H. von Dechend, *Hamlet's Mill*, David R. Godine, 1969.
30 This has a bearing on the so-called Saturn theory, which supposes an unnatural array of the solar system planets in order to account for the tradition of a fiery cataclysm in the north of the Sky. The more prosaic explanation is that the north became important symbolically when the Egyptians celebrated their interplanetary cult along the river Nile, which geographically ran south-north. This south-north symbolism was enhanced by the fact that the northern stars never set, and thus appeared to be immortal; the importance of the northern stars is well attested in Egyptian funerary cults, for the sacred adzes used in the Opening of the Mouth rebirth ceremony resembled the shape of the northern constellations Ursa Minor and Ursa Major.
31 Pyramid Texts, Utterance 694, para 2144.
32 Coffin Texts, Spell 172.
33 Coffin Texts, Spell 169.
34 Coffin Texts, Spell 1129.
35 A. Heidel, *The Gilgamesh Epic and Old Testament Parallels*, op. cit., p. 65.
36 In addition to the legends already cited, see the legend of Inanna, the farmer and the shepherd in S. N. Kramer, *History Begins at Sumer*, op. cit., p. 309; in the context of the sacred marriage of Heaven and Earth, we read: 'On the river bank, the shepherd (Dumuzi) rejoiced.'
37 Coffin Texts, Spells 353, 317.
38 *ANET*, op. cit., p. 372.
39 Ibid., p. 371. Other traditions confirmed that the source of the Nile was in Nun (Nu); see E. A. Wallis Budge, *From Fetish to God in Ancient Egypt*, op. cit., p. 235, and *Legends of the Egyptian Gods*, op. cit., p. 242 footnote 3; apparently, the Nile had flowed into Egypt through two breast-like openings known as *Qerti*, see *Legends of the Egyptian Gods*, op. cit., p.124 footnote 5.
40 This is a remarkable claim since the Eye of Horus can only be interpreted as being either the lost moon of Heaven, or its reincarnation in the Moon of the Earth; whichever way one interprets the text, the Nile-god had inundated the heavens.
41 E. A. Wallis Budge, *From Fetish to God in Ancient Egypt*, op. cit., p. 385: *A Hymn of Thanksgiving to the Nile*.
42 *ANET*, op. cit., p. 373.
43 G. de Santillana & H. von Dechend, *Hamlet's Mill*, op. cit., p. 253; compare Coffin Texts, Spell 318: 'the Nile came into being in the limits of the Earth'.
44 S. N. Kramer, *The Sumerians*, op. cit., p. 200; compare this *Huluppu*-tree to the mythical *styrax*-tree in the Epic of Etana, *ANET*, op. cit., pp. 114-15.
45 *ANET*, op. cit., p. 95; I have added 'in the distance' for poetic effect; Utnapishtim was known as 'the Distant One', see A. Heidel, *The Gilgamesh Epic and Old Testament Parallels*, op. cit., p. 79; the same epithet, 'the Far-Distant', was applied to his namesakes Ziusudra and Atra-Hasis, see S. Dalley, *Myths from Mesopotamia*, op. cit., p. 2.
46 *ANET*, op. cit., p. 373. See also *ANET*, p. 371: 'the true Nile comes from the underworld for Egypt'; also p. 370: 'Thou makest a Nile in the underworld'.
47 E. A. Wallis Budge, *From Fetish to God in Ancient Egypt*, op. cit., p. 256. See also E. A. Wallis Budge, *Legends of the Egyptian Gods*, op. cit., p. 125, and E. A. Wallis Budge, *Egyptian Religion*, op. cit., p. 131.
48 E. A. Wallis Budge, *Legends of the Egyptian Gods*, op. cit., p. 135.
49 Ibid., p. 125; see also *ANET*, op. cit., p. 31. Might Uaua represent the underworld?
50 Coffin Texts, Spell 318.
51 E. A. Wallis Budge, *Legends of the Egyptian Gods*, op. cit., p. 218; see also E. A. Wallis Budge, *From Fetish to God in Ancient Egypt*, op. cit., p. 179, and E. A. Wallis Budge, *Egyptian Religion*, op. cit., pp. 45-6.
52 E. A. Wallis Budge, *From Fetish to God in Ancient Egypt*, op. cit., p. 235: 'The Egyptians knew nothing about the true sources of the Nile, and the annual flooding or Inundation.'
53 According to A. Heidel, *The Gilgamesh Epic and Old Testament Parallels*, op. cit., p. 227, the name Ziusudra meant something like 'He who laid hold on life of distant days'. There may have been a connection to the goddess Sud, who was the tutelary deity of Shuruppak.
54 *ANET*, op. cit., p. 44; the text seems to treat Anu and Enlil as a singular deity, hence the

rendering 'Anu-and-Enlil'; I have paraphrased the translation in places, substituted 'Utu' for 'Sun', and used the alternative translation possibilities cited in *ANET*, p. 44 footnotes 59-60; hence 'the land of crossing' becomes 'the mountain of rulership', whilst 'the land of Dilmun' becomes the 'mountain of Dilmun'.

55 Some scholars locate Dilmun in Bahrein, others locate it in south-western Iran; see discussion in S. N. Kramer, *The Sumerians*, op. cit., pp. 281-4; see also D. Rohl, *Legend*, op. cit., ch. 8.

56 The translation is a composite of *ANET*, op. cit., p. 38, and H. Frankfort et al, *The Intellectual Adventure of Ancient Man*, op. cit., pp. 159-60.

57 Compare the poetic iterations in the legend entitled *The Dispute between Cattle and Grain*: prior to the lowering of cattle and grain from Heaven, 'there was no ewe, no lamb was dropped, there was no goat, no kid was dropped, the ewe did not give birth to its two lambs, the goat did not give birth to its three kids'; see S. N. Kramer, *The Sumerians*, op. cit., p. 220.

58 *ANET*, op. cit., p. 38.

59 D. Rohl, *Legend*, op. cit., pp. 246-7; the dwelling place was said to be at a distance of 30 *beru* (literally 'double-hours').

60 The translation is a composite of S. N. Kramer, *The Sumerians*, op. cit., p. 175, and T. Jacobsen, *The Treasures of Darkness*, op. cit., p. 110; as in many other instances, it is preferable to render 'the place where *the Sun* rises' as 'the place where *Utu* rises'.

61 *ANET*, op. cit., pp. 93, 95.

62 T. Jacobsen, *The Treasures of Darkness*, op. cit., p. 253 footnote 227: the omitted line relating to Imdugud reads 'fettered on knee and beak with Inanna's fetter'.

63 Pyramid Texts, Utterance 574, para 1485; note how the gods stand underneath the tree in the 'Lower Sky', i.e. the fallen Sky in the underworld.

64 S. N. Kramer, *History Begins at Sumer*, op. cit., p. 27.

65 The seven 'mountains' of the underworld probably correspond to the seven 'heavens', which had to be crossed to reach the abode of God, e.g. in the ascension of Muhammed. These seven 'mountains' should not be taken literally as seven planets that exploded; on the contrary, the number is most likely to be symbolic.

66 Lugalbanda fell deathly ill at the foot of Mount Hurrum, and was thus forced to abandon his journey to Heaven (Aratta); see S. N. Kramer, *The Sumerians*, op. cit., p. 275.

67 S. N. Kramer, *History Begins at Sumer*, op. cit., p. 27.

68 See Z. Sitchin, *Divine Encounters*, Avon Books, 1995, p. 170.

69 T. Jacobsen, *The Sumerian King List,* op. cit., pp. 86-7 footnote 115; compare S. N. Kramer, *The Sumerians*, op. cit., p. 270.

70 S. N. Kramer, *History Begins at Sumer*, op. cit., pp. 18-29; see also S. N. Kramer, *The Sumerians*, op. cit., pp. 270-1.

71 S. N. Kramer, *The Sumerians*, op. cit., p. 270. It is worth noting that the various minerals of Aratta were heaped up in the courtyard of the E.AN.NA temple at Uruk; when one reads the legend carefully, one realises that it is a tale of a mythical 'people' bringing minerals and stones down to Earth from a 'mountain' in the heavens: see S. N. Kramer, *History Begins at Sumer*, op. cit., pp. 24-5.

72 S. N. Kramer, *The Sumerians*, op. cit., pp. 270-4.

73 E. A. Wallis Budge, *Egyptian Religion*, op. cit., p. 190.

74 Coffin Texts, Spell 467.

75 Coffin Texts, Spell 335.

76 Coffin Texts, Spell 316.

77 E. A. Wallis Budge, *The Egyptian Heaven and Hell*, op. cit., III, pp. 65-6.

78 T. Jacobsen, *The Sumerian King List,* op. cit., pp. 77, 85, 93, 95.

79 *ANET*, op. cit., p. 47.

80 The sequence of the two cities has, of course, been reversed, but this can be explained very simply by political shenanigans on the part of the authors of the texts.

81 T. Jacobsen, *The Sumerian King List,* op. cit., pp. 71-7.

82 Ibid., pp. 61-2.

83 *ANET*, op. cit., p. 53.

84 T. Jacobsen, *The Sumerian King List,* op. cit., p. 62 footnote 116; 'abandoned' can also be translated as 'forsook', but in view of the context, a better verb would be 'fell'.

85 Concerning the first part, the number of planetary 'cities' – five – might well be symbolic; the

ancient Egyptians regarded '5' as symbolic of the creation owing to the difference between the actual calendar of 365 days and an imaginary perfect 'golden age' calendar of 360 days; thus it was supposed that Nut gave birth to five children of chaos, and thus the word *Duat* was written using a five-pointed star.

86 One must suppose that the opening lines of the pre-diluvial King List have been reworked from 'when kingship was in Heaven' to the formula of the post-diluvial King List, i.e. 'when kingship was *lowered from* Heaven', thus destroying the original meaning of the pre-diluvial tradition. This is all too plausible in my view. A later scribe seems to have stitched the two traditions back together, but without reinstating the original first line.

87 *ANET*, op. cit., p. 120.

88 See T. Jacobsen, *The Sumerian King List,* op. cit., p. 71.

89 D. Rohl, *Legend*, op. cit., p. 201; it is worth making the comparison to the legend of the Allallu-bird, whose pinions were broken, see J. G. Frazer, *The Golden Bough*, op. cit., p. 650.

90 *Mahabharata*, Drona Parva section, p. 690, verses 62-77; cited in E. von Daniken, *The Return of the Gods*, Element, 1997, pp. 76-7.

91 *Legendary Times* 1:1 (January 1999), pp. 6-7.

CHAPTER SEVEN: LIFE ON THE ARK

1 The translation is a composite of S. Dalley, *Myths from Mesopotamia*, op. cit., p. 18, *ANET*, op. cit., p. 104, and A. Heidel, *The Gilgamesh Epic and Old Testament Parallels*, op. cit., p. 107.

2 Genesis 7:11.

3 Genesis 6:1.

4 *ANET*, op. cit., p. 104; compare S. Dalley, *Myths from Mesopotamia*, op. cit., p. 2.

5 *ANET*, op. cit., p. 95 footnote 218.

6 The translation is a composite of S. Dalley, *Myths from Mesopotamia*, op. cit., pp. 26-7, and A. Heidel, *The Gilgamesh Epic and Old Testament Parallels*, op. cit., p. 111 & footnote 29.

7 S. Dalley, *Myths from Mesopotamia*, op. cit., p. 37 footnote 26.

8 Ibid., p. 28.

9 Ibid., p. 29.

10 The translation is a composite of S. Dalley, *Myths from Mesopotamia*, op. cit., pp. 29-30, *ANET*, op. cit., p. 105, and A. Heidel, *The Gilgamesh Epic and Old Testament Parallels*, op. cit., p. 109.

11 S. Dalley, *Myths from Mesopotamia*, op. cit., p. 31.

12 *ANET*, op. cit., p. 514; I prefer to render the last line '. . . destruction approaches mankind' slightly differently.

13 S. Dalley, *Myths from Mesopotamia*, op. cit., p. 31; I prefer to render 'went against' as 'overcame'.

14 Ibid., p. 32-3.

15 Ibid., p. 34.

16 Ibid., p. 30.

17 *ANET*, op. cit., p. 61; compare the legend entitled 'When Anu had created the heavens' in A. Heidel, *The Babylonian Genesis*, op. cit., p. 65.

18 *ANET*, op. cit., p. 93.

19 Ibid.

20 Ibid.; compare A. Heidel, *The Gilgamesh Epic and Old Testament Parallels*, op. cit., p. 81.

21 C. H. Gordon & G. A. Rendsburg, *The Bible and the Ancient Near East,* 4th edition, W. W. Norton & Co., 1997, p. 48.

22 Ibid.

23 *ANET*, op. cit., p. 93; the Deep is the Apsu.

24 J. Gardner & J. Maier, *Gilgamesh*, op. cit., p. 292.

25 Genesis 7:11, 8:2; see my comments in chapter 9 of this work.

26 Remember that Utnapishtim was told to abandon his possessions; see the note in J. Gardner & J. Maier, *Gilgamesh*, op. cit., p. 233. It strikes me, with hindsight, that this detail is a dead giveaway as to the original planetary nature of the legend; compare the piling up of minerals in Uruk by the mythical residents of the heavenly 'city' of Aratta (see earlier references).

27 Compare this boatman to the Mesopotamian traditions of the *Apkallu* – the fish-like beings

who brought the gods from Heaven to Earth.

28 The translation is a composite of *ANET*, op. cit., p. 94, and A. Heidel, *The Gilgamesh Epic and Old Testament Parallels*, op. cit., p. 85.

29 *ANET*, op. cit., pp. 103-4, 507-12.

30 The translation is a composite of *ANET*, op. cit., p. 94, A. Heidel, *The Gilgamesh Epic and Old Testament Parallels*, op. cit., p. 85, and J. Gardner & J. Maier, *Gilgamesh*, op. cit., p. 235. The word 'battle' was synonymous with 'the dance of Inanna'; see T. Jacobsen, *The Treasures of Darkness*, op. cit., p. 137. In one hymn, Inanna boasted: "when I begin moving at the end of the battle, I am an evilly rising flood." (Jacobsen, ibid., pp. 137-8), whilst in another legend Inanna fought a rather strange battle against a personified 'mountain', named 'Ebih' (Jacobsen, ibid., p. 137). In one text, Inanna was described as 'the great dread storm of Heaven', and in another as 'Mistress of E.AN.NA, who lay waste the mountains' (Jacobsen, ibid., pp. 136, 54). Inanna was probably the unnamed goddess who complained of being abducted on a boat, along with all her goods, 'on that day of mine on which I was destroyed' (Jacobsen, ibid., pp. 77-8); finally, it is worth citing the hymn to Inanna (Jacobsen, ibid., p. 136), which praised the goddess with the words:

> 'O destroyer of mountains, you lent the storm wings!...
> O beloved one of Enlil, you came flying into the land,
> Attended to the instructions of Anu.
> O my lady, at your roar you made the lands bow low...
> With the charging storm you charge, with the howling storm you howl,
> With Ishkur you roar, with all evil winds you rage!'

31 See footnotes 97 and 99 to chapter 3 of this work.

32 See A. F. Alford, *The Phoenix Solution*, op. cit., p. 156. It is generally acknowledged that there is a connection, too, between Tiamat and the watery *tehom* of Genesis 1; see S. H. Hooke, *Middle Eastern Mythology*, Penguin Books, 1963, p. 119.

33 H. Frankfort, *Kingship and the Gods*, op. cit., p. 328.

34 A. Heidel, *The Babylonian Genesis*, op. cit., p. 19; see also T. Jacobsen, *The Treasures of Darkness*, op. cit., p. 170, where he equated Tiamat's belly to 'the heart of Heaven's foundation'.

35 *ANET*, op. cit., p. 71, lines 89-90.

36 Ibid., p. 94, lines 127-30; compare the six days of creation in the book of Genesis.

37 The translation is a composite of J. Gardner & J. Maier, *Gilgamesh*, op. cit., p. 236, and *ANET*, op. cit., p. 94. Note also the idea that the Flood had swept *into* the land of Earth, *ANET*, p. 44 footnote 51.

38 S. Dalley, *Myths from Mesopotamia*, op. cit., p. 33.

39 The translation is a composite of J. Gardner & J. Maier, *Gilgamesh*, op. cit., p. 236, and *ANET*, op. cit., p. 94.

40 On the meaning of Mount Nisir, see A. Heidel, *The Gilgamesh Epic and Old Testament Parallels*, op. cit., p. 250.

41 Strictly speaking, the boat should have entered the underworld, but there is no suggestion of this in the Utnapishtim story (there is perhaps a slight hint of it in the Ziusudra story, when the god Utu opened up an aperture in the sunken boat). The original sacrifice scene would have been played out upon the fallen 'mountain' of the underworld.

42 J. Gardner & J. Maier, *Gilgamesh*, op. cit., p. 242.

43 Ibid., p. 239; see also their comment p. 242.

44 S. Dalley, *Myths from Mesopotamia*, op. cit., pp. 33-4; see also her comment p. 38 note 42.

45 Ibid., p. 38 footnote 42. It may be significant that, in the legend of Inanna's descent to the underworld, the creatures which were sent down to save her were compared to flies, flying around Ereshkigal's door, see S. N. Kramer, *History Begins at Sumer*, op. cit., p. 298.

46 J. Gardner & J. Maier, *Gilgamesh*, op. cit., p. 240.

47 *ANET*, op. cit., p. 95; the blame is similarly placed on the Igigi in the legend of Atra-Hasis, see S. Dalley, *Myths from Mesopotamia*, op. cit., p. 34.

48 *ANET*, op. cit., p. 95, partly paraphrased.

49 Ibid., p. 44; this legend, written in Sumerian, is dated to *c.* 1700 BC, a little earlier than the legend of Atra-Hasis.

50 S. N. Kramer, *History Begins at Sumer*, op. cit., p. 296.

51 *ANET*, op. cit., p. 619.
52 In support of this, the Mesopotamians suggested that the 'house' was a 'birth-hut', hence the goddess Mami/Ninharsag was known as Nintu (or Nintur), 'Lady Birth-hut'; see T. Jacobsen, *The Treasures of Darkness*, op. cit., p. 107.
53 It is evident that the significance of the reed-hut in the opening lines of *Enuma Elish* needs to be reconsidered; see *ANET*, op. cit., p. 61.
54 *ANET,* op. cit., p. 47.
55 S. N. Kramer, *The Sumerians*, op. cit., p. 195; see also *ANET*, op. cit., p. 49.
56 S. N. Kramer, *The Sumerians*, op. cit., pp. 195, 277; see also *ANET*, op. cit., p. 49.
57 S. N. Kramer, *The Sumerians*, op. cit., p. 176; it is linked, apparently, to a place called Meluhha, which would suggest a mythical as well as a geographical identity for that place.
58 Coffin Texts, Spells 132, 136.
59 On 'Mooring Post', see R. O. Faulkner, *The Ancient Egyptian Pyramid Texts*, op. cit., references listed on p. 321; see also Coffin Texts, for example Spells 50 & 68; the term is sometimes dual, implying a belief in two great Mooring Posts in the Sky.
60 The translation is a composite of J. Gardner & J. Maier, *Gilgamesh*, op. cit., p. 227, S. Dalley, *Myths from Mesopotamia*, op. cit., p. 110, and *ANET*, op. cit., p. 93.
61 Hence perhaps the odd statement by Utnapishtim: 'The land was gathered about me' (see *ANET*, op. cit., p. 93), a saying which is found also in *The Epic of Gilgamesh*, where the land of Uruk was gathered around the 'star' or 'pickaxe' which fell down from the sky.
62 A. Heidel, *The Gilgamesh Epic and Old Testament Parallels*, op. cit., p. 232.
63 Ibid.
64 J. Gardner & J. Maier, *Gilgamesh*, op. cit., p. 233.
65 S. N. Kramer, *History Begins at Sumer*, op. cit., p. 224.
66 See T. Jacobsen, *The Sumerian King List,* op. cit., p. 76 note 32.
67 Although the excessive 'noise' of the 'people' was largely a mythical idea (see later in this book), it is not unlikely that the cities of the ancient Near East would indeed have been afflicted by the noise of the rabble, which might have disturbed the kings who rested in their palaces.
68 S. N. Kramer, *History Begins at Sumer*, op. cit., p. 370.
69 Coffin Texts, Spell 80.
70 T. Jacobsen, *The Treasures of Darkness*, op. cit., pp. 95, 98.
71 Ibid., p. 110; see also S. N. Kramer, *The Sumerians*, op. cit., p. 175.
72 *ANET*, op. cit., p. 576.
73 Coffin Texts, Spell 317.
74 Coffin Texts, Spells 143, 153.
75 Coffin Texts, Spell 989; compare 'the ropes of iron' in Spell 62; it is a little-known fact that some older texts wrote Nut's name as *Hnw*, meaning 'vessel' or 'ship', see A. Gardiner, *Egyptian Grammar*, 3rd ed., p. 530.
76 *ANET*, op. cit., p. 71; see also S. Dalley, *Myths from Mesopotamia*, op. cit., p. 270.
77 *ANET*, op. cit., p. 616; on the same page we read of Damgalnunna, 'mother of the lofty house'; Utnapishtim, too, abandoned his possessions when he sailed away from heavenly Shuruppak towards the Apsu (underworld).
78 *ANET*, op. cit., p. 44.

CHAPTER EIGHT: THE BLACK-HEADED ONES

1 *ANET*, op. cit., p. 43; see also A. Heidel, *The Babylonian Genesis*, op. cit., p. 72.
2 Ibid.; see also S. N. Kramer, *The Sumerians*, op. cit., p. 286, and A. Heidel, *The Babylonian Genesis*, op. cit., p. 72.
3 *ANET*, op. cit., p. 44.
4 It should be noted, however, that the meaning of the term translated 'vegetation' is not certain.
5 *ANET*, op. cit., pp. 462-3.
6 The translation is a composite of *ANET*, op. cit., p. 94, and A. Heidel, *The Gilgamesh Epic and Old Testament Parallels*, op. cit., p. 85.
7 S. N. Kramer, *The Sumerians*, op. cit., p. 220; however, 'on' should be rendered as 'in'.
8 Ibid., p. 177.
9 S. Dalley, *Myths from Mesopotamia*, op. cit., pp. 9-10; see also T. Jacobsen, *The Treasures of*

Darkness, op. cit., p. 117.

10 S. N. Kramer, *The Sumerians*, op. cit., pp. 220-1.

11 Ibid., p. 221.

12 *ANET*, op. cit., p. 51 footnote 23; compare the legend of the barley gods, cited in chapter 7.

13 Hence perhaps the name Marduk, derived from *Mr* and *Duku*, meaning 'God of Ascending from the Underworld', as indeed he did during the Babylonian New Year Festival.

14 S. N. Kramer, *The Sumerians*, op. cit., p. 221.

15 A. Heidel, *The Babylonian Genesis*, op. cit., p. 70 footnote 56.

16 Ibid., p. 70.

17 *ANET*, op. cit., p. 99.

18 S. N. Kramer, *The Sumerians*, op. cit., p. 150; compare D. Rohl, *Legend*, op. cit., p. 204.

19 Ibid.; see also H. Frankfort et al, *The Intellectual Adventure of Ancient Man*, op. cit., p. 162.

20 Scholars usually translate 'Lullu' as 'savage man' or 'primitive man'; compare the state of Enkidu before he was initiated by the prostitute.

21 S. Dalley, *Myths from Mesopotamia*, op. cit., p. 13.

22 Ibid.

23 Ibid., p. 14; compare also p. 15, and *ANET*, op. cit., p. 99.

24 S. Dalley, *Myths from Mesopotamia*, op. cit., p. 13.

25 Ibid., p. 15; compare *ANET*, op. cit., p. 100.

26 S. N. Kramer, *The Sumerians*, op. cit., pp. 285, 243, 264; the repeated term LU meant 'man', whilst the particle NAM was used to form abstract nouns; LU could also mean 'those who are shepherded', hence mankind was like sheep, and the king like a shepherd.

27 S. Dalley, *Myths from Mesopotamia*, op. cit., p. 18.

28 Ibid., p. 16.

29 T. Jacobsen, *Toward the Image of Tammuz*, Harvard University Press, 1970, pp. 111-14.

30 Ibid.

31 E. A. Wallis Budge, *Legends of the Egyptian Gods*, op. cit., p. 17.

32 Ibid., p. 33, and compare *ANET*, op. cit., p. 8, where 'Land of Caves' is rendered 'Island of Baba' – a part of the underworld. The legend contains references to mankind being 'on the mountain' or 'in the desert land', terms which now appear to indicate the underworld.

33 *ANET*, op. cit., p. 368.

34 The saying might also allude to the distinction between man's physical body and his hidden element – his soul or life-breath.

35 R. Graves, *The Greek Myths*, op. cit., p. 36.

36 M. Eliade, *A History of Religious Ideas*, Volume 1, op. cit., pp. 253-4.

37 Ibid., p. 254.

38 Ibid. *Encyclopaedia Britannica* states that the silver race had an 'inordinately prolonged childhood'. According to another Greek tradition, 'mankind' was created from the ashes of Titans, who had been incinerated by a thunderbolt from Zeus; see M. Eliade, *A History of Religious Ideas*, Volume 1, op. cit., p 371.

39 M. Eliade, *A History of Religious Ideas*, Volume 1, op. cit., p. 257.

40 A. Heidel, *The Babylonian Genesis*, op. cit., pp. 69-71.

41 S. Dalley, *Myths from Mesopotamia*, op. cit., p. 13; we should not be put off by the suggestion that the Anunnaki were sitting there; this would have referred to their metaphysical doubles.

42 According to a variant tradition, mankind was created from the gods which came from Tiamat's insides; see *ANET*, op. cit., p. 71 lines 88-9.

43 The translation is a composite of A. Heidel, *The Babylonian Genesis*, op. cit., pp. 46-7, *ANET*, op. cit., p. 68, and S. Dalley, *Myths from Mesopotamia*, op. cit., pp. 260-1.

44 The translation is a composite of S. Dalley, *Myths from Mesopotamia*, op. cit., p. 15, and *ANET*, op. cit., pp. 99-100.

45 It is worth noting that the Akkadian word for 'clay' was *ti-it-tu*, literally meaning 'piece with life'; see C. & B. J. O'Brien, *The Shining Ones*, op. cit., p. 151.

46 See discussion in chapter 4 of this work.

47 *ANET*, op. cit., p. 43, with regard to footnote 4; the repetition seems to echo the repetition of LU, 'man', in the name for mankind, NAM.LU.LU; all of this seems to hint at the belief in Heaven falling to Earth on at least two occasions.

48 S. Dalley, *Myths from Mesopotamia*, op. cit., p. 276 footnote 41.

49 A. Heidel, *The Babylonian Genesis*, op. cit., p. 63.

50 S. N. Kramer, *The Sumerians*, op. cit., pp. 80, 317.

51 *ANET*, op. cit., p. 114; in respect of the ninth line, see also the Assyrian version on p. 115: 'the regions had not been created altogether'.

52 Ibid., p. 115.

53 Ibid., p. 517.

54 Etana was considered to be god-like, hence he reigned reputedly for 1,560 years, and was able to consolidate all lands, presumably by means of his famous ascent to Heaven on the back of an eagle; see T. Jacobsen, *The Sumerian King List,* op. cit., p. 81, and *ANET*, op. cit., p. 118.

55 L. W. King, *The Seven Tablets of Creation*, 1902, I, pp. 122-5.

56 A. Heidel, *The Babylonian Genesis*, op. cit., p. 64; see also the legend of the creation of the world by Marduk on pp. 61-3: 'he created the beasts of Sumuqan, and the living things of the *edinnu...* the city he made, living creatures he placed therein.'

57 Ibid., p. 64.

58 S. Dalley, *Myths from Mesopotamia*, op. cit., p. 328.

59 Ibid., pp. 286, 313.

60 See citation earlier in this chapter; note how the newly created mankind would 'make *the field of the Anunnaki* produce plentifully'.

CHAPTER NINE: GENESIS REVISITED

1 Many writers have identified 'Ur-of-the-Chaldeans' with the Sumerian city of Ur, but this is challenged by scholars such as Cyrus H. Gordon, who prefers the site of Urfa in northern Mesopotamia; see C. H. Gordon, 'Abraham and the Merchants of Ura' in *Journal of Near Eastern Studies* 17 (1958), pp. 28-31.

2 Genesis 15:13, though 430 years is specified in Exodus 12:40; it is a matter of dispute which is the correct figure, though I am now minded to agree with C. H. Gordon, who states: 'it is obvious that these numbers are not to be taken literally, for they are idealised figures very typical of the epic tradition'; see C. H. Gordon & G. A. Rendsburg, *The Bible and the Ancient Near East,* op. cit., p. 112.

3 Powerful evidence for the 12th century BC is cited in C. H. Gordon & G. A. Rendsburg, *The Bible and the Ancient Near East,* op. cit. The 17th century BC is favoured by those who wish to see in the Exodus tradition a recollection of the volcanic explosion of Thera.

4 C. H. Gordon & G. A. Rendsburg, *The Bible and the Ancient Near East,* op. cit., pp. 149-50.

5 K. Armstrong takes the view that the early Hebrews such as Abraham were probably pagans, and that Abraham's God was El, the High God of Canaan; see *A History of God*, op. cit., p. 98.

6 *ANET*, op. cit., pp. 140, 152.

7 A. F. Alford, unpublished research.

8 K. Armstrong, *A History of God*, op. cit., p. 31, stated: 'It is very difficult to find a single monotheistic statement in the whole of the Pentateuch'; in other words, the existence of other gods was taken for granted.

9 Scholars have noted that the Hebrew legends have a particularly close connection to the legends of the Canaanites – the so-called Ugaritic literature; see C. H. Gordon & G. A. Rendsburg, *The Bible and the Ancient Near East,* op. cit., pp. 88-9.

10 There is an amazing parallel here to the story of the Flood in *The Epic of Gilgamesh*; the Flood, we are told, raged for six days and six nights, and then 'broke from its battle' on the 7th day.

11 Genesis 5:24; Enoch was thus 365 years old, a figure which was undoubtedly based on the Earth's solar year of 365 days. Enoch was the *seventh patriarch*, and there is a parallel here to one of the Sumerian pre-diluvial king lists, where the *seventh king*, Enmeduranki, was selected to be taken up to Heaven to sit before the gods Shamash and Adad.

It may be significant that Enoch's father was Jared, and the name Jared meant 'descent'; according to the Book of Enoch, two hundred entities known as the Watchers had descended from Heaven to Earth 'in the days of Jared'; it was Enoch who testified against the sins of these Watchers, which were seemingly committed in the underworld (compare the Nephilim).

12 See also the apocryphal legends in the Book of Enoch, of 'the Watchers' who descended from Heaven to Mount Hermon, fornicated with human women, and thus produced a race of giants.

13 Noah 950 years; Shem 600 years; Arphaxad 438 years; Shelah 433 years; Eber 464 years;

Peleg 239 years; Reu 239 years; Serug 230 years; Nahor 148 years; Terah 205 years.

14 Genesis 15.

15 Compare the tradition recorded in Jeremiah 34:18-19.

16 Genesis 22:17.

17 Genesis 32:22-32.

18 R. Alter, *Genesis*, op. cit., p. 182; according to C. H. Gordon & G. A. Rendsburg in *The Bible and the Ancient Near East*, op. cit., p. 138, the name 'Israel' appears as the name of a warrior in the Ugaritic literature.

19 Genesis 32:28. The meaning is very uncertain, especially since *elohim* is ambiguous (it can refer to 'God' or 'gods'); this translation is my own interpretation, inspired partly by R. Alter, *Genesis*, op. cit., p. 182; it makes sense to imagine Israel having striven to overcome both pagan gods and men.

20 Genesis 1:1-3. The biblical translations in this book are generally based on the King James Version of the Bible (as opposed to the New International Version, in which many fine points of detail, often significant, have been obscured). The language of the KJV, however, is at times archaic, and so I have not hesitated to paraphrase where necessary in order to elucidate the meaning for modern readers. Quotations from Genesis have also benefited from comparison to R. Alter, *Genesis*, op. cit.

21 Genesis 19:28.

22 Joshua 10:11: 'more were those who died from the hailstones than those who were slain by the swords of the children of Israel'.

23 See, for example: Exodus 19:18; Kings I 18:38; Kings I 19:11-12; Kings II 1:10; Job 1:16; Job 36:29-33; Job 38:1.

24 Deuteronomy 32:22.

25 Job 9:5.

26 Psalm 89:8-10. Compare translation in A. Heidel, *The Babylonian Genesis*, op. cit., p. 103.

27 Isaiah 51:9.

28 Job 26:6-13. The 'fleeing serpent' can also be rendered 'crooked serpent'. Compare translation in A. Heidel, *The Babylonian Genesis*, op. cit., p. 103, and note how the meaning of the passage can be altered by changing 'heavens' (per KJV) to 'sky'; similarly pp. 104-5. This clearance of the heavens echoes the manner in which the Egyptian god Re facilitated the resurrection of the deceased king by causing the Sky to be cleared like a road, see Coffin Texts, Spell 50; one Egyptian legend describes how the 'paths of Re' were obscured on 'the day when the Sky became choked and stifled', see Book of the Dead, Spell 110; another Egyptian legend refers to a day 'when the Sky was big with gods', see D. Meeks & C. Favard-Meeks, *Daily Life of the Egyptian Gods*, op. cit., p. 78. Why, then, ignore the obvious meaning of Job 26:6-13? Note the reference in Job 26:6 to Sheol being 'the Place of Destruction' (*Abaddon*); both terms referred to the underworld, which is exactly where the vanquished Rahab would have ended up.

29 A. Heidel, *The Babylonian Genesis*, op. cit., pp. 104-5, acknowledges that the fleeing serpent is a feature in the Sky, but neuters the meaning by pulling the old trick of making the Sky no higher than the troposphere.

30 Psalm 74:13-14. See also Job 9:13 (NIV) 'the cohorts of Rahab cowered at God's feet'.

31 The multiple-headed Leviathan had its counterpart in Ugaritic literature – the seven-headed 'Lotan', who was also described as 'the fleeing serpent'; see A. Heidel, *The Babylonian Genesis*, op. cit., pp. 107-8.

32 This would make sense if the vanquished Leviathan was cast down out of the Sky into the underworld like the Babylonian sea-dragon, Tiamat; see *ANET*, op. cit., pp. 71, 501-2.

33 Job 41:14-21.

34 Luke 10:18; see also Revelations 12:7-9 & 20:1-3.

35 Job 41:34.

36 Revelations 12:7-9.

37 The same tendency is notable in ancient Egypt in the worship of non-violent gods such as Atum and Ptah; and in the Mesopotamian legends it is difficult to find any legends of the supreme god Anu engaged directly in battle. Instead, it would seem that the battle scenes were, in time, delegated to the younger generation of gods.

38 This is probably the 'day of battle' remembered in Zechariah 14:3.

39 Genesis 1:1-3.

40 Psalm 104:1-2.

41 This is supported by Job 26:10: 'He marks out the horizon on the face of the waters for a boundary between light and darkness.' (NIV) See also Proverbs 8:27: 'I [Wisdom] was there when he set the Heaven(s) in place, when he marked out the horizon upon the face of the Deep.' (NIV)

42 The Jehovah's Witnesses, for example, suppose that the Sun, Moon and stars were created on Day 1 when God created 'the heavens'; the apparent second creation of the Sun, Moon and stars on Day 4 thus implied a removal of 'whatever had formerly obstructed the Sun's rays from reaching this planet'. See *Insight on the Scriptures*, Volume I, p. 528 & Volume II, p. 253. This seems a contrived explanation, indeed a non-explanation, in the sense that nowhere in the Bible is it made clear what the obstruction was which prevented the light from reaching the Earth (and in any event, no creature had yet been made on the Earth, making the supposed distinction between Days 1 and 4 entirely academic). Furthermore, it must be stressed that the belief of the Jehovah's Witnesses rests on the assumption that the *shamayim* which were created on Day 1 were 'heavens' (plural), when the term can equally well be rendered 'Heaven' (singular); see R. Alter, *Genesis*, op. cit., p. 3. The latter option fits neatly with my own explanation that the book of Genesis begins post-catastrophe with God's creation (sic) of the combined 'mountain' of Heaven-and-Earth.

43 Genesis 1:6-8.

44 These were the physical heavens, with God seated above them in a supernatural, spiritual abode. One wonders whether this idea might have been inspired by the ancient Egyptian belief that the realm of the gods in the Sky-*Duat* could be accessed via the stars of Orion and Sirius.

45 Genesis 1:17.

46 Compare this idea to the ancient Egyptian Coffin Texts, Spell 38A, where the creator-god Atum exclaimed: "I am Atum who ascended from the celestial waters to the celestial waters, I have taken my seat in the West".

47 Psalm 29:10.

48 Job 38:34.

49 Proverbs 3:19-20. Hence the waters above the Expanse and the waters below the Expanse; see Genesis 1:6-7.

50 See A. Heidel, *The Gilgamesh Epic and Old Testament Parallels*, op. cit., p. 243.

51 A possible translation of *shamayim* is 'where the waters were' (from *sham-maim*); another possible translation, rather intriguingly, is 'planted highlands', see C. & B. J. O'Brien, *The Shining Ones*, op. cit., pp. 57, 109; note the idea on p. 58 that Genesis 1 might allude to the gods felling timbers in Heaven and Earth – a very Mesopotamian idea. Compare Ezekiel 31:18 "Thou shalt be brought down with the trees of Eden unto the nether parts of the Earth".

52 These seven heavens are not to be taken literally as seven planets, but purely as symbolic of God's ascent to the highest heights. Eventually, on the seventh day, God finished his work and rested in the seventh band of the *shamayim*, otherwise known as 'the Seventh Heaven', 'Heaven', 'the highest heavens' or 'the Heaven of heavens'. See, for example, Deuteronomy 10:14; Kings I 8:27; Nehemiah 9:6. One particularly striking passage is in Psalm 68:33, where God is 'him that rideth upon the ancient Heaven of heavens'.

53 The death of God, the creation of a multiplicity of gods therefrom, the fall to the Earth, and the resurrection to Heaven. The passage benefits greatly from an understanding of Heaven-and-Earth as a single, combined entity. The idea of a Father-of-Beginning falling to Earth is evocative of the Egyptian belief in God falling from Heliopolis to either Abydos (the 'Mountain of Beginning') or to Elephantine (the 'City of Beginning').

54 S. N. Kramer, *The Sumerians*, op. cit., p. 150; the ancient Egyptians had a similar idea, see the 'Building Inscription' of Amenhotep III, in which Amen-Re declared the king to be "my son, of my body, my beloved, my living image" (*ANET*, op. cit., p. 376). See also Coffin Texts, Spell 906, where the king was said to be 'the eldest son of Atum, the image of him'.

55 It is ironic that some modern writers, including myself, have suggested that a flesh-and-blood God might have created a flesh-and-blood mankind in his own image, using genetic science.

56 This would explain why Adam created Seth 'in his own likeness, in his own image'; see Genesis 5:3.

57 Genesis 2:6-7; the word translated 'mist' is of very uncertain meaning per S. H. Hooke, *Middle Eastern Mythology*, op. cit., pp. 110-11.

58 Ezekiel 28:2 & 28:12-18. Compare this idea of a 'covering cherub' to the theme in Genesis 3:24, where the cherubim effectively covered the access to the Tree of Life in the underworld Garden of Eden.

59 Lamentations 2:1.

60 E. Pagels, *The Gnostic Gospels*, op. cit., p. 57.

61 Psalm 139:15. One wonders whether such a belief might explain the Hebrew custom of humbling oneself by sitting in ashes. See, for example, Jonah 3:6. See also *ANET*, op. cit., p. 139, re the Ugaritic legend of El pouring dust on his head in mourning.

62 Genesis 2:18-22; translation based on R. Alter, *Genesis*, op. cit., p. 9; 'rib' can also mean 'side' per S. H. Hooke, *Middle Eastern Mythology*, op. cit., p. 112; Hooke also pointed out, correctly, that the sleep of Adam was a 'supernatural slumber'.

63 This makes more sense. As has been noted by scholars, the biblical legend of the creation of Adam and Eve inverts the usual biological sequence of female giving birth to male; see E. Pagels, *The Gnostic Gospels*, op. cit., p. 77.

64 Genesis 3:20, and see R. Alter, *Genesis*, op. cit., p. 15 note 20; Eve's name is derived from the Hebrew verb *hayah*, meaning 'to make live'.

65 The Jewish Talmud. Legends of serpents falling from Heaven and entering the underworld are not hard to find; in ancient Egyptian lore, the god Seth entered the Earth as a hissing serpent, see E. A. Wallis Budge, *Legends of the Egyptian Gods*, op. cit., p. 77; and in ancient Greek lore, the great serpent Ophion was expelled from Mount Olympus into the dark caves beneath the Earth, see R. Graves, *The Greek Myths*, op. cit., pp. 27-8; oddly enough Ophion was expelled by having his head bruised by the heel of the goddess Eurynome – a theme which turns up in Genesis 3:15. The plot thickens when we read in R. Alter, *Genesis*, op. cit., p. 15 note 20, that the Hebrew word for Eve, *hawah*, sounds like the Aramaic word for 'serpent'.

66 Coffin Texts, Spell 269; see also Spell 405, where the 'river-bank' of Heaven was described as 'Backbone of Geb, and Ribs of Isis, on which are the repellers of the Serpent'.

67 Genesis 2:21. Compare the legend of Ea and Apsu in *Enuma Elish*, see *ANET*, op. cit., p. 61; as we shall see, Abram, too, was a descending god who was put into a deep sleep.

68 See R. Alter, *Genesis*, op. cit., p. 38; also A. Heidel, *The Babylonian Genesis*, op. cit., p. 46.

69 Genesis 2:24.

70 Coffin Texts, Spell 111.

71 Coffin Texts, Spell 686.

72 S. N. Kramer, *History Begins at Sumer*, op. cit., pp. 72-4, 353; it all happened 'one day' when Inanna happened to be 'crossing Heaven, crossing Earth', evidently a descent from Heaven into the underworld.

73 D. Rohl, *Legend*, op. cit., p. 57.

74 *ANET*, op. cit., p. 613.

75 On the crushed mountain motif, there is an interesting legend which recounts how king Naram-Sin forged mighty axes in order 'to turn the E.KUR into dust, like a mountain mined for silver, to cut it to pieces like a mountain of lapis lazuli'; see S. N. Kramer, *History Begins at Sumer*, op. cit., p. 293; although referring to the temple at Nippur, it uses words which evoke the archetypal disintegration of the heavenly 'mountain'.

76 See *ANET*, op. cit., p. 43, S. N. Kramer, *The Sumerians*, op. cit., p. 286, or A. Heidel, *The Babylonian Genesis*, op. cit., p. 72.

77 S. N. Kramer, *History Begins at Sumer*, op. cit., p. 177; see also *ANET*, op. cit., p. 48.

78 In this respect, there is a very interesting Armenian legend reported in G. Massey, *The Natural Genesis*, 1883, Vol. 2, p. 231; the legend suggests that the garden where Adam and Eve were raised is now at the bottom of Lake Van, having been submerged there at the time of the Flood. Compare Ezekiel 31:18 "Thou shalt be brought down with the trees of Eden unto the nether parts of the Earth", i.e. the trees of Eden had fallen into the underworld.

79 Genesis 2:18-19; translation based on R. Alter, *Genesis*, op. cit., p. 9.

80 I use the conventional term 'Garden *of* Eden', although it is worth noting that C. & B. J. O'Brien, in *The Shining Ones*, op. cit., p. 60, suggest that the term should really be translated 'Garden *in* Eden'.

81 Genesis 2:10 (King James Version, though the NIV translation amounts to the same thing).

82 It would seem that this celestial river split into 'four heads', having entered the underworld. This mythical explanation of the river in Genesis 2:10 might well supply the solution to the

mysterious identification of the four sub-rivers, the Pishon, the Gihon, the Hiddekel and the Euphrates. Of these four, the last three can easily be identified as the Nile, the Tigris and the Euphrates; might the other river, Pishon, which wound its way through the land of Havilah – a land full of gold, bdellium and lapis lazuli – be a mythical river of the underworld? The idea of Eden above and below is confirmed by a gnostic work attributed to Simon Magus, which states: 'Grant Paradise to be the womb... Moses using allegory had declared Paradise to be the womb... and Eden the placenta...'; see E. Pagels, *The Gnostic Gospels*, op. cit., p. 75.

83 Genesis 2:8-9.

84 Genesis 2:15.

85 Genesis 3:22-24. Compare Coffin Texts, Spell 76: 'O Lord of the Flame guarding the doors of the Sky [or of Nun]'. According to R. Alter, *Genesis*, op. cit., p. 15, the root of the word 'cherub' means either 'hybrid' or 'mount/steed'. It is generally acknowledged that the 'cherub' is related etymologically to the Babylonian *karibu* – the huge winged guardians which protected the entrances to temples. C. & B. J. O'Brien, *The Shining Ones*, op. cit., p. 140, trace the term *karibu* to the ideas of crying out, flying, and barbed spears.

86 Genesis 7:11.

87 *ANET*, op. cit., p. 104, or A. Heidel, *The Gilgamesh Epic and Old Testament Parallels*, op. cit., pp. 107-8; compare Genesis 5:29 & 8:21.

88 S. Dalley, *Myths from Mesopotamia*, op. cit., pp. 18, 20, 23. The references in Genesis 5:29 & 8:21 seem to suggest that the ground was cursed by Yahweh for a period of 600 years. The name of Noah, meaning 'rest', 'respite' or 'comfort', seems to be related primarily to what happened when he was 600 years old.

89 On the 7-day countdown, compare Genesis 7:4 to S. Dalley, *Myths from Mesopotamia*, op. cit., p. 30 (also to the Utnapishtim legend in *ANET*, op. cit., p. 94). On the sacrifice scene and pleasing smell, compare Genesis 8:20-21 to S. Dalley, *Myths from Mesopotamia*, op. cit., p. 33.

90 Genesis 6:3. It is evident from the *Kebra Nagast*, op. cit., p. 148, that this 120-year period was *not* allotted to man, as is commonly presumed, but primarily to the giants.

91 Genesis 6:7.

92 Genesis 7:11. It may well be that these waters originally fell in Genesis 1, hence the need for the separation of the waters in Genesis 1:6-7; here, then, the waters which God took back up to the highest heights seem to have come cascading back down to Earth once again.

93 Job 38:8-9 states that God shut the sea beneath doors after it 'broke forth, as if issued out of the womb'; the Dead Sea Scrolls state that this was a reference to 'the womb of the Deep' (see L. H. Schiffman, *Reclaiming the Dead Sea Scrolls*, Doubleday, 1994, p. 215). This is a remarkable parallel to the Mesopotamian idea that the Flood came forth from the womb of the *Sky*-goddess. Although scholars have assumed that the springs broke forth in the underworld, this is merely an assumption, and the expression could apply equally to the springs of the 'mountain' in the Sky. In support of this latter interpretation, see Genesis 8:2, where the first two clauses of the sentence seem to support the third clause: 'the rain stopped falling from the Sky'; see also Kings II 7:2 & Isaiah 24:18, where the floodgates of Heaven are mentioned in isolation, without any mention of the springs of the great Deep.

94 See *ANET*, op. cit., p. 61.

95 See, for example, Proverbs 3:19-20: 'by his knowledge the Deeps were divided'.

96 It has traditionally been assumed that the passage was presenting poetic opposites; see R. Alter, *Genesis*, op. cit., p. 32, which also discusses the possibility that the lines are from an old epic poem; it seems equally possible, however, that the lines would be reinforcing one another.

97 R. Alter, *Genesis*, op. cit., pp. xxxv-xxxvi.

98 See Coffin Texts, Spells 62, 225, 488, 491, 508, 611, 626, 637.

99 Coffin Texts, Spell 344.

100 A. Heidel, *The Gilgamesh Epic and Old Testament Parallels*, op. cit., p. 233.

101 Z. Sitchin, *Divine Encounters*, op. cit., p. 95.

102 One of the oddities of the biblical Flood story is that Noah's Ark came to rest on the mountains of Ararat after 150 days, (Genesis 8:3-4) and yet the tops of the mountains only became visible three months later (Genesis 8:5), and the waters covered the face of the whole Earth for another forty days after that. Might the explanation be that the biblical story draws upon the Mesopotamian idea of a celestial boat, which came down from Heaven and landed *on the waters of* the 'mountain' of Ararat after 150 days?

103 R. Eisenman & M. Wise, *Dead Sea Scrolls Uncovered*, Penguin Books, 1992, p. 36.
104 Ibid., pp. 33-4, 36.
105 Ibid., p. 243.
106 Note the manner in which 'the Foundations of the Universe' would 'shout out judgement'; see R. Eisenman & M. Wise, *Dead Sea Scrolls Uncovered*, op. cit., p. 250. In the Book of Enoch, Noah experienced earthquakes in the Lowlands, and was afraid of being killed; there was a great commotion, a voice out of Eden, and Noah then fell on his face; see C. & B. J. O'Brien, *The Shining Ones*, op. cit., p. 174.
107 C. & B. J. O'Brien, *The Shining Ones*, op. cit., p. 156.
108 Ibid.
109 One cannot help wondering whether there were two different legends of Noah in circulation: one in which an adult Noah sailed down from Heaven to Earth; and one in which Noah was a child born in the underworld as the result of a heavenly impregnation of the Earth.
110 Genesis 9:20-25.
111 The vine motif features in the legends of Joseph, and also of Jesus Christ. It is also important in the Greek legend of Deucalion, and in the legends of the Holy Grail.
112 See Psalm 75:8; Isaiah 51:17, 21; Jeremiah 25:15 & 49:12; Ezekiel 23:31; the reasoning behind this idiom should be entirely evident to anyone who has taken one tipple too many; compare Psalm 60:3 'you have given us wine that makes us stagger'.
113 M. Eliade, *A History of Religious Ideas*, Volume 1, op. cit., p. 248.
114 As an example of how the word 'tent' can be used idiomatically, see Psalm 19, where there is a 'tent for the Sun' in the heavens. The tent-peg is also a very interesting motif in the Bible; for example, there may well be a celestial archetype behind the legend in Judges 5:26, where Jael used a tent-peg to pierce the head of Sisera, nailing it into the ground; in Judges 5:20 we read: 'They fought from Heaven; the stars in their courses fought against Sisera. The river of Kishon swept them away, that ancient river, the river Kishon.' Was this a celestial river?
115 The idea is prompted by the line in Genesis 9:24: 'what his younger son had done to him'.
116 Ham was the ancestor of the African peoples per The Table of Nations, Genesis 10:6-20.
117 R. Graves, *The Greek Myths*, op. cit., p. 141 note 3.
118 Ibid., p. 139; also A. Heidel, *The Gilgamesh Epic and Old Testament Parallels*, op. cit., p. 260.
119 Ibid. Hence the reason the Greek words for 'people' (*laos*) and 'a stone' (*laas*) were so similar. The idea seems to have found its way into the New Testament, for in Matthew 3:9 and Luke 3:8, we read: 'out of these stones God can raise up children'.
120 Compare, in particular, the legends of the lapis lazuli flies, decoded in chapter 7 of this work.
121 Exodus 3:6.
122 Exodus 33:20.
123 Exodus 33:23.
124 *Kebra Nagast*, op. cit., p. 134. Compare a similar motif in Isaiah 30:26, in the context of God's cataclysmic judgement of the Earth.
125 Genesis 9:28-9; there seems to be a curious connection between Noah's life span and the numbers 600 and 350; compare the reference from the Dead Sea Scrolls, cited earlier, where Noah was 'born in the night' and 'came out perfect', with 'a weight of 350 shekels'. Might it be that two Noahs have been combined into one (see footnote 109 above)?

CHAPTER TEN: PARTING THE WATERS

1 There are some exceptions to this, e.g. Psalm 16, Psalm 49, and possibly Psalm 23. Many other passages in the Psalms are ambiguous, perhaps deliberately so. Perhaps we see here the traces of the Hebrews' pagan past. In any event, it is always difficult to maintain an absolute orthodoxy, and the debate about the afterlife was certainly a live one, as witnessed by Ecclesiastes 3:21: 'Who knows if the spirit of man rises upwards and if the spirit of the animal goes down into the earth?'.
2 Psalm 115:16.
3 Genesis 3:19.
4 Job 7:9, 14:7-10. This is the orthodoxy through most of the Old Testament. The most dramatic change to this theology came in the book of Daniel, where eternity in Sheol was replaced by the idea of an End of Days resurrection to life eternal or eternal contempt; see Daniel 12:2-4.

As noted in C. H. Gordon & G. A. Rendsburg, *The Bible and the Ancient Near East,* op. cit., pp. 296-7, 'the Hebrew Bible is an anthology... We need not expect and of course we do not find.. a monolithic view on theological issues.'

5   Exodus 3:2.

6   Psalm 105:26-36; the passage does contain slight differences to the account of the ten plagues in Exodus.

7   Exodus 12:33-36; one is reminded of the manner in which Utnapishtim brought silver and gold to Earth out of the heavenly 'city' of Shuruppak, and the manner in which the residents of the heavenly 'city' of Aratta were required to heap up minerals in the courtyard of Uruk. This transference of minerals between Heaven and Earth was an important motif in ancient mythology, and it may well be echoed here in Exodus 12:33-36.

8   Exodus 13:21; compare Exodus 14:19.

9   Exodus 14:21-22.

10   Exodus 19:12. Presumably this strict punishment derived from the great sanctity of the mystery which was about to unfold. Note, too, the similar sanctity surrounding the Ark of the Covenant – that portable 'cosmic mountain'.

11   Exodus 19:16-19.

12   Exodus 24:10.

13   Exodus 24:12, 31:18, 32:15-16; see also Deuteronomy 4:13. Various factors cause me to suspect that these 'tablets of stone' were meteoric material.

14   Exodus 32:19, Deuteronomy 9:17. Compare the breaking of the tablets at the foot of the mountain to the various pagan creation myths, where the world began with the breaking of a stick, or a pot, or a god, or the 'mountain' itself.

15   See C. H. Gordon & G. A. Rendsburg, *The Bible and the Ancient Near East,* op. cit., p. 318. The main quibble is whether the numbers of Israelites on the Exodus were as high as claimed, and whether they really spent a full forty years wandering around in the desert.

16   Exodus 34:28.

17   Deuteronomy 8:4. See also Nehemiah 9:21.

18   M. Eliade, *The Myth of the Eternal Return,* op. cit., p. 42.

19   Deuteronomy 34:10.

20   Acts 7:20 states that he was 'exceeding fair'; *Insight on the Scriptures,* Volume II, op. cit., p. 434, states that he was 'divinely beautiful'.

21   Exodus 1:15-22. A similar theme recurs in the New Testament, at the time of the birth of Jesus; see, for example, Matthew 2:16.

22   The name Moses sounds like the Hebrew for 'draw out'.

23   E. von Daniken, *Chariots of the Gods?,* Souvenir Press, 1969, pp. 77-8.

24   Compare the Mesopotamian legend of Damu, 'the child who comes out of the river' (at the time of the flood); see T. Jacobsen, *The Treasures of Darkness,* op. cit., p. 69.

25   R. Graves, *The Greek Myths,* op. cit., pp. 373-7.

26   *ANET,* op. cit., p. 119; the translation 'changeling mother' comes from G. Roux, *Ancient Iraq,* op. cit., p. 152.

27   A. Heidel, *The Gilgamesh Epic and Old Testament Parallels,* op. cit., p. 233. See also C. H. Gordon & G. A. Rendsburg, *The Bible and the Ancient Near East,* op. cit., p. 48 footnote 34.

28   Isaiah 63:11.

29   The lapis lazuli palace of the Sumerian goddess Ereshkigal; see A. Heidel, *The Gilgamesh Epic and Old Testament Parallels,* op. cit., p. 172.

30   Jeremiah 46:8.

31   R. Alter, *Genesis,* op. cit., p. 217.

32   *Insight on the Scriptures,* Volume II, op. cit., p. 728.

33   *ANET,* op. cit., pp. 67, 71, 501-2.

34   Luke 10:18, Revelations 20:1-3.

35   Job 41:31.

36   Psalm 74:14.

37   G. de Santillana & H. von Dechend, *Hamlet's Mill,* op. cit., p. 253.

38   Jeremiah 46:22-23.

39   See, for example, Deuteronomy 4:20; Kings I 8:51; Jeremiah 11:4.

40   I. Shaw & P. Nicholson, *British Museum Dictionary of Ancient Egypt,* op. cit., p. 141.

41 Ezekiel 16:5-7. Compare Ezekiel 16:22: 'Thou hast not remembered the days of thy youth, when thou wast naked and bare, and wast polluted in thy blood.'
42 The parallel should not, however, be taken too far, for there is one very significant difference between the two sets of legends. In the Mesopotamian version of the story, the parent deities, Anu and Ishtar, represent the popular ancient Near Eastern idea of two 'good' planets, one male and one female, which joined together in a sacred marriage in the Earth. Both are thus presented in a positive light, and the enslaving of the second emanation – 'mankind' – by the first emanation – the Anunnaki – had less to do with a battle between good and evil, and more to do with the matter of territorial rights in the underworld.
43 Or 'House of Bondage' (KJV). See Exodus 13:3, 13:14, 20:2; Deuteronomy 5:6, 6:12, 8:14, 13:5; Joshua 24:17; Judges 6:8.
44 Cited in B. Rux, *Architects of the Underworld*, Frog Ltd, 1996, p. 390.
45 Exodus 19:4.
46 E. von Daniken, *The Return of the Gods*, op. cit., p. 27.
47 *Insight on the Scriptures*, Volume II, op. cit., p. 763.
48 See A. F. Alford, *The Phoenix Solution*, op. cit., chapters 9-10.
49 Exodus 15:10, 15:5.
50 The Hebrew word *tehom* is widely recognised as alluding to Tiamat, the watery creature slain in battle by Marduk; see S. H. Hooke, *Middle Eastern Mythology*, op. cit., p. 119.
51 A. Heidel, *The Babylonian Genesis*, op. cit., p. 109 footnote 86.
52 Exodus 15:5. Compare Exodus 15:10 'they sank like lead'.
53 Exodus 14:30.
54 Even if 'shore' was a mistranslation for 'bed', the passage would not work, because the drowned Egyptians would not have been visible (they would have been covered by the waters).
55 Exodus 15:12.
56 Exodus 19:20.
57 Nehemiah 9:13.
58 Exodus 20:22.
59 Deuteronomy 4:36.
60 Deuteronomy 4:11.
61 Deuteronomy 4:36.
62 Exodus 19:16-19.
63 N. J. Dawood trans., *The Koran*, op. cit., p. 257 (traditional chapter number 7).
64 *ANET*, op. cit., p. 613.
65 Exodus 3:1, 33:6; Deuteronomy 4:10.
66 *Insight on the Scriptures*, Volume I, op. cit., p. 1141.
67 Exodus 3:1-5.
68 The name of Moses's father-in-law in Midian was 'Jethro', meaning 'abundance'; this fits well with the Mesopotamian idea of Heaven as a storehouse of an abundance of produce. Midian was also the name of a mythical son of Abraham, who was sent away 'eastward unto the east country'; see Genesis 25:6.
69 Book of Jubilees, cited in Z. Sitchin, *The Stairway to Heaven*, Avon Books, 1980, p. 296.
70 Although the Hebrew term for 'wilderness' could mean 'desert' in a conventional sense, it was often used metaphorically in the Bible to refer to a place that had been destroyed and turned into a desolate wasteland; see *Insight on the Scriptures*, Volume II, op. cit., p. 1185.
71 Psalm 68:16-18. I have rendered 'gifts for men' as 'men for gifts', which makes more sense.
72 Corinthians I 10:1-4.
73 I am very serious about this suggestion. Numerous examples could be cited of cases where the Old Testament seemingly struggles to present slightly different versions of a particular tale. My proposals concerning the Exodus story should be seen as part of an integrated approach to understanding the Old Testament as a whole.
74 Deuteronomy 33:2 (KJV); 'right' is translated as 'south' in NIV; my insertions in brackets are intended to elucidate the meaning of this particularly enigmatic line.
75 *Insight on the Scriptures*, Volume II, op. cit., p. 891.
76 It should be noted that the name Mount 'Sinai' might also allude to twin peaks, if it is based on the ancient Egyptian *Sn,* meaning 'two/dual'.
77 Judges 5:4-5 (compare similar words in Psalm 68:7-8). 'That Sinai from before' is my own

suggestion, based on the KJV translation. It reflects the ancient belief that God and the 'mountain' were one-and-the-same.

78   Psalm 114:1-7. Similar language is used in Psalm 29, where Yahweh broke the cedars with his voice, and ended up 'enthroned upon the Flood'.

79   Psalm 77:16-20.

80   Isaiah 51:9-10.

81   Habakkuk 3:3-13. This third chapter of Habakkuk seems to be a psalm, which has been appended on to the prophecies in Habakkuk 1-2; see C. H. Gordon & G. A. Rendsburg, *The Bible and the Ancient Near East*, op. cit., p. 325. The measuring of the Earth may be an idiomatic expression with an esoteric meaning, for 'to measure the Earth' was the Sumerian way of saying 'to love'; see S. N. Kramer, *The Sumerians*, op. cit., p. 250; note how God threatened Jerusalem with the measuring-line in Kings II 21:13.

82   Psalm 18:7-17 (compare Samuel II 22:8-18). Note the reference to 'the brightness before him'; I take this to mean the planet Earth.

83   Exodus 15:17. The redeemed would be planted on God's holy dwelling, the mountain of inheritance.

84   Lamentations 2:1.

85   Genesis 10:24-25. R. Alter, *Genesis*, op. cit., p. 44, stated: 'Eber is explicitly linked with the term that means "from the other side" (of the river)'.

86   Genesis 10:25. R. Alter, *Genesis*, op. cit., p. 44, notes that the verb translated 'split' is stronger than the usual translation 'to divide', and he suggests a connection to a cataclysmic event.

87   Genesis 14:13; see discussion in *Insight on the Scriptures*, Volume I, op. cit., pp. 1066-7. Scholars have generally assumed that the name commemorates the crossing of the terrestrial river Euphrates. Scholars have also suggested a connection to the earlier patriarch Eber (on whom see note 85 above).

88   *Insight on the Scriptures*, Volume I, op. cit., p. 28.

89   According to this legend, Abram emerged from the cave after three years. One suspects that this legend belonged in Genesis 15:5, where God 'took Abram outside', or 'brought him forth abroad', and asked him to look towards the heavens. Concerning the idea of Abram having fallen from Heaven, it may be significant that in the Dead Sea Scrolls Abraham was compared to a cedar-tree, about to be chopped down, with his wife Sarah compared to a palm-tree.

90   R. Eisenman & M. Wise, *Dead Sea Scrolls Uncovered*, op. cit., p. 89.

91   See Genesis 17:17-19. Note how Abraham 'fell upon his face and laughed'. On the laughter of Geb, see I. Shaw & P. Nicholson, *British Museum Dictionary of Ancient Egypt*, op. cit., p. 109.

92   Genesis 32:22-28.

93   Genesis 32:7-8, 10; note the connection with fear and distress.

94   The staff of Moses was able to become a serpent; then it turned the waters of the Nile into blood; then it brought thunder, hail and lightning upon Egypt; then it caused a wind to bring a plague of locusts upon Egypt; then it caused the waters of the Red Sea to part; then it caused water to come out of a solid rock; and finally it helped the Israelites to defeat the Amalekites. Similar feats were performed by the staff of Aaron, the brother of Moses. An old Jewish legend states that the staff of Moses had been brought out of the Garden of Eden by Adam.

95   C. H. Gordon & G. A. Rendsburg, *The Bible and the Ancient Near East*, op. cit., p. 168.

96   Genesis 37:9. Joseph was the son of Jacob who was born in Haran, a name which might be translated 'Mountain of Heaven'.

97   Genesis 41:28 'seven years of great abundance are coming throughout the land of Egypt' (this was admittedly preceded by an unspecified period during which Joseph was placed in charge of Potiphar's house, and then imprisoned). Once again, however, we are probably looking at two different versions of the story which have been woven together.

98   Deuteronomy 33:16-17 (compare Genesis 49:26). I have rendered 'ends of the Earth' as 'depths of the Earth'; the term is *apsei-eretz*, which is evocative of the Mesopotamian Apsu. In the Bible, the *apsei-eretz* was the place where Yahweh would rule and judge at the End of Days. And in the book of Enoch, the *apsei-eretz* was the place where Enoch became resident. All things considered, the *apsei-eretz* must be the underworld.

99   Genesis 45:5-7. The portrayal of Joseph as a wild ox and seed of Israel reminds one of the Mesopotamian tradition, where the wild ox was literally a 'mountain-bull'.

100 Exodus 1:7. Compare Genesis 47:27, 48:16.

101 Genesis 49:22 (NIV translation).

102 Jeremiah 2:21. Compare Isaiah 60:21, where Israel was a shoot planted by the hand of Yahweh.

103 Psalm 80:8.

104 The body of Moses belonged in the Earth, as did the bodies of all fallen gods. However, according to the ancient rules of the underworld, the bodily fall of one god could act as ransom for another; hence in Exodus 13:19 we read that Moses took the bones of Joseph with him out of Egypt (the underworld).

105 Deuteronomy 34; compare the 120-year period in Genesis 6:3. In the original story, Mount Nebo would have been a celestial 'mountain'.

106 Deuteronomy 34:5-7. Compare the mystery surrounding the true burial places of Isis and Osiris in Egypt.

CHAPTER ELEVEN: THE LAMB LIES DOWN

1 Exodus 12:26-7.

2 Corinthians I 5:7.

3 See Genesis 2:9, 3:3.

4 C. H. Gordon & G. A. Rendsburg, *The Bible and the Ancient Near East,* op. cit., p. 36.

5 Why had mankind missed out on the Tree of Life? This question gave rise to the idea that mankind had erred; the blame was put on Satan, or Eve, or Adam himself.

6 The fruit of the Tree of Knowledge was not an apple as many people suppose, but an unidentified fruit, the Hebrew term for which alludes to 'life-breath'.

7 T. Jacobsen, *The Treasures of Darkness,* op. cit., p. 59.

8 Genesis 17:1-6. Abraham then had a son at the age of 100 years. Note that Abram 'fell on his face', and compare the tradition in the Sumerian King List that Dumuzi ruled in the city of the underworld for 100 years, prior to the emergence of Gilgamesh as a human king; see T. Jacobsen, *The Sumerian King List,* op. cit., p. 89.

9 According to Herodotus, the practice of circumcision was inherited from Egypt.

10 Genesis 22:2.

11 Genesis 22:13; R. Alter, *Genesis,* op. cit., p. 106, noted that 'ram behind him' could be translated as 'a sole ram'.

12 *Kebra Nagast,* op. cit., p. 165.

13 One presumes that Ham, Shem and Japheth were the three sons who emerged from the underworld, after the incident of seeing Noah in his 'tent'.

14 Exodus 4:27 (KJV).

15 It is undeniable that the concept of the 'cosmic mountain' was known by the Hebrew scribes. In the Dead Sea Scrolls text *Testament of Levi,* the chief priest, Levi, stated: "Then I was shown visions . . . in the vision of visions, and I saw Heaven opened and I saw the mountain beneath me, as high as to reach to Heaven, and I was on it. Then the gates of Heaven were opened to me, and an angel spoke to me: 'Levi, enter...'"; see R. Eisenman & M. Wise, *Dead Sea Scrolls Uncovered,* op. cit., p. 140.

16 Exodus 12:3-7.

17 Exodus 12:7-11.

18 Incidentally, there is a passage in the Old Testament (Amos 9:7) which states that Yahweh also brought the Philistines on an exodus out of Caphtor (Crete) and the Arameans out of Kir. The exodus-from-the-underworld motif is thus more widespread than is generally realised.

19 J. G. Frazer, *The Golden Bough,* op. cit., pp. 268-9.

20 Judges 11:29-39.

21 Kings II 16:3, 21:6 (compare Kings II 23:10).

22 Ezekiel 16:20-21, 23:37-39; the children were to be 'food' for the idols (literally 'to be devoured'); a specific reference to the first-born is found in Ezekiel 20:26.

23 See, for example: Leviticus 18:21, 20:2; Deuteronomy 12:31, 18:10; Psalm 106:37.

24 Isaiah 57:5.

25 C. H. Gordon & G. A. Rendsburg, *The Bible and the Ancient Near East,* op. cit., p. 120; *Insight on the Scriptures,* Volume II, op. cit., p. 424.

26 See J. G. Frazer, *The Golden Bough,* op. cit., pp. 269-70; also R. Graves, *The Greek Myths,* op. cit., pp. 42, 119, 141. The custom also seems to have been commonplace in ancient South

America and Meso-america.

27 Kings II 3:27.

28 Joshua 6:26.

29 Kings I 16:34.

30 M. Eliade, *The Myth of the Eternal Return*, op. cit., p. 35.

31 *Insight on the Scriptures*, Volume I, op. cit., p. 213. The goat was traditionally associated with deception by the Hebrews; see R. Alter, *Genesis*, op. cit., pp. 139, 164, 214, 220. Compare the reference to goats in the New Testament, Matthew 25:31.

32 The *kapporeth* was the 'cover' of the Ark, not the 'mercy seat'; L. H. Schiffman, *Reclaiming the Dead Sea Scrolls*, op. cit., p. 214.

33 On Jerusalem as the Bond of Heaven-and-Earth, see M. Eliade, *The Myth of the Eternal Return*, op. cit., pp. 15-18, 77-8.

34 *Insight on the Scriptures*, Volume II, op. cit., p. 733. The Hebrew word for 'ransom', *kopher*, stems from the noun *kaphar*, which literally means 'a cover, or covering'. It is possible that *kaphar* stems from the Akkadian *kpr*, meaning 'brimstone'.

35 Micah 6:7.

36 In ancient Egypt, the first-born meant literally 'the opener of the womb'.

37 A. Ellegard, *Jesus – One Hundred Years Before Christ*, Century, 1999, p. 178.

38 Exodus 13:14-15.

39 Genesis 17:10-13. The passage specifies that the child should be circumcised when 8 days old.

40 Exodus 4:24-26.

41 The name Zipporah meant 'female bird' (*Oxford Concordance to the Bible*) and Jewish tradition asserts that she had talons on her feet; see E. C. M. Begg, *The Cult of the Black Virgin*, Arkana, 1985, p. 38.

42 See Z. Sitchin, *Divine Encounters*, op. cit., p. 311; hence the Sumerian astronomical tablets known as the MUL.APIN.

43 Hence ancient priests would castrate themselves in honour of the Goddess. See, for example, J. G. Frazer, *The Golden Bough*, op. cit., p. 348.

44 John 1:29, 1:36.

45 Of particular interest is the reference in Revelations 13:8 to 'the Lamb slain from the foundation of the world. If any man have an ear, let him hear.'

46 Matthew 27:46; Mark 15:34.

47 Psalm 22:6-7.

48 In Job 25:6, man is described as 'a maggot, a son of the soil, who is only a worm'. In Mark 9:48, there is a reference to people being thrown into hell, where 'their worm does not die'.

49 Psalm 22:12-15.

50 Psalm 22:16-18.

51 Matthew 27:35.

52 T. Jacobsen, *The Treasures of Darkness*, op. cit., p. 53.

53 Although apparently St Jerome said that Jesus was lame.

54 Isaiah 52:13-15 (I have reversed the order in order to make the text flow). The reference to the disfigured and repulsive appearance of this 'man' reminds one of the writings of Berossus, where he referred to mythical amphibious creatures, which came up out of the waters (celestial waters I suggest) onto the Earth; the leader of these creatures was Musarus Oannes the Annedotus; Musarus meant 'abomination', whilst Annedotus meant 'repulsive one'; see R. Temple, *The Sirius Mystery*, op. cit., pp. 276-8.

55 Isaiah 53:2-3.

56 *Kebra Nagast,* op. cit., p. 151.

57 Isaiah 53:4-6.

58 Isaiah 53:7-9.

59 Isaiah 53:10-11.

60 Isaiah 53:12.

61 Genesis 18. It is now apparent that Sodom and Gomorrah were 'cities' of the underworld; this is why they were called 'the cities of the plain'. According to Genesis 14:8, there were five such 'cities', which would tie in to the idea of the five 'cities' which were dropped from the heavens in the Sumerian Kings List. Furthermore, it should be noted that Revelations 11:8 refers to Jesus Christ ('our Lord') being crucified in 'the great city which is figuratively called

Sodom and Egypt'; both Sodom and Egypt, I suggest, were metaphors for the 'city' of the underworld.

The intercession of the Righteous Servant for the transgressors is also evocative of Enoch's intercession for the Watchers, who had sinned against God by sleeping with human women and teaching forbidden knowledge to mankind (see the Book of Enoch); these events, too, took place in the underworld.

62 John 1:29; Matthew 20:28.

63 Matthew 27:12-14.

64 Matthew 2:15.

65 Hosea 11:1.

66 John 8:58.

67 John 17:5.

68 John 1:14; Jesus (the Lamb) was also called 'the Word of God' in Revelations 19:13.

69 John 1:1-2. I prefer to translate 'the Word was a god' although 'the Word was God' is also a valid translation; in the beginning the Father and the Son were one, pre-catastrophe.

70 In ancient times, the enigmatic figure known as 'Wisdom' was identified frequently with Jesus Christ; see A. Ellegard, *Jesus – One Hundred Years Before Christ*, op. cit., pp. 17-18, 75. The *Kebra Nagast*, op. cit., p. 158, equated Wisdom with Solomon, but identified Solomon, in turn, with Christ. A 2nd century BC work by Jesus ben Sira asserted that Wisdom had come forth from the mouth of the Most High as the divine Word by which God created the world (see K. Armstrong, *A History of God*, op. cit., p. 82.).

71 Proverbs 8:22-29.

72 Genesis 1:26; see A. Ellegard, *Jesus – One Hundred Years Before Christ*, op. cit., pp. 71, 76.

73 Hebrews 1:2.

74 Colossians 1:15-16.

75 John 1:3.

76 Book of the Dead, trans. by Normandi Ellis, in R. Bauval & G. Hancock, *Keeper of Genesis*, op. cit., p. 283.

77 John 8:56.

78 Genesis 22:14; this is my translation, based on the KJV translation and the comments in R. Alter, *Genesis*, op. cit., p. 106.

79 Compare how Aaron met Moses *in* the mountain of God (Exodus 4:27, KJV).

80 John 5:46.

81 Isaiah 63:11.

82 Corinthians I 10:1-5. The next line refers to the bodies of the Israelites being scattered over the desert; the word 'desert' is a metaphor for the celestial wilderness. Anthony T. Hanson, former professor of Theology at Hull University, has commented that 'Paul believed that the Messiah was in some form present with the people during this critical period in the wilderness'; see A. T. Hanson, *Jesus in the Old Testament*, 1965.

83 Matthew 26:26; John 6:53-58.

84 Matthew 20:28; see also Mark 10:45.

85 Only the flesh of the lamb was taken into the stomachs of the Israelites who ascended; the bones of the lamb were left behind in the underworld. Moreover, it was important that not one of these bones was to be broken; see Exodus 12:46; Psalm 34:20; John 19:33-36. This permitted an eventual resurrection of the body. Note how Moses gave himself as a ransom for Joseph, by carrying his bones out of Egypt (the underworld); see Genesis 50:25, Exodus 13:19.

86 John 15:18, 15:25; and see John 7:7: 'the world hates me because I testify that its way are evil'.

87 Psalm 69:1-4.

88 Samuel II 22:5-19.

89 Ezekiel 16:5-7.

90 Habakkuk 3:12-14 (KJV). The third line sounds like an idiomatic expression for decapitation.

91 As we shall see in chapter 13 of this work, the Messiah of the End of Days was known by many different names, of which Jesus Christ was only one.

92 The ancient 'universe' consisted of Heaven and Earth. In Colossians 1:15-16, we read that 'all things are held together' in Jesus Christ. This idea can be traced back to the pagan religions of ancient Egypt and Mesopotamia; it was believed that the awesome destruction of the creation was kept in check in the underworld; the one in the underworld was thus the sustainer and

saviour of Heaven and Earth; if he came up out of the underworld, the chaos of the beginning would be unleashed once again.

93 *ANET*, op. cit., p. 55. A further detail, added by the Akkadian version of this tale, notes that Inanna was afflicted with 'sixty miseries', which raged against every part of her body (*ANET*, p. 108). It is remarkable that the 'stake' on which Inanna was hung in the underworld recurs in the New Testament story as the *stauros*, literally a 'torture stake', on which Jesus Christ was nailed; see *Insight on the Scriptures*, Volume II, op. cit., pp. 1116-17.

CHAPTER TWELVE: HE RAISED THE DEAD

1 *Ben Adamah* is the term most often translated as 'Son of Man' in the Hebrew Old Testament, although occasionally the term is its Aramaic equivalent, *Bar Enash*. The New Testament is, of course, written in Greek, but there is no evidence to suggest that Jesus actually spoke in Greek. It would seem most likely that, when Jesus spoke of himself as the *Ben Adamah*, he did so using an equivalent term in Aramaic or a popular form of 1st century Hebrew.

2 K. Armstrong, *A History of God*, op. cit., p. 98.

3 Matthew 13:34-5. Compare Psalm 78:2.

4 Mark 4:10-12.

5 John 1:51.

6 Matthew 24:27, 24:30-31.

7 R. Alter, *Genesis*, op. cit., p. 31. This was the 'seed' which Noah saved at the time of the Flood, the 'seed' of Noah with whom God made his covenant (Genesis 9:9), and the 'seed' of Abram to whom God promised the land of Canaan (Genesis 12:7 and 13:15-16).

8 The term can also be translated 'son of the soil', such is the delicious ambiguity of both components in the expression. And there are many instances in the Old Testament where 'son of the soil' is obviously the intended meaning; see, for example, Job 25:6.

9 John 1:3.

10 Colossians 1:15-16.

11 Matthew 13:37, the Parable of the Weeds.

12 In further support of the esoteric meaning 'Seed of Mankind', consider the following enigmatic verses from the *Gospel of Philip* (Nag Hammadi scrolls): 'There is the Son of Man and there is the son of the Son of Man. The Lord [Christ] is the Son of Man, and the son of the Son of Man is he who is created through the Son of Man.' See M. Baigent et al, *The Holy Blood and the Holy Grail*, op. cit., p. 404.

13 Luke 8:5-8.

14 Luke 8:11. *Insight on the Scriptures*, Volume II, op. cit., p. 1201, states: 'God's word or message is like seed'. Indeed it is.

15 John 1:1-2. I prefer to translate 'the Word was a god' although 'the Word was God' is also a valid translation; in the beginning the Father and the Son were one, pre-catastrophe.

16 John 1:14; Jesus (the Lamb) was also called 'the Word of God' in Revelations 19:13.

17 A. Ellegard, *Jesus – One Hundred Years Before Christ*, op. cit., p. 205; compare the Sumerian goddess Aruru: the Lady of the Word, but also the Lady of Silence.

18 John 1:3; Colossians 1:15-16.

19 Jeremiah 23:29. See also Jeremiah 50:23, where Babylon was compared to 'the hammer of the whole Earth'.

20 T. Jacobsen, *The Treasures of Darkness*, op. cit., p. 108.

21 Ibid., pp. 102-3.

22 D. Meeks & C. Favard-Meeks, *Daily Life of the Egyptian Gods*, op. cit., pp. 79, 103-4. A similar belief is found in the Book of the Dead, Spell 17, which records that the underworld-god Anubis had prepared places inside the Earth for 'Seven Spirits' during the primeval age of *Zep Tepi*, in readiness for their arrival at a time known cryptically as 'The Day of Come Thence'; decoded, this means 'The Day of Coming from Heaven to Earth'.

23 Coffin Texts, Spells 1080 & 1087.

24 See chapter 3 of this work.

25 Matthew 21:33-42; Mark 12:1-10; Luke 20:9-17.

26 Matthew 21:42.

27 Ephesians 2:20; see also Peter I 2:4-6.

28 Job 38:4-6.

29 Isaiah 28:16.

30 Jeremiah 51:25-26.

31 Luke 20:18.

32 Matthew 13:34-5. Compare Psalm 78:2.

33 L. H. Schiffman, *Reclaiming the Dead Sea Scrolls*, op. cit., p. 151; S. N. Kramer, *The Sumerians*, op. cit., p. 128 (which adds 'a sinless youth has not existed from of old'). In Hebrew, to sin meant literally to err by missing the mark.

34 Matthew 1:21.

35 The translation is a composite of *ANET*, op. cit., p. 94, A. Heidel, *The Gilgamesh Epic and Old Testament Parallels*, op. cit., p. 85, and J. Gardner & J. Maier, *Gilgamesh*, op. cit., p. 235.

36 Ibid.

37 *ANET*, op. cit., p. 104. S. Dalley, *Myths from Mesopotamia*, op. cit., pp. 18, 20, 23-4.

38 T. Jacobsen, *The Sumerian King List*, op. cit., p. 60 footnote 113.

39 Digging out the canals: see S. Dalley, *Myths from Mesopotamia*, op. cit., pp. 13-14, 16, 18.

40 S. Dalley, *Myths from Mesopotamia*, op. cit., p. 32.

41 *ANET*, op. cit., p. 61, Tablet I, line 8 says it all; see also Tablet I lines 23, 29.

42 The translation is a composite of *ANET*, op. cit., p. 61, S. Dalley, *Myths from Mesopotamia*, op. cit., p. 233, and A. Heidel, *The Babylonian Genesis*, op. cit., p. 19.

43 The translation is a composite of *ANET*, op. cit., p. 61, and A. Heidel, *The Babylonian Genesis*, op. cit., p. 19.

44 See, for example, S. Dalley, *Myths from Mesopotamia*, op. cit., p. 288: 'the Anunnaki who love silence'. And in the ancient Egyptian Coffin Texts, Spell 37, we read: 'the detestation of Osiris is a shouter'; because Osiris was 'foremost among the Silent Ones', 'the god of reckoning in the Garden of the Silent One', Spell 111. Silence was thus a great virtue for one seeking the afterlife; see 'A Prayer to Thoth' in *ANET*, op. cit., p. 379; also 'The Instruction of Ani' in *ANET*, p. 420.

45 *ANET*, op. cit., pp. 63-4; for *huburu* = 'noise', see T. Jacobsen, *The Sumerian King List*, op. cit., p. 60 footnote 113.

46 See *ANET*, op. cit., p. 600. The river Hubur was also known as 'the River of the Night', 'the River of the Underworld', 'the River of Creation', and 'the River of Fishes and Birds'.

47 *ANET*, op. cit., p. 71.

48 Isaiah 53:4-6.

49 Isaiah 53:7-8.

50 Isaiah 53:10-11.

51 Isaiah 53:12.

52 Matthew 20:28; Mark 10:45.

53 John 6:51.

54 Ibid.

55 See, for example, Coffin Texts, Spells 76, 79, 94, 237, 519, 828, 1129.

56 Coffin Texts, Spell 94.

57 John 1:14.

58 Revelations 1:5.

59 R. Graves, *The Greek Myths*, op. cit., p. 37. Compare the Egyptian legend of the gods springing into being from the drops of blood which dripped from the phallus of Re (E. A. Wallis Budge, *From Fetish to God in Ancient Egypt*, op. cit., p. 150). Compare also the Dogon legend of the mutilation of the Fox; the blood of its genitals fell on ground, but was then raised up to the heavens to become four satellites of Jupiter (R. Temple, *The Sirius Mystery*, op. cit., pp. 71-2).

60 R. Graves, *The Greek Myths*, op. cit., p. 240.

61 E. A. Wallis Budge, *From Fetish to God in Ancient Egypt*, op. cit., p. 143.

62 John 19:34. Incidentally, Osiris, too, was said to have had a wound in his side, from which water gushed forth; see Coffin Texts, Spell 74: "Come, that we may make a dam in his side... there drips the efflux which has issued from this Spirit."

63 The translation is a composite of S. Dalley, *Myths from Mesopotamia*, op. cit., p. 15, and *ANET*, op. cit., pp. 99-100.

64 John 3:22; see also John 3:26 and the contradictory statement in John 4:1-2.

65 Acts 22:16; it must be stressed that ancient baptisms involved complete immersion.
66 Corinthians I 15:45-49.
67 The translation is a composite of *ANET*, op. cit., p. 68, S. Dalley, *Myths from Mesopotamia*, op. cit., pp. 260-1, and A. Heidel, *The Babylonian Genesis*, op. cit., p. 46; however, for the fifth line I have gone with the rather appealing translation from T. Jacobsen, *The Treasures of Darkness*, op. cit., p. 181, for a 'ball' is a perfect description of the form in which the gods were once held together. See also the further references in lines 39-44 and 143-5 of *Enuma Elish* Tablet VI.
68 The translation is a composite of *ANET*, op. cit., p. 68, S. Dalley, *Myths from Mesopotamia*, op. cit., pp. 260-1, and A. Heidel, *The Babylonian Genesis*, op. cit., p. 46. Note that the Anunnaki in their totality were known as 'mighty gods of Heaven and Earth'; see *ANET*, p. 180.
69 *ANET*, op. cit., pp. 58-9, 164.
70 Ibid., p. 503, Tablet VII.
71 T. Jacobsen, *The Treasures of Darkness*, op. cit., p. 59.
72 The translation is a composite of *ANET*, op. cit., p. 70, & S. Dalley, *Myths from Mesopotamia*, op. cit., p. 268.
73 The translation is a composite of *ANET*, op. cit., p. 70, S. Dalley, *Myths from Mesopotamia*, op. cit., p. 266, and A. Heidel, *The Babylonian Genesis*, op. cit., pp. 53-4.
74 Matthew 27:51-3. Mark 15:38 and Luke 23:45 mention the splitting veil but not the ascension; the 'holy city' might well mean the heavenly Jerusalem.
75 It would also explain the legend in Luke 23:44-45 of the Sun being darkened for three hours.
76 E. Pagels, *The Gnostic Gospels*, op. cit., p. 107.

CHAPTER THIRTEEN: THE END OF DAYS

1 *The History of Christianity*, Lion Publishing, op. cit., pp. 116-7.
2 Just as the god Re (or the Phoenix) would raise his body (Osiris) from the dead.
3 Compare Matthew 8:10, which suggests that the little children have angelic counterparts already in Heaven and beholding the face of God.
4 As Mircea Eliade wrote in *The Myth of the Eternal Return*, op. cit., p. 59, 'on the cosmic level, it [baptism] is equivalent to the Deluge'. See also Peter I 3:20-21, which suggests a symbolic link between baptism and the Flood of Noah.
5 John 3:5.
6 Matthew 3:11. Compare Mark 1:7-8 and Luke 3:16. I had previously supposed that 'he that comes after me' might have been God himself; I now reject that idea. John 1:26-30 strongly suggests that Jesus Christ was intended.
7 Peter II 3:5-7.
8 Psalms 111:10. Compare Proverbs 9:10.
9 Isaiah 24:1, 24:18-20.
10 Isaiah 13:6, 13:9-13. The words are highly evocative of passages in the Mesopotamian legend entitled *Erra and Ishum*; see S. Dalley, *Myths from Mesopotamia*, op. cit., pp. 285-312.
11 El Shaddai is usually footnoted where it appears (NIV Bible), for example in Genesis 17:1, 35:11, 43:14; Exodus 6:3; and numerous other instances.
12 A related word, *shadad*, meant 'to be strong or powerful'.
13 Exodus 19:3. El resided within the seven chambers and eight enclosures of his mountain-like *Shad*; see ANET, op. cit., p. 137.
14 This may refer to the mountain-split-in-two, or to the dual mountains of Heaven and Earth, or to the two separate mountains of the heavens. Incidentally, there is a good biblical parallel to the mountain-split-in-two in Zechariah 6:1 'I looked and behold, there came four chariots out from between two mountains, and the mountains were mountains of bronze'.
15 Isaiah 13:4-5. This is in the context of a prophecy supposedly about Babylon. A similar army is compared to something like a swarm of locusts in Joel 2:25.
16 The words are very reminiscent of Mesopotamian lamentations concerning the dreaded mountain-people, the Guti, who would be brought down by Enlil to cause utter desolation to the land of Sumer; see ANET, op. cit., pp. 613, 649.
17 Joel 1:15, 2:1-5, 2:10-11. See also Joel 2:30-31 'the Sun will be turned into darkness, and the Moon into blood, before the great and terrible day of the LORD'.

18   Jeremiah 4:23.

19   Isaiah 40:3-5.

20   *Insight on the Scriptures*, Volume I, op. cit., p. 963. Compare the heaviness of God's *Shem* ('Name') in Isaiah 30:27 (KJV). Note the connection of heaviness and Heaven via 'to heave'.

21   R. Eisenman & M. Wise, *Dead Sea Scrolls Uncovered*, op. cit., p. 240. Numerous other passages in the Old Testament support my interpretation; for example, those passages which speak of the 'Glory of the LORD' (or his Name) filling the tabernacle, or the temple of Jerusalem, can be understood as referring to those sacred centres as microcosms of the planet Earth being filled by the heaviness of God; see Numbers 14:21; Kings I 8:11; Chronicles II 5:14; Psalm 8:1; Isaiah 6:3.

22   All ancient acts of creation began with a pre-existing watery abyss, which was in most cases already occupied by the 'islands' of Heaven and Earth, in their original pristine condition.

23   Isaiah 65:17.

24   Isaiah 34:4. Compare the Mesopotamian legend of *Erra and Ishum* in S. Dalley, *Myths from Mesopotamia*, op. cit., p. 308.

25   Isaiah 24:21.

26   Joel 3:14, 3:2, 3:12. The valley was supernaturally vast and is unlikely to have been a mundane valley; more likely it was a metaphorical allusion to the underworld.

27   Malachi 4:1.

28   Jeremiah 25:29-33.

29   Isaiah 27:13, 43:2-3.

30   Zechariah 8:3.

31   Revelations 21:2. Note here the recurrence of the city = planet metaphor, which was vital to our earlier decoding of ancient Egyptian and Mesopotamian legends. Ironically, this passage (from the *New* Testament) seems to follow the *Old* Testament philosophy of the new Heaven being experienced on Earth. A similar idea is found in the Dead Sea Scrolls, where we read that Heaven would be made to dwell with David for ever, rather than David being made to dwell in Heaven for ever; see R. Eisenman & M. Wise, *Dead Sea Scrolls Uncovered*, op. cit., pp. 90-2.

32   In the Dead Sea Scrolls, the New Jerusalem appears as a city ready and waiting in Heaven (complete with its temple), which would descend to the Earth; see H. Stegemann, *The Library of Qumran*, op. cit., pp. 98, 209. The *Sibylline Oracles* (2nd century BC) refer to New Jerusalem as having 'a temple... with a giant tower touching the very clouds'; see M. Eliade, *The Myth of the Eternal Return*, op. cit., pp. 8-9.

33   Micah 4:1.

34   Isaiah 31:4-5.

35   Isaiah 4:5.

36   Isaiah 32:15; Joel 2:28; Ezekiel 11:17, 12:23, 13:9, 16:60, 20:40, 28:25, 36:26, 36:33.

37   Isaiah 32:1.

38   Micah 4:1-5; Joel 3:10.

39   Isaiah 11:6-8, 33:24.

40   Isaiah 4:2.

41   Isaiah 66:22-23.

42   The Old Testament seems to give the impression that people would retain their flesh-and-blood bodies, yet slip out of the present world dimension into a rather surreal new world; this remarkable belief arose undoubtedly from the establishment's rejection of the idea that the afterlife would continue in Heaven.

43   Isaiah 52:13, 53:12.

44   The Hebrew underworld was known as Sheol, but also as *Abaddon*, meaning 'the Place of Destruction'; see Job 26:6. As observed in the notes to chapter 10, the Hebrew term for 'wilderness' did not simply mean 'desert' in a conventional sense, but was also used metaphorically to refer to a place that had been utterly destroyed and turned into a desolate wasteland; see for example Song of Songs 3:6. In the context of the exploded planet cult, the site of Mount Sinai was a wilderness (hence the name Horeb), the celestial sea was a wilderness (hence Psalm 106:9 'He led them through the depths [of the Red Sea] as through a wilderness'), and the underworld was a wilderness (hence the Righteous Servant, and hence the idea that Joseph was cast into a pit in the wilderness). The 'wilderness', then, stretched all the way from the site of the exploded planet, through space, and into the underworld, and this

explains, incidentally, why Yahweh was a god of deserts as well as a god of mountains. This same ambiguity of the term 'wilderness' is found in Mesopotamian legends, where characters such as Damu or Dumuzi were stolen away from a heavenly desert – often termed 'the high desert', and then imprisoned in an underworld 'desert' – termed 'the low desert'; see T. Jacobsen, *The Treasures of Darkness*, op. cit., pp. 55, 66, 70.

45 Isaiah 40:3-5.

46 The Old Testament philosophy was that God was the one who would descend catastrophically to the Earth; having done so, he would either appoint a Messiah-figure to act as saviour and king of the world, or take on that role himself; see for example, Isaiah 33:22.

47 Matthew 24:8.

48 Matthew 24:21.

49 Matthew 24:29-30. Compare the Day of the LORD in Isaiah 13:10.

50 Matthew 26:64.

51 John 1:51.

52 Matthew 24:27. Compare Luke 17:24.

53 Revelations 1:13-16.

54 Matthew 24:29-31.

55 Joshua 6. The name Jericho possibly means 'Moon City' (could it be 'City *with* the Moon'?), and it is referred to elsewhere as 'the city of palm trees'. It is highly significant that a prostitute named Rahab lived in the city's wall; Rahab was the name of the sea monster who was vanquished by Yahweh; using the metaphors decoded in this work, Rahab would indeed have been flung down to become part of the 'wall' of the 'city'; in other words, the city of Jericho symbolised the planet Earth.

56 Peter II 3:5-7.

57 Peter II 3:10.

58 Matthew 5:17-18.

59 Peter II 3:13.

60 Matthew 24:35.

61 Matthew 5:5.

62 Matthew 13:40-42.

63 John 14:2-3.

64 John 12:32. This statement is very evocative of the reconstruction of the exploded planet; compare the legend of Zeus and Mount Olympus referred to in chapter 4 of this work.

65 Matthew 22:30, 13:43.

66 Matthew 25:34.

67 Matthew 25:46. See also Matthew 19:29, referring to the inheritance of eternal life, and Matthew 13:42, referring to the fiery judgement of the wicked.

68 E. Pagels, *The Gnostic Gospels*, op. cit., p. 109. In the gnostic context, this statement probably refers to the imagined fall of man's soul or spirit from Heaven (the gnostics did not speak openly of the fall of the physical body).

69 Genesis 49:10; the omitted line reads 'nor the ruler's [or commander's] staff from between his feet'; this allegory is explained in the Dead Sea Scrolls, see R. Eisenman & M. Wise, *Dead Sea Scrolls Uncovered*, op. cit., p. 89.

70 The name Shiloh refers not only to the Messiah but also to the original Bond of Heaven-and-Earth in Israel. The Ark of the Covenant and the Tabernacle were first installed at Shiloh; see, for example: Joshua 18:1, 18:8-10, 19:51; Judges 18:31, 21:19; Samuel I 3:21, 4:3-4; Psalm 78:60; Jeremiah 7:12-14, 26:6, 26:9.

71 Numbers 24:17-19.

72 Isaiah 9:6-7.

73 Isaiah 4:2, 11:1.

74 Isaiah 11:1-2, 11:10-11. See also Zechariah 3:8: "Behold, I am going to bring forth my servant, the Branch." and Zechariah 6:12 "Behold the man whose name is 'the Branch'; and he shall grow up out of his place, and build the temple of the LORD."

75 Jeremiah 23:5-6. See also Jeremiah 33:15-16.

76 Ezekiel 37:24; David is referred to as 'a shepherd'. See also Ezekiel 34:23.

77 Daniel 7:13-14.

78 Daniel 7:18, 7:22, 7:25-27. The Ancient of Days is described in Daniel 7:9-10.

79 Micah 5:2. Bethlehem-Ephrathah is the old name of Bethlehem ('the house of bread'). This was the home town of the original king David.

80 Malachi 4:1-2.

81 L. H. Schiffman, *Reclaiming the Dead Sea Scrolls*, op. cit., pp. 342-4. See also R. Eisenman & M. Wise, *Dead Sea Scrolls Uncovered*, op. cit., p. 70.

82 Isaiah 11:1.

83 *Insight on the Scriptures*, Volume I, op. cit., p. 362.

84 R. Eisenman & M. Wise, *Dead Sea Scrolls Uncovered*, op. cit., pp. 83-4, 89. Ancient Jewish traditions in the Talmud and Targums asserted categorically that Shiloh was the Messiah; see *Insight on the Scriptures*, Volume II, op. cit., p. 929. Despite this, some modern commentators prefer to split the name Shiloh into *shai-lo*, which gives a completely different, non-messianic reading to Genesis 49:10; see R. Alter, *Genesis*, op. cit., p. 295.

85 *Thanksgiving Hymns*, 3:6-10; see L. H. Schiffman, *Reclaiming the Dead Sea Scrolls*, op. cit., p. 141. Compare Micah 5:2-3 'when she who is in labour gives birth'; also Micah 4:8-10 where the Daughter of Zion will give birth to a king or counsellor with the pains of labour (she is seemingly compared to a 'hill' per NIV footnote).

86 John 3:5.

87 Matthew 3:11. Compare Mark 1:7-8 and Luke 3:16.

88 Revelations 1:17. See also Revelations 22:13 (although it is not clear whether this latter statement was spoken by Jesus Christ or God).

89 Revelations 1:8. See also Revelations 21:6.

90 Isaiah 44:6.

91 Isaiah 48:12.

92 N. J. Dawood trans., *The Koran*, op. cit., p. 107 (traditional chapter number 57).

93 See H. Stegemann, *The Library of Qumran*, op. cit., p. 248: 'The messianic version of the *War Rule* from Qumran (4Q285) cites the coming execution of a death sentence *by* the Messiah – not, as so fondly supposed, *of* the Messiah'; similar views are expressed in L. H. Schiffman, *Reclaiming the Dead Sea Scrolls*, op. cit., pp. 344-7, and R. Eisenman & M. Wise, *Dead Sea Scrolls Uncovered*, op. cit., pp. 24, 29, 84-5, 171.

94 The view expressed is mine; see also H. Stegemann, *The Library of Qumran*, op. cit., p. 248.

95 John 12:34.

96 Malachi 4:5 expresses the idea that Elijah would come *before* the day of the LORD, to remind man of his wickedness and give him a last chance to change his ways.

97 Matthew 20:18, 17:22, 12:40.

98 John 15:25. Compare Psalm 69:1-4 and Samuel II 22:5-19.

99 Mark 9:13.

100 Mark 9:12.

101 Luke 18:31.

102 Matthew 26:24. Compare Mark 14:21. It was indeed written of the Righteous Servant that he would depart from this world by being lifted up (from the underworld) at the End of Days.

103 John 17:12. See also John 13:18 'this is to fulfil the scripture: He who shares my bread has lifted up his heel against me'. As we shall see, the gospels describe a re-enactment of the death of a Sky-god, and the lifting of the heel against the head was the means by which the god was cast down into the Earth out of Heaven; see the Greek legend of Eurynome and Ophion (which is echoed in the expulsion from Eden incident, Genesis 3:15).

104 Matthew 26:53-54. See also Matthew 26:56.

105 John 18:31-32.

106 Matthew 27:35 (KJV; and NIV footnote). Compare John 19:24.

107 John 19:28.

108 John 19:33-36. See also John 19:37 'and as another scripture says "They will look on the one they have pierced."'

109 Luke 24:44-46.

110 Matthew 27:51-3; Mark 15:38; Luke 23:45.

111 We appear to be faced with a crucifixion of the primeval Christ in Heaven, followed by a second crucifixion of the primeval Christ in the underworld, and it is quite plausible that this should be the case, in line with the old maxim 'as above so below'. Alternatively, one might take the view that the original legend concerned only the crucifixion in Heaven, and that the

writers of the Old Testament reworked the story to describe a crucifixion in the underworld.

112 Matthew 27:51-3. Compare the gnostic text *Testimony of Truth* in E. Pagels, *The Gnostic Gospels*, op. cit., p. 107.

113 Matthew 12:40. Compare Luke 11:29-32.

114 Jonah 1. The calming-of-the-sea motif appears also in the legend of Jesus calming the storm; see Matthew 8:23-26.

115 Jonah 1:17.

116 Jonah 2:1-2, 2:6. Compare the legend of the phallus of Osiris, which was cast into a river and swallowed by a fish (i.e. the flood of meteorite-seeds was swallowed by the Earth). Compare also the Abtu Fish of Abydos, which ordered what was to be, rather like a creator-god; see E. A. Wallis Budge, *Legends of the Egyptian Gods*, op. cit., pp. 155, 167. Elsewhere, Wallis Budge noted that Abtu meant 'ancestors'. In some legends, the 'fish' appears as a metaphor not for the Earth, but for the flood of meteorites which 'swam' from Heaven to Earth; see S. N. Kramer, *History Begins at Sumer*, op. cit., pp. 348-50.

117 Hence perhaps the comment of Jesus in Matthew 12:41 "now something greater than Jonah is here." In other words, Jonah I had become Jonah II – a king born of the Earth – whereas Christ had been born in Heaven.

118 It is interesting to note that the First Book of Enoch (deliberately excluded from the canonised books of the Bible) recorded a tradition that the Son of Man (i.e. Christ) had been 'concealed since the beginning'; see A. Ellegard, *Jesus – One Hundred Years Before Christ*, op. cit., p. 134. This wording implies, to my ears at least, the idea of a concealment in the underworld rather than a concealment in Heaven.

119 Psalm 90:4. See also Peter II 3:8.

120 N. J. Dawood trans., *The Koran*, op. cit., p. 57 (traditional chapter number 70). Alternatively, one thousand years is specified on p. 187 (traditional chapter number 32).

121 John 2:19. Compare Matthew 26:61, 27:40; Mark 14:58, 15:29.

122 Matthew 24:36 "No-one knows about that day or hour, not even the angels in Heaven, nor the Son, but only the Father."

123 Something had convinced the people of the 1st century that the End of Days would occur during their lifetimes. The New Testament indicates repeatedly that the events of the End Days were imminent. In Matthew 4:7, for example, Jesus preached: "Repent, for the kingdom of Heaven is near.", whilst in Matthew 24:34, Jesus stated: "this generation will certainly not pass away until all these things have happened."

124 God was in Heaven 'enthroned over the Flood' (see Psalm 29:10) and was often imagined to descend to Earth in a thick cloud of waters; see Exodus 19:9; Psalm 18:11; Samuel II 22:12.

125 A. Ellegard, *Jesus – One Hundred Years Before Christ*, op. cit., pp. 66-7, 257-8, argues the point that the earliest Christians never saw Jesus in the flesh, but encountered him in visions and revelations as a spiritual being.

126 The gnostics, quite rightly, had a problem with the idea of the bodily resurrection of Christ, referring to it as 'a very great error' and 'the faith of fools'; see E. Pagels, *The Gnostic Gospels*, op. cit., pp. 41-3, 50.

127 Revelations 1:5. See also Corinthians I 15:20 'Christ has indeed been raised from the dead, the first fruits of them that slept. For since death came through a man [Adam] the resurrection of the dead comes also through a man [Christ]'. See also Colossians 1:18.

128 Jeremiah 23:29. Compare Matthew 16:18 "You are Peter [*petros*, i.e. a *piece* of rock] and on this Rock [*petra*, i.e. a *mass* of rock] I will build my church, and the gates of Hell shall not prevail against it.' The specific wording, as well as the general context, make it clear that the 'Rock', in this case, meant the entire planet of Earth (*in addition to and beyond* the symbolism of Jesus Christ being the Rock; see Corinthians I 10:4).

129 Matthew 6:10; Peter II 3:13.

CHAPTER FOURTEEN: A FAREWELL TO FAIRY TALES

1 See V. Clube & B. Napier, *The Cosmic Winter*, Basil Blackwell, 1990.

2 Job 11:7-8.

3 Cited in *Meta Research Bulletin* 7:4 (December 1998), p. 60.

4 See references to 'eyes' and 'head' in A. F. Alford, *The Phoenix Solution*, op. cit., Index.

5 For example, according to one ancient Egyptian legend, the god Re one day summoned all the gods and goddesses to an assembly, whereupon he swallowed them and took them into his stomach; the gods then engaged in battle until every last god was killed, at which point Re spat the gods out of his mouth in the form of fishes and birds; see D. Meeks & C. Favard-Meeks, *Daily Life of the Egyptian Gods*, op. cit., p. 25. Readers should note the connection to the underworld River Hubur, the 'River of Fishes and Birds', also the similarity to the Greek legend of Cronus, who swallowed 'children' but was tricked into vomiting them back up.

6 See T. Van Flandern, *Dark Matter, Missing Planets & New Comets*, North Atlantic Books, 1993 (or updated 2nd edition, 1999). See also the following key articles in *Meta Research Bulletin*: 'A Revision of the Exploded Planet Hypothesis' in *MRB* 4:3 (1995), pp. 33-42; 'Summary of the Exploded Planet Hypothesis' in *MRB* 6:1 (1997), pp. 2-4; 'The Original Solar System' in *MRB* 6:2 (1997), pp. 17-29; and 'Dark Matter... 1999 Edition' in *MRB* 7:4 (1998), p. 2. For further information, or to subscribe to *Meta Research Bulletin*, write to Meta Research, P. O. Box 15186, Chevy Chase, MD 20825-5186, USA; or go to the website (http://www.metaresearch.org).

7 The most recent evidence (1999) is the surprising discovery of salt water in meteorites.

8 The first of these missions is the NEAR spacecraft, which will hopefully go into orbit around the asteroid Eros in February 2000. The Japanese space agency have plans to send a spacecraft to asteroid Nereus in 2002/3.

9 On the Gaea hypothesis, see the works of J. E. Lovelock in the 1970s: *Gaia – a New Look at Life on Earth*, and *The Ages of Gaia: A Biography of Our Living Earth*.

10 To the trained eye, the Father Christmas story has obvious exploded planet connotations. A thorough study of this possibility, however, has not been carried out as at the time of writing.

11 S. N. Kramer, *The Sumerians*, op. cit., p. 39.

12 Corinthians I 13:11. At present we do indeed 'see through a glass darkly'.

APPENDIX A: THE EMISSARIES OF GOD

1 See, for example, Numbers 22:23, 22:31; Chronicles I 21:16.

2 See, for example, Judges 13:20.

3 Genesis 19:12-13.

4 Kings II 19:35.

5 R. Alter, *Genesis*, op. cit., p. 69.

6 Although commonly translated as 'Almighty', the name Sabaoth literally means 'hosts', or 'multitudes', either in the context of human armies or in the context of the starry hosts of the heavens. See Preface to NIV Bible.

7 Kings I 22:19.

8 John 1:3; Colossians 1:16.

9 D. Meeks & C. Favard-Meeks, *Daily Life of the Egyptian Gods*, op. cit., p. 14. See also E. A. Wallis Budge, *Legends of the Egyptian Gods*, op. cit., p. 9.

10 Coffin Texts, Spell 76. See also Spell 79.

11 D. Meeks & C. Favard-Meeks, *Daily Life of the Egyptian Gods*, op. cit., p. 33.

12 *ANET*, op. cit., p. 371.

13 Ibid., p. 4.

14 E. A. Wallis Budge, *The Egyptian Heaven and Hell*, op. cit., three volumes in one. On the 'place of destruction', see I, p. 19.

15 Ibid., I, pp. 18-19.

16 *ANET*, op. cit., p. 13.

17 E. A. Wallis Budge, *The Egyptian Heaven and Hell*, op. cit., II, p. 82. Compare Coffin Texts, Spell 50: 'Osiris has come safely to the West with all the gods in his train'.

18 S. N. Kramer, *The Sumerians*, op. cit., p. 220.

19 The translation is a composite of *ANET*, op. cit., p. 94, and A. Heidel, *The Gilgamesh Epic and Old Testament Parallels*, op. cit., p. 85.

20 The translation is a composite of *ANET*, op. cit., p. 94, A. Heidel, *The Gilgamesh Epic and Old Testament Parallels*, op. cit., p. 85, and J. Gardner & J. Maier, *Gilgamesh*, op. cit., p. 235. As noted in chapter 8, Utnapishtim's story of the Flood in *The Epic of Gilgamesh* is an amalgam of two separate Flood stories, indeed two separate explosions – one of Anu, and one of Ishtar.

21 Genesis 1:26-27.
22 Genesis 6:4.
23 Psalm 82:1-2, 5-7. Some authorities have suggested that *elohim* here refers to men. In my view this is quite erroneous, and stems from a rather obscure and ambiguous reference in John 10:35.
24 E. A. Wallis Budge, *Egyptian Religion*, op. cit., p. 20. This is only one of a large number of ancient Egyptian sayings concerning God which parallel the various statements made about God in the Bible. See ibid., pp. 19-22.
25 Jeremiah 2:3, 31:9 (KJV).
26 Isaiah 63:8; Hosea 1:10.
27 Jeremiah 31:9.
28 Exodus 4:22-23.
29 Psalm 77:15, 77:20.
30 K. Armstrong, *A History of God*, op. cit., p. 91.
31 An amazing parallel to this scheme may be found in the theory known as 'the breaking of the vessels', which was proposed by Isaac Luria during the 16th century. Luria began with the idea of the Godhead, En Sof, which had been expressed in the 13th century Jewish text, the Zohar. Luria, referring to the Godhead as Adam Kadmon, 'Primordial Man', taught that the first three *sefiroth* ('numerations') had formed inside the Godhead, and had been released in turn through the 'nose', 'ears' and 'mouth' of Adam Kadmon. These *sefiroth* issued forth successfully within 'vessels' which protected and segregated them. But then a catastrophe occurred. When the next six *sefiroth* issued forth from Adam Kadmon's 'eyes', their vessels broke, and the divine light within them was scattered. Some of this light rose upwards and returned to the Godhead, whilst some of the 'divine sparks' fell into an empty wasteland and were trapped there. All was chaos. Even the first three *sefiroth* had fallen to a 'lower sphere' as a result of the catastrophe. Luria explained this esoteric symbolism by equating the breaking of the vessels to the fall of Adam, whose sin had introduced disharmony into God's created order. Luria also suggested that the divine sparks of light which had fallen from the Godhead, Adam Kadmon, were the Jews. The Jews were thus regarded as the scattered parts of Adam's fallen soul, which had become trapped in matter. The upshot of all this was that the Jews were instrumental in restoring the glorious, harmonious order of God. In short, the Jews were required to help rebuild a new Godhead. For further information, see K. Armstrong, *A History of God*, op. cit., pp. 307-11; see also pp. 285-7.
32 Deuteronomy 32:3-4, 15, 18.
33 Isaiah 51:1.
34 Daniel 2:31, 2:34-35.
35 E. Pagels, *The Gnostic Gospels*, op. cit., p. 56.
36 See C. & B. J. O'Brien, *The Shining Ones*, op. cit., pp. 45, 103.
37 Job 38:4, 38:6-7. It seems to me that the two terms 'morning stars' and 'Sons-of-God' are used in parallel, referring to the same group of entities. In ancient legends, the term translated 'star' could be used very loosely indeed, and in this context 'morning stars' seems to evoke the idea of the birth of the meteorites amid the breaking of light. The shouting for joy reminds one of the Egyptian texts where the rejoicing of the gods was more literally a 'rising up' from their abodes. Incidentally, the references in Job 1:6 (etc) probably refer to the rather unusual idea of the Sons-of-God and Satan appearing before God in the underworld.
38 Genesis 28:12-13. The term translated 'ladder' might better be rendered 'ramp'; see R. Alter, *Genesis*, op. cit., p. 149.
39 *ANET*, op. cit., pp. 503, 68-9. I realise, of course, that the proper sequence of descending and ascending angels has been reversed in Genesis 28:12. Perhaps the expression 'ascending and descending' was intended idiomatically rather than literally in that sequence.
40 Hence in Joshua 5:14, an angel announced that he was 'prince of the army of Yahweh'.
41 Psalm 68:16-17 (KJV).
42 *ANET*, op. cit., p. 58; Deuteronomy 33:2 (KJV).
43 R. Eisenman & M. Wise, *Dead Sea Scrolls Uncovered*, op. cit., p. 250: 'angels of Heaven whose inheritance is eternal life... abundant radiance dwells with them'.
44 *ANET*, op. cit., pp. 58-9; Psalm 104:4.
45 Exodus 3.
46 We should not be misled by the fact that these spiritual emissaries were able to have physical

effects on the Earth. See the discussion concerning God and the Second Coming of Christ in chapter 13 of this work. Nor should we rule out the possibility that some legends might bear traces of man's encounters with genuine astronomical objects such as meteorites, cometary debris, or comets (in this respect, readers should consider carefully Chronicles I 21:16 and possibly the pillars of cloud and fire in the book of Exodus).

47 E. von Daniken, *The Return of the Gods*, op. cit., p. 51.
48 Z. Sitchin, *Divine Encounters*, op. cit., p. 62.
49 John 10:14-15, 30, 38.
50 John 6:54, 14:19-20.
51 E. Pagels, *The Gnostic Gospels*, op. cit., p. 109. In the gnostic context, this statement probably refers to the imagined fall of man's soul or spirit from Heaven (the gnostics did not speak openly of the fall of the physical body).
52 The *Atra-Hasis Epic*; see S. Dalley, *Myths from Mesopotamia*, op. cit., p. 32.

APPENDIX B: MARY, MARY, QUITE CONTRARY

1 Luke 1:34-35. Mary's expression was literally "I know not a man" (KJV).
2 S. N. Kramer, *History Begins at Sumer*, op. cit., pp. 303-4.
3 B. Watterson, *Gods of Ancient Egypt*, Sutton Publishing, 1996 ed., p. 80; see the photograph in the Plates section of this book.
4 J. G. Frazer, *The Golden Bough*, op. cit., p. 389.
5 Coffin Texts, Spell 334. Compare the legend of the phallus of Osiris being swallowed by a fish.
6 Coffin Texts, Spell 148.
7 E. Pagels, *The Gnostic Gospels*, op. cit., p. 75; see also p. 15.
8 Ibid., p. 75.
9 Ibid. The implication seems to be that the Spirit was male, although elsewhere it was female.
10 Ibid. The passage highlights the fact that the matters alluded to were part of the Mysteries.
11 Ibid.
12 *Kebra Nagast*, op. cit., p. 136. The reference is supposedly to Ezekiel 43:1, but in fact differs considerably. It seems likely that there was once an Ezekiel prophecy which was excluded from the canonised book of Ezekiel. The reference to 'the Lord of hosts' echoes the saying in John 3:13: 'No man has gone up to Heaven except he that came down from Heaven – the Seed of Mankind which is in Heaven'.
13 This possibly refers to the belief that Christ had been resurrected to Heaven in the beginning, and had then descended to the Earth during the 1st century AD. Hence the statement elsewhere that Christ had 'put on our body from her [Mary]'; see *Kebra Nagast*, op. cit., p. 136 (and similar p. 140).
14 *Kebra Nagast*, op. cit., p. 136.
15 *Kebra Nagast*, op. cit., pp. 140, 129, 139, 166.
16 The rod or staff symbolised the flesh of the gods which had fallen from Heaven and sprouted in the Earth – hence the old Jewish legend which stated that the staff of Moses had been brought out of the Garden of Eden by Adam. It is also pertinent to note that the Virgin Mary was known by the epithet 'Star of the Sea'; see J. G. Frazer, *The Golden Bough*, op. cit., p. 389, and L. Gardner, *Bloodline of the Holy Grail*, Element, 1996, pp. 126-30.
17 *Kebra Nagast*, op. cit., p. 140.
18 See John 2:19; Matthew 26:61, 27:40; Mark 14:58, 15:29.
19 The *Kebra Nagast* contains a confusing mixture of orthodox and non-orthodox Christian legends, but some parts of it are suggestive of Mary having brought Jesus Christ with her (in her womb) to the Earth. This legend of course challenges the gender of the 'God' from whom Christ came forth in John 1.
20 See A. F. Alford, *The Phoenix Solution*, op. cit., p. 287. *Ta-Meri* can also mean 'the Beloved Land'. Some authorities state that Mary derives from the Hebrew name Miriam; but Miriam, in turn, can be traced to the Egyptian *Mr*.
21 Ibid., pp. 291-3. I had not at that time realised that the ancients imagined Heaven to be the exact image of the Earth.
22 Ibid., p. 286.
23 In the Gospel of Philip we read: 'the companion of the Saviour is Mary Magdalene. But Christ

loved her more than any of the disciples and used to kiss her often on the mouth.' See E. Pagels, *The Gnostic Gospels*, op. cit., p. 84.

24 Luke 8:2; Mark 16:9. Compare Spell 17 of the ancient Egyptian Book of the Dead, where the underworld-god Anubis had prepared places inside the Earth for 'Seven Spirits' during the primeval age of *Zep Tepi*, in readiness for their arrival at a time known cryptically as 'The Day of Come Thence', i.e. 'The Day of Coming from Heaven to Earth'.
It should also be noted that the name Magdalene meant something like 'castle', 'fortress' or 'tower' – all terms which evoked the idea of the fortified palace of the underworld and its imaginary tower which reached up to Heaven.

25 J. Gardner & J. Maier, *Gilgamesh*, op. cit., p. 77, and notes on pp. 79-80; I prefer to render 'courtesan' as 'harlot', 'wind' as 'life-force', and 'ravaging' to the unnecessarily crude term used by Gardner & Maier.

26 See *ANET*, op. cit., p. 94 (6 days & 6 nights), p. 95 (6 days & 7 nights), and p. 44 (7 days & 7 nights).

27 My source of information is *Encyclopaedia Britannica* (1999 CD).

28 The importance of the she-wolf to the story is demonstrated by the fact that the names of Romulus and Remus (and hence Rome) stem from the word *ruma*, meaning the dug or teat of a creature's breast.

29 See even the most basic Latin-English dictionary.

30 The Jews seem to have picked up a similar idea, hence the legend that a prostitute Rahab lived in the wall of the city of Jericho. Rahab was of course the Sky-deity vanquished by Yahweh and cast down into the Earth; Jericho symbolised the Earth, with its city wall symbolising the surface of the Earth, within which the prostitute Rahab came to reside.
Incidentally, the Mandaean people of southern Iraq have a tradition of a loose woman called Miriai, who sat on a throne at the mouth of the Euphrates, and read from a 'Book of Truth'.
And the gnostic legends of Simon Magus refer to his companion, Helen, as a former prostitute; she was the First Thought of God (*Ennoia*) who had directed the creation of the Earth but subsequently become imprisoned in the material world.

31 See, for example, L. Picknett & C. Prince, *The Templar Revelation*, Bantam Press, 1997. It is worth citing here an extract from *Le serpent rouge* (a 20th century mystery school text) which reads: 'the one that I must release... Long ago her name was Isis, queen of the benevolent springs... others knew her as Magdalene with the celebrated vase full of healing balm. The initiated knew her to be Notre Dame des Cross.' See D. Wood, *Genisis*, op. cit., p. 300.

32 The first story has precedents in the birth legend of Sargon, and the biblical legend of Moses in the ark. The second story has a precedent in the Mesopotamian legends of the sacred marriage between Inanna and Dumuzi.

33 Isaiah 23:16.

34 E. Pagels, *The Gnostic Gospels*, op. cit., p. 77.

APPENDIX C: JESUS OF NAZARETH

1 For 'Jesus of Nazareth', see Matthew 26:71; Mark 1:24, 10:47, 14:67, 16:6; Luke 4:34, 18:37, 24:19; John 1:45, 18:5-7, 19:19. For 'Jesus of Nazareth of Galilee', see Matthew 21:11.

2 Luke 1:26-31.

3 John 7:41-42.

4 Would Joseph really have taken Mary on the journey to Bethlehem when she was within days of going into labour? The idea seems a little far-fetched unless they were deliberately attempting to fulfil the Jewish prophecy of the Messiah from Bethlehem, in which case it is an astonishing coincidence that the birth coincided with the Roman census. Everything seems just a little too convenient, and Luke 2:4 seems to stress Joseph's Davidic connections a little too hard. Furthermore, the whole episode is steeped in mythological symbolism; see note 5 below.

5 Compare Luke 2:12 'You shall find a baby wrapped in swaddling clothes, lying in a manger'. This motif of the discovery of the child in a protective box echoes the discovery of the baby Moses in his ark, the discovery of the baby Sargon in the 'basket of reeds', the discovery of Oedipus locked in a chest and washed up on the shore, and the discovery of Romulus and Remus in their 'trough' on the bank of the flooding river Tiber. Furthermore, the story of Joseph and Mary finding no room at the inn echoes the story of Adam and Eve's expulsion

from the underworld – all four of these characters being planetary or ex-planetary deities, and the inn symbolising the underworld in the story of Moses (Exodus 4:24).

6 Luke 2:39-40.
7 See, for example, Luke 2:39, 4:29.
8 A. Ellegard, *Jesus – One Hundred Years Before Christ*, op. cit., p. 239.
9 Ibid., pp. 238-41. See also Matthew 2:23 which refers to an unknown prophecy: "He will be called a Nazarene."
10 A. Gardiner, *Egyptian Grammar*, 3rd ed., op. cit., p. 576.
11 R. O. Faulkner, *The Ancient Egyptian Coffin Texts*, Volume III, op. cit., pp. 11-12.
12 On *Abaddon*, see, for example, Job 26:6; the word is footnoted frequently in the NIV Bible. On *Nsrt*, see *ANET*, op. cit., p. 148.
13 It is surely no coincidence that the ancients linked immortality to purification by fire. See, for example, the legend of the Greek goddess Demeter and the queen's son.
14 There is another possible etymology for Nazareth, which leads to similar conclusions. It is said that the name Nazareth might derive from the Hebrew root *netser*, meaning 'to sprout'. Nazareth would thus be 'Sprout-town'; see *Insight on the Scriptures*, Volume II, op. cit., p. 476. Compare the legend of Gilgamesh and the meaning of his name 'MES which is the sprouting seed of a new tree' (see chapter 5 of this work).
15 *Insight on the Scriptures*, Volume I, op. cit., p. 883. As might be expected, Nazareth was supposedly built upon a hill or mountain; see Luke 4:29.
16 It may be significant that the Egyptian god associated with the birth and rebirth of the planet which exploded was Khoprer (the birth form of Re), whose name literally meant 'he who rolls'; see E. A. Wallis Budge, *Egyptian Religion*, op. cit., pp. 99-100. The Egyptian text entitled 'The History of Creation' begins with the words: 'The book of knowing the rollings of the god Re', i.e. knowing the things which came into being through the rollings of the ball of the god Re; see E. A. Wallis Budge, *Legends of the Egyptian Gods*, op. cit., pp. 2-3.
17 Matthew 28:7, 10, 16. Note also the theme of rolling away the stone from Jesus's tomb; see Matthew 27:60, 28:2; Mark 15:46, 16:4; Luke 24:2.
18 T. Jacobsen, *The Sumerian King List*, op. cit., p. 87.
19 On Bethlehem as the 'House of Bread', see *Insight on the Scriptures*, Volume I, op. cit., p. 299.
20 The possibility that Bethlehem and Nazareth *both* symbolised the underworld does not present us with a problem. A precedent for such confusion exists in the Nile-based schemes set up by the ancient Egyptians, whereby Abydos and Elephantine both symbolised the Earth.
21 John 19:34. The same injury is also referred to in John 20:19, where Jesus appeared to his disciples with wounds in his hands *and his side*.
22 Coffin Texts, Spell 74.
23 John 1:46. The initiate's answer would have been "yes, but only at the End of Days".

APPENDIX D: JESUS AND JOHN THE BAPTIST

1 Matthew 3:1, 11.
2 Matthew 4:17.
3 Matthew 11:11. This interpretation is supported by the subsequent statement: 'he who is least in the kingdom of Heaven is greater than he [i.e. John].'
4 Matthew 11:14, 17:11-13; Luke 1:17. The prophecy of the future Elijah occurs at Malachi 4:5.
5 John 1:21-22.
6 John 1:23. Compare Isaiah 40:3-5.
7 John 1:6-7.
8 In this regard, note the worship of John the Baptist as 'John of the Sea'; see J. G. Frazer, *The Golden Bough*, op. cit., p. 341.
9 John 5:35.
10 John 1:4-5, 8-9.
11 Luke 1:5-25, 36. The name Elisabeth meant 'My God is Plenty', although it might also be read as 'House of Elisha', i.e. 'House of God is Salvation' (Elisha being the successor to Elijah, and the subject of some very interesting legends). According to the religion of the Mandaeans, John was born after a star hovered over Elisabeth; see Picknett & Prince, *The Templar Revelation*, op. cit., p. 328.

12 Luke 1:80. The same was said of Jesus in Luke 2:40.

13 Matthew 14:6-11; Mark 6:21-28.

14 A severed head on a platter features in the Celtic legend of the hero Peredur (part of the Welsh folk tales known as the *Mabinogion*).

15 Mark 6:23. The text states '*up to* half of my kingdom'. It is my suggestion that the head equated to the full half.

16 Such sources included 'the Clementine Recognitions' and the apocryphal Book of James.

17 H. Schonfield, *The Essene Odyssey*, Element, 1984, p. 58.

18 Ibid., p. 40.

19 See L. Picknett & C. Prince, *The Templar Revelation*, op. cit., p. 312. The theme of fleeing into the hills (or mountains) is a recurring motif in ancient mythology and has celestial connotations. In the Egyptian legend known as *The Contendings of Horus and Seth*, we read that Horus 'cut off the head of his mother Isis, took it up in his arms and climbed up into the mountain'; see R. T. Rundle Clark, *Myth and Symbol in Ancient Egypt*, op. cit., p. 204.

20 L. Picknett & C. Prince, *The Templar Revelation*, op. cit., pp. 313-14.

21 On the last point see Matthew 17:11-13 where Jesus stated: "Elijah [meaning John] has already come, and they knew him not, but have done to him whatsoever they wished. Likewise shall the Seed of Mankind [i.e. myself, Jesus] suffer at their hands."

22 L. Picknett & C. Prince, *The Templar Revelation*, op. cit., pp. 231-5.

23 Luke 1:39-41.

24 I refer here to such things as the raised forefinger signal among followers of John the Baptist, esoteric sayings such as the one cited at the end of Appendix D, the occasional depictions of John in a feminine form, and the celestial identifications of both Jesus and John.

25 A. F. Alford, *The Phoenix Solution*, Hodder & Stoughton, 1998.

26 L. Picknett & C. Prince, *The Templar Revelation*, op. cit., p. 359.

27 E. A. Wallis Budge, *Legends of the Egyptian Gods*, op. cit., p. 5. A second version of the legend informs us that Neber-Djer accomplished this task by bestowing 'the uraeus of fire' upon the first Eye, ibid., p. 11. Shu and Tefnut personified the fiery breath and moisture expelled by Atum in his catastrophic moment of glory. This text apparently refers to another Shu and Tefnut who were associated with the Eye; i.e. Shu and Tefnut seem to represent the twin principles of hot breath and moisture arising from the explosion of *any* celestial body.

APPENDIX E: PONTIUS PILATE

1 Joseph of Arimathea was a secret disciple of Jesus, and it may be significant that he had the body of Jesus Christ buried in his own tomb. The gospels also identify Joseph of Arimathea as one who 'waited for the kingdom of God'. It should be noted that the name Arimathea derives from *ha-Rama-Theo*, meaning 'the Divine Highness'; see L. Gardner, *Genesis of the Grail Kings*, Bantam Press, 1999, p. 212. Note, too, that Joseph of Arimathea played a prominent role in Grail literature.

2 E. Pagels, *The Gnostic Gospels*, op. cit., p. 89.

3 According to *Encyclopaedia Britannica* (1999 CD).

4 Compare the title 'pontiff', once used by the pagan high priests at Rome, and now held by the Pope.

5 *Collins English Dictionary*, op. cit., p. 1112.

6 See any Latin-English dictionary.

7 *Collins English Dictionary*, op. cit., p. 1517.

8 Ibid., p. 1111.

9 See, for example, D. Rohl, *Legend*, op. cit., pp. 200-1. The *apkallu* conducted 'kings', but these kings were gods. Note the tradition by which 'the *apkallu* of Enmerkar made Inanna descend from Heaven'; see T. Jacobsen, *The Sumerian King List,* op. cit., pp. 86-7. It is also pertinent to note that the Grand Master of the Priory de Sion (a so-called secret society) is the 'Nautonnier', i.e. the Navigator.

10 The translation is a composite of A. Heidel, *The Babylonian Genesis*, op. cit., p. 57, and *ANET*, op. cit., p. 71.

* * * * *

INDEX

* * * * *